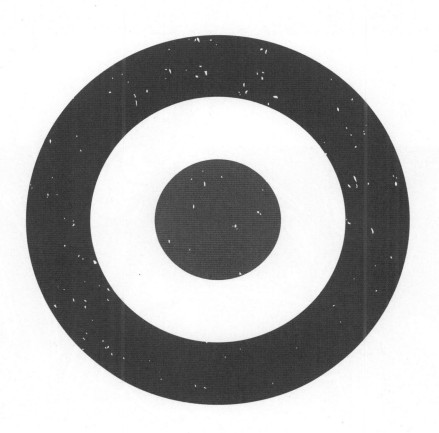

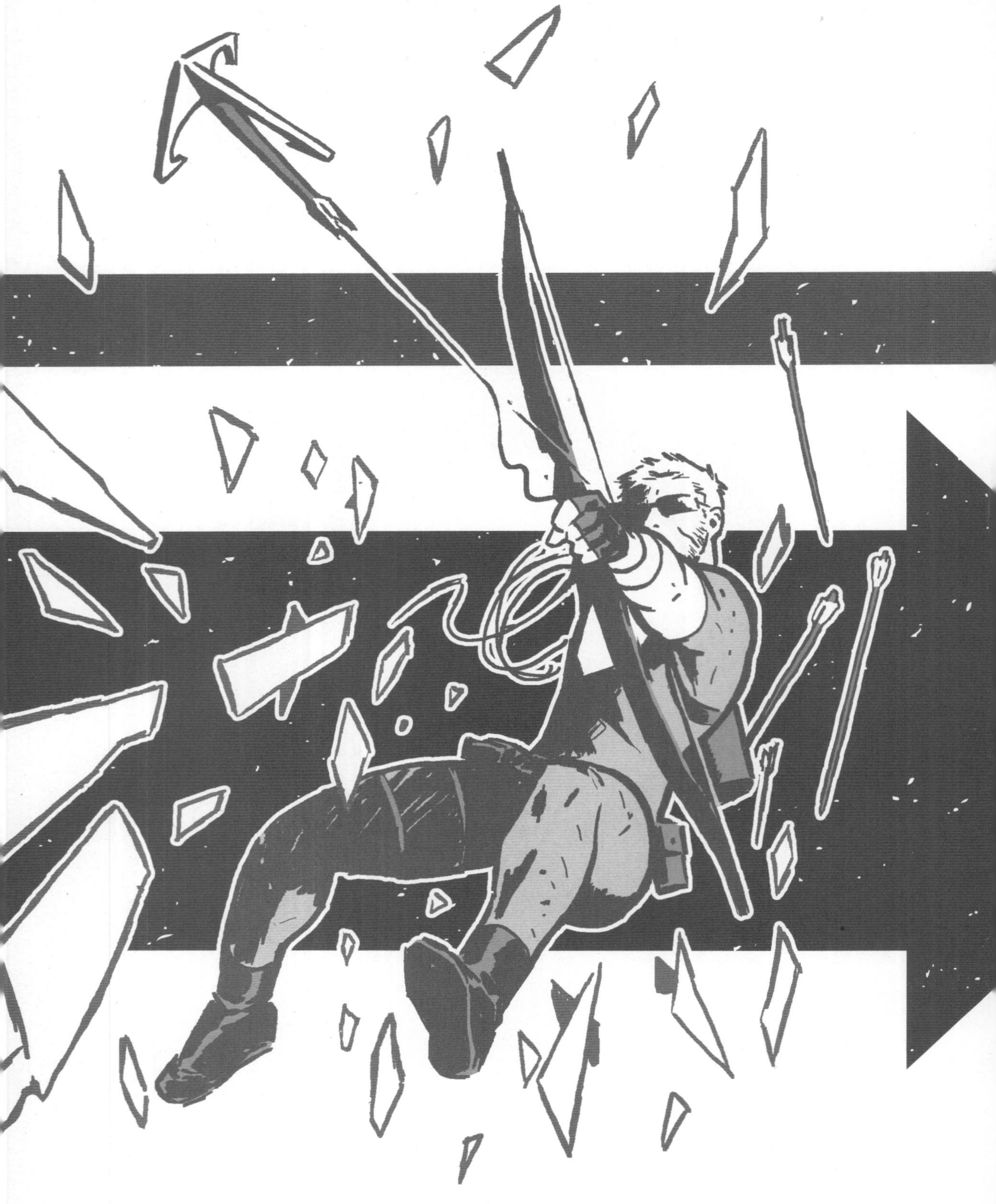

COLLECTION EDITOR: **JENNIFER GRÜNWALD** • ASSISTANT EDITORS: **ALEX STARBUCK & NELSON RIBEIRO**
EDITOR, SPECIAL PROJECTS: **MARK D. BEAZLEY** • SENIOR EDITOR, SPECIAL PROJECTS: **JEFF YOUNGQUIST**
SVP OF PRINT & DIGITAL PUBLISHING SALES: **DAVID GABRIEL** • BOOK DESIGN: **JEFF POWELL**

EDITOR IN CHIEF: **AXEL ALONSO** • CHIEF CREATIVE OFFICER: **JOE QUESADA**
PUBLISHER: **DAN BUCKLEY** • EXECUTIVE PRODUCER: **ALAN FINE**

**HAWKEYE VOL. 1.** Contains material originally published in magazine form as HAWKEYE #1-11 and YOUNG AVENGERS PRESENTS #6. First printing 2013. ISBN# 978-0-7851-8487-4. Published by MARVEL WORLDWIDE, INC., a subsidiary of MARVEL ENTERTAINMENT, LLC. OFFICE OF PUBLICATION: 135 West 50th Street, New York, NY 10020.  **Printed in China.** ALAN FINE, EVP - Office of the President, Marvel Worldwide, Inc. and EVP & CMO Marvel Characters B.V.; DAN BUCKLEY, Publisher & President - Print, Animation & Digital Divisions; JOE QUESADA, Chief Creative Officer; TOM BREVOORT, SVP of Publishing; DAVID BOGART, SVP of Operations & Procurement, Publishing; C.B. CEBULSKI, SVP of Creator & Content Development; DAVID GABRIEL, SVP of Print & Digital Publishing Sales; JIM O'KEEFE, VP of Operations & Logistics; DAN CARR, Executive Director of Publishing Technology; SUSAN CRESPI, Editorial Operations Manager; ALEX MORALES, Publishing Operations Manager; STAN LEE, Chairman Emeritus. For information regarding advertising in Marvel Comics or on Marvel.com, please contact Niza Disla, Director of Marvel Partnerships, at ndisla@marvel.com. For Marvel subscription inquiries, please call 800-217-9158. **Manufactured between 7/19/2013 and 9/16/2013 by R.R. DONNELLEY ASIA PRINTING SOLUTIONS, CHINA.**

10 9 8 7 6 5 4 3 2 1

# hawkeye

## VOLUME 1

**MATT FRACTION**
WRITER

**DAVID AJA**
ARTIST, #1-3, #6, #8-9 & #11

**JAVIER PULIDO**
ARTIST, #4-5

**FRANCESCO FRANCAVILLA**
ART & COLOR, #10

**STEVE LIEBER & JESSE HAMM**
ARTISTS, #7

**ANNIE WU**
ROMANCE COMIC COVER PAGES, #8

**MATT HOLLINGSWORTH**
COLOR ARTIST, #1-9 & #11

**CHRIS ELIOPOULOS**
LETTERER

**DAVID AJA**
COVER ART, #1-9 & #11

**FRANCESCO FRANCAVILLA**
COVER ART, #10

**SANA AMANAT & TOM BRENNAN**
ASSOCIATE EDITORS

**STEPHEN WACKER**
EDITOR

## YOUNG AVENGERS PRESENTS #6

**MATT FRACTION**
WRITER

**ALAN DAVIS**
PENCILER

**MARK FARMER**
INKER

**PAUL MOUNTS**
COLORIST

**VC'S CORY PETIT**
LETTERER

**JIM CHEUNG, JOHN DELL & JUSTIN PONSOR**
COVER ART

**MOLLY LAZER**
ASSOCIATE EDITOR

**TOM BREVOORT**
EDITOR

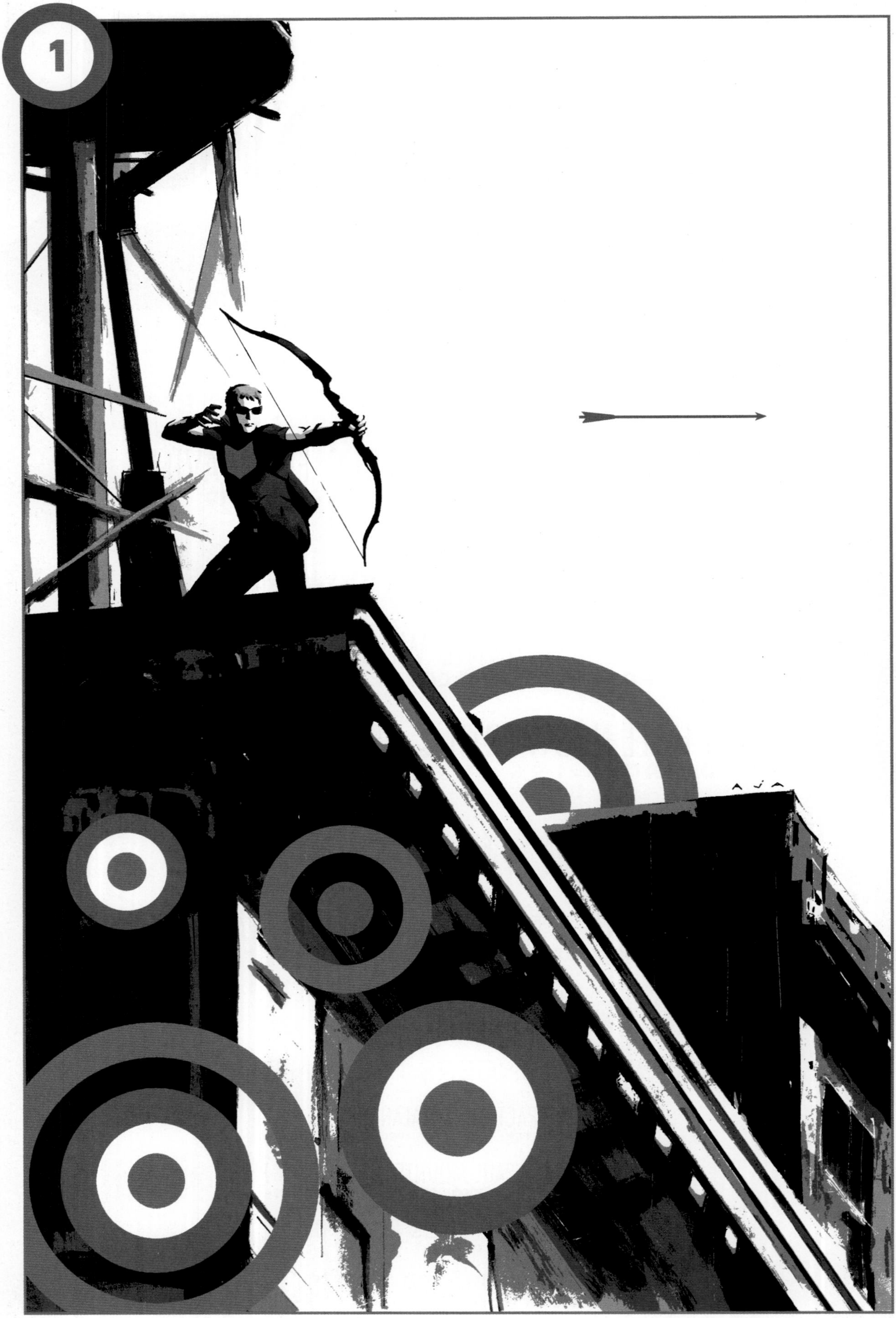
1

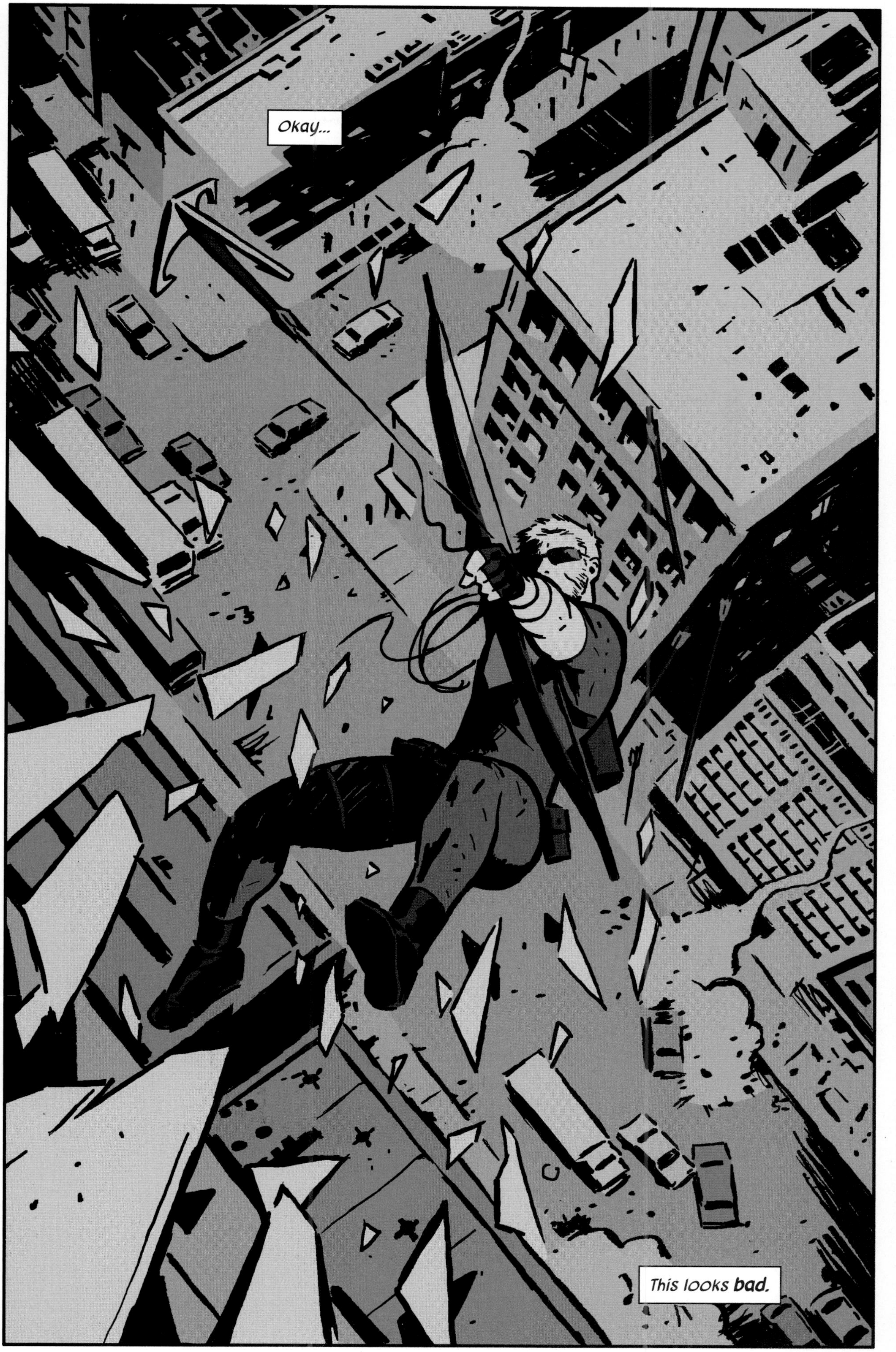
Okay...
This looks bad.

clint barton, a.k.a.

# hawkeye,

became the greatest sharp-shooter known to man.

he then joined the avengers.

this is what he does when he's not being an avenger.

that's all you need to know.

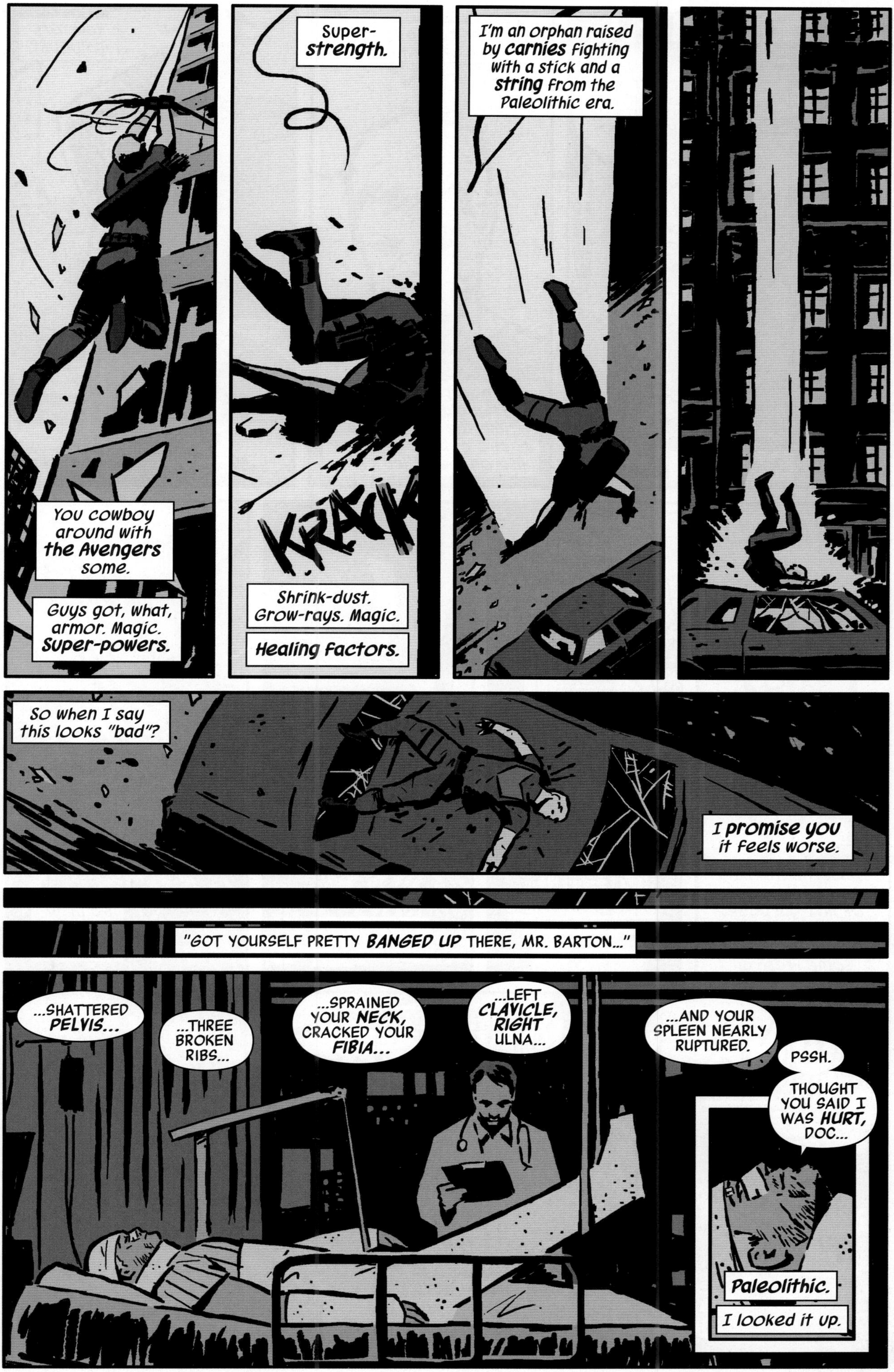
You cowboy around with the Avengers some.
Guys got, what, armor. Magic. Super-powers.
Super-strength.
KRACK
Shrink-dust. Grow-rays. Magic.
Healing factors.
I'm an orphan raised by carnies fighting with a stick and a string from the Paleolithic era.
So when I say this looks "bad"?
I promise you it feels worse.
"GOT YOURSELF PRETTY BANGED UP THERE, MR. BARTON..."
...SHATTERED PELVIS...
...THREE BROKEN RIBS...
...SPRAINED YOUR NECK, CRACKED YOUR FIBIA...
...LEFT CLAVICLE, RIGHT ULNA...
...AND YOUR SPLEEN NEARLY RUPTURED.
PSSH.
THOUGHT YOU SAID I WAS HURT, DOC...
Paleolithic.
I looked it up.

SIX WEEKS LATER:

I CAN **WALK.**

NO YOU CAN'T. YOU SLIP AND FALL, YOU **SUE US,** EVERYBODY LOSES.

*God.* This guy.

He don't stop talking the whole time.

I can **see** the sunshine on the glass and every time the doors slide open I catch a **whiff** of life on the other side--

New York in **August.**

S'just **perfect.**

Underneath that baked summer scent of **hot garbage,** wet pennies, and **pee** you can kinda smell some fresh air.

Already sweating.

Everything's perfect.

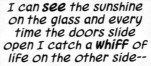

And for my **next trick--**

S'a little juvenile, I admit--

BEEEP BEEEP    BEEEP BEEEP

HONK HONNNNK

--but I've wanted to do that for months.

Now I'm going home and I'm gonna sleep like the **dead.**

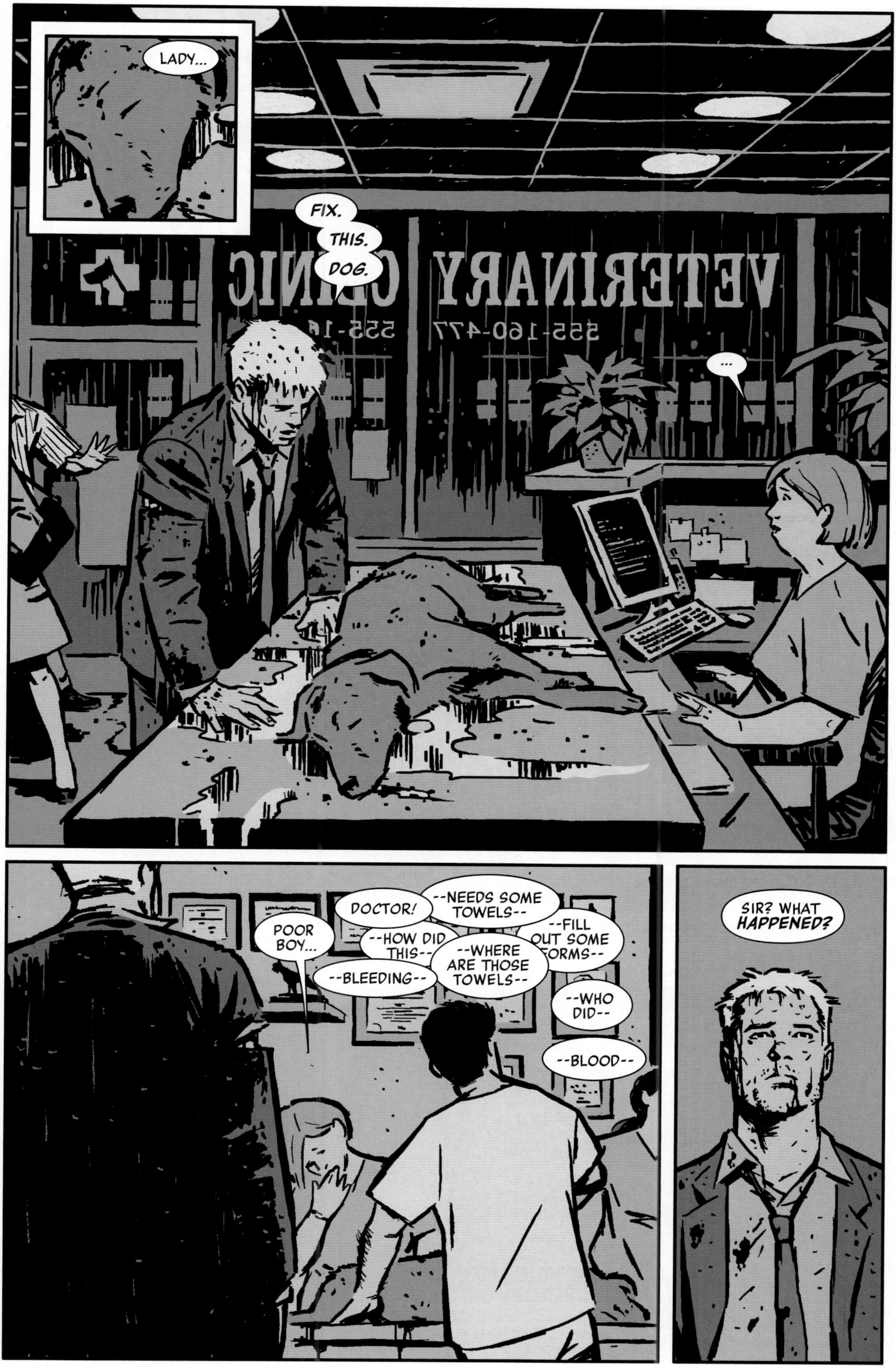
LADY...
FIX.
THIS.
DOG.
...
POOR BOY...
DOCTOR!
--NEEDS SOME TOWELS--
--HOW DID THIS--
--FILL OUT SOME FORMS--
--WHERE ARE THOSE TOWELS--
--BLEEDING--
--WHO DID--
--BLOOD--
SIR? WHAT **HAPPENED?**

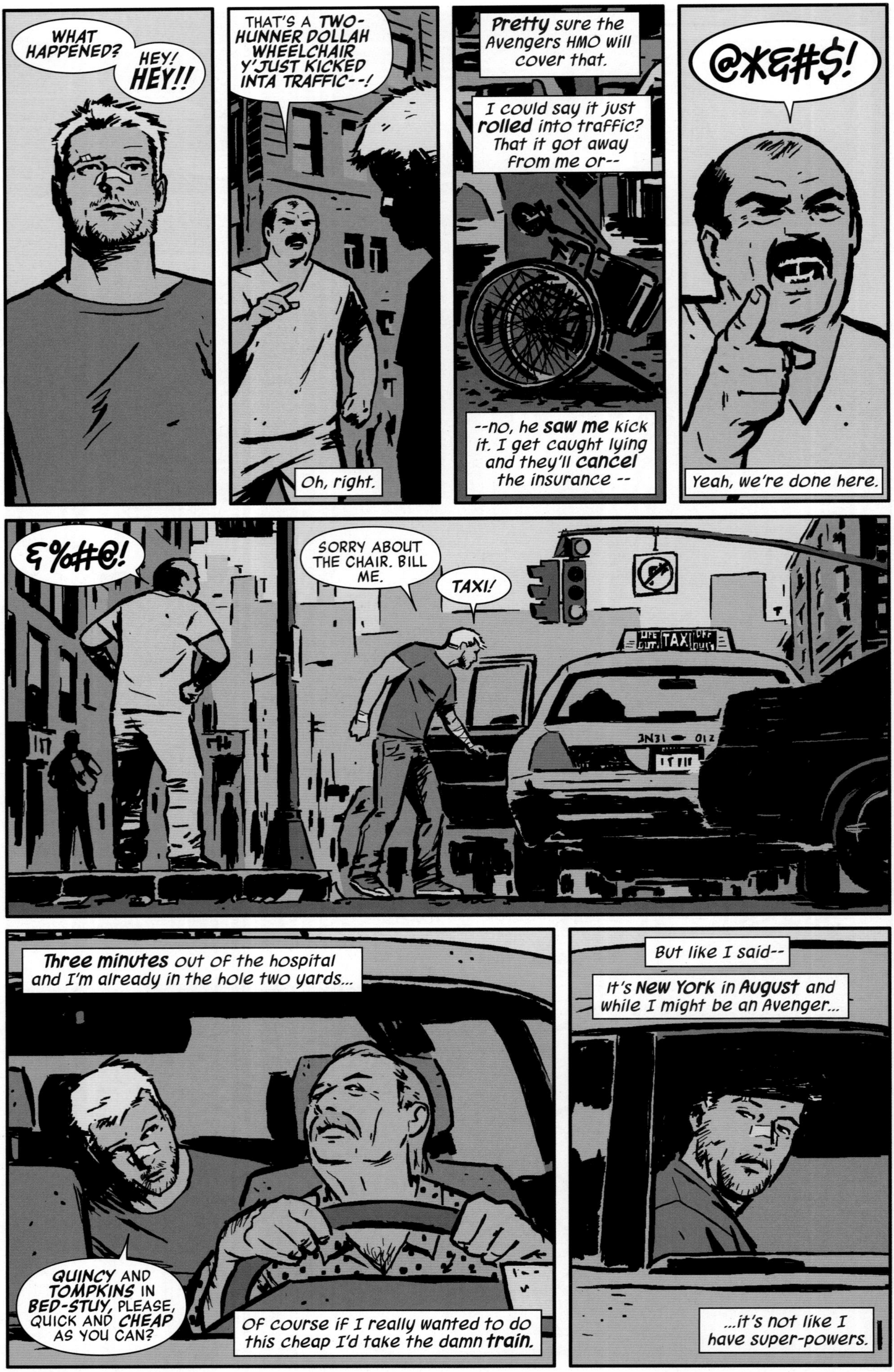
WHAT HAPPENED?
HEY! HEY!!
THAT'S A TWO-HUNNER DOLLAH WHEELCHAIR Y'JUST KICKED INTA TRAFFIC--!
Oh, right.
Pretty sure the Avengers HMO will cover that.
I could say it just rolled into traffic? That it got away from me or--
--no, he saw me kick it. I get caught lying and they'll cancel the insurance --
@✱&#$!
Yeah, we're done here.
&%#@!
SORRY ABOUT THE CHAIR. BILL ME.
TAXI!
TAXI
Three minutes out of the hospital and I'm already in the hole two yards...
QUINCY AND TOMPKINS IN BED-STUY, PLEASE, QUICK AND CHEAP AS YOU CAN?
Of course if I really wanted to do this cheap I'd take the damn train.
But like I said--
It's New York in August and while I might be an Avenger...
...it's not like I have super-powers.

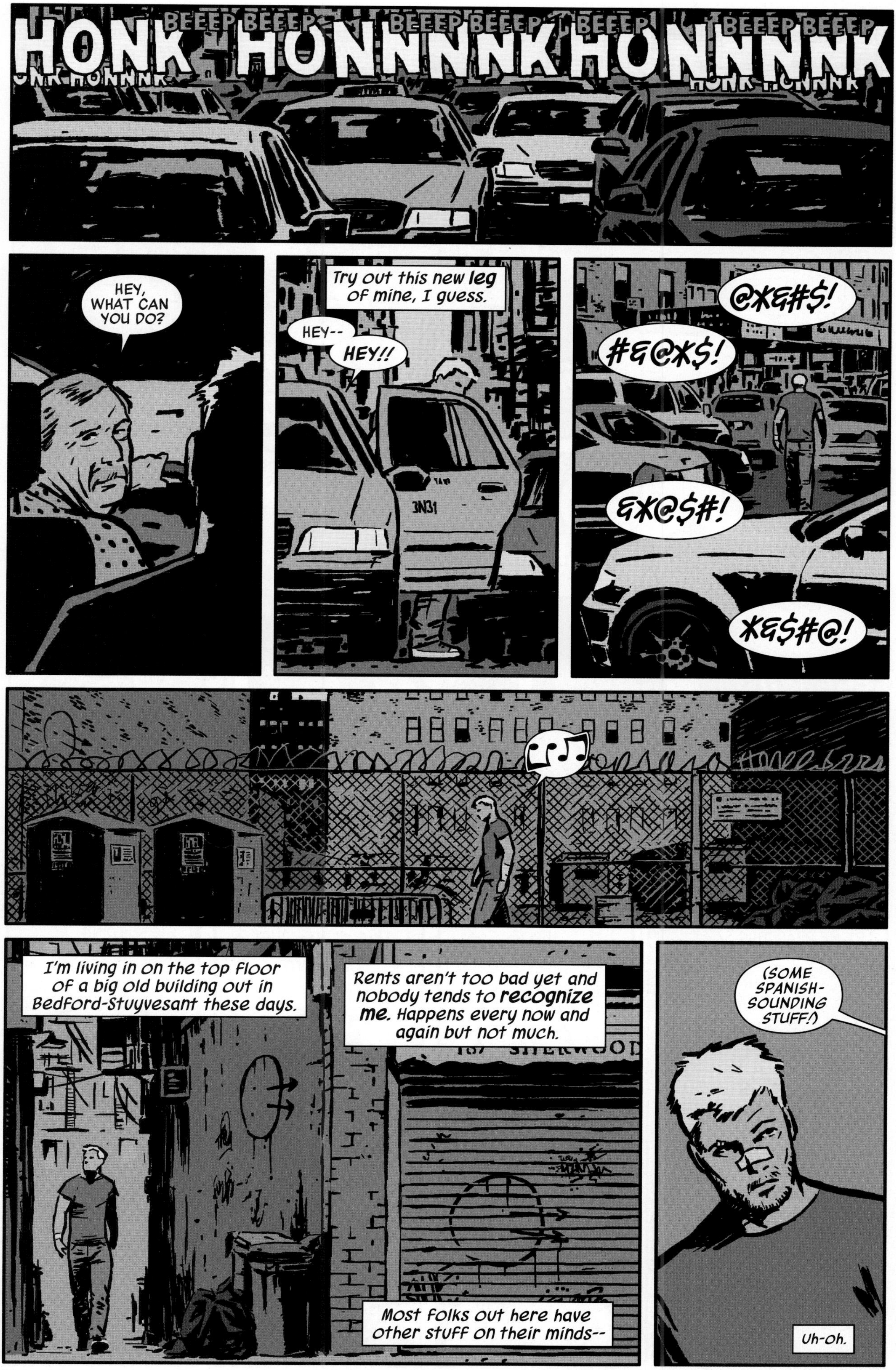
BEEEP BEEEP
BEEEP BEEEP BEEEP
BEEEP BEEEP
HONK HONNNNK HONNNNK
HEY, WHAT CAN YOU DO?
Try out this new **leg** of mine, I guess.
HEY--
HEY!!
3N31
@*&#$!
#&@*$!
&*@$#!
*&$#@!
I'm living in on the top floor of a big old building out in Bedford-Stuyvesant these days.
Rents aren't too bad yet and nobody tends to **recognize me.** Happens every now and again but not much.
137 SHERWOOD
Most folks out here have other stuff on their minds--
(SOME SPANISH-SOUNDING STUFF!)
Uh-oh.

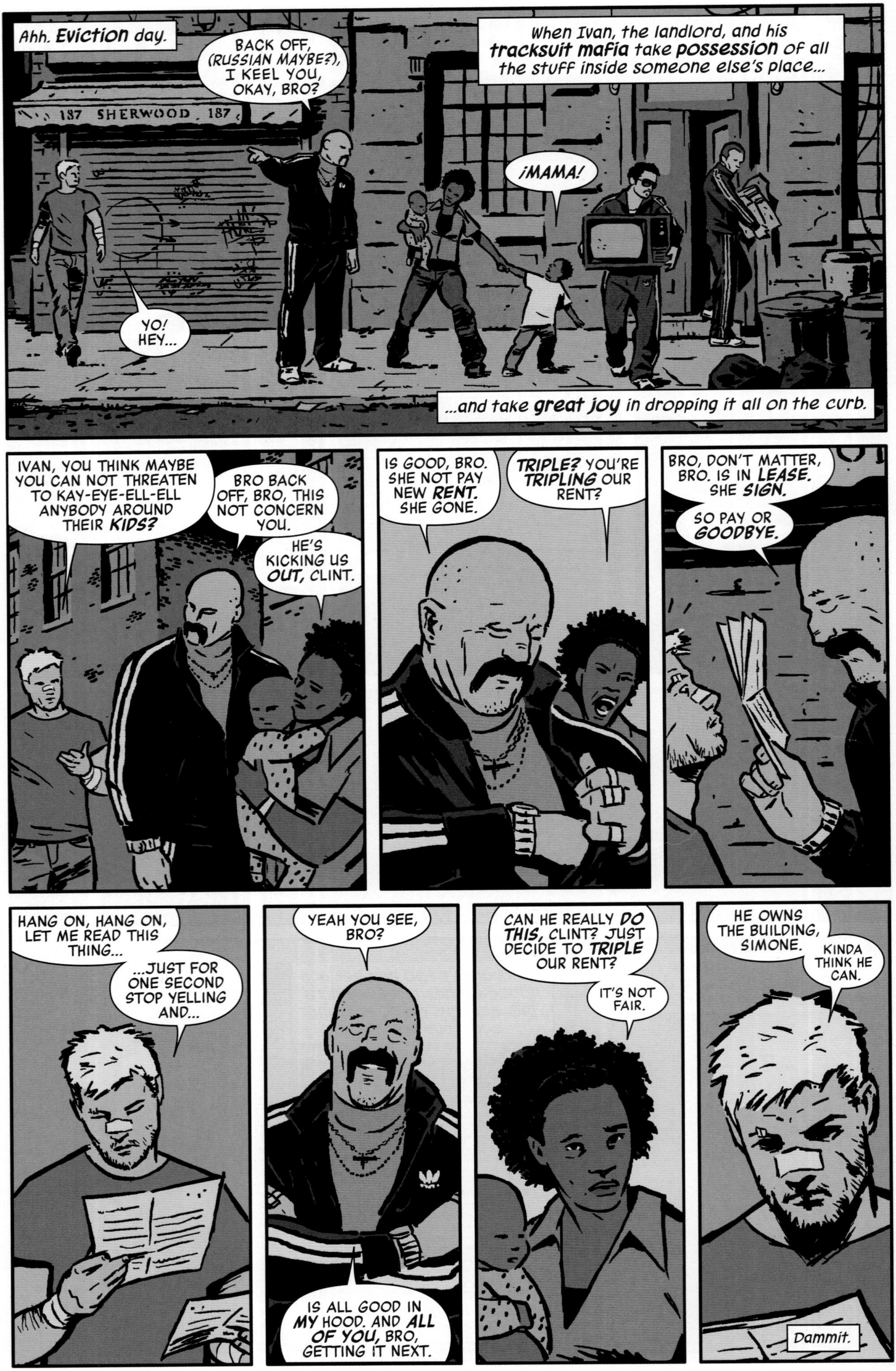
Ahh. **Eviction** day.
BACK OFF, (RUSSIAN MAYBE?), I KEEL YOU, OKAY, BRO?
When Ivan, the landlord, and his **tracksuit mafia** take **possession** of all the stuff inside someone else's place...
187 SHERWOOD 187
YO! HEY...
¡MAMA!
...and take **great joy** in dropping it all on the curb.
IVAN, YOU THINK MAYBE YOU CAN NOT THREATEN TO KAY-EYE-ELL-ELL ANYBODY AROUND THEIR ***KIDS?***
BRO BACK OFF, BRO, THIS NOT CONCERN YOU.
HE'S KICKING US ***OUT,*** CLINT.
IS GOOD, BRO. SHE NOT PAY NEW ***RENT.*** SHE GONE.
***TRIPLE?*** YOU'RE ***TRIPLING*** OUR RENT?
BRO, DON'T MATTER, BRO. IS IN ***LEASE.*** SHE ***SIGN.***
SO PAY OR ***GOODBYE.***
HANG ON, HANG ON, LET ME READ THIS THING...
...JUST FOR ONE SECOND STOP YELLING AND...
YEAH YOU SEE, BRO?
IS ALL GOOD IN ***MY*** HOOD. AND ***ALL OF YOU,*** BRO, GETTING IT NEXT.
CAN HE REALLY ***DO THIS,*** CLINT? JUST DECIDE TO ***TRIPLE*** OUR RENT?
IT'S NOT FAIR.
HE OWNS THE BUILDING, SIMONE.
KINDA THINK HE CAN.
Dammit.

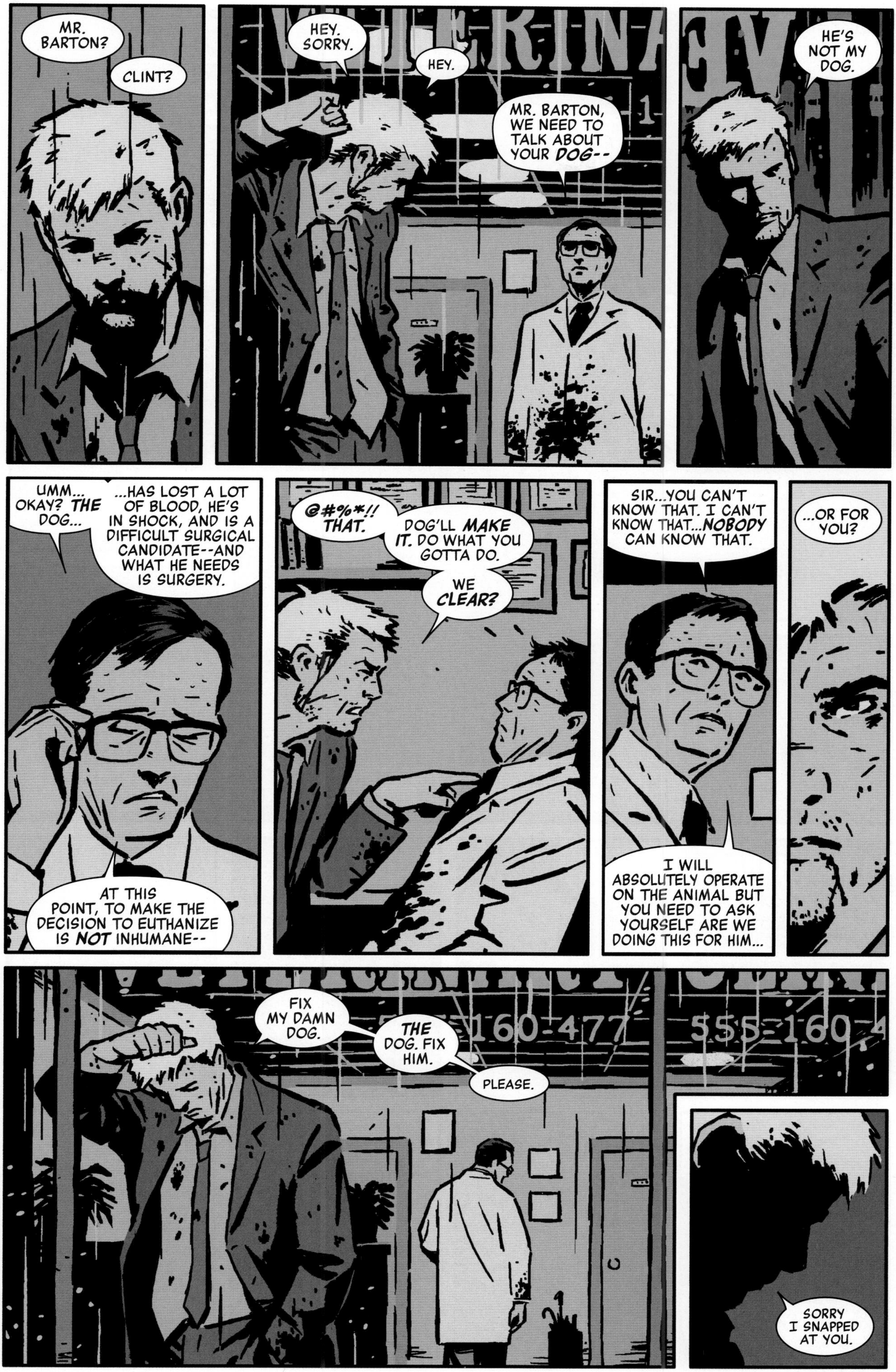
MR. BARTON?
CLINT?
HEY. SORRY.
HEY.
MR. BARTON, WE NEED TO TALK ABOUT YOUR DOG--
HE'S NOT MY DOG.
UMM... OKAY? THE DOG...
...HAS LOST A LOT OF BLOOD, HE'S IN SHOCK, AND IS A DIFFICULT SURGICAL CANDIDATE--AND WHAT HE NEEDS IS SURGERY.
AT THIS POINT, TO MAKE THE DECISION TO EUTHANIZE IS NOT INHUMANE--
@#%*!! THAT.
DOG'LL MAKE IT. DO WHAT YOU GOTTA DO.
WE CLEAR?
SIR...YOU CAN'T KNOW THAT. I CAN'T KNOW THAT...NOBODY CAN KNOW THAT.
I WILL ABSOLUTELY OPERATE ON THE ANIMAL BUT YOU NEED TO ASK YOURSELF ARE WE DOING THIS FOR HIM...
...OR FOR YOU?
555-160-477
555-160-4
FIX MY DAMN DOG.
THE DOG. FIX HIM.
PLEASE.
SORRY I SNAPPED AT YOU.

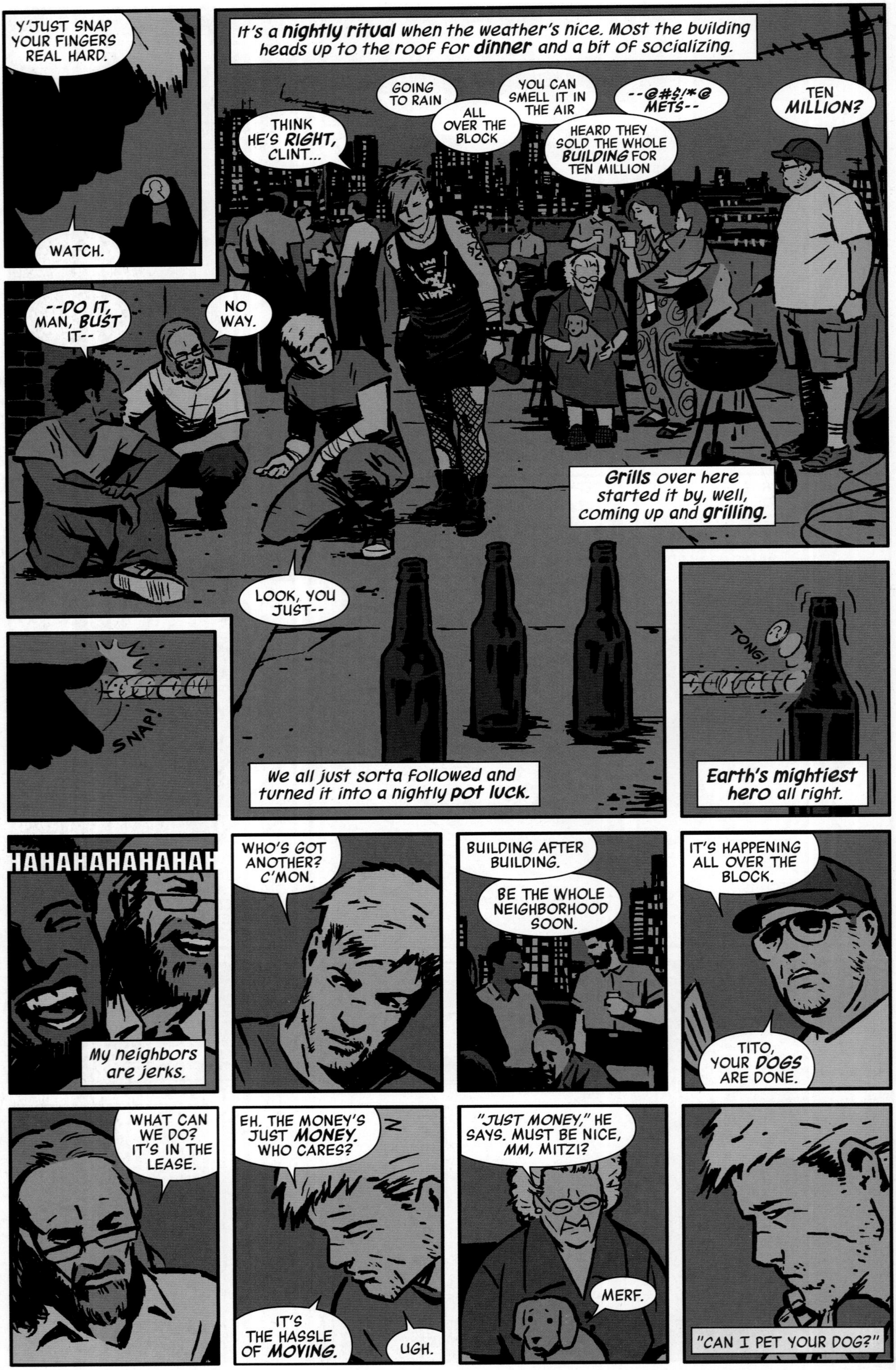
Y'JUST SNAP YOUR FINGERS REAL HARD.
WATCH.
It's a nightly ritual when the weather's nice. Most the building heads up to the roof for dinner and a bit of socializing.
GOING TO RAIN
THINK HE'S RIGHT, CLINT...
ALL OVER THE BLOCK
YOU CAN SMELL IT IN THE AIR
HEARD THEY SOLD THE WHOLE BUILDING FOR TEN MILLION
--@#$!*@ METS--
TEN MILLION?
--DO IT, MAN, BUST IT--
NO WAY.
Grills over here started it by, well, coming up and grilling.
LOOK, YOU JUST--
SNAP!
We all just sorta followed and turned it into a nightly pot luck.
TONG!
Earth's mightiest hero all right.
HAHAHAHAHAHAH
My neighbors are jerks.
WHO'S GOT ANOTHER? C'MON.
BUILDING AFTER BUILDING.
BE THE WHOLE NEIGHBORHOOD SOON.
IT'S HAPPENING ALL OVER THE BLOCK.
TITO, YOUR DOGS ARE DONE.
WHAT CAN WE DO? IT'S IN THE LEASE.
EH. THE MONEY'S JUST MONEY. WHO CARES?
IT'S THE HASSLE OF MOVING.
UGH.
"JUST MONEY," HE SAYS. MUST BE NICE, MM, MITZI?
MERF.
"CAN I PET YOUR DOG?"

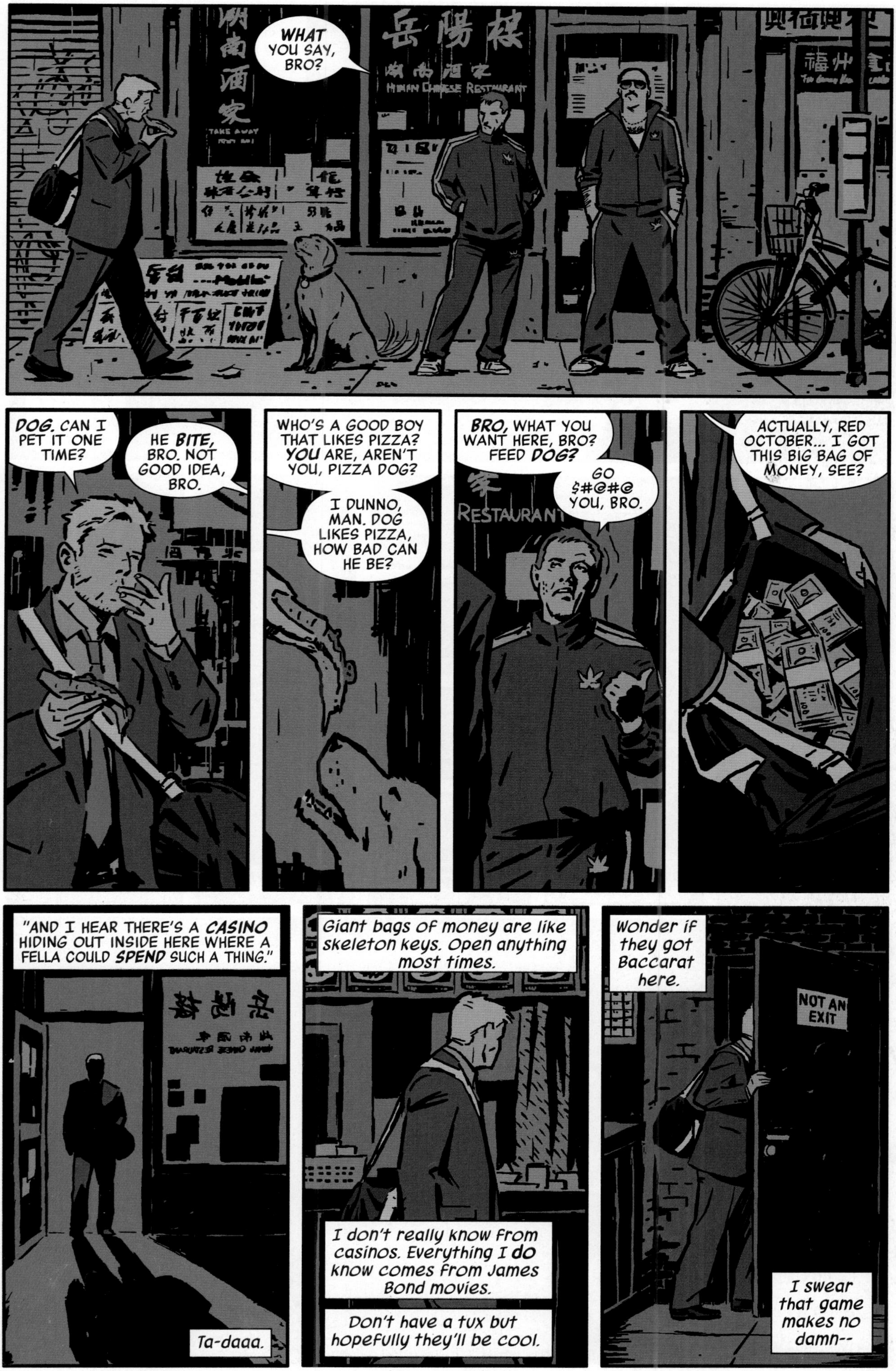
WHAT YOU SAY, BRO?
岳陽樓
湖南酒家
HUNAN CHINESE RESTAURANT
TAKE AWAY
DOG. CAN I PET IT ONE TIME?
HE BITE, BRO. NOT GOOD IDEA, BRO.
WHO'S A GOOD BOY THAT LIKES PIZZA? YOU ARE, AREN'T YOU, PIZZA DOG?
I DUNNO, MAN. DOG LIKES PIZZA, HOW BAD CAN HE BE?
BRO, WHAT YOU WANT HERE, BRO? FEED DOG?
GO $#@#@ YOU, BRO.
RESTAURANT
ACTUALLY, RED OCTOBER... I GOT THIS BIG BAG OF MONEY, SEE?
"AND I HEAR THERE'S A CASINO HIDING OUT INSIDE HERE WHERE A FELLA COULD SPEND SUCH A THING."
Ta-daaa.
Giant bags of money are like skeleton keys. Open anything most times.
I don't really know from casinos. Everything I do know comes from James Bond movies.
Don't have a tux but hopefully they'll be cool.
Wonder if they got Baccarat here.
NOT AN EXIT
I swear that game makes no damn--

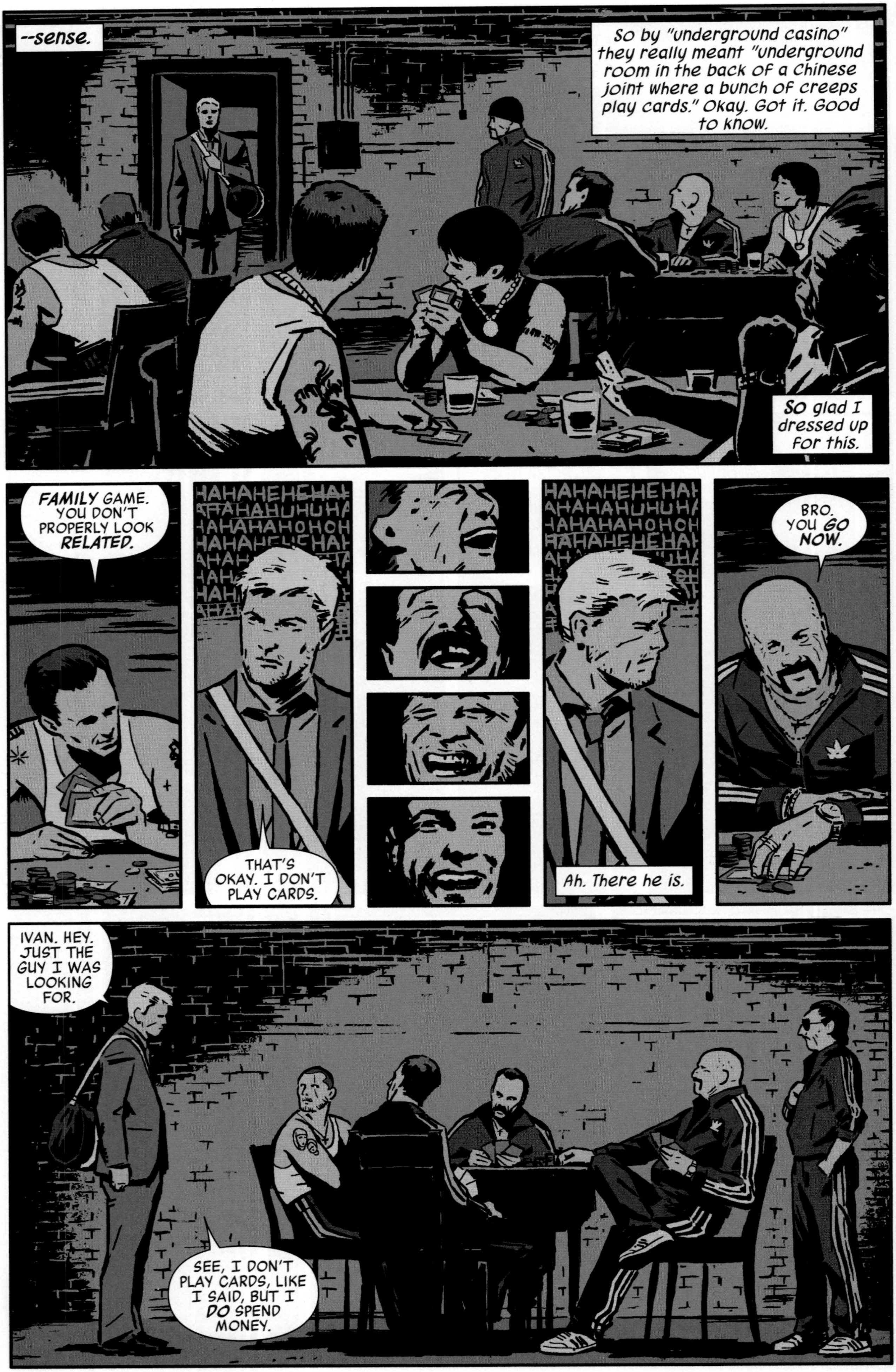
--sense.
So by "underground casino" they really meant "underground room in the back of a Chinese joint where a bunch of creeps play cards." Okay. Got it. Good to know.
SO glad I dressed up for this.
FAMILY GAME. YOU DON'T PROPERLY LOOK RELATED.
THAT'S OKAY. I DON'T PLAY CARDS.
Ah. There he is.
BRO. YOU GO NOW.
IVAN. HEY. JUST THE GUY I WAS LOOKING FOR.
SEE, I DON'T PLAY CARDS, LIKE I SAID, BUT I DO SPEND MONEY.

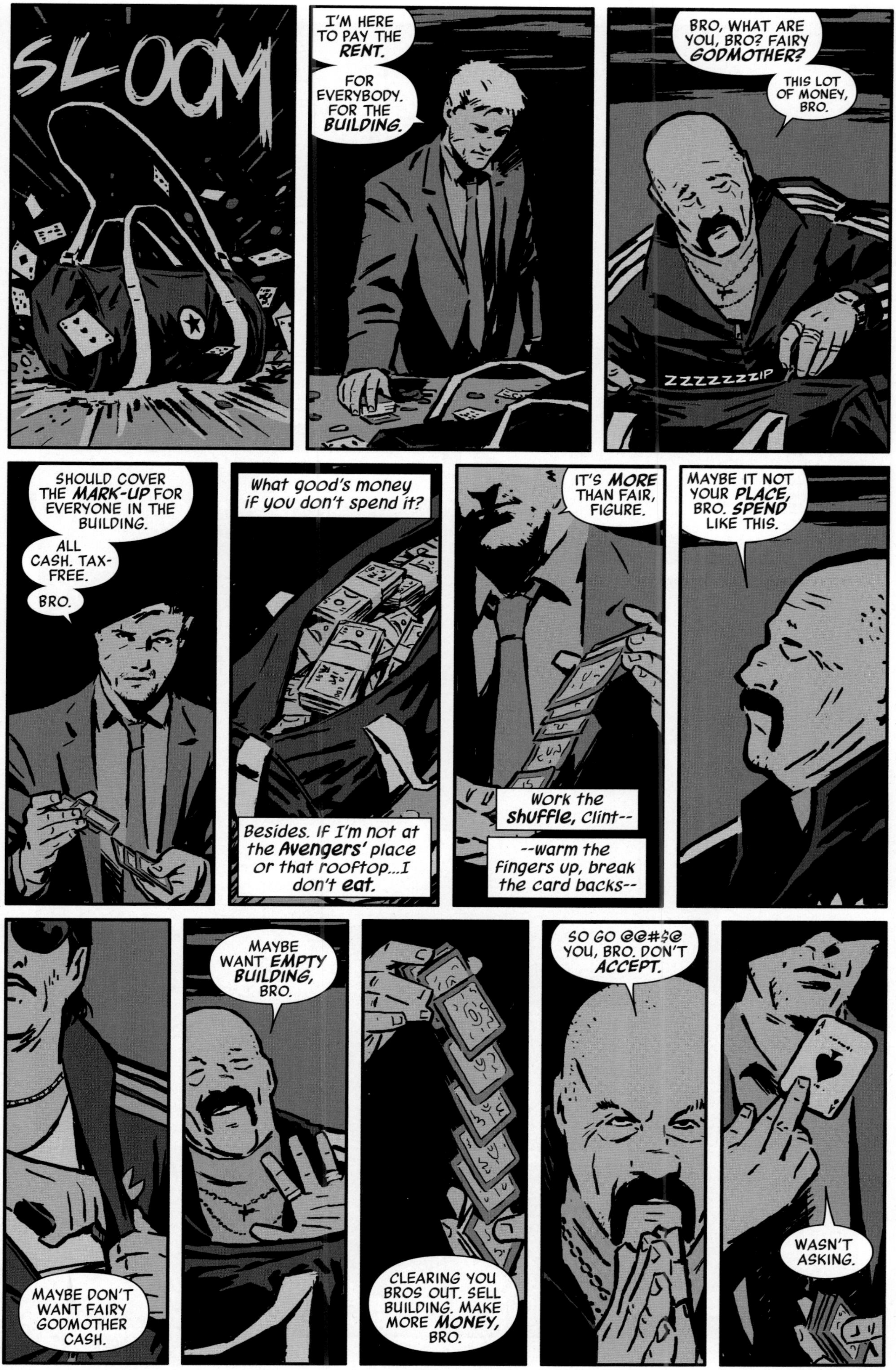
SLOOM
I'M HERE TO PAY THE RENT.
FOR EVERYBODY. FOR THE BUILDING.
BRO, WHAT ARE YOU, BRO? FAIRY GODMOTHER?
THIS LOT OF MONEY, BRO.
ZZZZZZZIP
SHOULD COVER THE MARK-UP FOR EVERYONE IN THE BUILDING.
ALL CASH. TAX-FREE.
BRO.
What good's money if you don't spend it?
Besides. If I'm not at the Avengers' place or that rooftop...I don't eat.
IT'S MORE THAN FAIR, FIGURE.
Work the shuffle, Clint--
--warm the fingers up, break the card backs--
MAYBE IT NOT YOUR PLACE, BRO. SPEND LIKE THIS.
MAYBE DON'T WANT FAIRY GODMOTHER CASH.
MAYBE WANT EMPTY BUILDING, BRO.
CLEARING YOU BROS OUT. SELL BUILDING. MAKE MORE MONEY, BRO.
SO GO @@#$@ YOU, BRO. DON'T ACCEPT.
WASN'T ASKING.

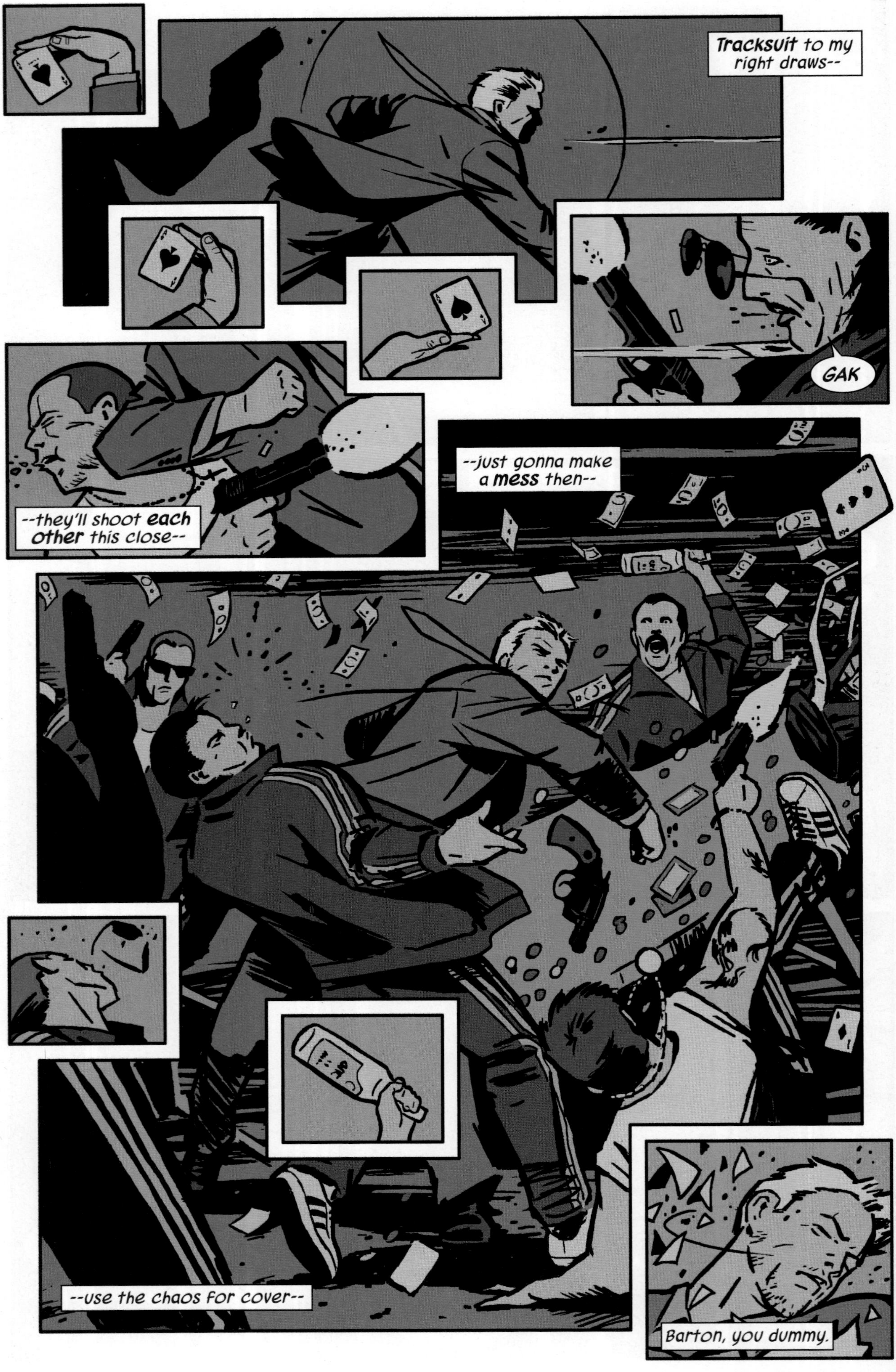
Tracksuit to my right draws--
GAK
--they'll shoot each other this close--
--just gonna make a mess then--
--use the chaos for cover--
Barton, you dummy.

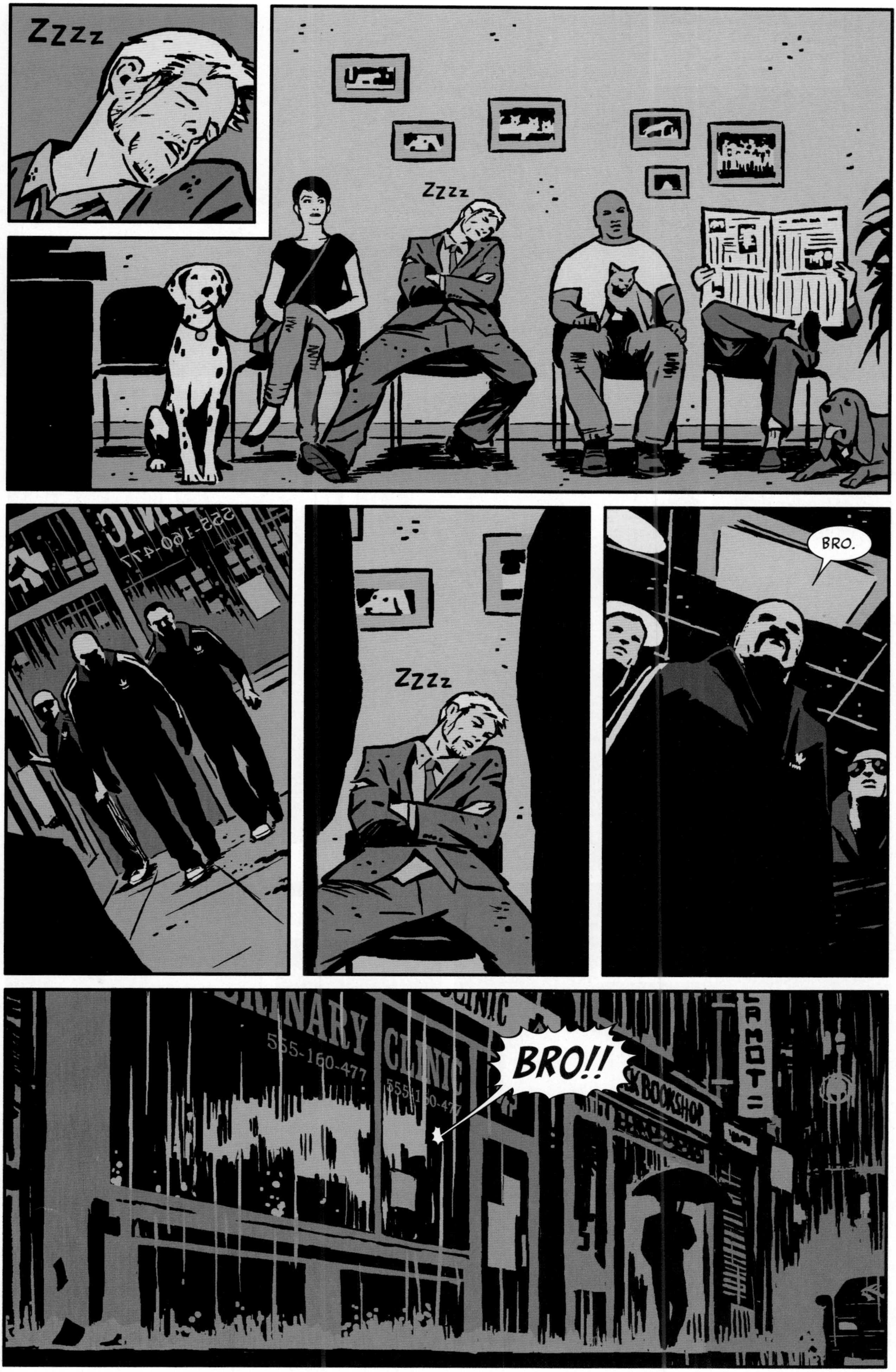
Zzzz
Zzzz
Zzzz
BRO.
BRO!!
555-160-477
CLINIC
BOOKSHOP

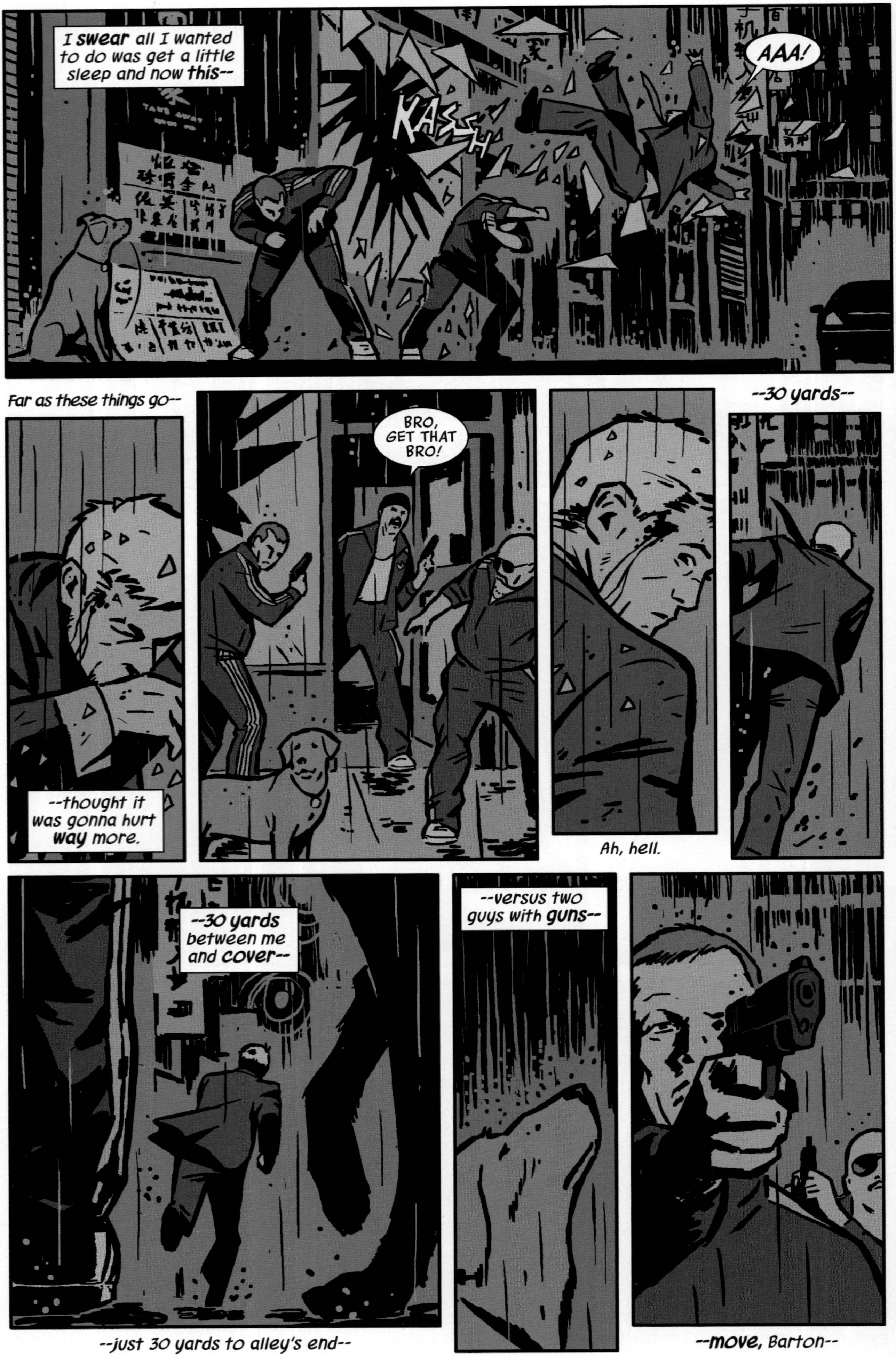

I swear all I wanted to do was get a little sleep and now this--
KASSH
AAA!
Far as these things go--
--thought it was gonna hurt way more.
BRO, GET THAT BRO!
Ah, hell.
--30 yards--
--30 yards between me and cover--
--just 30 yards to alley's end--
--versus two guys with guns--
--move, Barton--

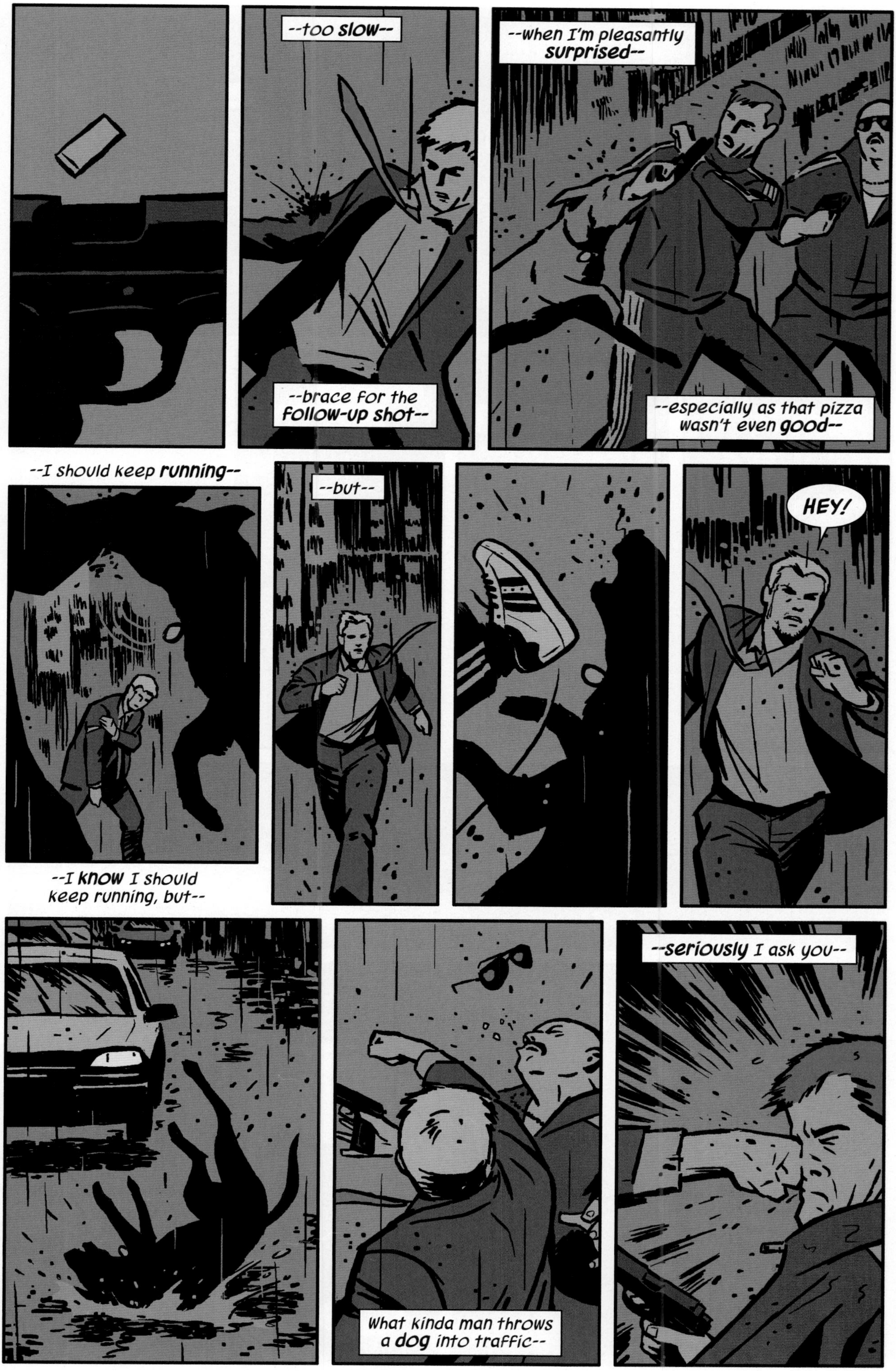
--too slow--
--brace for the follow-up shot--
--when I'm pleasantly surprised--
--especially as that pizza wasn't even good--
--I should keep running--
--I know I should keep running, but--
--but--
HEY!
What kinda man throws a dog into traffic--
--seriously I ask you--

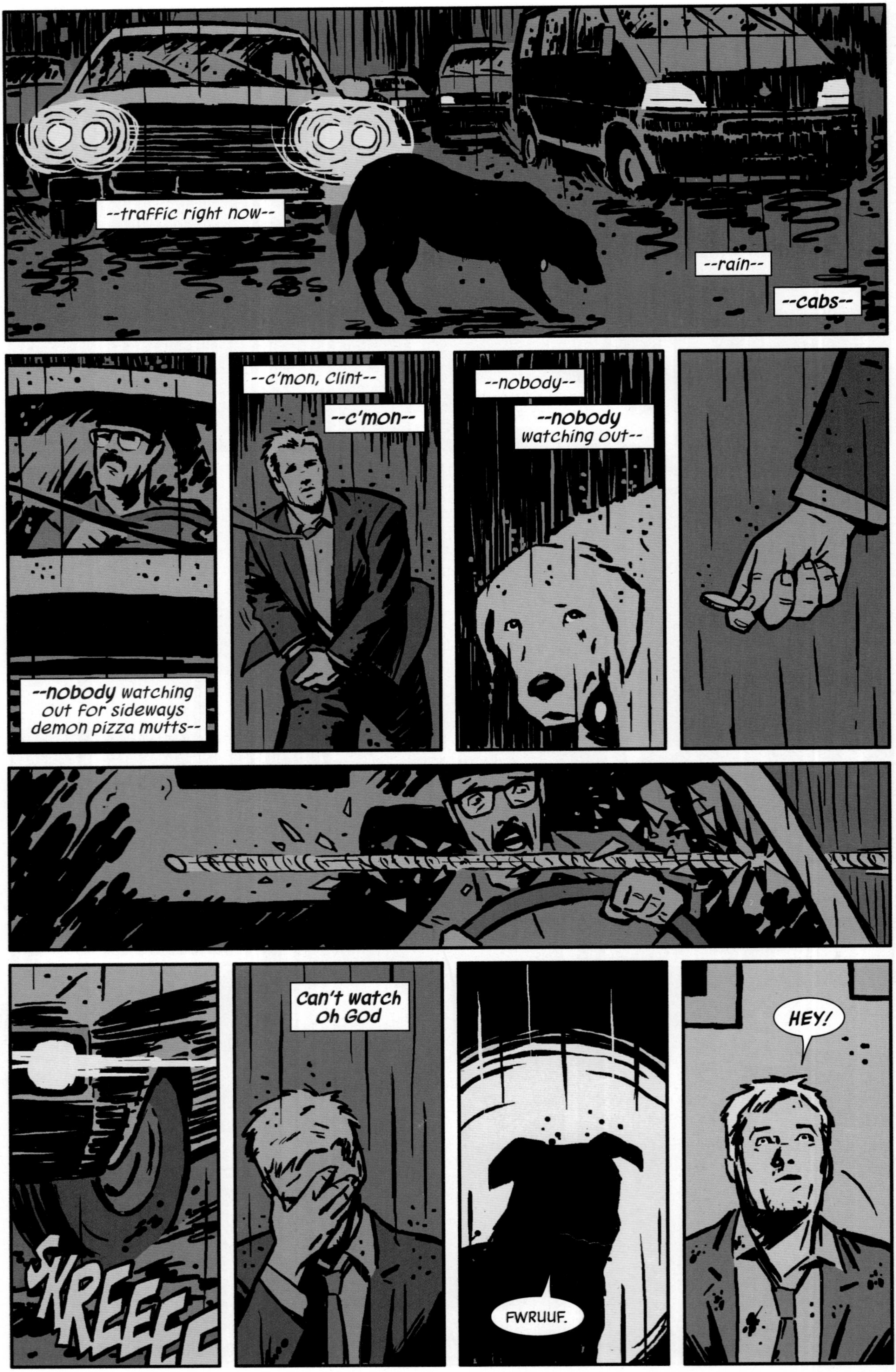
--traffic right now--
--rain--
--cabs--
--nobody watching out for sideways demon pizza mutts--
--c'mon, Clint--
--c'mon--
--nobody--
--nobody watching out--
SKREEEE
Can't watch oh God
FWRUUF.
HEY!

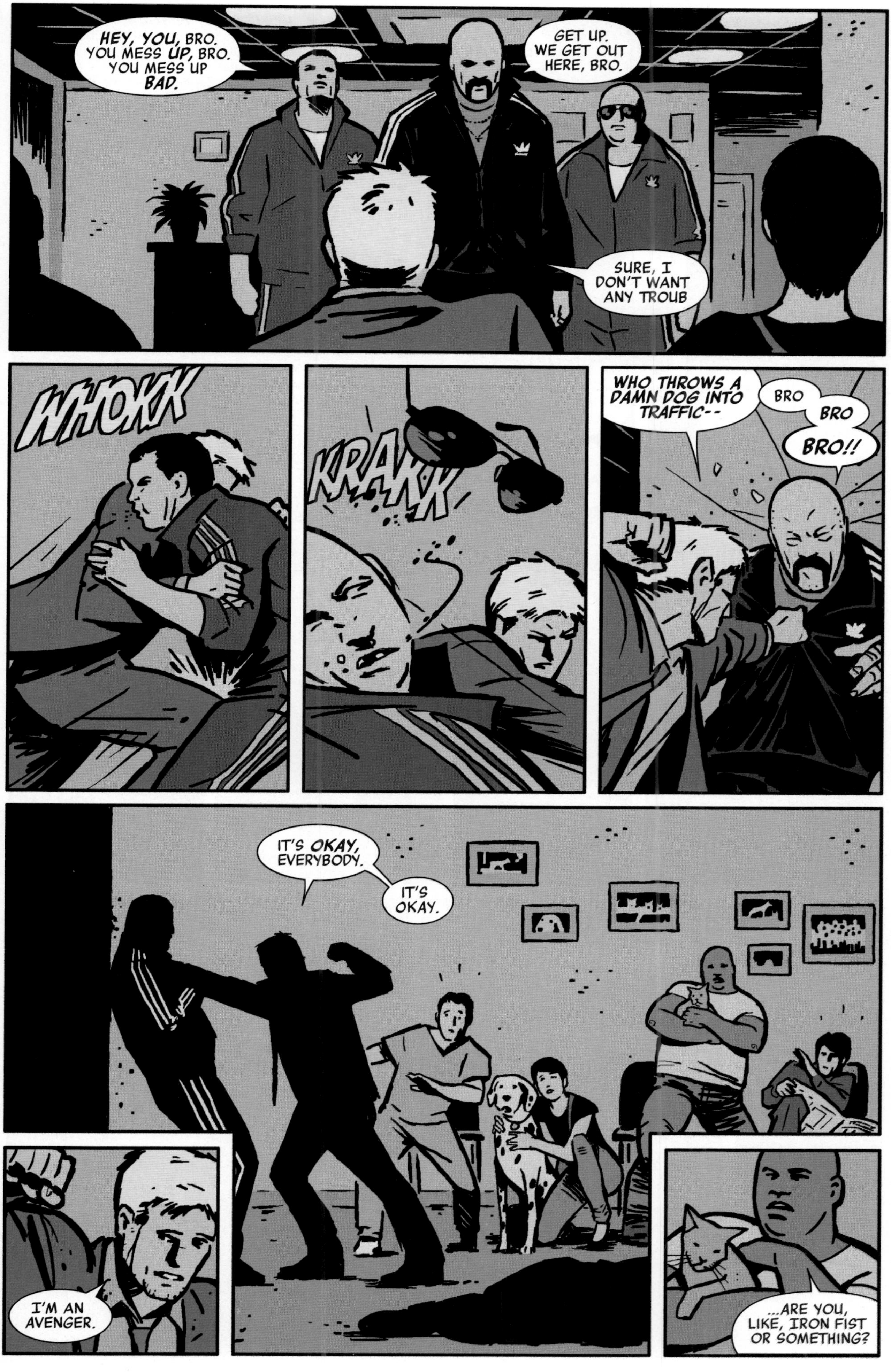
HEY, YOU, BRO. YOU MESS UP, BRO. YOU MESS UP BAD.
GET UP. WE GET OUT HERE, BRO.
SURE, I DON'T WANT ANY TROUB
WHOKK
KRAKK
WHO THROWS A DAMN DOG INTO TRAFFIC--
BRO
BRO
BRO!!
IT'S OKAY, EVERYBODY.
IT'S OKAY.
I'M AN AVENGER.
...ARE YOU, LIKE, IRON FIST OR SOMETHING?

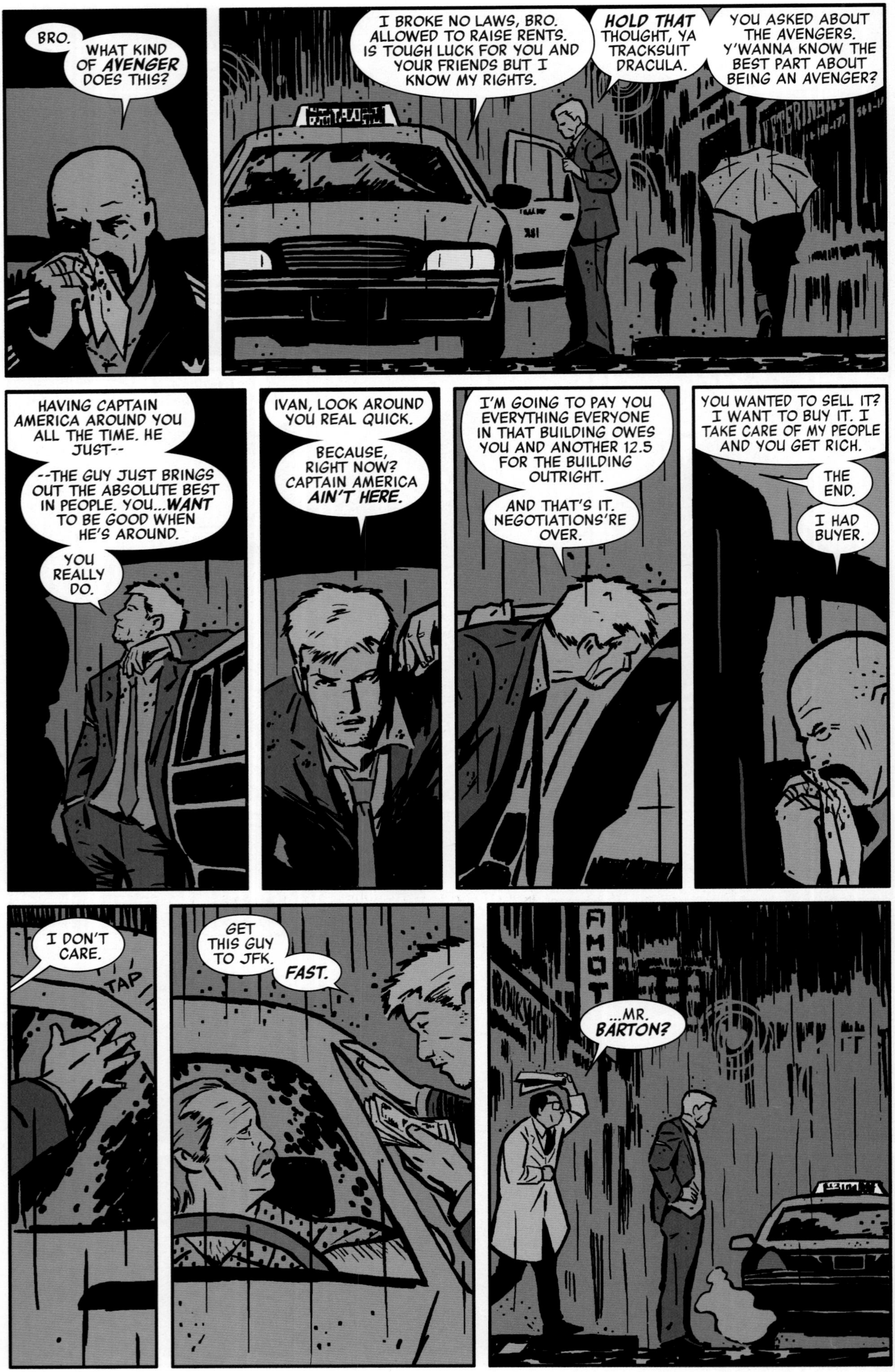
BRO.
WHAT KIND OF AVENGER DOES THIS?
I BROKE NO LAWS, BRO. ALLOWED TO RAISE RENTS. IS TOUGH LUCK FOR YOU AND YOUR FRIENDS BUT I KNOW MY RIGHTS.
HOLD THAT THOUGHT, YA TRACKSUIT DRACULA.
YOU ASKED ABOUT THE AVENGERS. Y'WANNA KNOW THE BEST PART ABOUT BEING AN AVENGER?
HAVING CAPTAIN AMERICA AROUND YOU ALL THE TIME. HE JUST--
--THE GUY JUST BRINGS OUT THE ABSOLUTE BEST IN PEOPLE. YOU...WANT TO BE GOOD WHEN HE'S AROUND.
YOU REALLY DO.
IVAN, LOOK AROUND YOU REAL QUICK.
BECAUSE, RIGHT NOW? CAPTAIN AMERICA AIN'T HERE.
I'M GOING TO PAY YOU EVERYTHING EVERYONE IN THAT BUILDING OWES YOU AND ANOTHER 12.5 FOR THE BUILDING OUTRIGHT.
AND THAT'S IT. NEGOTIATIONS'RE OVER.
YOU WANTED TO SELL IT? I WANT TO BUY IT. I TAKE CARE OF MY PEOPLE AND YOU GET RICH.
THE END.
I HAD BUYER.
I DON'T CARE.
TAP
GET THIS GUY TO JFK.
FAST.
...MR. BARTON?

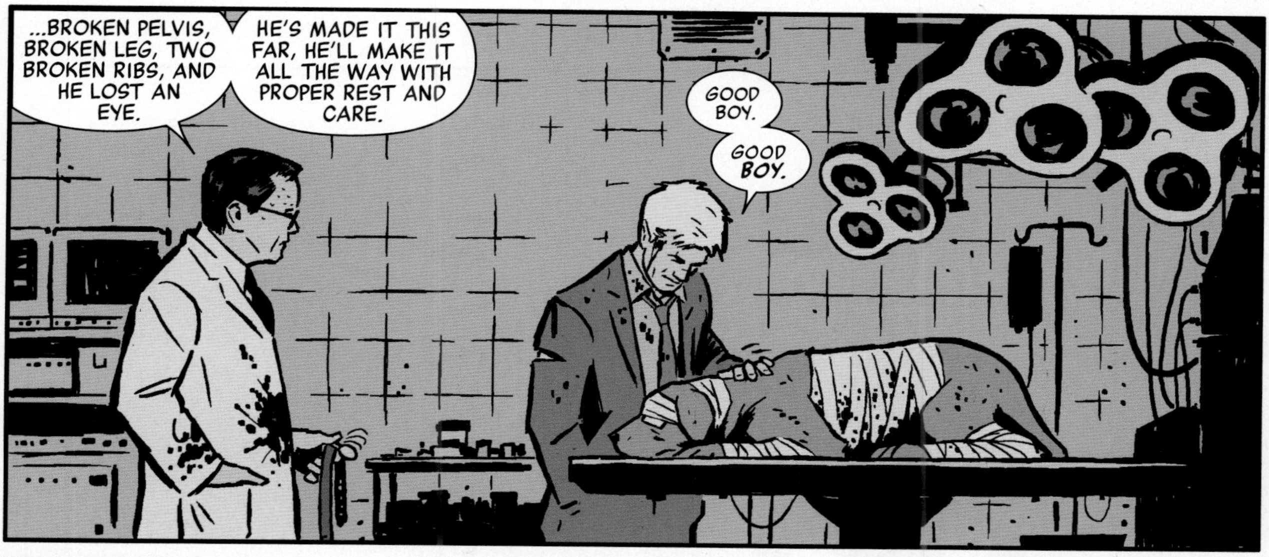
...BROKEN PELVIS, BROKEN LEG, TWO BROKEN RIBS, AND HE LOST AN EYE.
HE'S MADE IT THIS FAR, HE'LL MAKE IT ALL THE WAY WITH PROPER REST AND CARE.
GOOD BOY.
GOOD BOY.

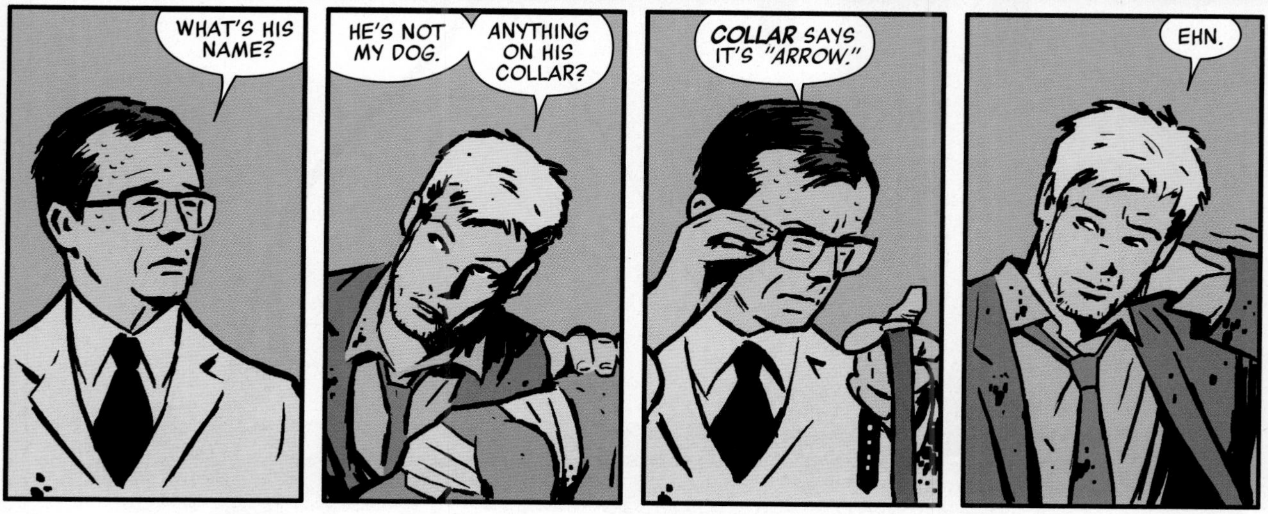
WHAT'S HIS NAME?
HE'S NOT MY DOG.
ANYTHING ON HIS COLLAR?
COLLAR SAYS IT'S "ARROW."
EHN.

# lucky

a clint barton **hawkeye** adventure

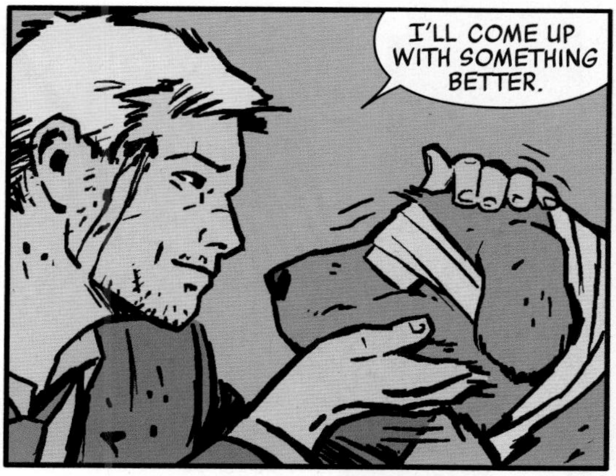
I'LL COME UP WITH SOMETHING BETTER.

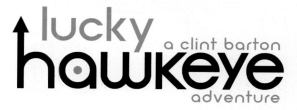

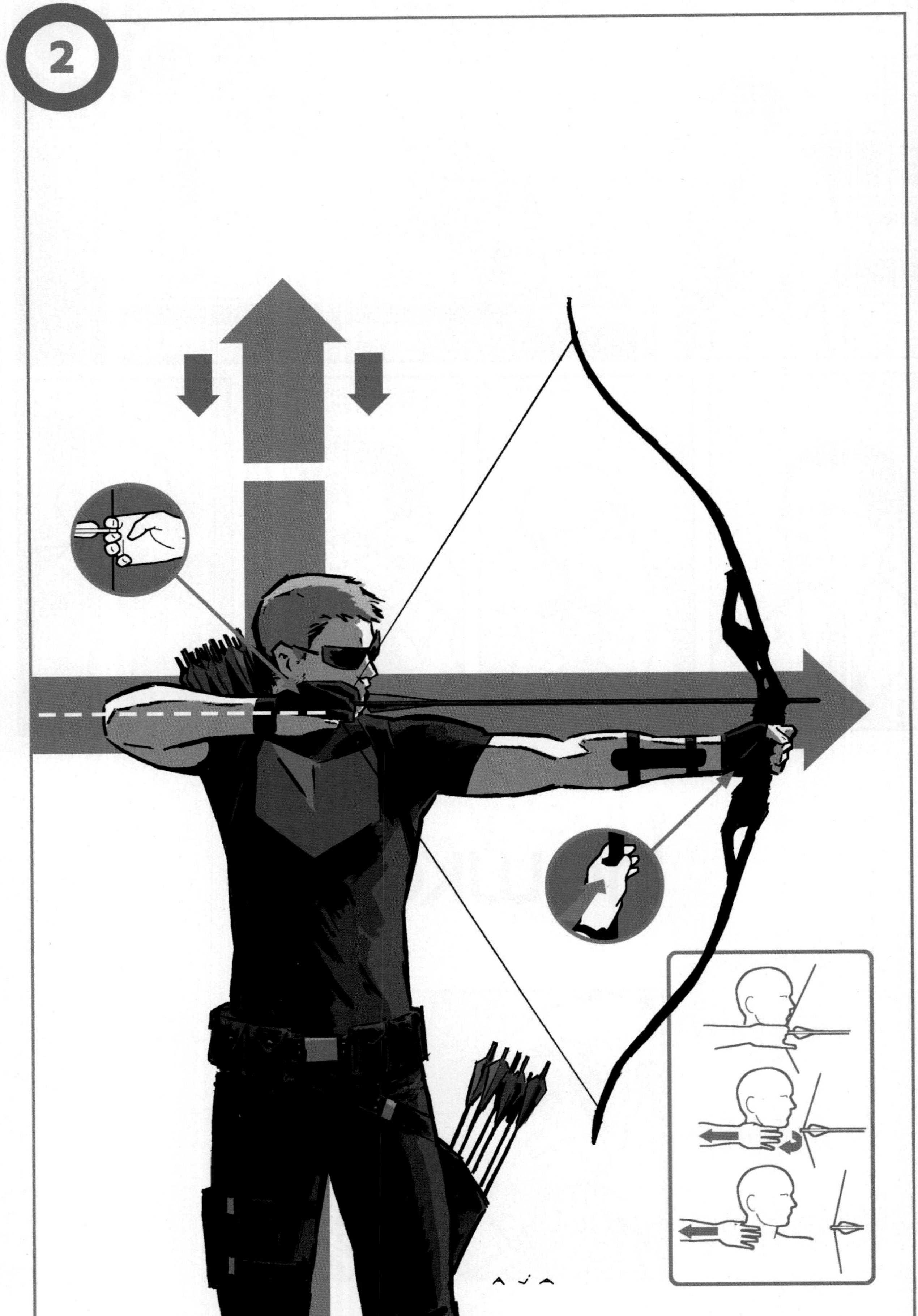
2
AJA

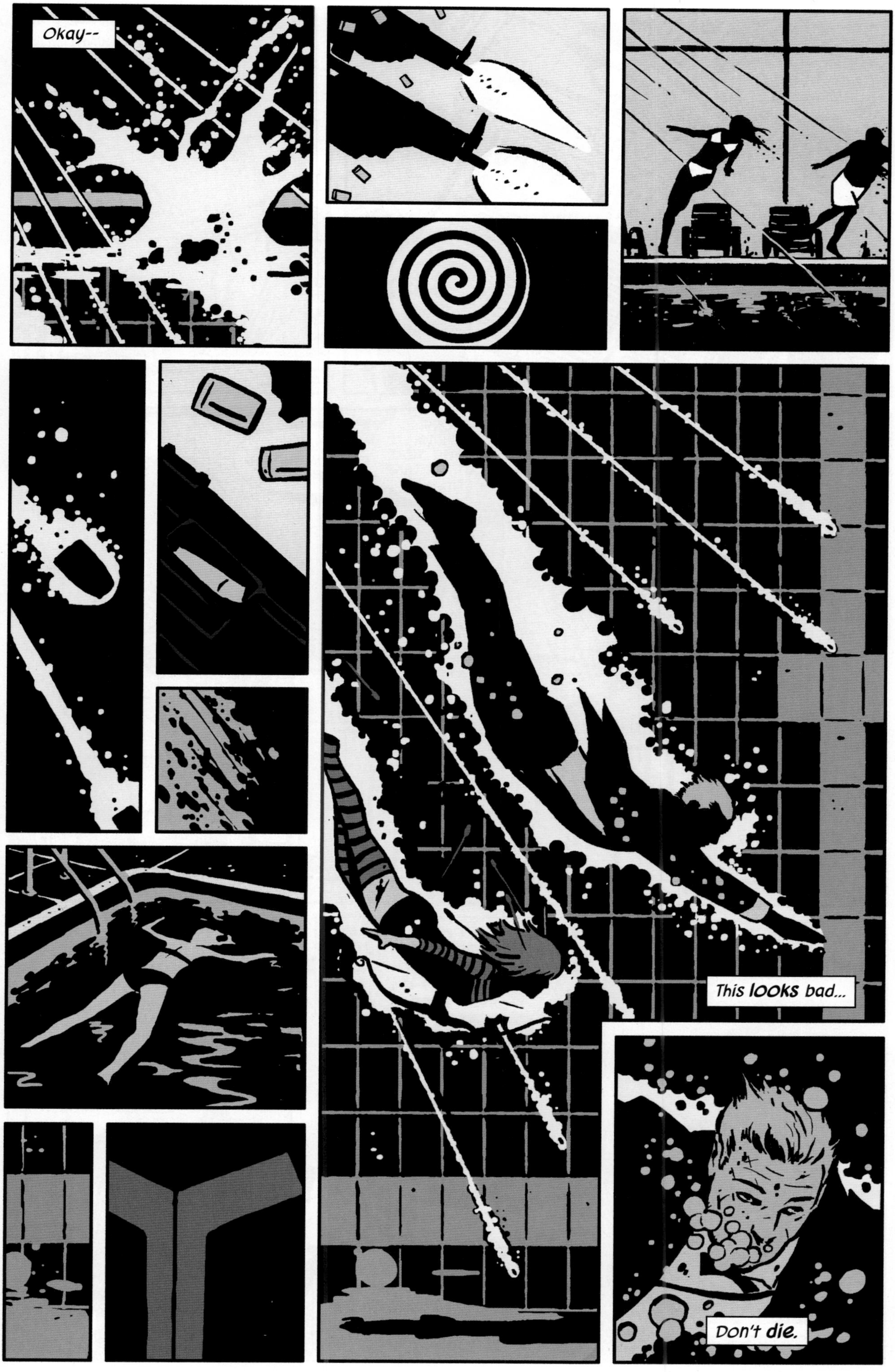
Okay--
This looks bad...
Don't die.

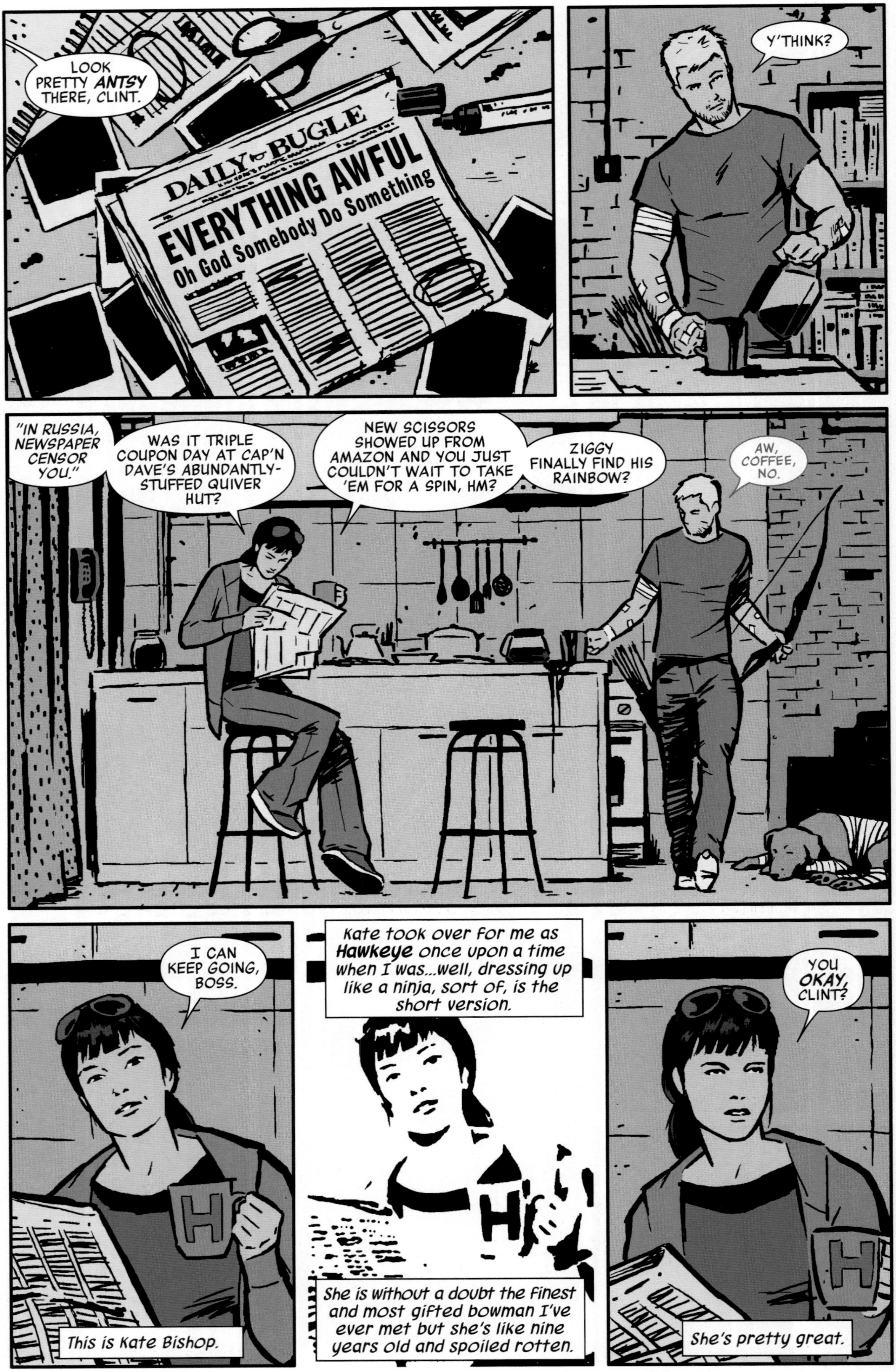

LOOK PRETTY ANTSY THERE, CLINT.
DAILY BUGLE
EVERYTHING AWFUL
Oh God Somebody Do Something
Y'THINK?
"IN RUSSIA, NEWSPAPER CENSOR YOU."
WAS IT TRIPLE COUPON DAY AT CAP'N DAVE'S ABUNDANTLY-STUFFED QUIVER HUT?
NEW SCISSORS SHOWED UP FROM AMAZON AND YOU JUST COULDN'T WAIT TO TAKE 'EM FOR A SPIN, HM?
ZIGGY FINALLY FIND HIS RAINBOW?
AW, COFFEE, NO.
I CAN KEEP GOING, BOSS.
This is Kate Bishop.
Kate took over for me as Hawkeye once upon a time when I was...well, dressing up like a ninja, sort of, is the short version.
She is without a doubt the finest and most gifted bowman I've ever met but she's like nine years old and spoiled rotten.
YOU OKAY, CLINT?
She's pretty great.

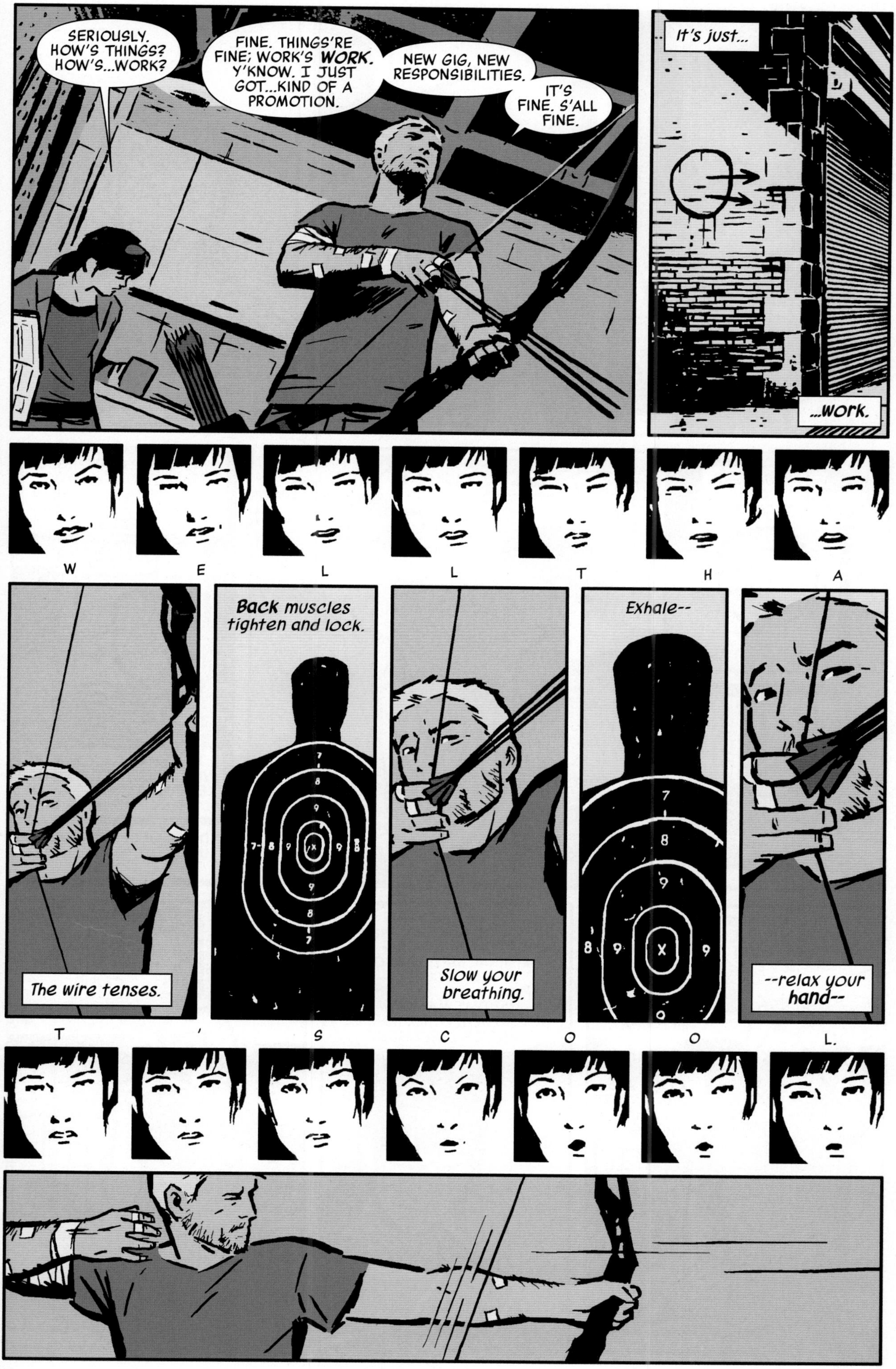

SERIOUSLY. HOW'S THINGS? HOW'S...WORK?
FINE. THINGS'RE FINE; WORK'S **WORK.** Y'KNOW. I JUST GOT...KIND OF A PROMOTION.
NEW GIG, NEW RESPONSIBILITIES.
IT'S FINE. S'ALL FINE.
It's just...
...work.
W E L L T H A
*The wire tenses.*
***Back*** *muscles tighten and lock.*
*Slow your breathing.*
*Exhale--*
*--relax your* ***hand--***
T ' S C O O L.

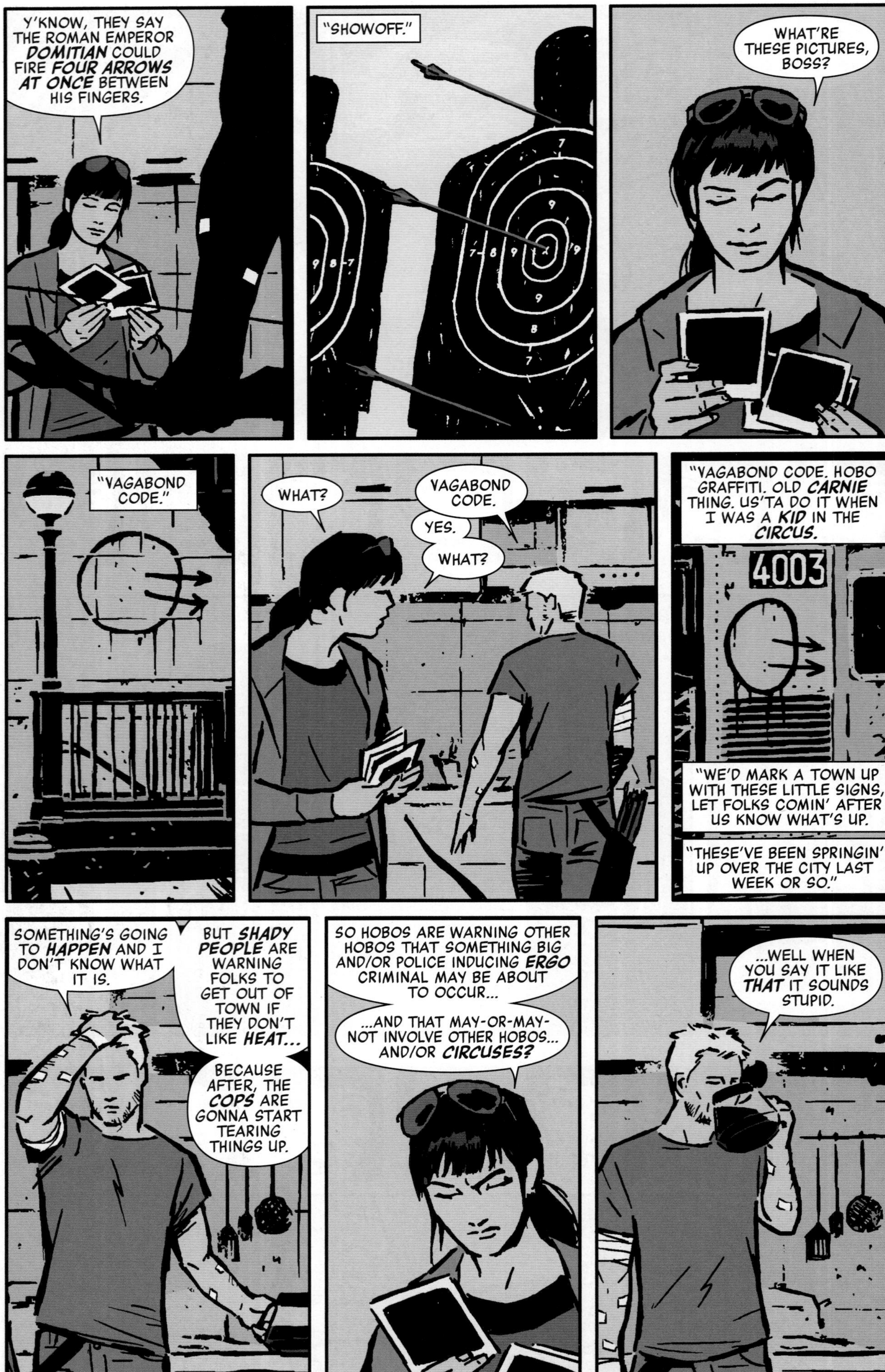
Y'KNOW, THEY SAY THE ROMAN EMPEROR DOMITIAN COULD FIRE FOUR ARROWS AT ONCE BETWEEN HIS FINGERS.
"SHOWOFF."
WHAT'RE THESE PICTURES, BOSS?
"VAGABOND CODE."
WHAT?
VAGABOND CODE.
YES.
WHAT?
"VAGABOND CODE. HOBO GRAFFITI. OLD CARNIE THING. US'TA DO IT WHEN I WAS A KID IN THE CIRCUS.
4003
"WE'D MARK A TOWN UP WITH THESE LITTLE SIGNS, LET FOLKS COMIN' AFTER US KNOW WHAT'S UP.
"THESE'VE BEEN SPRINGIN' UP OVER THE CITY LAST WEEK OR SO."
SOMETHING'S GOING TO HAPPEN AND I DON'T KNOW WHAT IT IS.
BUT SHADY PEOPLE ARE WARNING FOLKS TO GET OUT OF TOWN IF THEY DON'T LIKE HEAT...
BECAUSE AFTER, THE COPS ARE GONNA START TEARING THINGS UP.
SO HOBOS ARE WARNING OTHER HOBOS THAT SOMETHING BIG AND/OR POLICE INDUCING ERGO CRIMINAL MAY BE ABOUT TO OCCUR...
...AND THAT MAY-OR-MAY-NOT INVOLVE OTHER HOBOS... AND/OR CIRCUSES?
...WELL WHEN YOU SAY IT LIKE THAT IT SOUNDS STUPID.

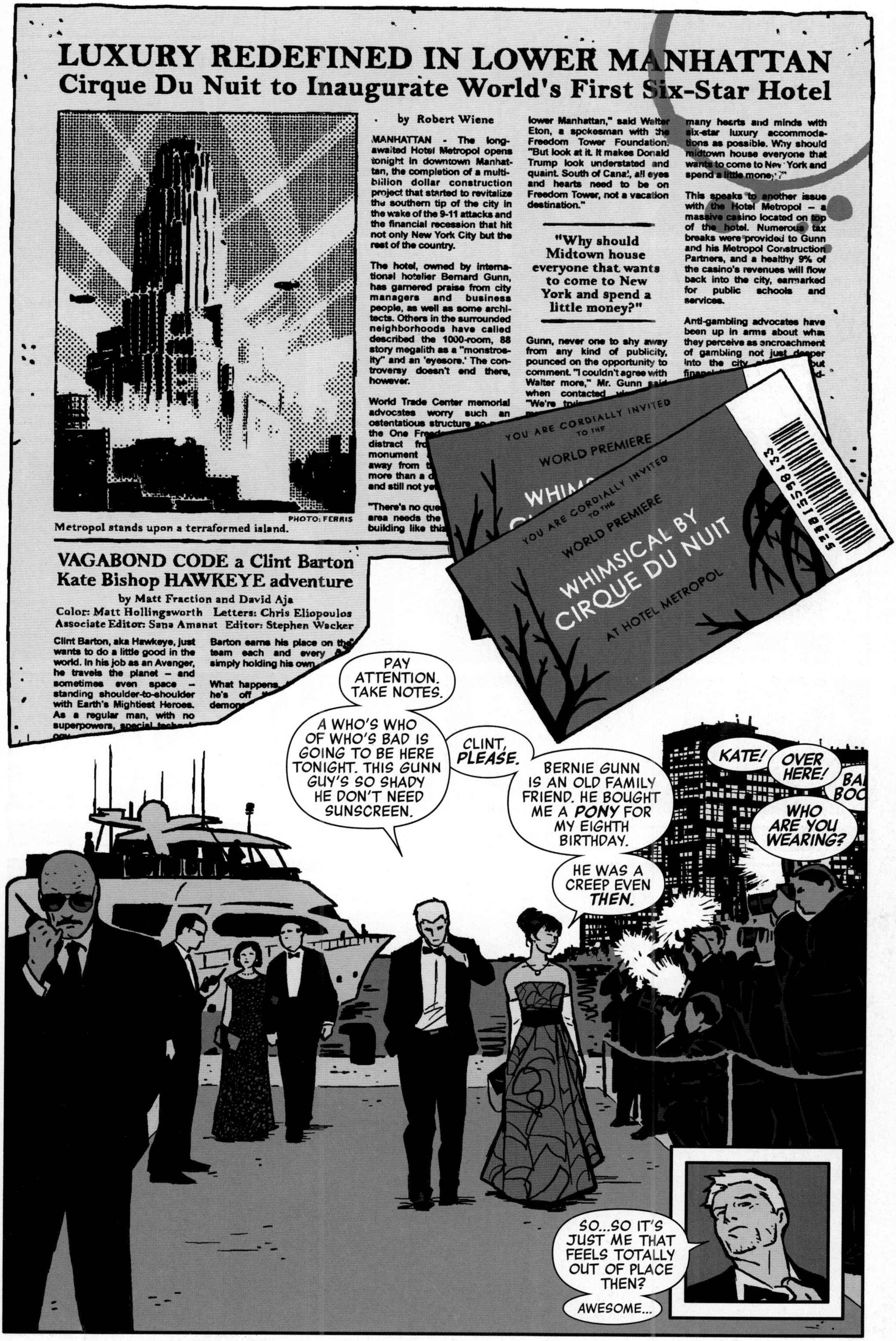

# LUXURY REDEFINED IN LOWER MANHATTAN
## Cirque Du Nuit to Inaugurate World's First Six-Star Hotel

by Robert Wiene

MANHATTAN - The long-awaited Hotel Metropol opens tonight in downtown Manhattan, the completion of a multi-billion dollar construction project that started to revitalize the southern tip of the city in the wake of the 9-11 attacks and the financial recession that hit not only New York City but the rest of the country.

The hotel, owned by international hotelier Bernard Gunn, has garnered praise from city managers and business people, as well as some architects. Others in the surrounded neighborhoods have called described the 1000-room, 88 story megalith as a "monstrosity" and an 'eyesore.' The controversy doesn't end there, however.

World Trade Center memorial advocates worry such an ostentatious structure so n the One Freed distract fro monument away from t more than a d and still not ye

"There's no que area needs the building like this

lower Manhattan," said Walter Eton, a spokesman with the Freedom Tower Foundation. "But look at it. It makes Donald Trump look understated and quaint. South of Canal, all eyes and hearts need to be on Freedom Tower, not a vacation destination."

"Why should Midtown house everyone that wants to come to New York and spend a little money?"

Gunn, never one to shy away from any kind of publicity, pounced on the opportunity to comment. "I couldn't agree with Walter more," Mr. Gunn said when contacted "We're tr

many hearts and minds with six-star luxury accommodations as possible. Why should midtown house everyone that wants to come to New York and spend a little money?"

This speaks to another issue with the Hotel Metropol – a massive casino located on top of the hotel. Numerous tax breaks were provided to Gunn and his Metropol Construction Partners, and a healthy 9% of the casino's revenues will flow back into the city, earmarked for public schools and services.

Anti-gambling advocates have been up in arms about what they perceive as encroachment of gambling not just deeper into the city but financ d-

PHOTO: FERRIS

Metropol stands upon a terraformed island.

## VAGABOND CODE a Clint Barton Kate Bishop HAWKEYE adventure

by Matt Fraction and David Aja

Color: Matt Hollingsworth Letters: Chris Eliopoulos

Associate Editor: Sana Amanat Editor: Stephen Wacker

Clint Barton, aka Hawkeye, just wants to do a little good in the world. In his job as an Avenger, he travels the planet – and sometimes even space – standing shoulder-to-shoulder with Earth's Mightiest Heroes. As a regular man, with no superpowers, special techn

Barton earns his place on the team each and every simply holding his own.

What happens he's off demons


YOU ARE CORDIALLY INVITED TO THE
WORLD PREMIERE
WHIMSICAL BY CIRQUE DU NUIT
AT HOTEL METROPOL
PAY ATTENTION. TAKE NOTES.
A WHO'S WHO OF WHO'S BAD IS GOING TO BE HERE TONIGHT. THIS GUNN GUY'S SO SHADY HE DON'T NEED SUNSCREEN.
CLINT, PLEASE.
BERNIE GUNN IS AN OLD FAMILY FRIEND. HE BOUGHT ME A PONY FOR MY EIGHTH BIRTHDAY.
HE WAS A CREEP EVEN THEN.
KATE!
OVER HERE!
WHO ARE YOU WEARING?
SO...SO IT'S JUST ME THAT FEELS TOTALLY OUT OF PLACE THEN?
AWESOME...

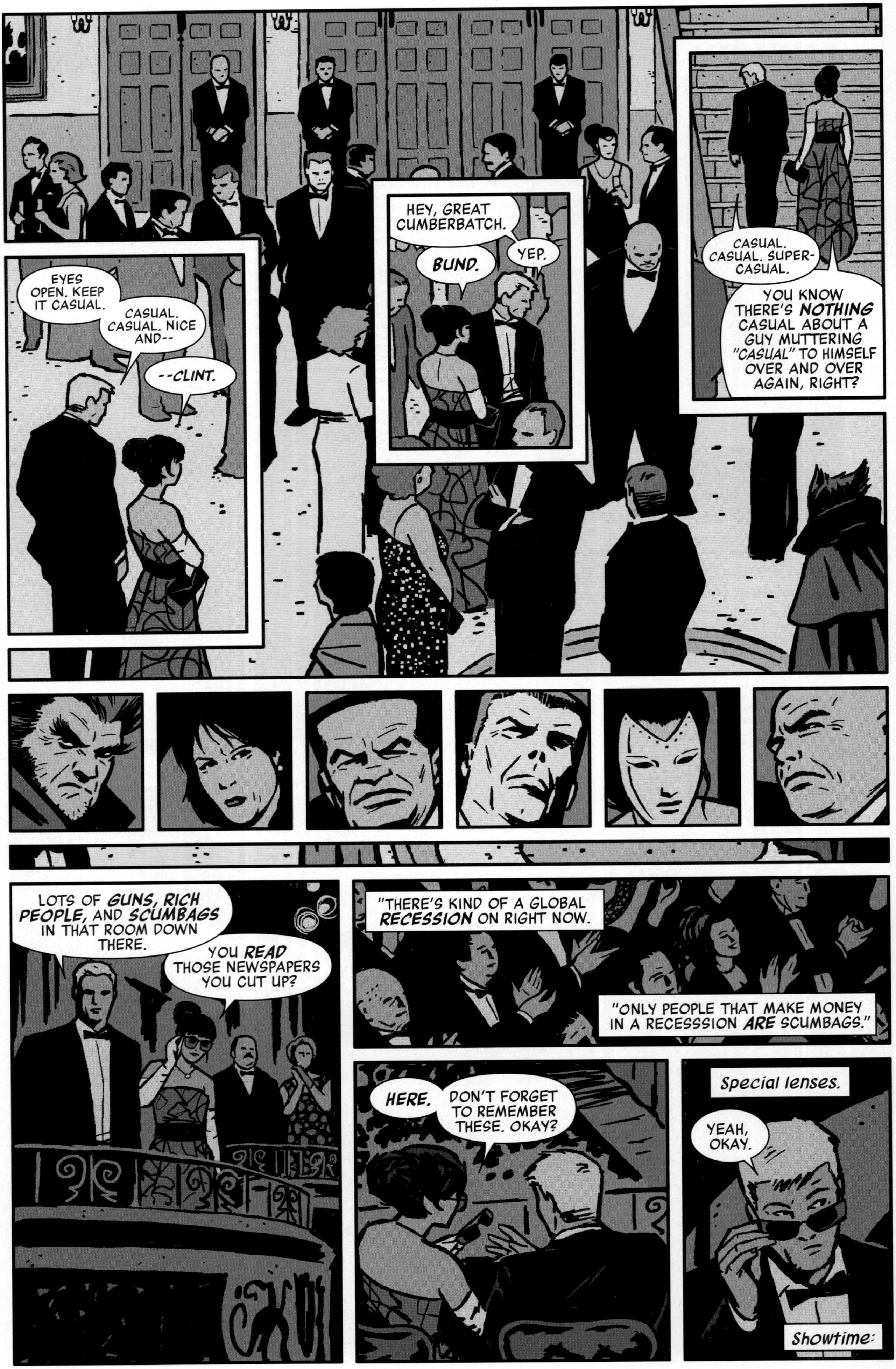

EYES OPEN. KEEP IT CASUAL.
CASUAL. CASUAL. NICE AND--
--CLINT.
HEY, GREAT CUMBERBATCH.
BUND.
YEP.
CASUAL. CASUAL. SUPER-CASUAL.
YOU KNOW THERE'S NOTHING CASUAL ABOUT A GUY MUTTERING "CASUAL" TO HIMSELF OVER AND OVER AGAIN, RIGHT?
LOTS OF GUNS, RICH PEOPLE, AND SCUMBAGS IN THAT ROOM DOWN THERE.
YOU READ THOSE NEWSPAPERS YOU CUT UP?
"THERE'S KIND OF A GLOBAL RECESSION ON RIGHT NOW.
"ONLY PEOPLE THAT MAKE MONEY IN A RECESSSION ARE SCUMBAGS."
HERE.
DON'T FORGET TO REMEMBER THESE. OKAY?
Special lenses.
YEAH, OKAY.
Showtime:

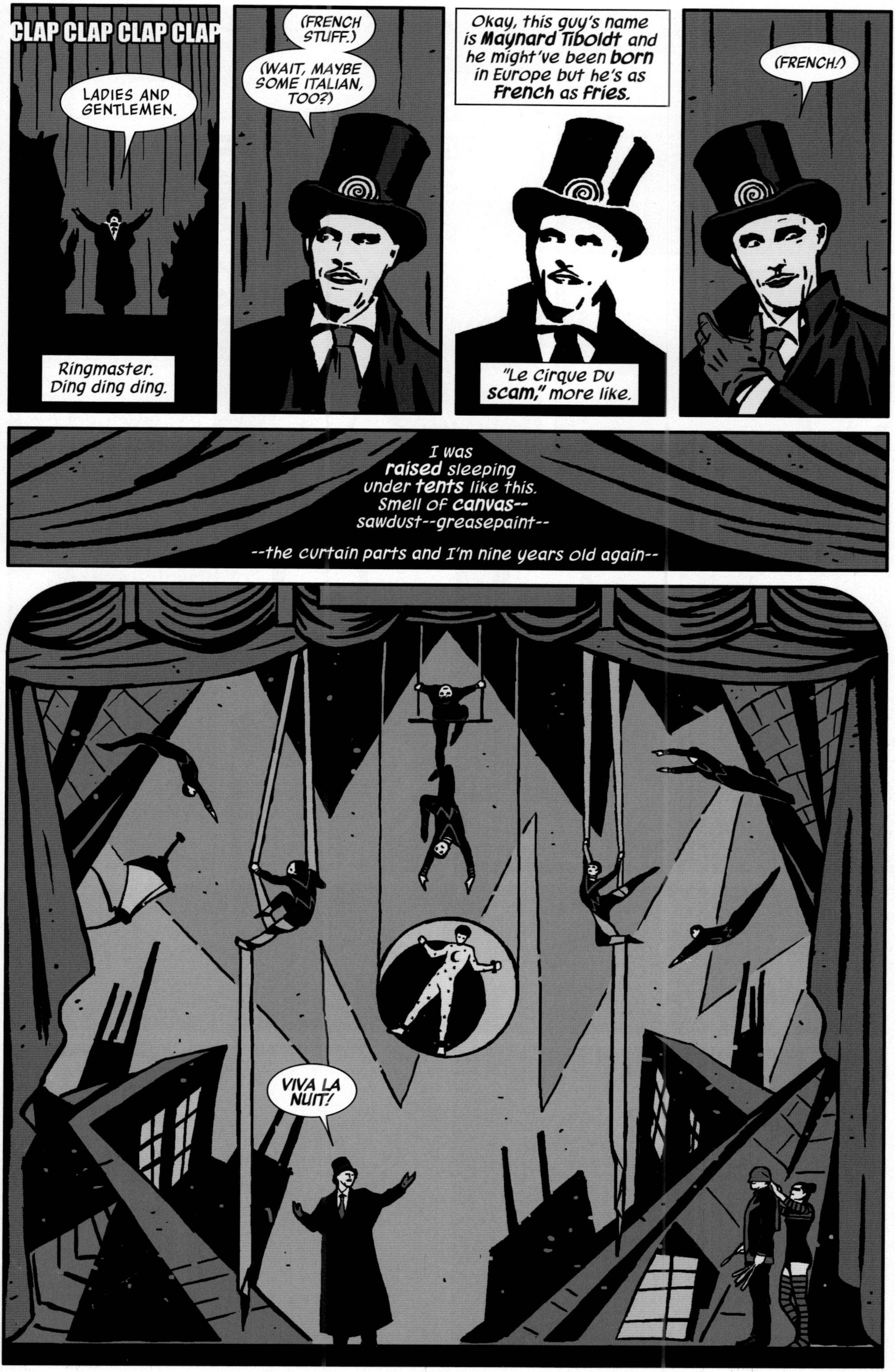
CLAP CLAP CLAP CLAP
LADIES AND GENTLEMEN.
Ringmaster. Ding ding ding.
(FRENCH STUFF.)
(WAIT, MAYBE SOME ITALIAN, TOO?)
Okay, this guy's name is Maynard Tiboldt and he might've been born in Europe but he's as French as fries.
"Le Cirque Du scam," more like.
(FRENCH!)
I was raised sleeping under tents like this. Smell of canvas-- sawdust--greasepaint--
--the curtain parts and I'm nine years old again--
VIVA LA NUIT!

There's a **thing** that happens when a **pro** is around the work of another pro.

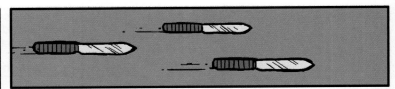

You spot the style...

...even without a signature.

I know before the knives hit the boards the face of the man that **taught** this guy.

This guy--and me-- we share the same **mentor**. The same man that taught this guy how to throw...

MERCI.

...taught me how to be a living **weapon**.

Students of the **Swordsman**.

And it was the Swordsman that taught me how to **steal**.

MERCI. MERCI BEAUCOUP.

THEY'RE THIEVES. THEY'RE ALL @#$%!€ING THIEVES.

MERCI, MERCI.

(SOMETHING FRENCH.)

Phonies. All of 'em.

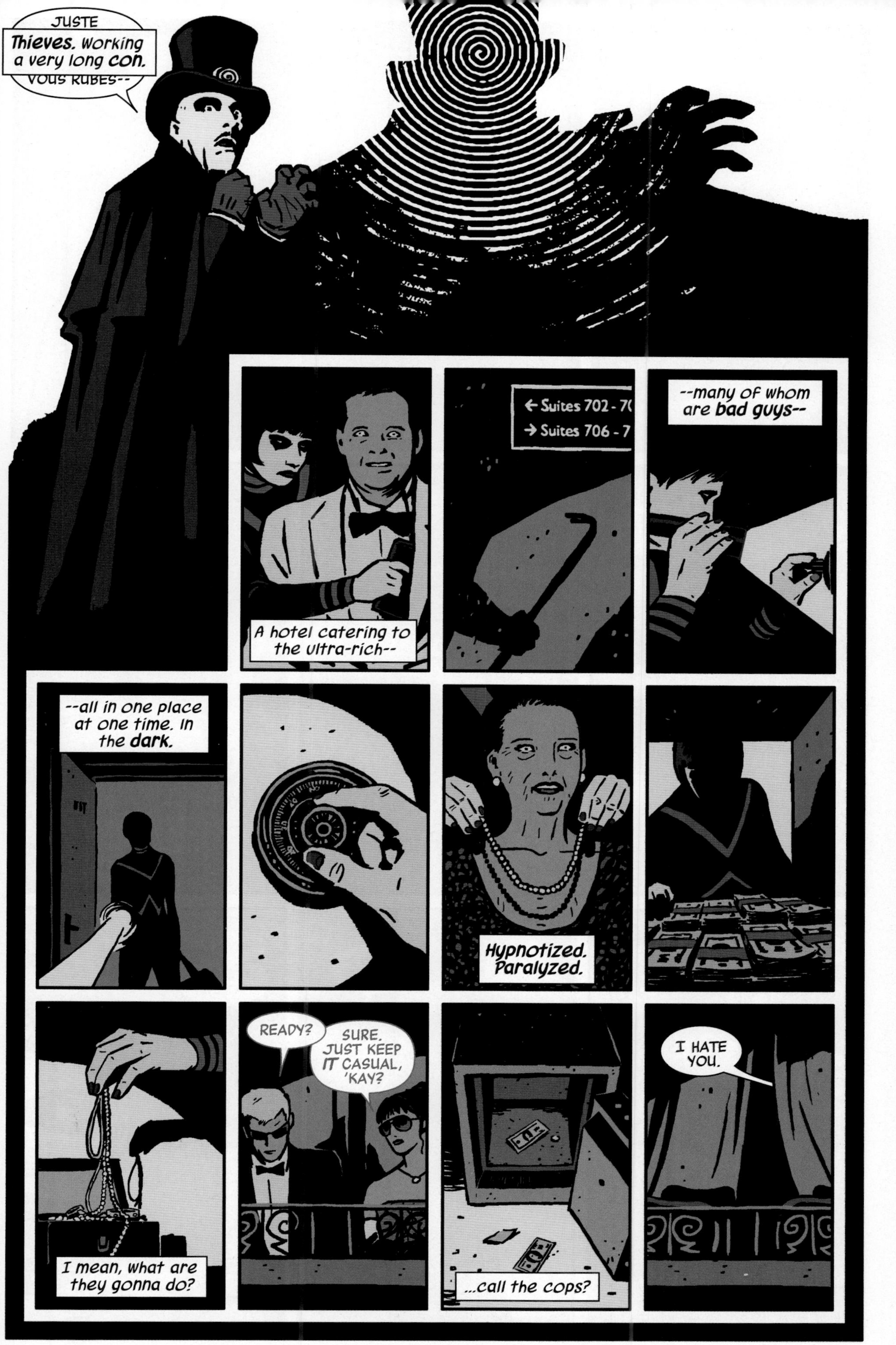
JUSTE
Thieves. Working a very long con.
VOUS RUBES--
A hotel catering to the ultra-rich--
← Suites 702 - 70
→ Suites 706 - 7
--many of whom are bad guys--
--all in one place at one time. In the dark.
Hypnotized. Paralyzed.
I mean, what are they gonna do?
READY?
SURE. JUST KEEP IT CASUAL, 'KAY?
...call the cops?
I HATE YOU.

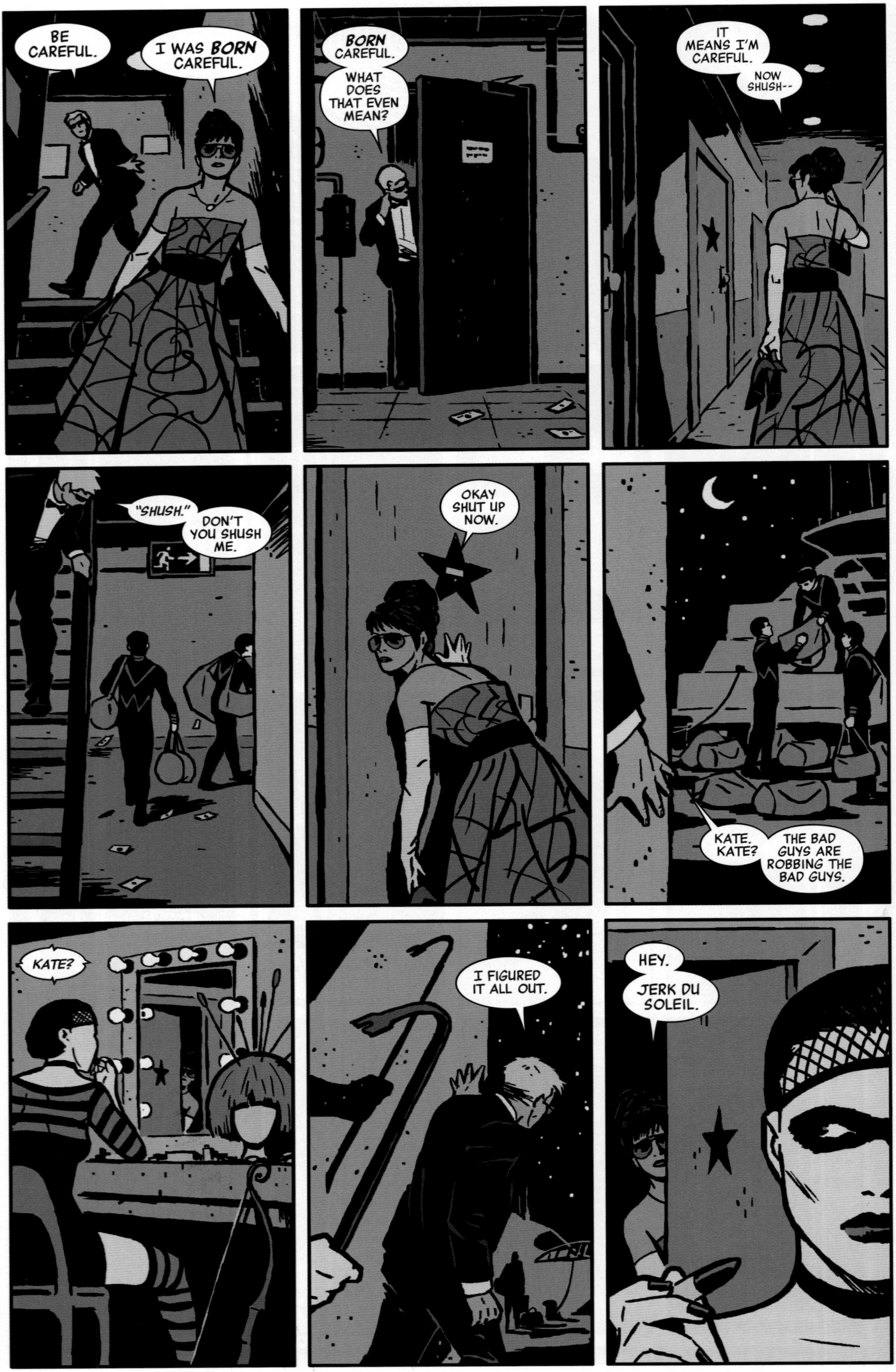
BE CAREFUL.
I WAS BORN CAREFUL.
BORN CAREFUL.
WHAT DOES THAT EVEN MEAN?
IT MEANS I'M CAREFUL.
NOW SHUSH--
"SHUSH."
DON'T YOU SHUSH ME.
OKAY SHUT UP NOW.
KATE. KATE?
THE BAD GUYS ARE ROBBING THE BAD GUYS.
KATE?
I FIGURED IT ALL OUT.
HEY.
JERK DU SOLEIL.

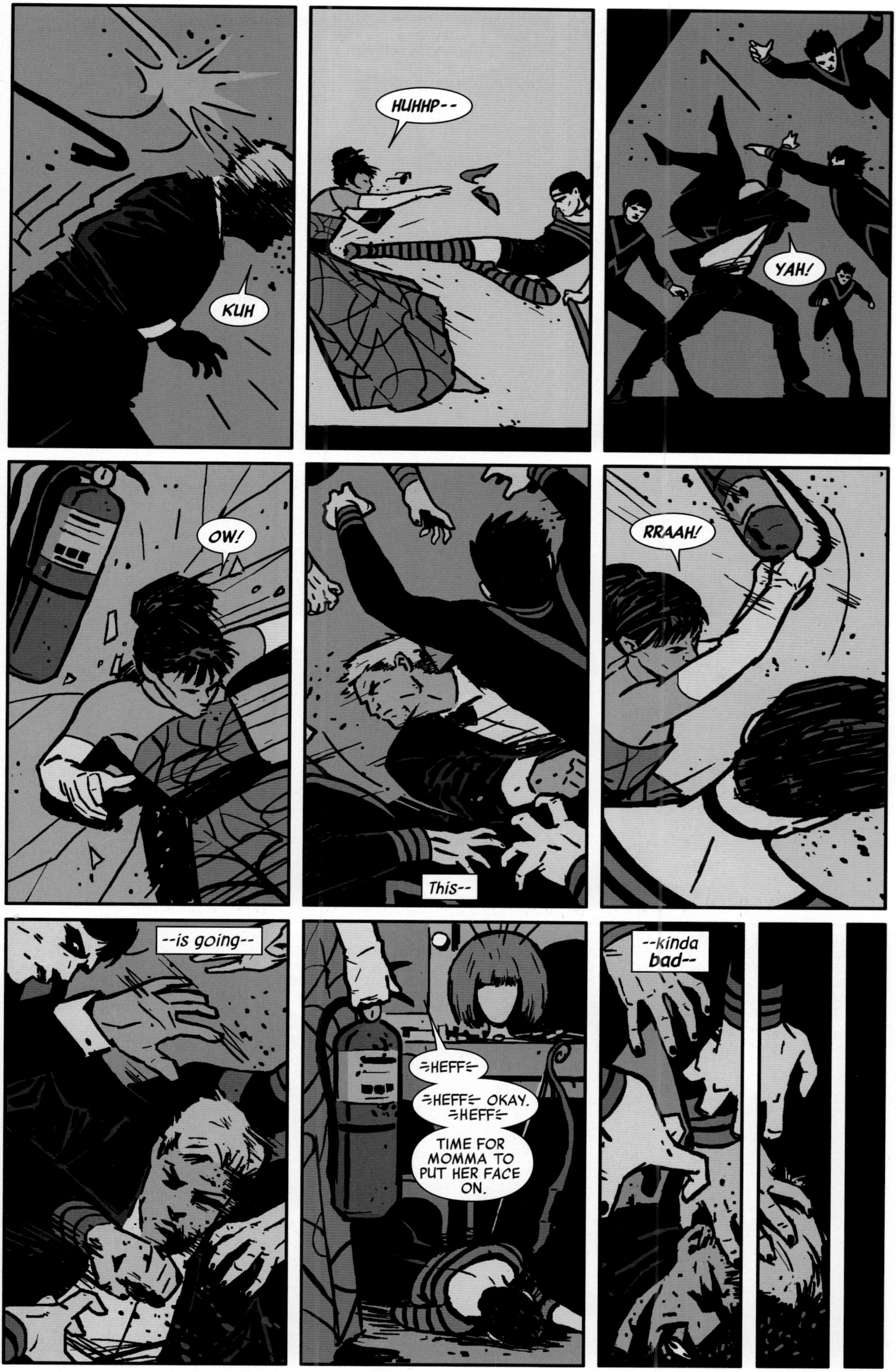
KUH
HUHHP--
YAH!
OW!
This--
RRAAH!
--is going--
≡HEFF≡
≡HEFF≡ OKAY. ≡HEFF≡
TIME FOR MOMMA TO PUT HER FACE ON.
--kinda bad--

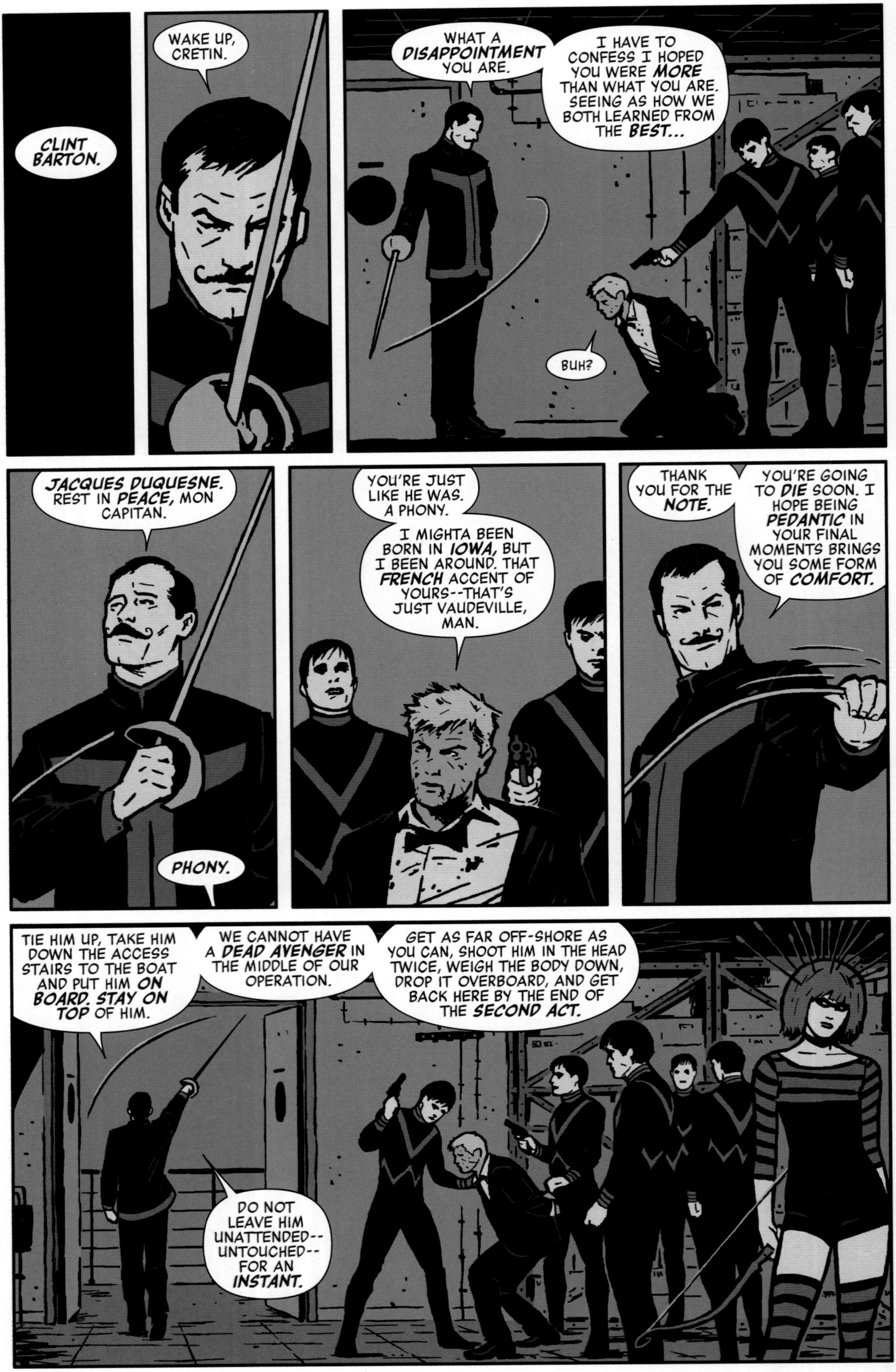
CLINT BARTON.
WAKE UP, CRETIN.
WHAT A DISAPPOINTMENT YOU ARE.
I HAVE TO CONFESS I HOPED YOU WERE MORE THAN WHAT YOU ARE. SEEING AS HOW WE BOTH LEARNED FROM THE BEST...
BUH?
JACQUES DUQUESNE. REST IN PEACE, MON CAPITAN.
PHONY.
YOU'RE JUST LIKE HE WAS. A PHONY.
I MIGHTA BEEN BORN IN IOWA, BUT I BEEN AROUND. THAT FRENCH ACCENT OF YOURS--THAT'S JUST VAUDEVILLE, MAN.
THANK YOU FOR THE NOTE.
YOU'RE GOING TO DIE SOON. I HOPE BEING PEDANTIC IN YOUR FINAL MOMENTS BRINGS YOU SOME FORM OF COMFORT.
TIE HIM UP, TAKE HIM DOWN THE ACCESS STAIRS TO THE BOAT AND PUT HIM ON BOARD. STAY ON TOP OF HIM.
WE CANNOT HAVE A DEAD AVENGER IN THE MIDDLE OF OUR OPERATION.
GET AS FAR OFF-SHORE AS YOU CAN, SHOOT HIM IN THE HEAD TWICE, WEIGH THE BODY DOWN, DROP IT OVERBOARD, AND GET BACK HERE BY THE END OF THE SECOND ACT.
DO NOT LEAVE HIM UNATTENDED--UNTOUCHED--FOR AN INSTANT.

Did I ever tell you why I love Kate Bishop?

NOPE.

I mean, look at her.

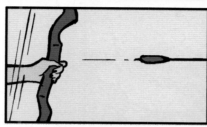

KATIE...

BWWOOOF

KATIE--!

She's perfect.

THANK YOU--

KILL 'EM ALL!

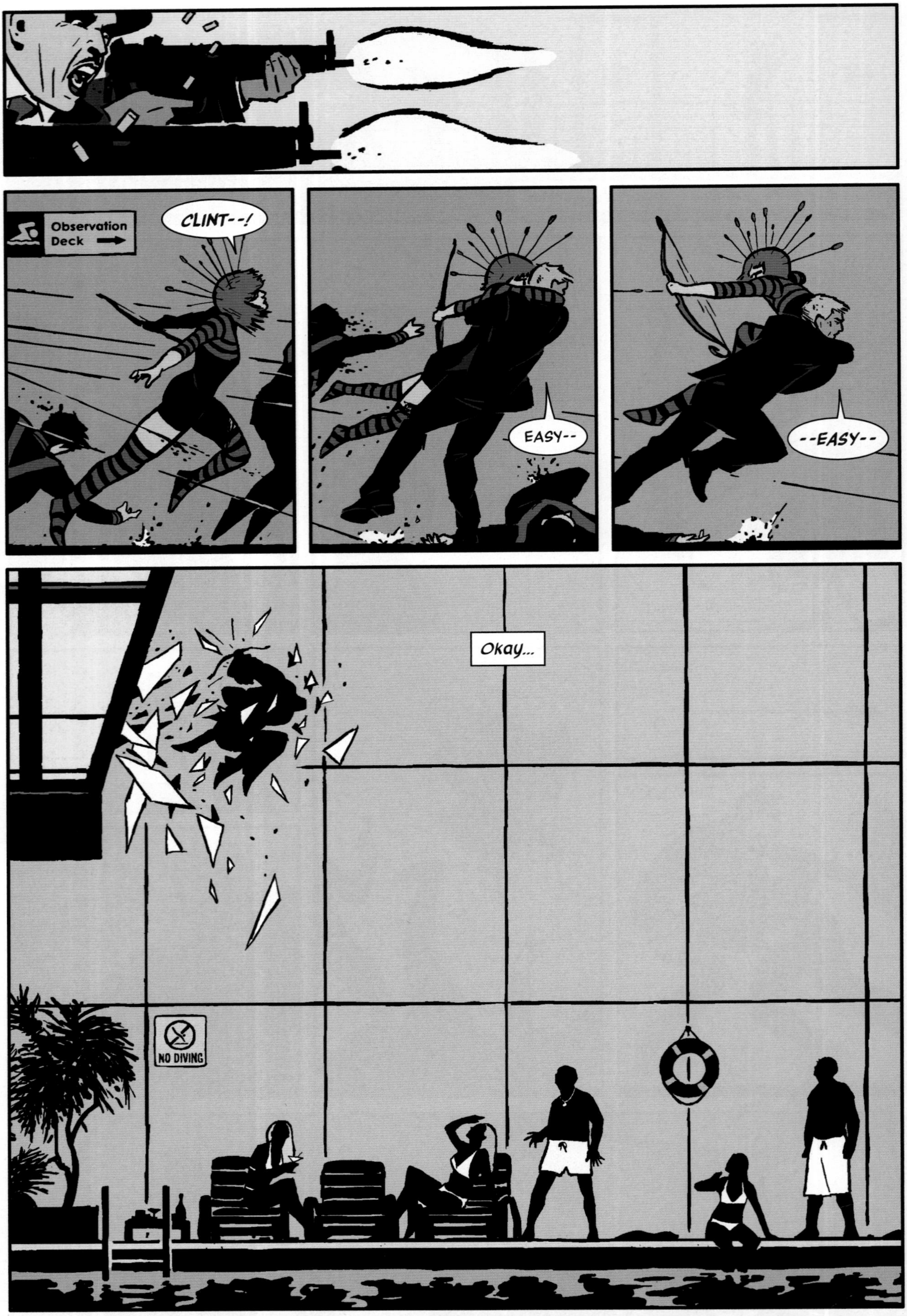
Observation Deck
CLINT--!
EASY--
--EASY--
Okay...
NO DIVING
...this looks bad.

Katie, don't you die down here.

I'll never **forgive** myself if you do.

CLINT. SHUSH.

GAHHHHHHHHHH THAT **SUCKED**.

The wire tenses.

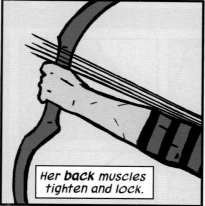

Her **back** muscles tighten and lock.

She slows her **breathing**...

...exhales...

And **just** as she relaxes her hand--

SUCK IT, DOMITIAN.

See?

She's perfect.

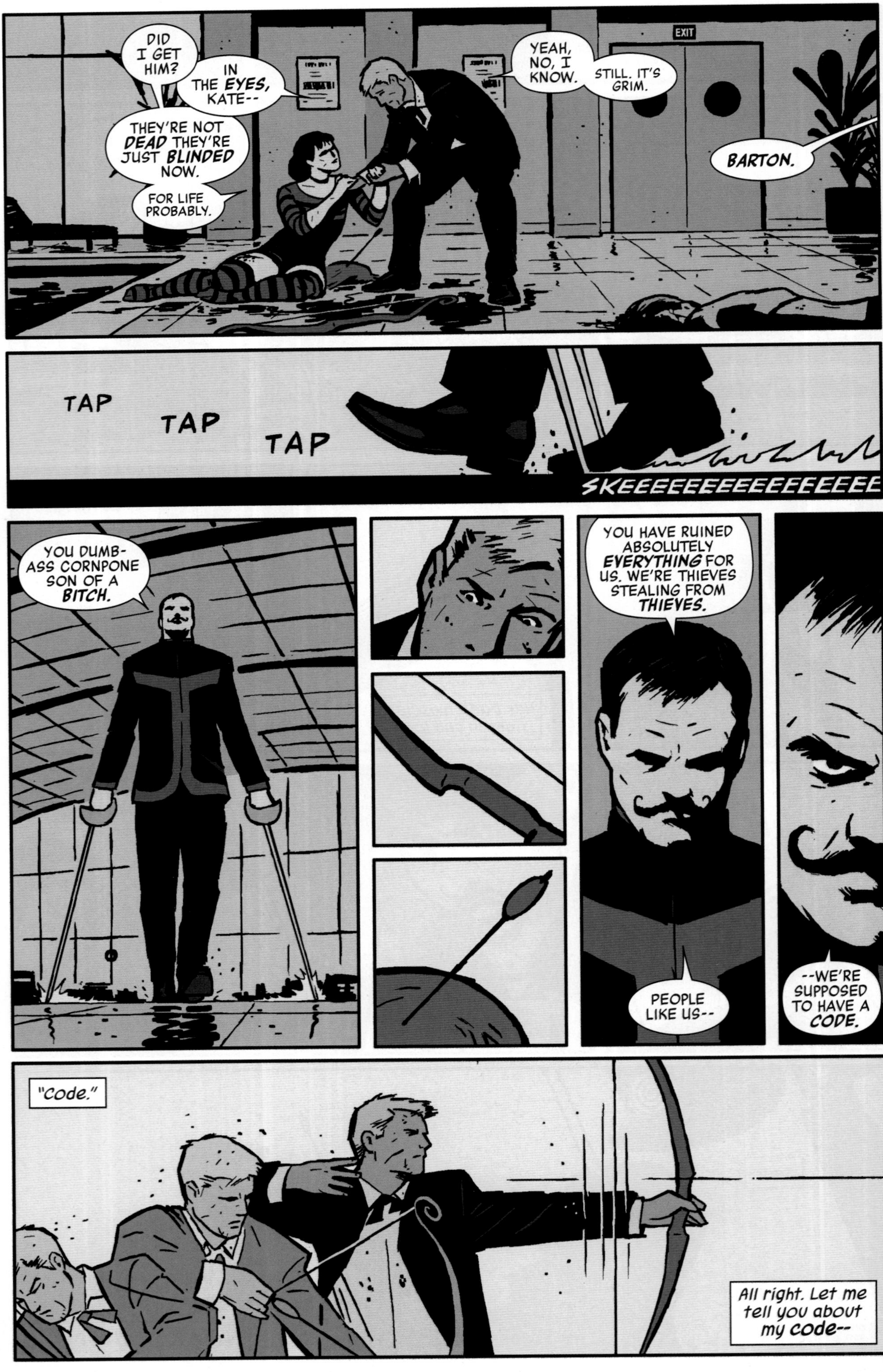
EXIT
DID I GET HIM?
IN THE EYES, KATE--
THEY'RE NOT DEAD THEY'RE JUST BLINDED NOW.
FOR LIFE PROBABLY.
YEAH, NO, I KNOW.
STILL. IT'S GRIM.
BARTON.
TAP
TAP
TAP
SKEEEEEEEEEEEEEEEEE
YOU DUMB-ASS CORNPONE SON OF A BITCH.
YOU HAVE RUINED ABSOLUTELY EVERYTHING FOR US. WE'RE THIEVES STEALING FROM THIEVES.
PEOPLE LIKE US--
--WE'RE SUPPOSED TO HAVE A CODE.
"Code."
All right. Let me tell you about my code--

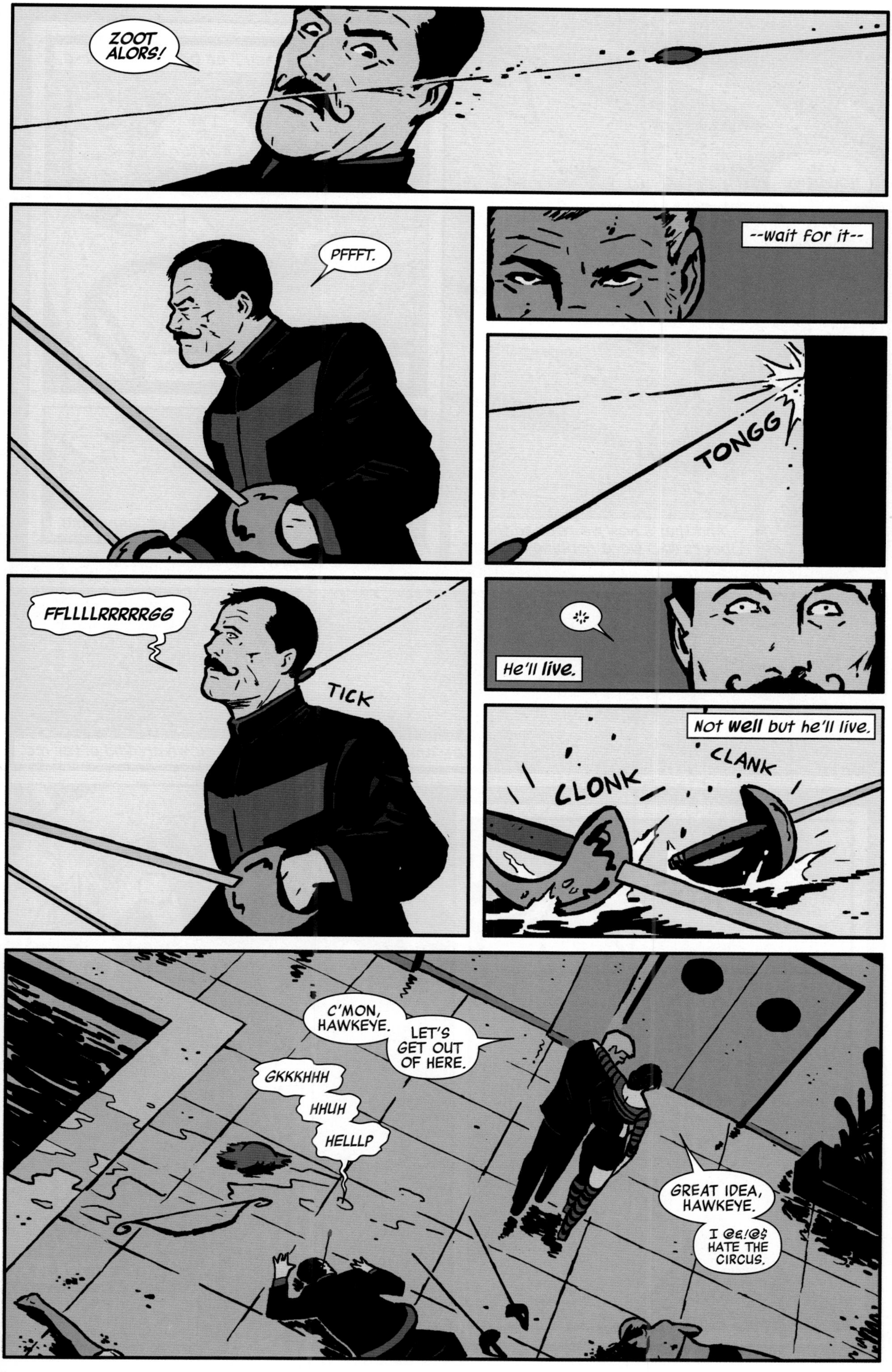
ZOOT ALORS!
PFFFT.
--wait for it--
TONGG
FFLLLLRRRRRGG
TICK
He'll **live.**
Not **well** but he'll live.
CLONK
CLANK
C'MON, HAWKEYE.
LET'S GET OUT OF HERE.
GKKKHHH
HHUH
HELLLP
GREAT IDEA, HAWKEYE.
I @&!@$ HATE THE CIRCUS.

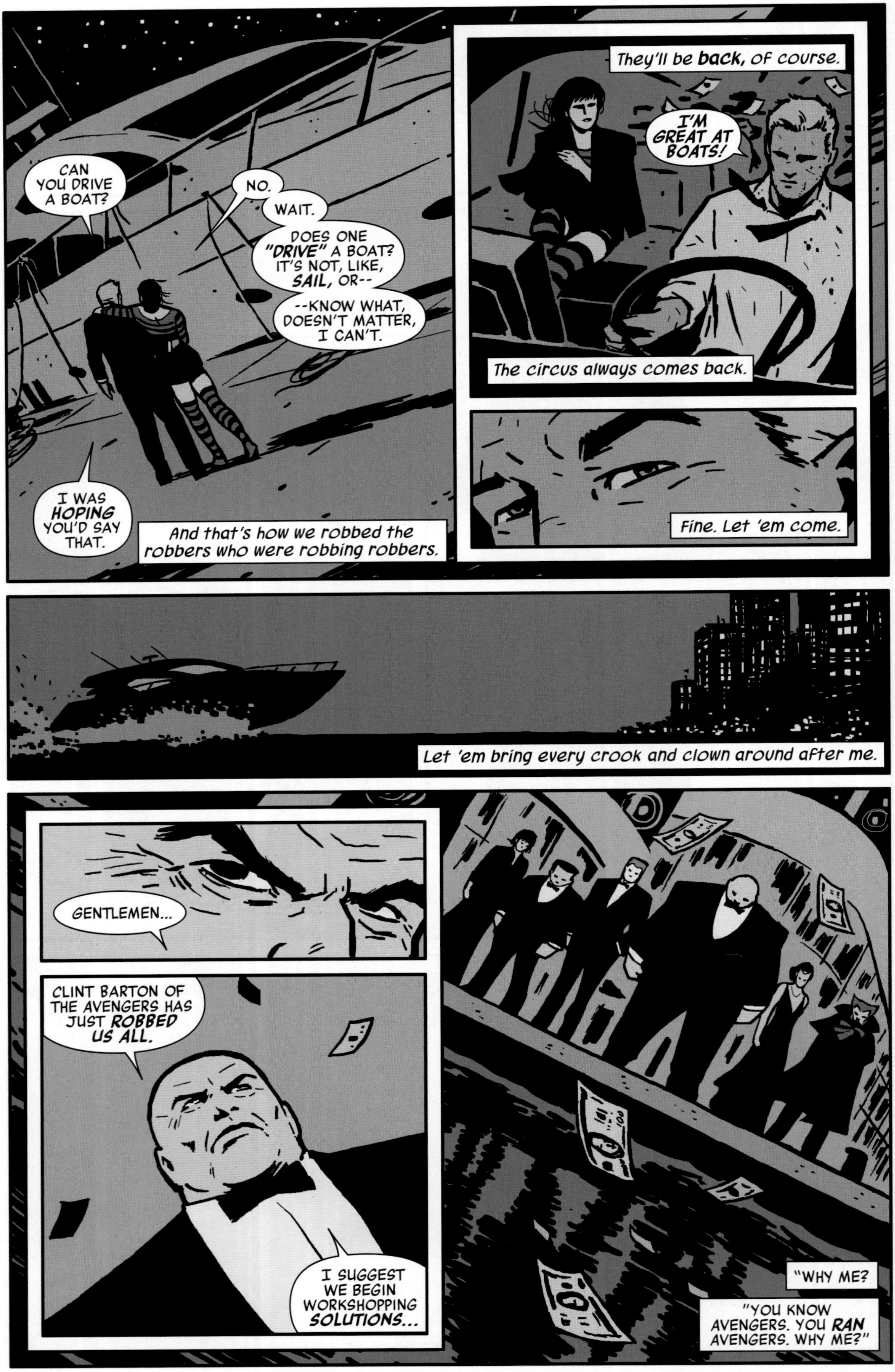
CAN YOU DRIVE A BOAT?
NO.
WAIT.
DOES ONE "DRIVE" A BOAT? IT'S NOT, LIKE, SAIL, OR--
--KNOW WHAT, DOESN'T MATTER, I CAN'T.
I WAS HOPING YOU'D SAY THAT.
And that's how we robbed the robbers who were robbing robbers.
They'll be back, of course.
I'M GREAT AT BOATS!
The circus always comes back.
Fine. Let 'em come.
Let 'em bring every crook and clown around after me.
GENTLEMEN...
CLINT BARTON OF THE AVENGERS HAS JUST ROBBED US ALL.
I SUGGEST WE BEGIN WORKSHOPPING SOLUTIONS...
"WHY ME?
"YOU KNOW AVENGERS. YOU RAN AVENGERS. WHY ME?"

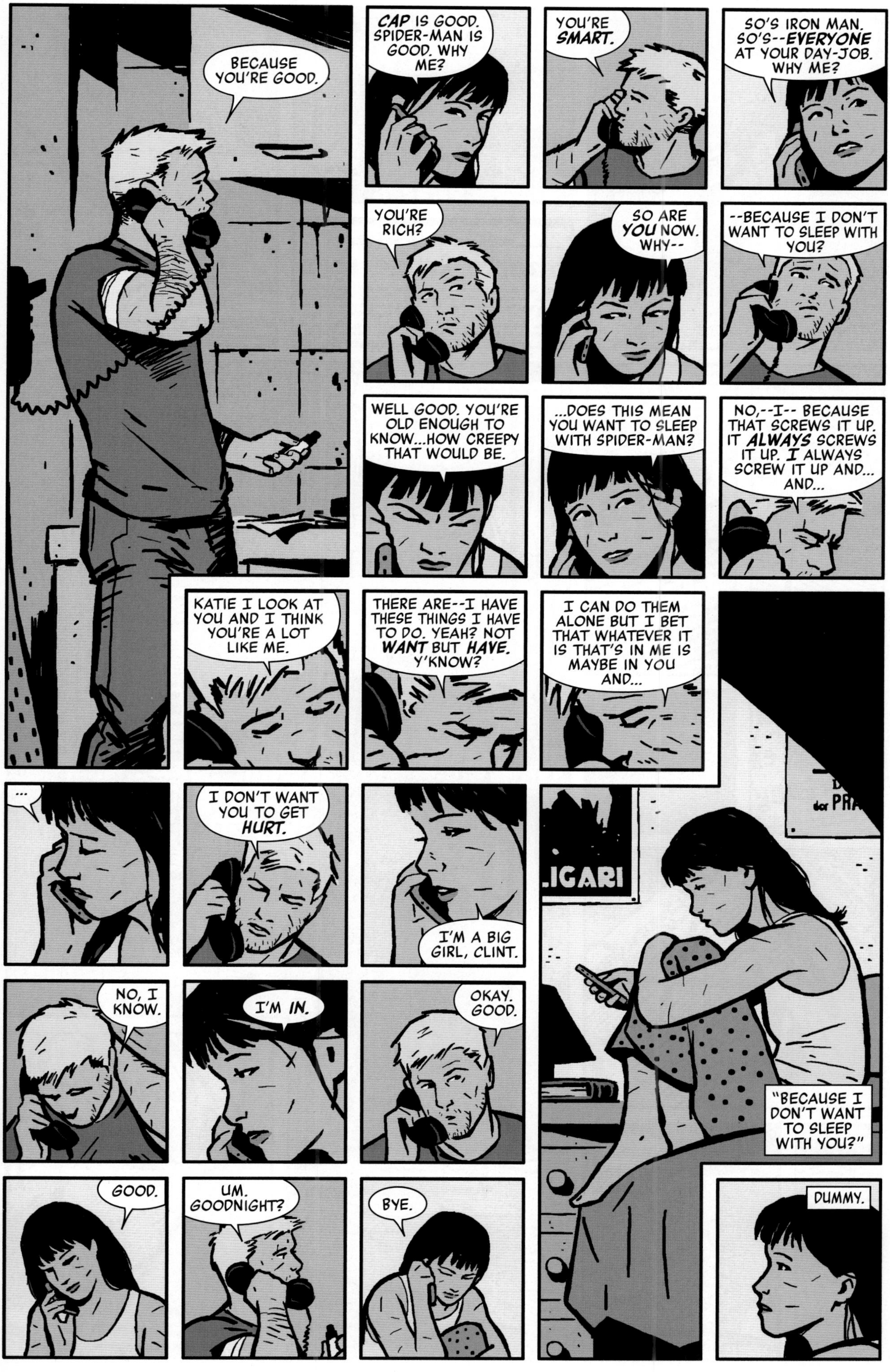
BECAUSE YOU'RE GOOD.
CAP IS GOOD. SPIDER-MAN IS GOOD. WHY ME?
YOU'RE SMART.
SO'S IRON MAN. SO'S--EVERYONE AT YOUR DAY-JOB. WHY ME?
YOU'RE RICH?
SO ARE YOU NOW. WHY--
--BECAUSE I DON'T WANT TO SLEEP WITH YOU?
WELL GOOD. YOU'RE OLD ENOUGH TO KNOW...HOW CREEPY THAT WOULD BE.
...DOES THIS MEAN YOU WANT TO SLEEP WITH SPIDER-MAN?
NO,--I-- BECAUSE THAT SCREWS IT UP. IT ALWAYS SCREWS IT UP. I ALWAYS SCREW IT UP AND... AND...
KATIE I LOOK AT YOU AND I THINK YOU'RE A LOT LIKE ME.
THERE ARE--I HAVE THESE THINGS I HAVE TO DO. YEAH? NOT WANT BUT HAVE. Y'KNOW?
I CAN DO THEM ALONE BUT I BET THAT WHATEVER IT IS THAT'S IN ME IS MAYBE IN YOU AND...
...
I DON'T WANT YOU TO GET HURT.
I'M A BIG GIRL, CLINT.
NO, I KNOW.
I'M IN.
OKAY. GOOD.
"BECAUSE I DON'T WANT TO SLEEP WITH YOU?"
GOOD.
UM. GOODNIGHT?
BYE.
DUMMY.

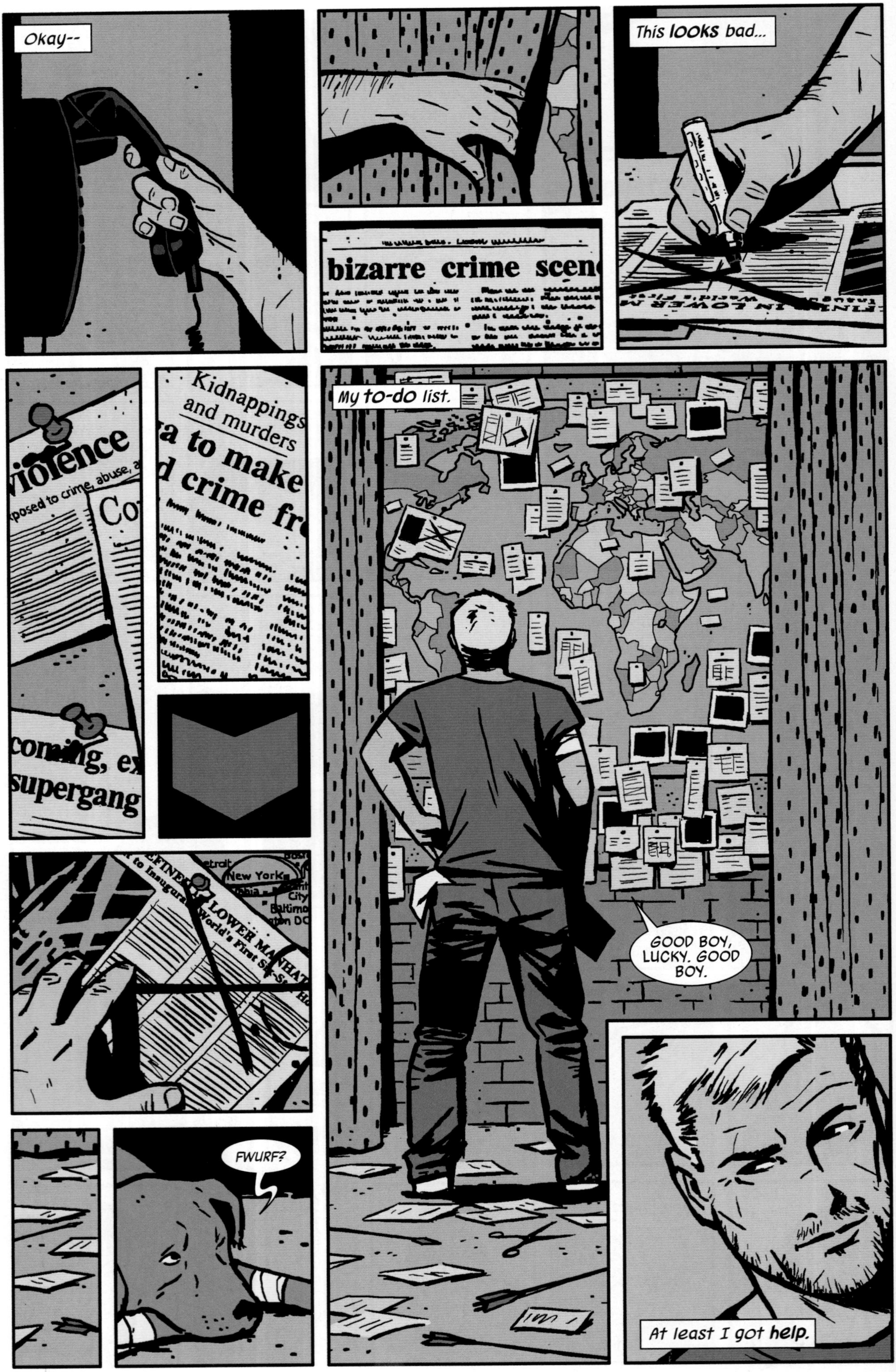
Okay--
bizarre crime scen
This looks bad...
violence
posed to crime, abuse, a
coming, ex
supergang
Kidnappings
and murders
a to make
d crime fr
New York
My to-do list.
GOOD BOY, LUCKY. GOOD BOY.
FWURF?
At least I got help.

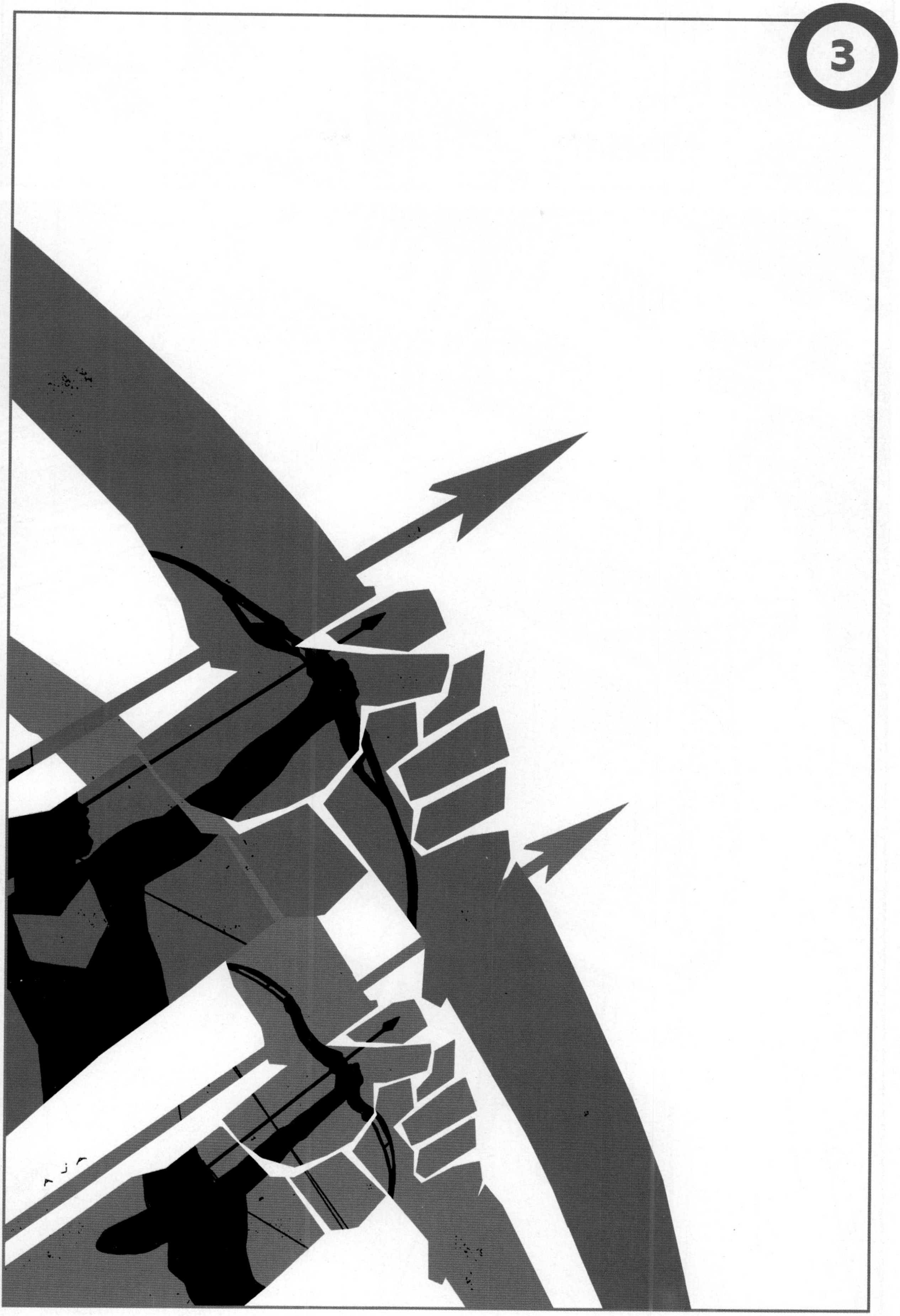
3

Okay...

This looks bad.

Really...

...really bad.

But believe it or not--

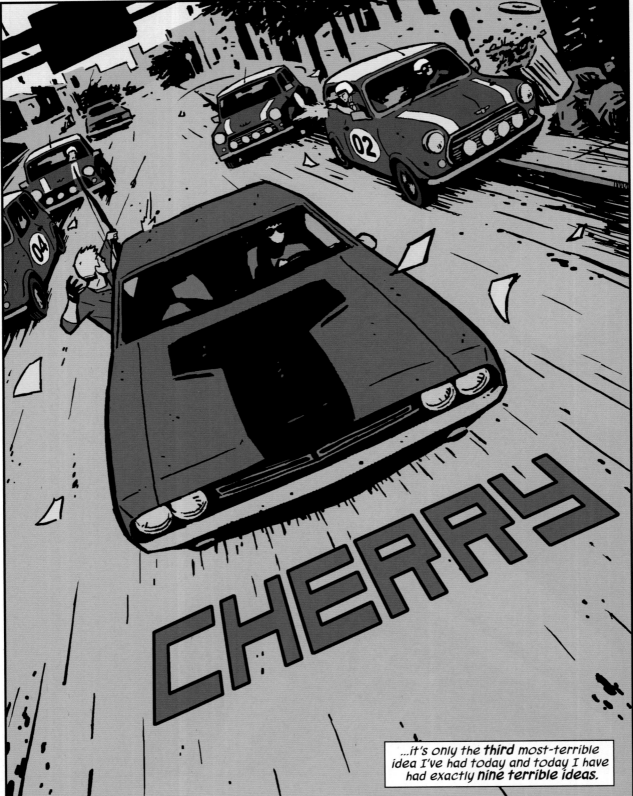

CHERRY

...it's only the **third** most-terrible idea I've had today and today I have had exactly **nine** terrible ideas.

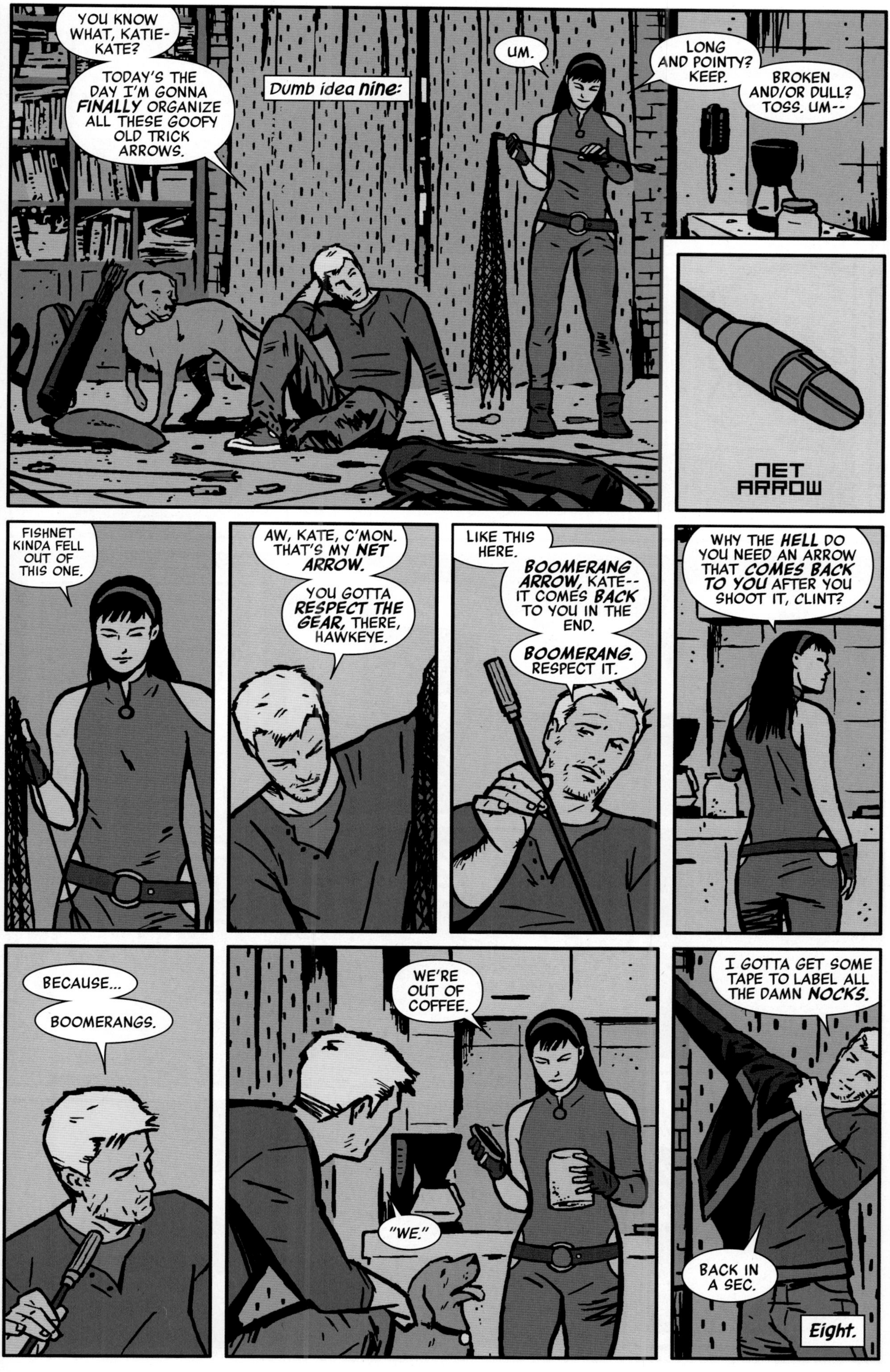

YOU KNOW WHAT, KATIE-KATE?
TODAY'S THE DAY I'M GONNA FINALLY ORGANIZE ALL THESE GOOFY OLD TRICK ARROWS.
Dumb idea nine:
UM.
LONG AND POINTY? KEEP.
BROKEN AND/OR DULL? TOSS. UM--
NET ARROW
FISHNET KINDA FELL OUT OF THIS ONE.
AW, KATE, C'MON. THAT'S MY NET ARROW.
YOU GOTTA RESPECT THE GEAR, THERE, HAWKEYE.
LIKE THIS HERE.
BOOMERANG ARROW, KATE--IT COMES BACK TO YOU IN THE END.
BOOMERANG. RESPECT IT.
WHY THE HELL DO YOU NEED AN ARROW THAT COMES BACK TO YOU AFTER YOU SHOOT IT, CLINT?
BECAUSE...
BOOMERANGS.
WE'RE OUT OF COFFEE.
"WE."
I GOTTA GET SOME TAPE TO LABEL ALL THE DAMN NOCKS.
BACK IN A SEC.
Eight.

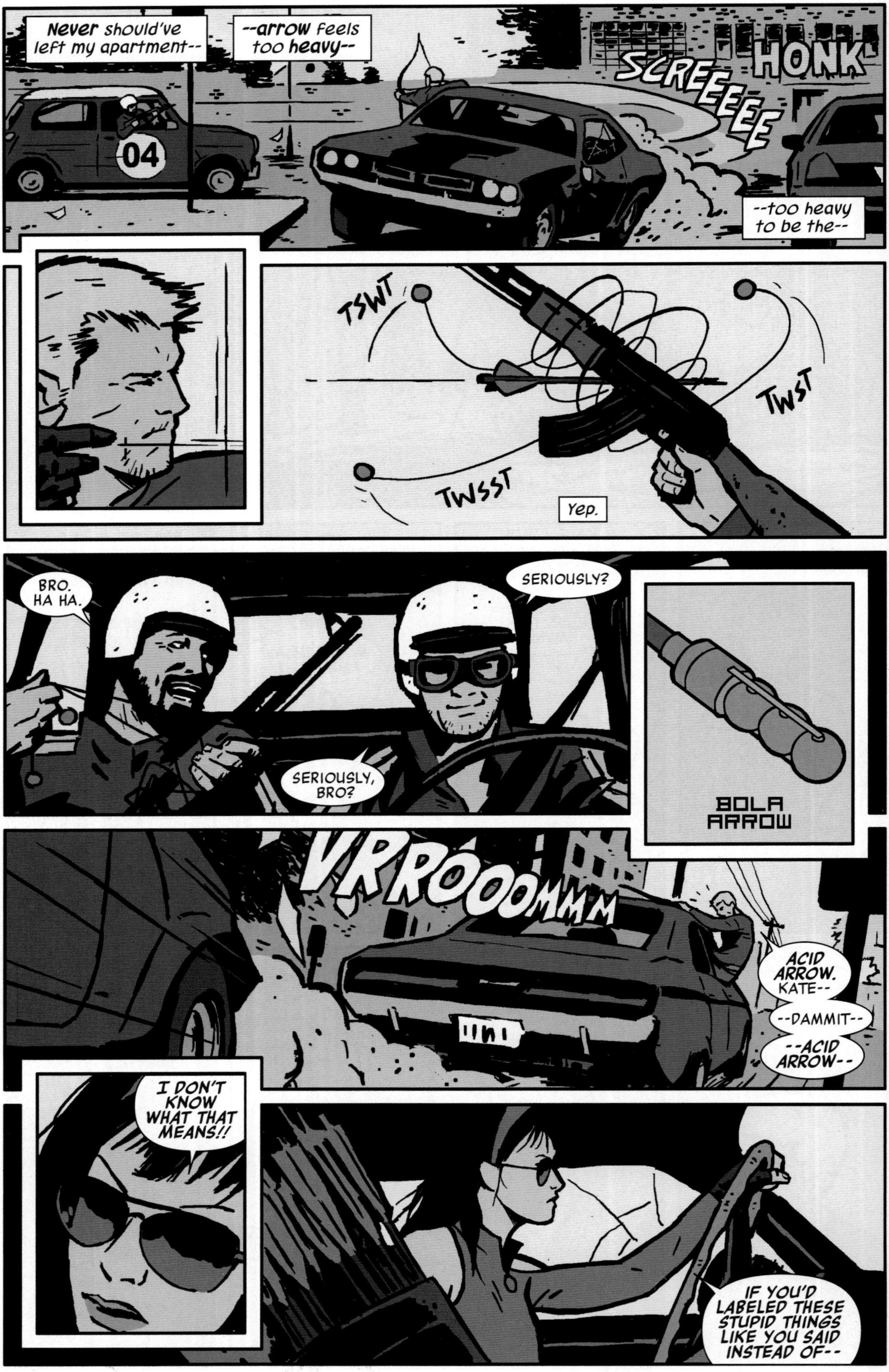
Never should've left my apartment--
--arrow feels too heavy--
SCREEEEEE
HONK
04
--too heavy to be the--
TSWT
TWST
TWSST
Yep.
BRO. HA HA.
SERIOUSLY?
SERIOUSLY, BRO?
BOLA ARROW
VRROOOMMM
ACID ARROW. KATE--
--DAMMIT--
--ACID ARROW--
I DON'T KNOW WHAT THAT MEANS!!
IF YOU'D LABELED THESE STUPID THINGS LIKE YOU SAID INSTEAD OF--

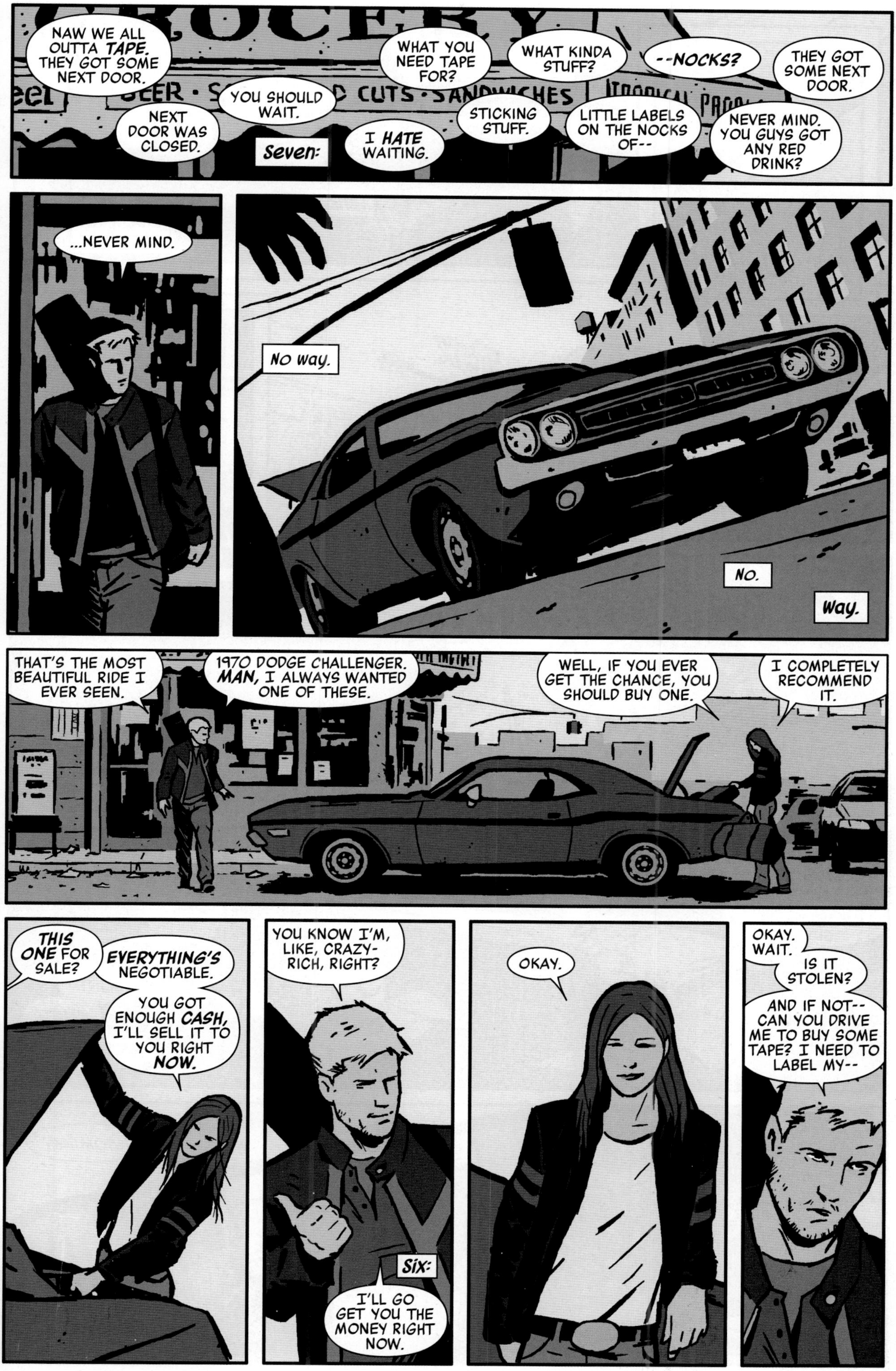
NAW WE ALL OUTTA TAPE. THEY GOT SOME NEXT DOOR.
NEXT DOOR WAS CLOSED.
YOU SHOULD WAIT.
Seven:
I HATE WAITING.
WHAT YOU NEED TAPE FOR?
STICKING STUFF.
WHAT KINDA STUFF?
LITTLE LABELS ON THE NOCKS OF--
--NOCKS?
THEY GOT SOME NEXT DOOR.
NEVER MIND. YOU GUYS GOT ANY RED DRINK?
...NEVER MIND.
No way.
No.
Way.
THAT'S THE MOST BEAUTIFUL RIDE I EVER SEEN.
1970 DODGE CHALLENGER. MAN, I ALWAYS WANTED ONE OF THESE.
WELL, IF YOU EVER GET THE CHANCE, YOU SHOULD BUY ONE.
I COMPLETELY RECOMMEND IT.
THIS ONE FOR SALE?
EVERYTHING'S NEGOTIABLE.
YOU GOT ENOUGH CASH, I'LL SELL IT TO YOU RIGHT NOW.
YOU KNOW I'M, LIKE, CRAZY-RICH, RIGHT?
Six:
I'LL GO GET YOU THE MONEY RIGHT NOW.
OKAY.
OKAY. WAIT.
IS IT STOLEN?
AND IF NOT-- CAN YOU DRIVE ME TO BUY SOME TAPE? I NEED TO LABEL MY--

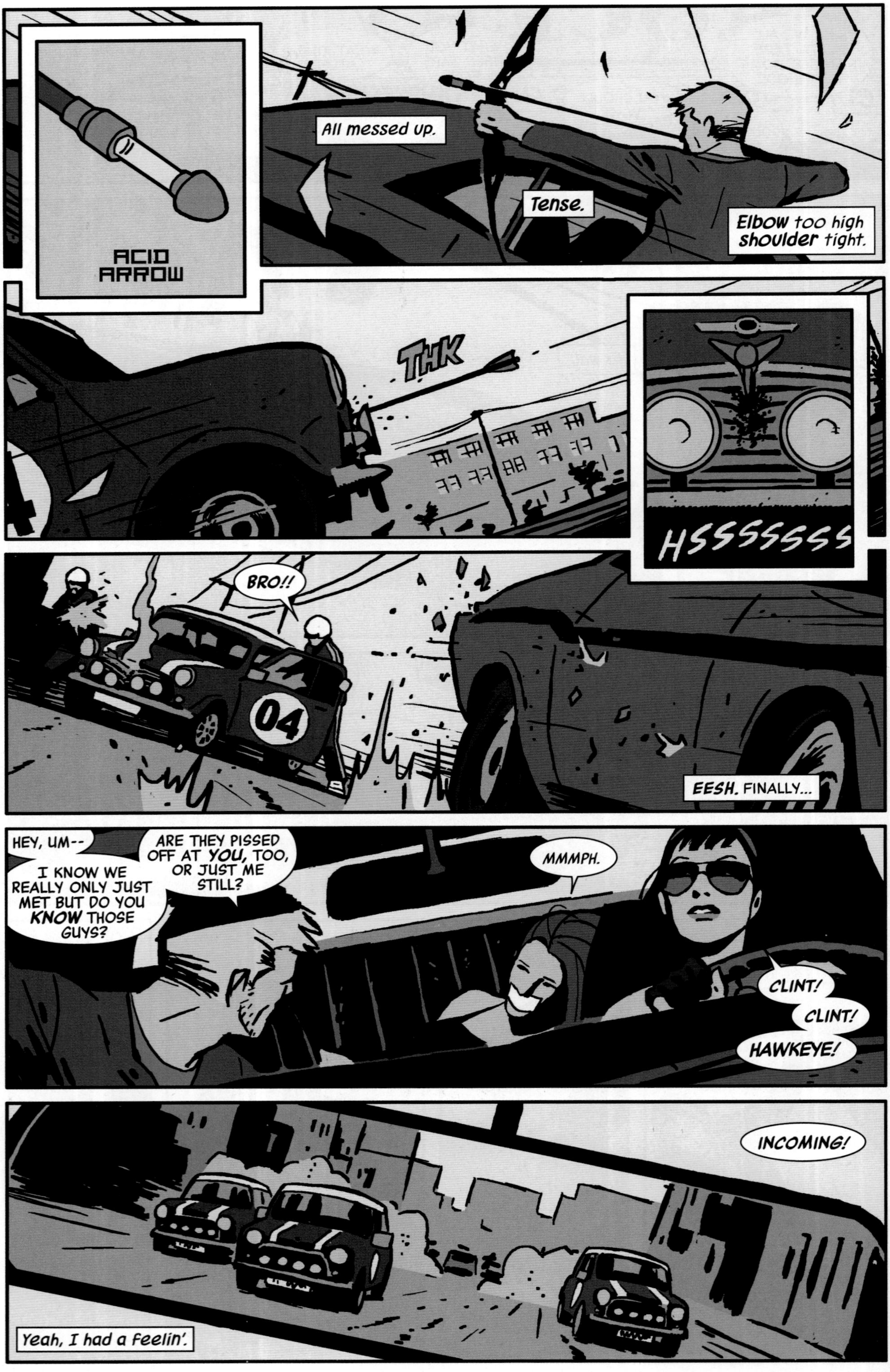

ACID ARROW
All messed up.
Tense.
Elbow too high shoulder tight.
THK
HSSSSSSS
BRO!!
EESH. FINALLY...
HEY, UM--
I KNOW WE REALLY ONLY JUST MET BUT DO YOU KNOW THOSE GUYS?
ARE THEY PISSED OFF AT YOU, TOO, OR JUST ME STILL?
MMMPH.
CLINT!
CLINT!
HAWKEYE!
INCOMING!
Yeah, I had a feelin'.

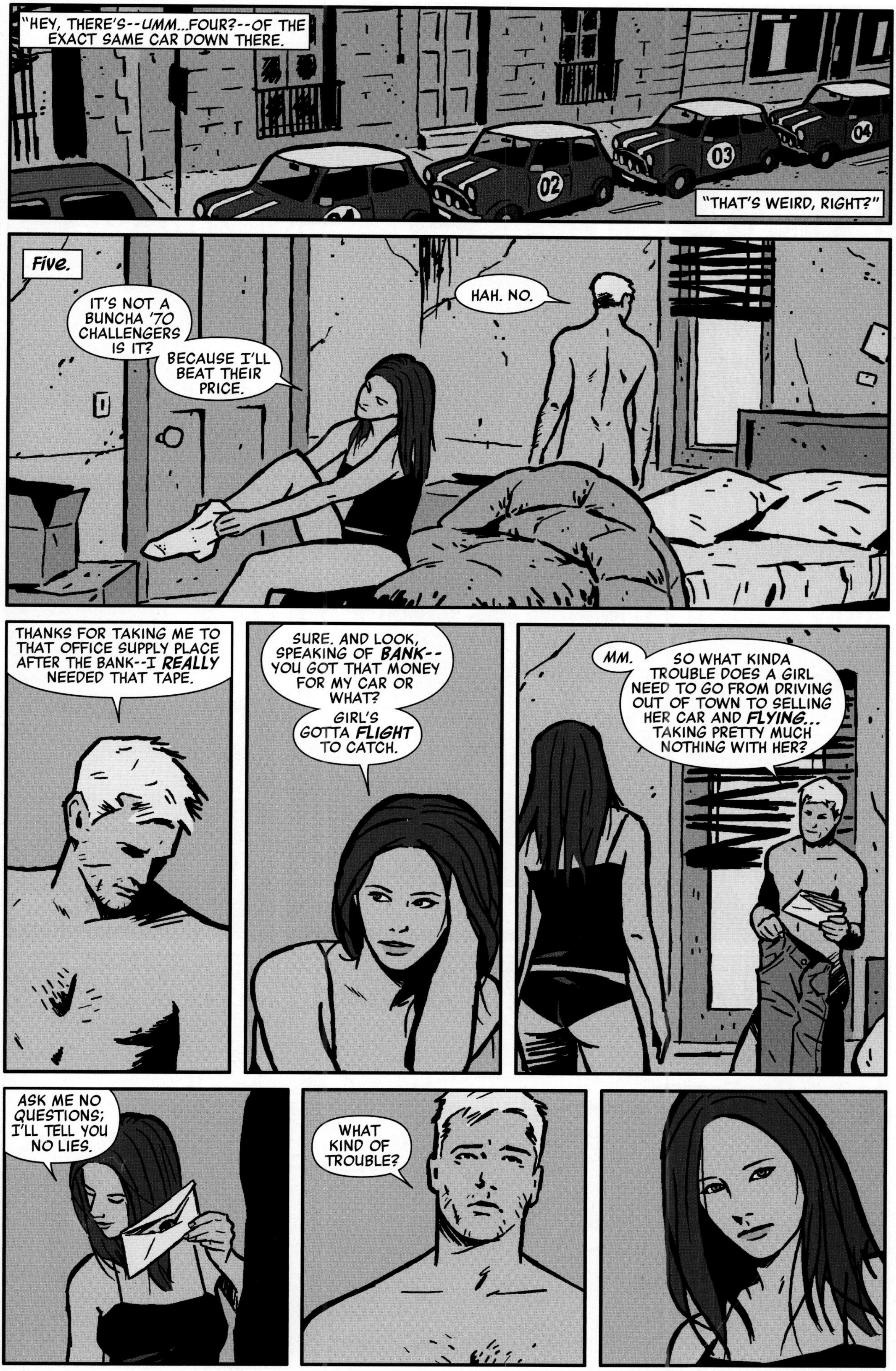
"HEY, THERE'S--UMM...FOUR?--OF THE EXACT SAME CAR DOWN THERE.
02
03
04
"THAT'S WEIRD, RIGHT?"
Five.
IT'S NOT A BUNCHA '70 CHALLENGERS IS IT?
BECAUSE I'LL BEAT THEIR PRICE.
HAH. NO.
THANKS FOR TAKING ME TO THAT OFFICE SUPPLY PLACE AFTER THE BANK--I REALLY NEEDED THAT TAPE.
SURE. AND LOOK, SPEAKING OF BANK--YOU GOT THAT MONEY FOR MY CAR OR WHAT?
GIRL'S GOTTA FLIGHT TO CATCH.
MM.
SO WHAT KINDA TROUBLE DOES A GIRL NEED TO GO FROM DRIVING OUT OF TOWN TO SELLING HER CAR AND FLYING... TAKING PRETTY MUCH NOTHING WITH HER?
ASK ME NO QUESTIONS; I'LL TELL YOU NO LIES.
WHAT KIND OF TROUBLE?

KRAK

--NO--

AW, BRO.

CHK

SUP, BROS?

BRAKA

WHOKK

BRAKABRAKABRA

Well the **bad news** is the Tracksuit Draculas are no longer playing around.

ABRAKABRA

The **good** news is...

RAKABRAKABRAKABRAKABRAKABRAKABR

Scratch that.

No good news.

Everything sucks.

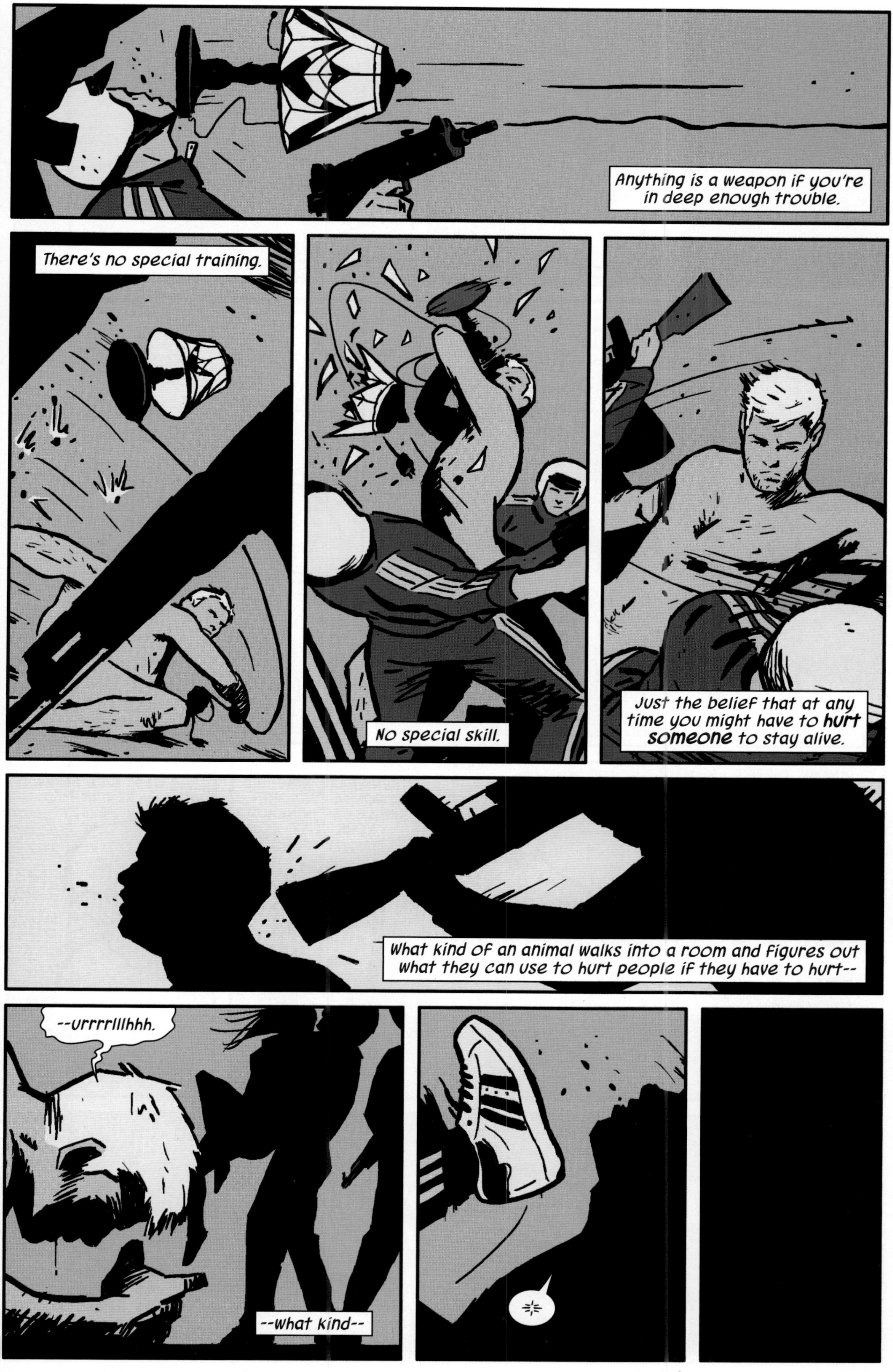
Anything is a weapon if you're in deep enough trouble.
There's no special training.
No special skill.
Just the belief that at any time you might have to **hurt someone** to stay alive.
What kind of an animal walks into a room and figures out what they can use to hurt people if they have to hurt--
--urrrrlllhhh.
--what kind--

AAOOWW

Okay, *this...*

...this is *bad.*

RNNGGG RNNGGG

WHY DO YOU STILL HAVE A PHONE WITH A CORD ON A WALL?

HOW DID YOU KNOW IT WAS ME?

WHO *ELSE* WOULD BE CALLING YOUR SAD ASS?

I-- WHAT?

*LOTS* OF PEOPLE.

*CAPTAIN AMERICA,* ONE TIME.

DID YOU HAVE TO GO TO *GOWANUS* FOR TAPE OR--

*KATE, SHUT UP AND COME GET ME RIGHT NOW.* I GOT *KNOCKED* OUT AND THIS GIRL--

GIRL'S BEEN KIDNAPPED AND WE GOTTA FOLLOW 'EM.

DUMMY, THERE'S 1.4 MILLION CARS IN NYC. *HOW LONG* HAVE YOU BEEN OUT?

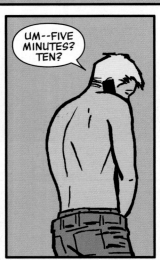

UM--FIVE MINUTES? TEN?

MIGHT AS WELL BE LIKE FIFTEEN YEARS. HOW ARE WE GONNA FIND ONE SINGLE CAR IN NEW YORK CITY?

THEY'RE ON THE WEST SIDE HIGHWAY HEADING TO JERSEY.

"THE HELL DO YOU KNOW *THAT?*"

"MY STUFF IS IN HER CAR.

"INCLUDING A *TRACER ARROW.*"

C'MON, KATIE. COME ON--

HONK

SCREEEE

GO GO GO!

COME ON--!

Bad idea FOUR:

REALLY.

KATE...

REALLY. WITH THE ABS AND THE--

DRIIIIVE!!

YEAH, YEAH.

KEEP YOUR SHIRT ON.

VVRRROOMM

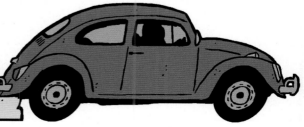

AHH, BRO.

BRO, BRO, BRO.

CAUSE LOTS TROUBLE, BRO.

OF ALL *CARS* TO STEAL, BRO.

AND, BRO, IF YOU GOT IT SCRATCHED, BRO?

HE KILL YOU EVEN MORE THAN ALREA

K-KLACK

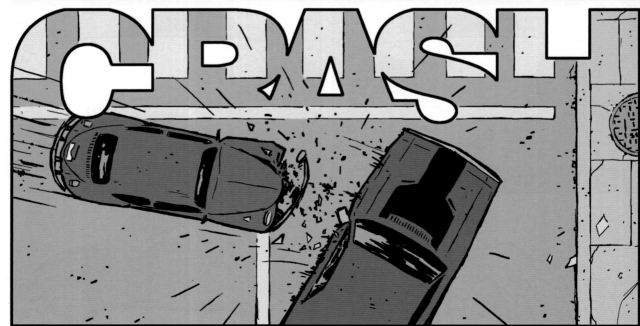

AW, MAN.

HEY, LOOK, IT'S A METAPHOR FOR YOUR LOVE-LIFE.

GET OUT OF MY DAMN CAR, *ASS.*

HOW'S IT GONNA FEEL DEEP DOWN IN YOUR *MAN-BITS* WHEN I DRIVE THIS CAR BETTER THAN YOU EVER DREAMED WAS POSSIBLE?

'CAUSE I'M ABOUT TO.

DON'T DANGLE YOUR *PREPOSITIONS* LIKE THAT, GIRLY-GIRL.

AND GIMME AN *ARROW* OUT THE QUIVER.

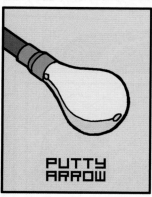

PUTTY ARROW

PUTTY ARROW, BRO!!!

VRRM VRRM

Where were we?

VRRRROOOOMMMM

VRROOM

VRROOM

04

02

Right. Worst idea number *three:*

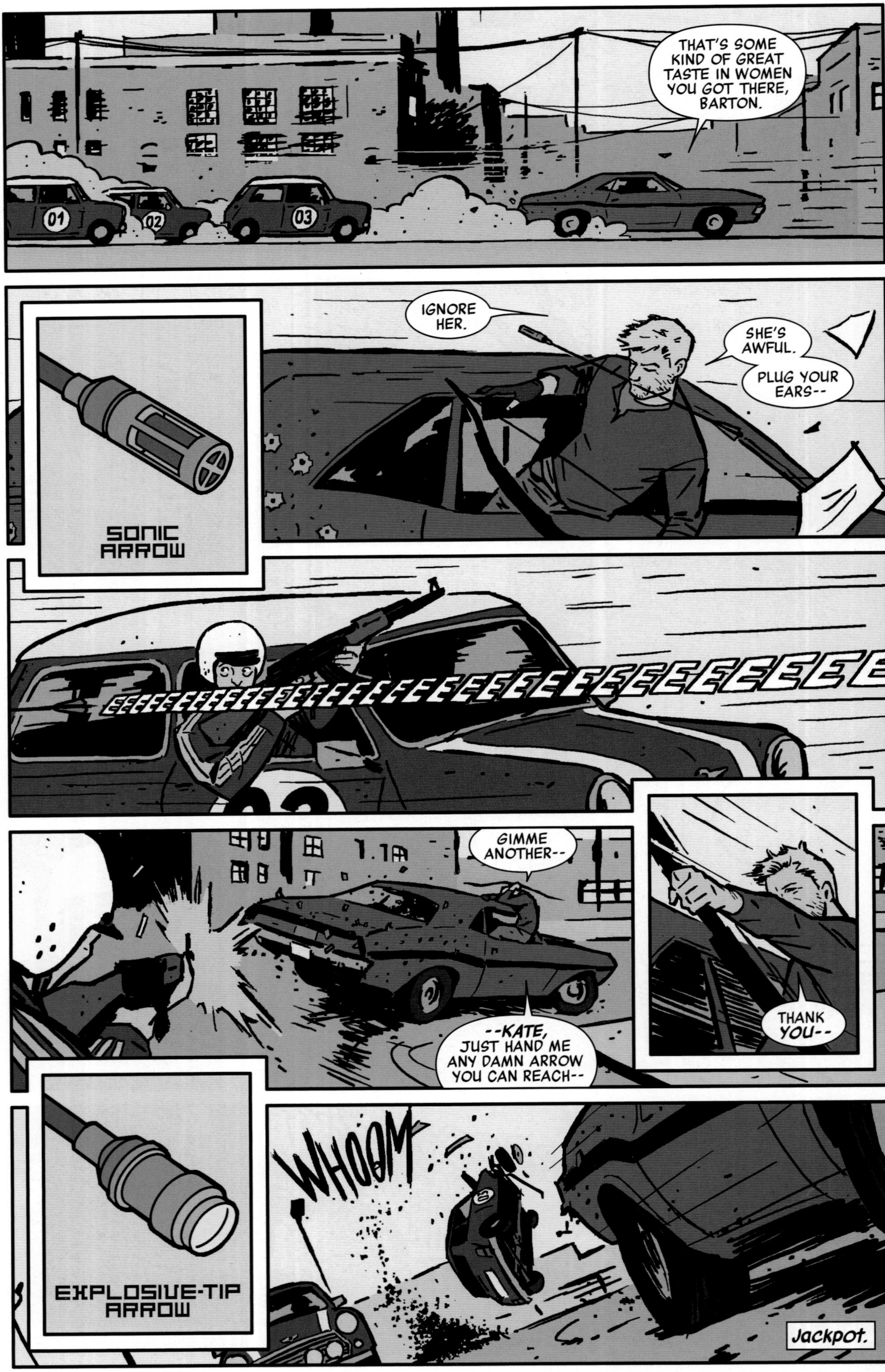
THAT'S SOME KIND OF GREAT TASTE IN WOMEN YOU GOT THERE, BARTON.
01
02
03
SONIC ARROW
IGNORE HER.
SHE'S AWFUL.
PLUG YOUR EARS--
EEEEEEEEEEEEEEEEEEEEEEEEEEEEEEEEEEEE
GIMME ANOTHER--
--KATE, JUST HAND ME ANY DAMN ARROW YOU CAN REACH--
THANK YOU--
EXPLOSIVE-TIP ARROW
WHOOM
Jackpot.

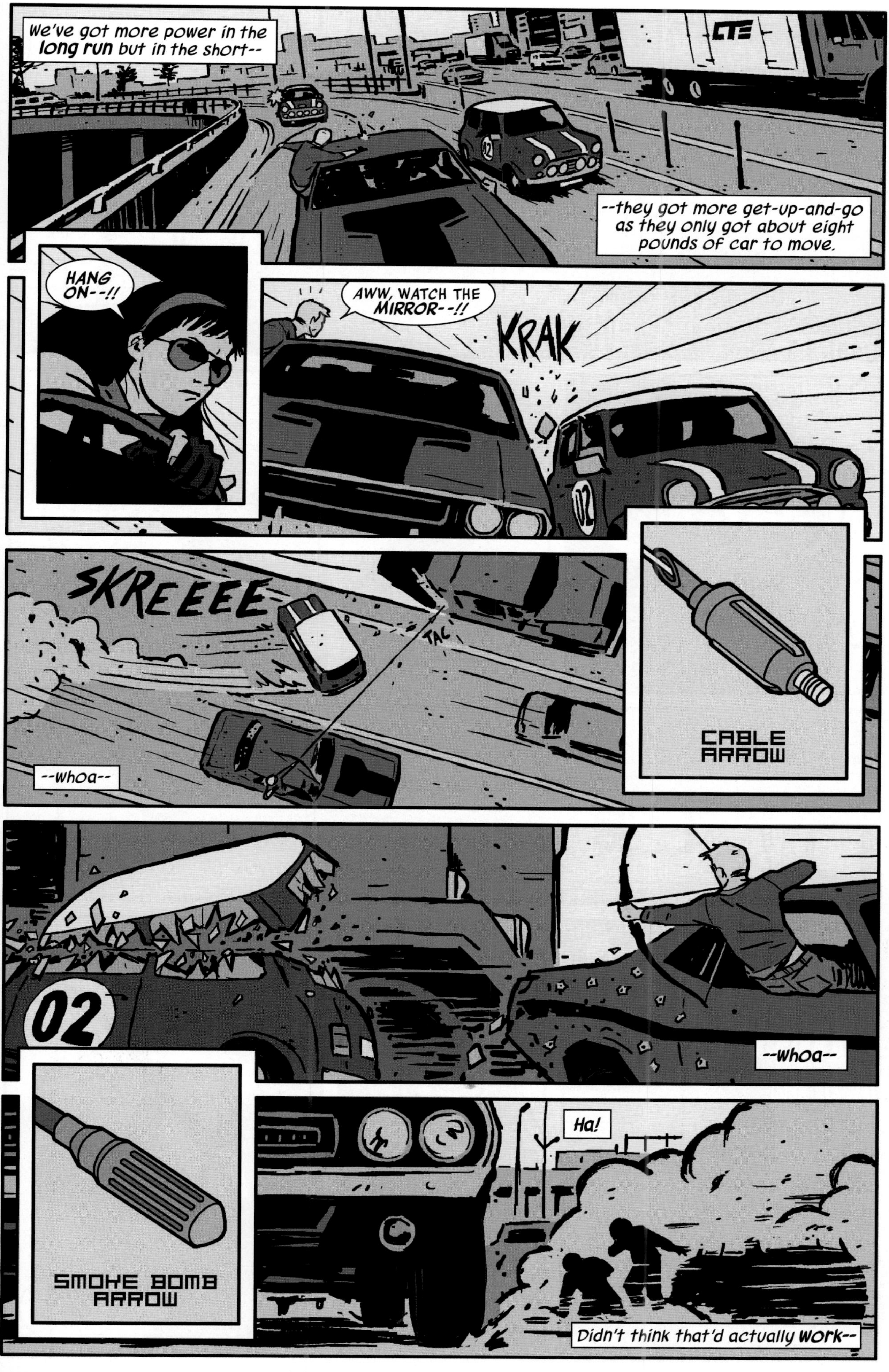
We've got more power in the long run but in the short--
--they got more get-up-and-go as they only got about eight pounds of car to move.
HANG ON--!!
AWW, WATCH THE MIRROR--!!
KRAK
SKREEEEE
TAC
--whoa--
CABLE ARROW
--whoa--
SMOKE BOMB ARROW
Ha!
Didn't think that'd actually work--

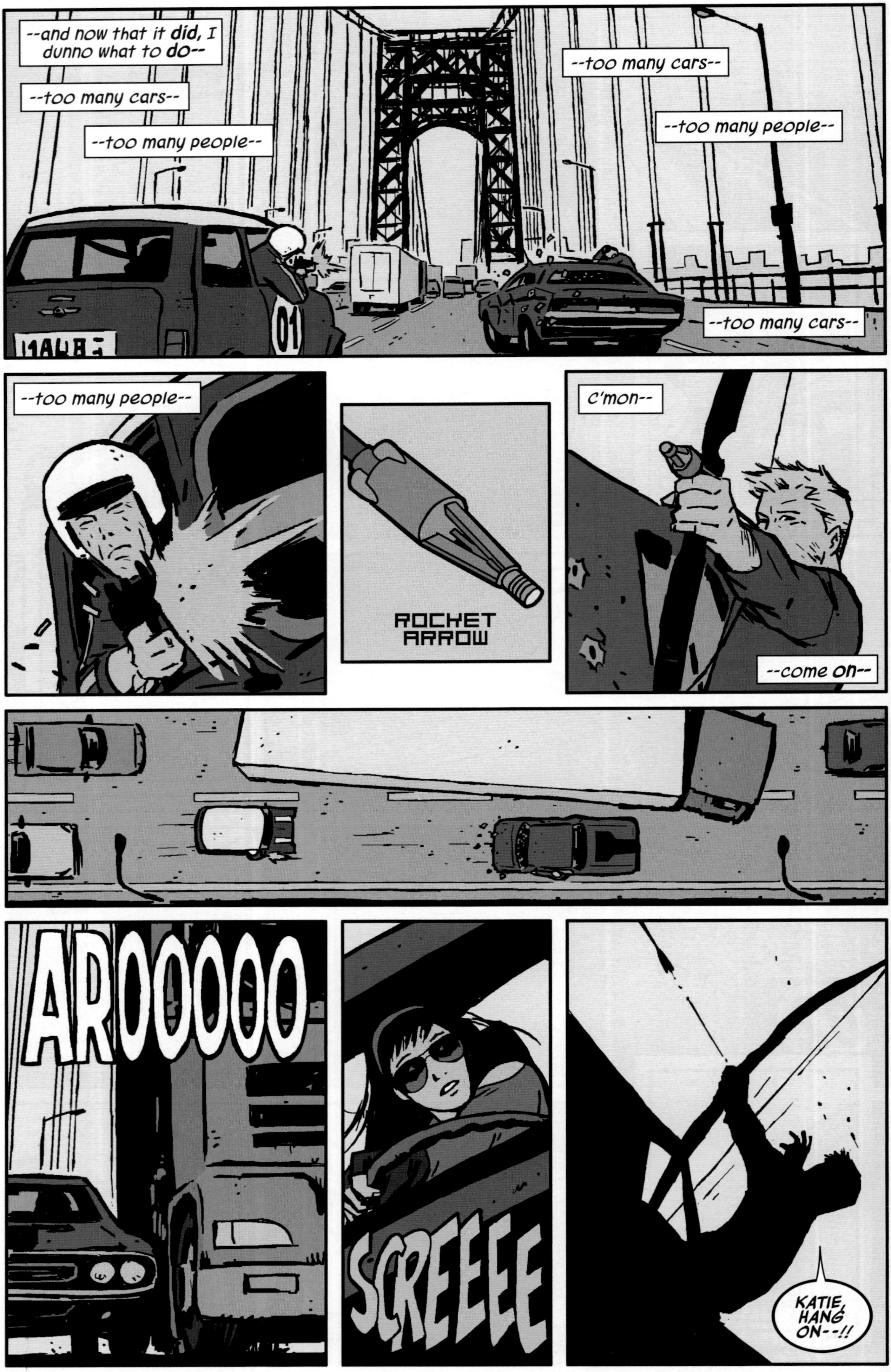
--and now that it did, I dunno what to do--
--too many cars--
--too many people--
--too many cars--
--too many people--
--too many cars--
--too many people--
ROCKET ARROW
C'mon--
--come on--
AROOOOO
SCREEEE
KATIE, HANG ON--!!

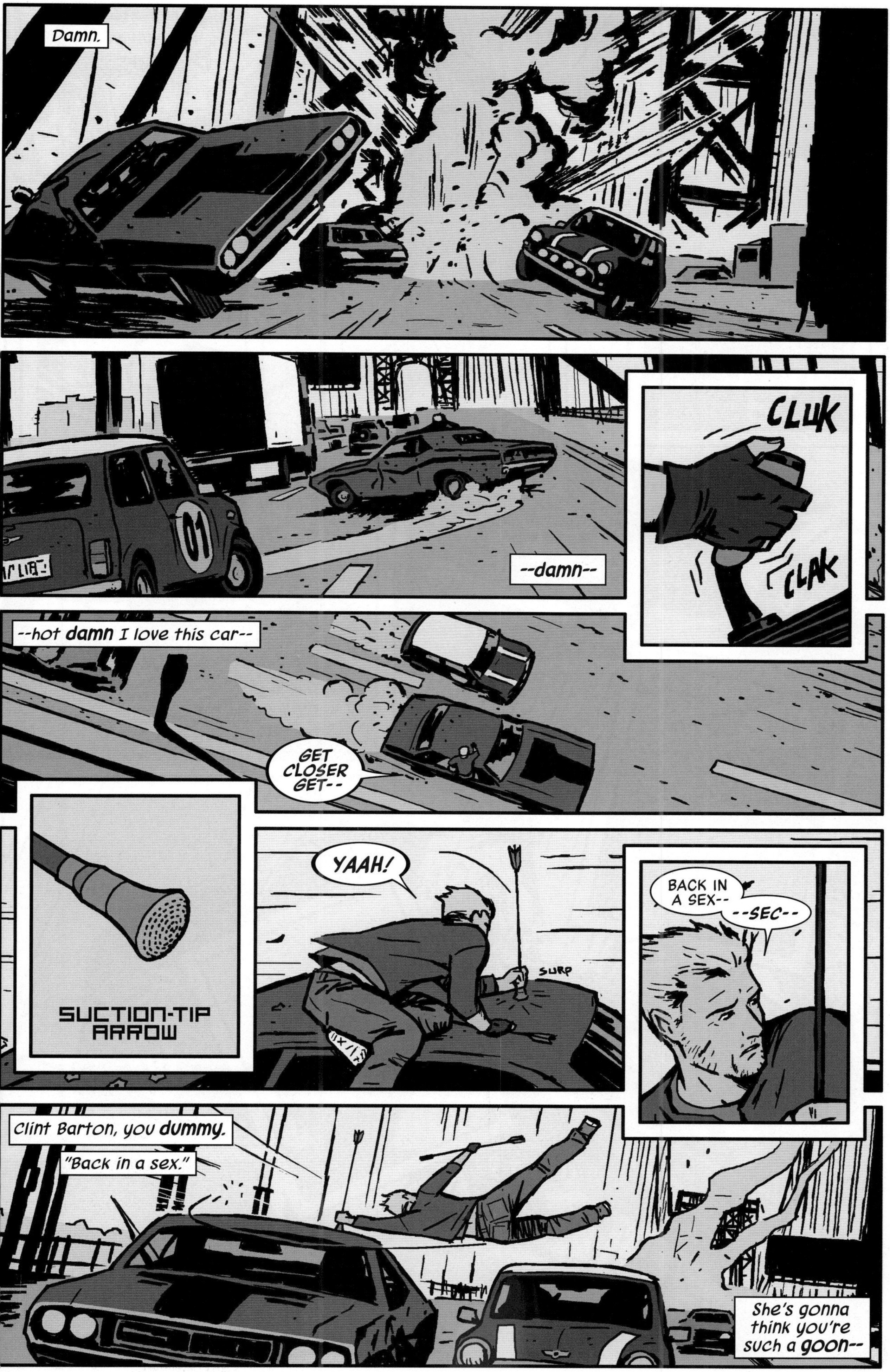
Damn.
--damn--
CLUK
CLAK
--hot damn I love this car--
GET CLOSER GET--
SUCTION-TIP ARROW
YAAH!
SURP
BACK IN A SEX--
--SEC--
Clint Barton, you dummy.
"Back in a sex."
She's gonna think you're such a goon--

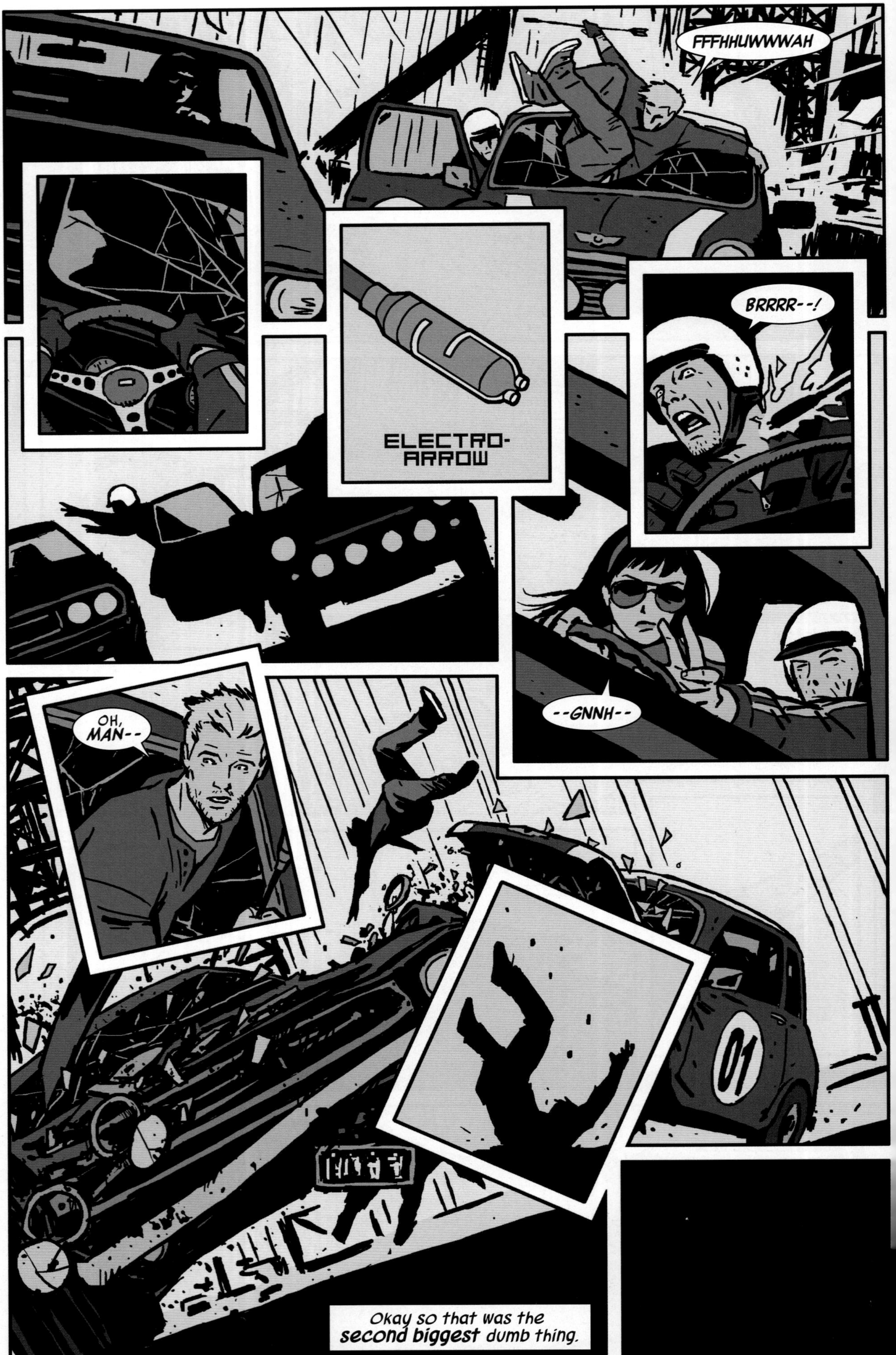
FFFHHUWWWAH
ELECTRO-
ARROW
BRRRR--!
--GNNH--
OH, MAN--
Okay so that was the
**second biggest** dumb thing.

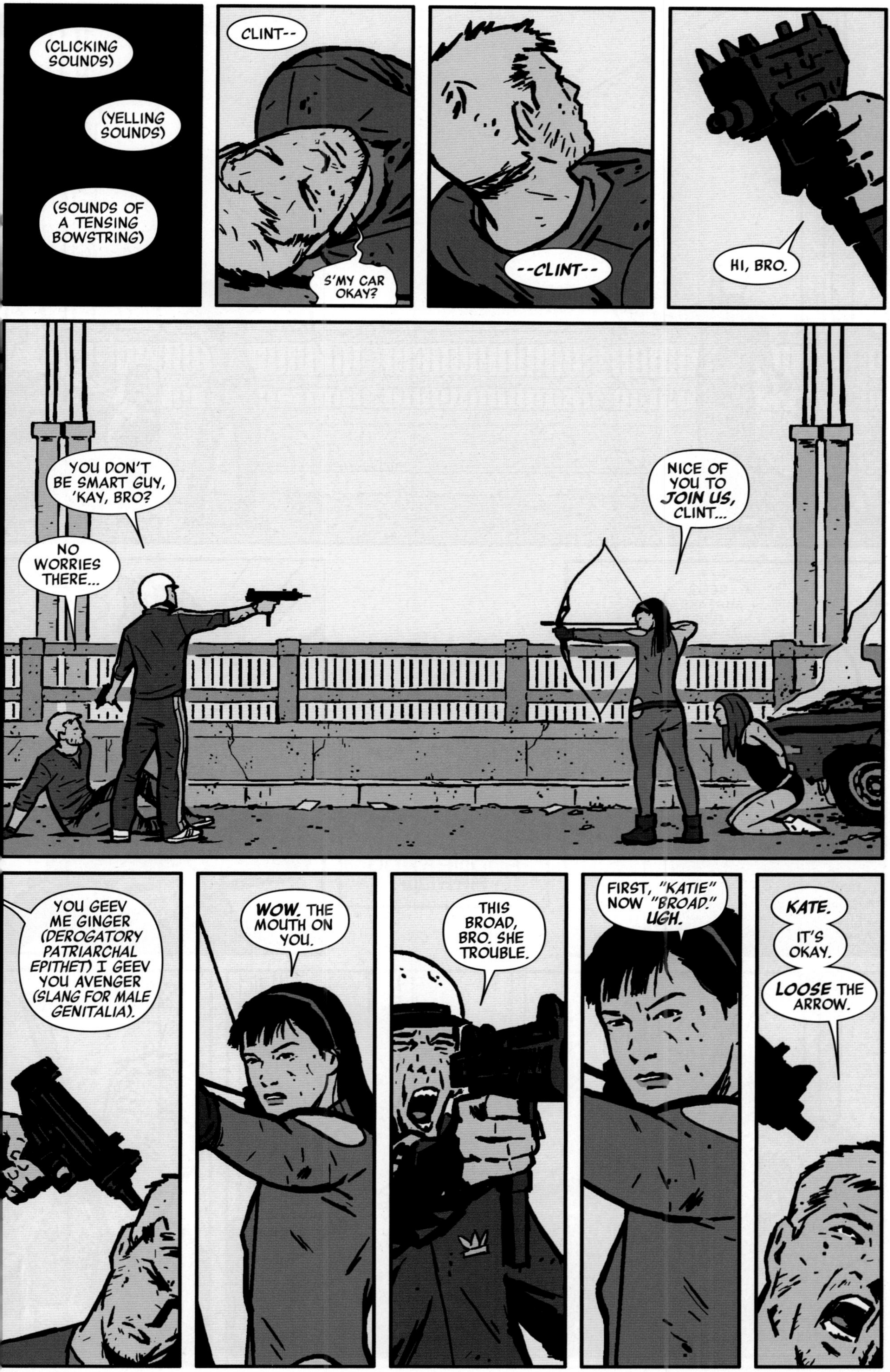
(CLICKING SOUNDS)
(YELLING SOUNDS)
(SOUNDS OF A TENSING BOWSTRING)
CLINT--
S'MY CAR OKAY?
--CLINT--
HI, BRO.
YOU DON'T BE SMART GUY, 'KAY, BRO?
NO WORRIES THERE...
NICE OF YOU TO JOIN US, CLINT...
YOU GEEV ME GINGER (DEROGATORY PATRIARCHAL EPITHET) I GEEV YOU AVENGER (SLANG FOR MALE GENITALIA).
WOW. THE MOUTH ON YOU.
THIS BROAD, BRO. SHE TROUBLE.
FIRST, "KATIE" NOW "BROAD." UGH.
KATE.
IT'S OKAY.
LOOSE THE ARROW.

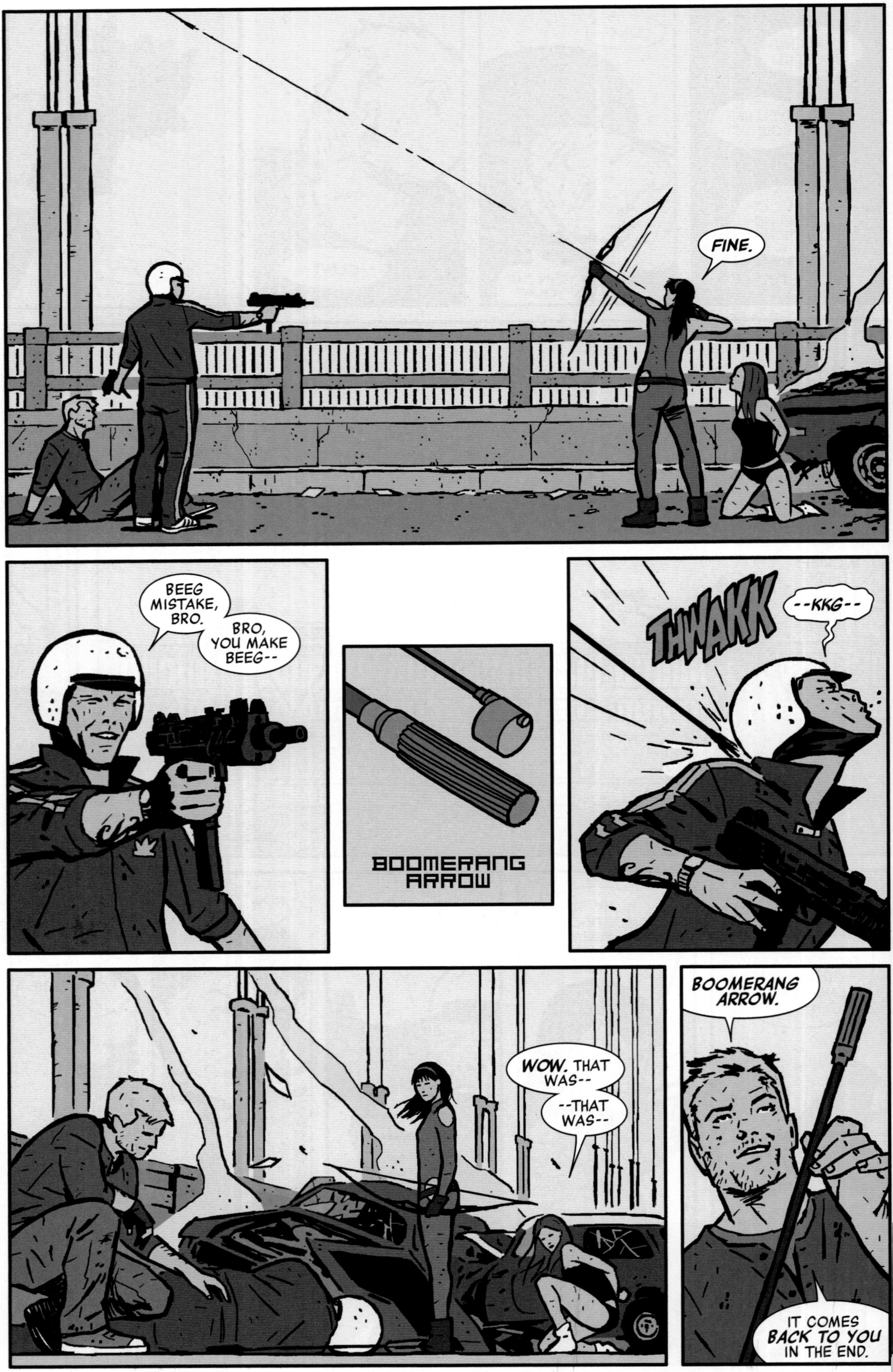
FINE.
BEEG MISTAKE, BRO.
BRO, YOU MAKE BEEG--
BOOMERANG ARROW
THWAKK
--KKG--
WOW. THAT WAS--
--THAT WAS--
BOOMERANG ARROW.
IT COMES BACK TO YOU IN THE END.

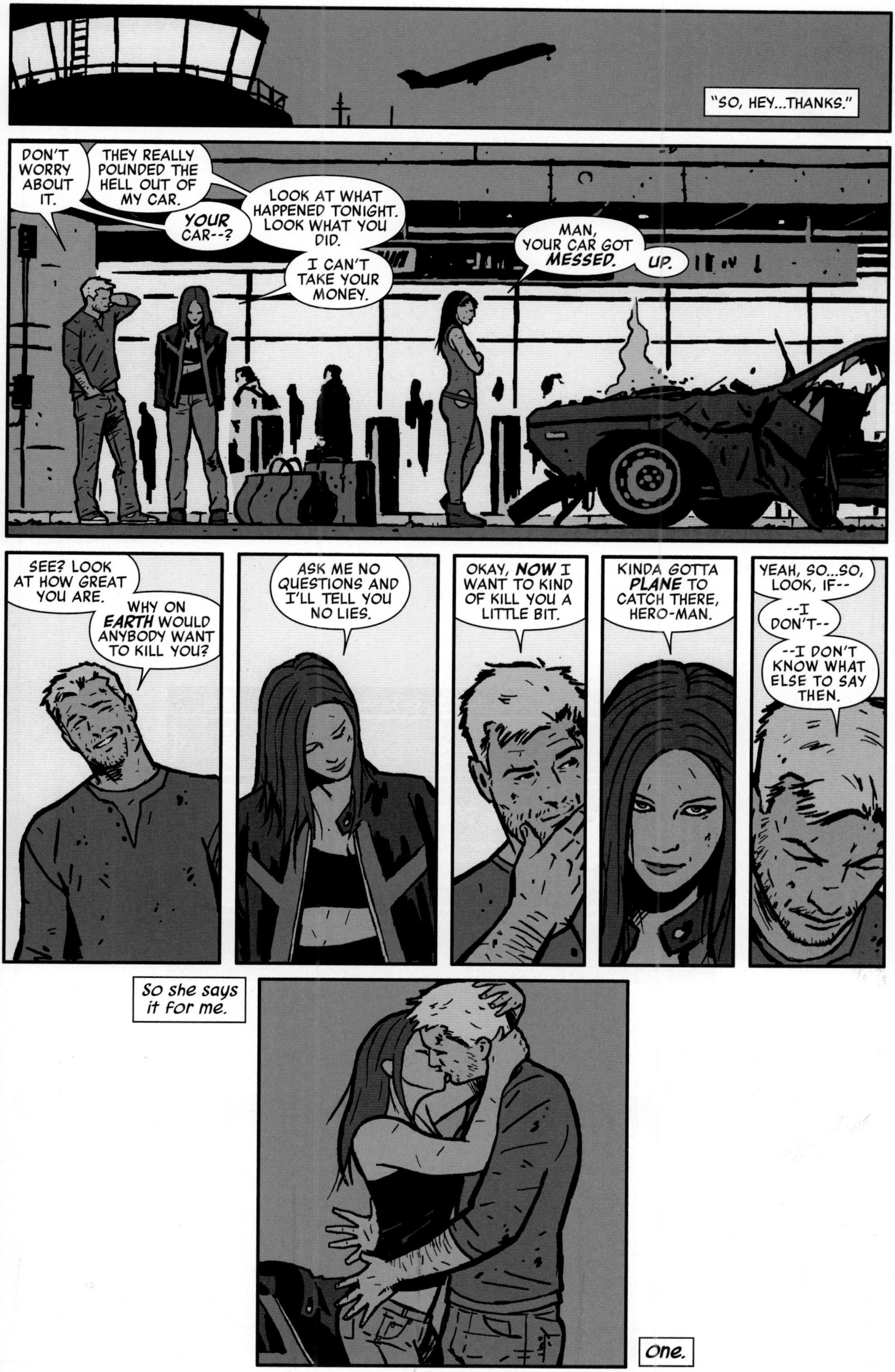
"SO, HEY...THANKS."
DON'T WORRY ABOUT IT.
THEY REALLY POUNDED THE HELL OUT OF MY CAR.
YOUR CAR--?
LOOK AT WHAT HAPPENED TONIGHT. LOOK WHAT YOU DID.
I CAN'T TAKE YOUR MONEY.
MAN, YOUR CAR GOT MESSED.
UP.
SEE? LOOK AT HOW GREAT YOU ARE.
WHY ON EARTH WOULD ANYBODY WANT TO KILL YOU?
ASK ME NO QUESTIONS AND I'LL TELL YOU NO LIES.
OKAY, NOW I WANT TO KIND OF KILL YOU A LITTLE BIT.
KINDA GOTTA PLANE TO CATCH THERE, HERO-MAN.
YEAH, SO...SO, LOOK, IF--
--I DON'T--
--I DON'T KNOW WHAT ELSE TO SAY THEN.
So she says it for me.
One.

# 4

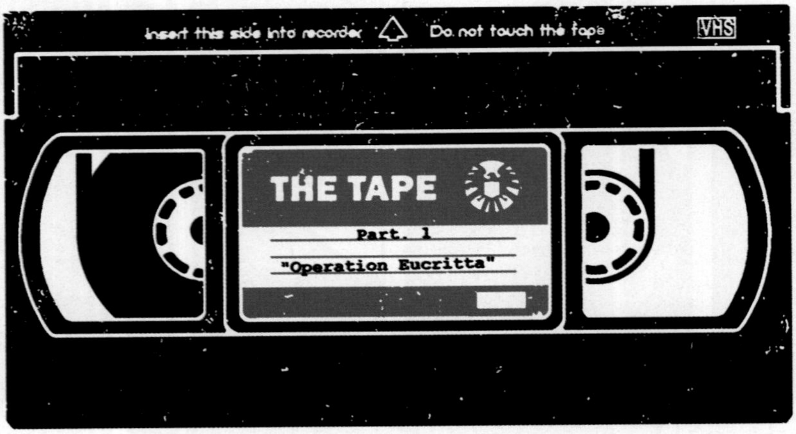
Insert this side into recorder
Do not touch the tape
VHS
THE TAPE
Part. 1
"Operation Eucritta"

clint barton is

# hawkeye

# THE TAPE

## 1 OF 2

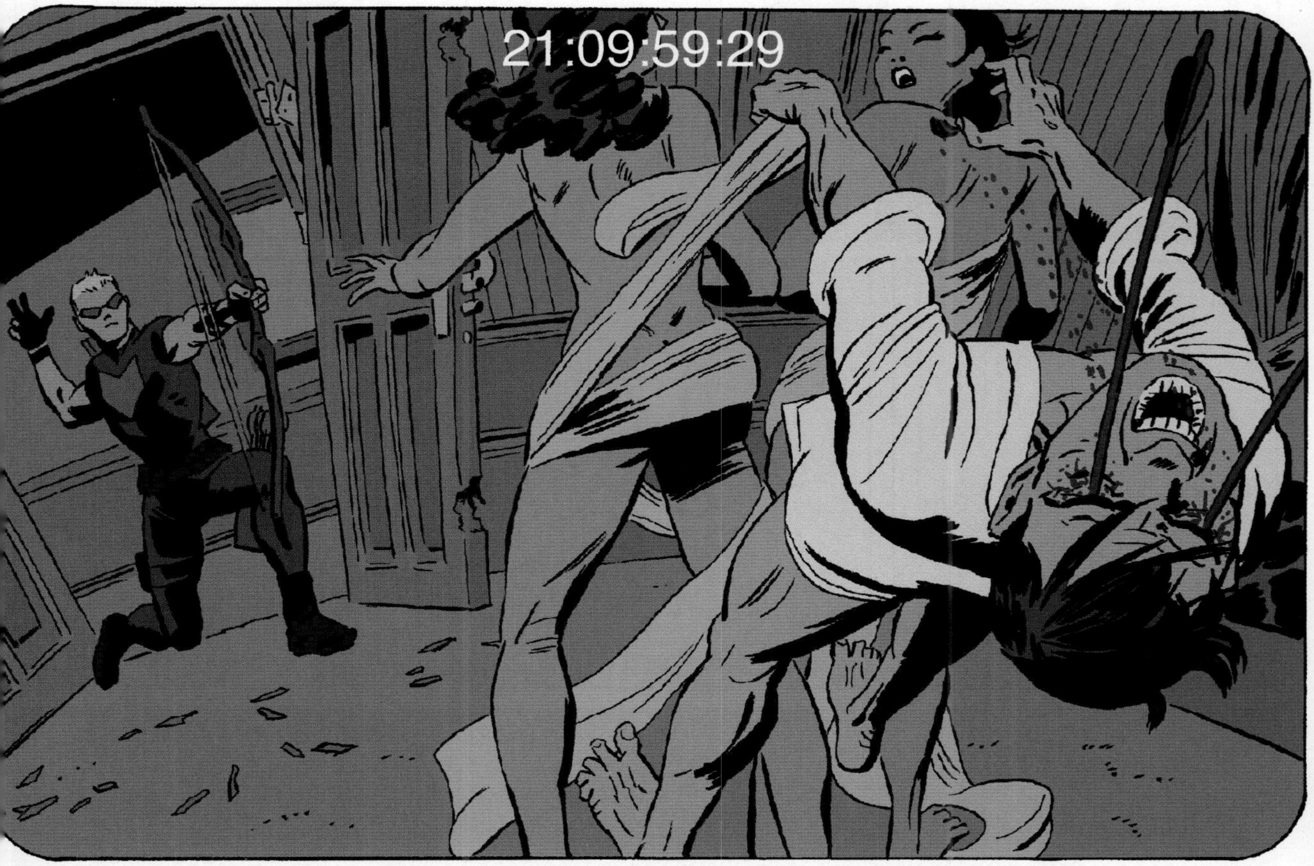
21:09:59:29

"YOU EVER KILL ANYBODY, CLINT?"

PPPFFFFWWWSSSHHH

'SCUSE ME?

DID YOU EVER **KILL** ANYBODY?

KATIE. THE HELL'S THE MATTER WITH YOU?

WHAT? NOTHING. I HAD SOME STUFF. MY GUYS AND ME.

HELL **NO** THAT BOY NEVER KILLED ANYBODY. THEY DON'T LET YOU IN **THE AVENGERS** IF YOU KILL PEOPLE.

I'M NOT AN AVENGER.

I'M NOBODY.

...

WHAT?

LOOK AT ME, DO I HAVE SUPER-POWERS OR ANY OF THAT KINDA--

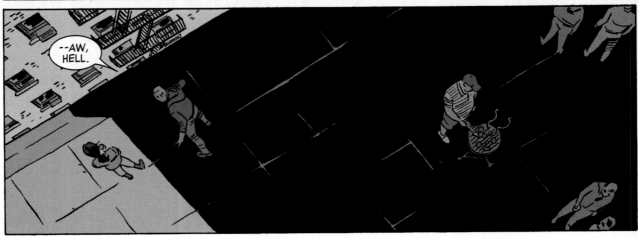

--AW, HELL.

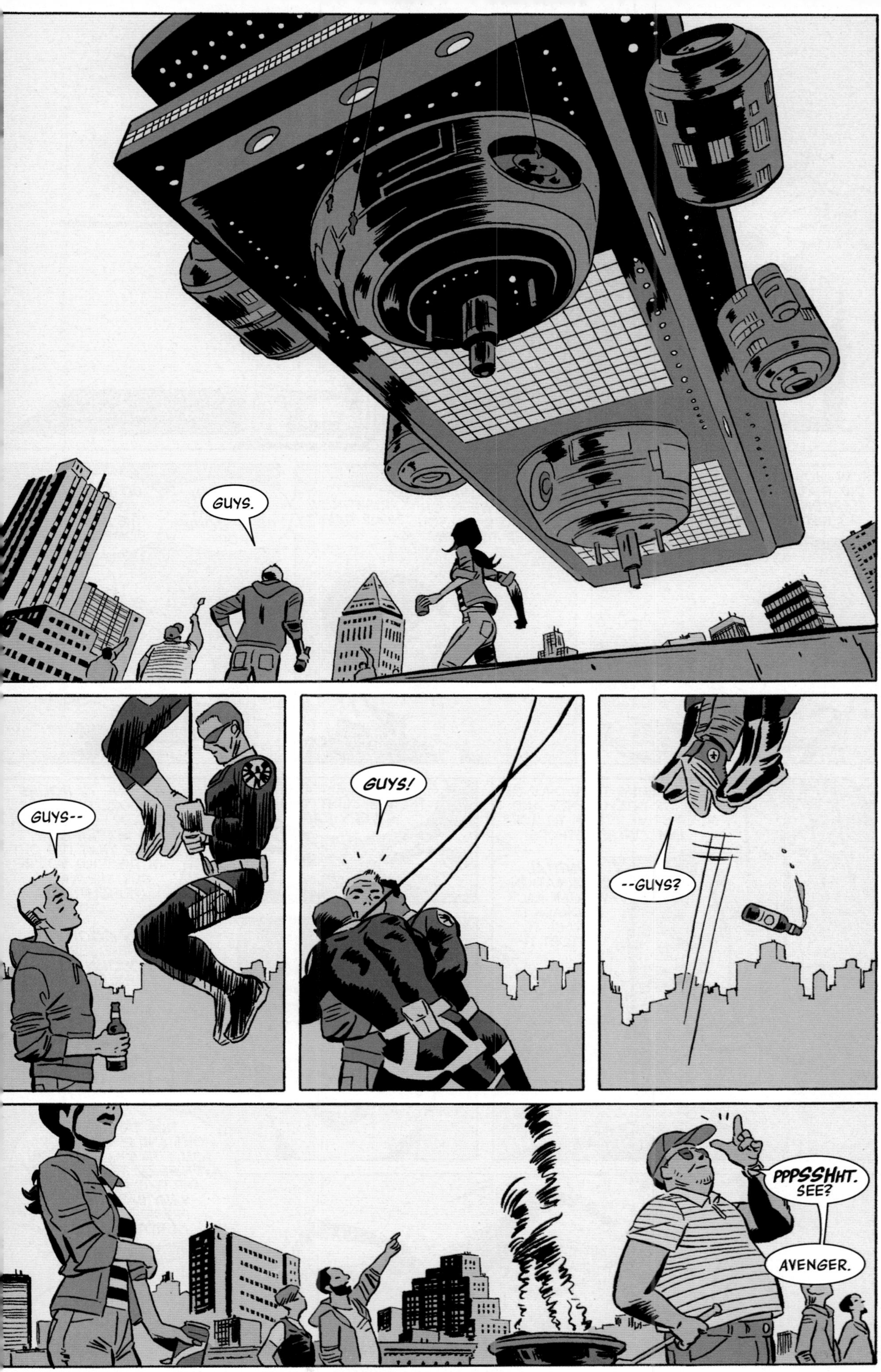
GUYS.
GUYS--
GUYS!
--GUYS?
PPPSSHHT.
SEE?
AVENGER.

THE **TAPE** GOT OUT, CLINT. IT'S OUT. IT'S OUT THERE.

THE VIDEOTAPED RECORD OF **OPERATION: EUCRITTA.**

HOW...HOW DID THAT **HAPPEN,** MS. HILL?

BECAUSE I THOUGHT THE WHOLE THING WAS THAT THAT **COULDN'T** HAPPEN. YOU GUYS **PROMISED,** IN FACT.

WELL THAT'S ON **US** AND WE'RE ON **IT.** THAT'S ALL YOU NEED TO KNOW.

RIGHT NOW YOUR **SAFETY** IS--

HOW **MANY** TAPES? ARE THERE **COPIES** OR--

DO I NEED TO GO ON THE **LAM** OR SOMETHING?

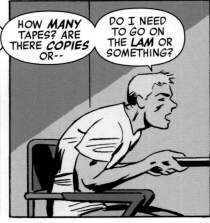

WE'RE SEEING THE WORLD OF TERROR INTELLIGENCE AND SUPER-CRIME RETURN TO MORE **ANALOGUE** METHODS.

**DIGITAL** INFORMATION... WE CAN HACK IT, CRACK IT, TRACK IT, DISTORT IT--

--BUT **ONE** TAPE IS JUST ONE THING TO KEEP TRACK OF. SO IF THERE'S **GOOD NEWS,** IT'S THAT.

MAKE NO MISTAKE THOUGH, CLINT. THIS IS **VERY BAD.**

WE HAVE **72 HOURS** BEFORE THE TAPE GOES UP FOR AUCTION IN **MADRIPOOR. AFTER THAT** IT'S OUT IN THE WILD. YOU'RE OUT. THE WHOLE **OPERATION** IS OUT.

ANY **GOON** WITH A NINE-FIGURE **BANK ACCOUNT** OR AN **AMEX BLACK** WILL BE THERE. SO WE'RE GIVING YOU OURS AND HOPING FOR THE BEST.

DON'T **LOSE IT,** BUTTERCUP.

THIS TAPE GETS OUT AND IT'S BAD FOR **YOU,** FOR S.H.I.E.L.D., THE **AVENGERS,** THE **MILITARY,** AND IT IS PERSONALLY **VERY** BAD FOR THE PRESIDENT OF THE UNITED STATES.

I'M SORRY--

--DID YOU SAY **"AUCTION"?**

"KATIE? THE HELL ARE YOU DOING HERE?"

"IT'S LIKE THREE IN THE MORNING."

YOU'RE COMING AT *ME* WITH THE QUESTIONS?

*YOU'RE* THE ONE THAT GOT KIDNAPPED BY THE AVENGERS FROM A--

THOSE WEREN'T THE AVENGERS, KATIE.

AH. OH. SO-- SO...

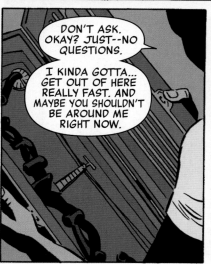

DON'T ASK. OKAY? JUST--NO QUESTIONS.

I KINDA GOTTA... GET OUT OF HERE REALLY FAST. AND MAYBE YOU SHOULDN'T BE AROUND ME RIGHT NOW.

WHOA, HOW COME I'VE NEVER SEEN *THIS ONE* BEFORE?

SORRY. QUESTION.

CLINT, LET ME *HELP* YOU. I TRADE ON YOUR NAME. WHAT KIND OF *YOU* WOULD I BE IF I DIDN'T HELP?

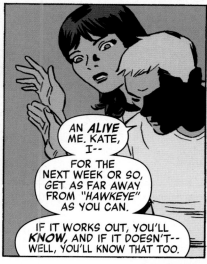

AN *ALIVE* ME. KATE, I--

FOR THE NEXT WEEK OR SO, GET AS FAR AWAY FROM "HAWKEYE" AS YOU CAN.

IF IT WORKS OUT, YOU'LL *KNOW*, AND IF IT DOESN'T-- WELL, YOU'LL KNOW THAT TOO.

CLINT...

CAN I HAVE YOUR STUFF, WHEN YOU'RE DEAD?

HELL NO. YOU'RE RICH. BUY YOUR OWN STUFF.

BESIDES, S.H.I.E.L.D. WILL PROBABLY HAVE TO CONFISCATE IT FOR EVIDENCE.

OH, C'MON!

TELL YOU WHAT, IF I DIE, YOU CAN HAVE THE CASE. IT'S GOOD FOR TRAVEL.

THINK I HAVE QUITE ENOUGH OF YOUR BAGGAGE ALREADY, THANKS."--

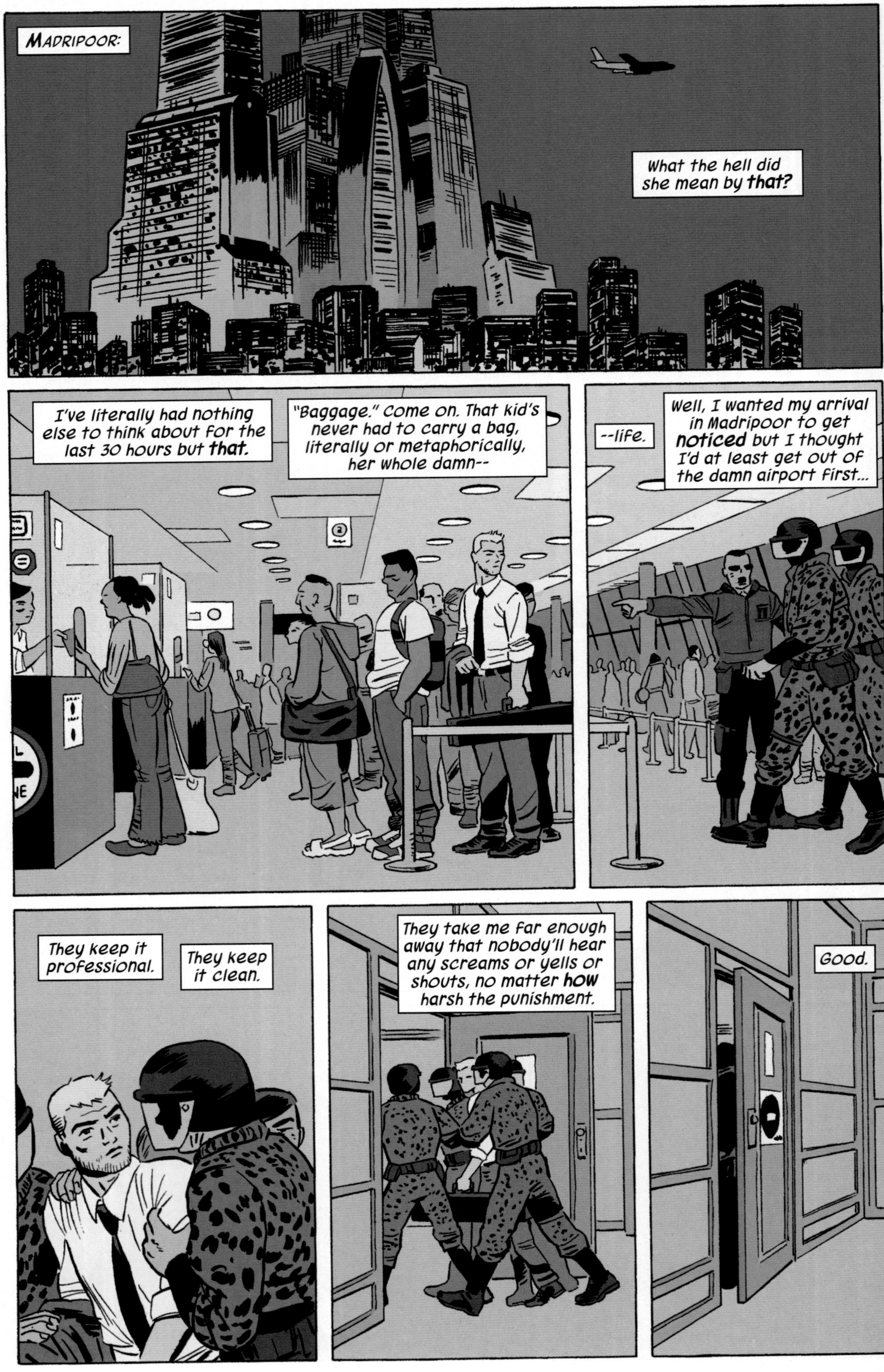
MADRIPOOR:
What the hell did she mean by that?
I've literally had nothing else to think about for the last 30 hours but that.
"Baggage." Come on. That kid's never had to carry a bag, literally or metaphorically, her whole damn--
--life.
Well, I wanted my arrival in Madripoor to get noticed but I thought I'd at least get out of the damn airport first...
They keep it professional.
They keep it clean.
They take me far enough away that nobody'll hear any screams or yells or shouts, no matter how harsh the punishment.
Good.

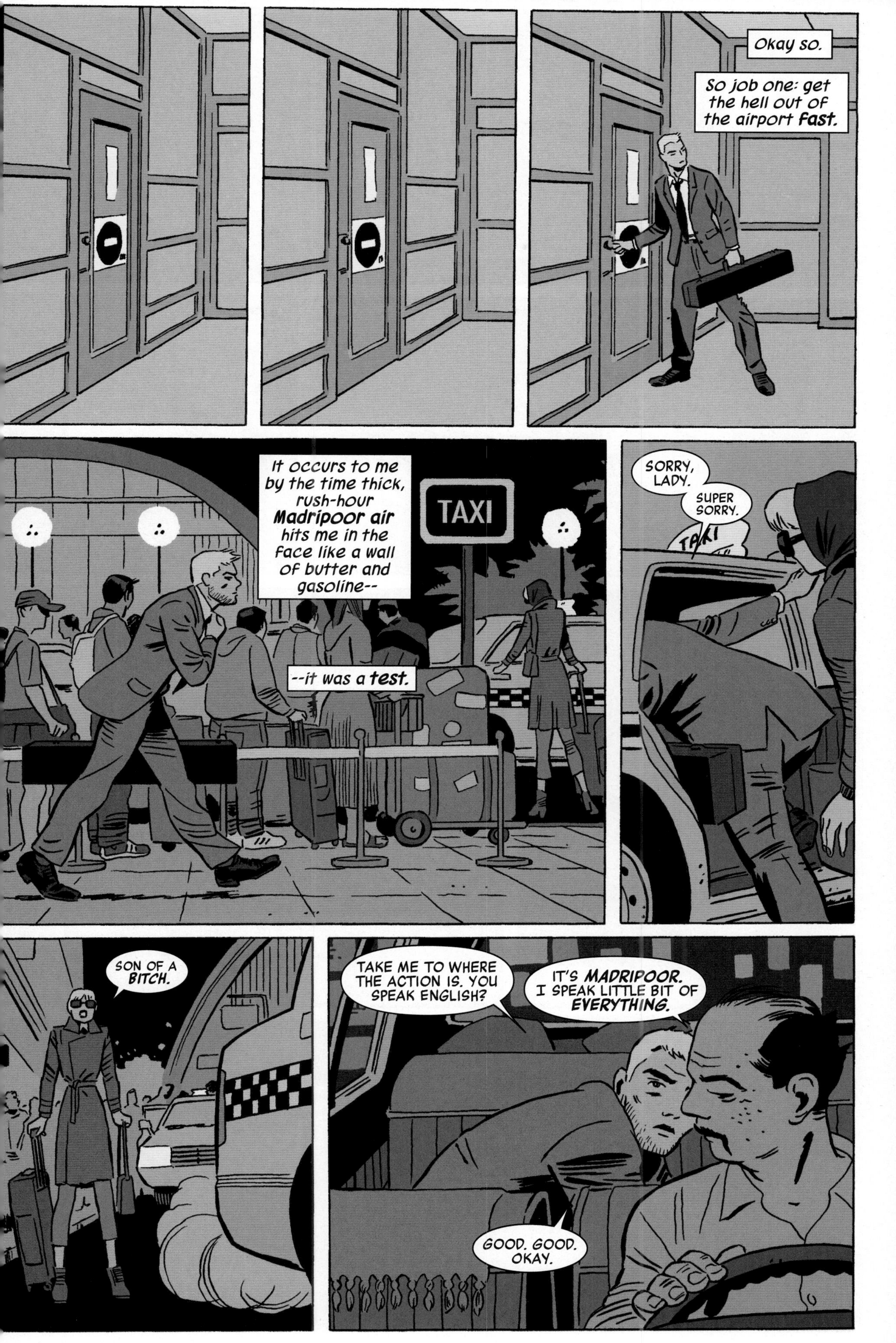
Okay so.
So job one: get the hell out of the airport fast.
It occurs to me by the time thick, rush-hour Madripoor air hits me in the face like a wall of butter and gasoline--
--it was a test.
TAXI
SORRY, LADY.
SUPER SORRY.
SON OF A BITCH.
TAKE ME TO WHERE THE ACTION IS. YOU SPEAK ENGLISH?
IT'S MADRIPOOR. I SPEAK LITTLE BIT OF EVERYTHING.
GOOD. GOOD. OKAY.

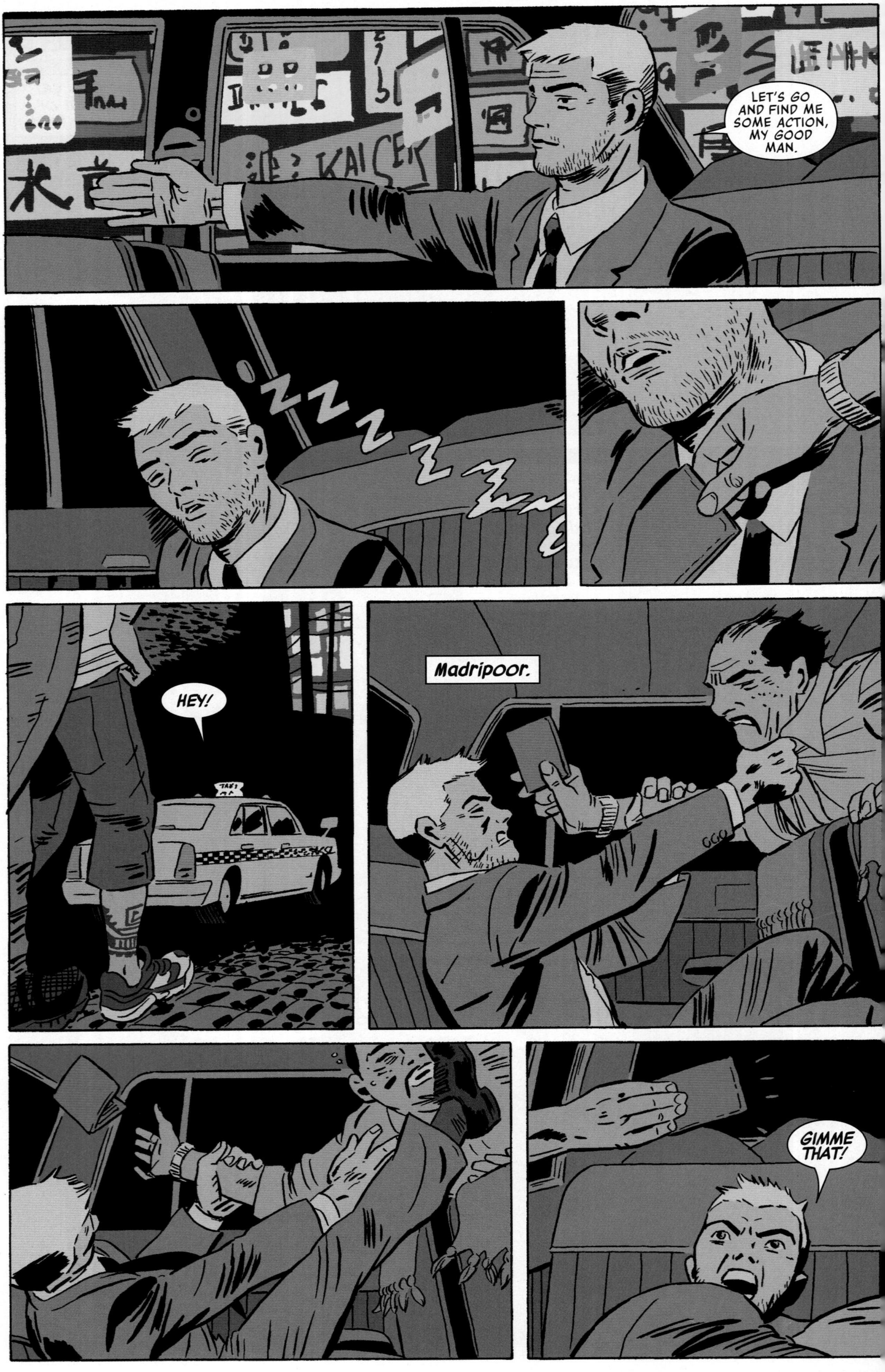
LET'S GO AND FIND ME SOME ACTION, MY GOOD MAN.
KAISER
ZZZZZ
HEY!
Madripoor.
GIMME THAT!

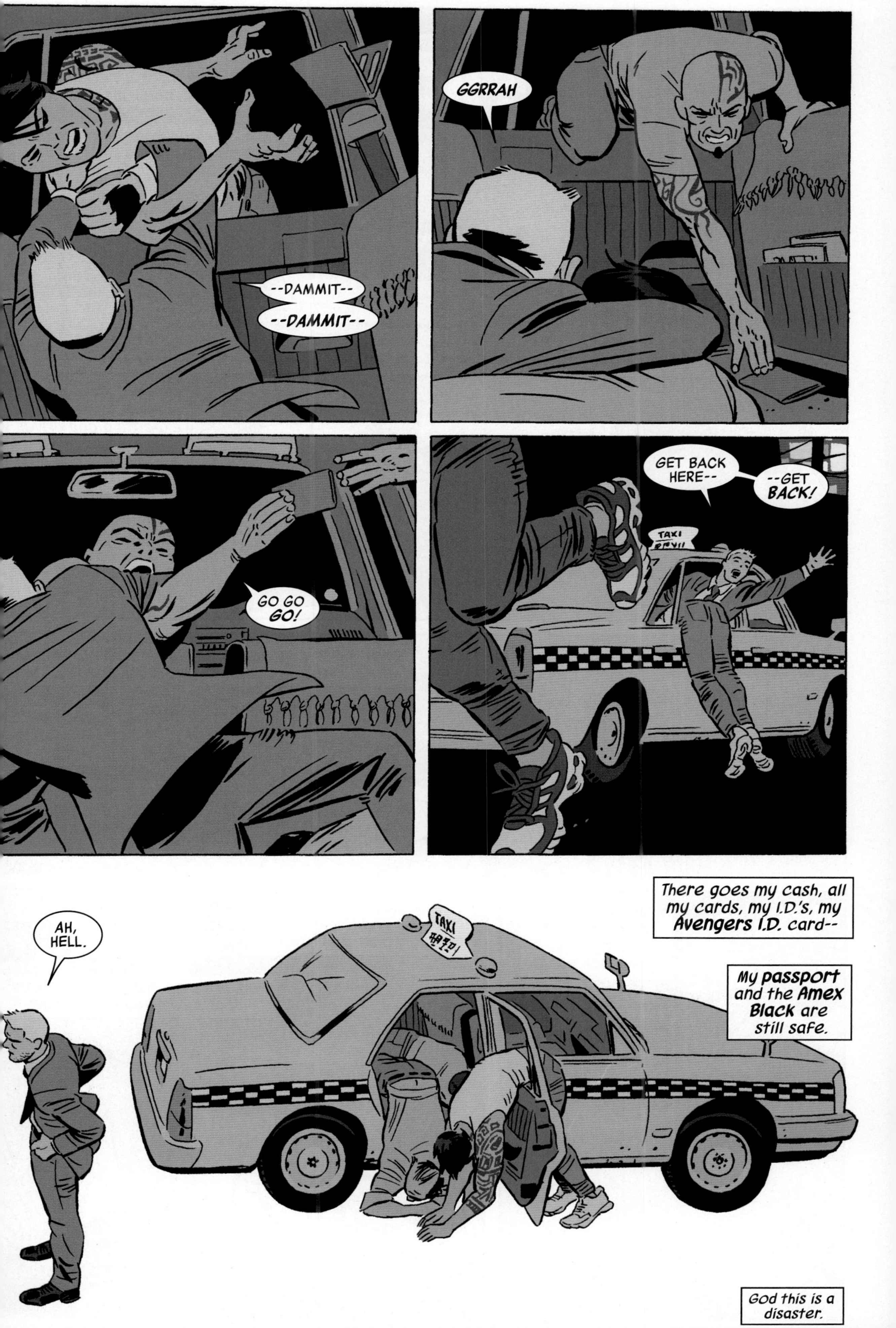
--DAMMIT--
--DAMMIT--
GGRRAH
GO GO GO!
GET BACK HERE--
--GET BACK!
TAXI
There goes my cash, all my cards, my I.D.'s, my Avengers I.D. card--
AH, HELL.
TAXI
My passport and the Amex Black are still safe.
God this is a disaster.

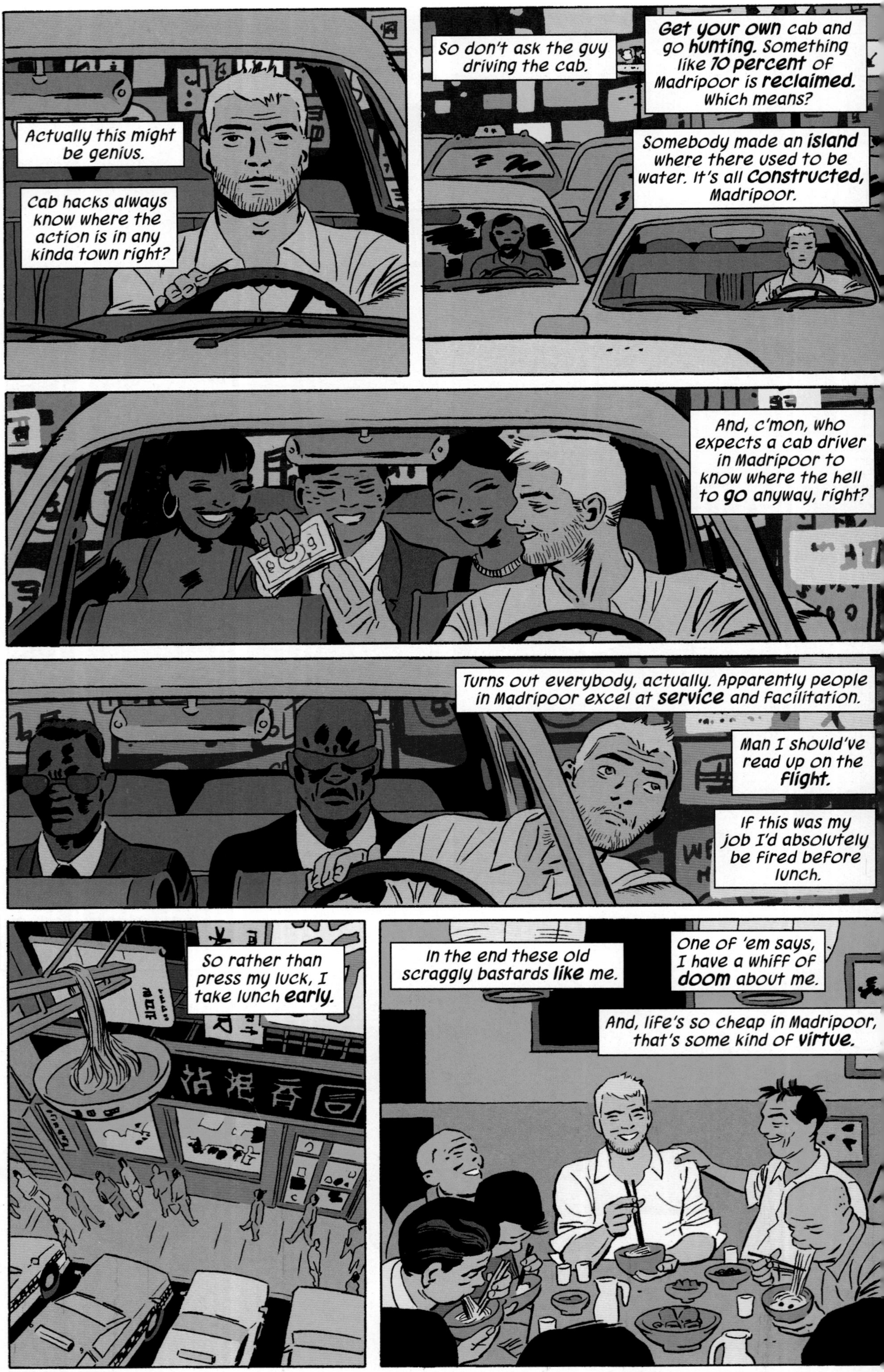
Actually this might be genius.
Cab hacks always know where the action is in any kinda town right?
So don't ask the guy driving the cab.
Get your own cab and go hunting. Something like 70 percent of Madripoor is reclaimed. Which means?
Somebody made an island where there used to be water. It's all constructed, Madripoor.
And, c'mon, who expects a cab driver in Madripoor to know where the hell to go anyway, right?
Turns out everybody, actually. Apparently people in Madripoor excel at service and facilitation.
Man I should've read up on the flight.
If this was my job I'd absolutely be fired before lunch.
So rather than press my luck, I take lunch early.
In the end these old scraggly bastards like me.
One of 'em says, I have a whiff of doom about me.
And, life's so cheap in Madripoor, that's some kind of virtue.

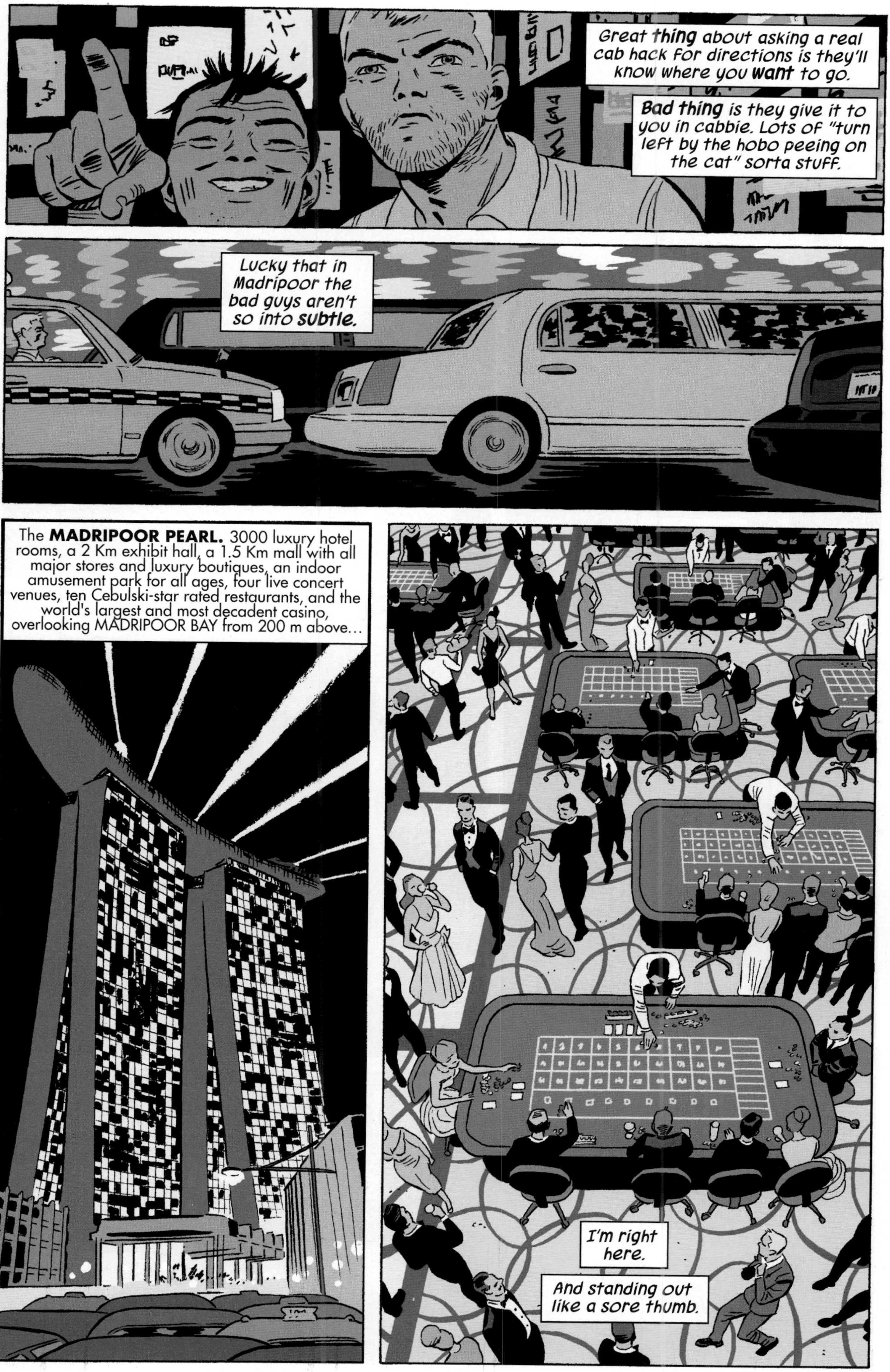
Great thing about asking a real cab hack for directions is they'll know where you want to go.
Bad thing is they give it to you in cabbie. Lots of "turn left by the hobo peeing on the cat" sorta stuff.
Lucky that in Madripoor the bad guys aren't so into subtle.
The MADRIPOOR PEARL. 3000 luxury hotel rooms, a 2 Km exhibit hall, a 1.5 Km mall with all major stores and luxury boutiques, an indoor amusement park for all ages, four live concert venues, ten Cebulski-star rated restaurants, and the world's largest and most decadent casino, overlooking MADRIPOOR BAY from 200 m above...
I'm right here.
And standing out like a sore thumb.

WHOA WHOA WHOA--

Not a *single* raised voice.

Not a *gasp.*

It's Madripoor. People get black-bagged all the time and nobody cares.

The crowd noise dims. A door shuts.

Echoes of heels on tile floor in a hallway like Lee Marvin in *Point Blank.*

Whispers, barks. A left, two rights. Another door shut. I'm held down. Tied up.

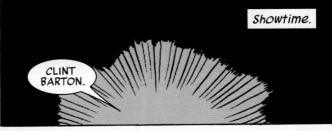

Showtime.

CLINT BARTON.

"HAWKEYE."

HI.

YOU GUYS FANS? I LOVE MEETING--

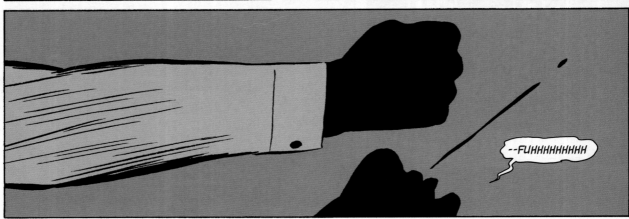

--FUHHHHHHHHH

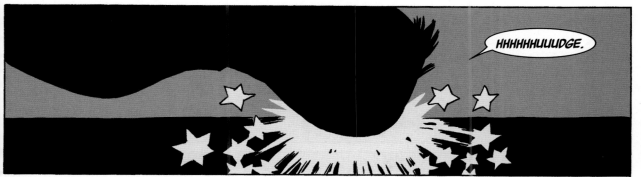

HHHHHHUUUDGE.

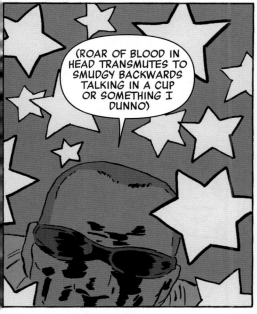

(ROAR OF BLOOD IN HEAD TRANSMUTES TO SMUDGY BACKWARDS TALKING IN A CUP OR SOMETHING I DUNNO)

GOTCHER PASSPORT, MAN. NO WEAPONS THOUGH? THAT'S CRAZY.

IN THE CAR. HE HAD HIS BOW IN THE CAR.

DON'T TAKE THE AMEX BLACK-- PLEASE--HILL WILL KILL ME--

AFTER WE MAIL YOUR HEAD TO CAPTAIN AMERICA, I'M GONNA SELL THIS THING ON eBAY--

A-HEM.

YOU'LL DO NO SUCH THING.

YES, MADAME MASQUE.

LIGHTS OUT. TAKE HIM UP TO MY ROOM NOW.

YOU GOT IT, MADAME MASQUE.

OH COME ON I

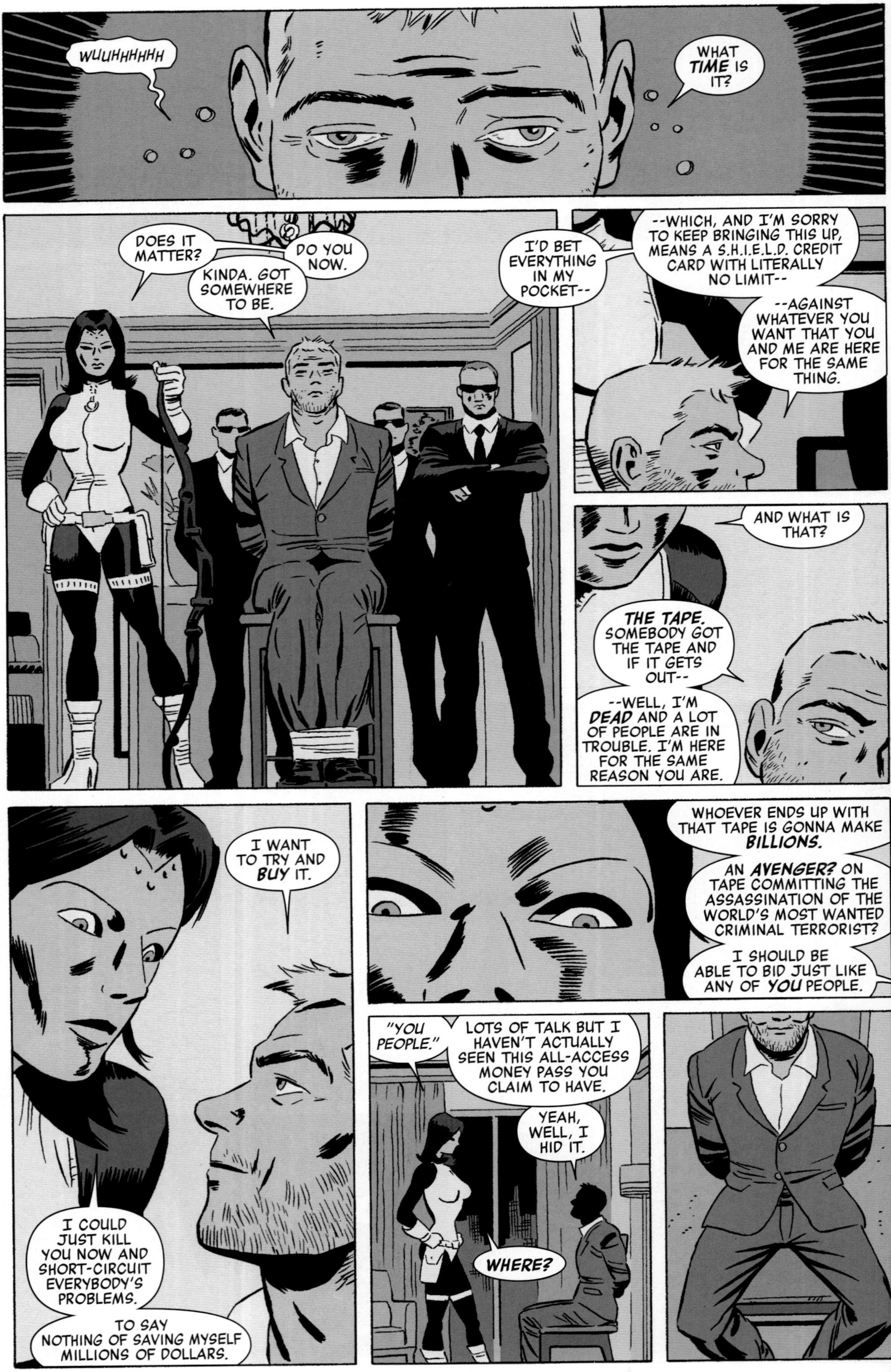
WUUHHHHHH
WHAT TIME IS IT?
DOES IT MATTER?
KINDA. GOT SOMEWHERE TO BE.
DO YOU NOW.
I'D BET EVERYTHING IN MY POCKET--
--WHICH, AND I'M SORRY TO KEEP BRINGING THIS UP, MEANS A S.H.I.E.L.D. CREDIT CARD WITH LITERALLY NO LIMIT--
--AGAINST WHATEVER YOU WANT THAT YOU AND ME ARE HERE FOR THE SAME THING.
AND WHAT IS THAT?
THE TAPE. SOMEBODY GOT THE TAPE AND IF IT GETS OUT--
--WELL, I'M DEAD AND A LOT OF PEOPLE ARE IN TROUBLE. I'M HERE FOR THE SAME REASON YOU ARE.
I WANT TO TRY AND BUY IT.
I COULD JUST KILL YOU NOW AND SHORT-CIRCUIT EVERYBODY'S PROBLEMS.
TO SAY NOTHING OF SAVING MYSELF MILLIONS OF DOLLARS.
WHOEVER ENDS UP WITH THAT TAPE IS GONNA MAKE BILLIONS.
AN AVENGER? ON TAPE COMMITTING THE ASSASSINATION OF THE WORLD'S MOST WANTED CRIMINAL TERRORIST?
I SHOULD BE ABLE TO BID JUST LIKE ANY OF YOU PEOPLE.
"YOU PEOPLE."
LOTS OF TALK BUT I HAVEN'T ACTUALLY SEEN THIS ALL-ACCESS MONEY PASS YOU CLAIM TO HAVE.
YEAH, WELL, I HID IT.
WHERE?

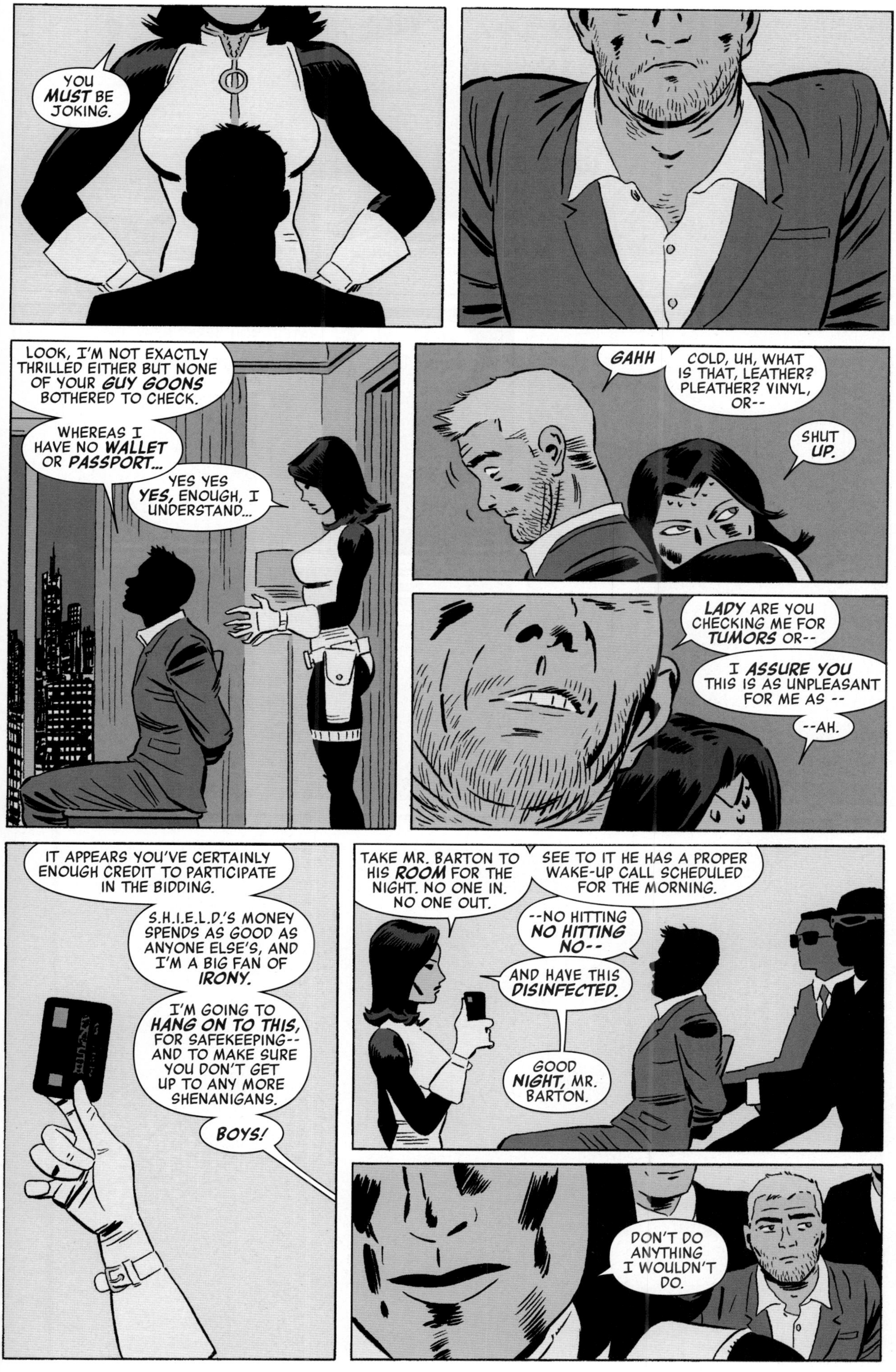
YOU MUST BE JOKING.
LOOK, I'M NOT EXACTLY THRILLED EITHER BUT NONE OF YOUR GUY GOONS BOTHERED TO CHECK.
WHEREAS I HAVE NO WALLET OR PASSPORT...
YES YES YES, ENOUGH, I UNDERSTAND...
GAHH
COLD, UH, WHAT IS THAT, LEATHER? PLEATHER? VINYL, OR--
SHUT UP.
LADY ARE YOU CHECKING ME FOR TUMORS OR--
I ASSURE YOU THIS IS AS UNPLEASANT FOR ME AS --
--AH.
IT APPEARS YOU'VE CERTAINLY ENOUGH CREDIT TO PARTICIPATE IN THE BIDDING.
S.H.I.E.L.D.'S MONEY SPENDS AS GOOD AS ANYONE ELSE'S, AND I'M A BIG FAN OF IRONY.
I'M GOING TO HANG ON TO THIS, FOR SAFEKEEPING-- AND TO MAKE SURE YOU DON'T GET UP TO ANY MORE SHENANIGANS.
BOYS!
TAKE MR. BARTON TO HIS ROOM FOR THE NIGHT. NO ONE IN. NO ONE OUT.
SEE TO IT HE HAS A PROPER WAKE-UP CALL SCHEDULED FOR THE MORNING.
--NO HITTING NO HITTING NO--
AND HAVE THIS DISINFECTED.
GOOD NIGHT, MR. BARTON.
DON'T DO ANYTHING I WOULDN'T DO.

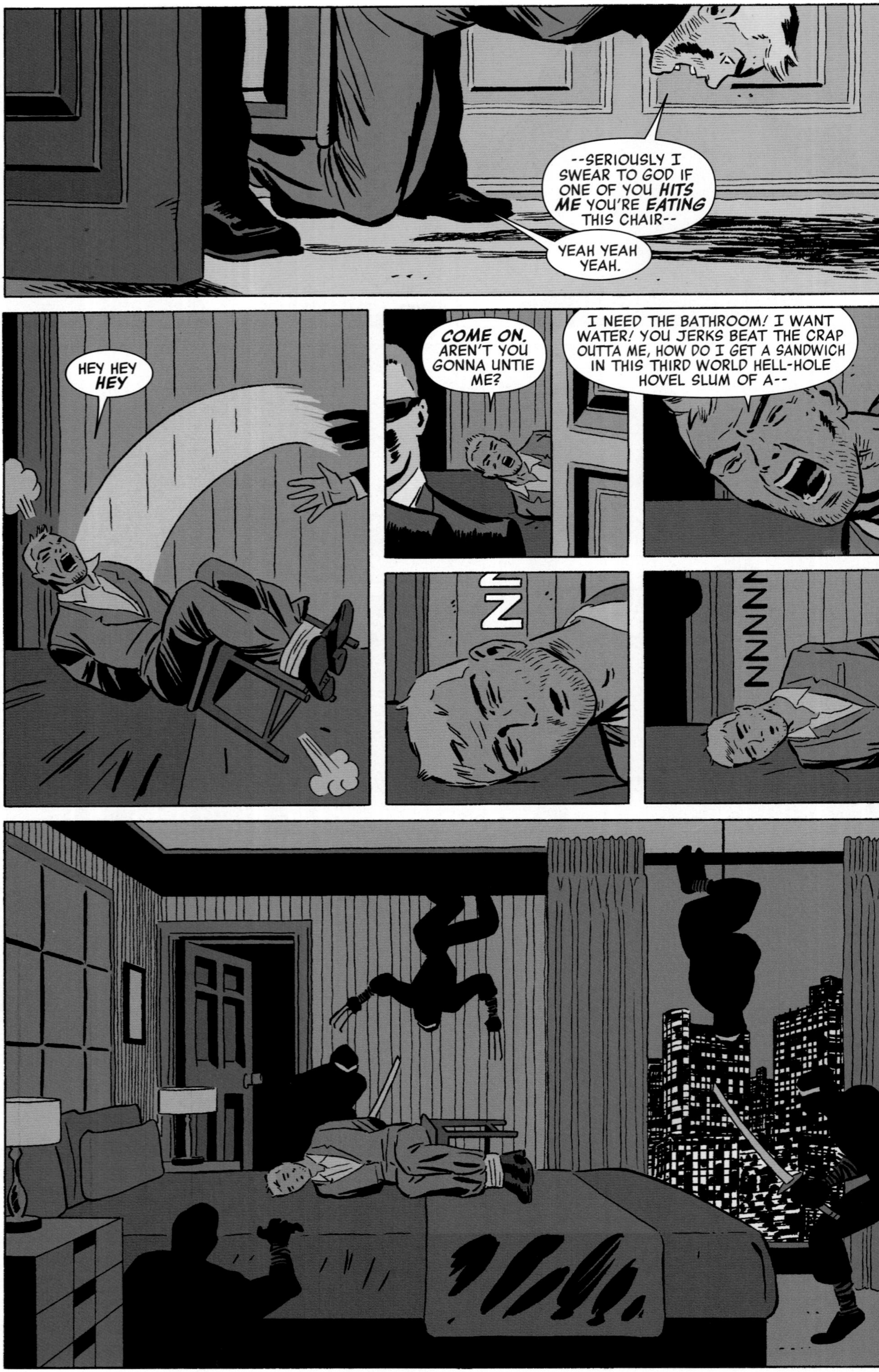
--SERIOUSLY I SWEAR TO GOD IF ONE OF YOU HITS ME YOU'RE EATING THIS CHAIR--
YEAH YEAH YEAH.
HEY HEY HEY
COME ON. AREN'T YOU GONNA UNTIE ME?
I NEED THE BATHROOM! I WANT WATER! YOU JERKS BEAT THE CRAP OUTTA ME, HOW DO I GET A SANDWICH IN THIS THIRD WORLD HELL-HOLE HOVEL SLUM OF A--
ZZ
ZZZZZZ

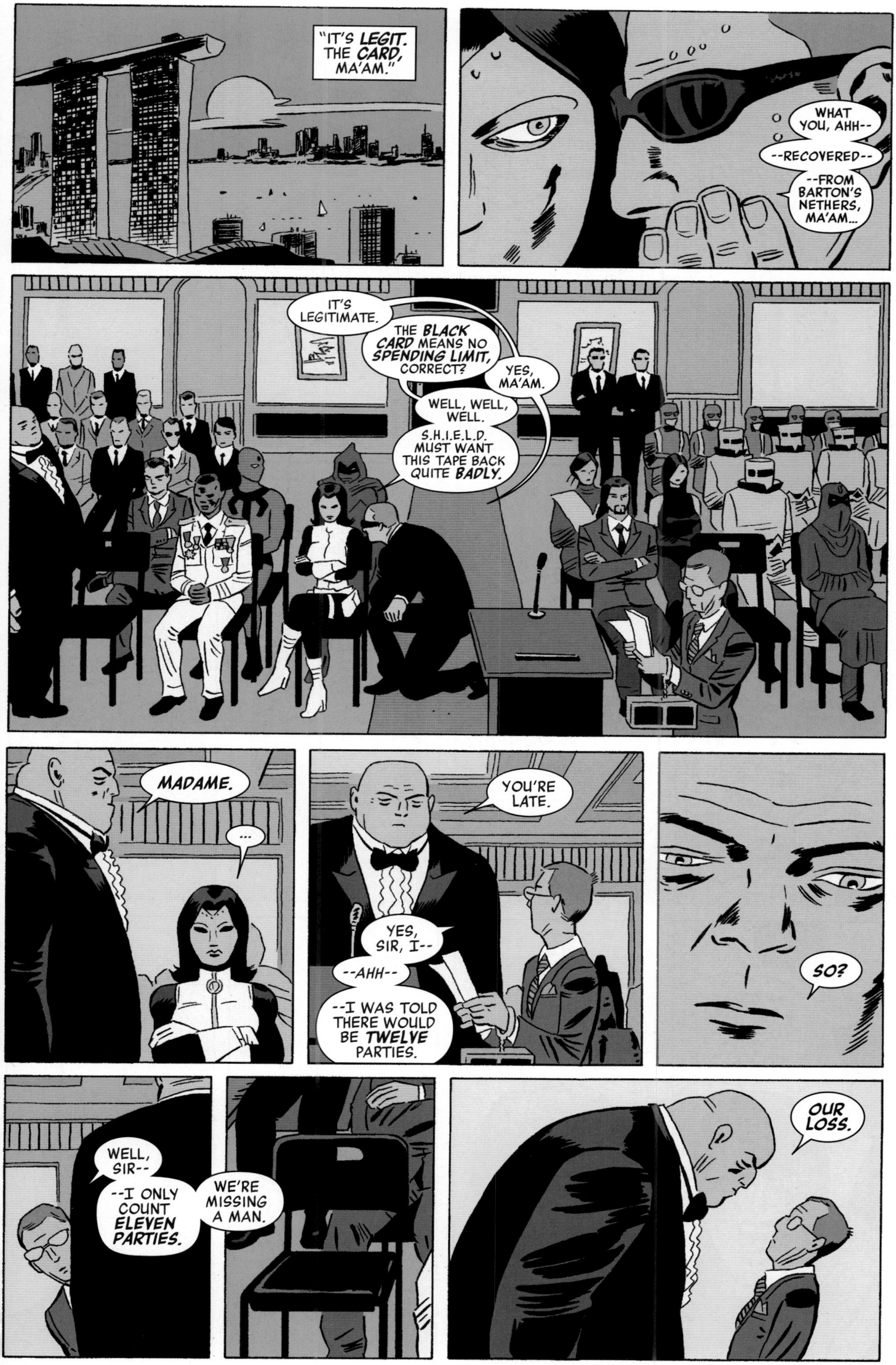
"IT'S LEGIT. THE CARD, MA'AM."
WHAT YOU, AHH--
--RECOVERED--
--FROM BARTON'S NETHERS, MA'AM...
IT'S LEGITIMATE.
THE BLACK CARD MEANS NO SPENDING LIMIT, CORRECT?
YES, MA'AM.
WELL, WELL, WELL.
S.H.I.E.L.D. MUST WANT THIS TAPE BACK QUITE BADLY.
MADAME.
...
YOU'RE LATE.
YES, SIR, I--
--AHH--
--I WAS TOLD THERE WOULD BE TWELVE PARTIES.
SO?
WELL, SIR--
--I ONLY COUNT ELEVEN PARTIES.
WE'RE MISSING A MAN.
OUR LOSS.

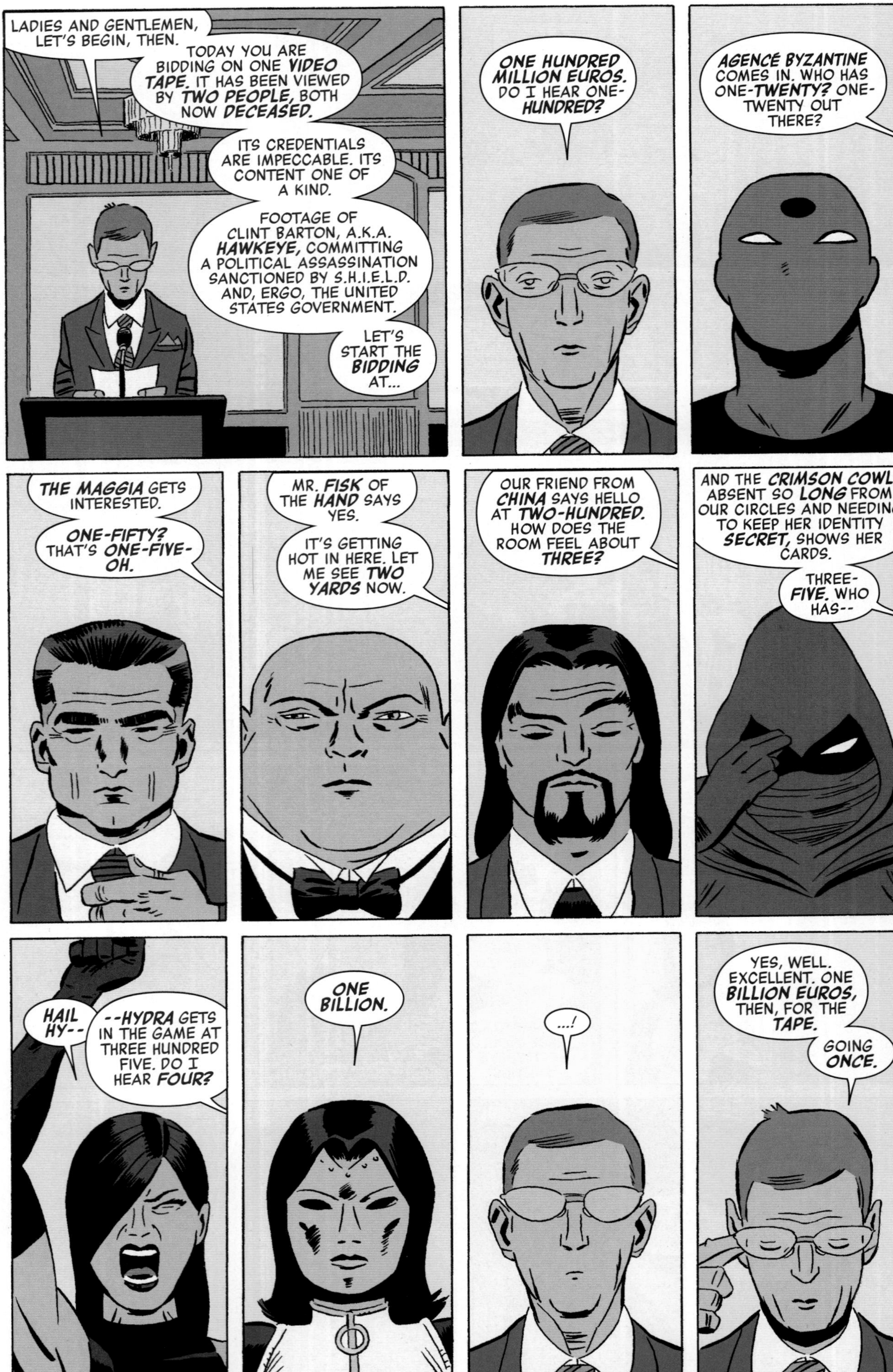
LADIES AND GENTLEMEN, LET'S BEGIN, THEN.
TODAY YOU ARE BIDDING ON ONE VIDEO TAPE. IT HAS BEEN VIEWED BY TWO PEOPLE, BOTH NOW DECEASED.
ITS CREDENTIALS ARE IMPECCABLE. ITS CONTENT ONE OF A KIND.
FOOTAGE OF CLINT BARTON, A.K.A. HAWKEYE, COMMITTING A POLITICAL ASSASSINATION SANCTIONED BY S.H.I.E.L.D. AND, ERGO, THE UNITED STATES GOVERNMENT.
LET'S START THE BIDDING AT...
ONE HUNDRED MILLION EUROS. DO I HEAR ONE-HUNDRED?
AGENCE BYZANTINE COMES IN. WHO HAS ONE-TWENTY? ONE-TWENTY OUT THERE?
THE MAGGIA GETS INTERESTED.
ONE-FIFTY? THAT'S ONE-FIVE-OH.
MR. FISK OF THE HAND SAYS YES.
IT'S GETTING HOT IN HERE. LET ME SEE TWO YARDS NOW.
OUR FRIEND FROM CHINA SAYS HELLO AT TWO-HUNDRED. HOW DOES THE ROOM FEEL ABOUT THREE?
AND THE CRIMSON COWL, ABSENT SO LONG FROM OUR CIRCLES AND NEEDING TO KEEP HER IDENTITY SECRET, SHOWS HER CARDS.
THREE-FIVE. WHO HAS--
HAIL HY--
--HYDRA GETS IN THE GAME AT THREE HUNDRED FIVE. DO I HEAR FOUR?
ONE BILLION.
...!
YES, WELL. EXCELLENT. ONE BILLION EUROS, THEN, FOR THE TAPE.
GOING ONCE.

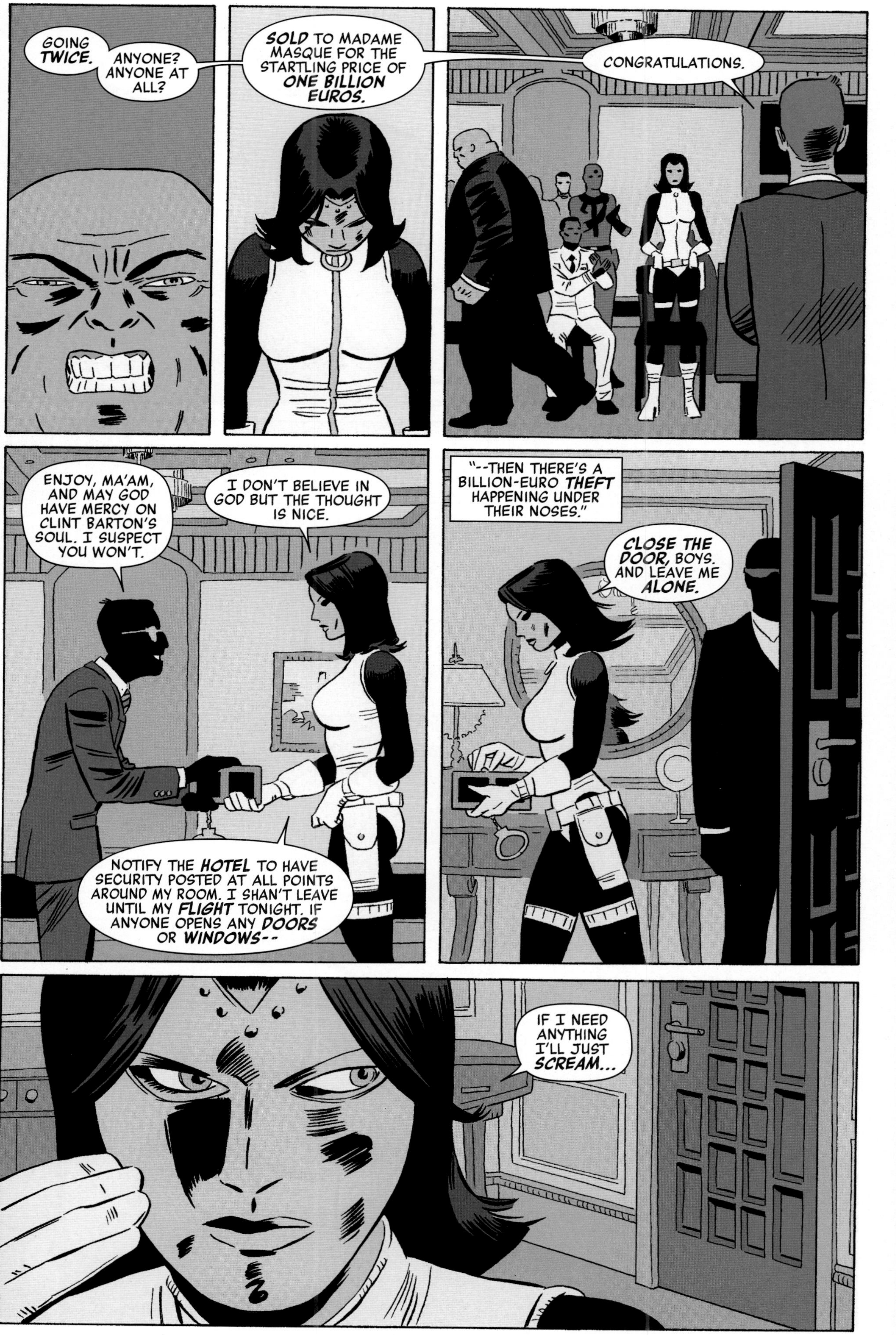
GOING TWICE.
ANYONE? ANYONE AT ALL?
SOLD TO MADAME MASQUE FOR THE STARTLING PRICE OF ONE BILLION EUROS.
CONGRATULATIONS.
ENJOY, MA'AM, AND MAY GOD HAVE MERCY ON CLINT BARTON'S SOUL. I SUSPECT YOU WON'T.
I DON'T BELIEVE IN GOD BUT THE THOUGHT IS NICE.
NOTIFY THE HOTEL TO HAVE SECURITY POSTED AT ALL POINTS AROUND MY ROOM. I SHAN'T LEAVE UNTIL MY FLIGHT TONIGHT. IF ANYONE OPENS ANY DOORS OR WINDOWS--
"--THEN THERE'S A BILLION-EURO THEFT HAPPENING UNDER THEIR NOSES."
CLOSE THE DOOR, BOYS. AND LEAVE ME ALONE.
IF I NEED ANYTHING I'LL JUST SCREAM...

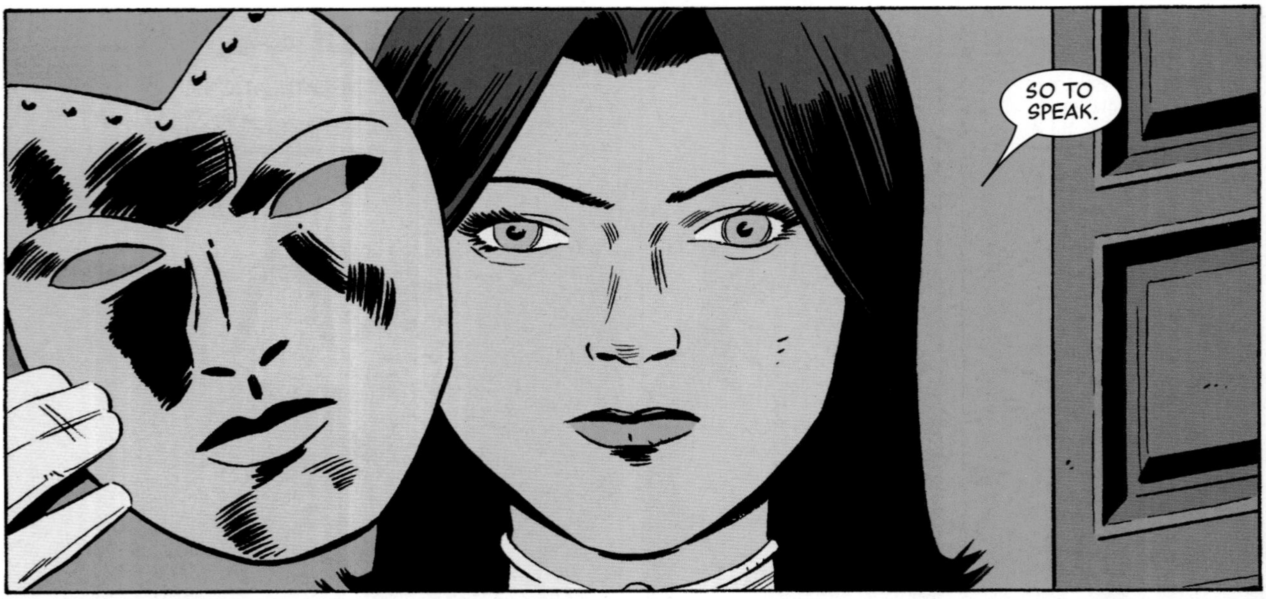
SO TO SPEAK.

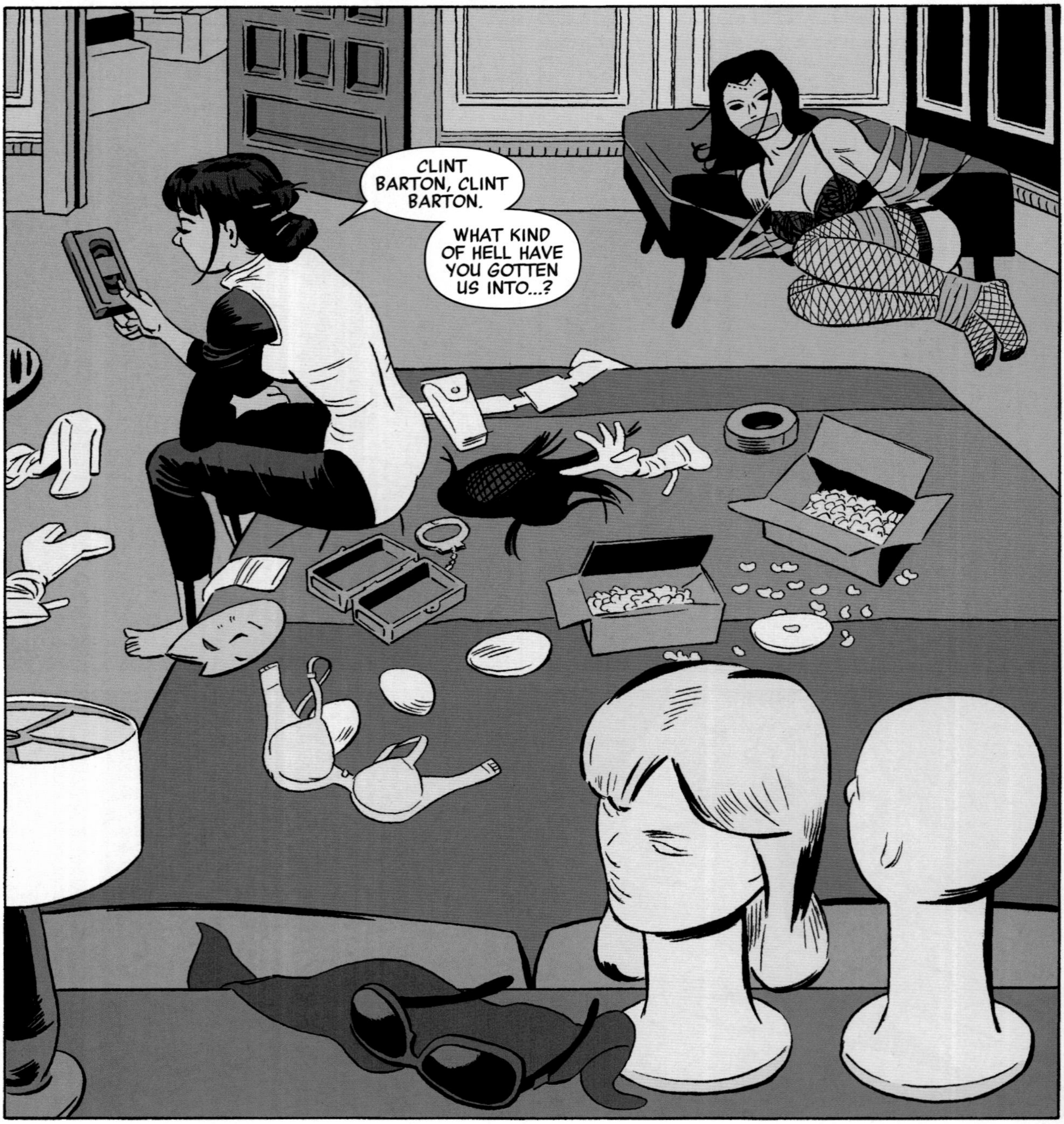
CLINT BARTON, CLINT BARTON.
WHAT KIND OF HELL HAVE YOU GOTTEN US INTO...?

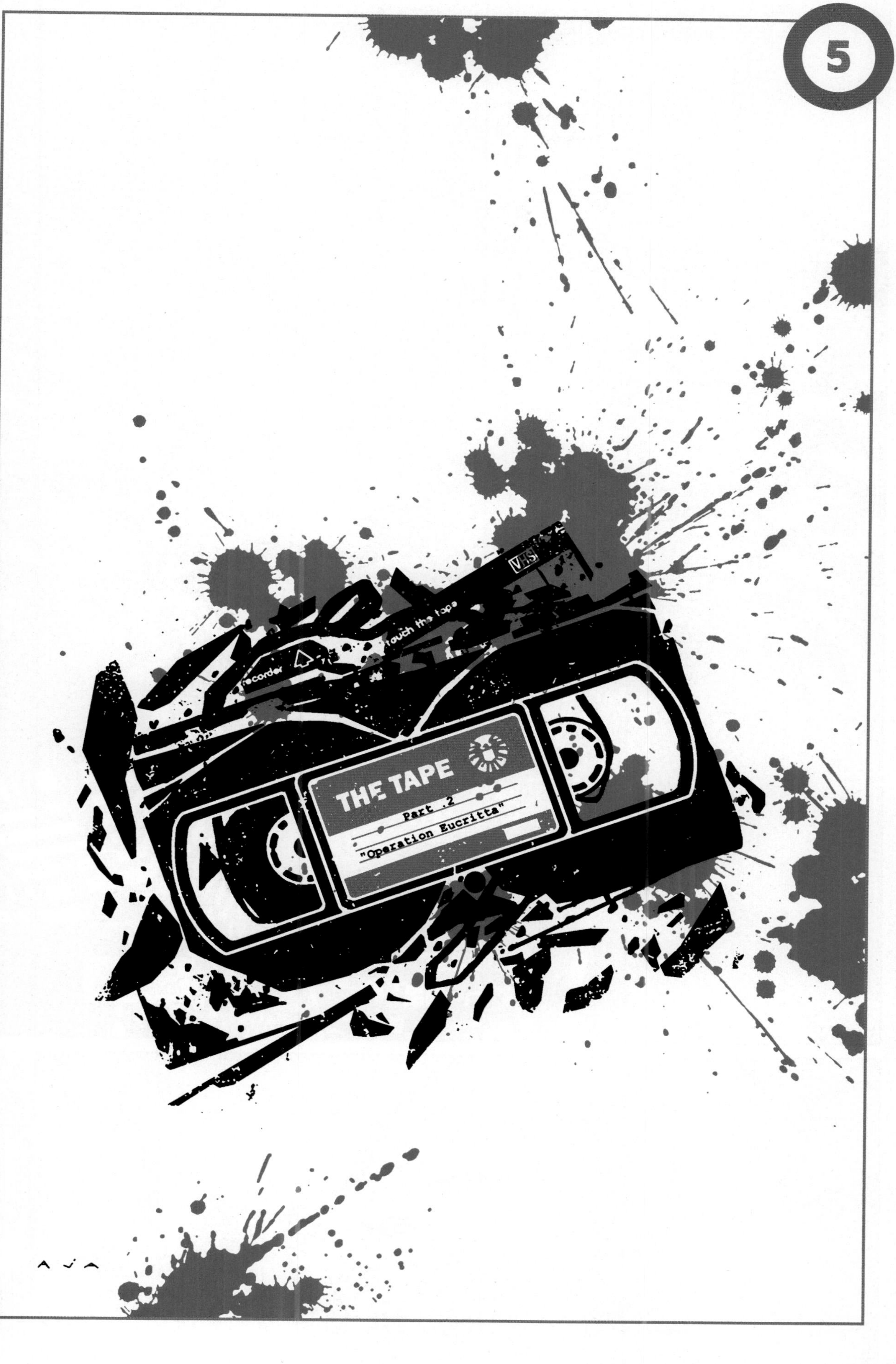
5
THE TAPE
Part .2
"Operation Eucritta"

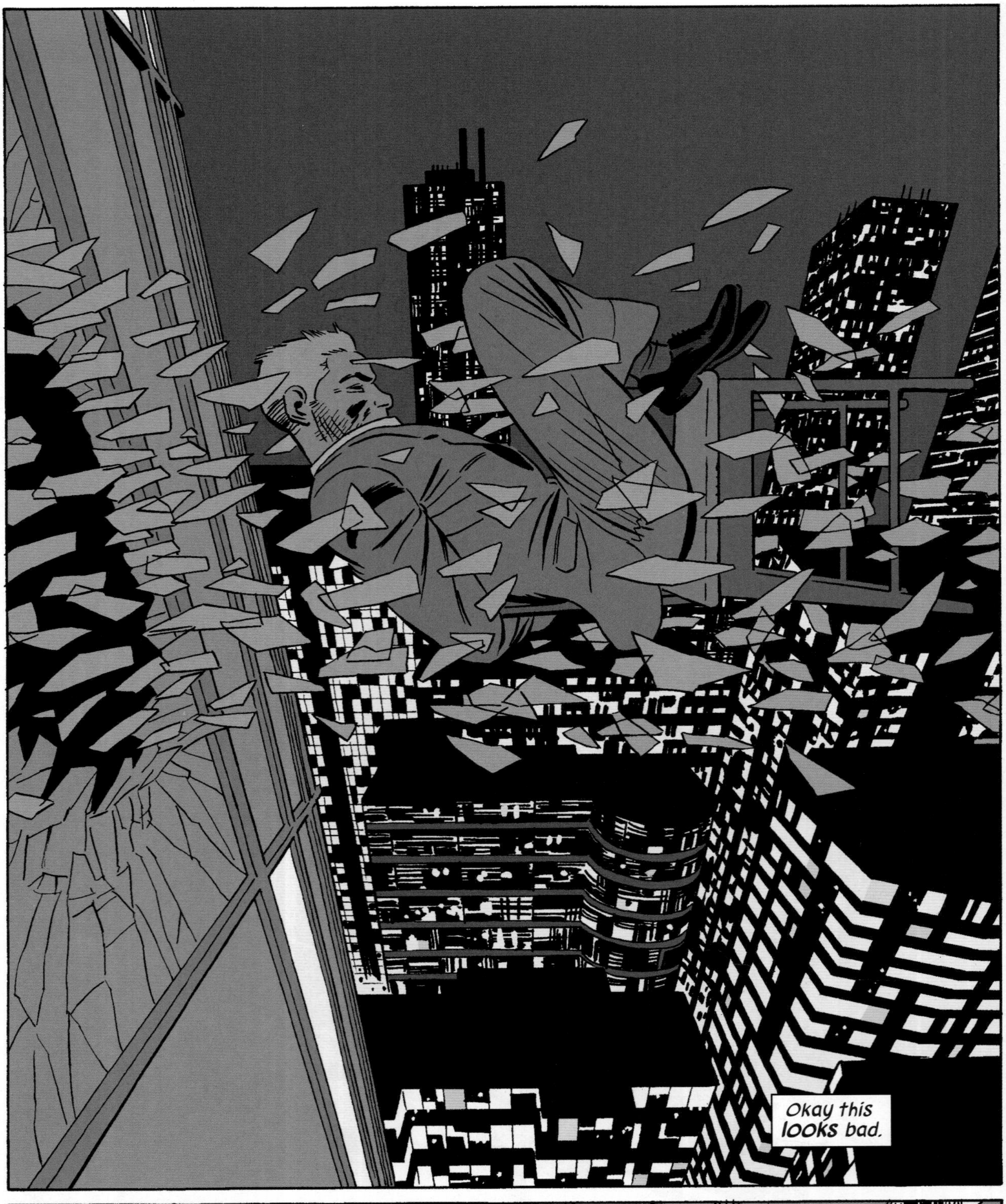
Okay this **looks** bad.

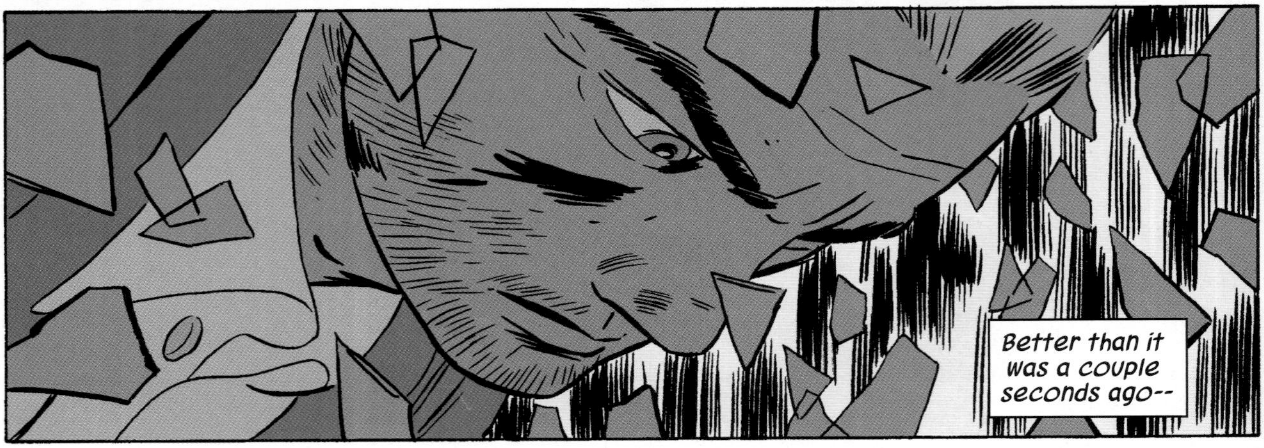
Better than it was a couple seconds ago--

A COUPLE SECONDS AGO:

UM. HELLO?

--Uh-Oh--

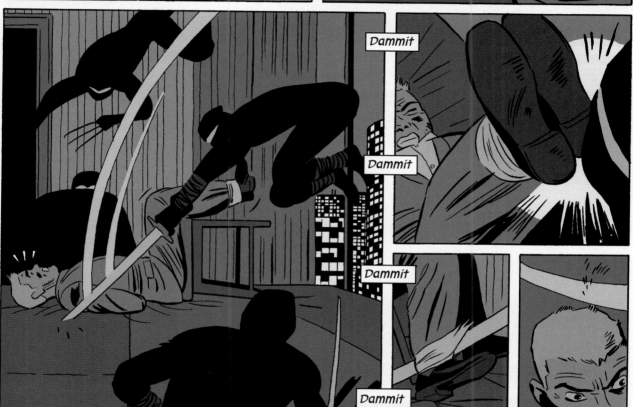

Dammit

Dammit

Dammit

Dammit

Dammit--

MAN does this look bad.

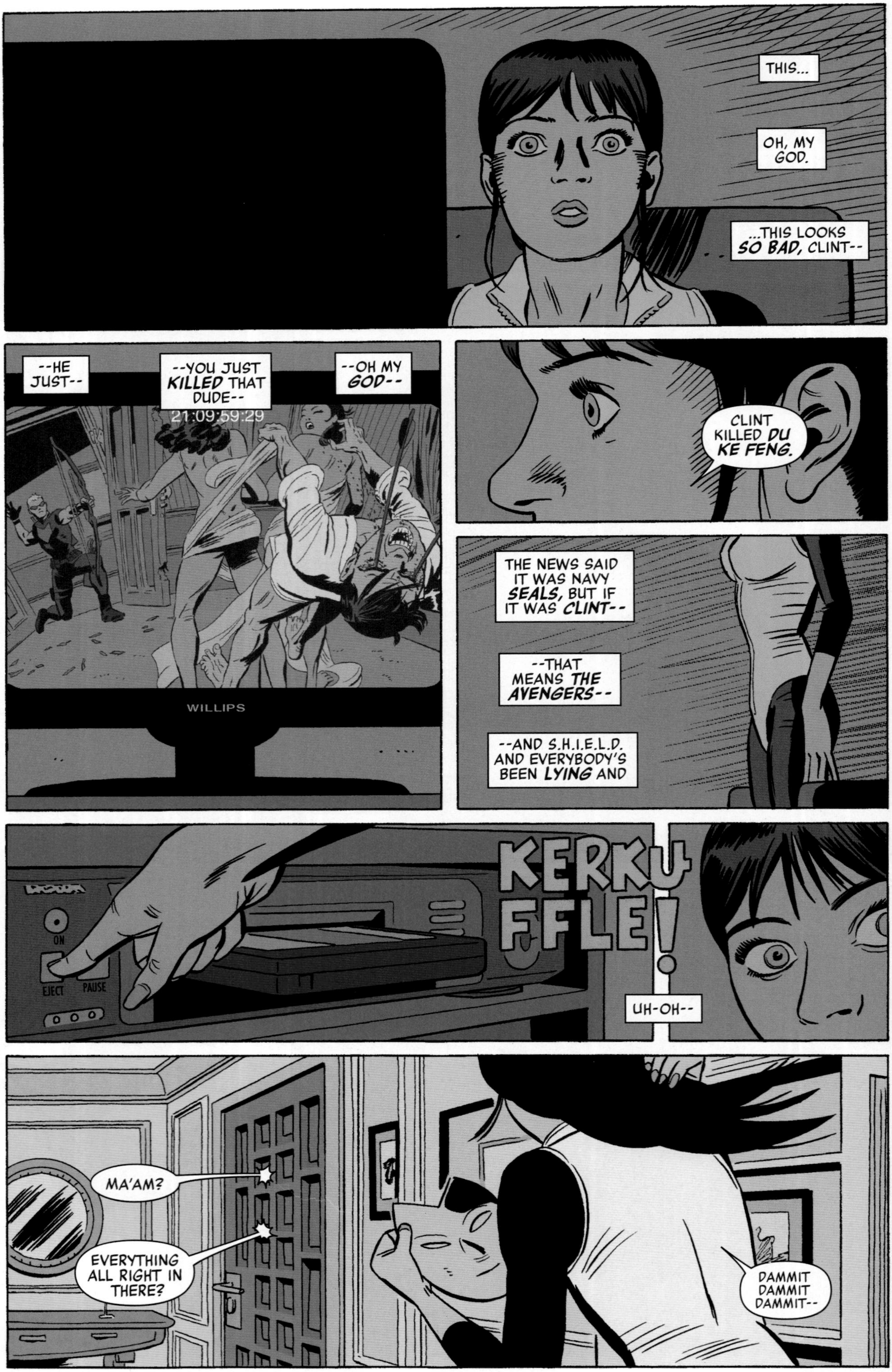
THIS...
OH, MY GOD.
...THIS LOOKS SO BAD, CLINT--
--HE JUST--
--YOU JUST KILLED THAT DUDE--
--OH MY GOD--
21:09:59:29
WILLIPS
CLINT KILLED DU KE FENG.
THE NEWS SAID IT WAS NAVY SEALS, BUT IF IT WAS CLINT--
--THAT MEANS THE AVENGERS--
--AND S.H.I.E.L.D. AND EVERYBODY'S BEEN LYING AND
ON
EJECT
PAUSE
KERKUFFLE!
UH-OH--
MA'AM?
EVERYTHING ALL RIGHT IN THERE?
DAMMIT DAMMIT DAMMIT--

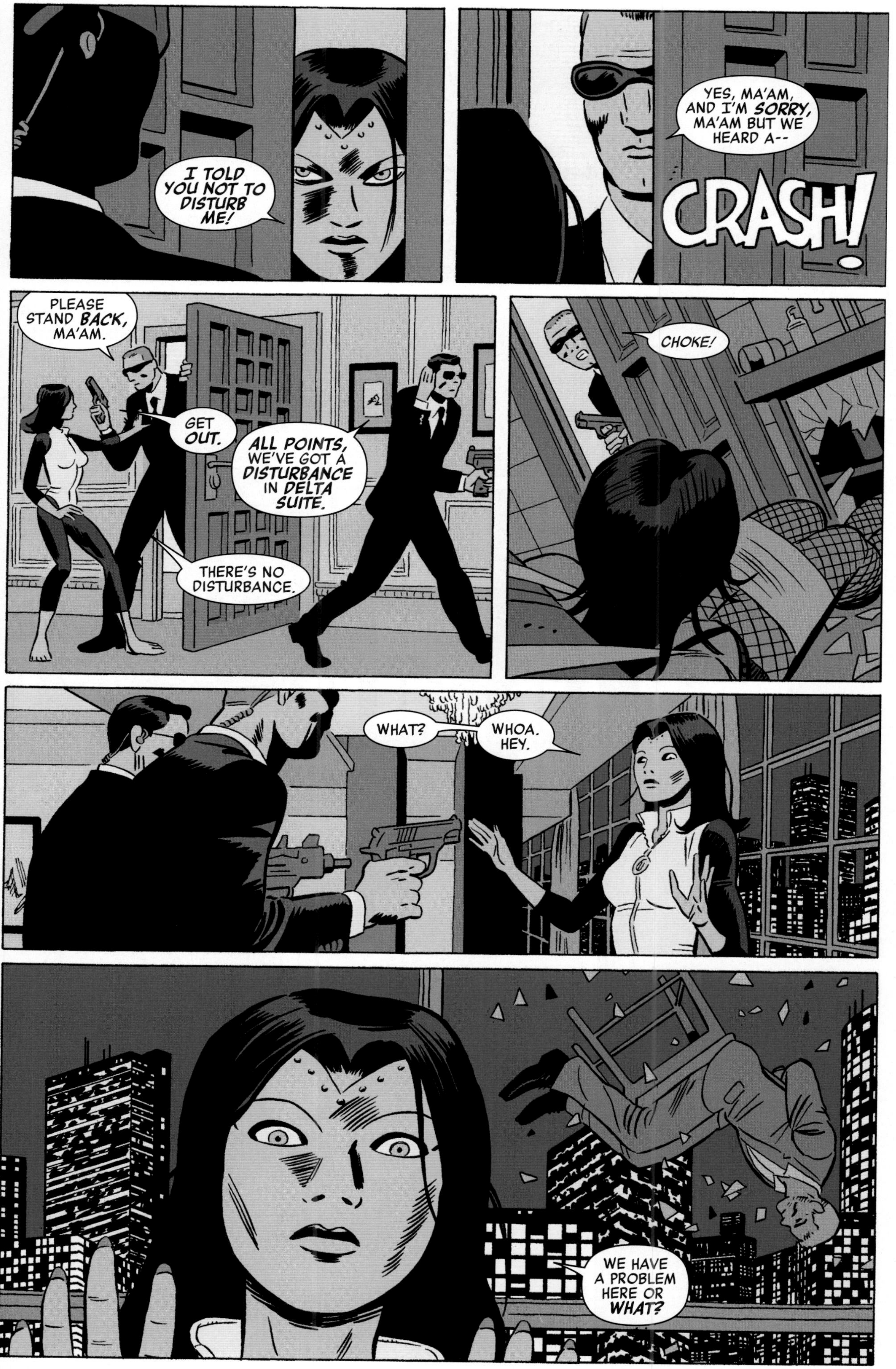
I TOLD YOU NOT TO DISTURB ME!
YES, MA'AM, AND I'M SORRY, MA'AM BUT WE HEARD A--
CRASH!
PLEASE STAND BACK, MA'AM.
GET OUT.
ALL POINTS, WE'VE GOT A DISTURBANCE IN DELTA SUITE.
THERE'S NO DISTURBANCE.
CHOKE!
WHAT?
WHOA. HEY.
WE HAVE A PROBLEM HERE OR WHAT?

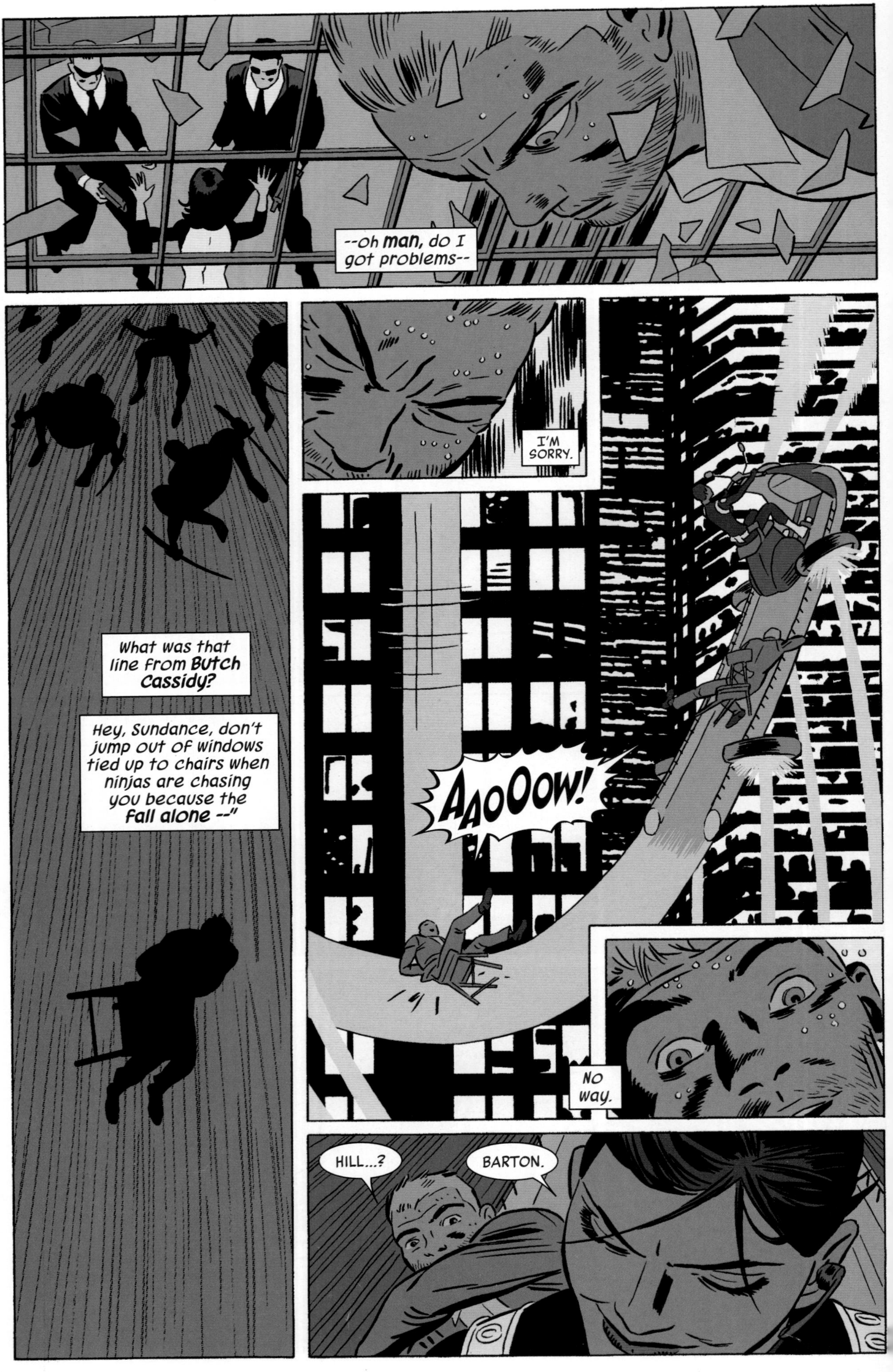
--oh man, do I got problems--
I'M SORRY.
What was that line from Butch Cassidy?
Hey, Sundance, don't jump out of windows tied up to chairs when ninjas are chasing you because the fall alone --"
AAOOOW!
No way.
HILL...?
BARTON.

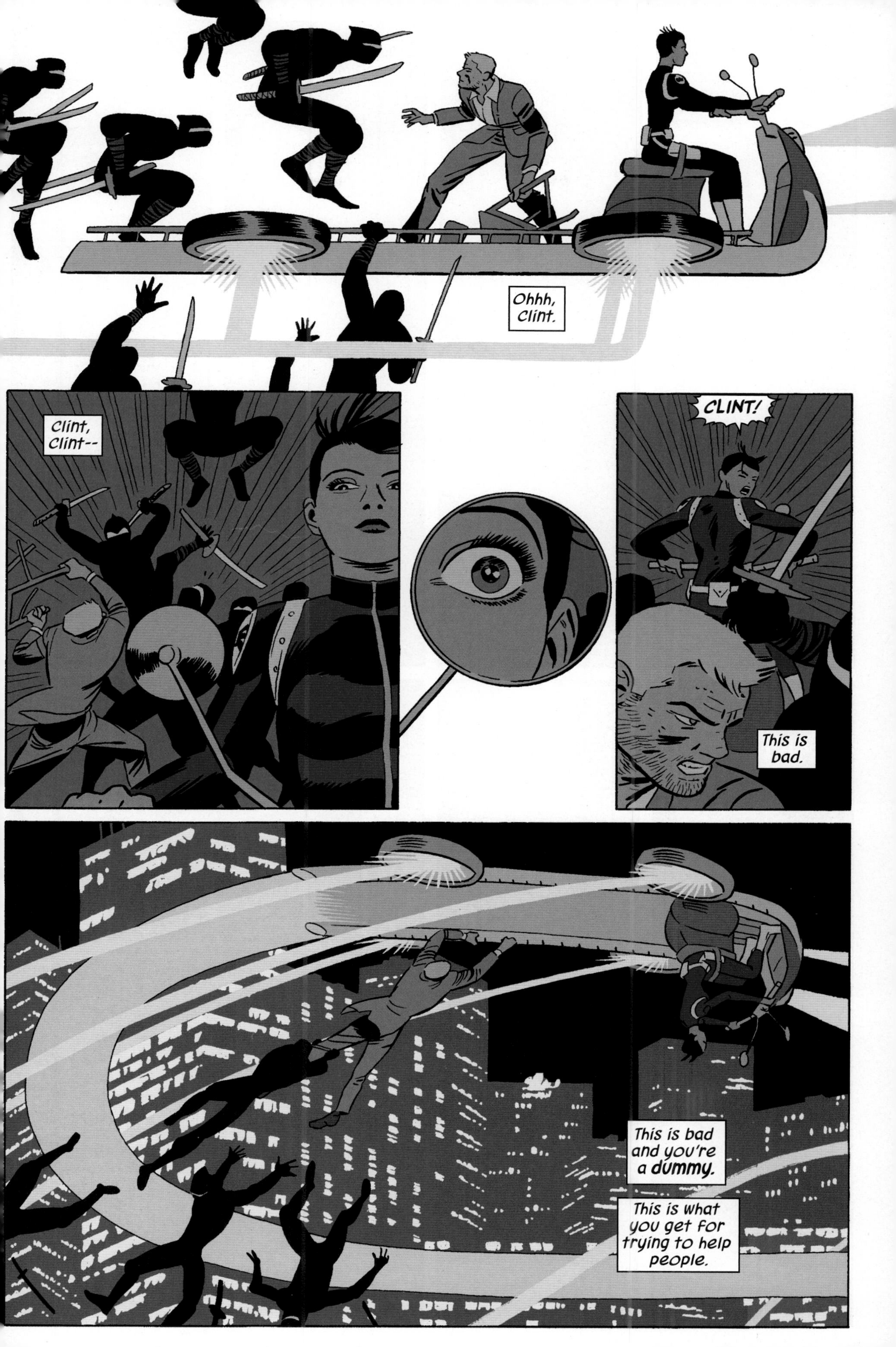
Ohhh, Clint.
Clint, Clint--
CLINT!
This is bad.
This is bad and you're a dummy.
This is what you get for trying to help people.

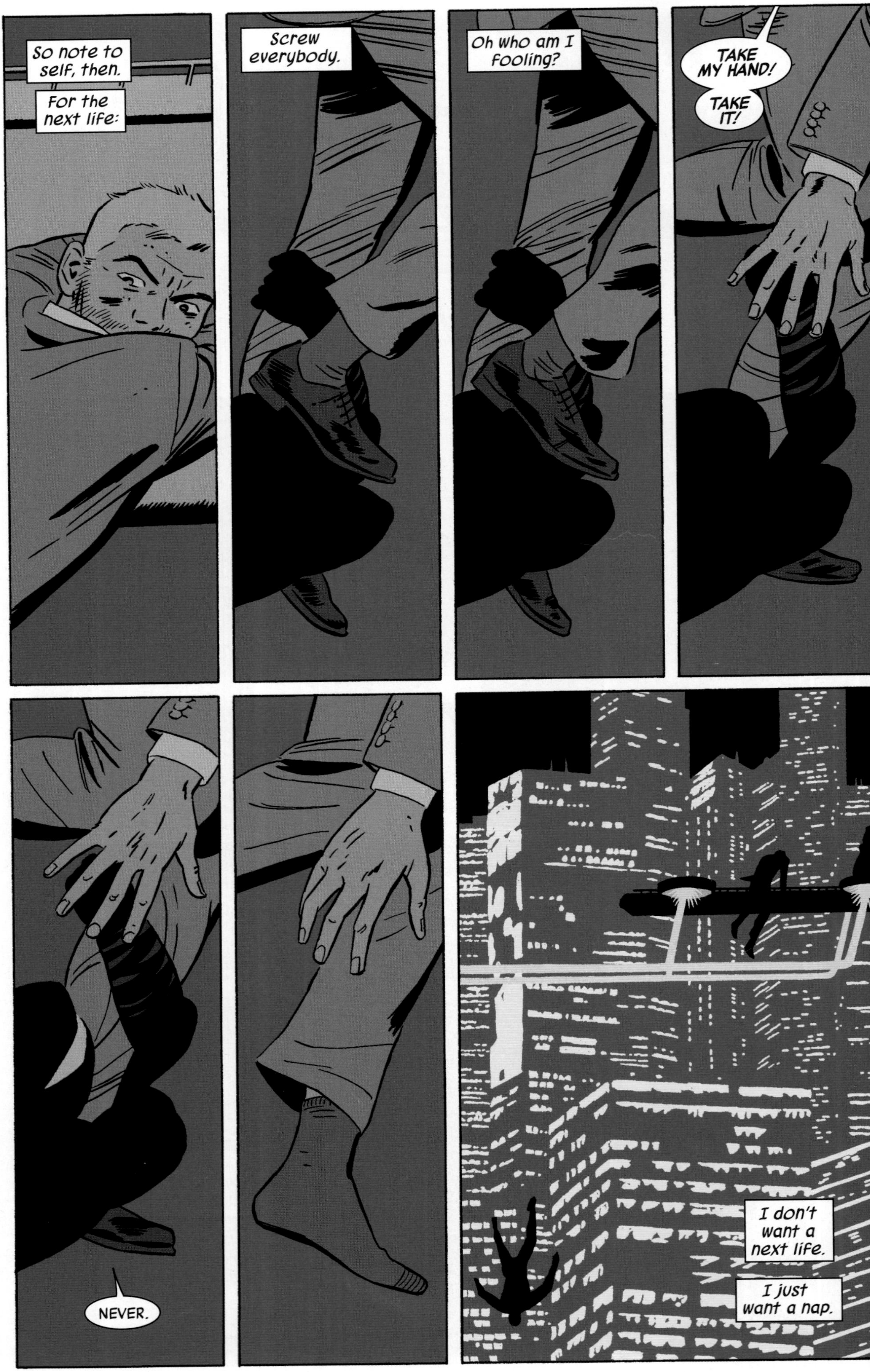
So note to self, then.
For the next life:
Screw everybody.
Oh who am I fooling?
TAKE MY HAND!
TAKE IT!
NEVER.
I don't want a next life.
I just want a nap.

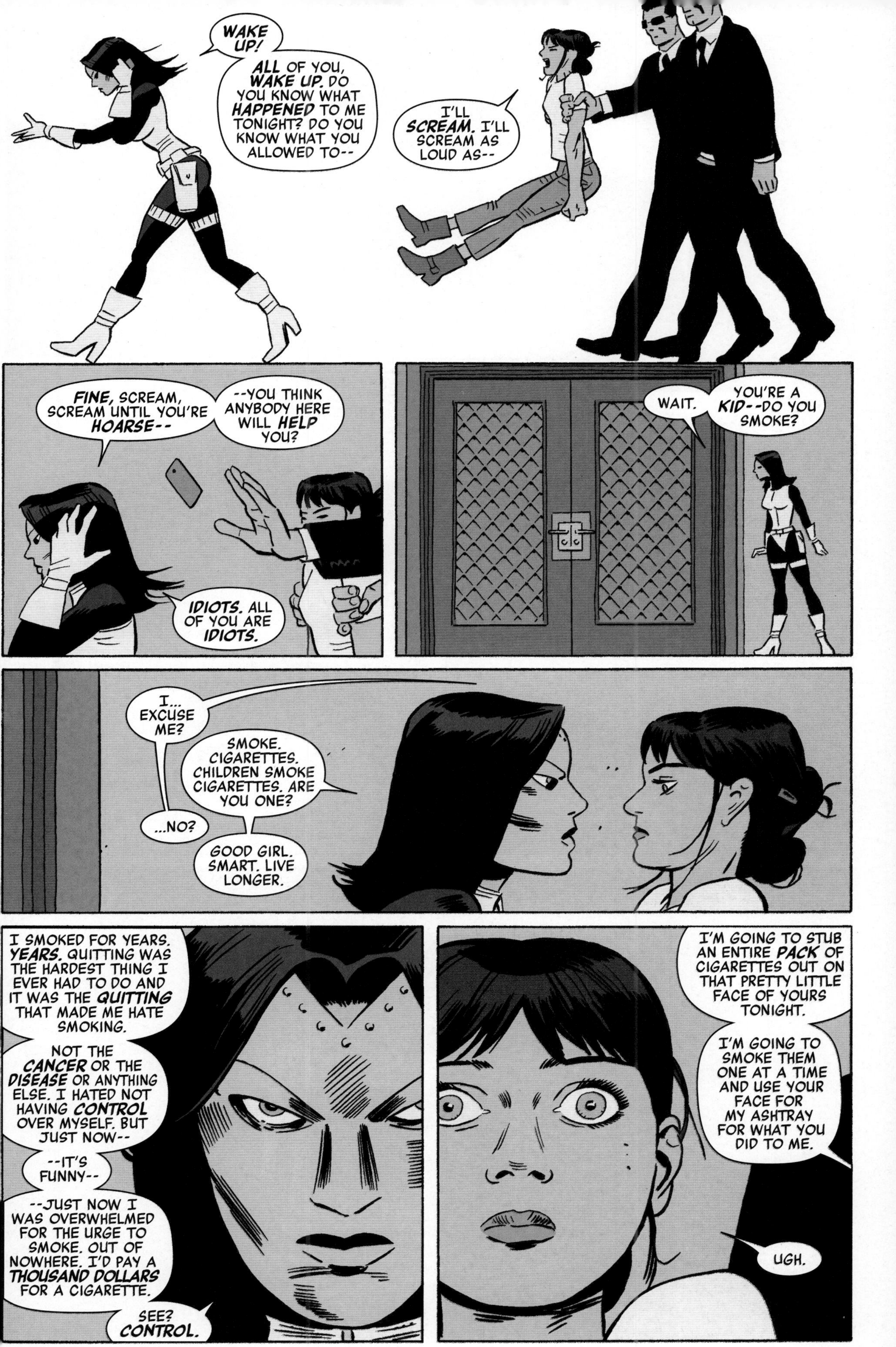

WAKE UP!
ALL OF YOU, WAKE UP. DO YOU KNOW WHAT HAPPENED TO ME TONIGHT? DO YOU KNOW WHAT YOU ALLOWED TO--
I'LL SCREAM. I'LL SCREAM AS LOUD AS--
FINE, SCREAM, SCREAM UNTIL YOU'RE HOARSE--
--YOU THINK ANYBODY HERE WILL HELP YOU?
IDIOTS. ALL OF YOU ARE IDIOTS.
WAIT.
YOU'RE A KID--DO YOU SMOKE?
I... EXCUSE ME?
SMOKE. CIGARETTES. CHILDREN SMOKE CIGARETTES. ARE YOU ONE?
...NO?
GOOD GIRL. SMART. LIVE LONGER.
I SMOKED FOR YEARS. YEARS. QUITTING WAS THE HARDEST THING I EVER HAD TO DO AND IT WAS THE QUITTING THAT MADE ME HATE SMOKING.
NOT THE CANCER OR THE DISEASE OR ANYTHING ELSE. I HATED NOT HAVING CONTROL OVER MYSELF. BUT JUST NOW--
--IT'S FUNNY--
--JUST NOW I WAS OVERWHELMED FOR THE URGE TO SMOKE. OUT OF NOWHERE. I'D PAY A THOUSAND DOLLARS FOR A CIGARETTE.
SEE? CONTROL.
I'M GOING TO STUB AN ENTIRE PACK OF CIGARETTES OUT ON THAT PRETTY LITTLE FACE OF YOURS TONIGHT.
I'M GOING TO SMOKE THEM ONE AT A TIME AND USE YOUR FACE FOR MY ASHTRAY FOR WHAT YOU DID TO ME.
UGH.

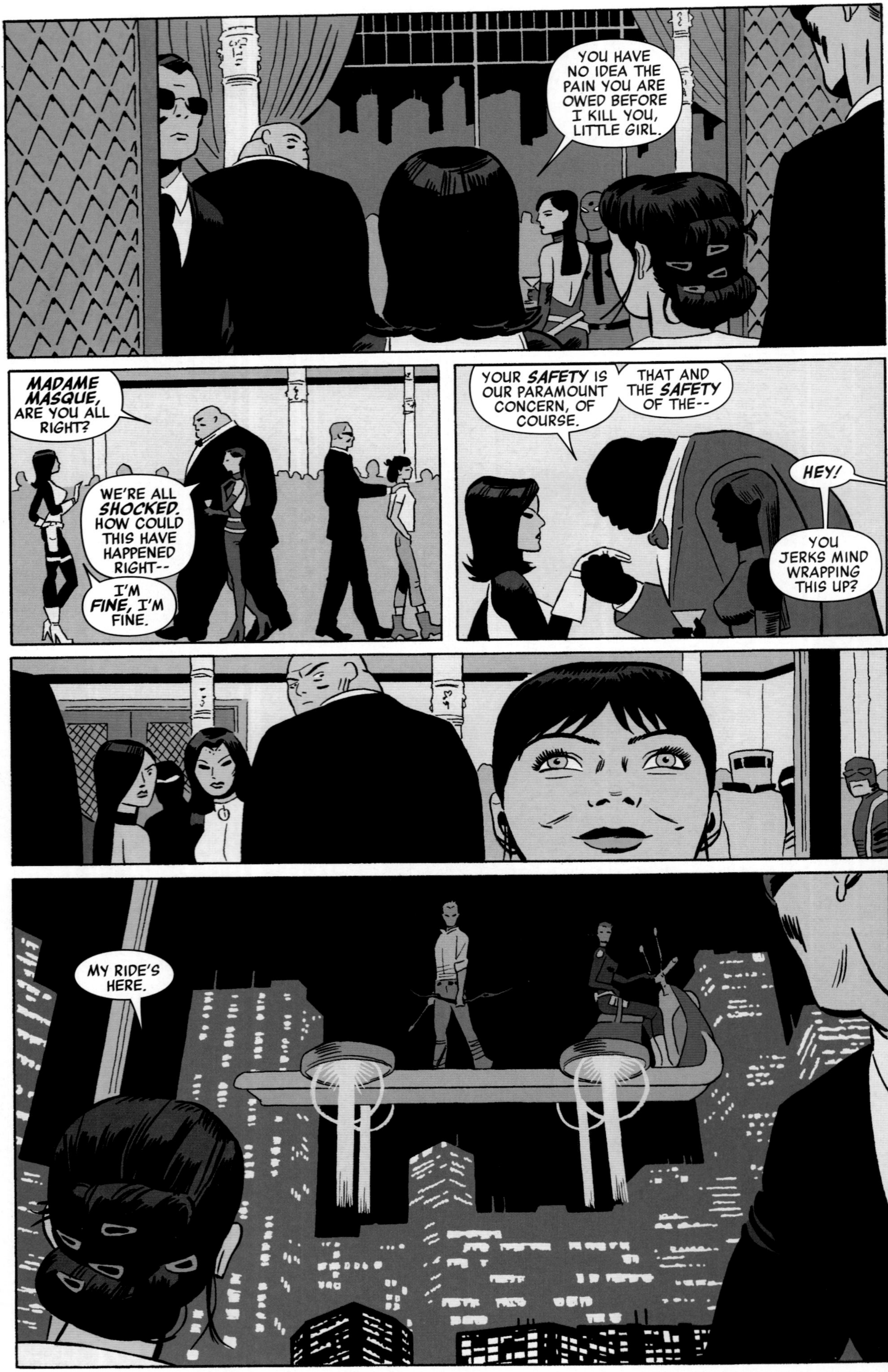

YOU HAVE NO IDEA THE PAIN YOU ARE OWED BEFORE I KILL YOU, LITTLE GIRL.
MADAME MASQUE, ARE YOU ALL RIGHT?
WE'RE ALL SHOCKED. HOW COULD THIS HAVE HAPPENED RIGHT--
I'M FINE, I'M FINE.
YOUR SAFETY IS OUR PARAMOUNT CONCERN, OF COURSE.
THAT AND THE SAFETY OF THE--
HEY!
YOU JERKS MIND WRAPPING THIS UP?
MY RIDE'S HERE.

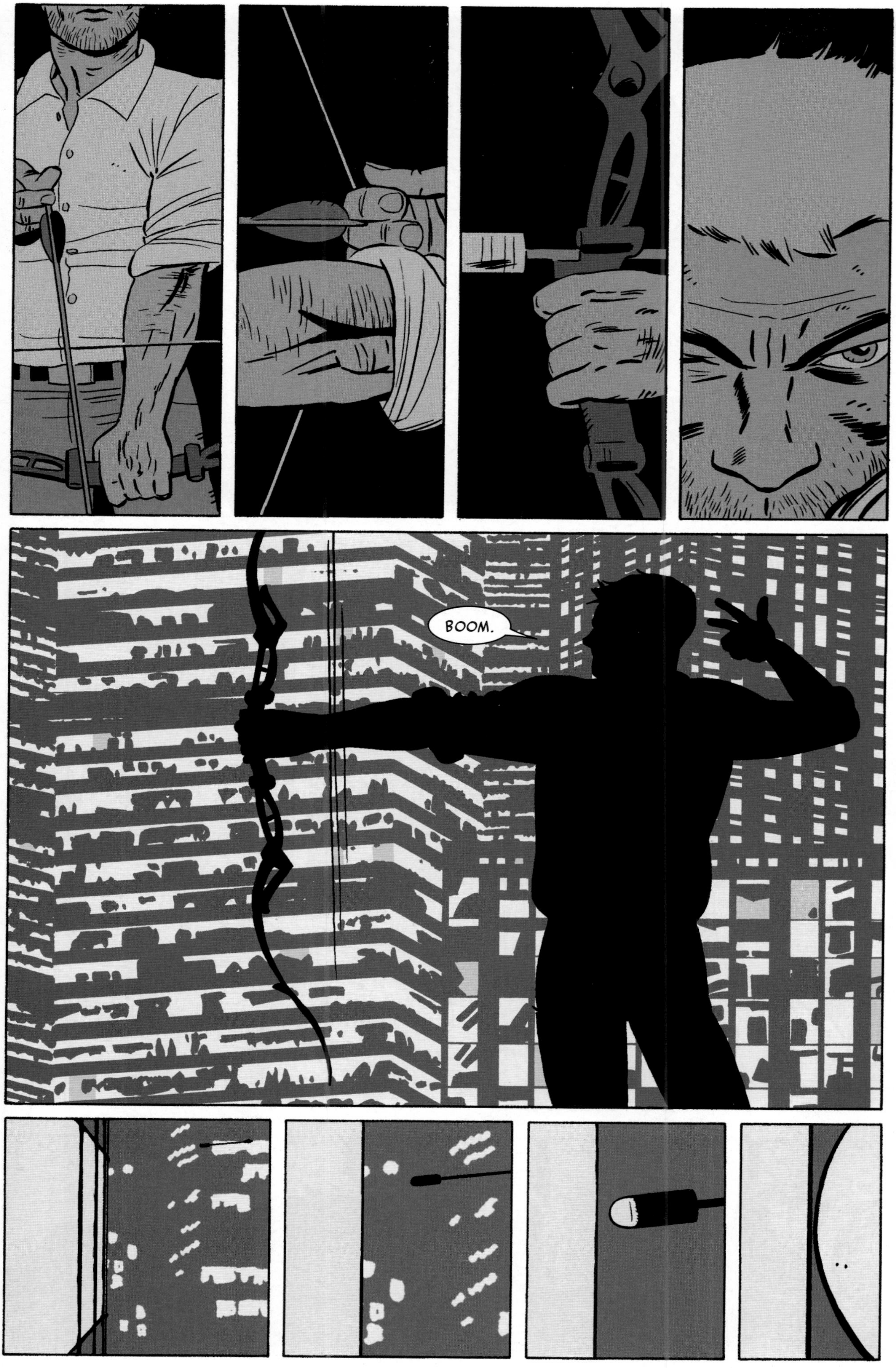
BOOM.

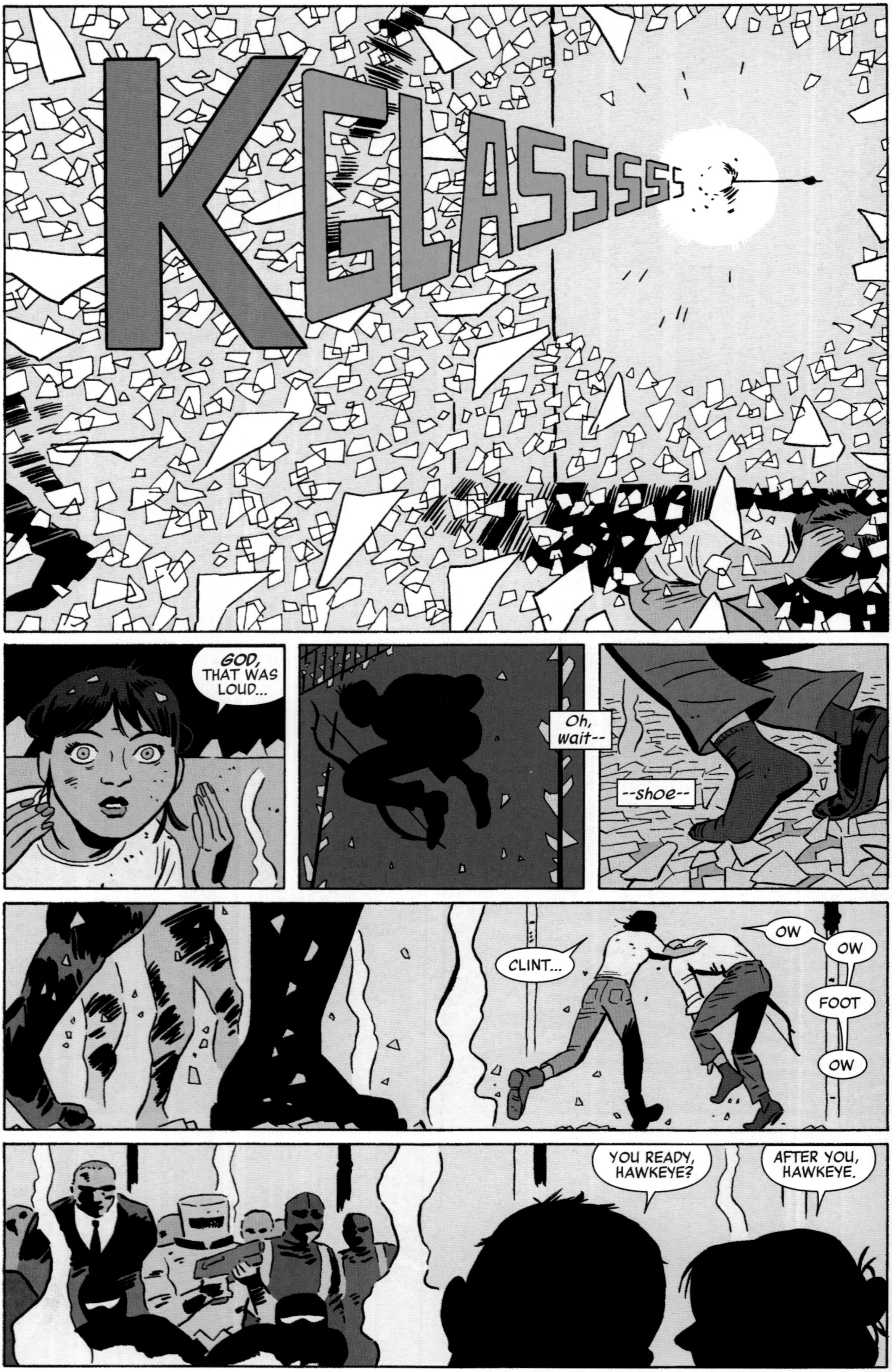
KGLASSSSSS
GOD, THAT WAS LOUD...
Oh, wait--
--shoe--
CLINT...
OW
OW
FOOT
OW
YOU READY, HAWKEYE?
AFTER YOU, HAWKEYE.

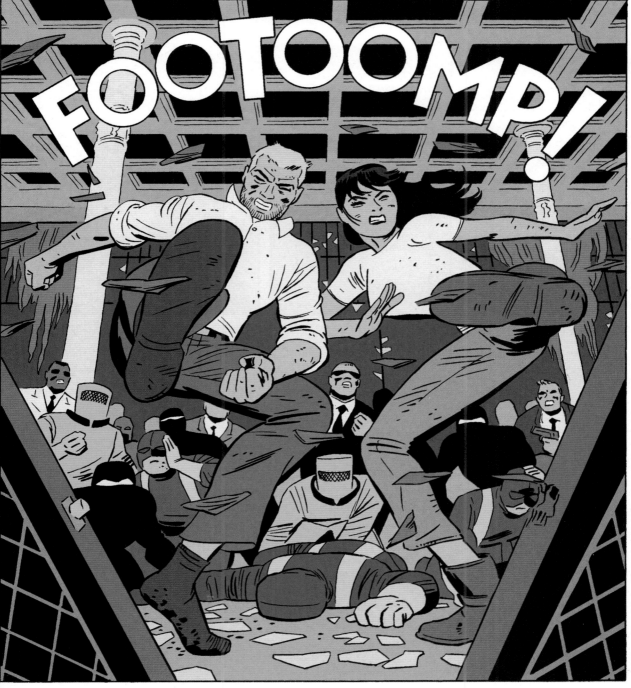

FOOTOOMP!

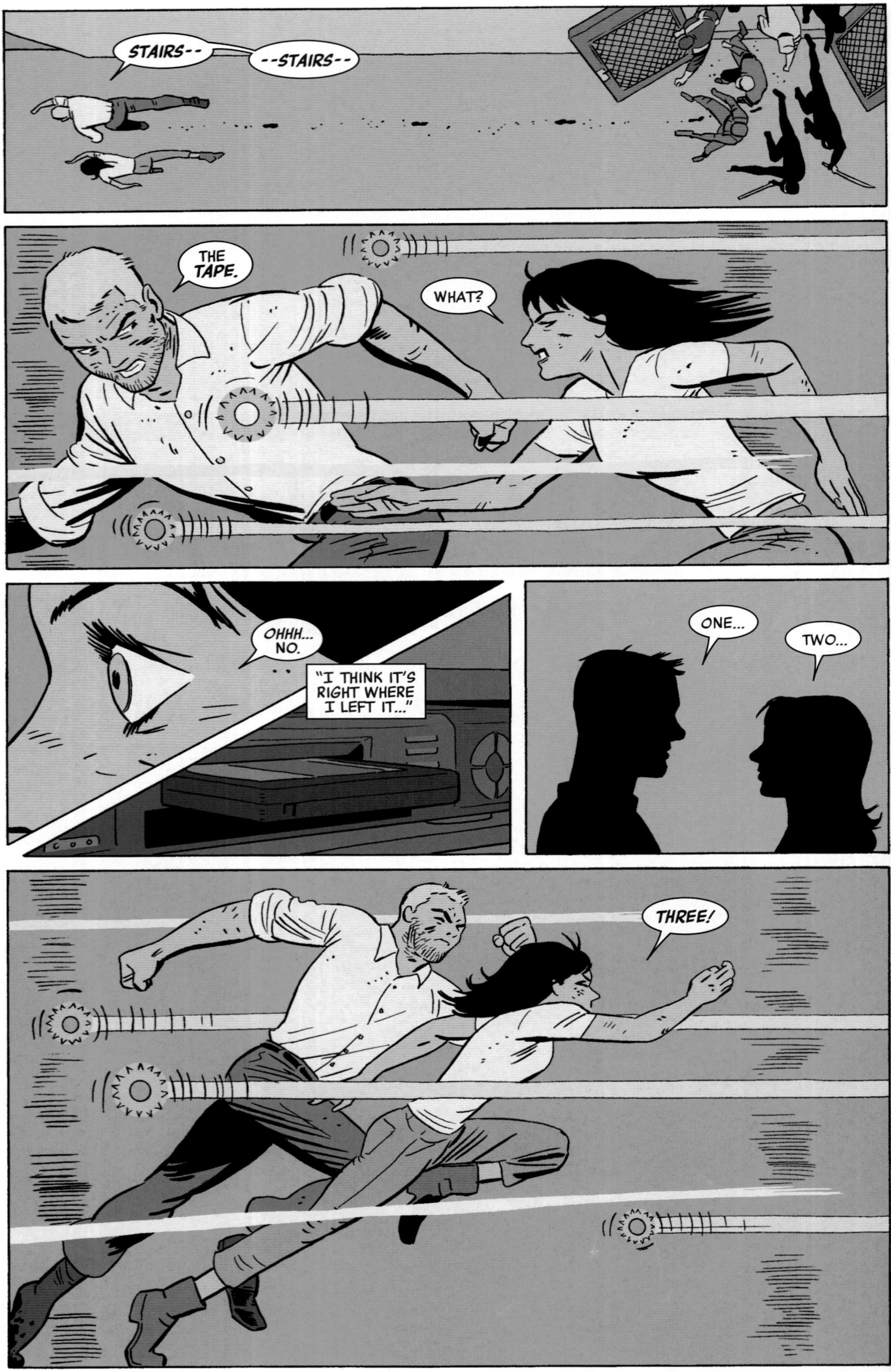
STAIRS--
--STAIRS--
THE TAPE.
WHAT?
OHHH... NO.
"I THINK IT'S RIGHT WHERE I LEFT IT..."
ONE...
TWO...
THREE!

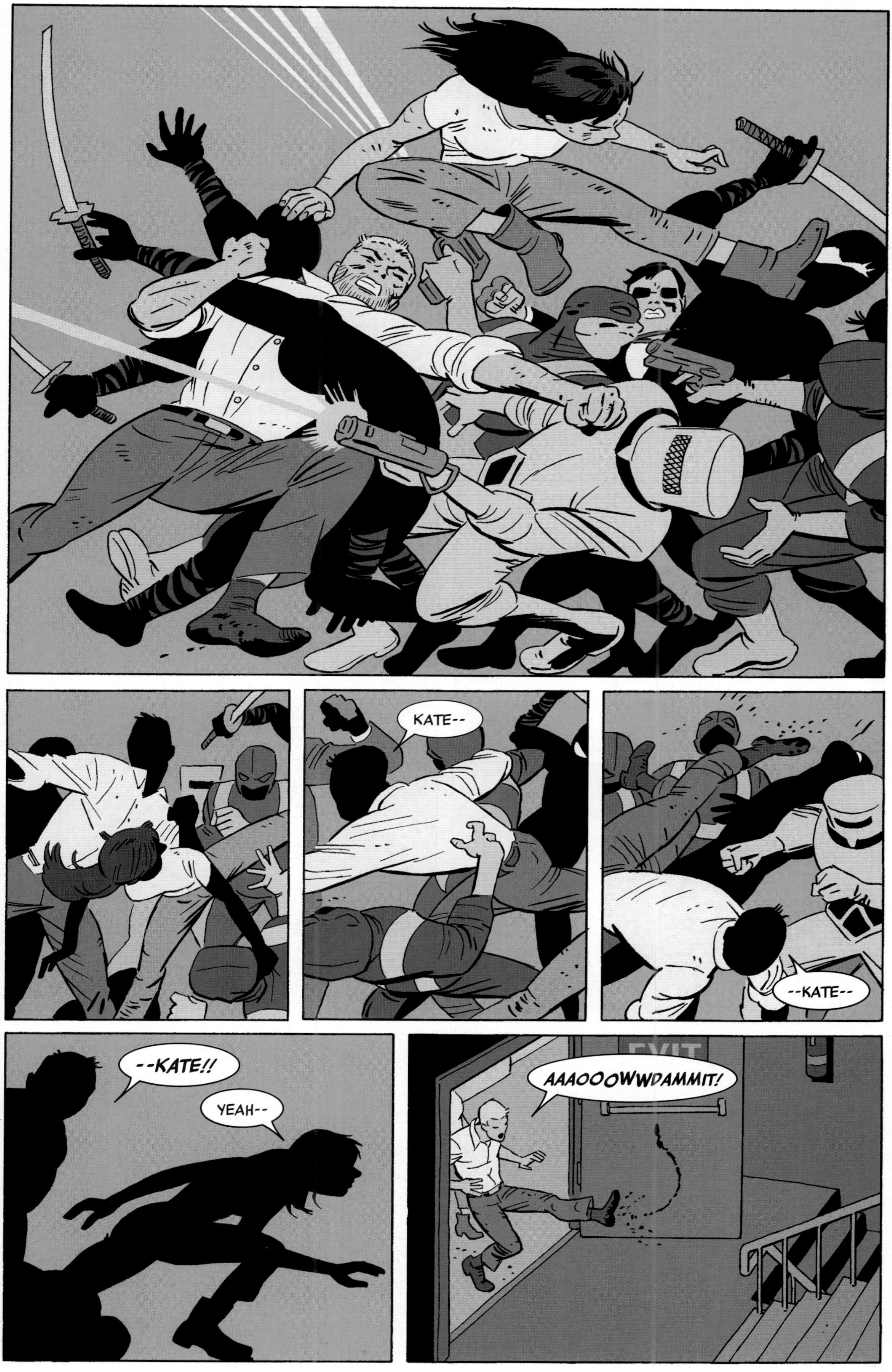
KATE--
--KATE--
--KATE!!
YEAH--
AAAOOOWWDAMMIT!
EXIT

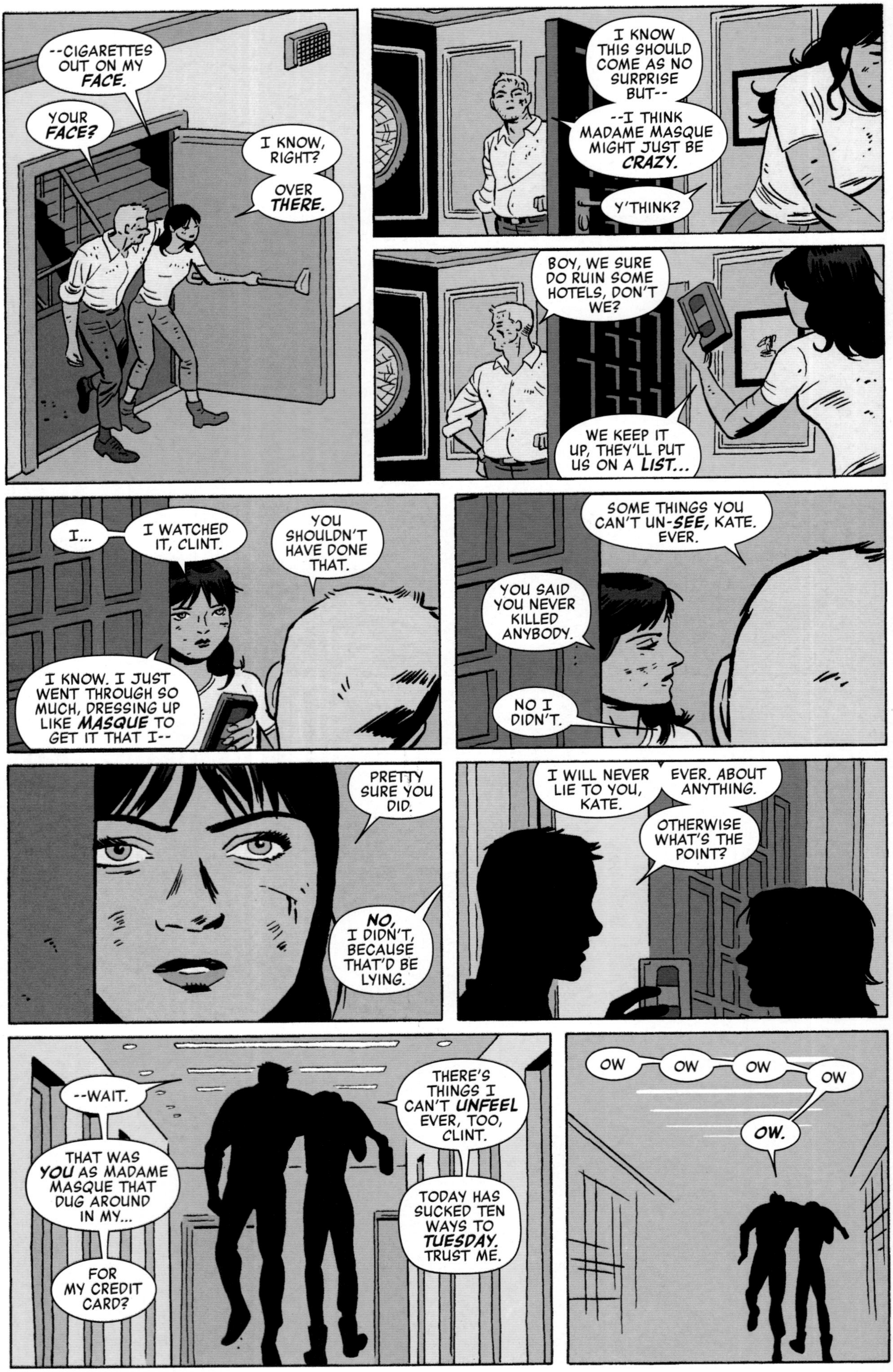
--CIGARETTES OUT ON MY FACE.
YOUR FACE?
I KNOW, RIGHT?
OVER THERE.
I KNOW THIS SHOULD COME AS NO SURPRISE BUT--
--I THINK MADAME MASQUE MIGHT JUST BE CRAZY.
Y'THINK?
BOY, WE SURE DO RUIN SOME HOTELS, DON'T WE?
WE KEEP IT UP, THEY'LL PUT US ON A LIST...
I...
I WATCHED IT, CLINT.
YOU SHOULDN'T HAVE DONE THAT.
I KNOW. I JUST WENT THROUGH SO MUCH, DRESSING UP LIKE MASQUE TO GET IT THAT I--
SOME THINGS YOU CAN'T UN-SEE, KATE. EVER.
YOU SAID YOU NEVER KILLED ANYBODY.
NO I DIDN'T.
PRETTY SURE YOU DID.
NO, I DIDN'T, BECAUSE THAT'D BE LYING.
I WILL NEVER LIE TO YOU, KATE.
EVER. ABOUT ANYTHING.
OTHERWISE WHAT'S THE POINT?
--WAIT.
THAT WAS YOU AS MADAME MASQUE THAT DUG AROUND IN MY...
FOR MY CREDIT CARD?
THERE'S THINGS I CAN'T UNFEEL EVER, TOO, CLINT.
TODAY HAS SUCKED TEN WAYS TO TUESDAY. TRUST ME.
OW
OW
OW
OW
OW.

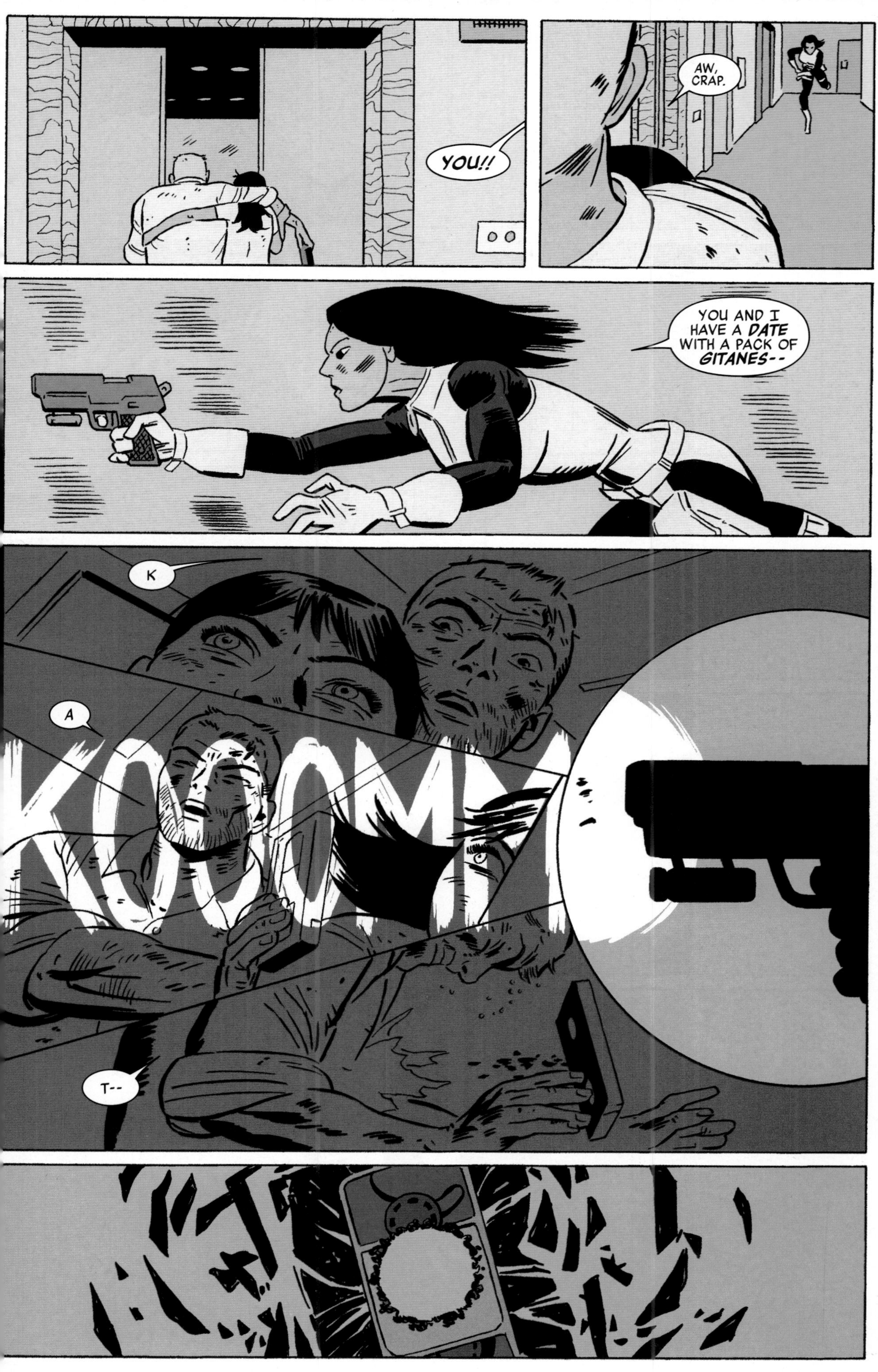

YOU!!
AW, CRAP.
YOU AND I HAVE A DATE WITH A PACK OF GITANES--
K
A
KOOOM
T--

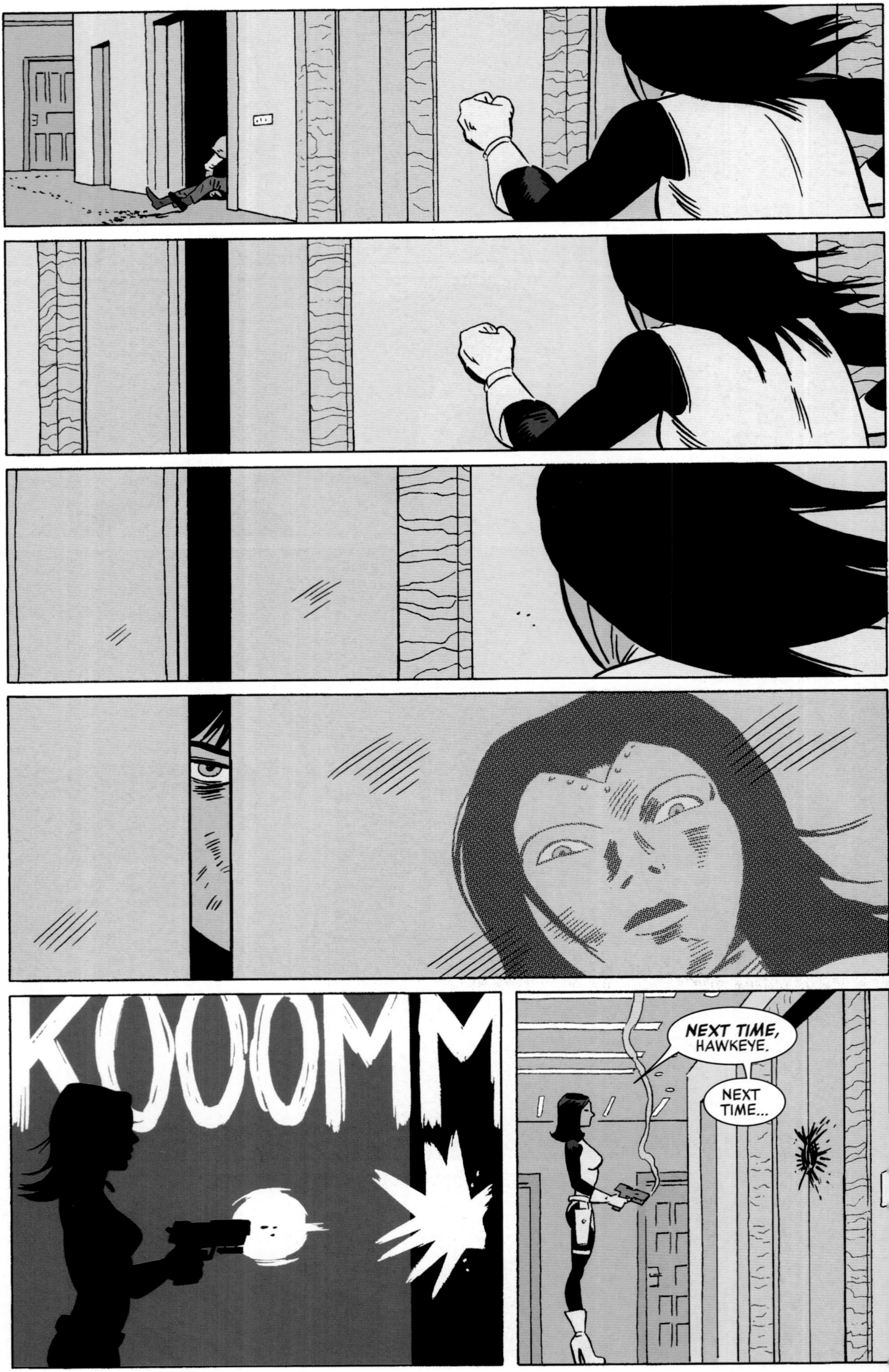
KOOOMM
NEXT TIME, HAWKEYE.
NEXT TIME...

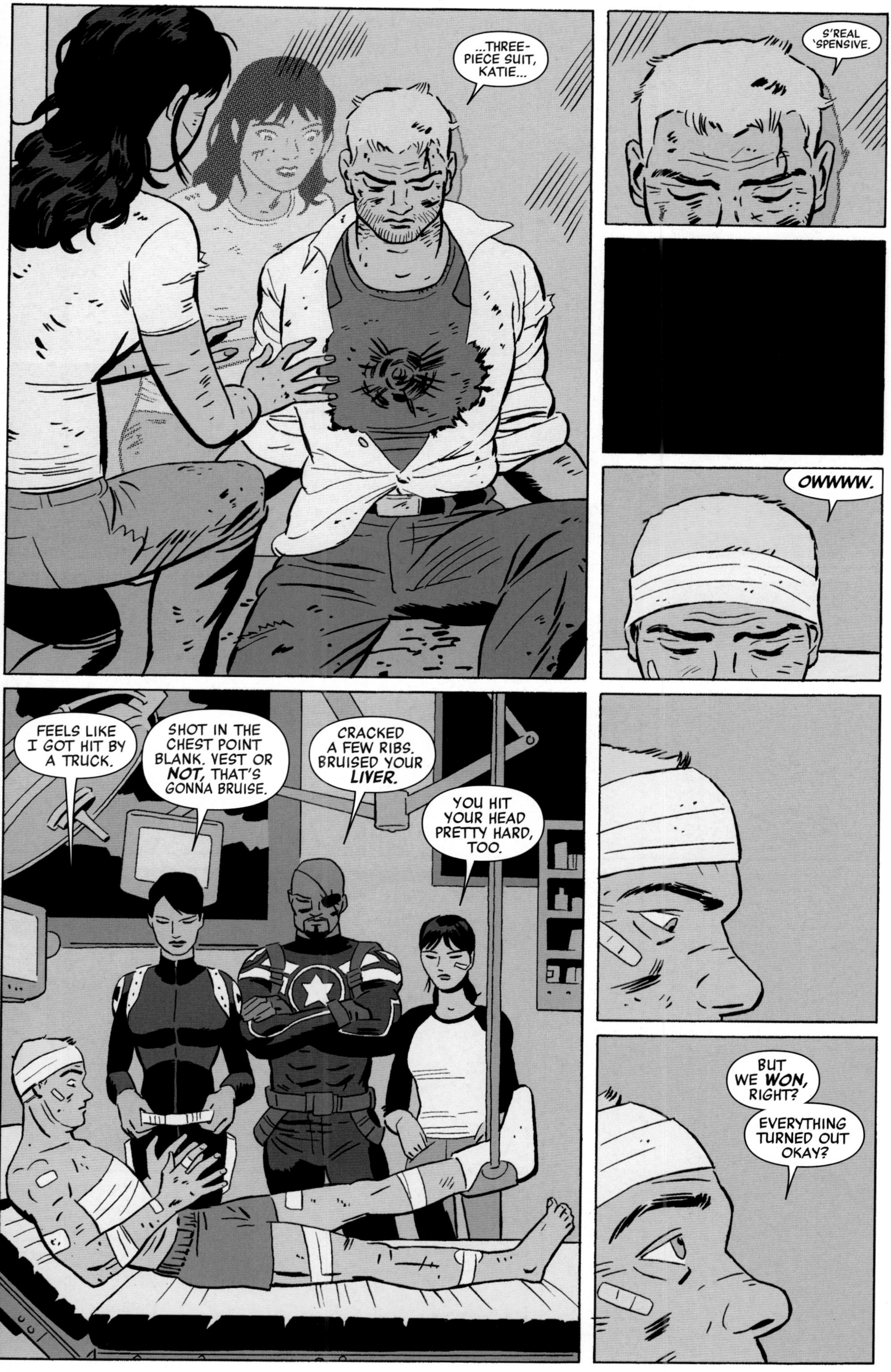
...THREE-PIECE SUIT, KATIE...
S'REAL 'SPENSIVE.
OWWWW.
FEELS LIKE I GOT HIT BY A TRUCK.
SHOT IN THE CHEST POINT BLANK. VEST OR NOT, THAT'S GONNA BRUISE.
CRACKED A FEW RIBS. BRUISED YOUR LIVER.
YOU HIT YOUR HEAD PRETTY HARD, TOO.
BUT WE WON, RIGHT?
EVERYTHING TURNED OUT OKAY?

THE **LEAK** WAS FOUND AND SEALED OFF.

THE IDENTITIES OF THE **NAVY SEALS** THAT KILLED **DU KE FENG** REMAIN **SAFE.**

S.H.I.E.L.D. THANKS YOU AND THE **AVENGERS** FOR YOUR PARTICIPATION IN HELPING US **SMOKE HIM OUT.**

WAIIIIIT **WHAT?**

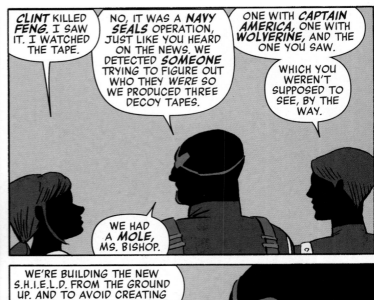

**CLINT** KILLED **FENG.** I SAW IT. I WATCHED THE TAPE.

NO, IT WAS A **NAVY SEALS** OPERATION, JUST LIKE YOU HEARD ON THE NEWS. WE DETECTED **SOMEONE** TRYING TO FIGURE OUT WHO THEY **WERE** SO WE PRODUCED THREE DECOY TAPES.

ONE WITH **CAPTAIN AMERICA,** ONE WITH **WOLVERINE,** AND THE ONE YOU SAW.

WHICH YOU **WEREN'T** SUPPOSED TO SEE, BY THE WAY.

WE HAD A **MOLE,** MS. BISHOP.

WE'RE BUILDING THE NEW S.H.I.E.L.D. FROM THE GROUND UP. AND TO AVOID CREATING SOMETHING LIKE MY **FATHER** MADE, WE...

I'M USING DIFFERENT METHODS. **MY** METHODS. AND THE ONLY WAY WE COULD FLUSH THE MOLE OUT WAS WITH **BAIT.**

THREE TAPES MADE SURREPTITIOUSLY "AVAILABLE" TO OUR THREE SUSPECTED MOLES. WHAT'S MORE SCANDALOUS AND VALUABLE THAN THE NAME OF SOME NAVY SEAL?

PROOF THE GOVERNMENT USED AN **AVENGER** AS ASSASSIN.

ONCE THE MOLE **HAD** THE TAPE WE HAD TO RESPOND APPROPRIATELY.

SO YOU WERE... ALL THIS WAS **THEATER?**

PEOPLE COULD'VE GOTTEN KILLED.

**WE** COULD HAVE GOTTEN KILLED.

LOOK, THEY ASKED, I SAID YES.

THE GUYS THAT **ACTUALLY** DID THIS-- THEY'RE DOING WHAT THEY THINK IS RIGHT. THEY DIDN'T SIGN UP TO GET THEIR FAMILIES AND FRIENDS KILLED AS **RETRIBUTION.**

SO I...

I DUNNO, I WANTED TO HELP.

JUST SEEMED LIKE THE RIGHT THING TO DO.

YOU'RE OKAY, BARTON.

ANYBODY EVER TELL YOU THAT?

"AS FAR AS PEOPLE GO, YOU'RE OKAY."

clint barton is

# hawkeye

# THE TAPE

## 2 OF 2

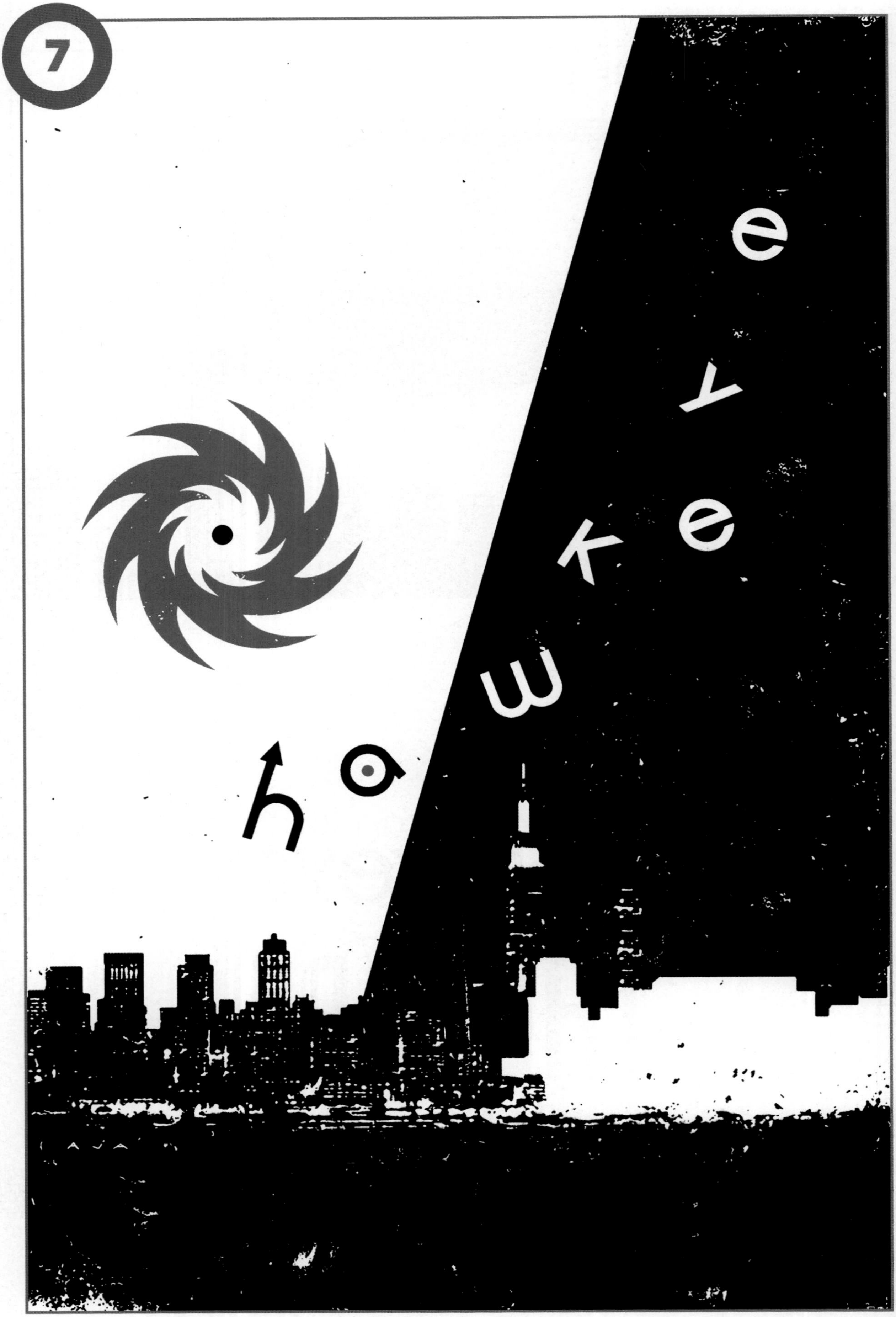
7
hawkeye

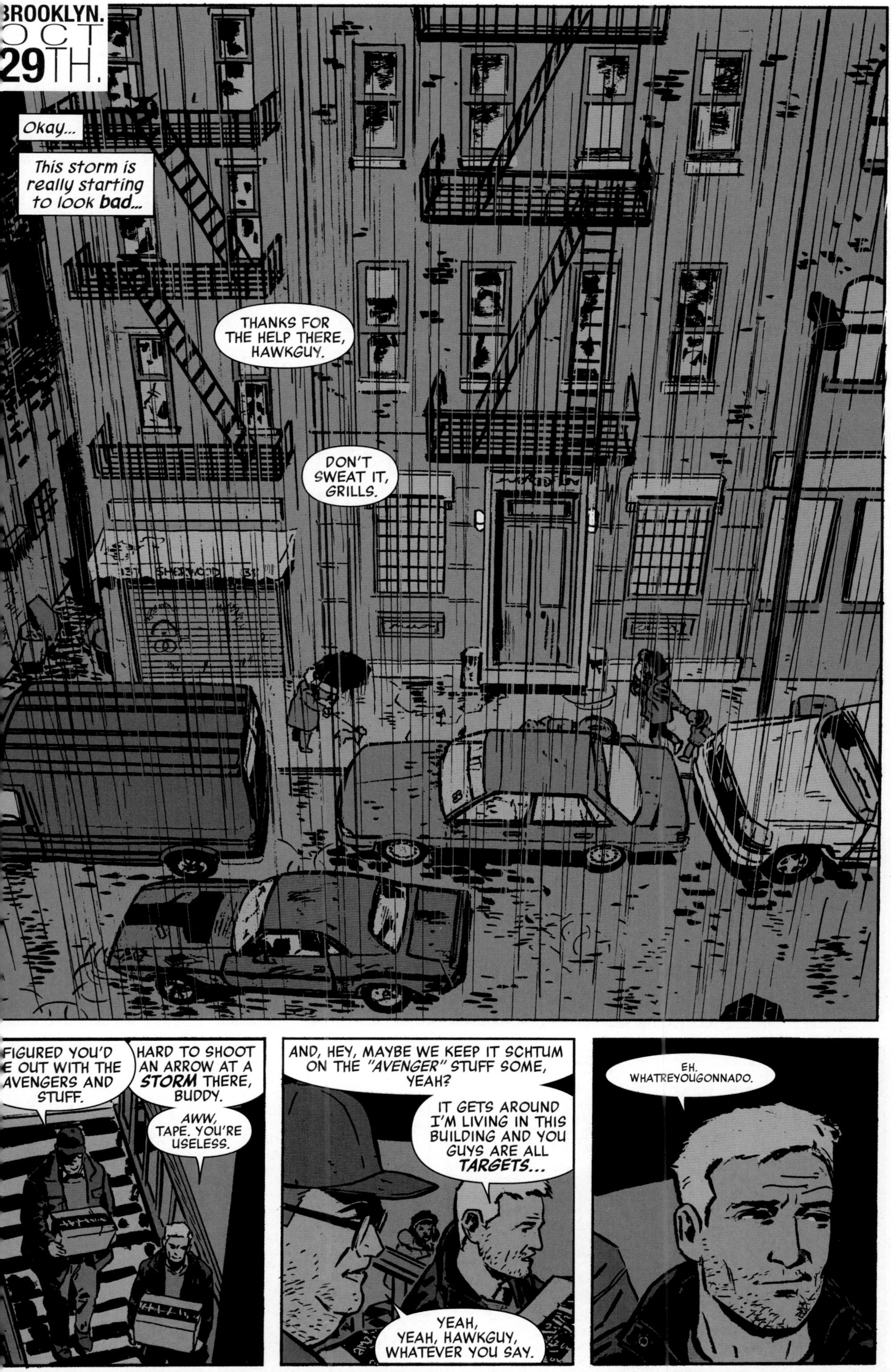
BROOKLYN. OCT 29TH.
Okay...
This storm is really starting to look **bad**...
THANKS FOR THE HELP THERE, HAWKGUY.
DON'T SWEAT IT, GRILLS.
FIGURED YOU'D E OUT WITH THE AVENGERS AND STUFF.
HARD TO SHOOT AN ARROW AT A **STORM** THERE, BUDDY.
AWW, TAPE. YOU'RE USELESS.
AND, HEY, MAYBE WE KEEP IT SCHTUM ON THE *"AVENGER"* STUFF SOME, YEAH?
IT GETS AROUND I'M LIVING IN THIS BUILDING AND YOU GUYS ARE ALL ***TARGETS...***
YEAH, YEAH, HAWKGUY, WHATEVER YOU SAY.
EH. WHATREYOUGONNADO.

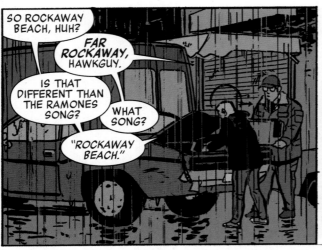
SO ROCKAWAY BEACH, HUH?

FAR ROCKAWAY, HAWKGUY.

IS THAT DIFFERENT THAN THE RAMONES SONG?

WHAT SONG?

"ROCKAWAY BEACH."

IT'S DOWN DERE, YEAH. THERE'S FAR ROCKAWAY, THEN ROCKAWAY PARK, THEN THE BEACH, THEN THE POINT. LOTSA ROCKAWAYS.

WHY AIN'T THIS SHUTTIN'?

SLAM

K-PUK

SLAM

YOU DON'T THINK THAT BROKE NONE OF THEM CANS IN THERE, DO YA?

OH... PROBABLY NOT.

PROBABLY.

HEY WHAT WAS THAT GUY'S NAME? THEIR SINGER THAT DIED.

JOEY SOMETHIN'.

JOEY RAMONE?

THAT GUY.

YEAH! YEAH. THAT GUY.

SO WHAT'S YOUR OLD MAN LIKE?

HE'S A MEAN OLD MAN AN' HE HATES MY GUTS, HAWKGUY. I AIN'T GONNA SUGAR-COAT IT.

HE KNOWS THE STORM'S COMIN' AND HE AIN'T LEAVIN'--NOT BECAUSE HE DON'T GOT NOWHERE TO GO, WHICH HE DON'T, BUT BECAUSE HE DON'T WANT NOTHING TO DO WITH ME.

I SHOULD LET THE STUBBORN OLD JERK DIE OUT THERE IN THAT HOUSE, BUT...

...

IT'S MY HOUSE. S'WHERE I GREW UP. YOU GOTTA TAKE CARE OF YOUR ROOTS, RIGHT? AND YOUR FAMILY, NO MATTER HOW BIGGA HEADACHE THEY ARE.

S'WHAT MY MA WOULDA WANTED, ANYWAY.

Real bad.

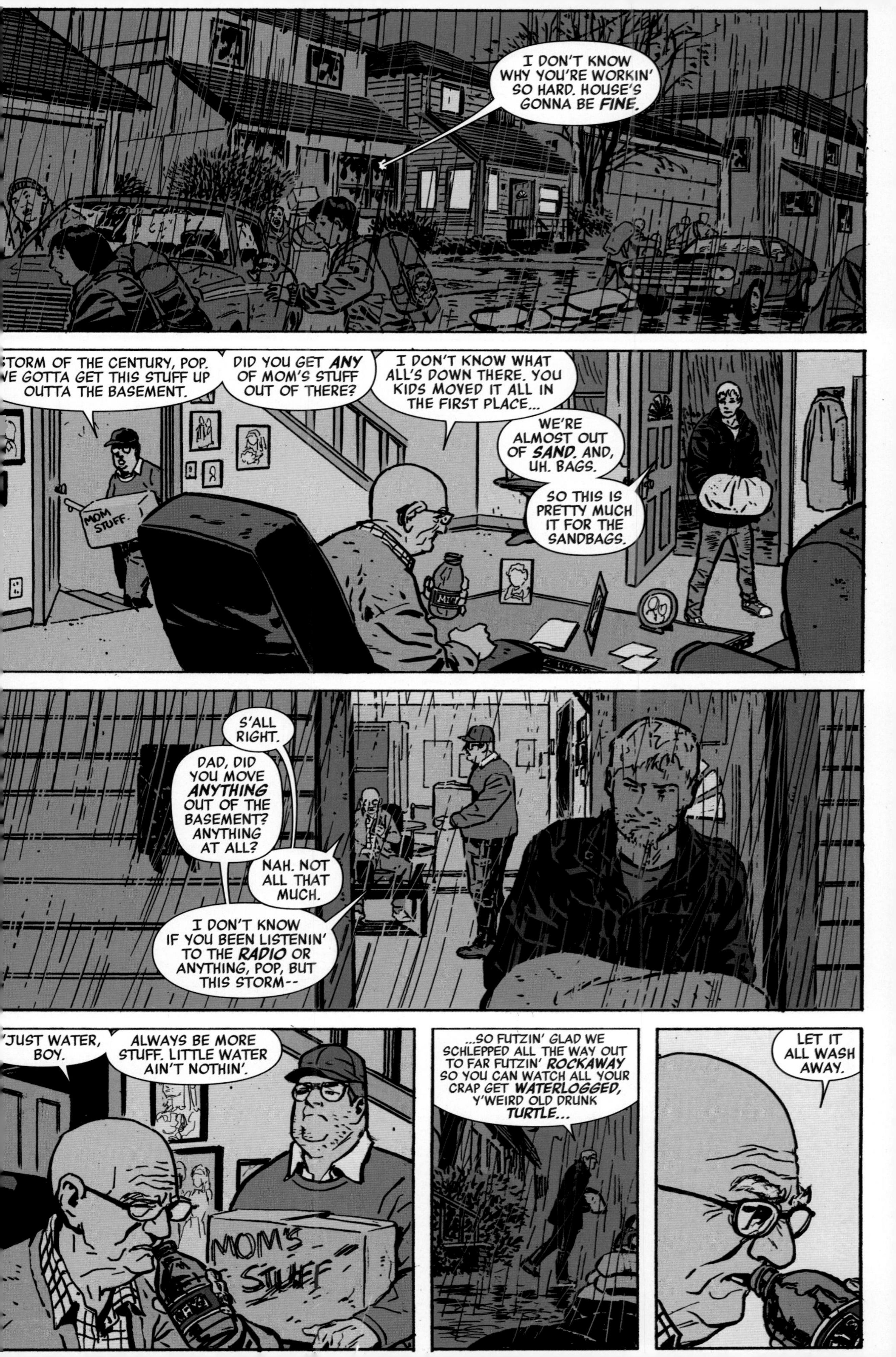
I DON'T KNOW WHY YOU'RE WORKIN' SO HARD. HOUSE'S GONNA BE FINE.
STORM OF THE CENTURY, POP. WE GOTTA GET THIS STUFF UP OUTTA THE BASEMENT.
DID YOU GET ANY OF MOM'S STUFF OUT OF THERE?
I DON'T KNOW WHAT ALL'S DOWN THERE. YOU KIDS MOVED IT ALL IN THE FIRST PLACE...
MOM STUFF.
WE'RE ALMOST OUT OF SAND. AND, UH. BAGS.
SO THIS IS PRETTY MUCH IT FOR THE SANDBAGS.
S'ALL RIGHT.
DAD, DID YOU MOVE ANYTHING OUT OF THE BASEMENT? ANYTHING AT ALL?
NAH. NOT ALL THAT MUCH.
I DON'T KNOW IF YOU BEEN LISTENIN' TO THE RADIO OR ANYTHING, POP, BUT THIS STORM--
'JUST WATER, BOY.
ALWAYS BE MORE STUFF. LITTLE WATER AIN'T NOTHIN'.
MOM'S STUFF
...SO FUTZIN' GLAD WE SCHLEPPED ALL THE WAY OUT TO FAR FUTZIN' ROCKAWAY SO YOU CAN WATCH ALL YOUR CRAP GET WATERLOGGED, Y'WEIRD OLD DRUNK TURTLE...
LET IT ALL WASH AWAY.

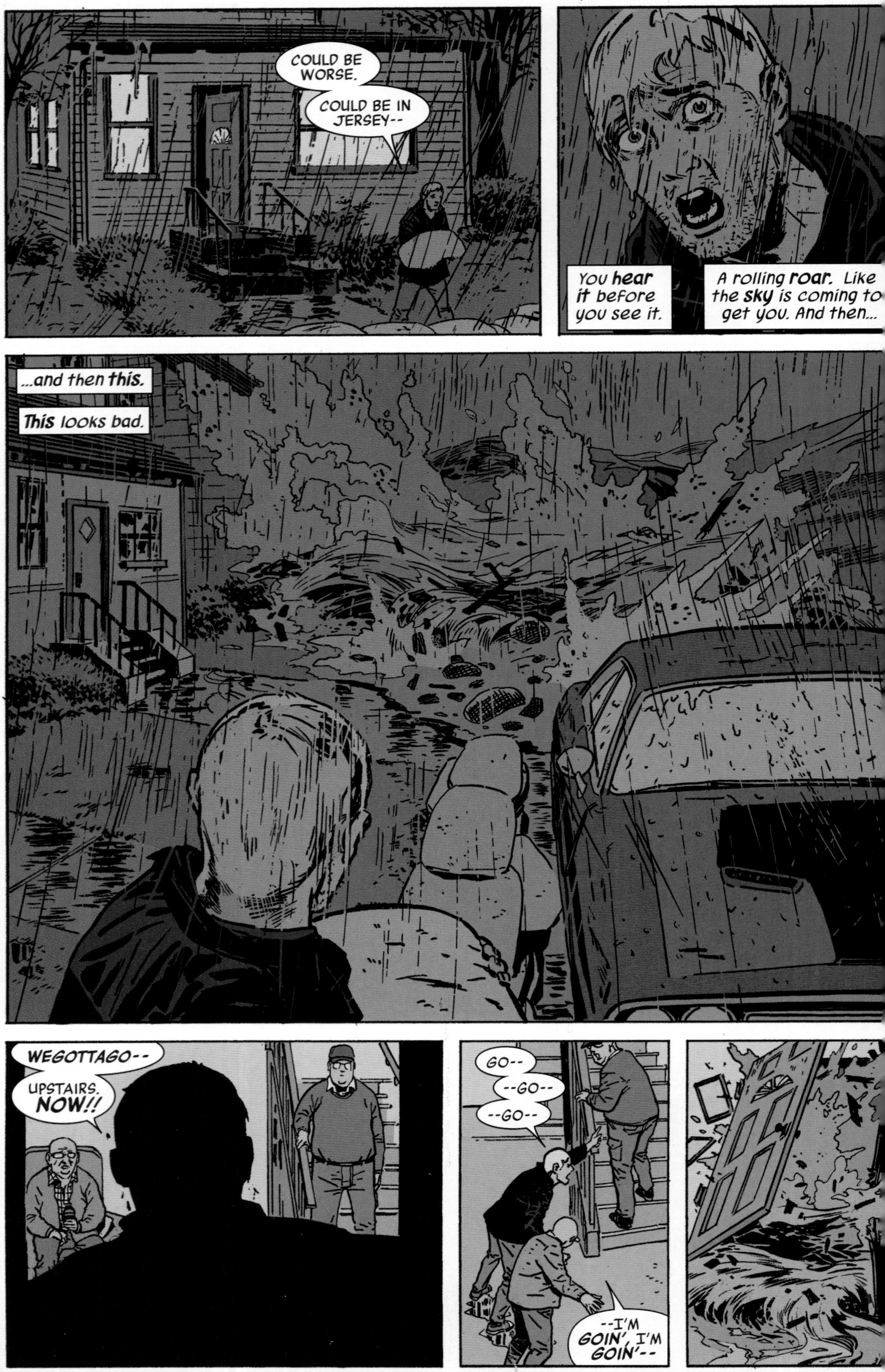

COULD BE WORSE.
COULD BE IN JERSEY--
You **hear it** before you see it.
A rolling **roar.** Like the **sky** is coming to get you. And then...
...and then **this.**
**This** looks bad.
WEGOTTAGO--
UPSTAIRS. NOW!!
GO--
--GO--
--GO--
--I'M GOIN', I'M GOIN'--

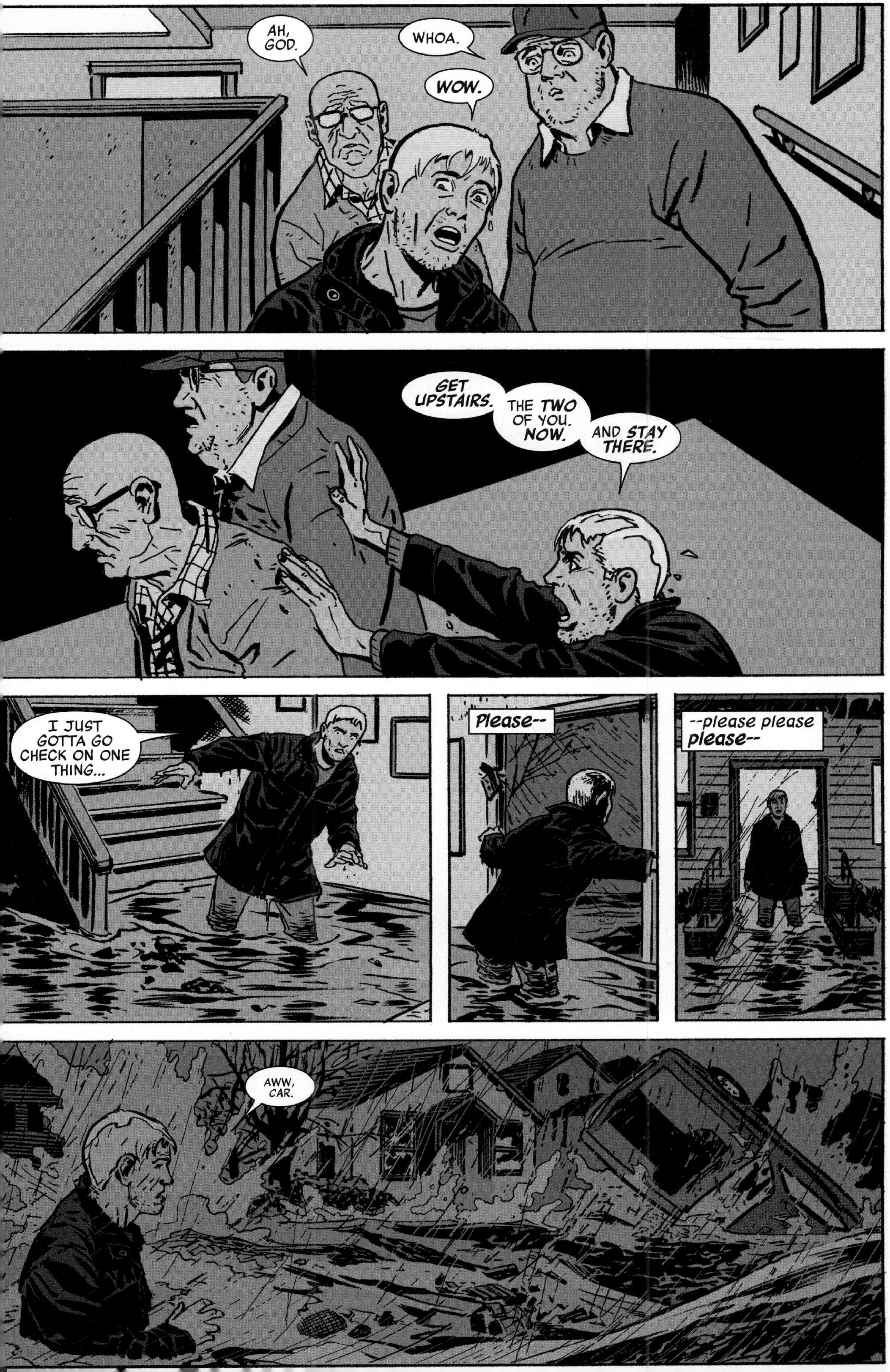
AH, GOD.
WHOA.
WOW.
GET UPSTAIRS.
THE TWO OF YOU. NOW.
AND STAY THERE.
I JUST GOTTA GO CHECK ON ONE THING...
Please--
--please please please--
AWW, CAR.

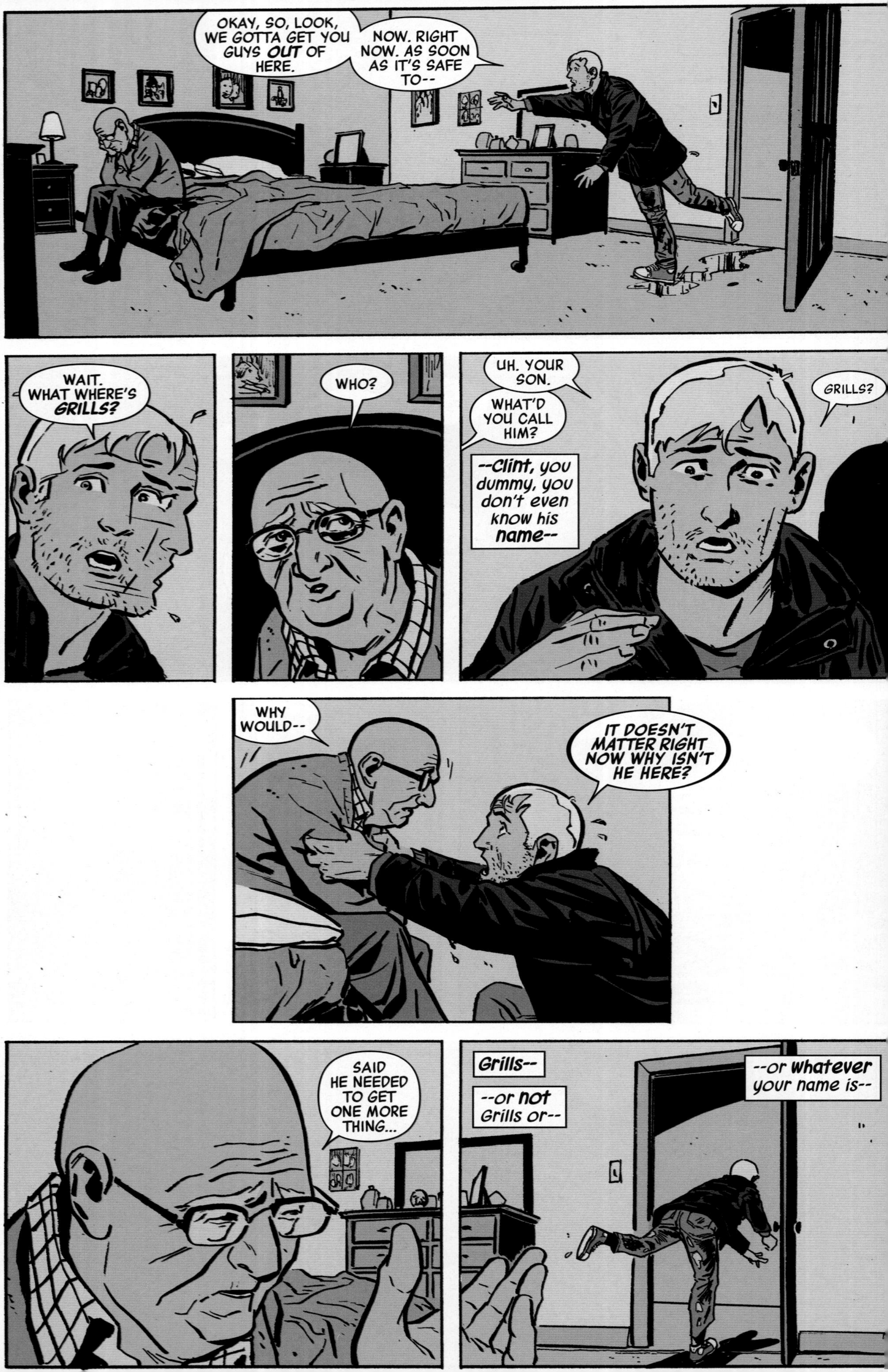
OKAY, SO, LOOK, WE GOTTA GET YOU GUYS OUT OF HERE.
NOW. RIGHT NOW. AS SOON AS IT'S SAFE TO--
WAIT. WHAT WHERE'S GRILLS?
WHO?
UH. YOUR SON.
WHAT'D YOU CALL HIM?
--Clint, you dummy, you don't even know his name--
GRILLS?
WHY WOULD--
IT DOESN'T MATTER RIGHT NOW WHY ISN'T HE HERE?
SAID HE NEEDED TO GET ONE MORE THING...
Grills--
--or not Grills or--
--or whatever your name is--

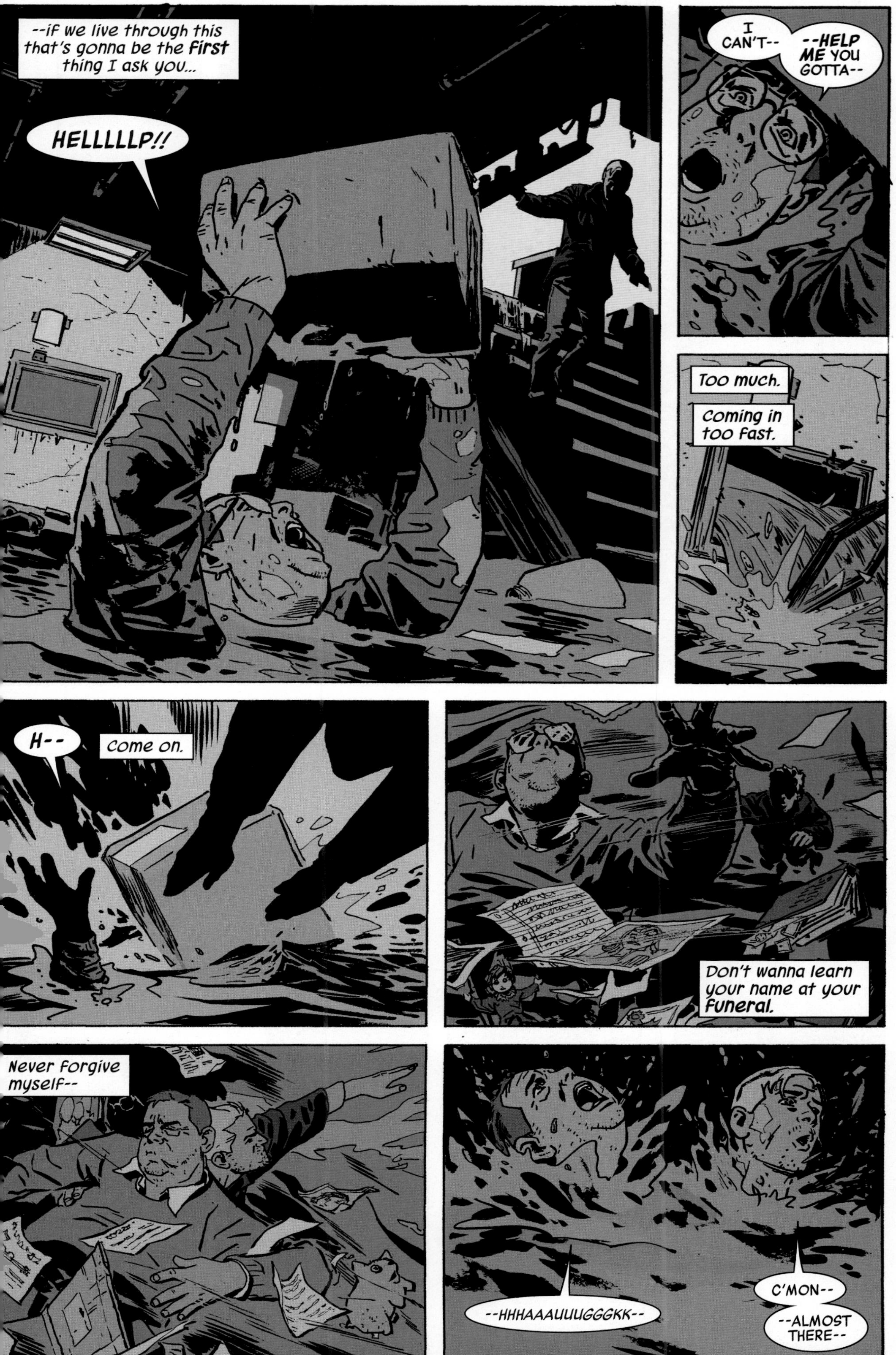
--if we live through this that's gonna be the first thing I ask you...
HELLLLLP!!
I CAN'T--
--HELP ME YOU GOTTA--
Too much.
Coming in too fast.
H--
Come on.
Don't wanna learn your name at your funeral.
Never forgive myself--
--HHHAAAUUUGGGKK--
C'MON--
--ALMOST THERE--

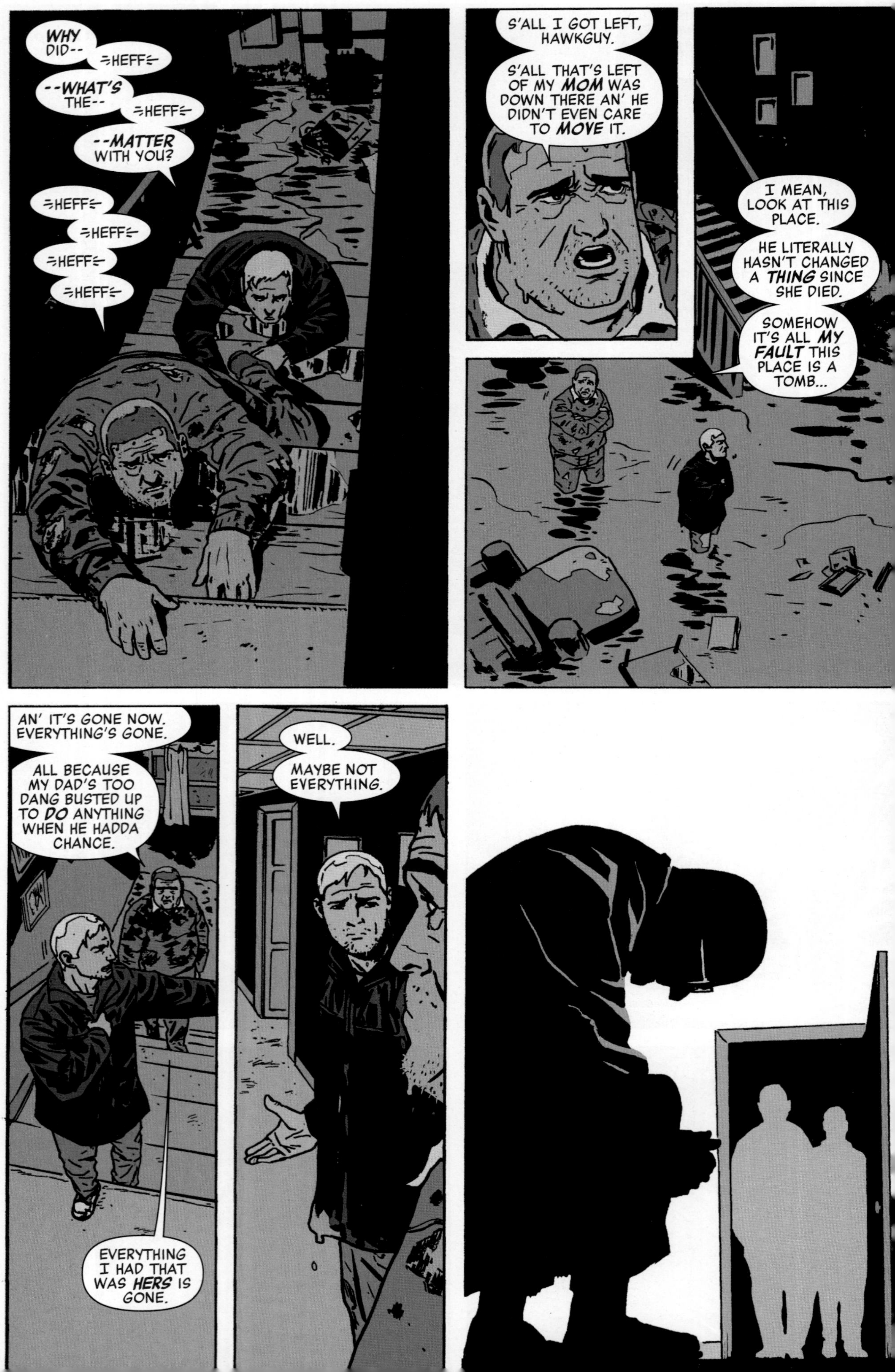

WHY DID--
=HEFF=
--WHAT'S THE--
=HEFF=
--MATTER WITH YOU?
=HEFF=
=HEFF=
=HEFF=
=HEFF=
S'ALL I GOT LEFT, HAWKGUY.
S'ALL THAT'S LEFT OF MY MOM WAS DOWN THERE AN' HE DIDN'T EVEN CARE TO MOVE IT.
I MEAN, LOOK AT THIS PLACE.
HE LITERALLY HASN'T CHANGED A THING SINCE SHE DIED.
SOMEHOW IT'S ALL MY FAULT THIS PLACE IS A TOMB...
AN' IT'S GONE NOW. EVERYTHING'S GONE.
ALL BECAUSE MY DAD'S TOO DANG BUSTED UP TO DO ANYTHING WHEN HE HADDA CHANCE.
EVERYTHING I HAD THAT WAS HERS IS GONE.
WELL.
MAYBE NOT EVERYTHING.

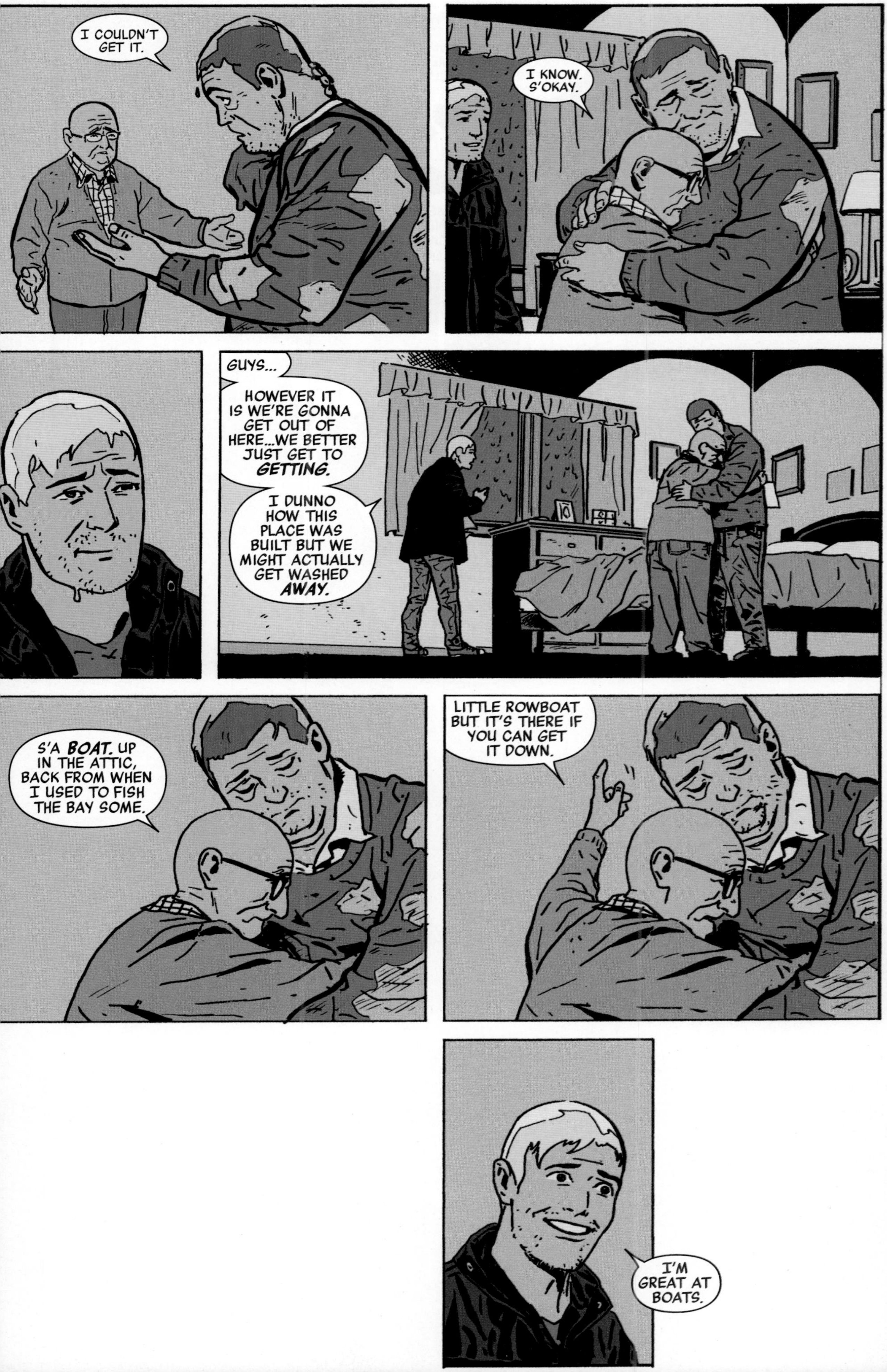
I COULDN'T GET IT.
I KNOW. S'OKAY.
GUYS...
HOWEVER IT IS WE'RE GONNA GET OUT OF HERE...WE BETTER JUST GET TO GETTING.
I DUNNO HOW THIS PLACE WAS BUILT BUT WE MIGHT ACTUALLY GET WASHED AWAY.
S'A BOAT. UP IN THE ATTIC, BACK FROM WHEN I USED TO FISH THE BAY SOME.
LITTLE ROWBOAT BUT IT'S THERE IF YOU CAN GET IT DOWN.
I'M GREAT AT BOATS.

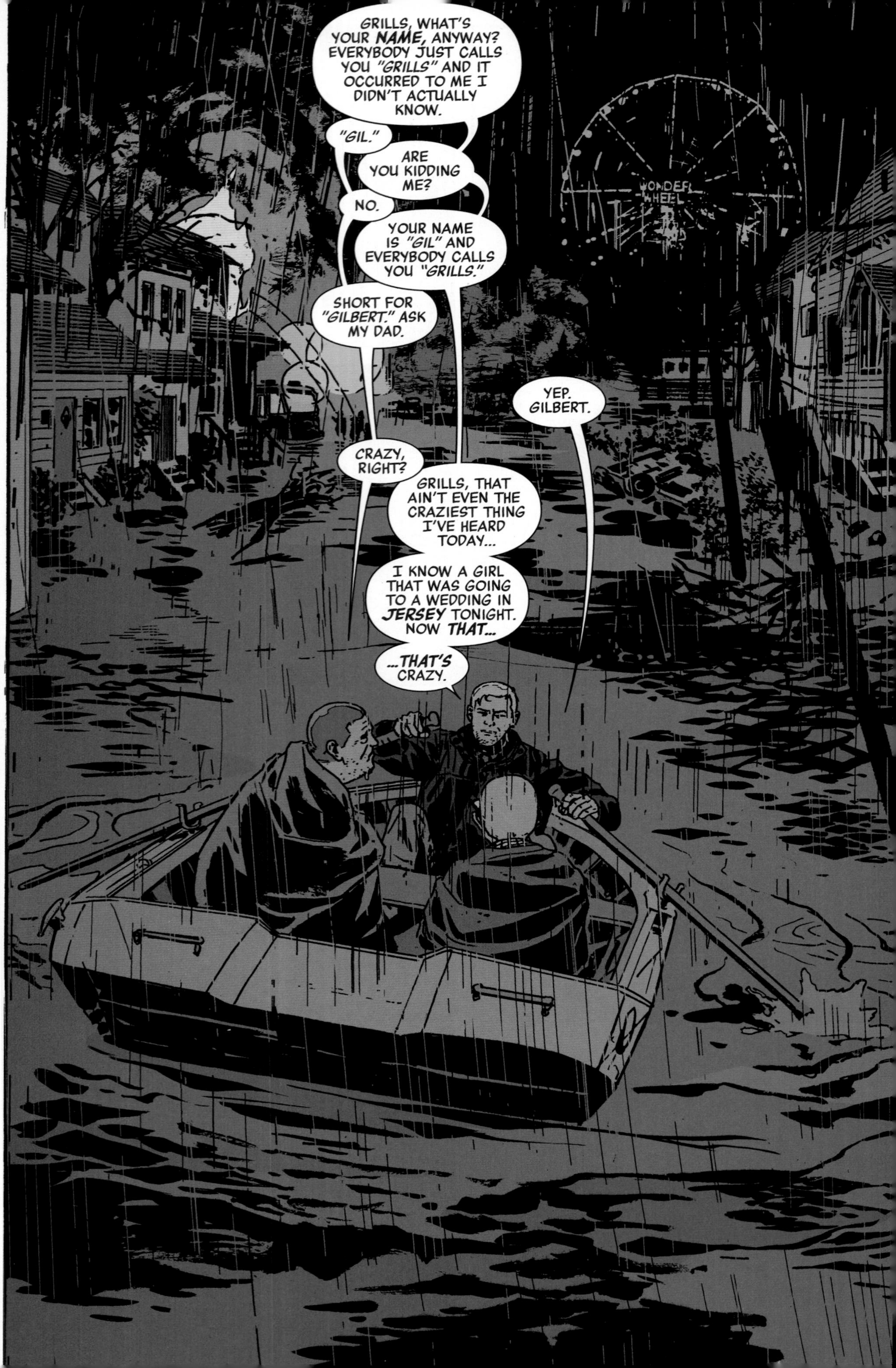
GRILLS, WHAT'S YOUR NAME, ANYWAY? EVERYBODY JUST CALLS YOU "GRILLS" AND IT OCCURRED TO ME I DIDN'T ACTUALLY KNOW.
"GIL."
ARE YOU KIDDING ME?
NO.
YOUR NAME IS "GIL" AND EVERYBODY CALLS YOU "GRILLS."
SHORT FOR "GILBERT." ASK MY DAD.
YEP. GILBERT.
CRAZY, RIGHT?
GRILLS, THAT AIN'T EVEN THE CRAZIEST THING I'VE HEARD TODAY...
I KNOW A GIRL THAT WAS GOING TO A WEDDING IN JERSEY TONIGHT. NOW THAT...
...THAT'S CRAZY.
WONDER WHEEL

AM I CRAZY? IS THIS CRAZY? CANNED GOODS?

IS THIS, LIKE, *Y2K*, CRAZY?

DID YOU GET ME THAT TAPE?

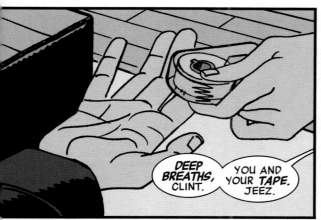

DEEP BREATHS, CLINT.

YOU AND YOUR *TAPE*. JEEZ.

THAT'S, UH. *THAT'S* SOME TINY TAPE Y'GOT ME THERE, KATIE-KATE.

I GOTTA CLOSE A *BOX* WITH THIS STUFF--

HELLO, NEIGHBOR.

GRILLS. C'MON IN. YOU KNOW KATE, MY WARD?

YOUR *WHAT*--?

MAYBE THAT WORD DOESN'T MEAN WHAT I THOUGHT.

YOU *STAYING HERE* OR GETTING OUT OF *TOWN* OR WHAT?

UM. HI THERE.

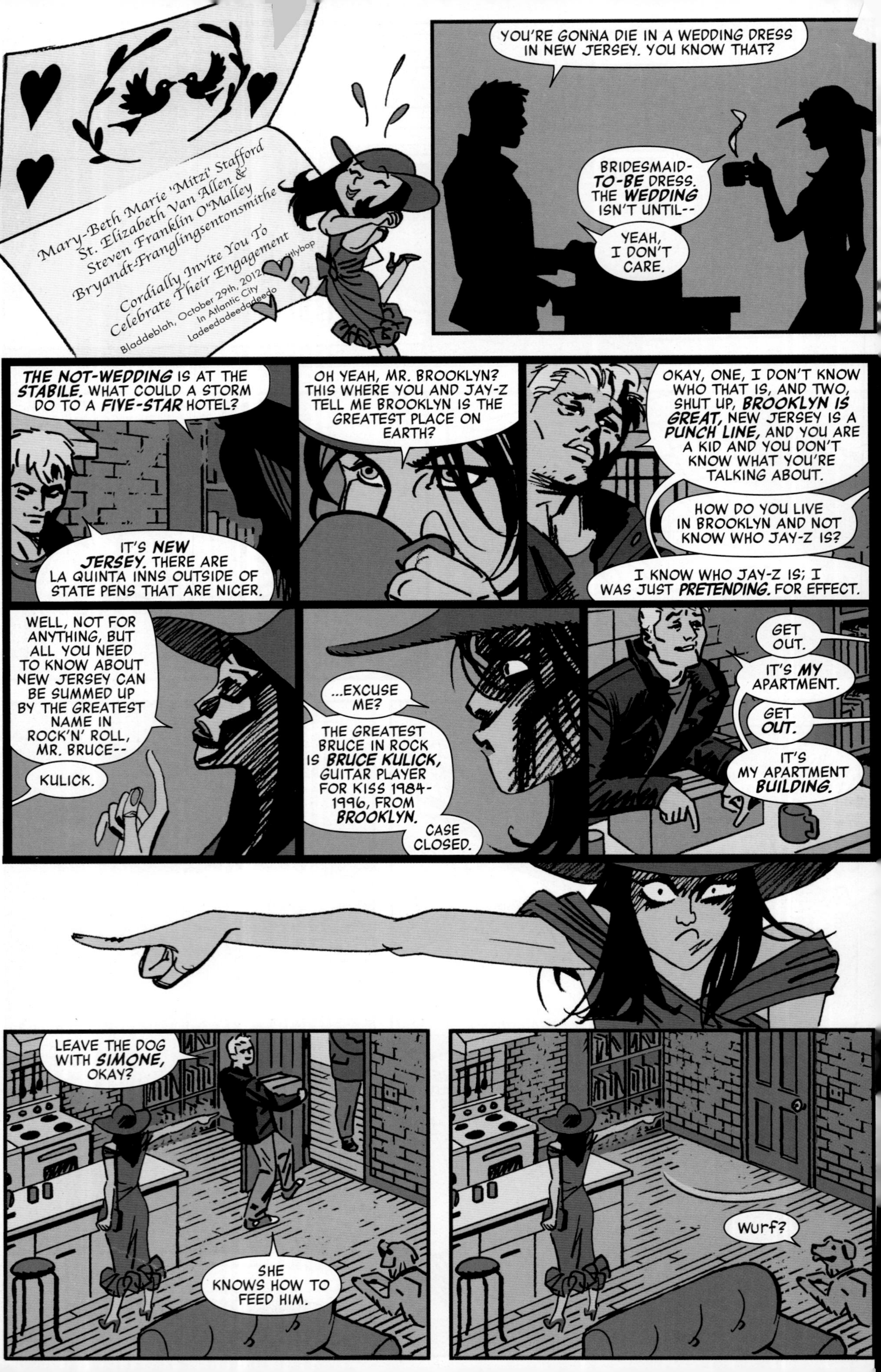
Mary-Beth Marie 'Mitzi' Stafford
St. Elizabeth Van Allen &
Steven Franklin O'Malley
Bryandt-Franglingsentonsmithe
Cordially Invite You To
Celebrate Their Engagement
Bladdeblah, October 29th, 2012,
In Atlantic City
Ladeedadeedadeedo
YOU'RE GONNA DIE IN A WEDDING DRESS IN NEW JERSEY. YOU KNOW THAT?
BRIDESMAID-TO-BE DRESS. THE WEDDING ISN'T UNTIL--
YEAH, I DON'T CARE.
THE NOT-WEDDING IS AT THE STABILE. WHAT COULD A STORM DO TO A FIVE-STAR HOTEL?
IT'S NEW JERSEY. THERE ARE LA QUINTA INNS OUTSIDE OF STATE PENS THAT ARE NICER.
OH YEAH, MR. BROOKLYN? THIS WHERE YOU AND JAY-Z TELL ME BROOKLYN IS THE GREATEST PLACE ON EARTH?
OKAY, ONE, I DON'T KNOW WHO THAT IS, AND TWO, SHUT UP, BROOKLYN IS GREAT, NEW JERSEY IS A PUNCH LINE, AND YOU ARE A KID AND YOU DON'T KNOW WHAT YOU'RE TALKING ABOUT.
HOW DO YOU LIVE IN BROOKLYN AND NOT KNOW WHO JAY-Z IS?
I KNOW WHO JAY-Z IS; I WAS JUST PRETENDING. FOR EFFECT.
WELL, NOT FOR ANYTHING, BUT ALL YOU NEED TO KNOW ABOUT NEW JERSEY CAN BE SUMMED UP BY THE GREATEST NAME IN ROCK'N' ROLL, MR. BRUCE--
KULICK.
...EXCUSE ME?
THE GREATEST BRUCE IN ROCK IS BRUCE KULICK, GUITAR PLAYER FOR KISS 1984-1996, FROM BROOKLYN.
CASE CLOSED.
GET OUT.
IT'S MY APARTMENT.
GET OUT.
IT'S MY APARTMENT BUILDING.
LEAVE THE DOG WITH SIMONE, OKAY?
SHE KNOWS HOW TO FEED HIM.
Wurf?

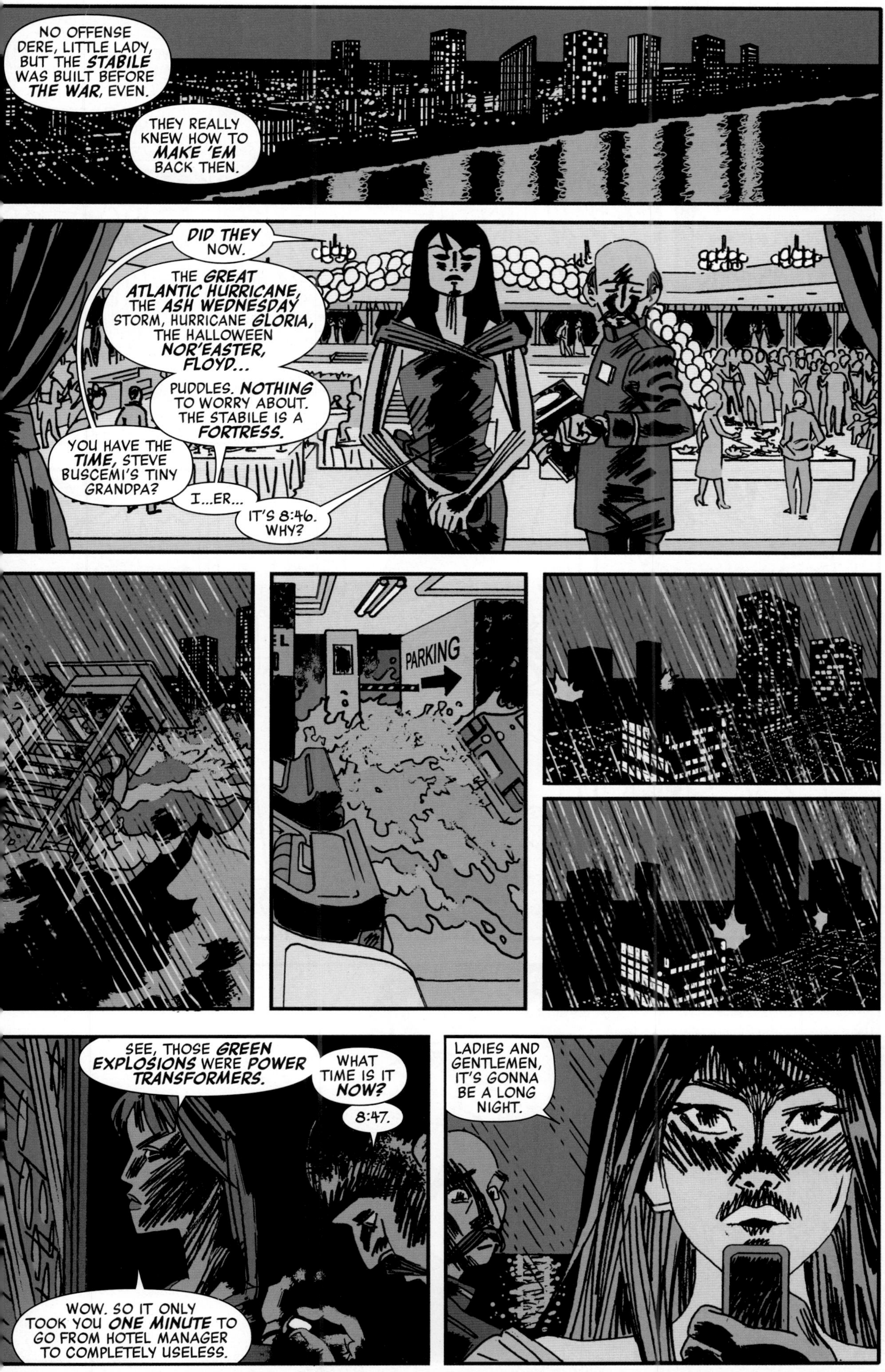
NO OFFENSE DERE, LITTLE LADY, BUT THE STABILE WAS BUILT BEFORE THE WAR, EVEN.
THEY REALLY KNEW HOW TO MAKE 'EM BACK THEN.
DID THEY NOW.
THE GREAT ATLANTIC HURRICANE, THE ASH WEDNESDAY STORM, HURRICANE GLORIA, THE HALLOWEEN NOR'EASTER, FLOYD...
PUDDLES. NOTHING TO WORRY ABOUT. THE STABILE IS A FORTRESS.
YOU HAVE THE TIME, STEVE BUSCEMI'S TINY GRANDPA?
I...ER...
IT'S 8:46. WHY?
PARKING
SEE, THOSE GREEN EXPLOSIONS WERE POWER TRANSFORMERS.
WHAT TIME IS IT NOW?
8:47.
WOW. SO IT ONLY TOOK YOU ONE MINUTE TO GO FROM HOTEL MANAGER TO COMPLETELY USELESS.
LADIES AND GENTLEMEN, IT'S GONNA BE A LONG NIGHT.

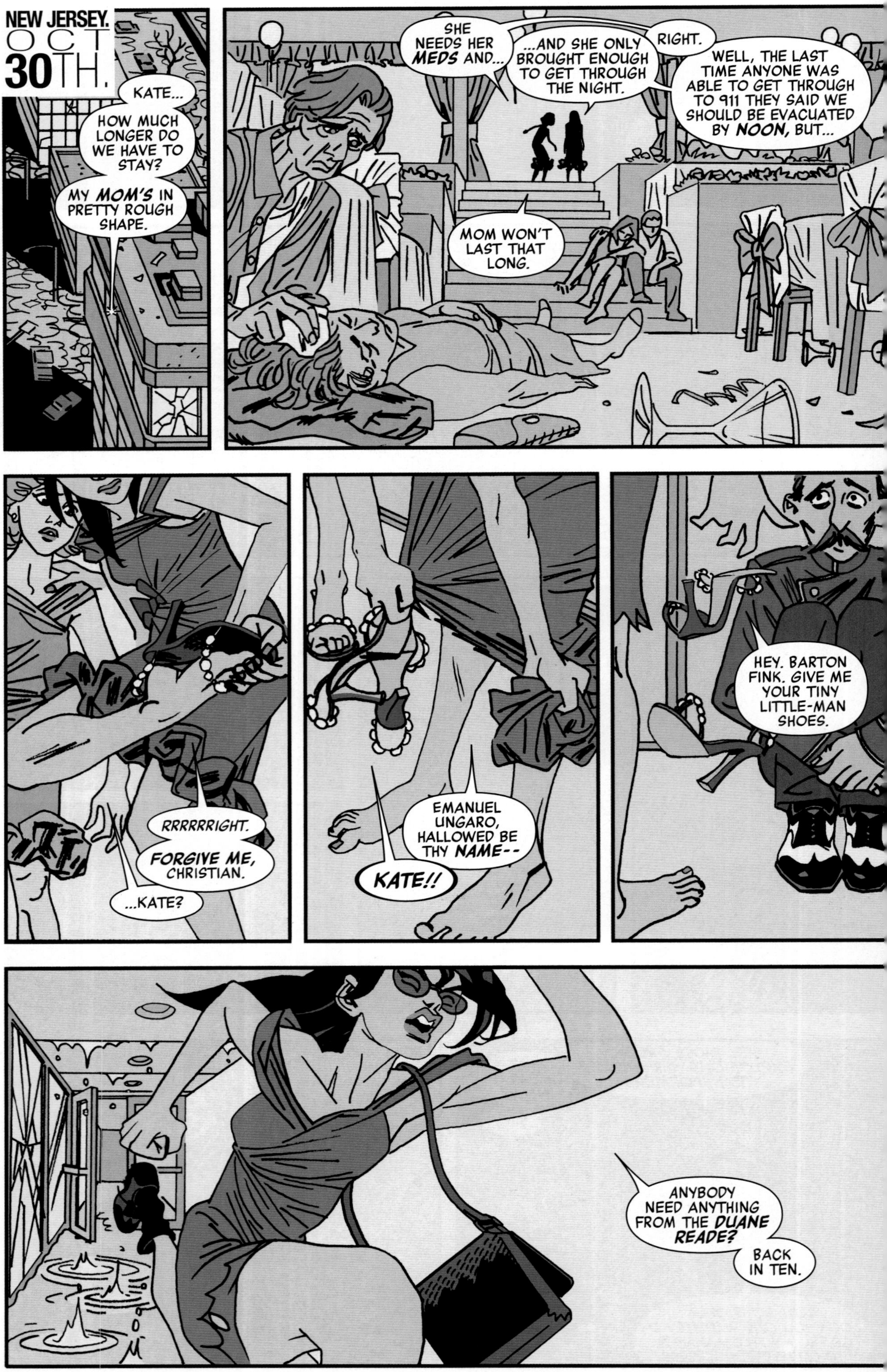
NEW JERSEY. OCT 30TH.
KATE...
HOW MUCH LONGER DO WE HAVE TO STAY?
MY MOM'S IN PRETTY ROUGH SHAPE.
SHE NEEDS HER MEDS AND...
...AND SHE ONLY BROUGHT ENOUGH TO GET THROUGH THE NIGHT.
RIGHT.
WELL, THE LAST TIME ANYONE WAS ABLE TO GET THROUGH TO 911 THEY SAID WE SHOULD BE EVACUATED BY NOON, BUT...
MOM WON'T LAST THAT LONG.
RRRRRRIGHT.
FORGIVE ME, CHRISTIAN.
...KATE?
EMANUEL UNGARO, HALLOWED BE THY NAME--
KATE!!
HEY. BARTON FINK. GIVE ME YOUR TINY LITTLE-MAN SHOES.
ANYBODY NEED ANYTHING FROM THE DUANE READE?
BACK IN TEN.

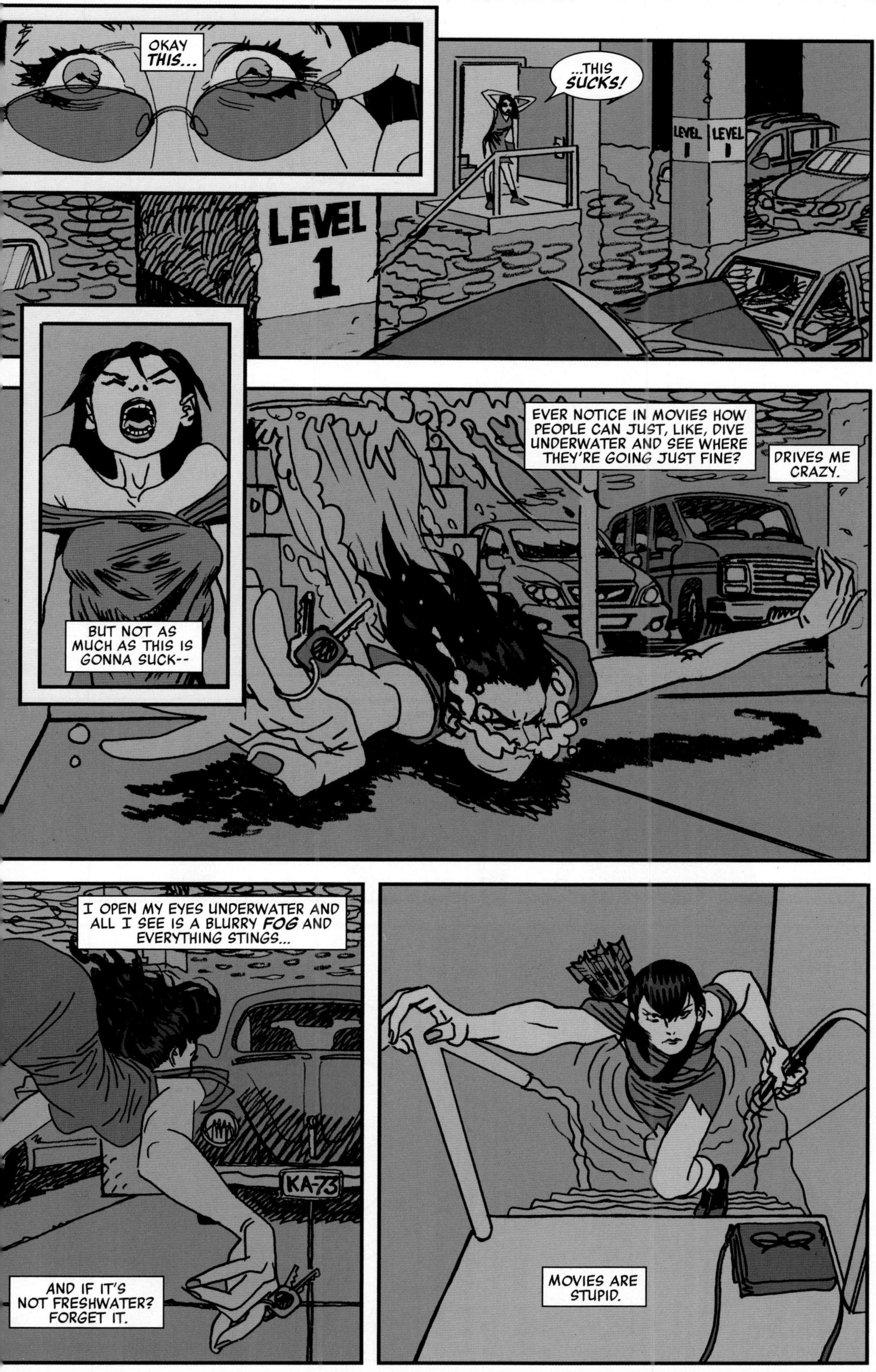
OKAY THIS...
...THIS SUCKS!
LEVEL 1
LEVEL 1
LEVEL 1
BUT NOT AS MUCH AS THIS IS GONNA SUCK--
EVER NOTICE IN MOVIES HOW PEOPLE CAN JUST, LIKE, DIVE UNDERWATER AND SEE WHERE THEY'RE GOING JUST FINE?
DRIVES ME CRAZY.
I OPEN MY EYES UNDERWATER AND ALL I SEE IS A BLURRY FOG AND EVERYTHING STINGS...
KA-73
AND IF IT'S NOT FRESHWATER? FORGET IT.
MOVIES ARE STUPID.

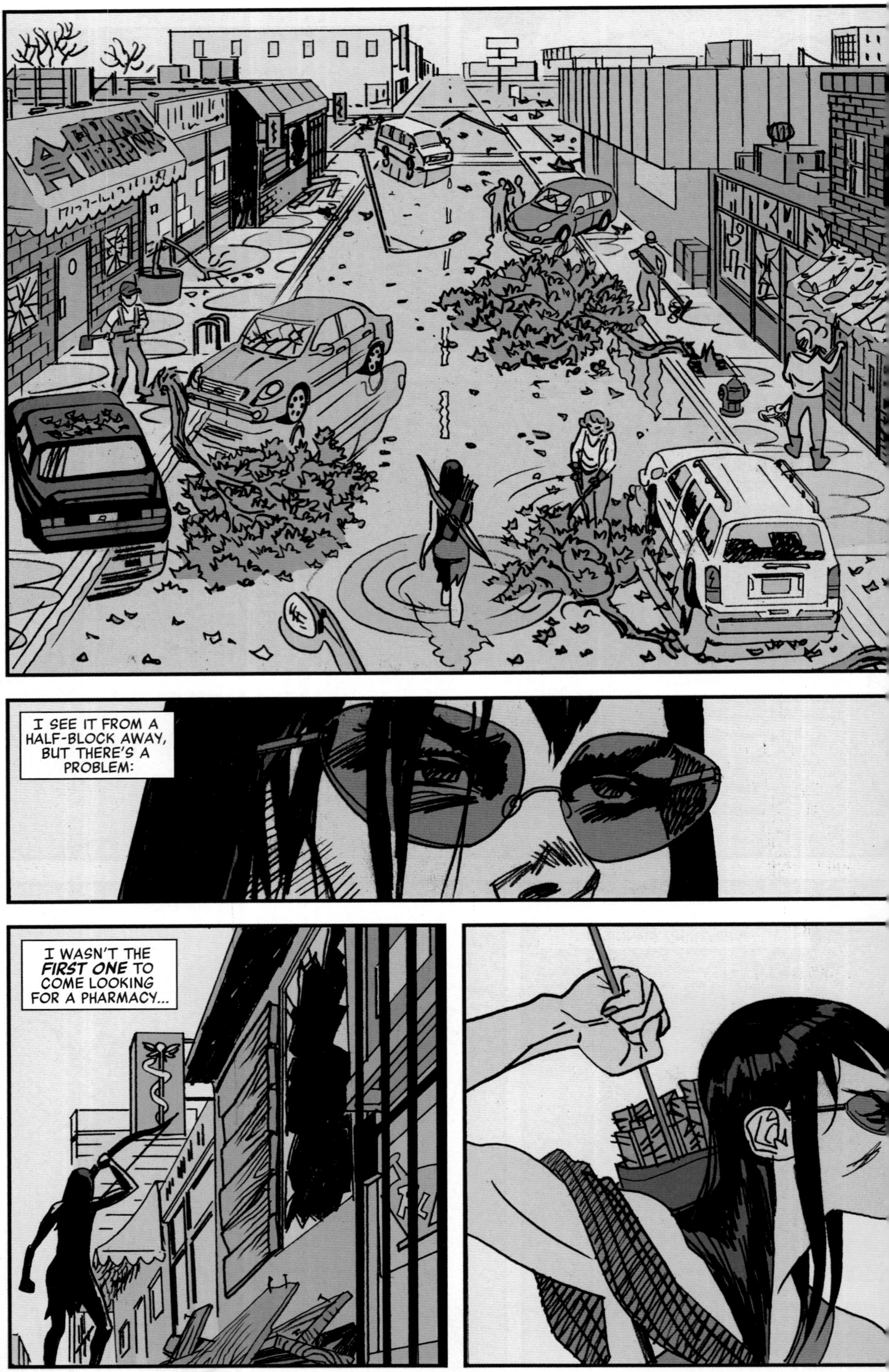
I SEE IT FROM A HALF-BLOCK AWAY, BUT THERE'S A PROBLEM:
I WASN'T THE ***FIRST ONE*** TO COME LOOKING FOR A PHARMACY...

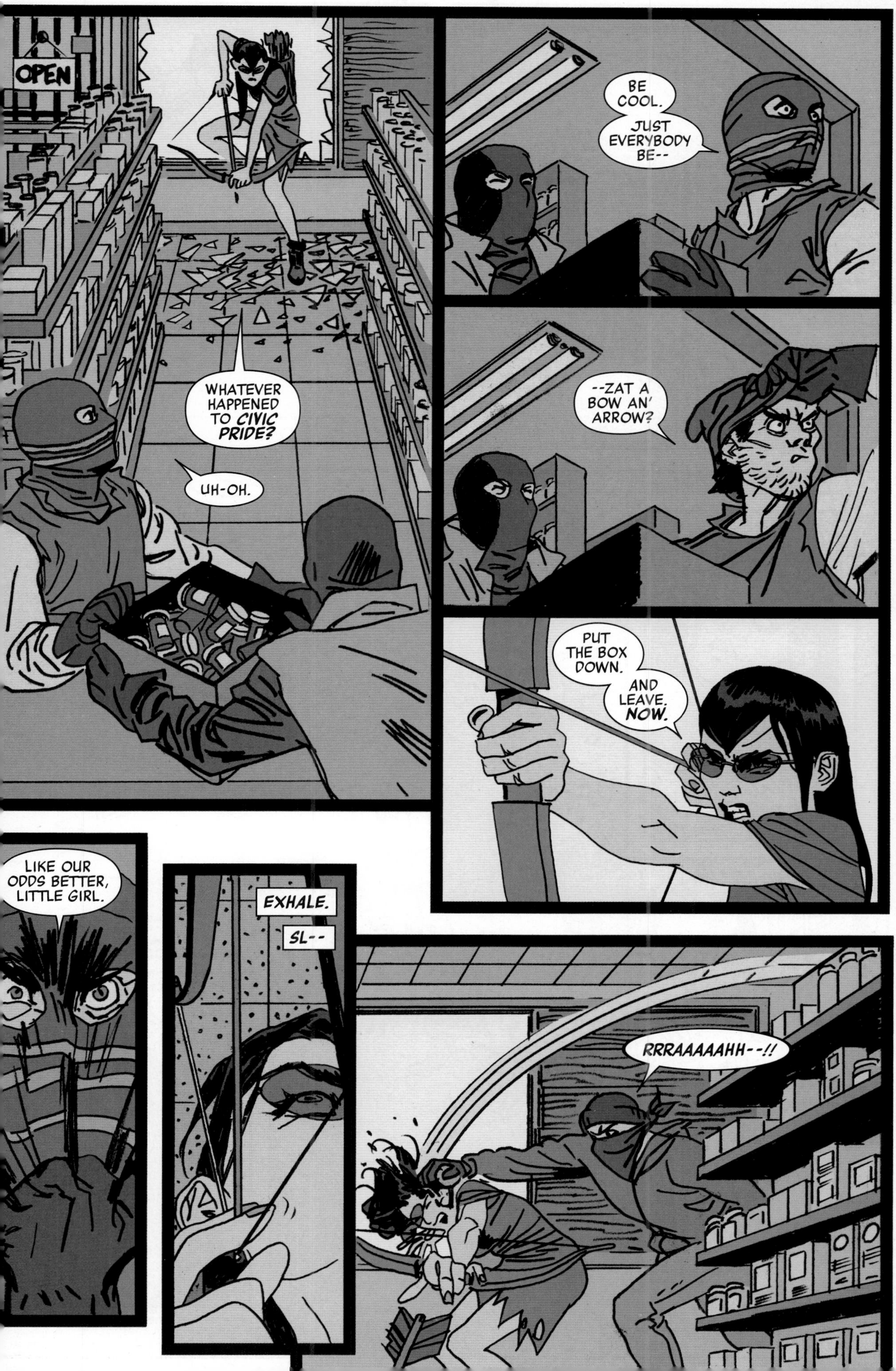
OPEN
WHATEVER HAPPENED TO CIVIC PRIDE?
UH-OH.
BE COOL.
JUST EVERYBODY BE--
--ZAT A BOW AN' ARROW?
PUT THE BOX DOWN.
AND LEAVE. NOW.
LIKE OUR ODDS BETTER, LITTLE GIRL.
EXHALE.
SL--
RRRAAAAAHH--!!

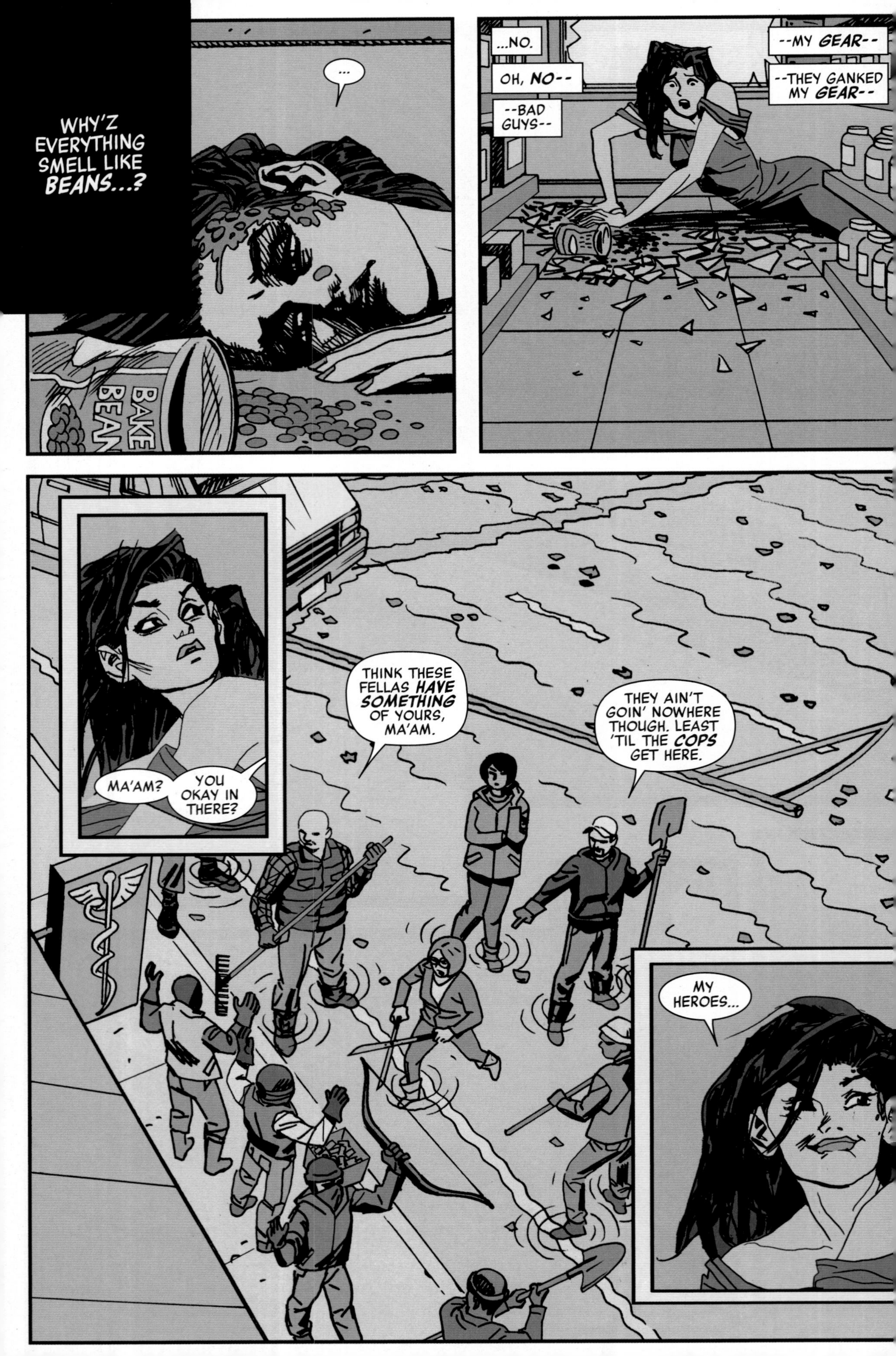
WHY'Z EVERYTHING SMELL LIKE BEANS...?
...
BAKE BEAN
...NO.
OH, NO--
--BAD GUYS--
--MY GEAR--
--THEY GANKED MY GEAR--
MA'AM?
YOU OKAY IN THERE?
THINK THESE FELLAS HAVE SOMETHING OF YOURS, MA'AM.
THEY AIN'T GOIN' NOWHERE THOUGH. LEAST 'TIL THE COPS GET HERE.
MY HEROES...

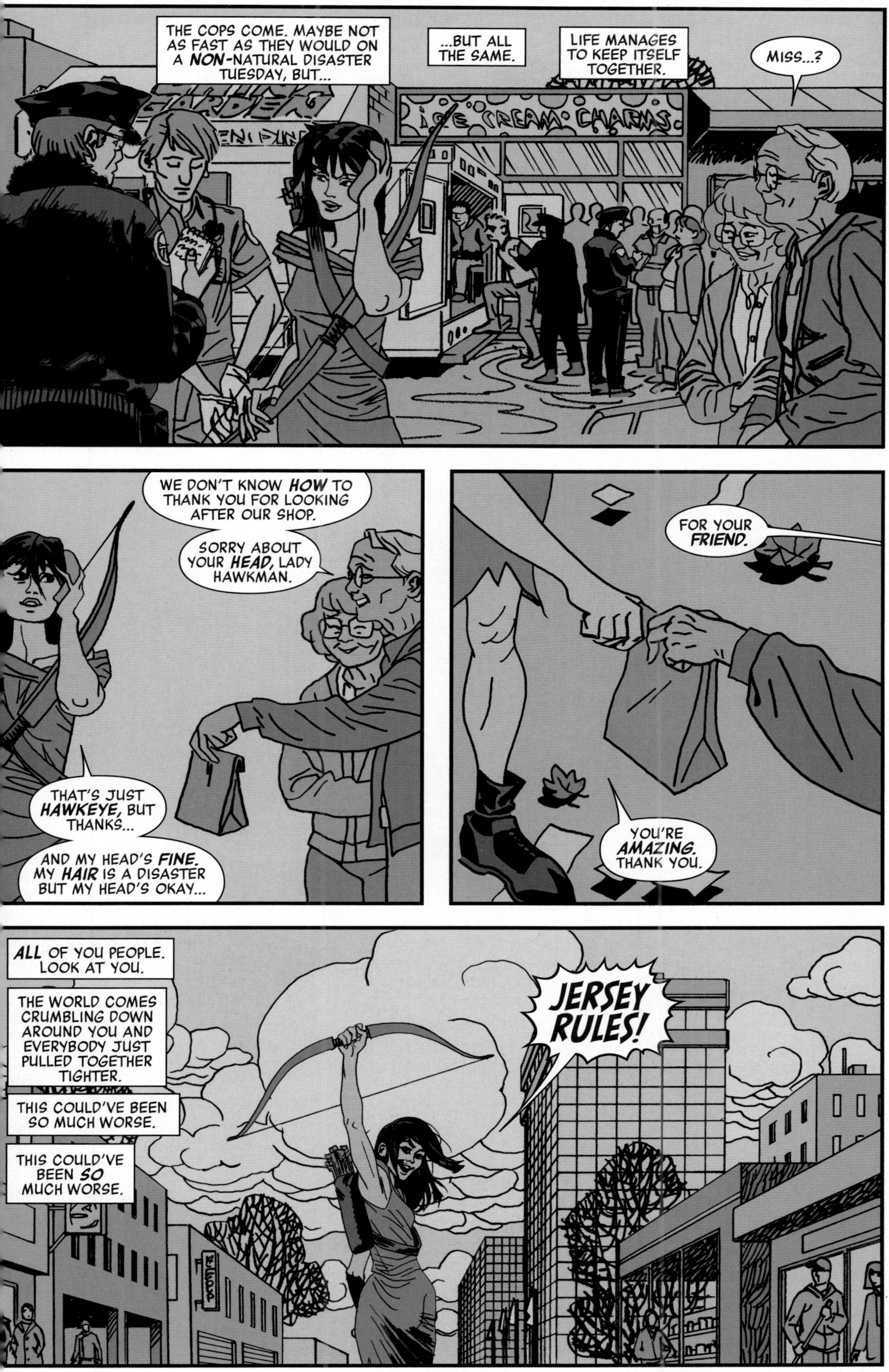
THE COPS COME. MAYBE NOT AS FAST AS THEY WOULD ON A NON-NATURAL DISASTER TUESDAY, BUT...
...BUT ALL THE SAME.
LIFE MANAGES TO KEEP ITSELF TOGETHER.
MISS...?
ICE CREAM CHARMS
WE DON'T KNOW HOW TO THANK YOU FOR LOOKING AFTER OUR SHOP.
SORRY ABOUT YOUR HEAD, LADY HAWKMAN.
THAT'S JUST HAWKEYE, BUT THANKS...
AND MY HEAD'S FINE. MY HAIR IS A DISASTER BUT MY HEAD'S OKAY...
FOR YOUR FRIEND.
YOU'RE AMAZING. THANK YOU.
ALL OF YOU PEOPLE. LOOK AT YOU.
THE WORLD COMES CRUMBLING DOWN AROUND YOU AND EVERYBODY JUST PULLED TOGETHER TIGHTER.
THIS COULD'VE BEEN SO MUCH WORSE.
THIS COULD'VE BEEN SO MUCH WORSE.
JERSEY RULES!

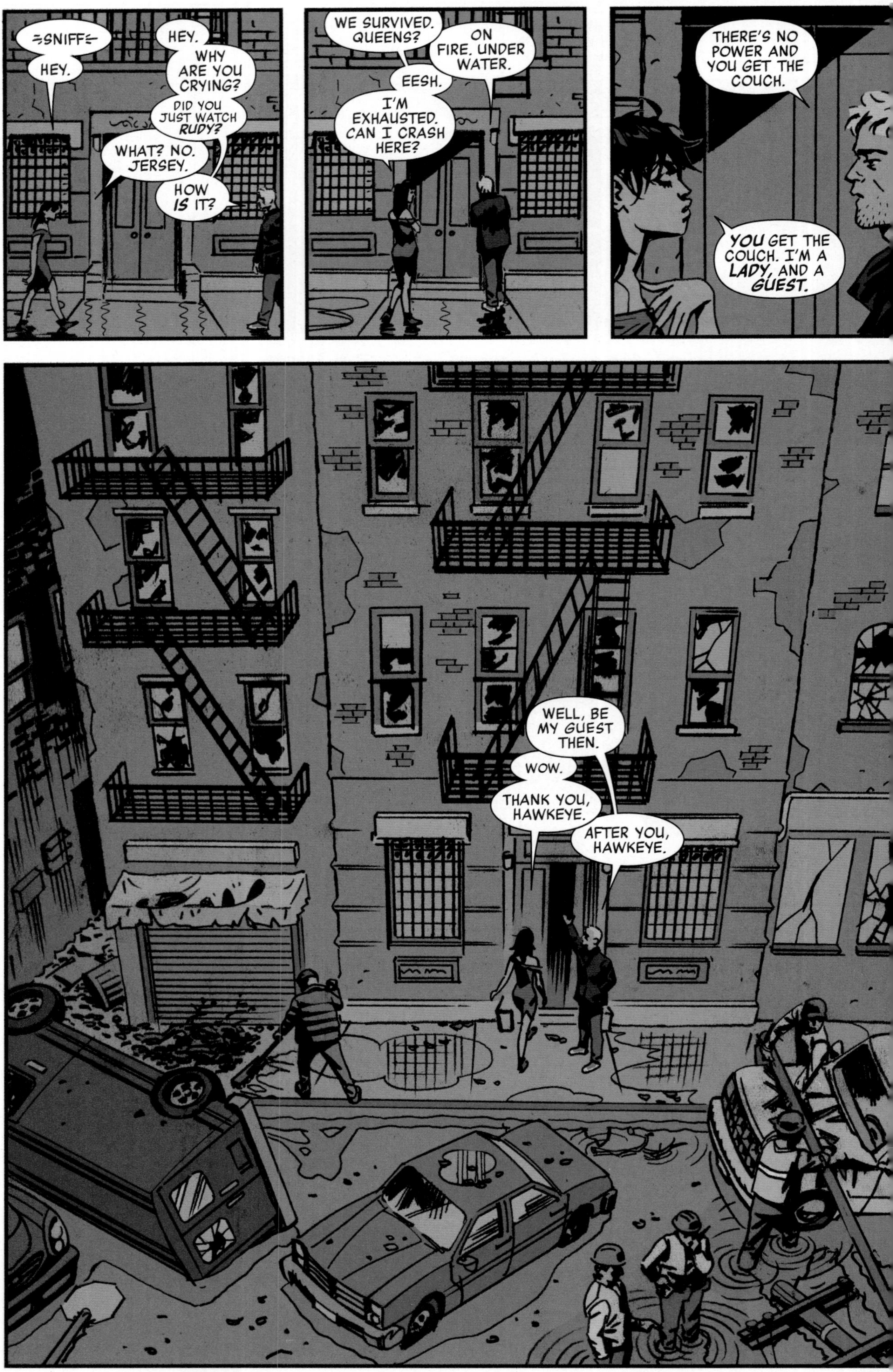

≈SNIFF≈
HEY.
HEY.
WHY ARE YOU CRYING?
DID YOU JUST WATCH RUDY?
WHAT? NO. JERSEY.
HOW IS IT?
WE SURVIVED. QUEENS?
ON FIRE. UNDER WATER.
EESH.
I'M EXHAUSTED. CAN I CRASH HERE?
THERE'S NO POWER AND YOU GET THE COUCH.
YOU GET THE COUCH. I'M A LADY, AND A GUEST.
WELL, BE MY GUEST THEN.
WOW.
THANK YOU, HAWKEYE.
AFTER YOU, HAWKEYE.

# TUESDAY
# DEC
# 18TH

Okay...

...this looks bad.

I don't know what to do with any of this stuff.

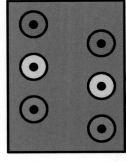

It's all knots.

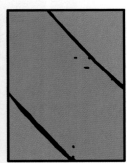

Screw this.

C'MON, CLINT.

I'M JUST GONNA *CUT* THE GREEN WIRE.

*CUT IT?*

WHAT?

THERE'S PROBABLY A BETTER WAY THAN THIS.

PROBABLY. AND YET.

CLINT--

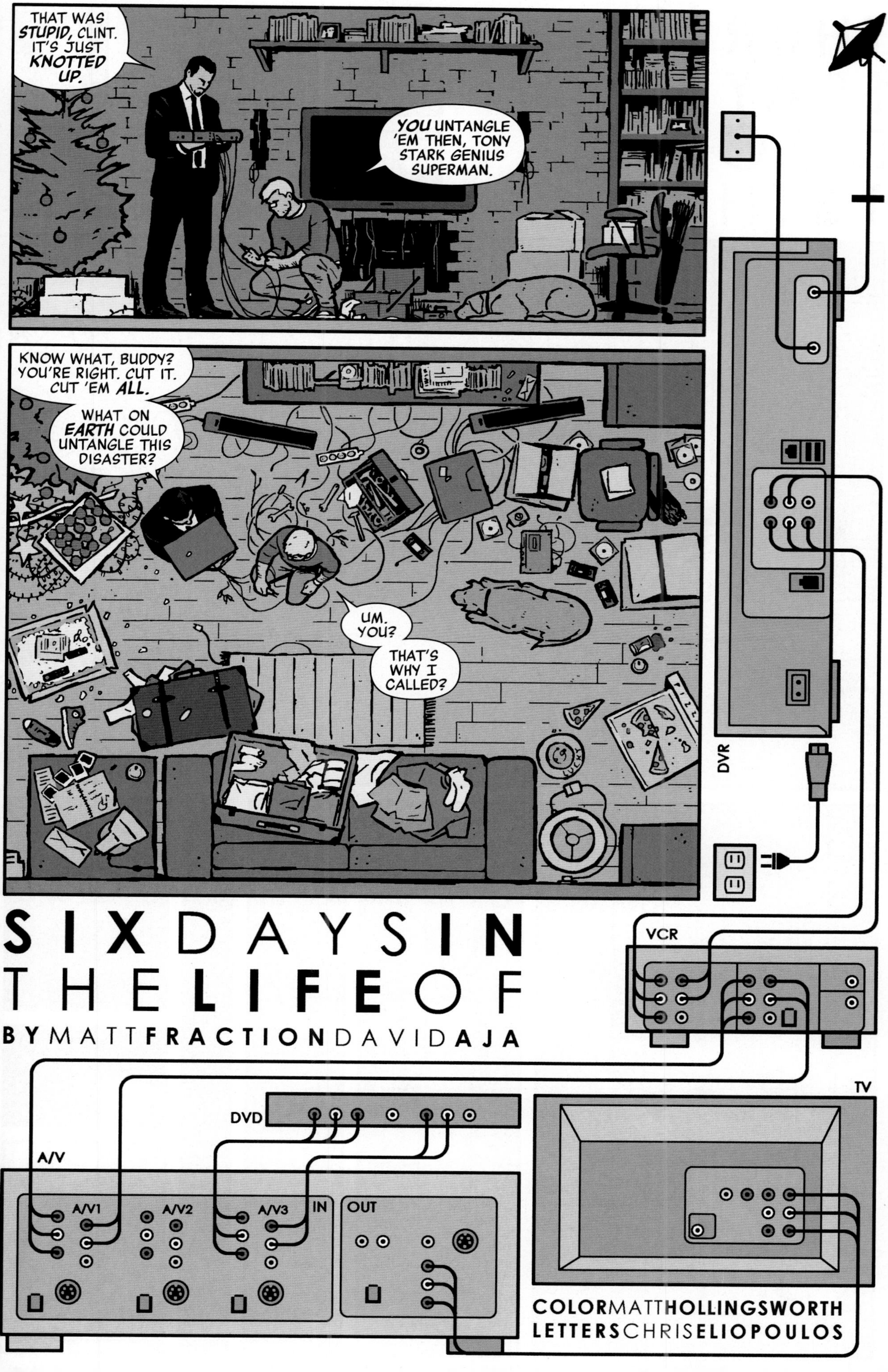

THAT WAS STUPID, CLINT. IT'S JUST KNOTTED UP.
YOU UNTANGLE 'EM THEN, TONY STARK GENIUS SUPERMAN.
KNOW WHAT, BUDDY? YOU'RE RIGHT. CUT IT. CUT 'EM ALL.
WHAT ON EARTH COULD UNTANGLE THIS DISASTER?
UM. YOU?
THAT'S WHY I CALLED?
DVR
VCR
DVD
TV
A/V
A/V1
A/V2
A/V3
IN
OUT
SIX DAYS IN THE LIFE OF
BY MATT FRACTION DAVID AJA
COLOR MATT HOLLINGSWORTH
LETTERS CHRIS ELIOPOULOS

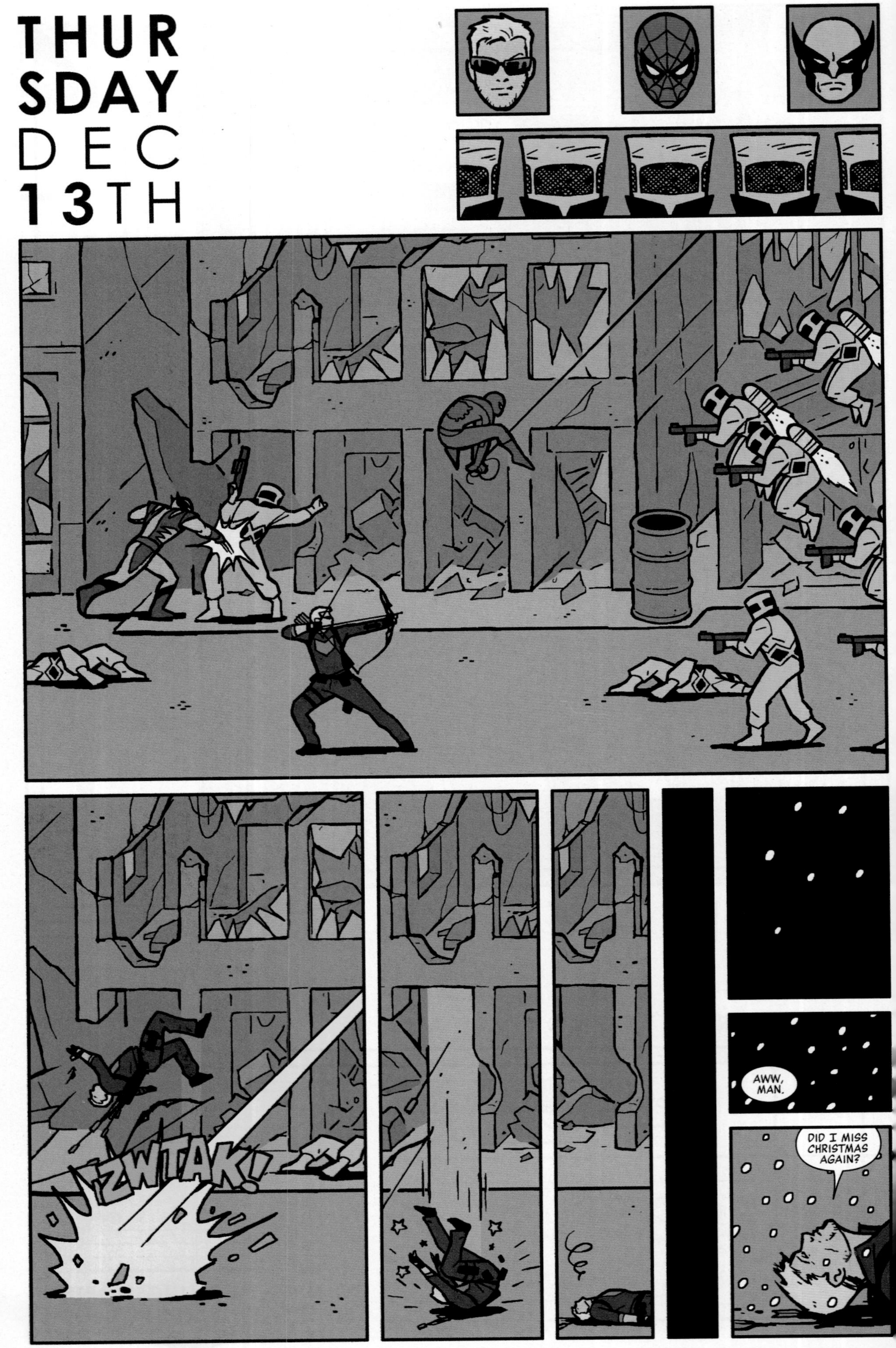

THURSDAY DEC 13TH
ZWTAK!
AWW, MAN.
DID I MISS CHRISTMAS AGAIN?

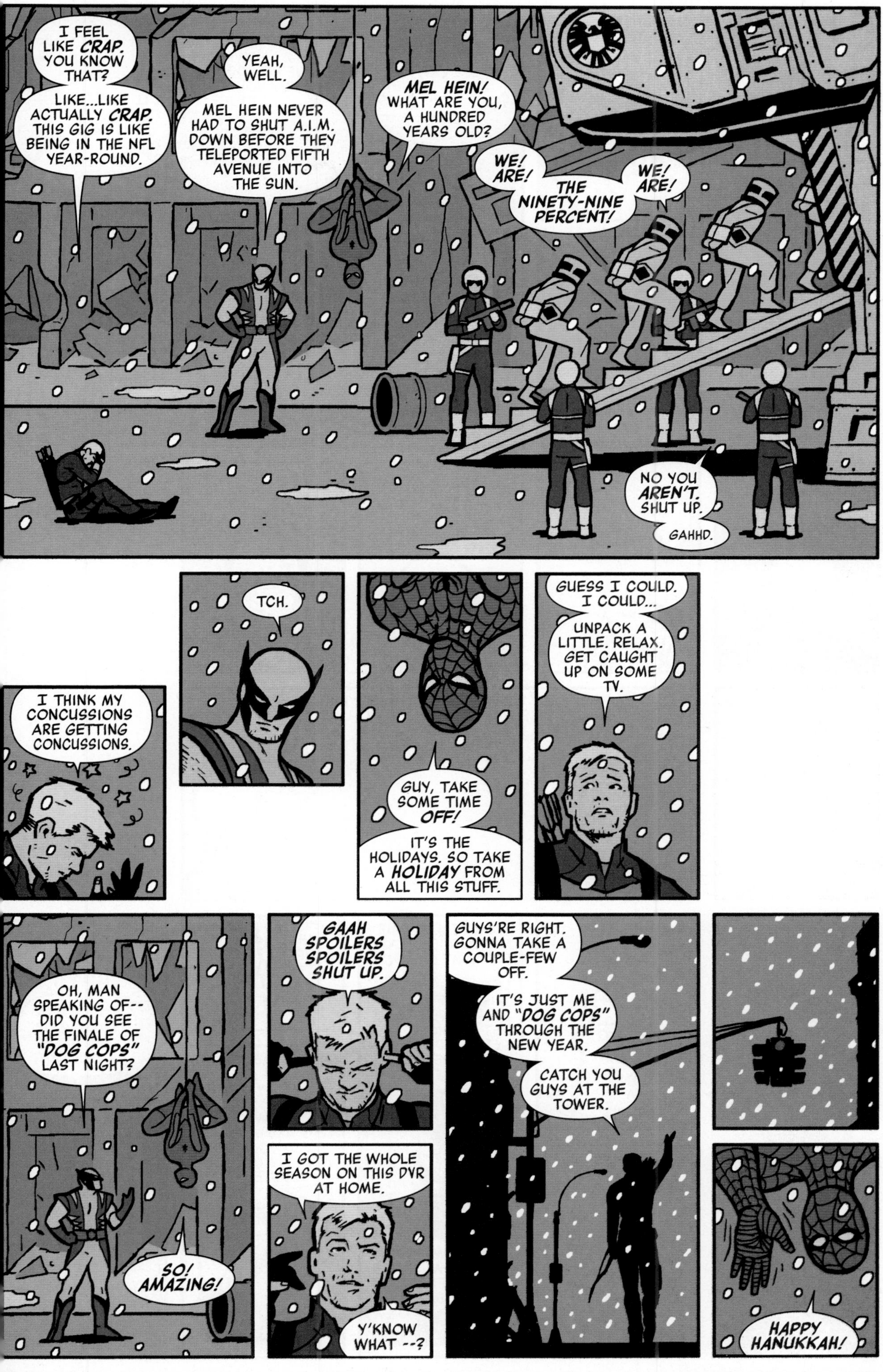
I FEEL LIKE CRAP. YOU KNOW THAT?
LIKE...LIKE ACTUALLY CRAP. THIS GIG IS LIKE BEING IN THE NFL YEAR-ROUND.
YEAH, WELL.
MEL HEIN NEVER HAD TO SHUT A.I.M. DOWN BEFORE THEY TELEPORTED FIFTH AVENUE INTO THE SUN.
MEL HEIN! WHAT ARE YOU, A HUNDRED YEARS OLD?
WE! ARE!
THE NINETY-NINE PERCENT!
WE! ARE!
NO YOU AREN'T. SHUT UP.
GAHHD.
I THINK MY CONCUSSIONS ARE GETTING CONCUSSIONS.
TCH.
GUY, TAKE SOME TIME OFF!
IT'S THE HOLIDAYS. SO TAKE A HOLIDAY FROM ALL THIS STUFF.
GUESS I COULD. I COULD...
UNPACK A LITTLE. RELAX. GET CAUGHT UP ON SOME TV.
OH, MAN SPEAKING OF-- DID YOU SEE THE FINALE OF "DOG COPS" LAST NIGHT?
SO! AMAZING!
GAAH SPOILERS SPOILERS SHUT UP.
I GOT THE WHOLE SEASON ON THIS DVR AT HOME.
Y'KNOW WHAT --?
GUYS'RE RIGHT. GONNA TAKE A COUPLE-FEW OFF.
IT'S JUST ME AND "DOG COPS" THROUGH THE NEW YEAR.
CATCH YOU GUYS AT THE TOWER.
HAPPY HANUKKAH!

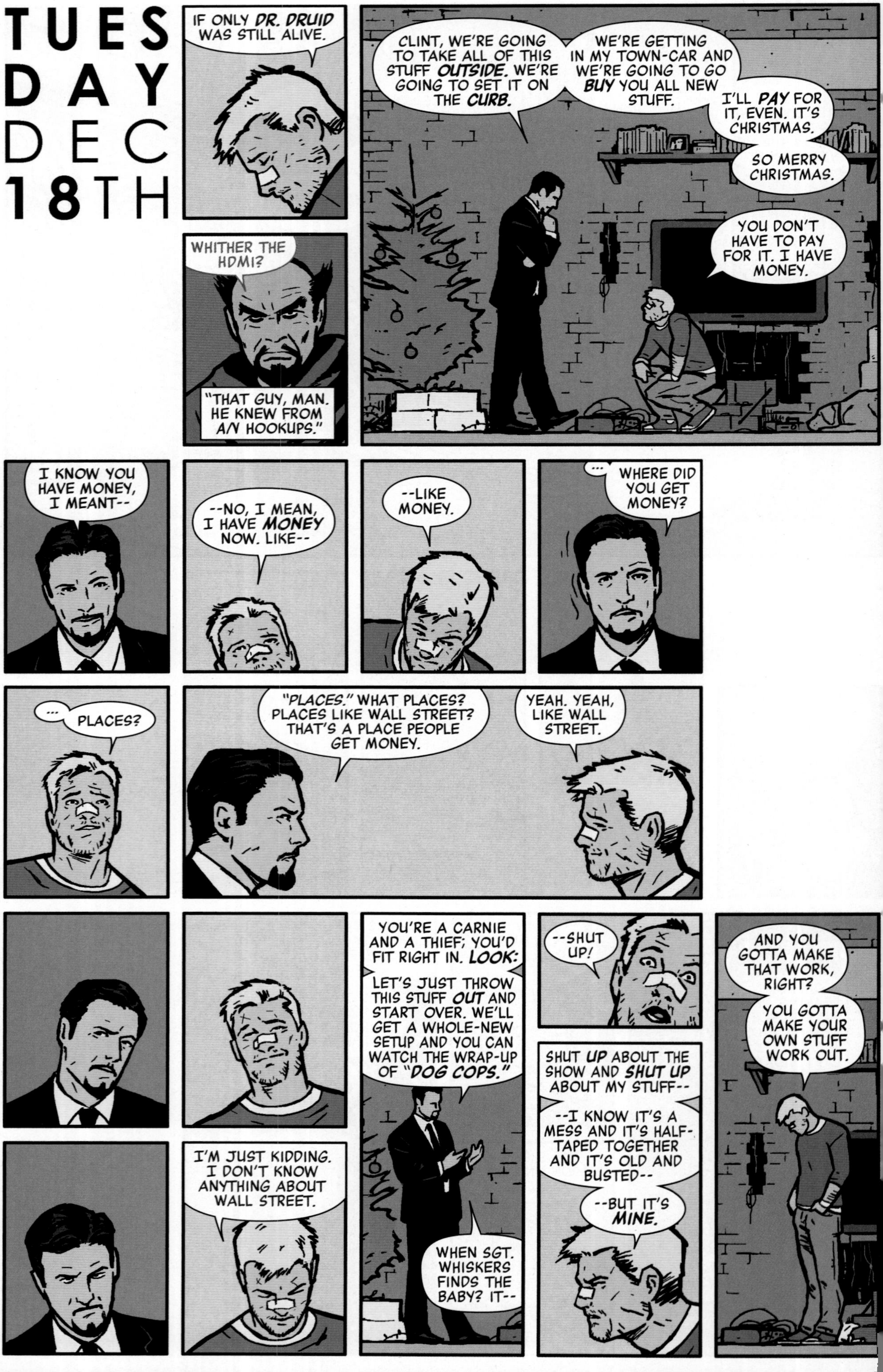
TUES DAY DEC 18TH
IF ONLY DR. DRUID WAS STILL ALIVE.
WHITHER THE HDMI?
"THAT GUY, MAN. HE KNEW FROM A/V HOOKUPS."
CLINT, WE'RE GOING TO TAKE ALL OF THIS STUFF OUTSIDE. WE'RE GOING TO SET IT ON THE CURB.
WE'RE GETTING IN MY TOWN-CAR AND WE'RE GOING TO GO BUY YOU ALL NEW STUFF.
I'LL PAY FOR IT, EVEN. IT'S CHRISTMAS.
SO MERRY CHRISTMAS.
YOU DON'T HAVE TO PAY FOR IT. I HAVE MONEY.
I KNOW YOU HAVE MONEY, I MEANT--
--NO, I MEAN, I HAVE MONEY NOW. LIKE--
--LIKE MONEY.
...
WHERE DID YOU GET MONEY?
...
PLACES?
"PLACES." WHAT PLACES? PLACES LIKE WALL STREET? THAT'S A PLACE PEOPLE GET MONEY.
YEAH. YEAH, LIKE WALL STREET.
I'M JUST KIDDING. I DON'T KNOW ANYTHING ABOUT WALL STREET.
YOU'RE A CARNIE AND A THIEF; YOU'D FIT RIGHT IN. LOOK:
LET'S JUST THROW THIS STUFF OUT AND START OVER. WE'LL GET A WHOLE-NEW SETUP AND YOU CAN WATCH THE WRAP-UP OF "DOG COPS."
WHEN SGT. WHISKERS FINDS THE BABY? IT--
--SHUT UP!
SHUT UP ABOUT THE SHOW AND SHUT UP ABOUT MY STUFF--
--I KNOW IT'S A MESS AND IT'S HALF-TAPED TOGETHER AND IT'S OLD AND BUSTED--
--BUT IT'S MINE.
AND YOU GOTTA MAKE THAT WORK, RIGHT?
YOU GOTTA MAKE YOUR OWN STUFF WORK OUT.

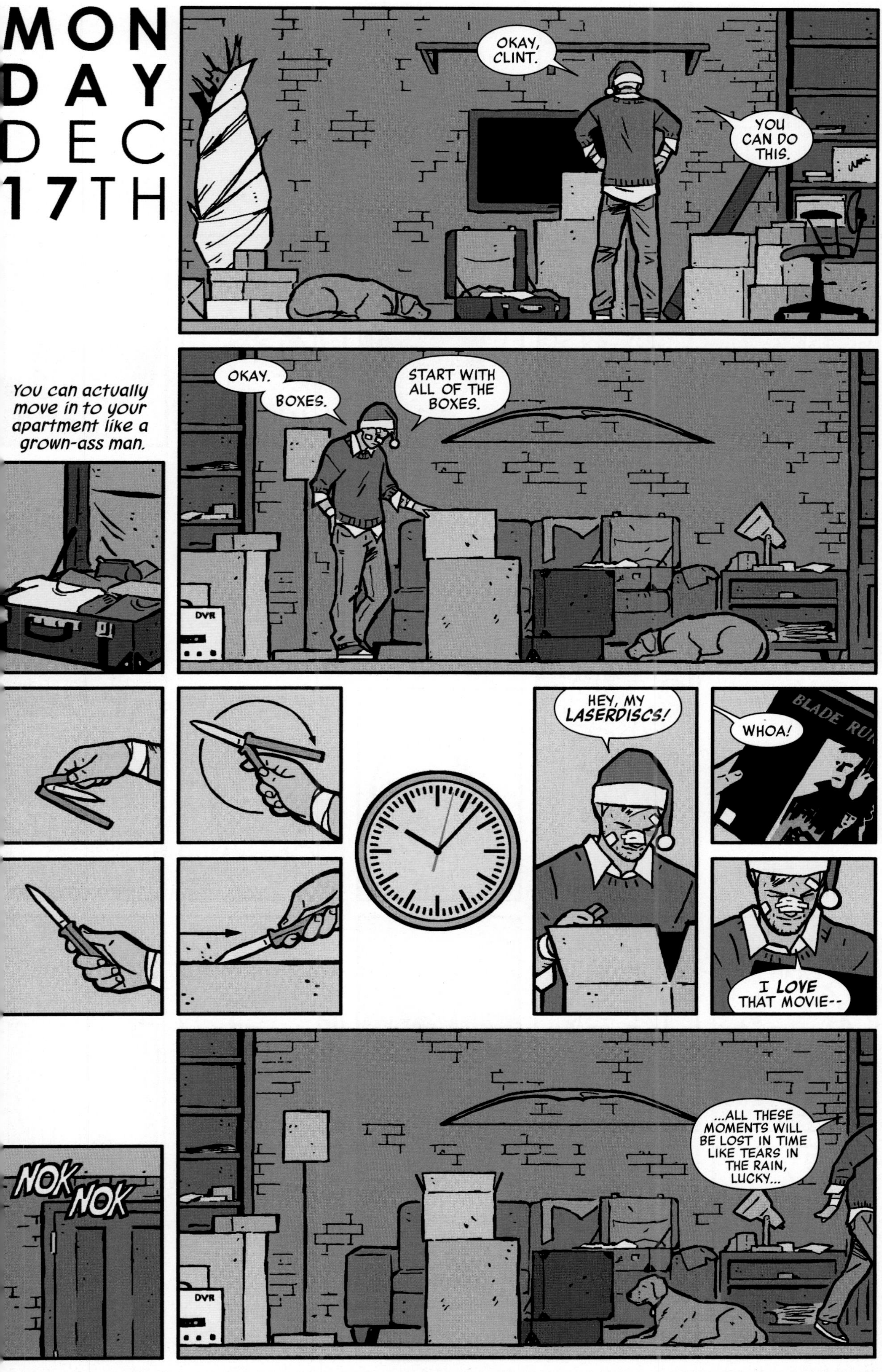
MON DAY DEC 17TH
OKAY, CLINT.
YOU CAN DO THIS.
You can actually move in to your apartment like a grown-ass man.
OKAY.
BOXES.
START WITH ALL OF THE BOXES.
DVR
HEY, MY LASERDISCS!
WHOA!
I LOVE THAT MOVIE--
NOK NOK
...ALL THESE MOMENTS WILL BE LOST IN TIME LIKE TEARS IN THE RAIN, LUCKY...
DVR

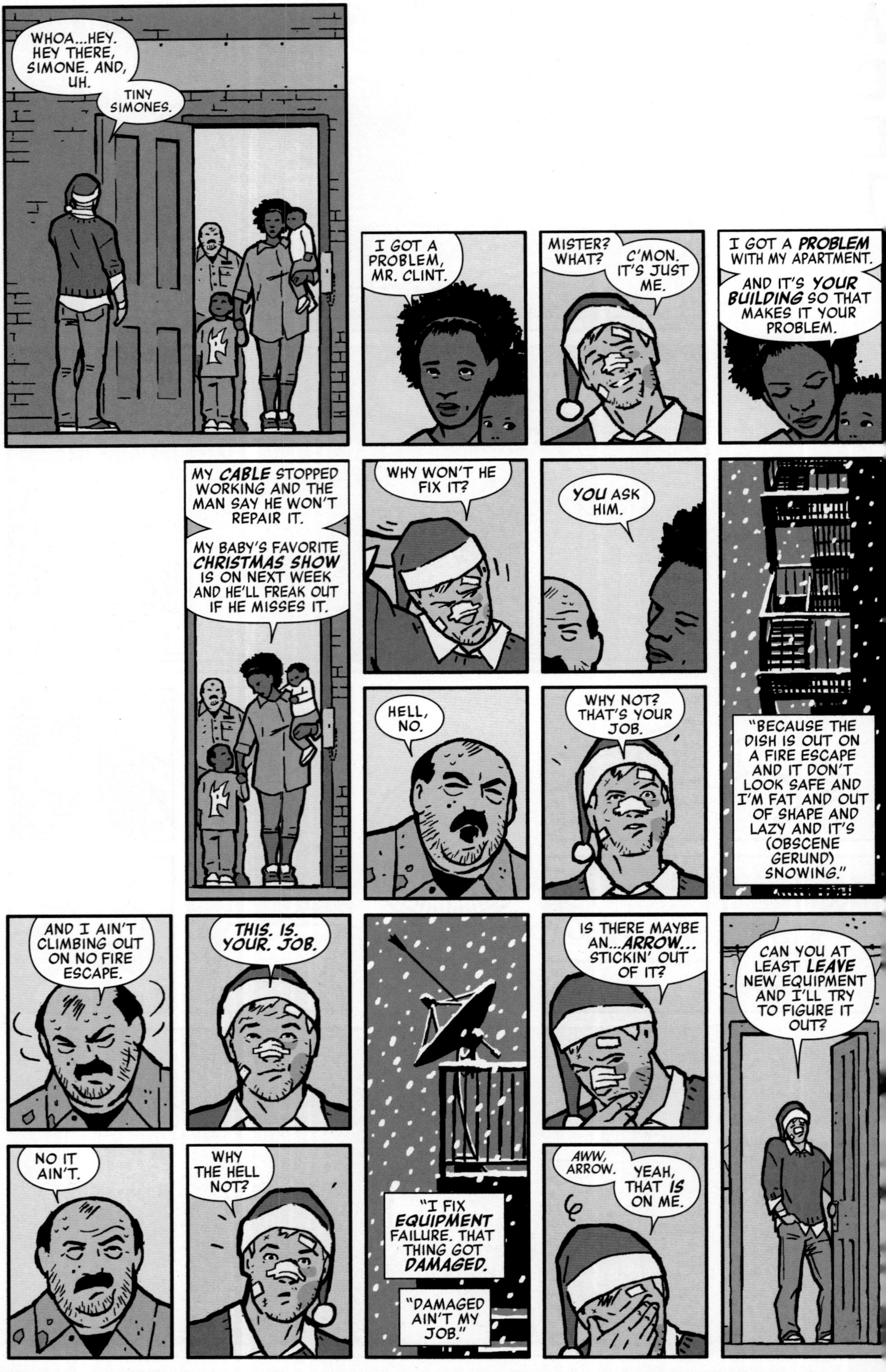
WHOA...HEY. HEY THERE, SIMONE. AND, UH.
TINY SIMONES.
I GOT A PROBLEM, MR. CLINT.
MISTER? WHAT?
C'MON. IT'S JUST ME.
I GOT A **PROBLEM** WITH MY APARTMENT.
AND IT'S **YOUR BUILDING** SO THAT MAKES IT YOUR PROBLEM.
MY **CABLE** STOPPED WORKING AND THE MAN SAY HE WON'T REPAIR IT.
MY BABY'S FAVORITE **CHRISTMAS SHOW** IS ON NEXT WEEK AND HE'LL FREAK OUT IF HE MISSES IT.
WHY WON'T HE FIX IT?
**YOU** ASK HIM.
HELL, NO.
WHY NOT? THAT'S YOUR JOB.
"BECAUSE THE DISH IS OUT ON A FIRE ESCAPE AND IT DON'T LOOK SAFE AND I'M FAT AND OUT OF SHAPE AND LAZY AND IT'S (OBSCENE GERUND) SNOWING."
AND I AIN'T CLIMBING OUT ON NO FIRE ESCAPE.
**THIS. IS. YOUR. JOB.**
NO IT AIN'T.
WHY THE HELL NOT?
"I FIX **EQUIPMENT** FAILURE. THAT THING GOT **DAMAGED.**
"DAMAGED AIN'T MY JOB."
IS THERE MAYBE AN...**ARROW...** STICKIN' OUT OF IT?
AWW, ARROW.
YEAH, THAT **IS** ON ME.
CAN YOU AT LEAST **LEAVE** NEW EQUIPMENT AND I'LL TRY TO FIGURE IT OUT?

# FRI DAY DEC 14TH

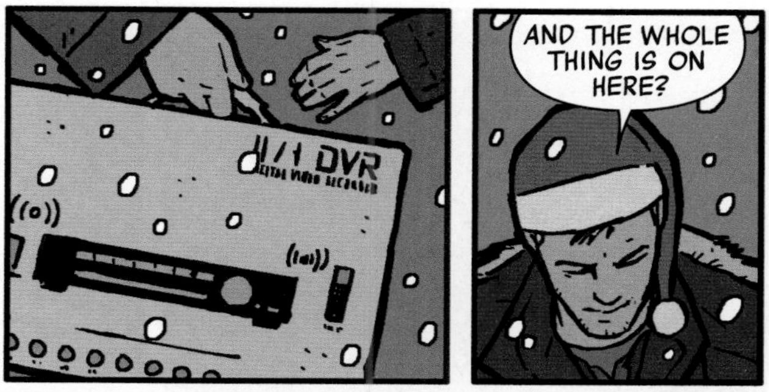

DVR
AND THE WHOLE THING IS ON HERE?


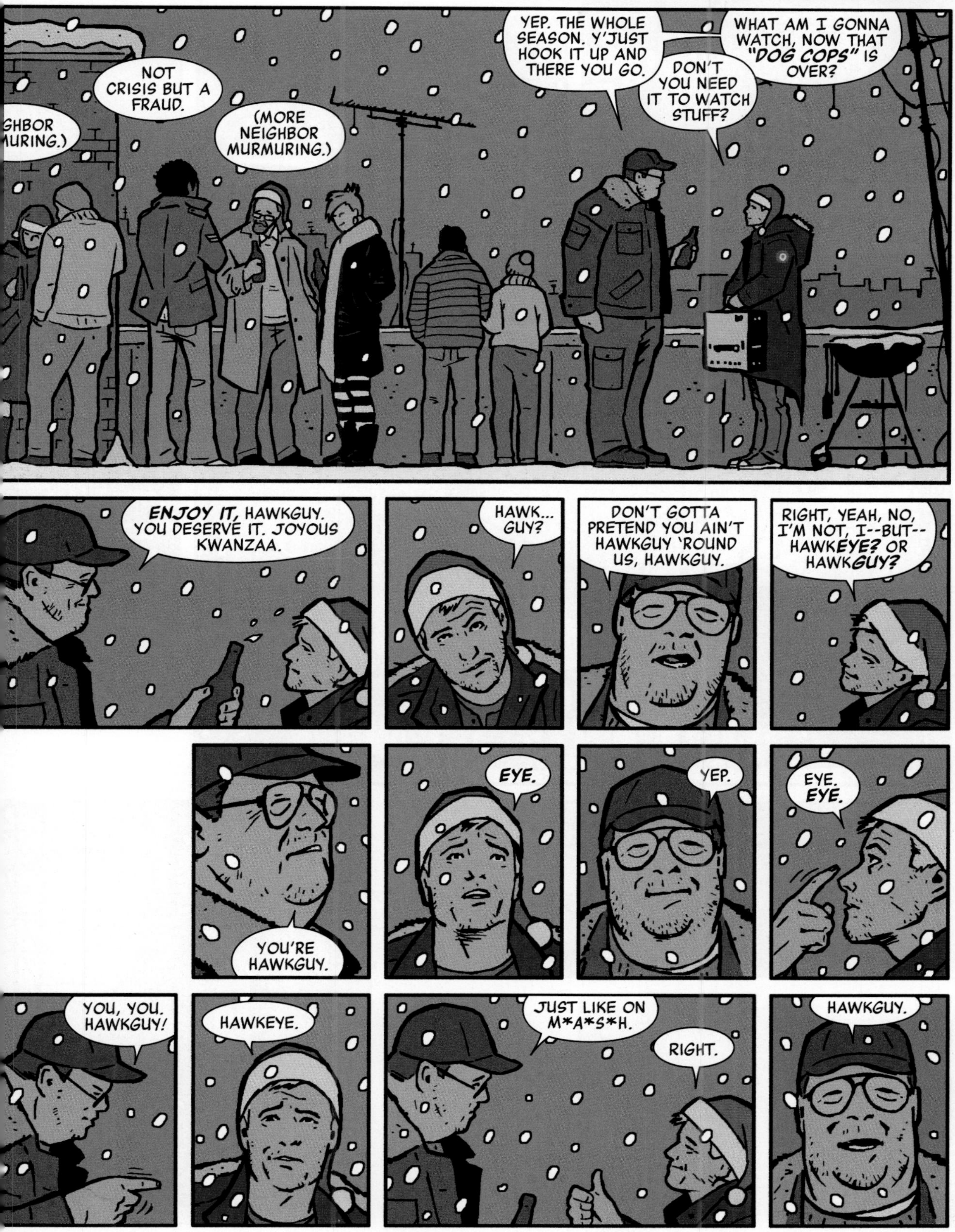

GHBOR MURING.)
NOT CRISIS BUT A FRAUD.
(MORE NEIGHBOR MURMURING.)
YEP. THE WHOLE SEASON. Y'JUST HOOK IT UP AND THERE YOU GO.
DON'T YOU NEED IT TO WATCH STUFF?
WHAT AM I GONNA WATCH, NOW THAT "DOG COPS" IS OVER?
ENJOY IT, HAWKGUY. YOU DESERVE IT. JOYOUS KWANZAA.
HAWK... GUY?
DON'T GOTTA PRETEND YOU AIN'T HAWKGUY 'ROUND US, HAWKGUY.
RIGHT, YEAH, NO, I'M NOT, I--BUT-- HAWKEYE? OR HAWKGUY?
YOU'RE HAWKGUY.
EYE.
YEP.
EYE. EYE.
YOU, YOU. HAWKGUY!
HAWKEYE.
JUST LIKE ON M*A*S*H.
RIGHT.
HAWKGUY.

'SUP?

YOU TALKIN' ABOUT HULK-GUY?

KWANZAA. JUST HAVIN' ONE JOYOUS-ASS KWANZAA.

WORD. YOU KNOW THERE'S GUYS DOWN FRONT WITH *BATS*, RIGHT?

HEY, BROOOOOOOOOOOOOOOOOOOOOO

HE *SEE* US, BRO?

HE *SAW* US, BRO. IS *ON NOW*, BRO.

BRO, *BRING IT*, BRO.

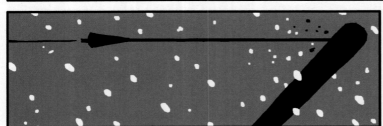

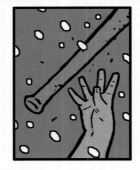

GET THE HELL AWAY FROM MY BUILDING.

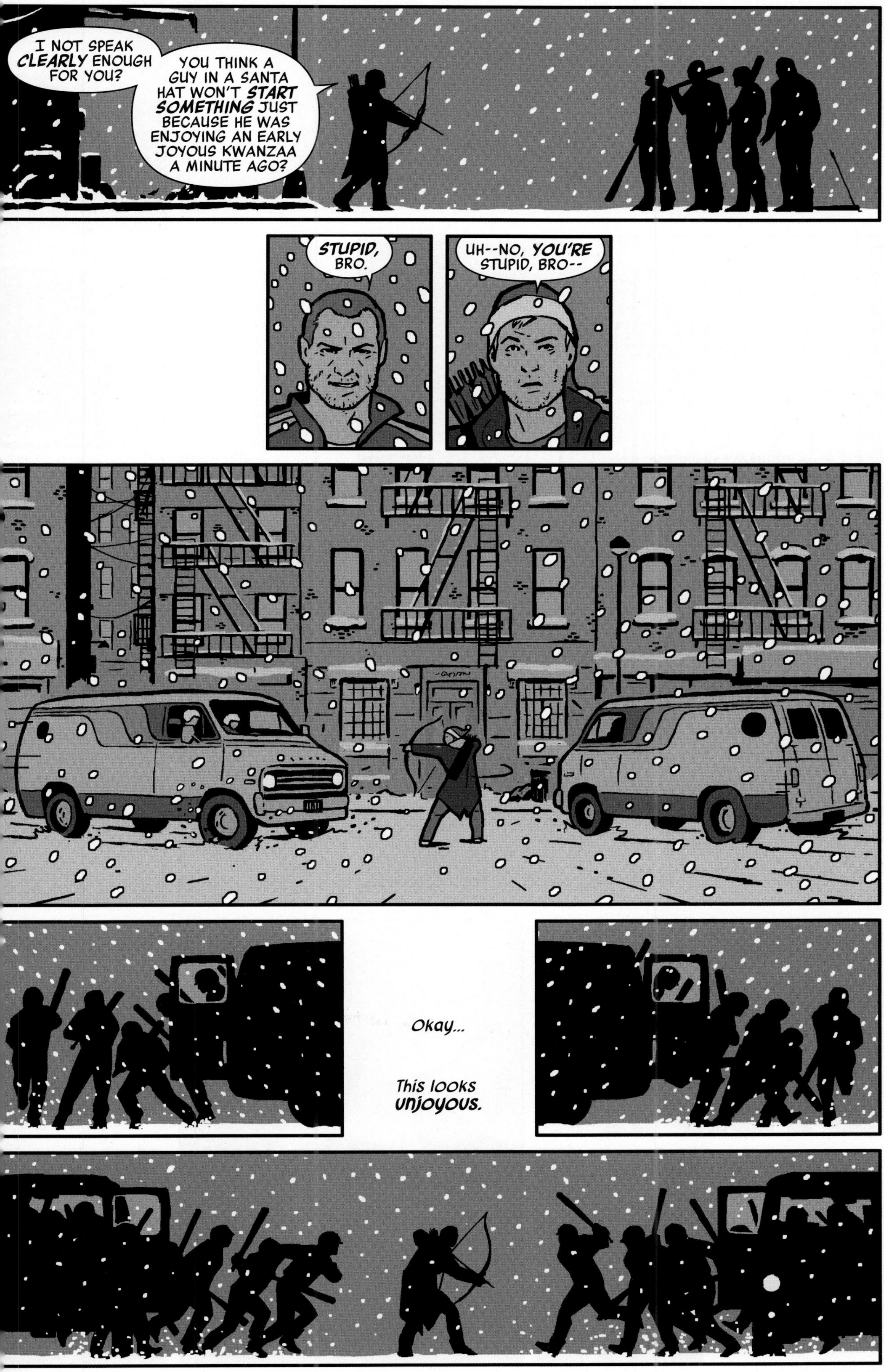

I NOT SPEAK CLEARLY ENOUGH FOR YOU?
YOU THINK A GUY IN A SANTA HAT WON'T START SOMETHING JUST BECAUSE HE WAS ENJOYING AN EARLY JOYOUS KWANZAA A MINUTE AGO?
STUPID, BRO.
UH--NO, YOU'RE STUPID, BRO--
Okay...
This looks unjoyous.

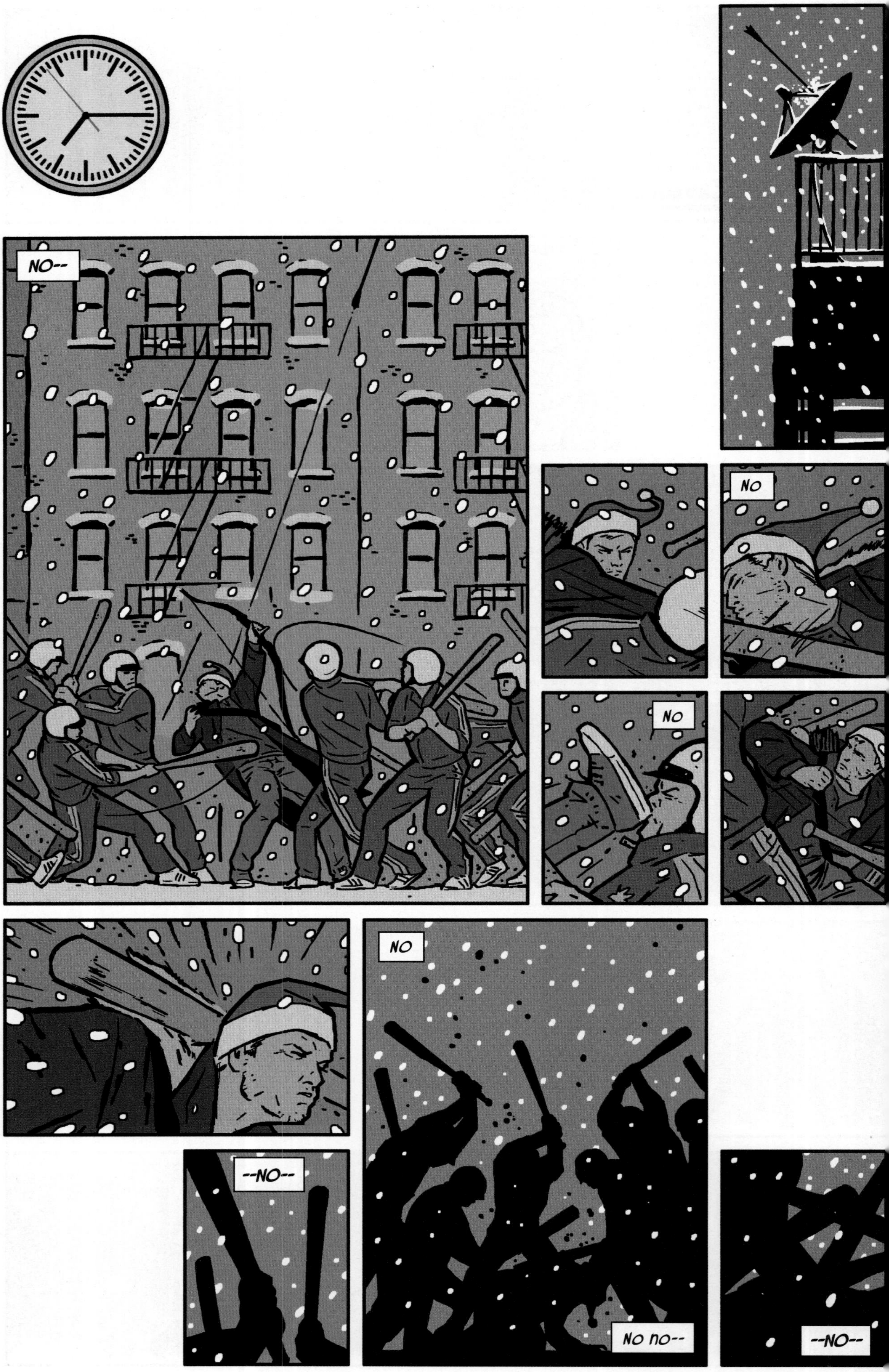

NO--
NO
NO
NO
--NO--
NO NO--
--NO--

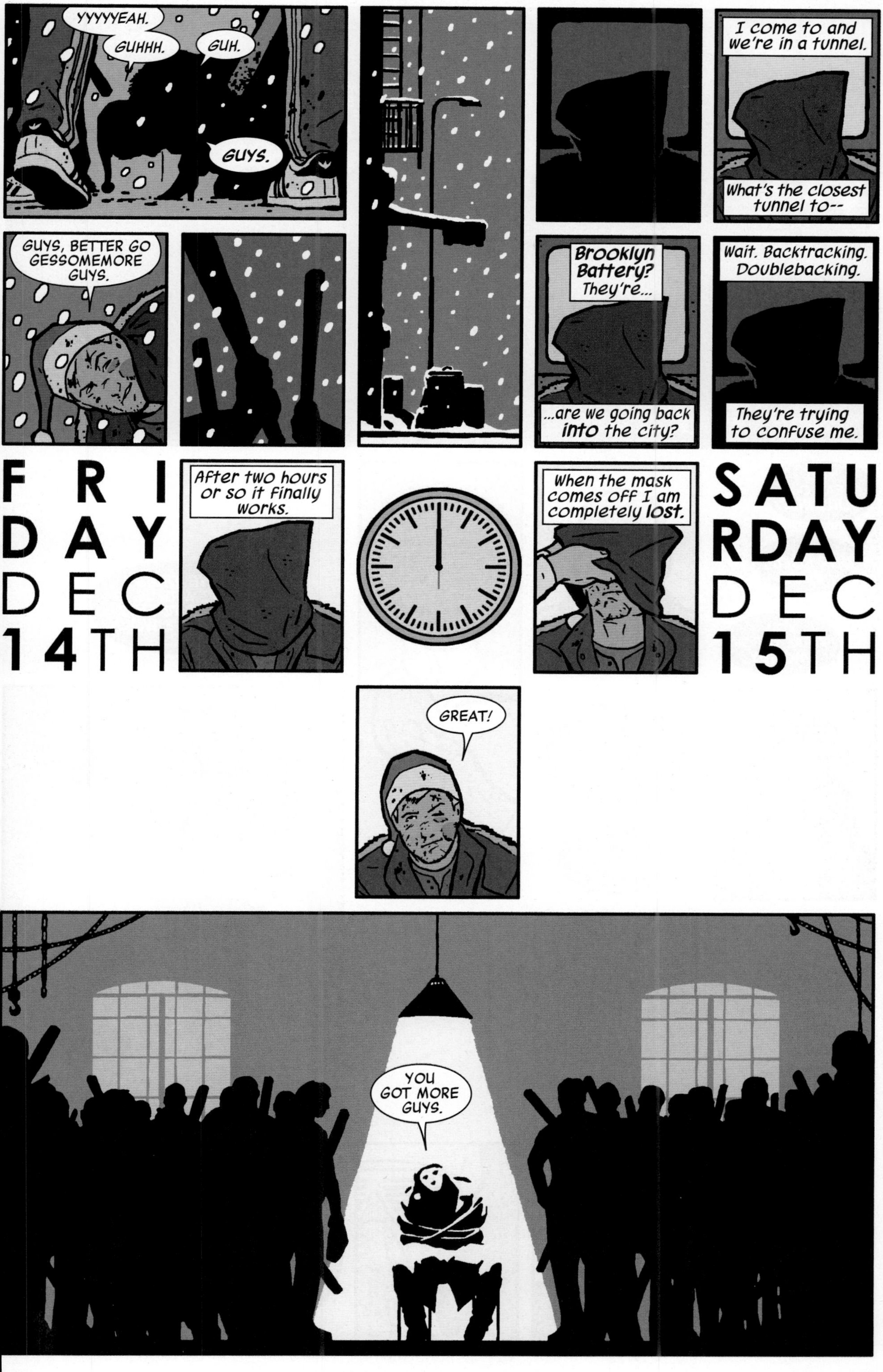

YYYYYEAH.
GUHHH.
GUH.
GUYS.
I come to and we're in a tunnel.
What's the closest tunnel to--
GUYS, BETTER GO GESSOMEMORE GUYS.
Brooklyn Battery? They're...
...are we going back into the city?
Wait. Backtracking. Doublebacking.
They're trying to confuse me.
FRIDAY DEC 14TH
After two hours or so it finally works.
When the mask comes off I am completely lost.
SATURDAY DEC 15TH
GREAT!
YOU GOT MORE GUYS.

BRO.

YOU MAKE LOT OF BIG BAD PEOPLE REAL MAD BRO.

YOU STEAL OUR **BUILDING.**

IN **OUR HOOD,** BRO.

YOU STEAL IT FOR **MONEY.**

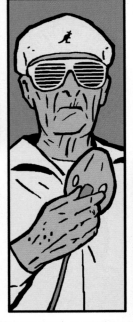

IS **ONE THING** TO **FUTZ** WITH US. IS **ANOTHER** TO **FUTZ** WITH GUYS WE **WORK FOR.**

YOU TAKE BRO'S **WIFE,** GET HER OUT OF TOWN? **FINE,** BRO. ALWAYS MORE WIFE.

BUT YOU STEAL FROM STEALERS, BRO?

AND, BRO, THOSE ARE SOME VERY SCARY FUTZING BROS, BRO.

THEY WANT US TELL YOU, THEY **DONE WITH** YOU, BRO.

YOU GO **WAY** NOW. YOU FUTZ OFF.

OR IS **WAR,** BRO. **TWENTY-FOUR HOURS,** BRO.

YOU **GONE** OR WE KEELING **EVERYBODY** IN YOU BUILDING, BRO.

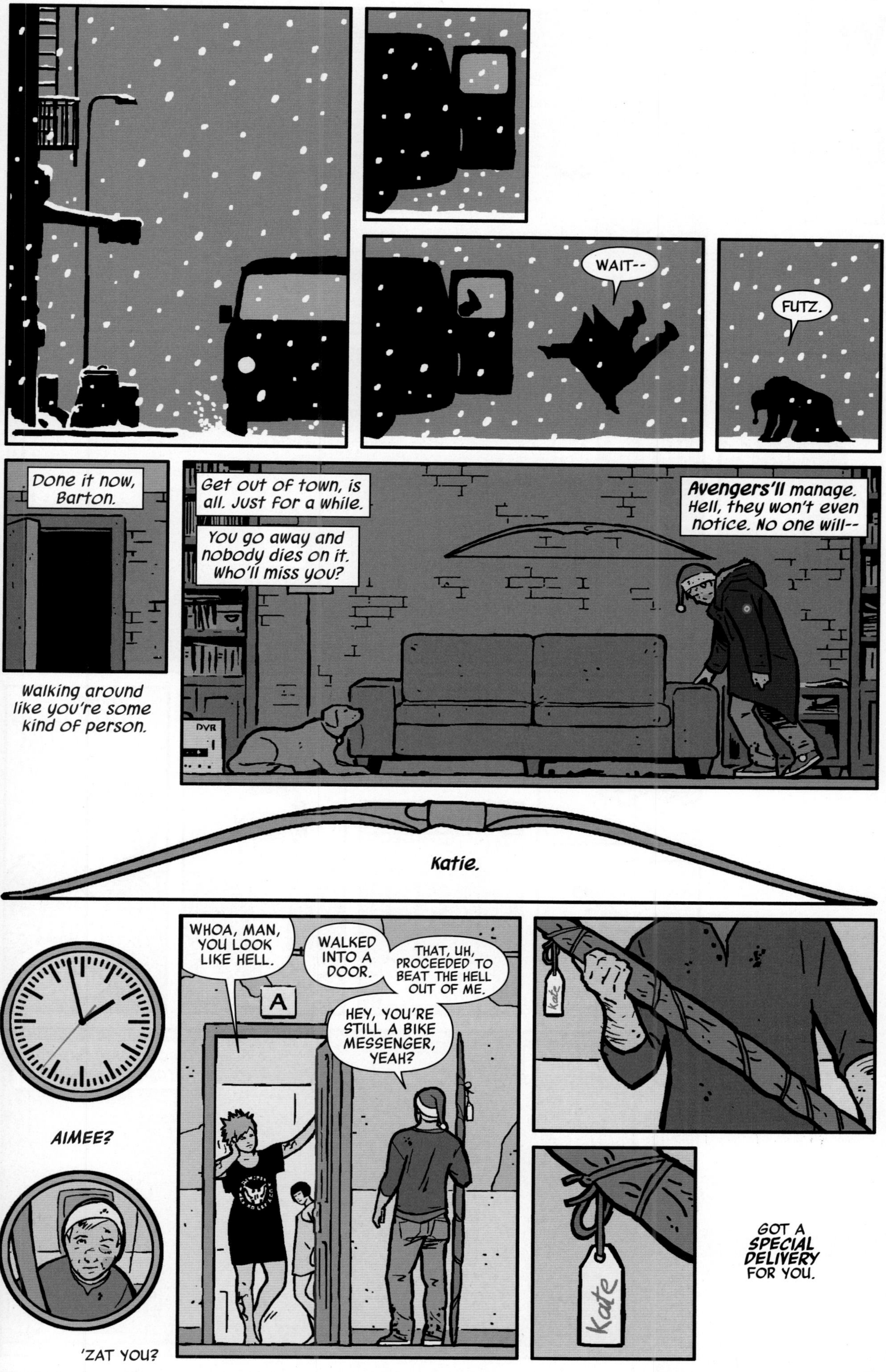
WAIT--
FUTZ.
Done it now, Barton.
Walking around like you're some kind of person.
Get out of town, is all. Just for a while.
You go away and nobody dies on it. Who'll miss you?
Avengers'll manage. Hell, they won't even notice. No one will--
DVR
Katie.
AIMEE?
'ZAT YOU?
WHOA, MAN, YOU LOOK LIKE HELL.
WALKED INTO A DOOR.
THAT, UH, PROCEEDED TO BEAT THE HELL OUT OF ME.
HEY, YOU'RE STILL A BIKE MESSENGER, YEAH?
A
Kate
GOT A SPECIAL DELIVERY FOR YOU.
Kate

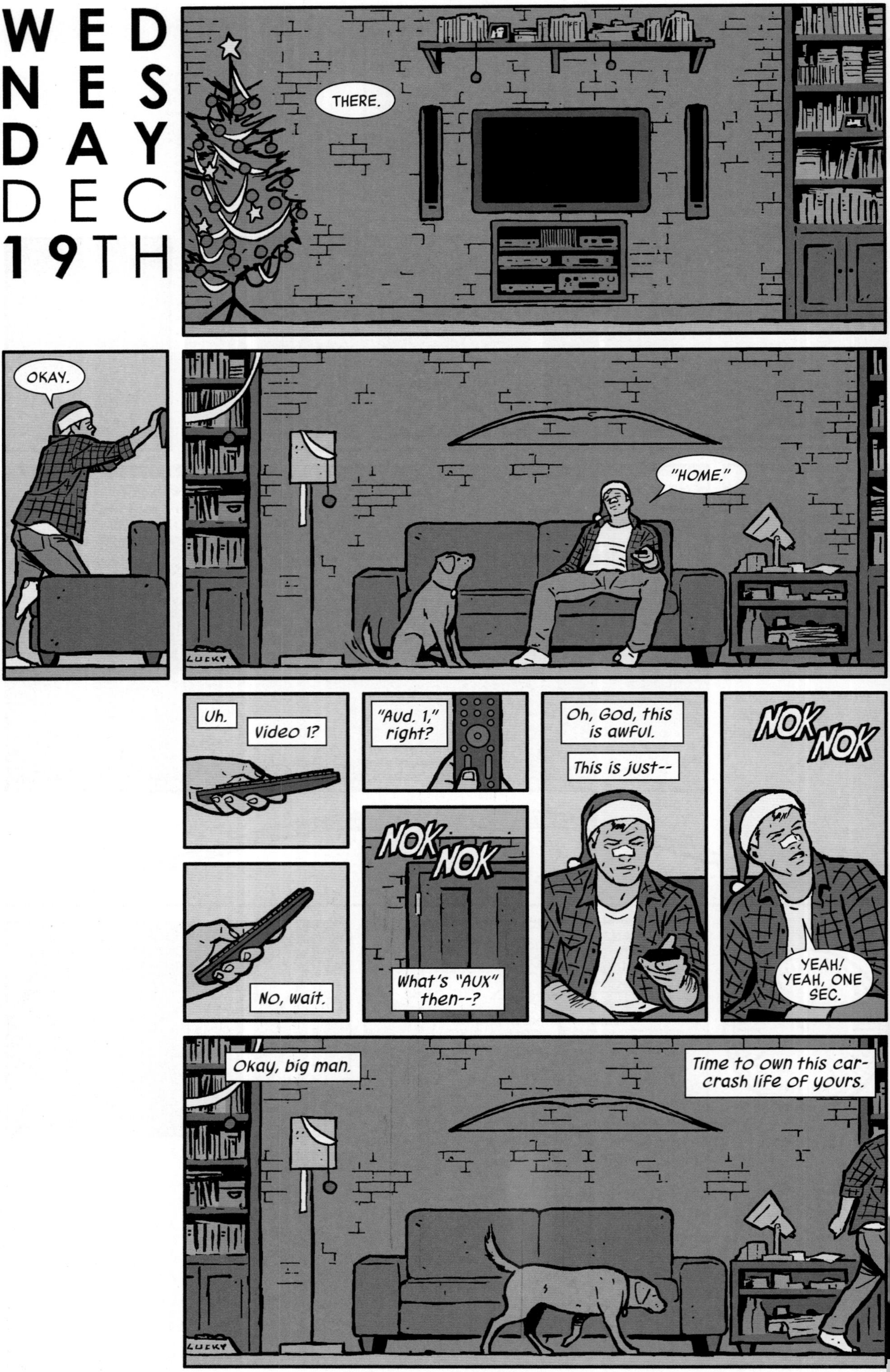
WEDNESDAY DEC 19TH
THERE.
OKAY.
"HOME."
LUCKY
Uh.
Video 1?
No, wait.
"Aud. 1," right?
NOK NOK
What's "AUX" then--?
Oh, God, this is awful.
This is just--
NOK NOK
YEAH! YEAH, ONE SEC.
Okay, big man.
Time to own this car-crash life of yours.
LUCKY

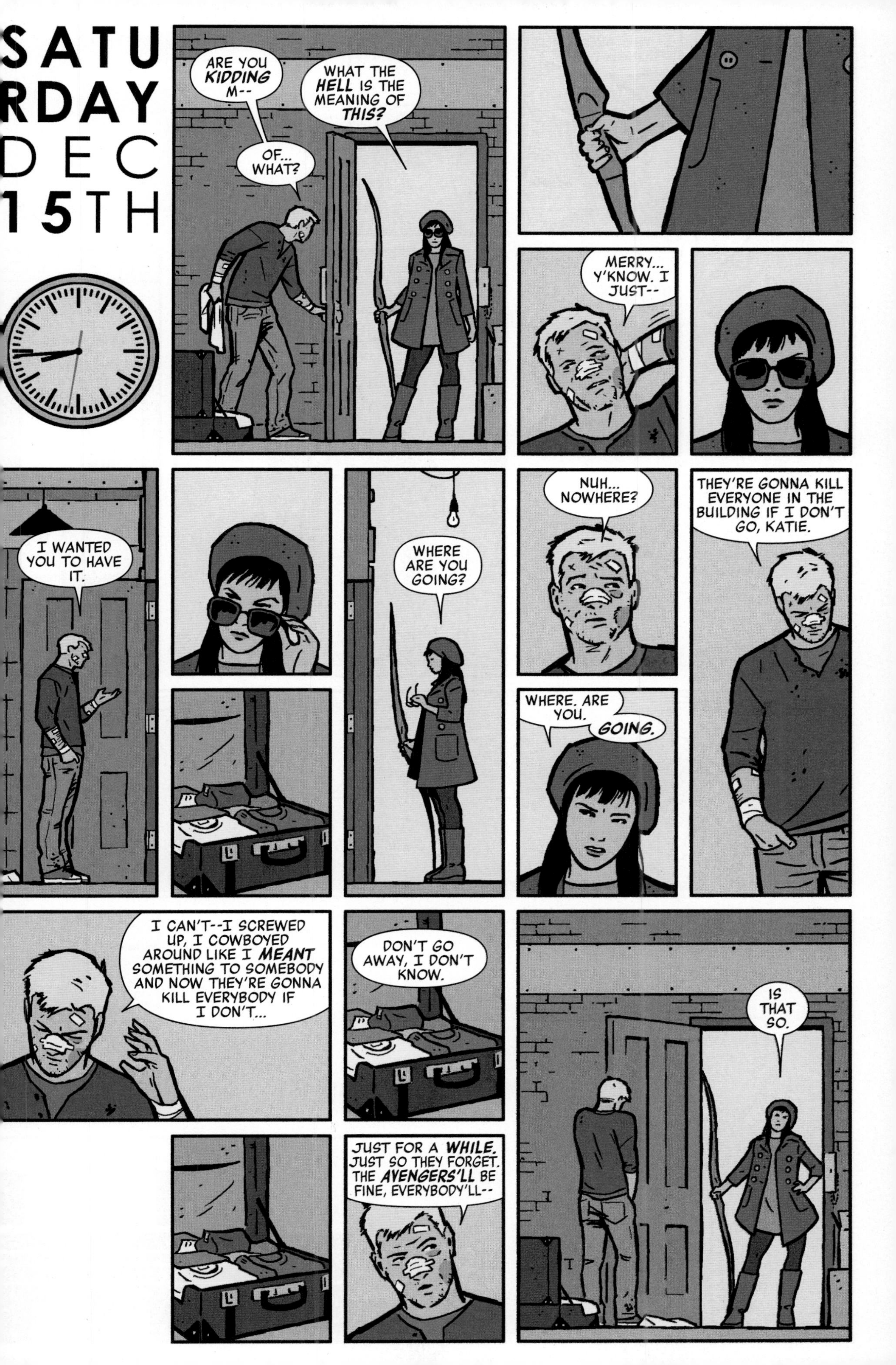
SATU
RDAY
DEC
15TH
ARE YOU KIDDING M--
OF... WHAT?
WHAT THE HELL IS THE MEANING OF THIS?
MERRY... Y'KNOW. I JUST--
I WANTED YOU TO HAVE IT.
WHERE ARE YOU GOING?
NUH... NOWHERE?
WHERE. ARE YOU. GOING.
THEY'RE GONNA KILL EVERYONE IN THE BUILDING IF I DON'T GO, KATIE.
I CAN'T--I SCREWED UP, I COWBOYED AROUND LIKE I MEANT SOMETHING TO SOMEBODY AND NOW THEY'RE GONNA KILL EVERYBODY IF I DON'T...
DON'T GO AWAY, I DON'T KNOW.
JUST FOR A WHILE. JUST SO THEY FORGET. THE AVENGERS'LL BE FINE, EVERYBODY'LL--
IS THAT SO.

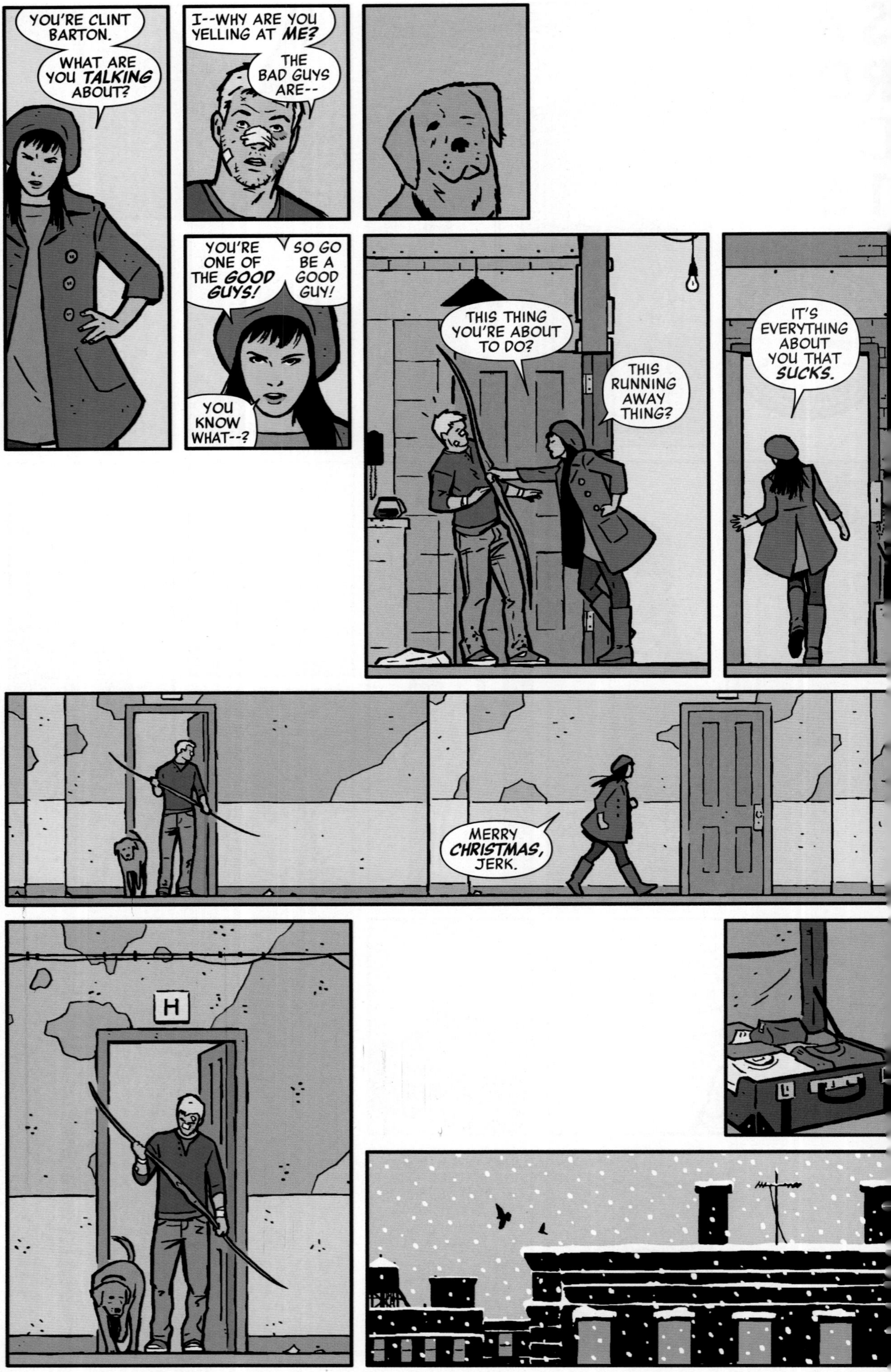
YOU'RE CLINT BARTON.
WHAT ARE YOU TALKING ABOUT?
I--WHY ARE YOU YELLING AT ME?
THE BAD GUYS ARE--
YOU'RE ONE OF THE GOOD GUYS!
SO GO BE A GOOD GUY!
YOU KNOW WHAT--?
THIS THING YOU'RE ABOUT TO DO?
THIS RUNNING AWAY THING?
IT'S EVERYTHING ABOUT YOU THAT SUCKS.
MERRY CHRISTMAS, JERK.
H

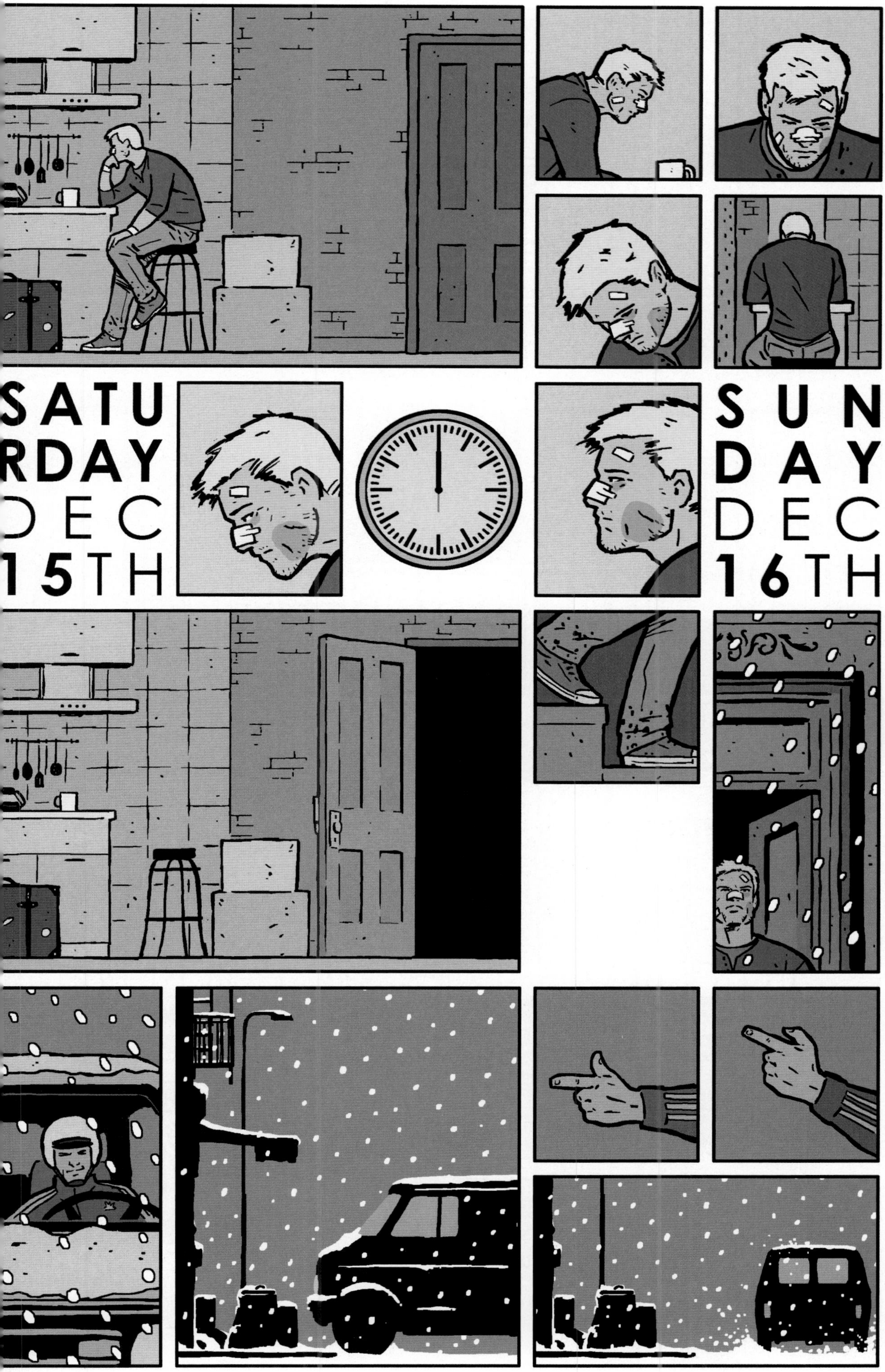
SATURDAY DEC 15TH
SUNDAY DEC 16TH

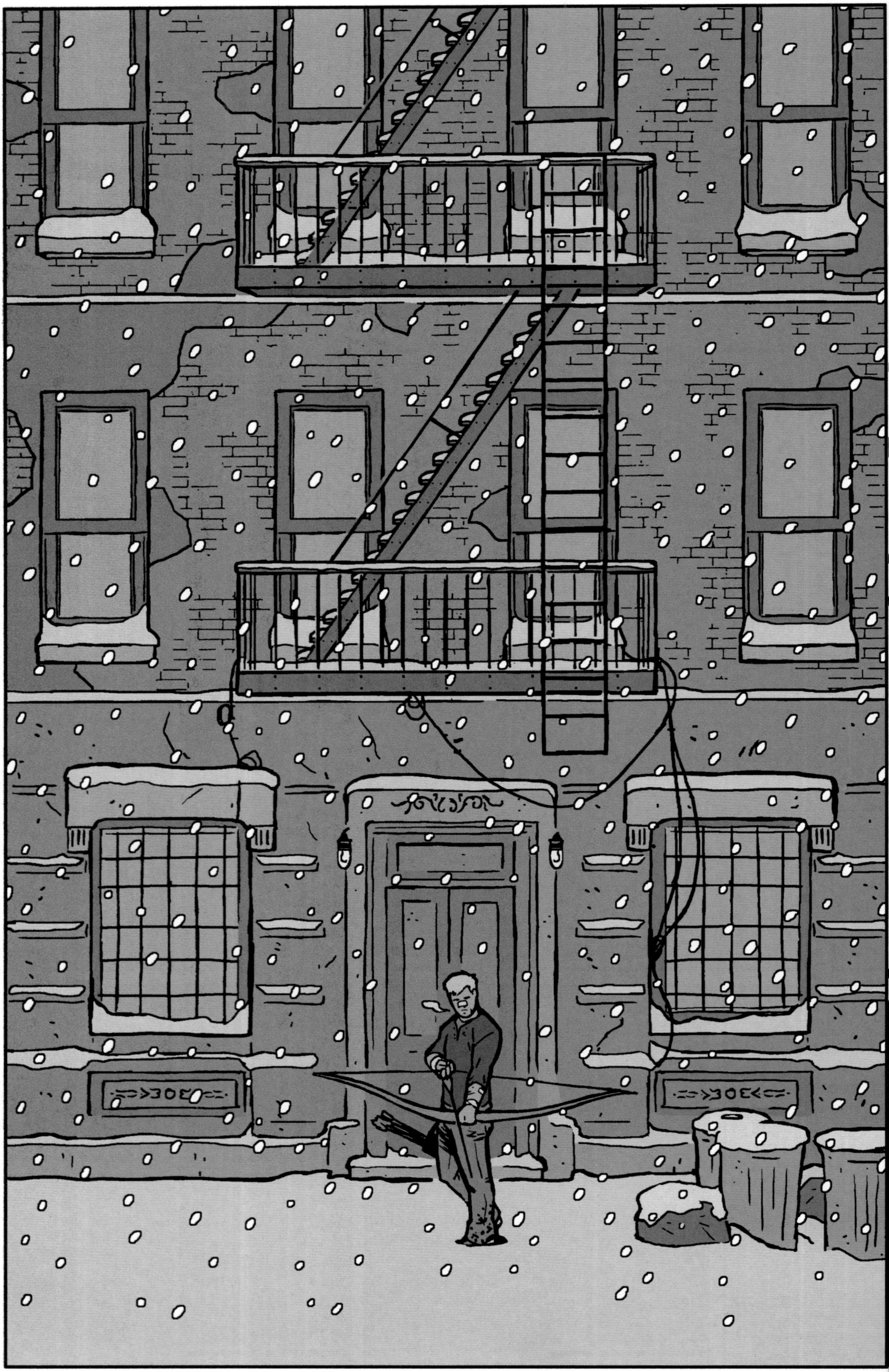

# WEDNESDAY
## DEC 19TH

MERRY CHRISTMAS!

IF, UH. IF THAT'S YOUR THING.

IT IS. HI, CLINT. SAY HI, KIDS.

(KID MUMBLE)

YOU *SURE* ABOUT THIS?

I HAVEN'T SEEN A *MINUTE* OF TV FOR GROWN-UPS IN FIVE YEARS. YOU DON'T HAVE TO DO THIS.

PLEASE! LEAST I CAN DO. S'MY ARROW IN YOUR DISH, RIGHT?

HAVE YOU EVER SEEN IT?

IT'S OUR FAVORITE.

I MADE POPCORN. CAN THEY HAVE POPCORN?

THEY CAN HAVE POPCORN.

GREAT.

IF YOU CAN FIGURE OUT HOW IT WORKS, WE CAN WATCH *CHRISTMAS SPECIALS* 'TIL YOUR MOM TELLS US TO STOP.

ARE YOU *SURE* THIS IS OKAY? DO YOU NEED TO *BE* SOMEWHERE?

NOPE.

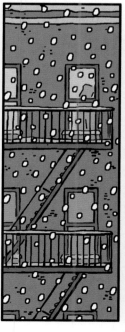

"I'M NOT GOING ANYWHERE."

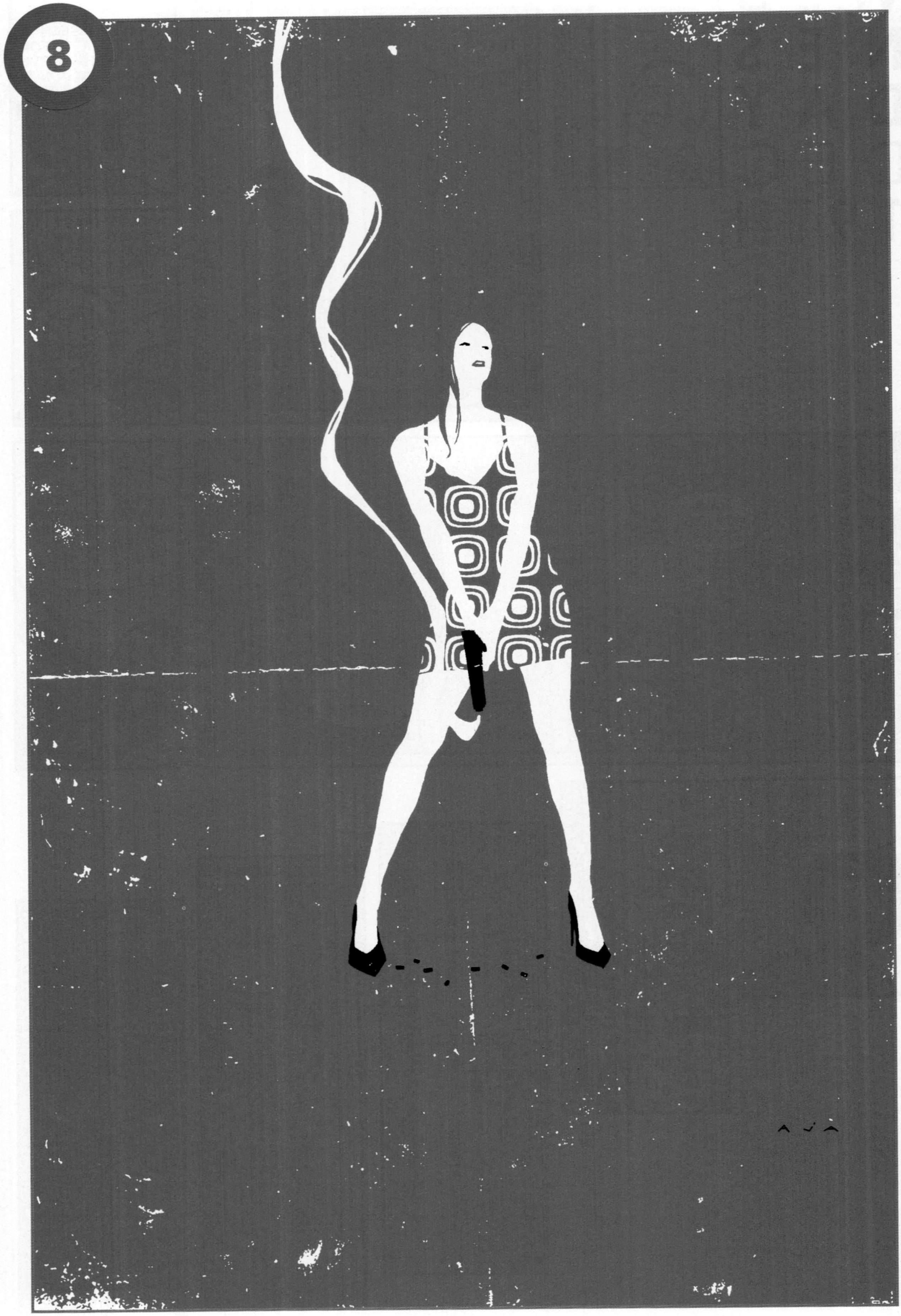
8

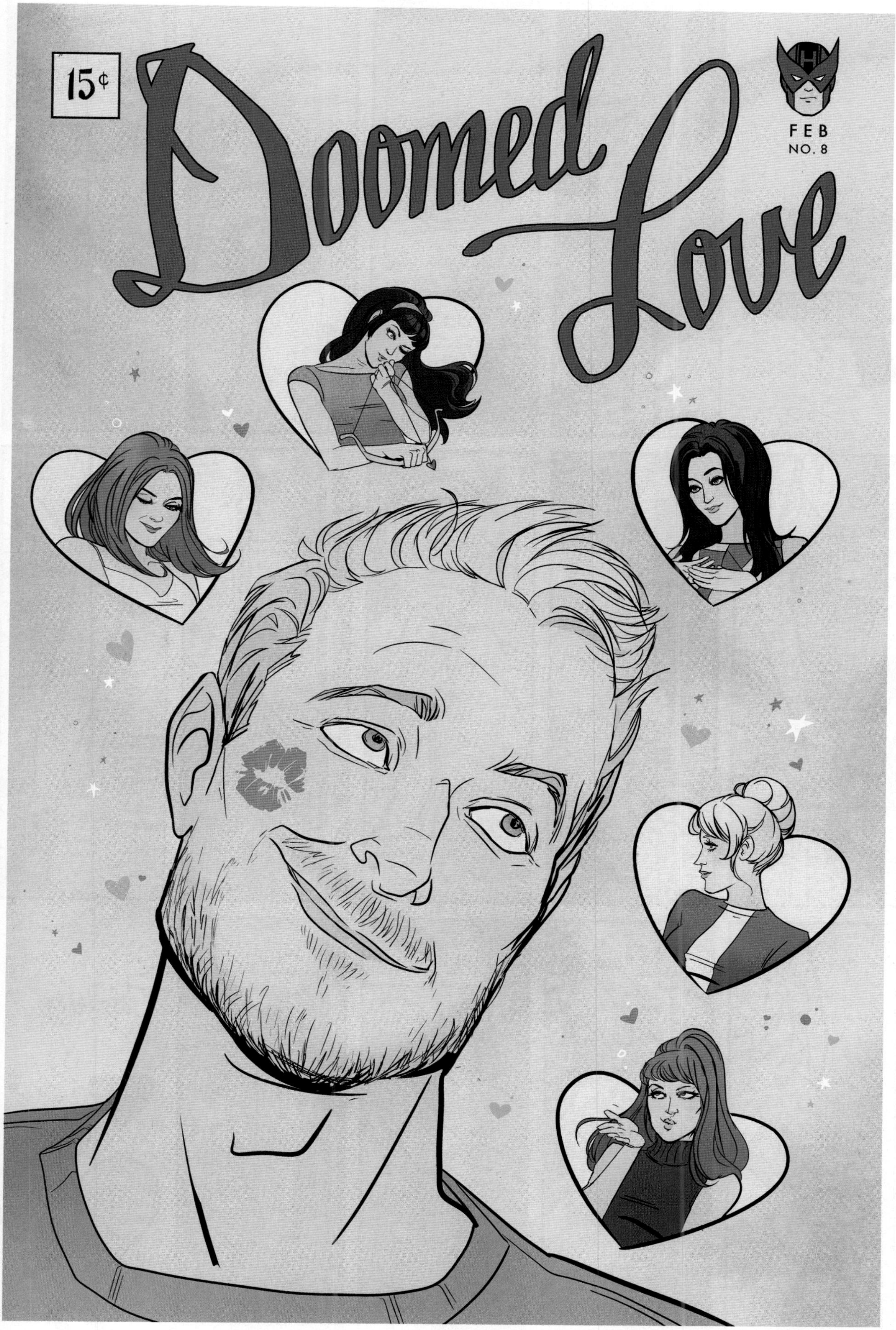
15¢
Doomed Love
FEB
NO. 8

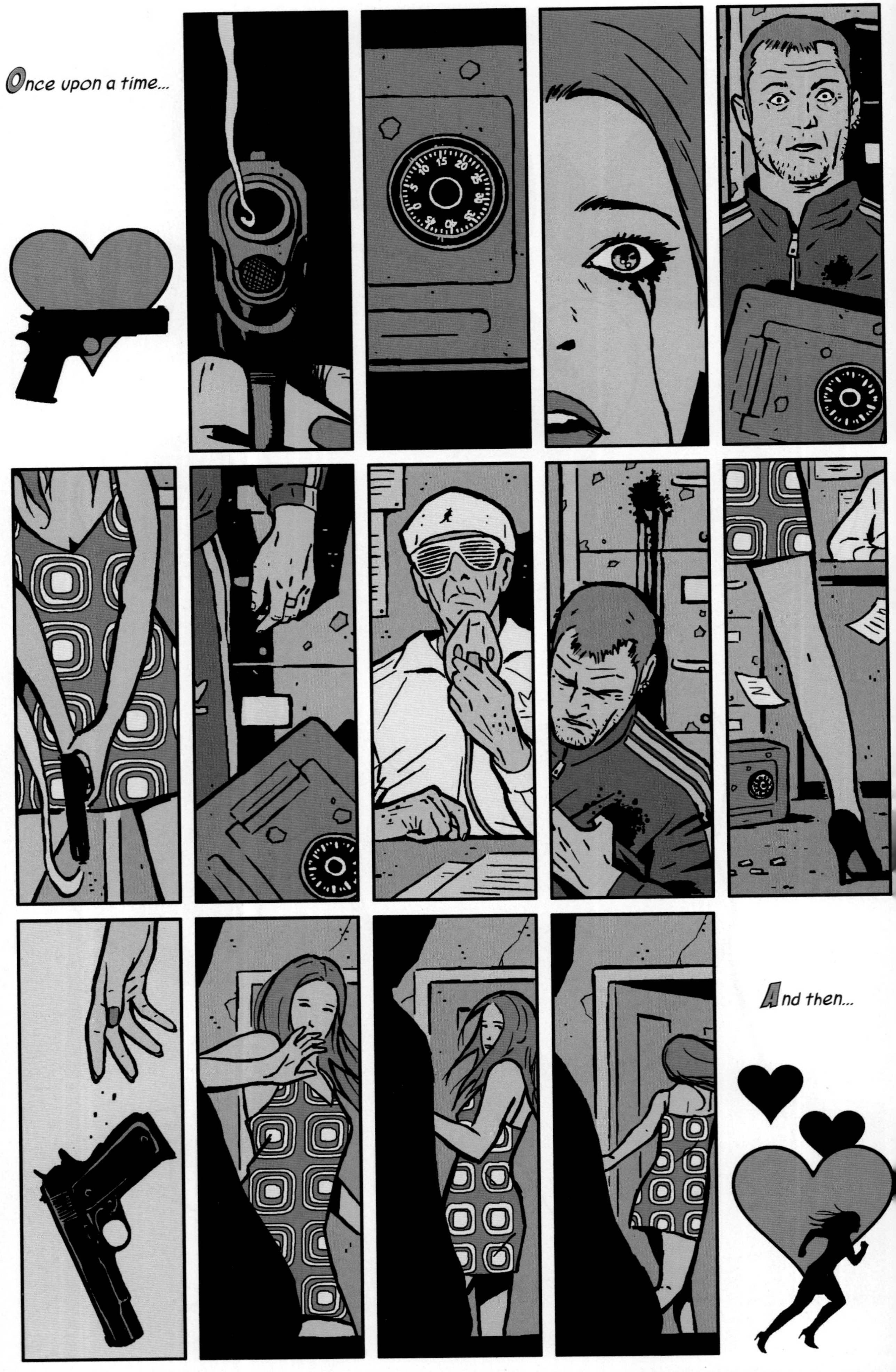
Once upon a time...
And then...

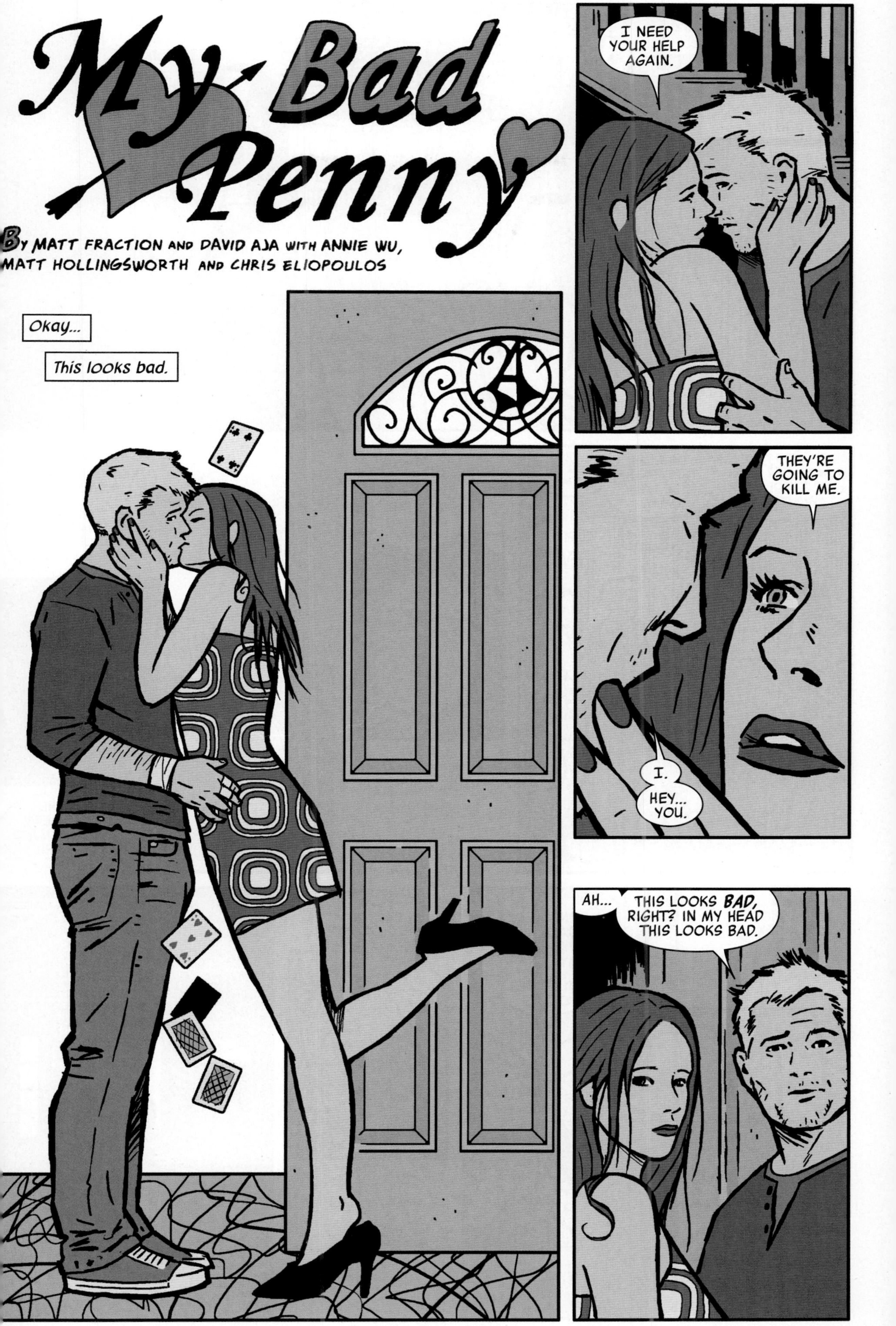

My Bad Penny
By Matt Fraction and David Aja with Annie Wu, Matt Hollingsworth and Chris Eliopoulos
Okay...
This looks bad.
I NEED YOUR HELP AGAIN.
THEY'RE GOING TO KILL ME.
I.
HEY... YOU.
AH...
THIS LOOKS BAD, RIGHT? IN MY HEAD THIS LOOKS BAD.

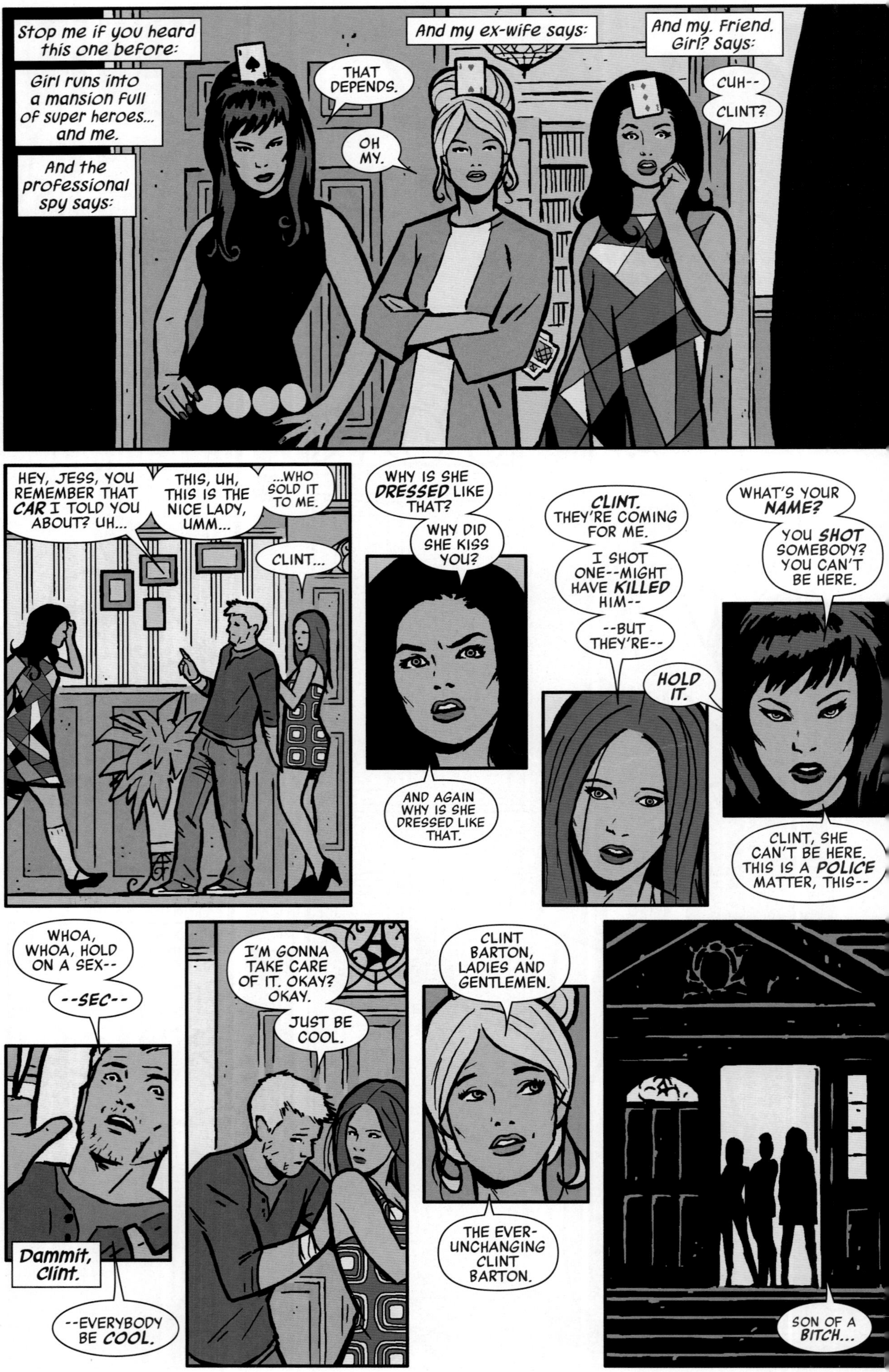
Stop me if you heard this one before:
Girl runs into a mansion full of super heroes... and me.
And the professional spy says:
THAT DEPENDS.
OH MY.
And my ex-wife says:
And my. Friend. Girl? Says:
CUH--
CLINT?
HEY, JESS, YOU REMEMBER THAT CAR I TOLD YOU ABOUT? UH...
THIS, UH, THIS IS THE NICE LADY, UMM...
...WHO SOLD IT TO ME.
CLINT...
WHY IS SHE DRESSED LIKE THAT?
WHY DID SHE KISS YOU?
AND AGAIN WHY IS SHE DRESSED LIKE THAT.
CLINT. THEY'RE COMING FOR ME.
I SHOT ONE--MIGHT HAVE KILLED HIM--
--BUT THEY'RE--
HOLD IT.
WHAT'S YOUR NAME?
YOU SHOT SOMEBODY? YOU CAN'T BE HERE.
CLINT, SHE CAN'T BE HERE. THIS IS A POLICE MATTER, THIS--
WHOA, WHOA, HOLD ON A SEX--
--SEC--
Dammit, Clint.
--EVERYBODY BE COOL.
I'M GONNA TAKE CARE OF IT. OKAY? OKAY.
JUST BE COOL.
CLINT BARTON, LADIES AND GENTLEMEN.
THE EVER-UNCHANGING CLINT BARTON.
SON OF A BITCH...

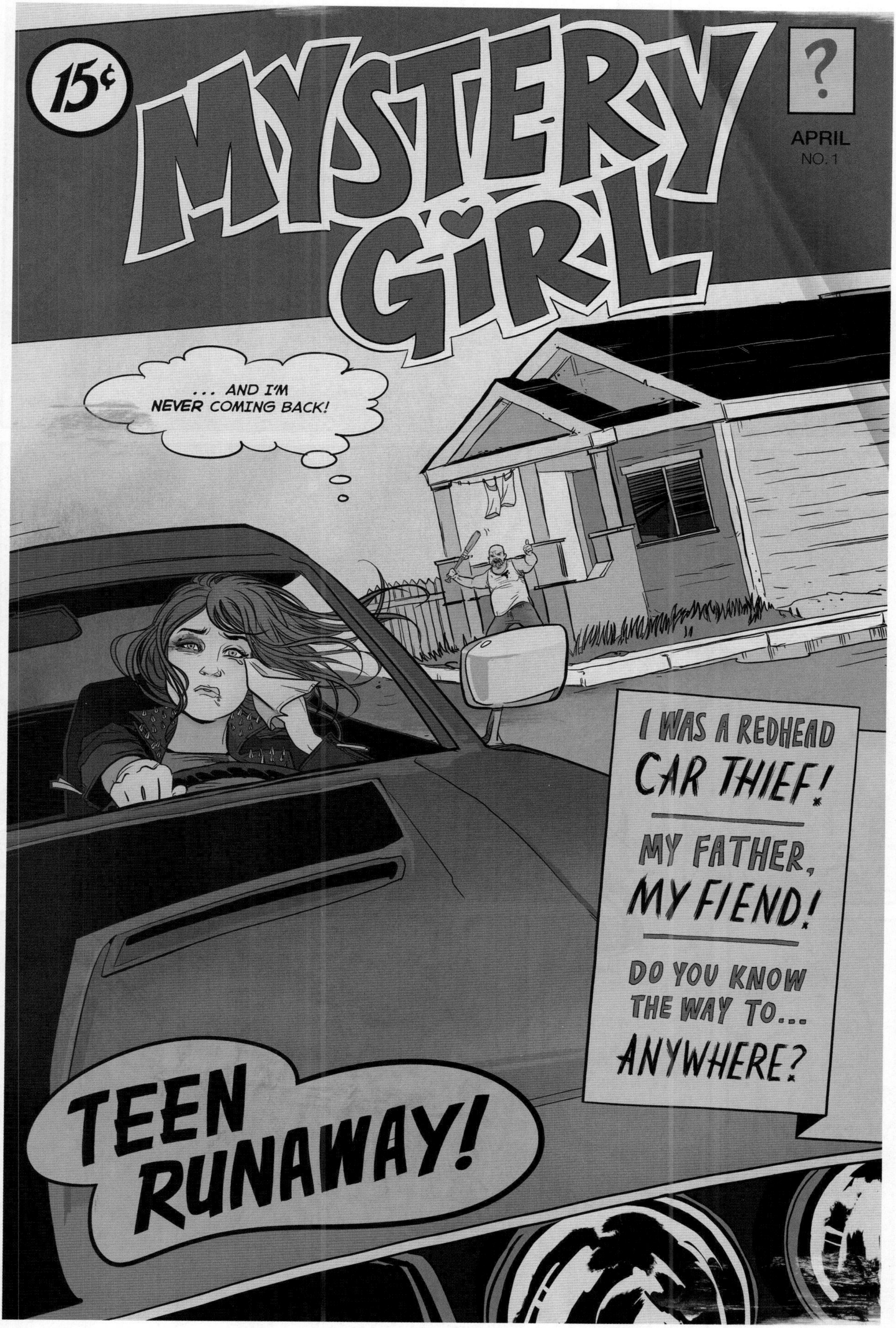
15¢
MYSTERY GIRL
?
APRIL
NO. 1
. . . AND I'M NEVER COMING BACK!
I WAS A REDHEAD CAR THIEF!
MY FATHER, MY FIEND!
DO YOU KNOW THE WAY TO... ANYWHERE?
TEEN RUNAWAY!

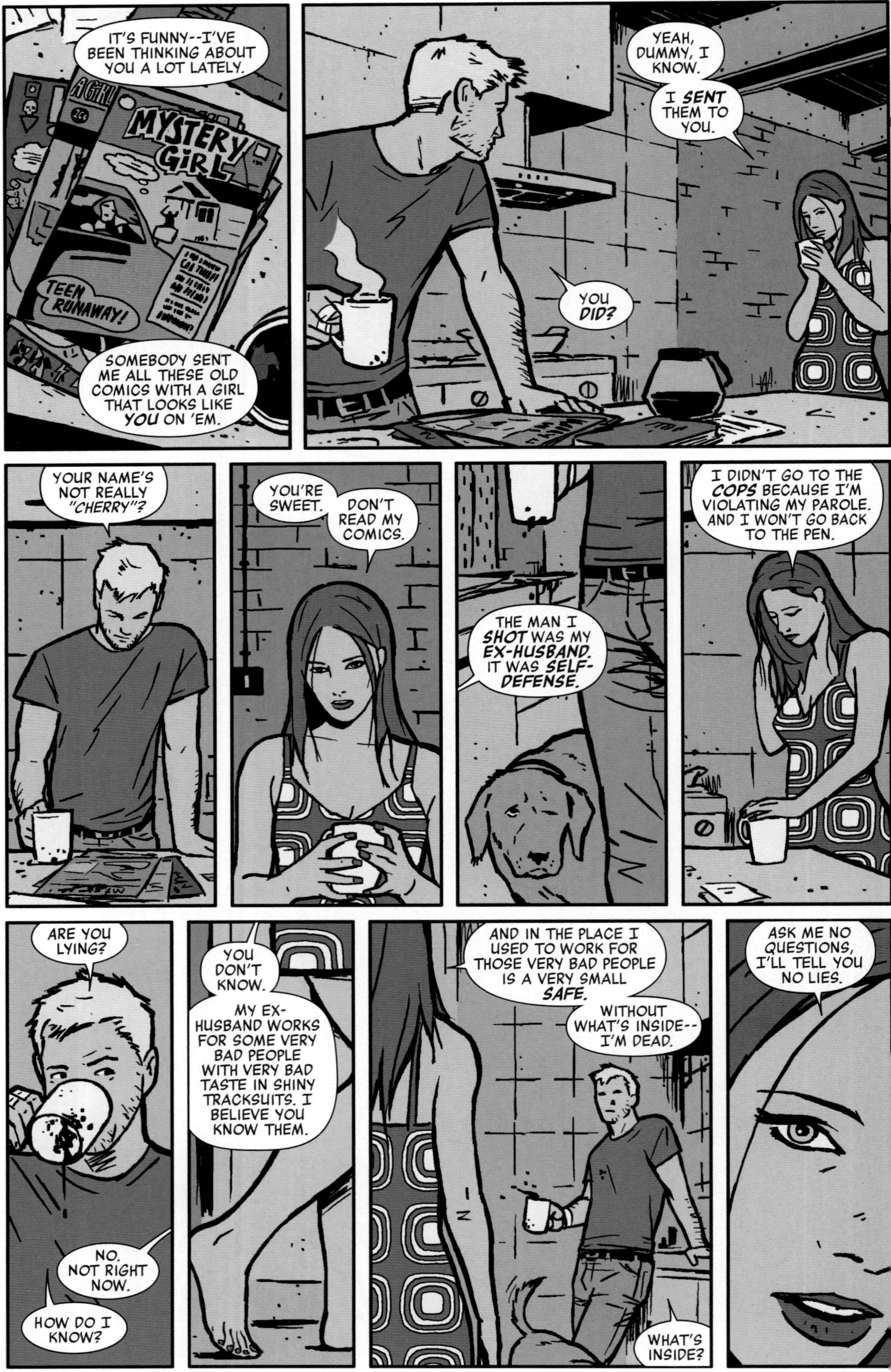
IT'S FUNNY--I'VE BEEN THINKING ABOUT YOU A LOT LATELY.
MYSTERY GIRL
TEEN RUNAWAY!
SOMEBODY SENT ME ALL THESE OLD COMICS WITH A GIRL THAT LOOKS LIKE YOU ON 'EM.
YEAH, DUMMY, I KNOW.
I SENT THEM TO YOU.
YOU DID?
YOUR NAME'S NOT REALLY "CHERRY"?
YOU'RE SWEET.
DON'T READ MY COMICS.
THE MAN I SHOT WAS MY EX-HUSBAND. IT WAS SELF-DEFENSE.
I DIDN'T GO TO THE COPS BECAUSE I'M VIOLATING MY PAROLE. AND I WON'T GO BACK TO THE PEN.
ARE YOU LYING?
NO. NOT RIGHT NOW.
HOW DO I KNOW?
YOU DON'T KNOW.
MY EX-HUSBAND WORKS FOR SOME VERY BAD PEOPLE WITH VERY BAD TASTE IN SHINY TRACKSUITS. I BELIEVE YOU KNOW THEM.
AND IN THE PLACE I USED TO WORK FOR THOSE VERY BAD PEOPLE IS A VERY SMALL SAFE.
WITHOUT WHAT'S INSIDE--I'M DEAD.
WHAT'S INSIDE?
ASK ME NO QUESTIONS, I'LL TELL YOU NO LIES.

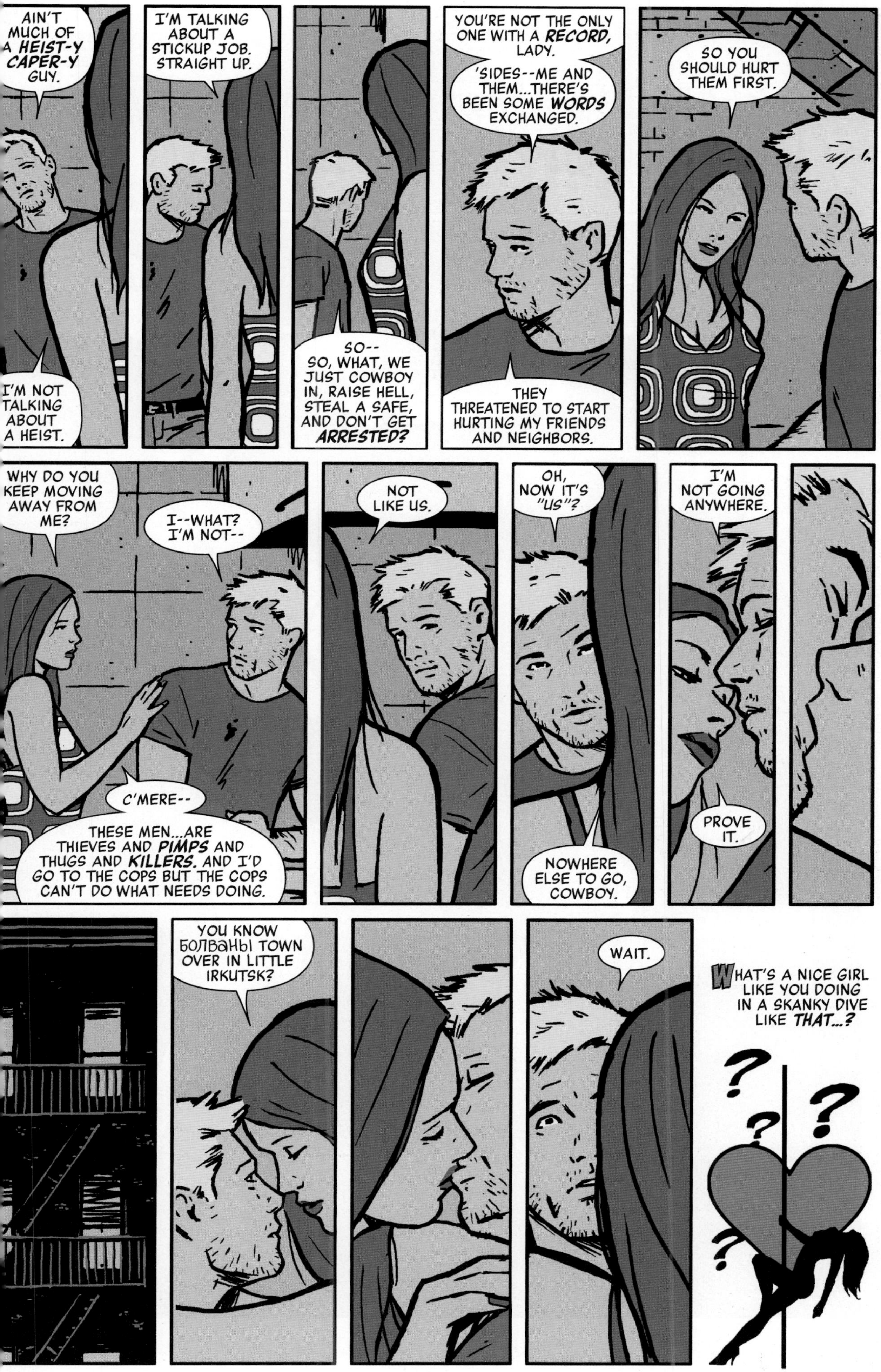

AIN'T MUCH OF A HEIST-Y CAPER-Y GUY.
I'M NOT TALKING ABOUT A HEIST.
I'M TALKING ABOUT A STICKUP JOB. STRAIGHT UP.
SO--
SO, WHAT, WE JUST COWBOY IN, RAISE HELL, STEAL A SAFE, AND DON'T GET ARRESTED?
YOU'RE NOT THE ONLY ONE WITH A RECORD, LADY.
'SIDES--ME AND THEM...THERE'S BEEN SOME WORDS EXCHANGED.
THEY THREATENED TO START HURTING MY FRIENDS AND NEIGHBORS.
SO YOU SHOULD HURT THEM FIRST.
WHY DO YOU KEEP MOVING AWAY FROM ME?
I--WHAT? I'M NOT--
C'MERE--
THESE MEN...ARE THIEVES AND PIMPS AND THUGS AND KILLERS. AND I'D GO TO THE COPS BUT THE COPS CAN'T DO WHAT NEEDS DOING.
NOT LIKE US.
OH, NOW IT'S "US"?
NOWHERE ELSE TO GO, COWBOY.
I'M NOT GOING ANYWHERE.
PROVE IT.
YOU KNOW БОЛВАНЫ TOWN OVER IN LITTLE IRKUTSK?
WAIT.
WHAT'S A NICE GIRL LIKE YOU DOING IN A SKANKY DIVE LIKE THAT...?

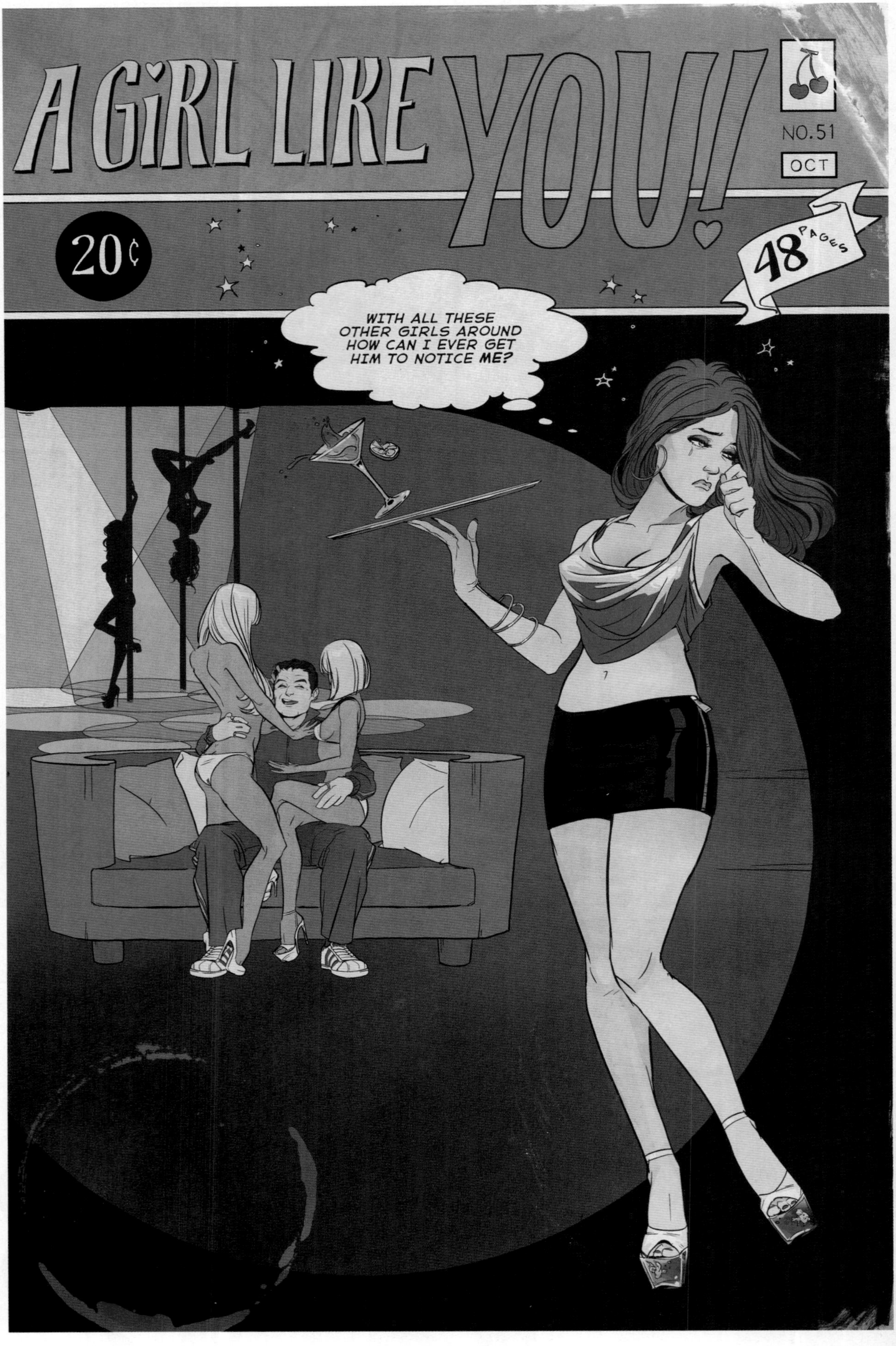
A GiRL LIKE YOU!
NO.51
OCT
20¢
48 PAGES
WITH ALL THESE OTHER GIRLS AROUND HOW CAN I EVER GET HIM TO NOTICE ME?

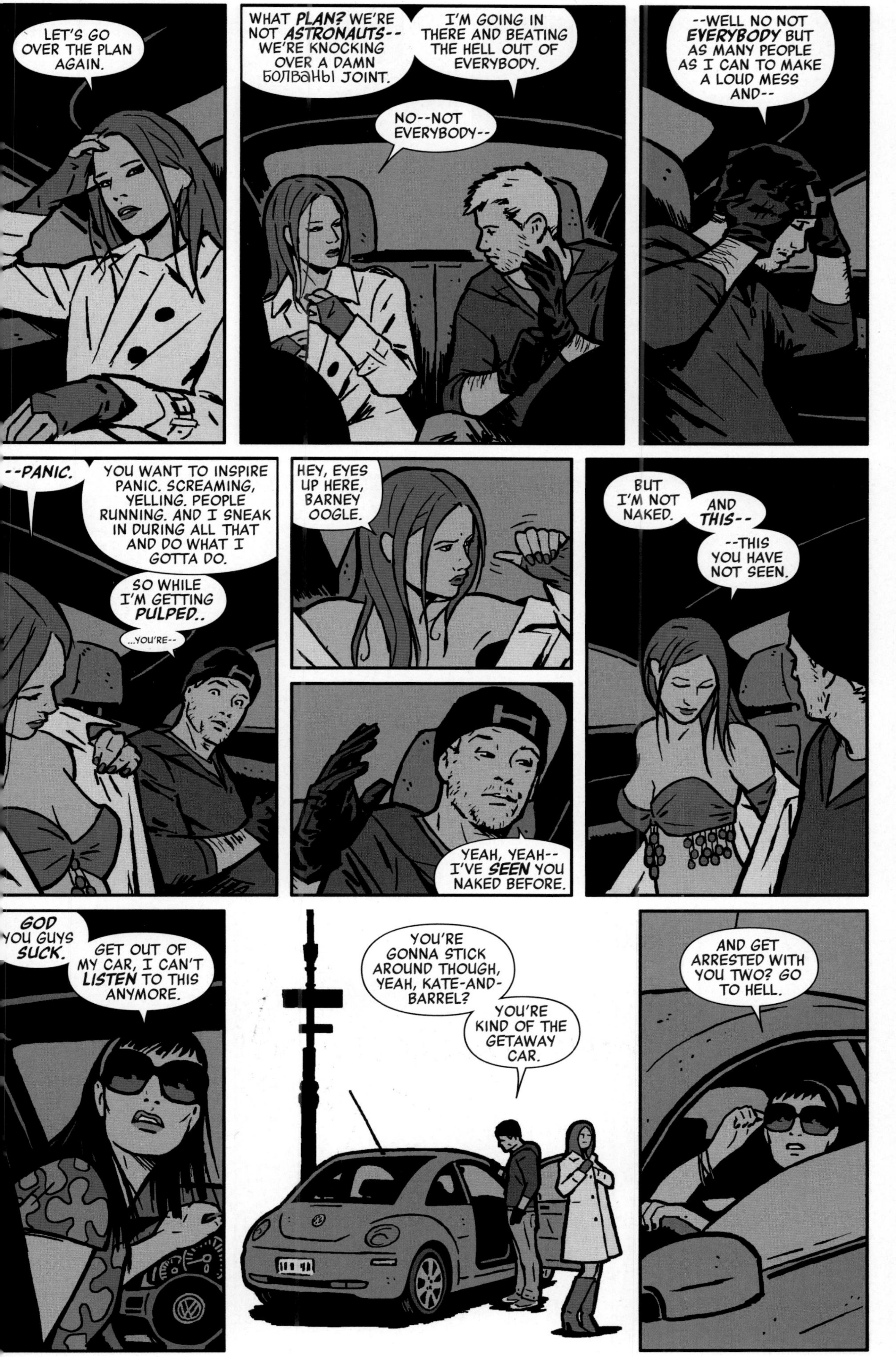
LET'S GO OVER THE PLAN AGAIN.
WHAT PLAN? WE'RE NOT ASTRONAUTS-- WE'RE KNOCKING OVER A DAMN БОЛВАНЫ JOINT.
I'M GOING IN THERE AND BEATING THE HELL OUT OF EVERYBODY.
NO--NOT EVERYBODY--
--WELL NO NOT EVERYBODY BUT AS MANY PEOPLE AS I CAN TO MAKE A LOUD MESS AND--
--PANIC.
YOU WANT TO INSPIRE PANIC. SCREAMING, YELLING. PEOPLE RUNNING. AND I SNEAK IN DURING ALL THAT AND DO WHAT I GOTTA DO.
SO WHILE I'M GETTING PULPED..
...YOU'RE--
HEY, EYES UP HERE, BARNEY OOGLE.
YEAH, YEAH-- I'VE SEEN YOU NAKED BEFORE.
BUT I'M NOT NAKED.
AND THIS--
--THIS YOU HAVE NOT SEEN.
GOD YOU GUYS SUCK.
GET OUT OF MY CAR, I CAN'T LISTEN TO THIS ANYMORE.
YOU'RE GONNA STICK AROUND THOUGH, YEAH, KATE-AND-BARREL?
YOU'RE KIND OF THE GETAWAY CAR.
AND GET ARRESTED WITH YOU TWO? GO TO HELL.

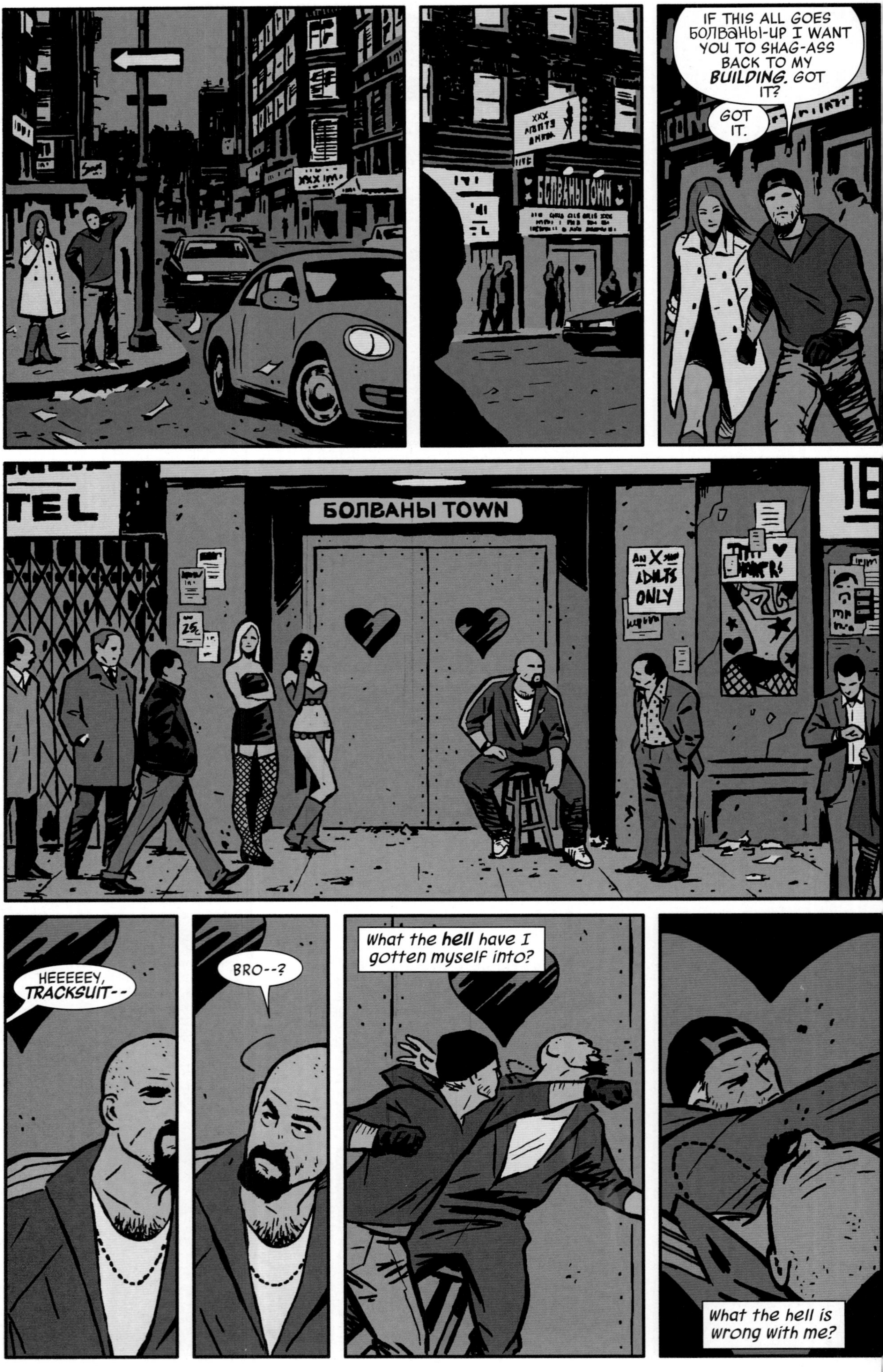

БОЛВАНЫ TOWN
IF THIS ALL GOES БОЛВАНЫ-UP I WANT YOU TO SHAG-ASS BACK TO MY **BUILDING.** GOT IT?
GOT IT.
TEL
БОЛВАНЫ TOWN
AN X ADULTS ONLY
HEEEEEY, **TRACKSUIT--**
BRO--?
What the **hell** have I gotten myself into?
What the hell is wrong with me?

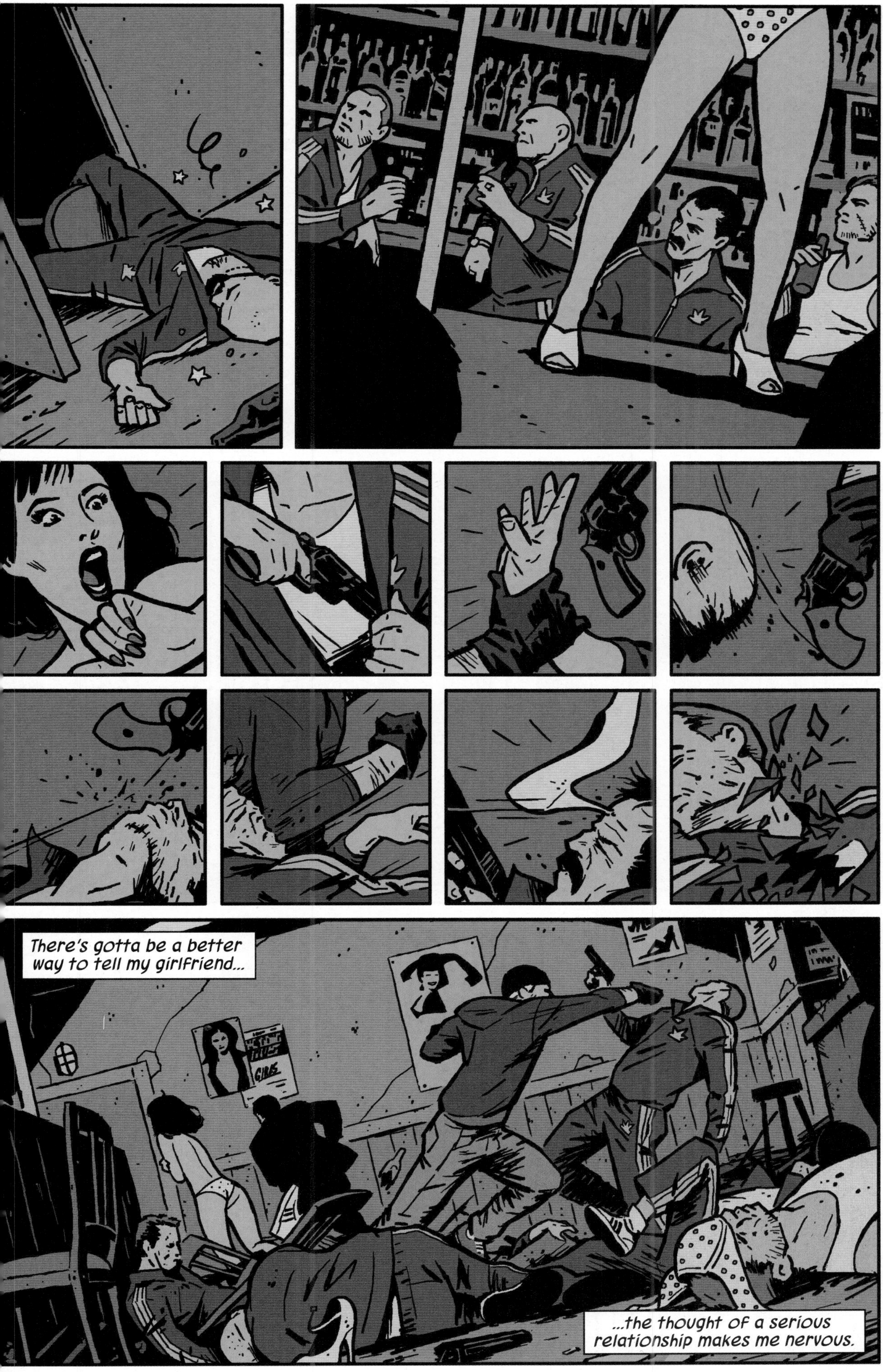
There's gotta be a better way to tell my girlfriend...
...the thought of a serious relationship makes me nervous.

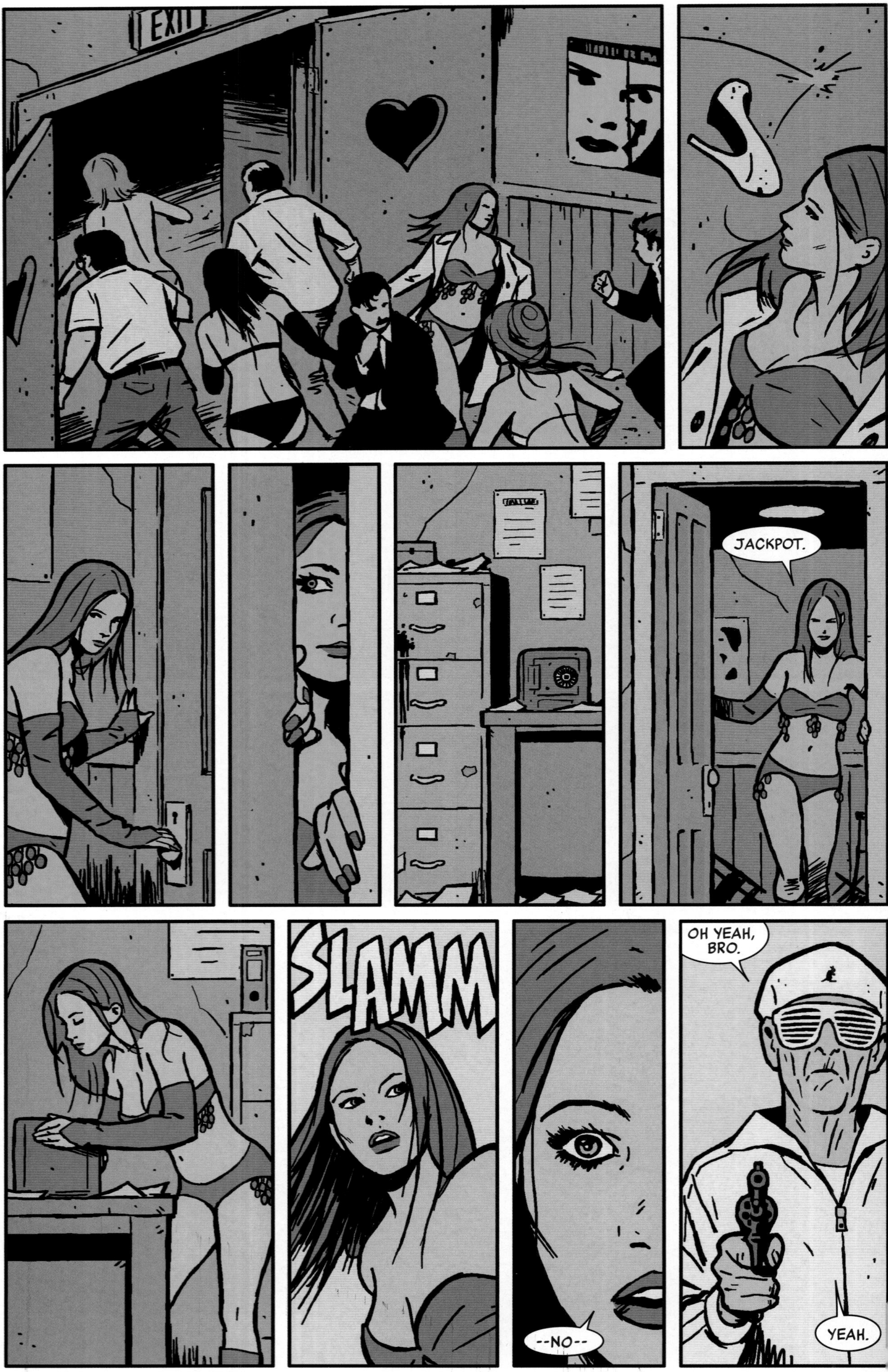
EXIT
JACKPOT.
SLAMM
--NO--
OH YEAH, BRO.
YEAH.

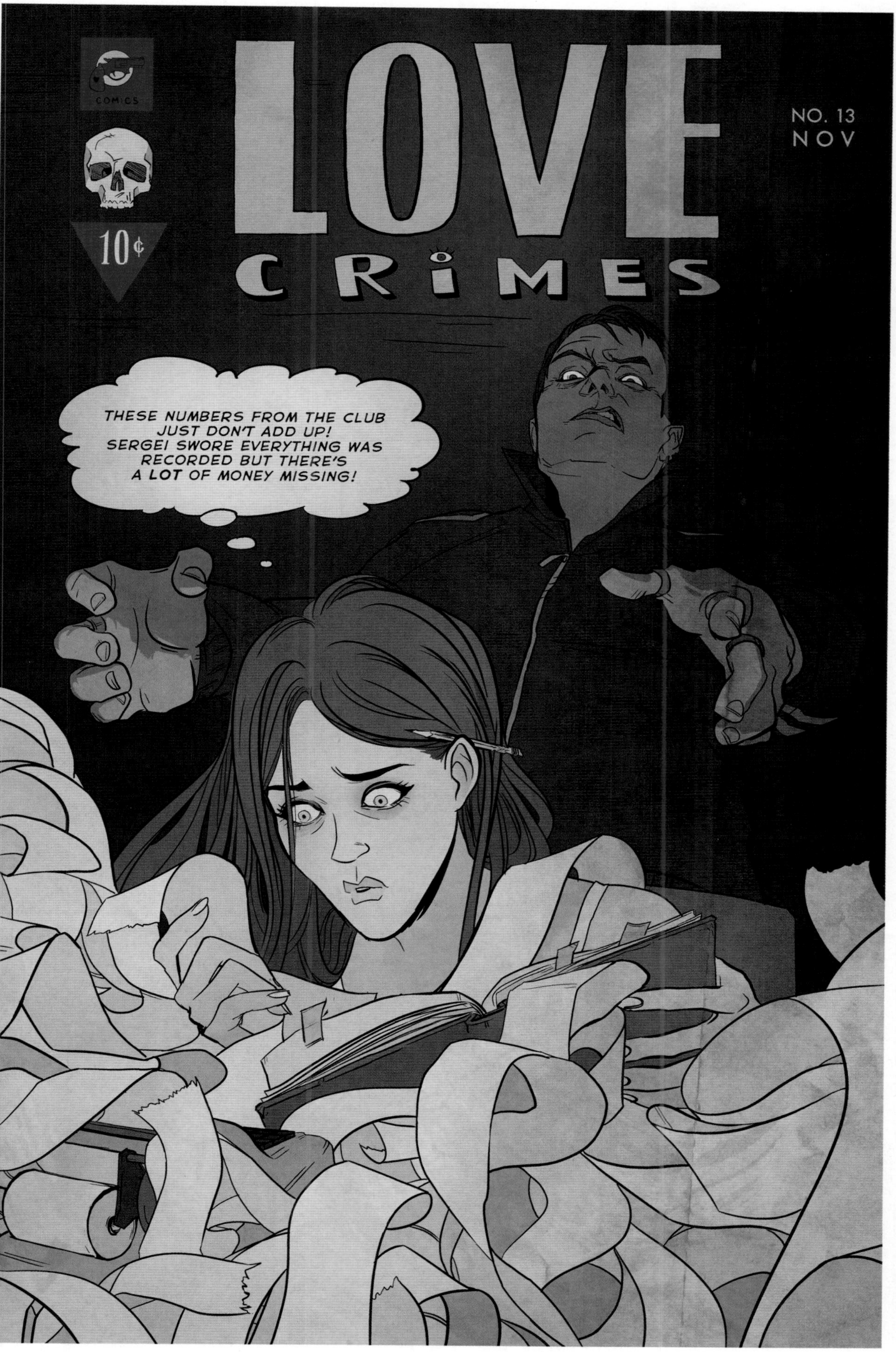
COMICS
LOVE CRIMES
10¢
NO. 13
NOV
THESE NUMBERS FROM THE CLUB JUST DON'T ADD UP! SERGEI SWORE EVERYTHING WAS RECORDED BUT THERE'S A LOT OF MONEY MISSING!

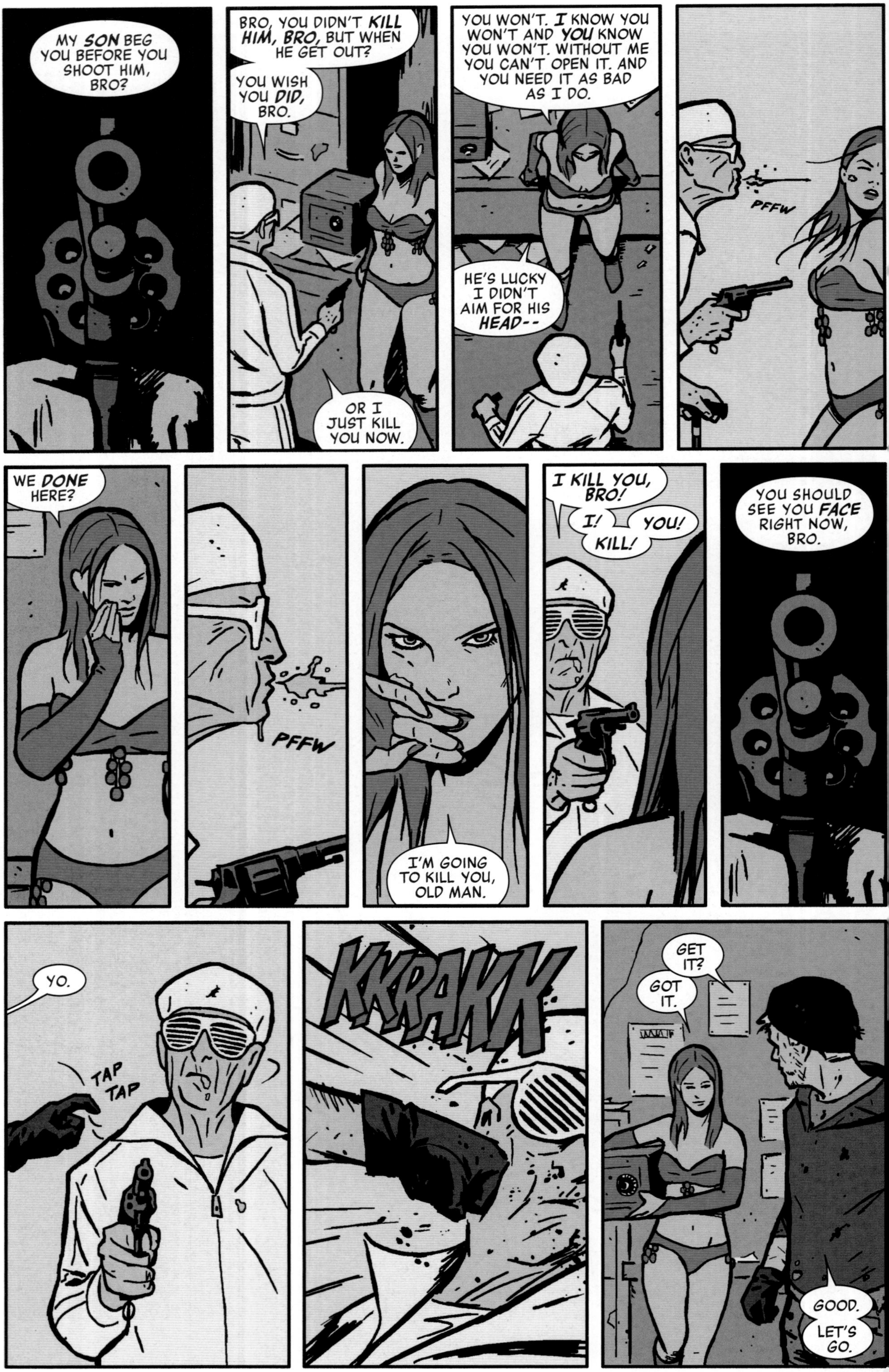
MY SON BEG YOU BEFORE YOU SHOOT HIM, BRO?
BRO, YOU DIDN'T KILL HIM, BRO, BUT WHEN HE GET OUT?
YOU WISH YOU DID, BRO.
OR I JUST KILL YOU NOW.
YOU WON'T. I KNOW YOU WON'T AND YOU KNOW YOU WON'T. WITHOUT ME YOU CAN'T OPEN IT. AND YOU NEED IT AS BAD AS I DO.
HE'S LUCKY I DIDN'T AIM FOR HIS HEAD--
PFFW
WE DONE HERE?
PFFW
I'M GOING TO KILL YOU, OLD MAN.
I KILL YOU, BRO!
I!
KILL!
YOU!
YOU SHOULD SEE YOU FACE RIGHT NOW, BRO.
YO.
TAP TAP
KKRAKK
GET IT?
GOT IT.
GOOD.
LET'S GO.

AHH, CRAP.

Now *this.*

DROP IT!

FREEZE!

HANDS UP!

This *looks bad.*

UM.

I'M AN AVENGER?

ARE YOU IRON FIST?

JEEZ WHY DOES EVERYBODY KEEP *ASKING* ME THAT--

GET DOWN!

OKAY, OKAY--

SERIOUSLY THOUGH I'M AN AVENGER.

I.D. AND EVERYTHING IS IN MY--

--WAAHHHH--

But it's okay.

It's all okay.

Good guys win.

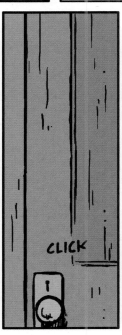

CLICK

...right?

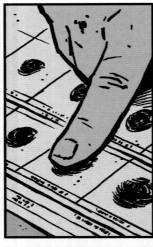

MALE    AJ 19261
-CLINTON F BARTON

MALE    AJ 19261
-CLINTON F BARTON

PRECINCT

"YOU READ MY COMICS?!"

DON'T THANK ME FOR GETTING ARRESTED FOR YOU *TOO* MUCH, OR PEOPLE WILL START TO TALK...

I'M IN TROUBLE WITH THIS. PLEASE DON'T *YELL* AT ME.

STARK ALREADY CALLED. *CAP* TOO. AS IN-- *AMERICA.*

I WONDER IF ANYBODY'S EVER BEEN *FIRED* FROM THE AVENGERS BEFORE.

STARK SAYS THERE'S A *BEHAVIOR* AND *MORALS CLAUSE* IN THE CONTRACT...

SHOULDA *READ* THIS BEFORE I SIGNED IT...

THEY WERE IN A CERTAIN ORDER!

THE SAFE-- --IT'S A VERY SPECIAL SAFE, SEE AND THE LOCK IS VERY SPECIAL.

YOU GET THREE CHANCES TO GET THE COMBO RIGHT AND IT SHUTS FOREVER AND DESTROYS ITS CONTENTS.

HOW DOES IT--

THE COMICS DIDN'T MATTER. BOUGHT 20 OF 'EM AT A SWAP MEET. IT WAS THE COVERS--

--THE NUMBERS, CLINT. THOSE COMICS, THAT ORDER--

--IT WAS THE COMBINATION.

IF THE AVENGERS WEREN'T ALL PISSED OFF AT ME MAYBE I COULD ASK THEM TO...

WHAT'S IN IT, ANYWAY?

DOESN'T MATTER NOW.

YOU CAN KEEP IT.

THE HELL AM I GONNA DO WITH A SAFE I CAN'T OPEN...?

UH.

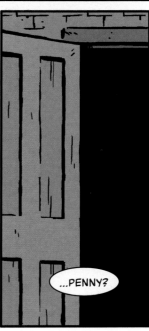

...PENNY?

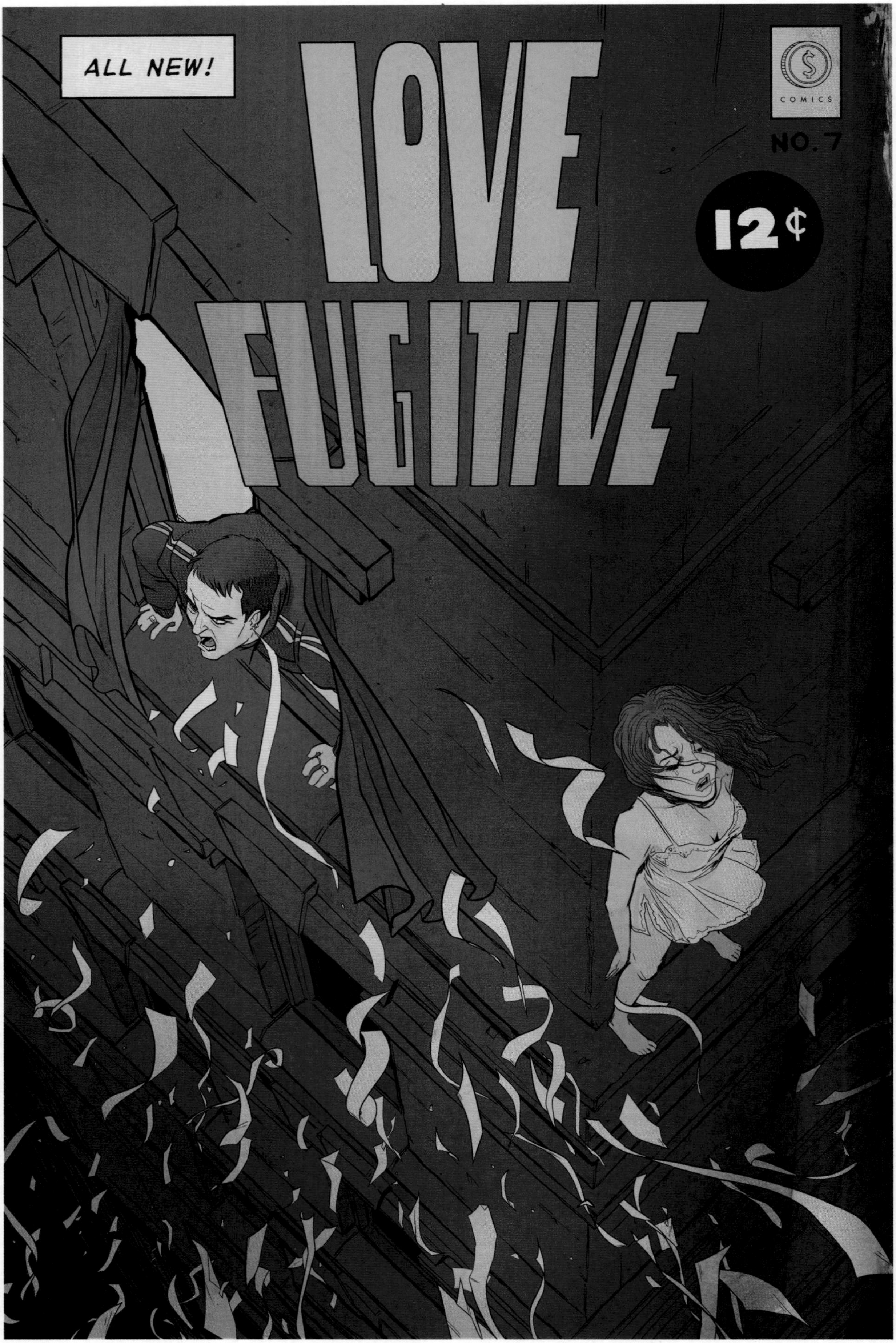
ALL NEW!
LOVE FUGITIVE
COMICS
NO. 7
12¢

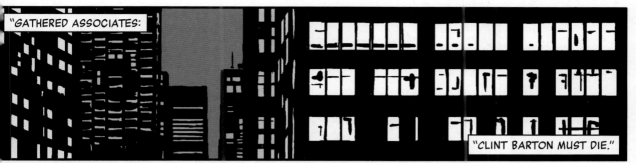

"GATHERED ASSOCIATES:

"CLINT BARTON MUST DIE."

ON THIS WE ALL AGREE.

AS ANNOYING AS HE MAY BE IN HIS... DAYTIME EMPLOYMENT, HIS CURRENT HABIT OF MEDDLING IN ALL OF OUR AFFAIRS HAS MADE HIM INSUFFERABLE.

HE HAS ROBBED US. EMBARRASSED US. ASSAULTED US.

HE HAS COST US MONEY.

CLINT BARTON MUST DIE.

AND OUR... JUNIOR ASSOCIATES... FROM LITTLE IRKUTSK WOULD LIKE TO MAKE THAT A REALITY.

LADIES AND GENTLEMEN. WE DO IT. WE TAKE HEAT. WE TAKE FALL. LESS YOU KNOW, IS BETTER. BUT GIVE US BEEG OKAY?

I GIVE YOU DEAD AVENGER.

NEVER BEEN DONE. AND WHO WOULD HE GET TO ACTUALLY DO IT? WHAT CAPABLE BUTTONMEN ARE ON THE OUTSIDE NOW?

NO. TOO MANY VARIABLES.

TOO MANY UNCERTAINTIES. NO.

RESPECTFULLY, SIR--LESS YOU KNOW IS BETTER.

WE HAVE OUR WAYS. AND WE HAVE THEM LONG TIME.

IT IS A LOT OF ATTENTION. POLICE. FEDERAL. SUPERPOWERED-- HEAT AND PRESSURE BROUGHT DOWN ON ALL OF US.

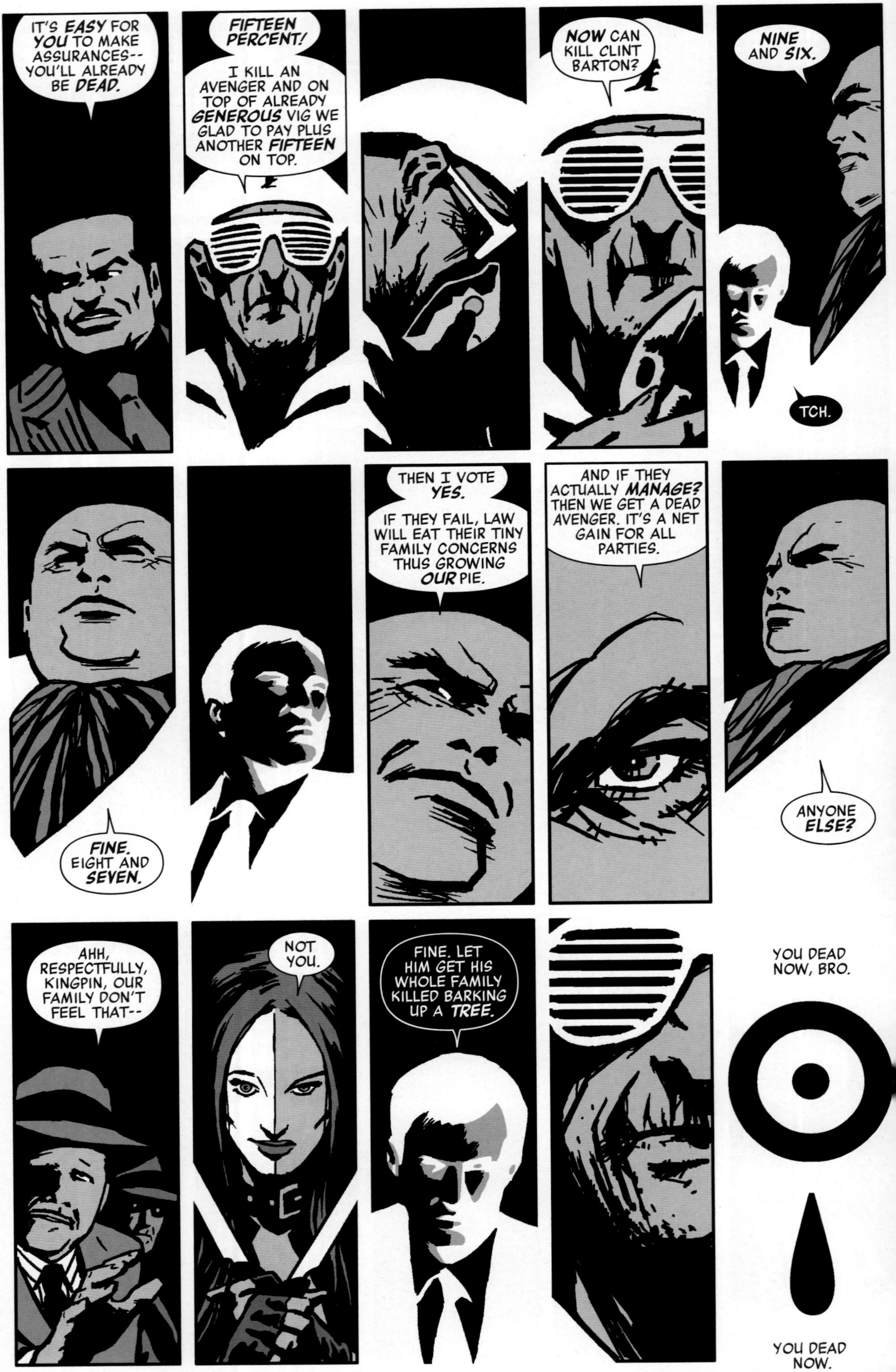
IT'S EASY FOR YOU TO MAKE ASSURANCES-- YOU'LL ALREADY BE DEAD.
FIFTEEN PERCENT!
I KILL AN AVENGER AND ON TOP OF ALREADY GENEROUS VIG WE GLAD TO PAY PLUS ANOTHER FIFTEEN ON TOP.
NOW CAN KILL CLINT BARTON?
NINE AND SIX.
TCH.
FINE. EIGHT AND SEVEN.
THEN I VOTE YES.
IF THEY FAIL, LAW WILL EAT THEIR TINY FAMILY CONCERNS THUS GROWING OUR PIE.
AND IF THEY ACTUALLY MANAGE? THEN WE GET A DEAD AVENGER. IT'S A NET GAIN FOR ALL PARTIES.
ANYONE ELSE?
AHH, RESPECTFULLY, KINGPIN, OUR FAMILY DON'T FEEL THAT--
NOT YOU.
FINE. LET HIM GET HIS WHOLE FAMILY KILLED BARKING UP A TREE.
YOU DEAD NOW, BRO.
YOU DEAD NOW.

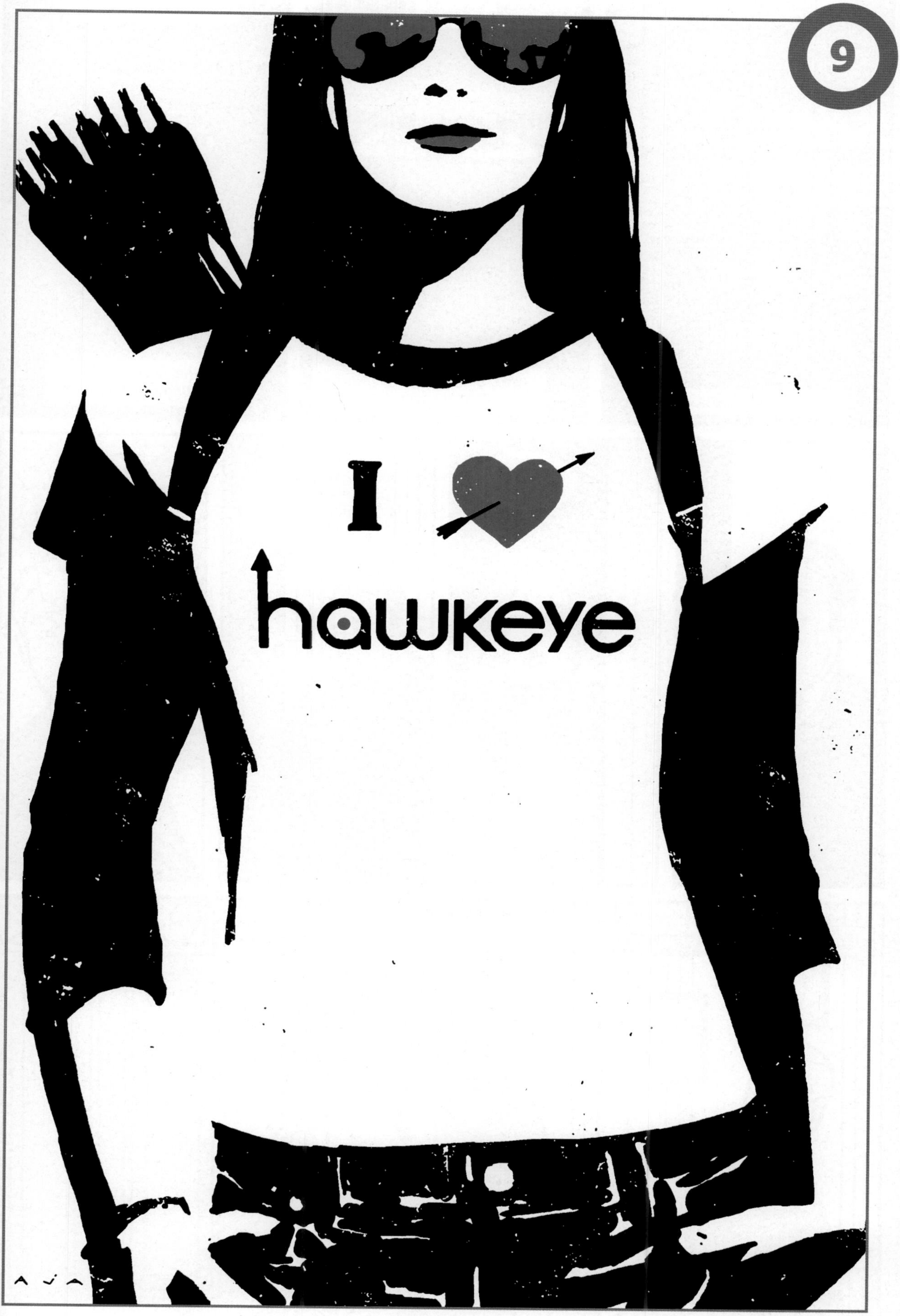
9
I ♥
hawkeye
AJA

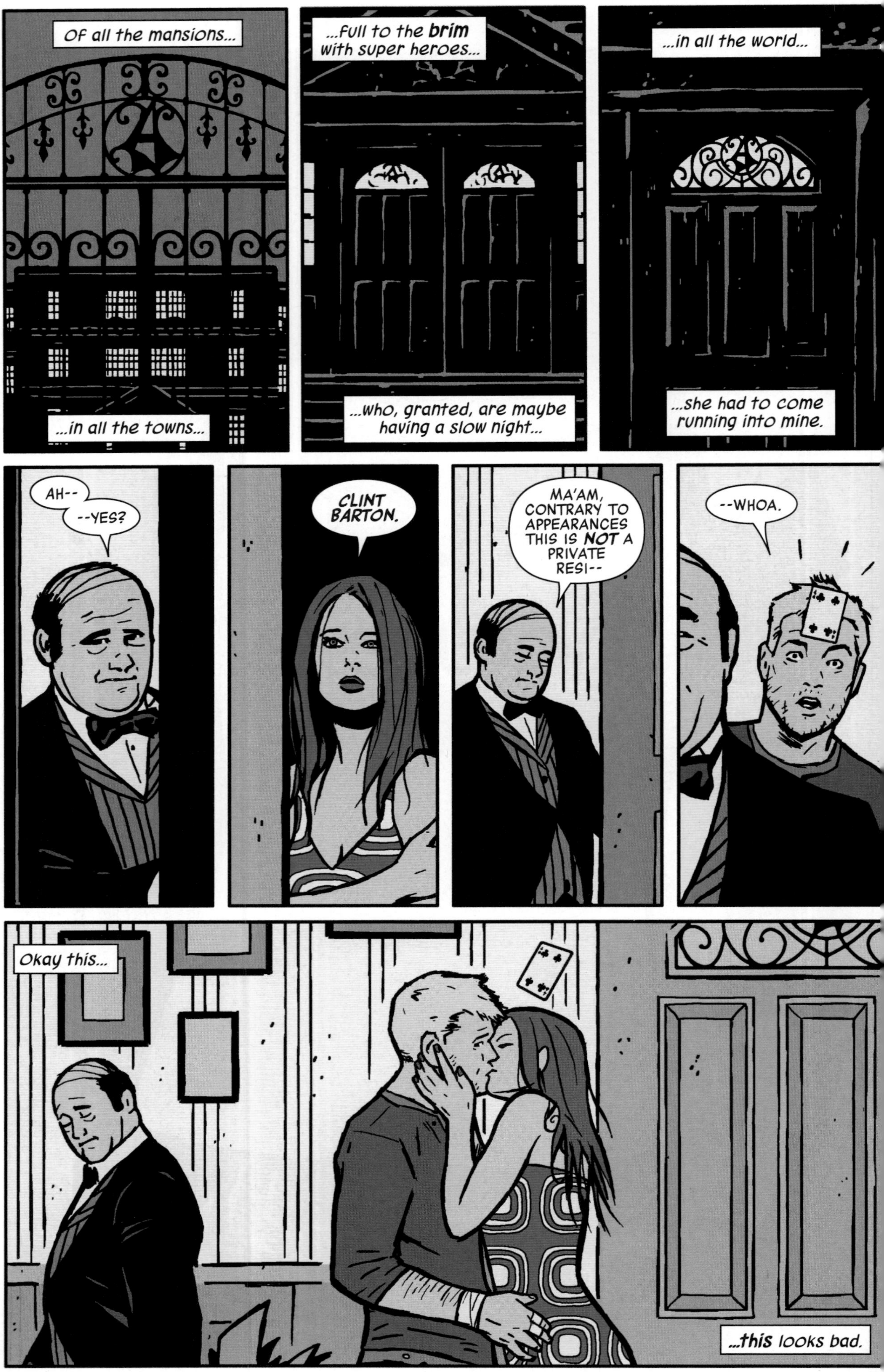

Of all the mansions...
...in all the towns...
...full to the **brim** with super heroes...
...who, granted, are maybe having a slow night...
...in all the world...
...she had to come running into mine.
AH--
--YES?
CLINT BARTON.
MA'AM, CONTRARY TO APPEARANCES THIS IS **NOT** A PRIVATE RESI--
--WHOA.
Okay this...
...**this** looks bad.

THEY'RE GOING TO KILL ME.

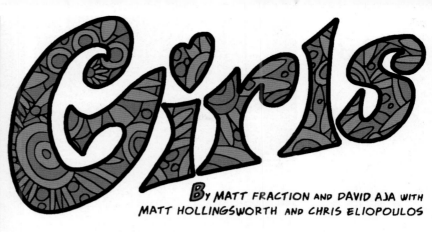

# Girls

BY MATT FRACTION AND DAVID AJA WITH MATT HOLLINGSWORTH AND CHRIS ELIOPOULOS

I NEED YOUR HELP AGAIN.

I... HEY... YOU.

THAT DEPENDS.

OH MY.

CUH-- CLINT?

AH...

THIS LOOKS BAD, RIGHT? IN MY HEAD THIS LOOKS BAD.

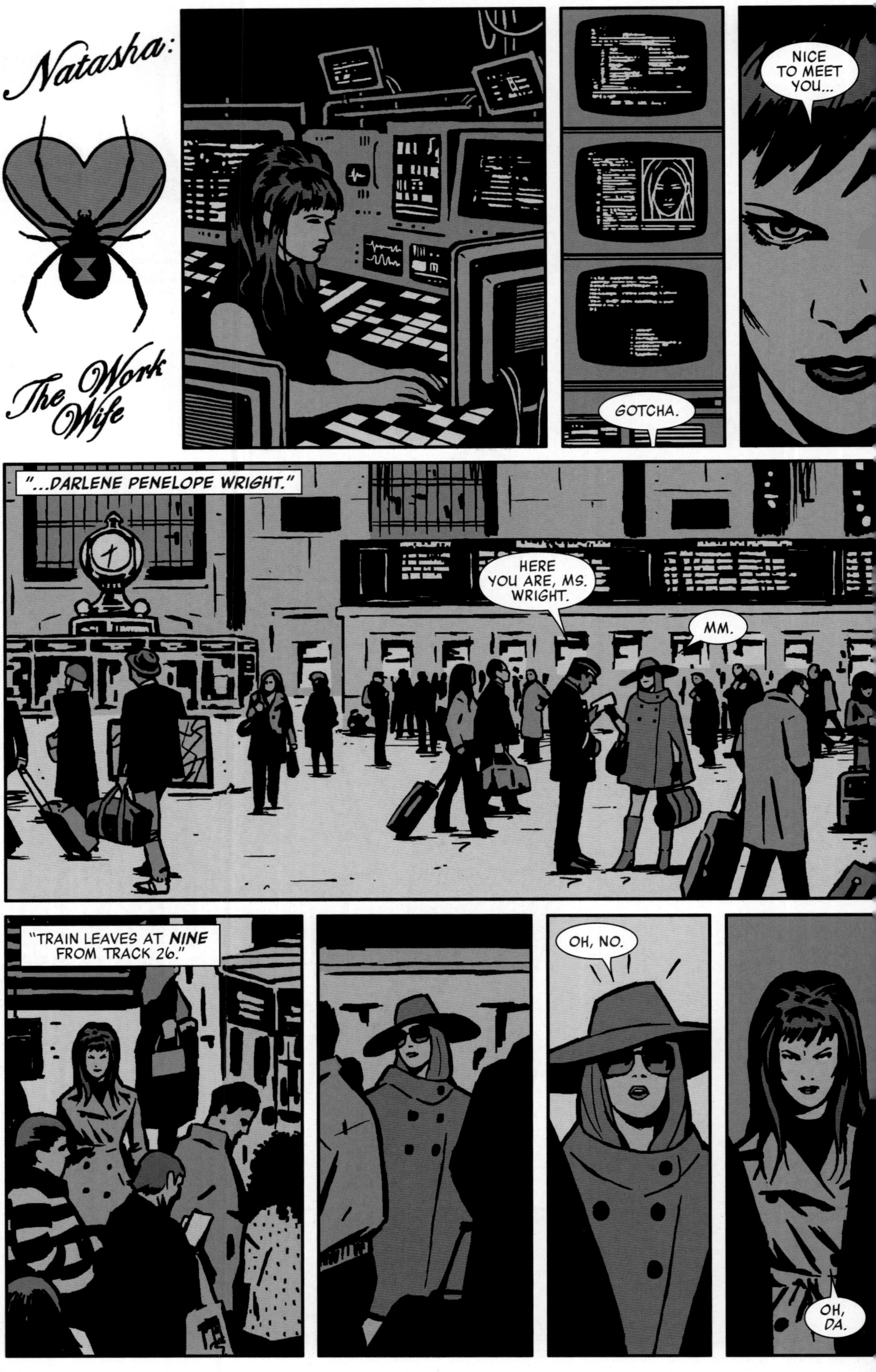
Natasha:
The Work Wife
NICE TO MEET YOU...
GOTCHA.
"...DARLENE PENELOPE WRIGHT."
HERE YOU ARE, MS. WRIGHT.
MM.
"TRAIN LEAVES AT NINE FROM TRACK 26."
OH, NO.
OH, DA.

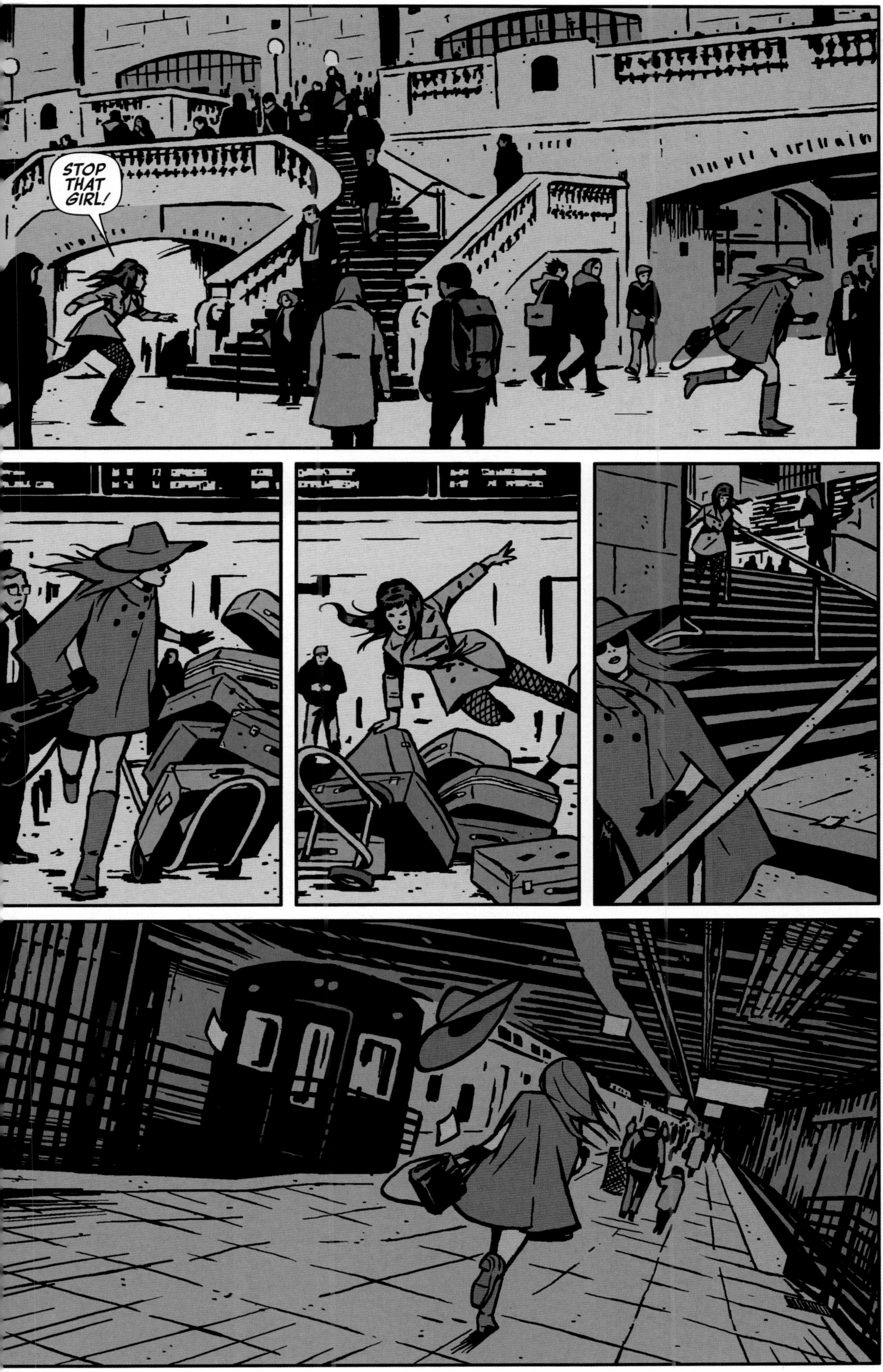
STOP THAT GIRL!

DARLENE. PENELOPE. WRIGHT.

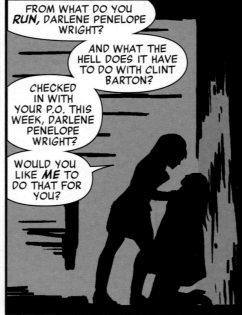

FROM WHAT DO YOU *RUN*, DARLENE PENELOPE WRIGHT?

AND WHAT THE HELL DOES IT HAVE TO DO WITH *CLINT BARTON*?

CHECKED IN WITH YOUR P.O. THIS WEEK, DARLENE PENELOPE WRIGHT?

WOULD YOU LIKE *ME* TO DO THAT FOR YOU?

YOUR TRAIN CROSSES STATE *LINES*, DARLENE PENELOPE WRIGHT. THAT VIOLATES YOUR PAROLE. TO SAY *NOTHING* OF THE SHOOTING YOU'VE ALREADY CONFESSED TO--

OKAY OKAY *OKAY--*

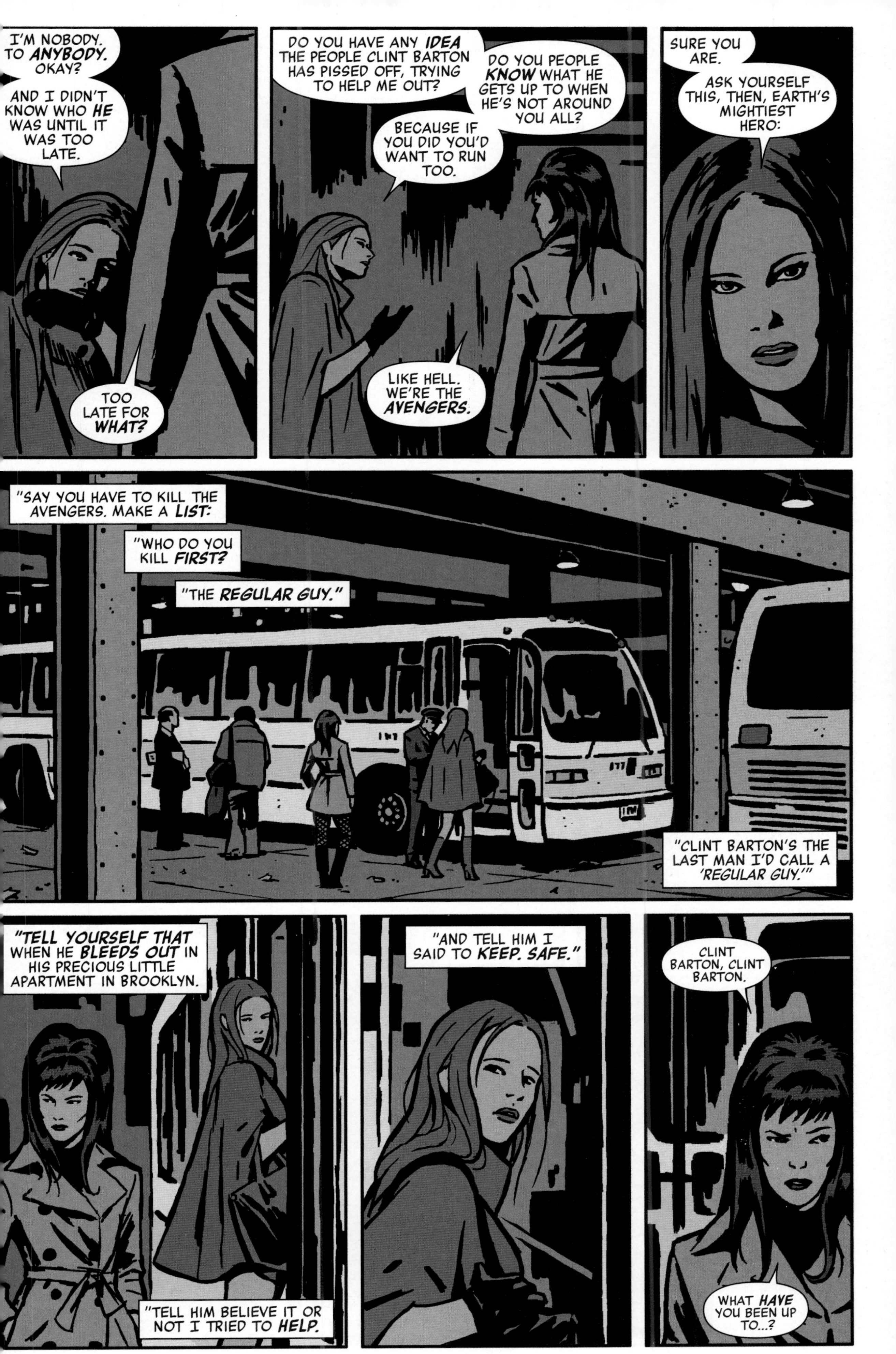
I'M NOBODY. TO *ANYBODY.* OKAY?
AND I DIDN'T KNOW WHO *HE* WAS UNTIL IT WAS TOO LATE.
TOO LATE FOR *WHAT?*
DO YOU HAVE ANY *IDEA* THE PEOPLE CLINT BARTON HAS PISSED OFF, TRYING TO HELP ME OUT?
DO YOU PEOPLE *KNOW* WHAT HE GETS UP TO WHEN HE'S NOT AROUND YOU ALL?
BECAUSE IF YOU DID YOU'D WANT TO RUN TOO.
LIKE HELL. WE'RE THE *AVENGERS.*
SURE YOU ARE.
ASK YOURSELF THIS, THEN, EARTH'S MIGHTIEST HERO:
"SAY YOU HAVE TO KILL THE AVENGERS. MAKE A *LIST:*
"WHO DO YOU KILL *FIRST?*
"THE *REGULAR GUY.*"
"CLINT BARTON'S THE LAST MAN I'D CALL A *'REGULAR GUY.'*"
*"TELL YOURSELF THAT* WHEN HE *BLEEDS OUT* IN HIS PRECIOUS LITTLE APARTMENT IN BROOKLYN.
"TELL HIM BELIEVE IT OR NOT I TRIED TO *HELP.*
"AND TELL HIM I SAID TO *KEEP. SAFE.*"
CLINT BARTON, CLINT BARTON.
WHAT *HAVE* YOU BEEN UP TO...?

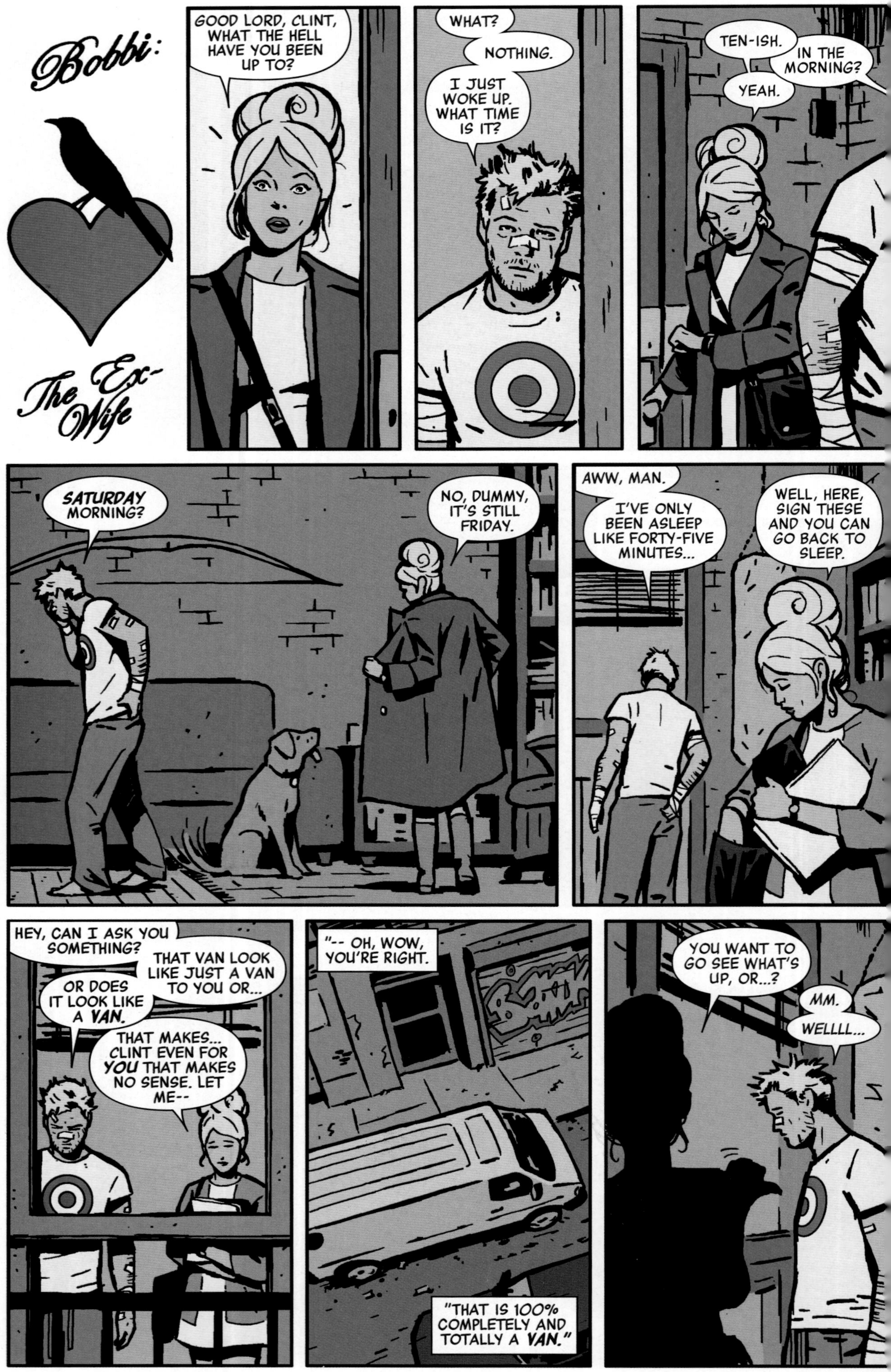

Bobbi:
The Ex-Wife
GOOD LORD, CLINT, WHAT THE HELL HAVE YOU BEEN UP TO?
WHAT?
NOTHING.
I JUST WOKE UP. WHAT TIME IS IT?
TEN-ISH.
IN THE MORNING?
YEAH.
SATURDAY MORNING?
NO, DUMMY, IT'S STILL FRIDAY.
AWW, MAN.
I'VE ONLY BEEN ASLEEP LIKE FORTY-FIVE MINUTES...
WELL, HERE, SIGN THESE AND YOU CAN GO BACK TO SLEEP.
HEY, CAN I ASK YOU SOMETHING?
THAT VAN LOOK LIKE JUST A VAN TO YOU OR...
OR DOES IT LOOK LIKE A VAN.
THAT MAKES... CLINT EVEN FOR YOU THAT MAKES NO SENSE. LET ME--
"-- OH, WOW, YOU'RE RIGHT.
"THAT IS 100% COMPLETELY AND TOTALLY A VAN."
YOU WANT TO GO SEE WHAT'S UP, OR...?
MM.
WELLLL...

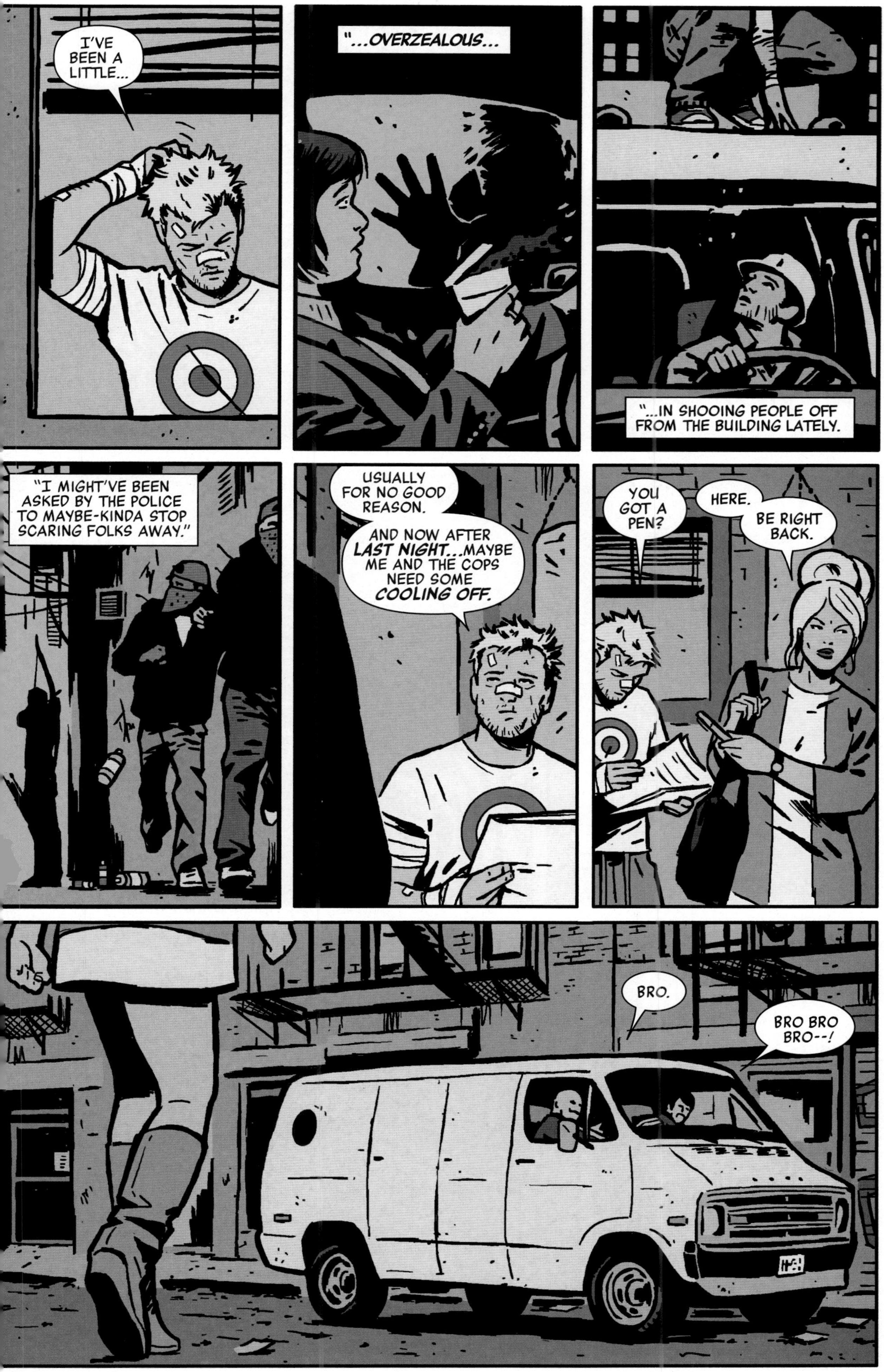
I'VE BEEN A LITTLE...
"...OVERZEALOUS...
"...IN SHOOING PEOPLE OFF FROM THE BUILDING LATELY.
"I MIGHT'VE BEEN ASKED BY THE POLICE TO MAYBE-KINDA STOP SCARING FOLKS AWAY."
USUALLY FOR NO GOOD REASON.
AND NOW AFTER LAST NIGHT...MAYBE ME AND THE COPS NEED SOME COOLING OFF.
YOU GOT A PEN?
HERE.
BE RIGHT BACK.
BRO.
BRO BRO BRO--!

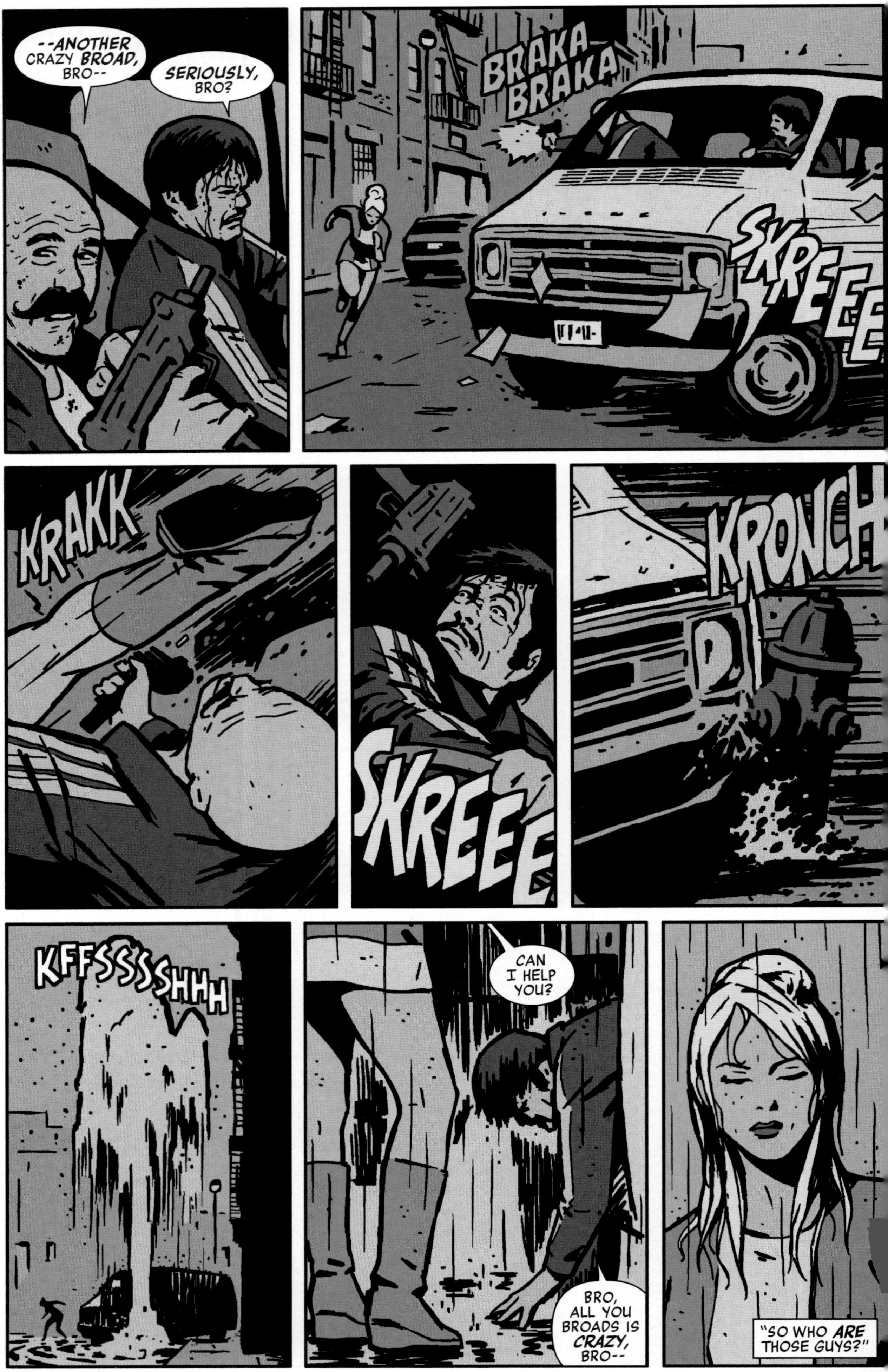
--ANOTHER CRAZY BROAD, BRO--
SERIOUSLY, BRO?
BRAKA BRAKA
SKREEEE
KRAKK
SKREEE
KRONCH
KFFSSSSSHHH
CAN I HELP YOU?
BRO, ALL YOU BROADS IS CRAZY, BRO--
"SO WHO ARE THOSE GUYS?"

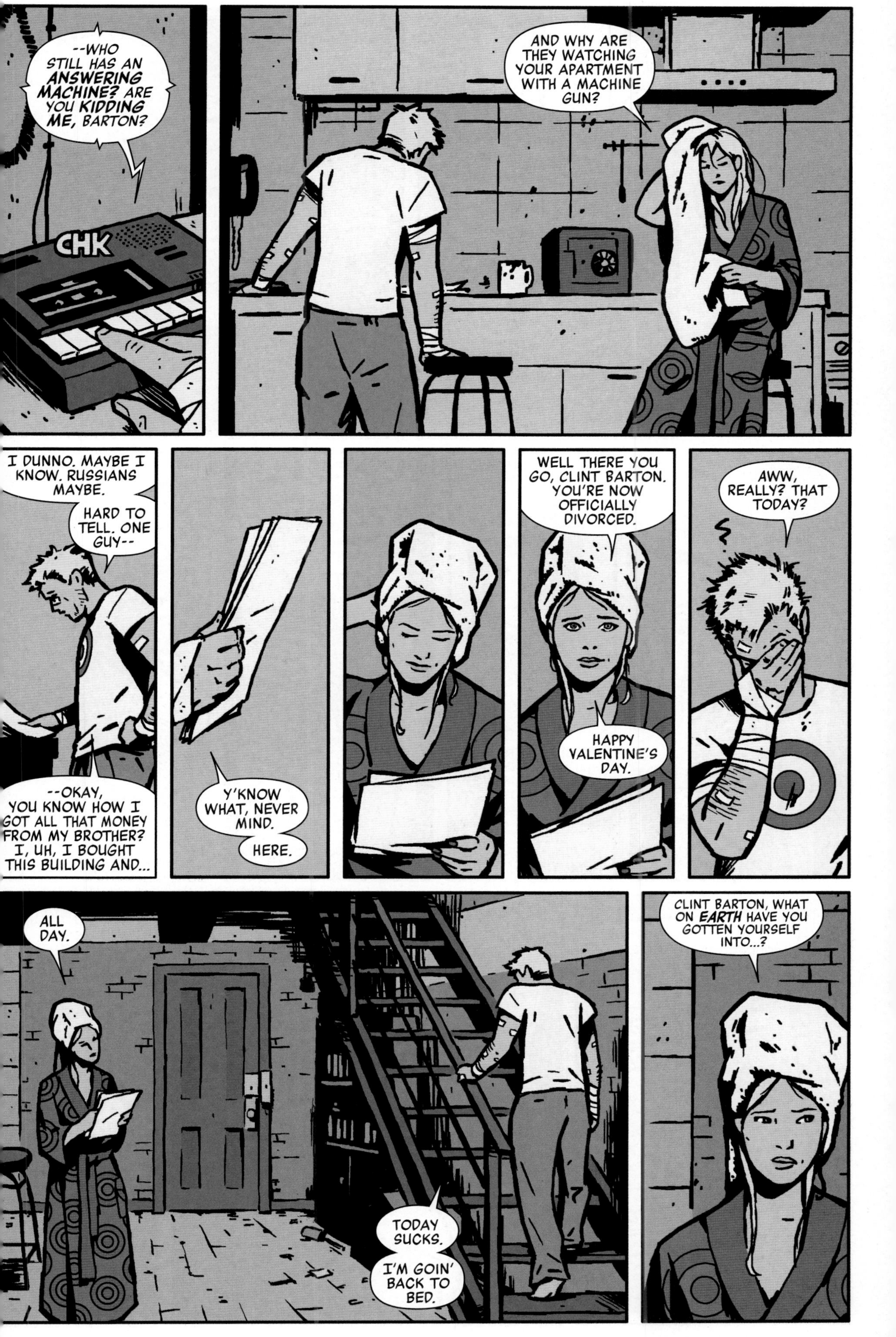
--WHO STILL HAS AN ANSWERING MACHINE? ARE YOU KIDDING ME, BARTON?
CHK
AND WHY ARE THEY WATCHING YOUR APARTMENT WITH A MACHINE GUN?
I DUNNO. MAYBE I KNOW. RUSSIANS MAYBE.
HARD TO TELL. ONE GUY--
--OKAY, YOU KNOW HOW I GOT ALL THAT MONEY FROM MY BROTHER? I, UH, I BOUGHT THIS BUILDING AND...
Y'KNOW WHAT, NEVER MIND.
HERE.
WELL THERE YOU GO, CLINT BARTON. YOU'RE NOW OFFICIALLY DIVORCED.
HAPPY VALENTINE'S DAY.
AWW, REALLY? THAT TODAY?
ALL DAY.
TODAY SUCKS.
I'M GOIN' BACK TO BED.
CLINT BARTON, WHAT ON EARTH HAVE YOU GOTTEN YOURSELF INTO...?

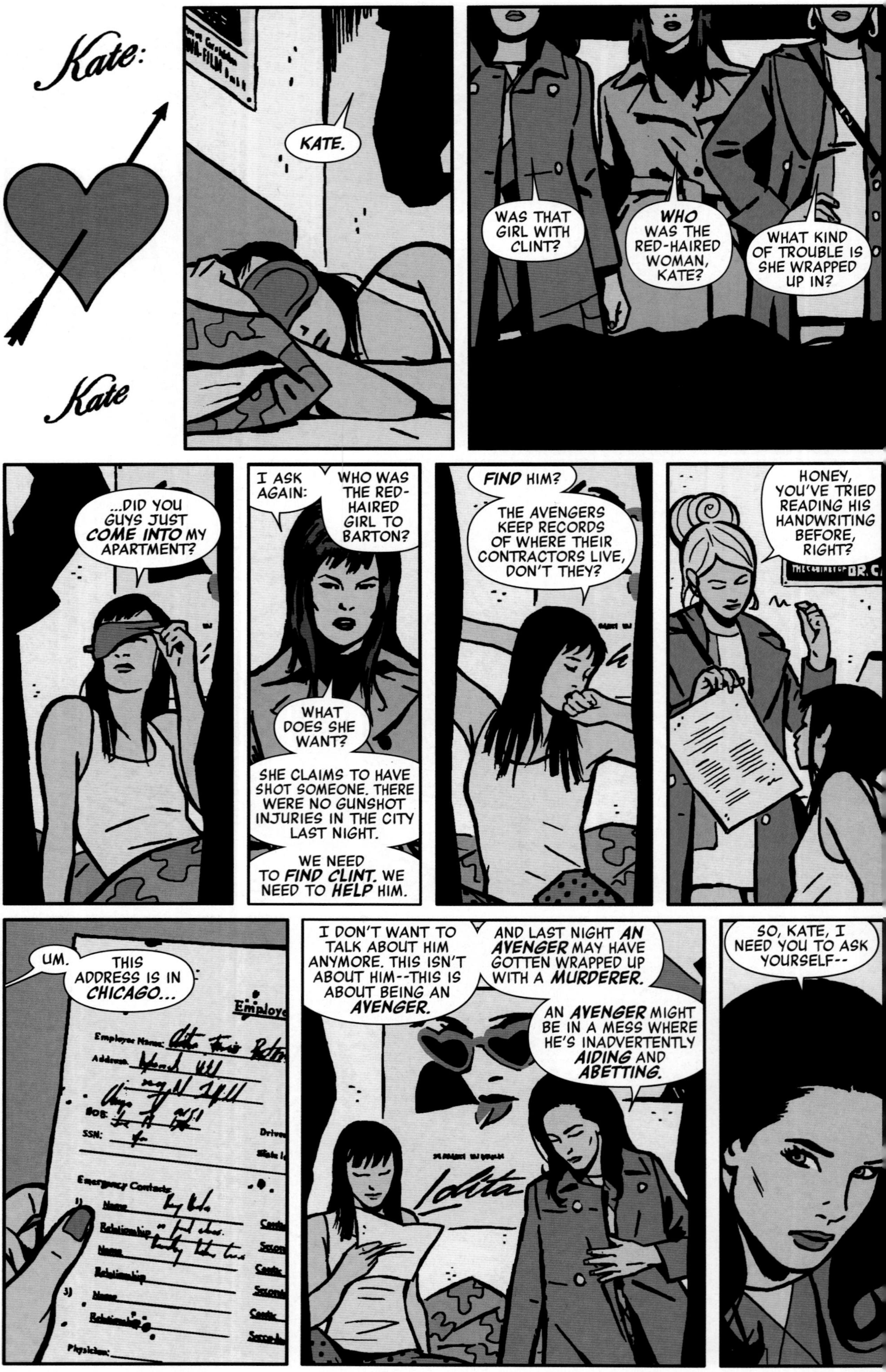
Kate:
Kate
KATE.
WAS THAT GIRL WITH CLINT?
WHO WAS THE RED-HAIRED WOMAN, KATE?
WHAT KIND OF TROUBLE IS SHE WRAPPED UP IN?
...DID YOU GUYS JUST COME INTO MY APARTMENT?
I ASK AGAIN:
WHO WAS THE RED-HAIRED GIRL TO BARTON?
WHAT DOES SHE WANT?
SHE CLAIMS TO HAVE SHOT SOMEONE. THERE WERE NO GUNSHOT INJURIES IN THE CITY LAST NIGHT.
WE NEED TO FIND CLINT. WE NEED TO HELP HIM.
FIND HIM?
THE AVENGERS KEEP RECORDS OF WHERE THEIR CONTRACTORS LIVE, DON'T THEY?
HONEY, YOU'VE TRIED READING HIS HANDWRITING BEFORE, RIGHT?
UM.
THIS ADDRESS IS IN CHICAGO...
Employee Name:
Address:
DOB:
SSN:
Emergency Contacts:
Name
Relationship
Physician:
I DON'T WANT TO TALK ABOUT HIM ANYMORE. THIS ISN'T ABOUT HIM--THIS IS ABOUT BEING AN AVENGER.
AND LAST NIGHT AN AVENGER MAY HAVE GOTTEN WRAPPED UP WITH A MURDERER.
AN AVENGER MIGHT BE IN A MESS WHERE HE'S INADVERTENTLY AIDING AND ABETTING.
Lolita
SO, KATE, I NEED YOU TO ASK YOURSELF--

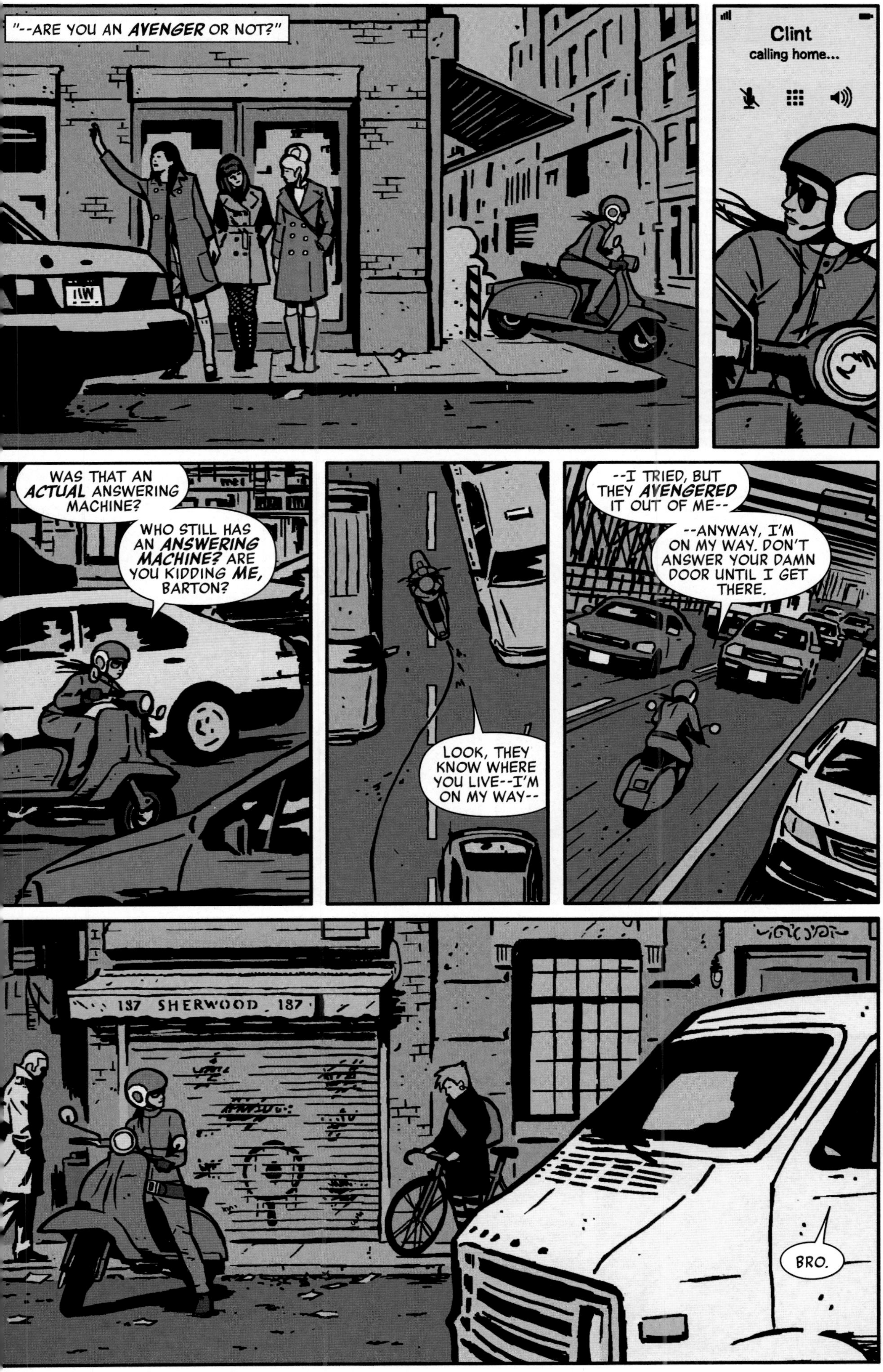
"--ARE YOU AN AVENGER OR NOT?"
Clint
calling home...
WAS THAT AN ACTUAL ANSWERING MACHINE?
WHO STILL HAS AN ANSWERING MACHINE? ARE YOU KIDDING ME, BARTON?
LOOK, THEY KNOW WHERE YOU LIVE--I'M ON MY WAY--
--I TRIED, BUT THEY AVENGERED IT OUT OF ME--
--ANYWAY, I'M ON MY WAY. DON'T ANSWER YOUR DAMN DOOR UNTIL I GET THERE.
187 SHERWOOD 187
BRO.

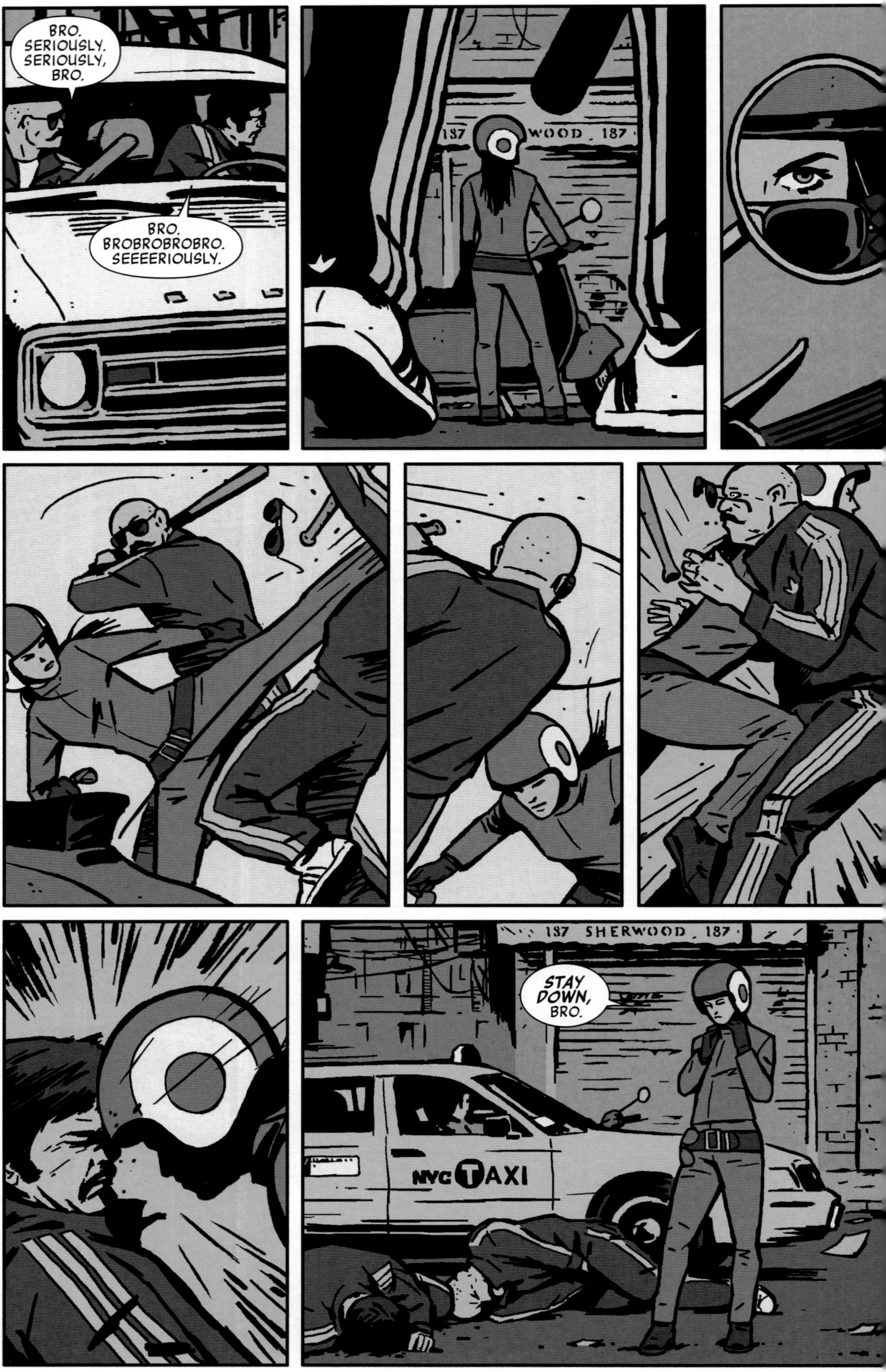
BRO. SERIOUSLY. SERIOUSLY, BRO.
BRO. BROBROBROBRO. SEEEERIOUSLY.
187 WOOD 187
187 SHERWOOD 187
STAY DOWN, BRO.
NYC TAXI

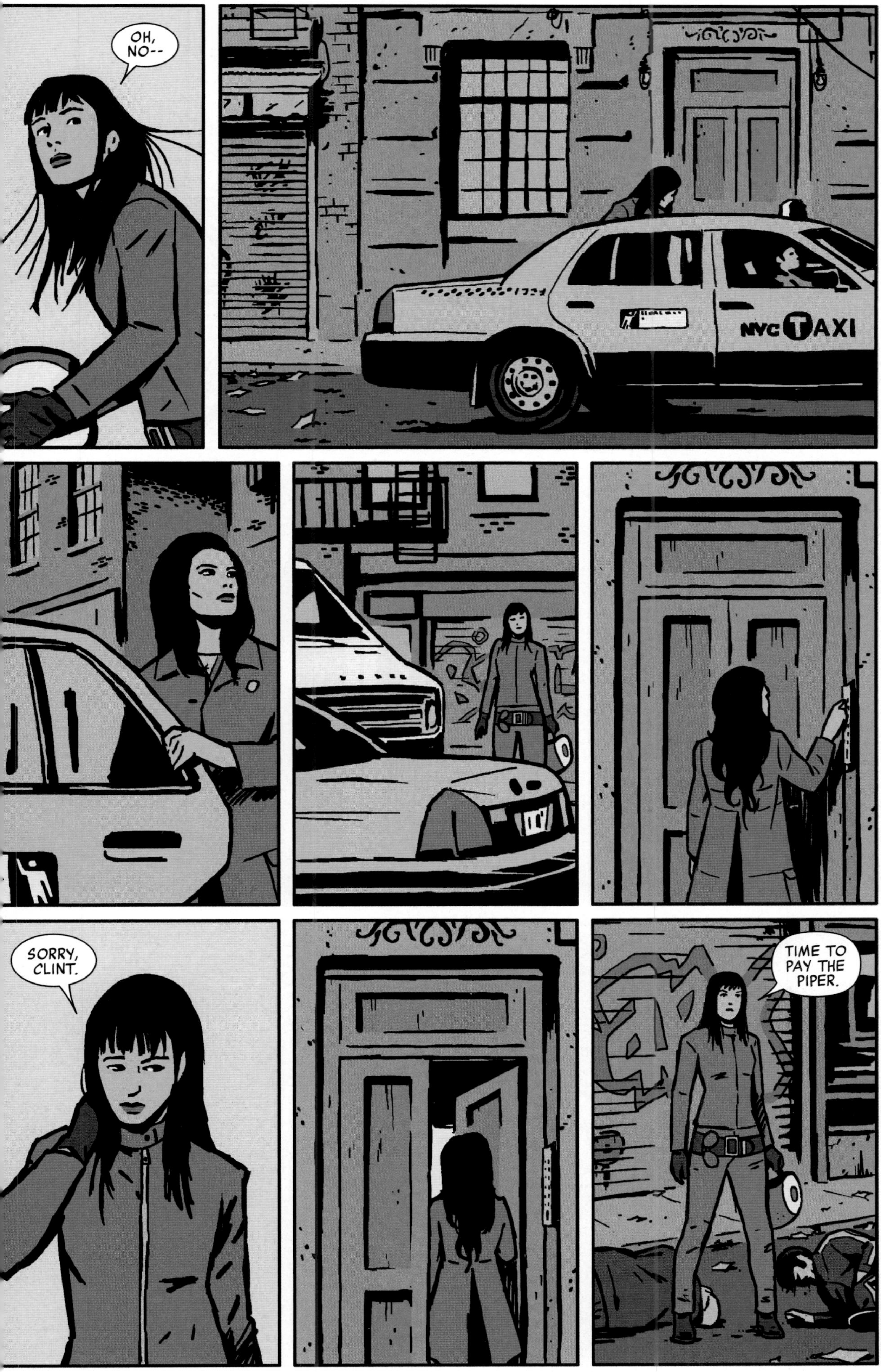
OH, NO--
NYC TAXI
SORRY, CLINT.
TIME TO PAY THE PIPER.

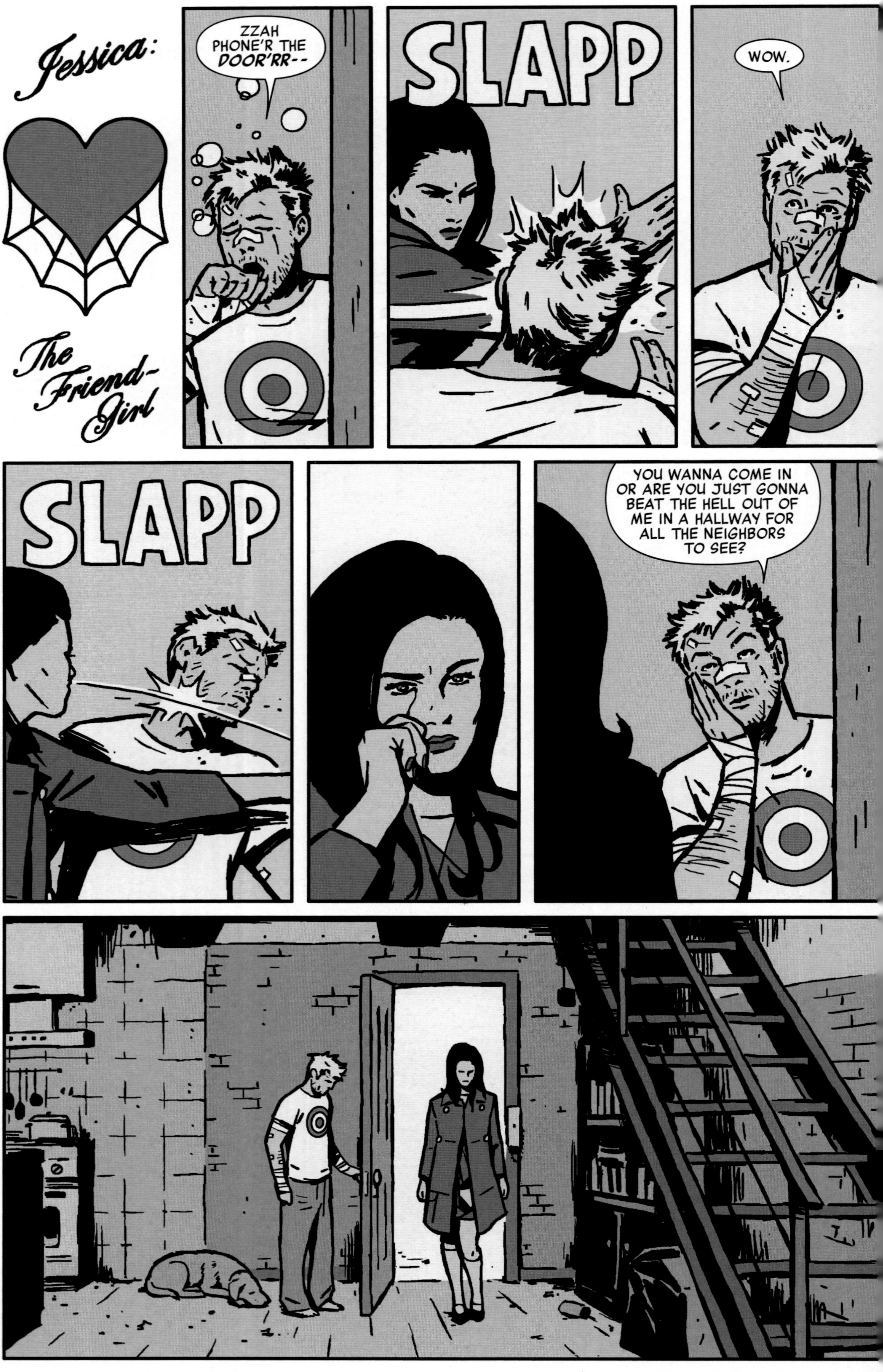
Jessica:
The Friend-Girl
ZZAH PHONE'R THE DOOR'RR--
SLAPP
WOW.
SLAPP
YOU WANNA COME IN OR ARE YOU JUST GONNA BEAT THE HELL OUT OF ME IN A HALLWAY FOR ALL THE NEIGHBORS TO SEE?

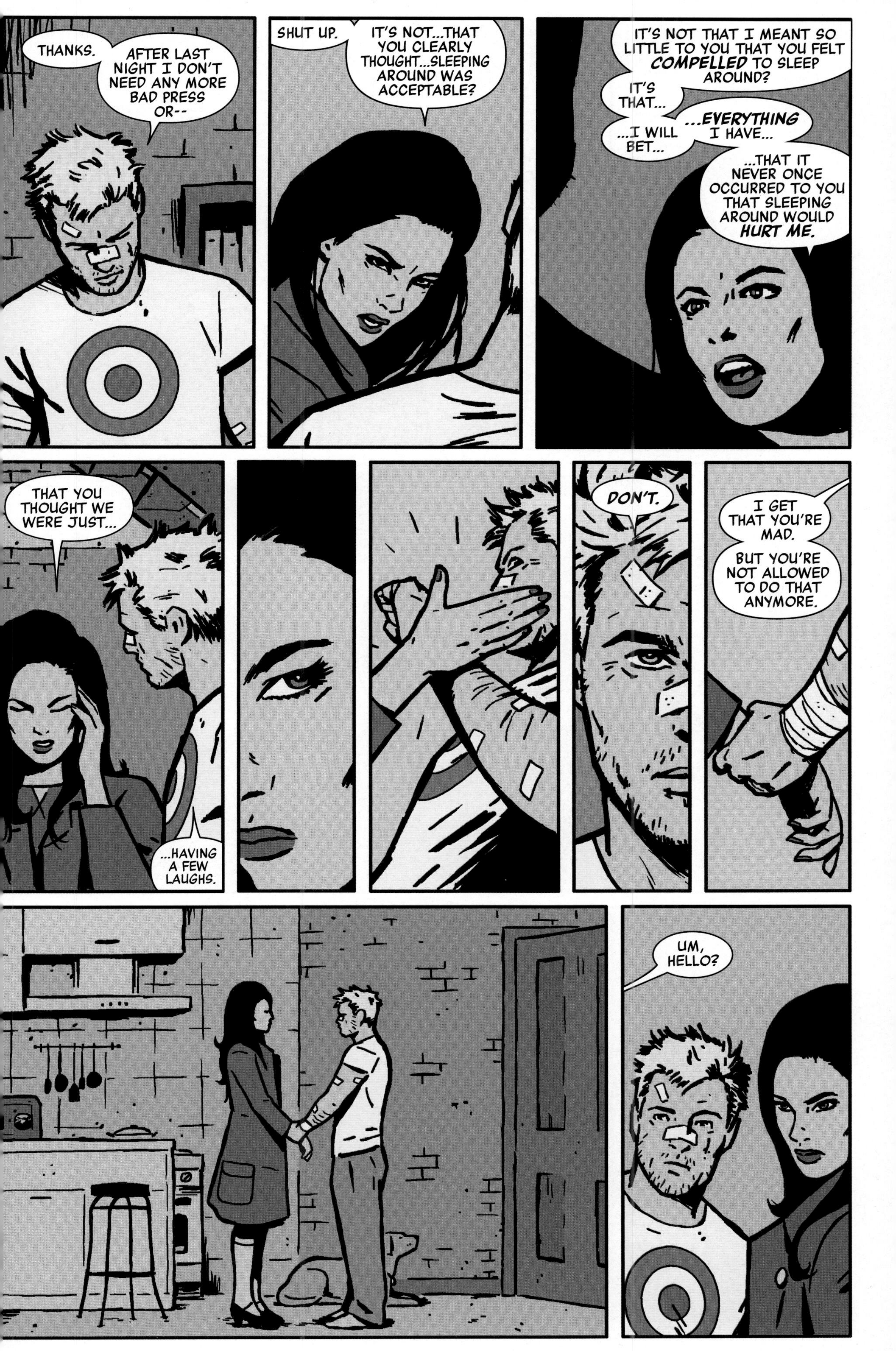
THANKS.
AFTER LAST NIGHT I DON'T NEED ANY MORE BAD PRESS OR--
SHUT UP.
IT'S NOT...THAT YOU CLEARLY THOUGHT...SLEEPING AROUND WAS ACCEPTABLE?
IT'S NOT THAT I MEANT SO LITTLE TO YOU THAT YOU FELT COMPELLED TO SLEEP AROUND?
IT'S THAT...
...I WILL BET...
...EVERYTHING I HAVE...
...THAT IT NEVER ONCE OCCURRED TO YOU THAT SLEEPING AROUND WOULD HURT ME.
THAT YOU THOUGHT WE WERE JUST...
...HAVING A FEW LAUGHS.
DON'T.
I GET THAT YOU'RE MAD.
BUT YOU'RE NOT ALLOWED TO DO THAT ANYMORE.
UM, HELLO?

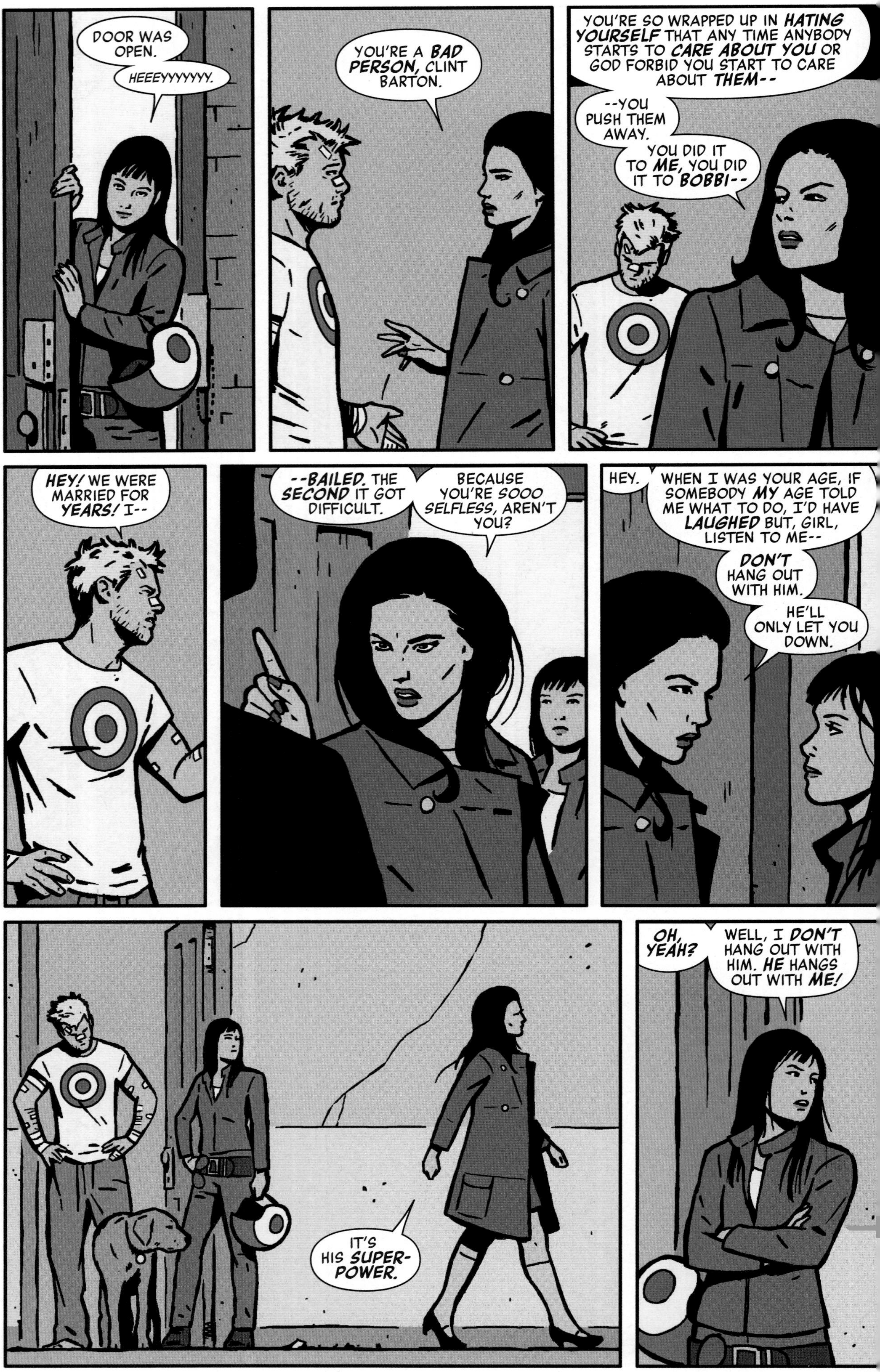

DOOR WAS OPEN.
HEEEYYYYYYY.
YOU'RE A BAD PERSON, CLINT BARTON.
YOU'RE SO WRAPPED UP IN HATING YOURSELF THAT ANY TIME ANYBODY STARTS TO CARE ABOUT YOU OR GOD FORBID YOU START TO CARE ABOUT THEM--
--YOU PUSH THEM AWAY.
YOU DID IT TO ME, YOU DID IT TO BOBBI--
HEY! WE WERE MARRIED FOR YEARS! I--
--BAILED. THE SECOND IT GOT DIFFICULT.
BECAUSE YOU'RE SOOO SELFLESS, AREN'T YOU?
HEY.
WHEN I WAS YOUR AGE, IF SOMEBODY MY AGE TOLD ME WHAT TO DO, I'D HAVE LAUGHED BUT, GIRL, LISTEN TO ME--
DON'T HANG OUT WITH HIM.
HE'LL ONLY LET YOU DOWN.
IT'S HIS SUPER-POWER.
OH, YEAH?
WELL, I DON'T HANG OUT WITH HIM. HE HANGS OUT WITH ME!

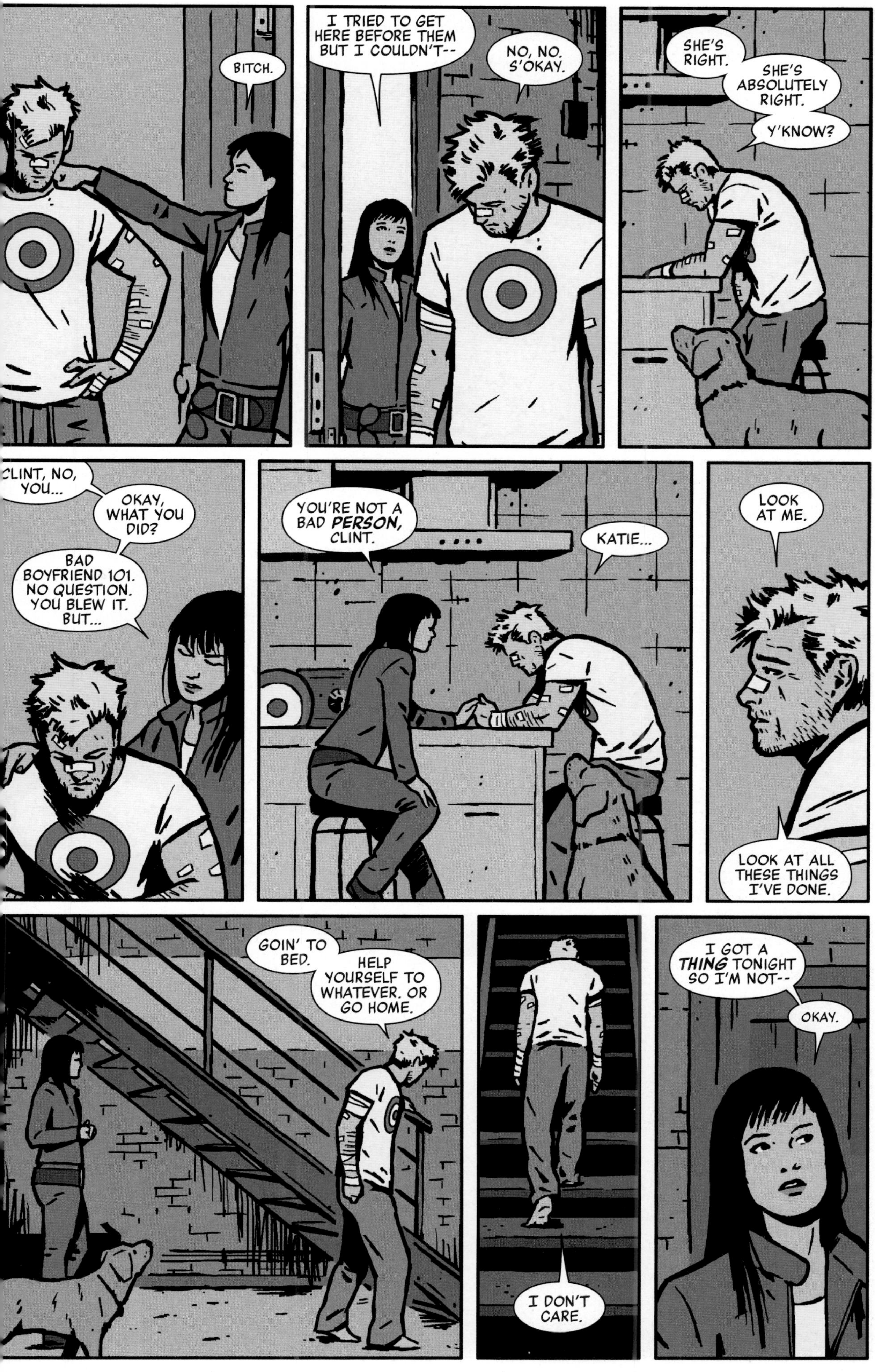

BITCH.
I TRIED TO GET HERE BEFORE THEM BUT I COULDN'T--
NO, NO. S'OKAY.
SHE'S RIGHT.
SHE'S ABSOLUTELY RIGHT.
Y'KNOW?
CLINT, NO, YOU...
OKAY, WHAT YOU DID?
BAD BOYFRIEND 101. NO QUESTION. YOU BLEW IT. BUT...
YOU'RE NOT A BAD PERSON, CLINT.
KATIE...
LOOK AT ME.
LOOK AT ALL THESE THINGS I'VE DONE.
GOIN' TO BED.
HELP YOURSELF TO WHATEVER. OR GO HOME.
I DON'T CARE.
I GOT A THING TONIGHT SO I'M NOT--
OKAY.

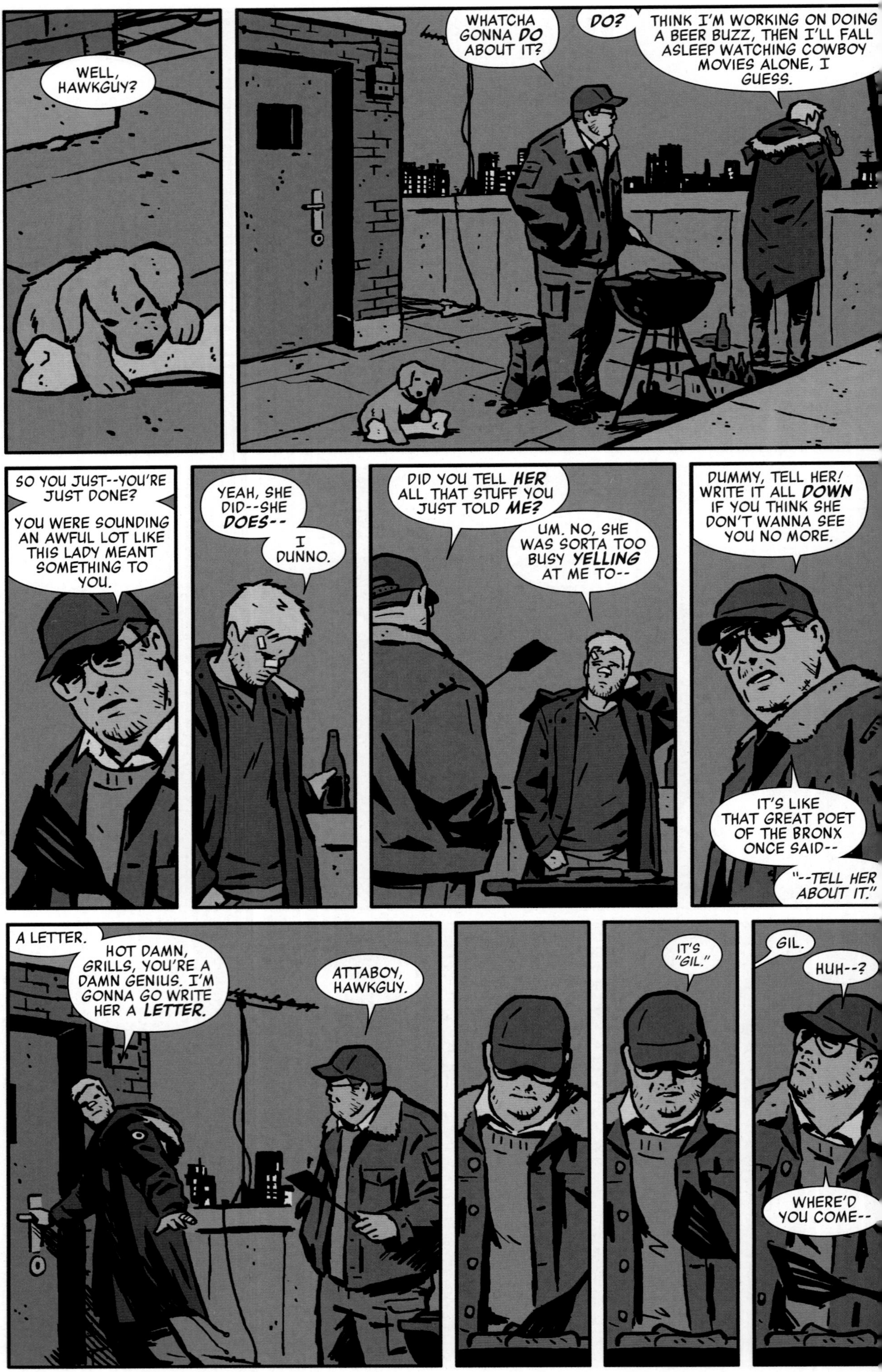
WELL, HAWKGUY?
WHATCHA GONNA DO ABOUT IT?
DO?
THINK I'M WORKING ON DOING A BEER BUZZ, THEN I'LL FALL ASLEEP WATCHING COWBOY MOVIES ALONE, I GUESS.
SO YOU JUST--YOU'RE JUST DONE?
YOU WERE SOUNDING AN AWFUL LOT LIKE THIS LADY MEANT SOMETHING TO YOU.
YEAH, SHE DID--SHE DOES--
I DUNNO.
DID YOU TELL HER ALL THAT STUFF YOU JUST TOLD ME?
UM. NO, SHE WAS SORTA TOO BUSY YELLING AT ME TO--
DUMMY, TELL HER! WRITE IT ALL DOWN IF YOU THINK SHE DON'T WANNA SEE YOU NO MORE.
IT'S LIKE THAT GREAT POET OF THE BRONX ONCE SAID--
"--TELL HER ABOUT IT."
A LETTER.
HOT DAMN, GRILLS, YOU'RE A DAMN GENIUS. I'M GONNA GO WRITE HER A LETTER.
ATTABOY, HAWKGUY.
IT'S "GIL."
GIL.
HUH--?
WHERE'D YOU COME--

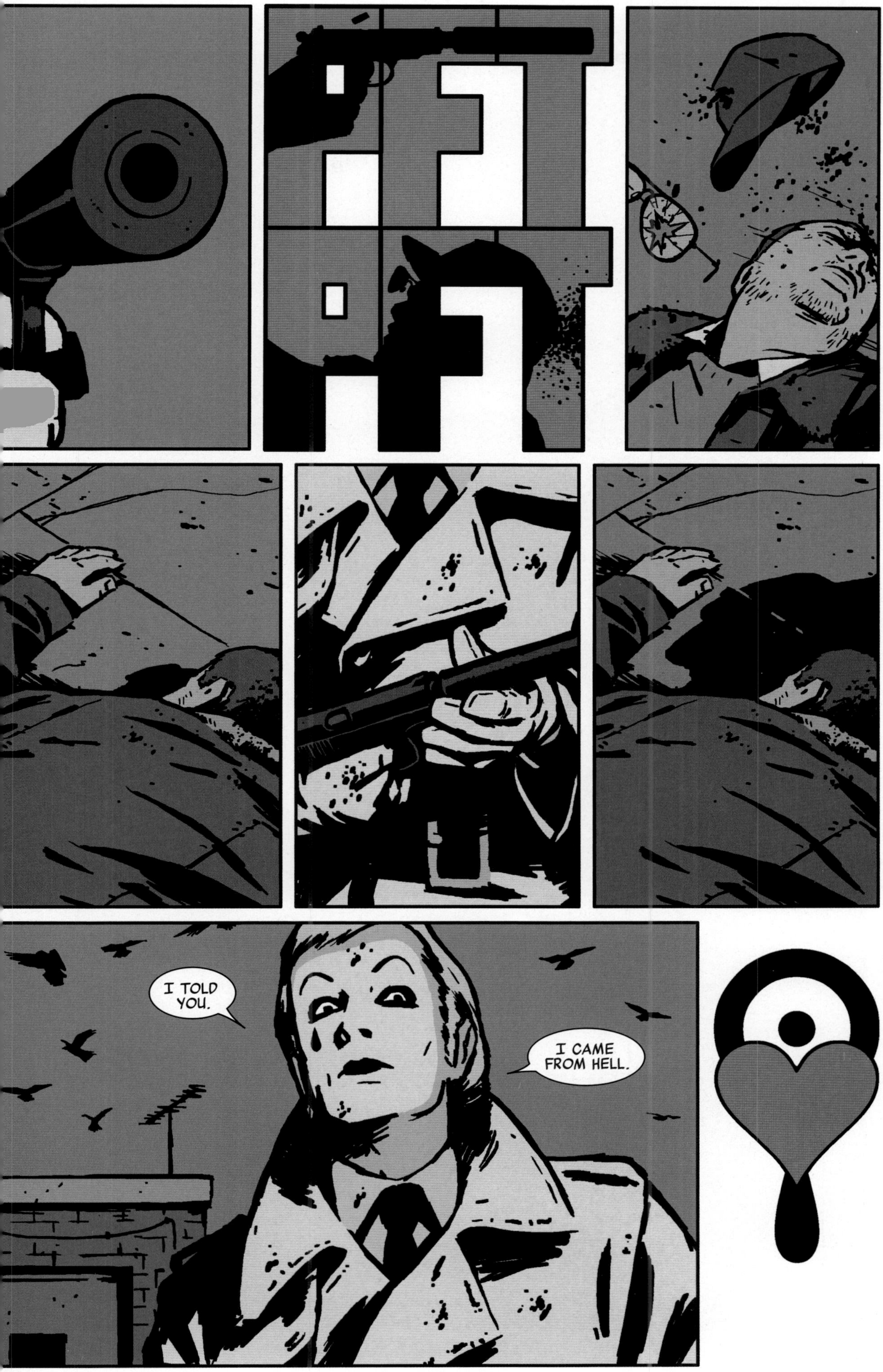
PFT
PFT
I TOLD YOU.
I CAME FROM HELL.

10

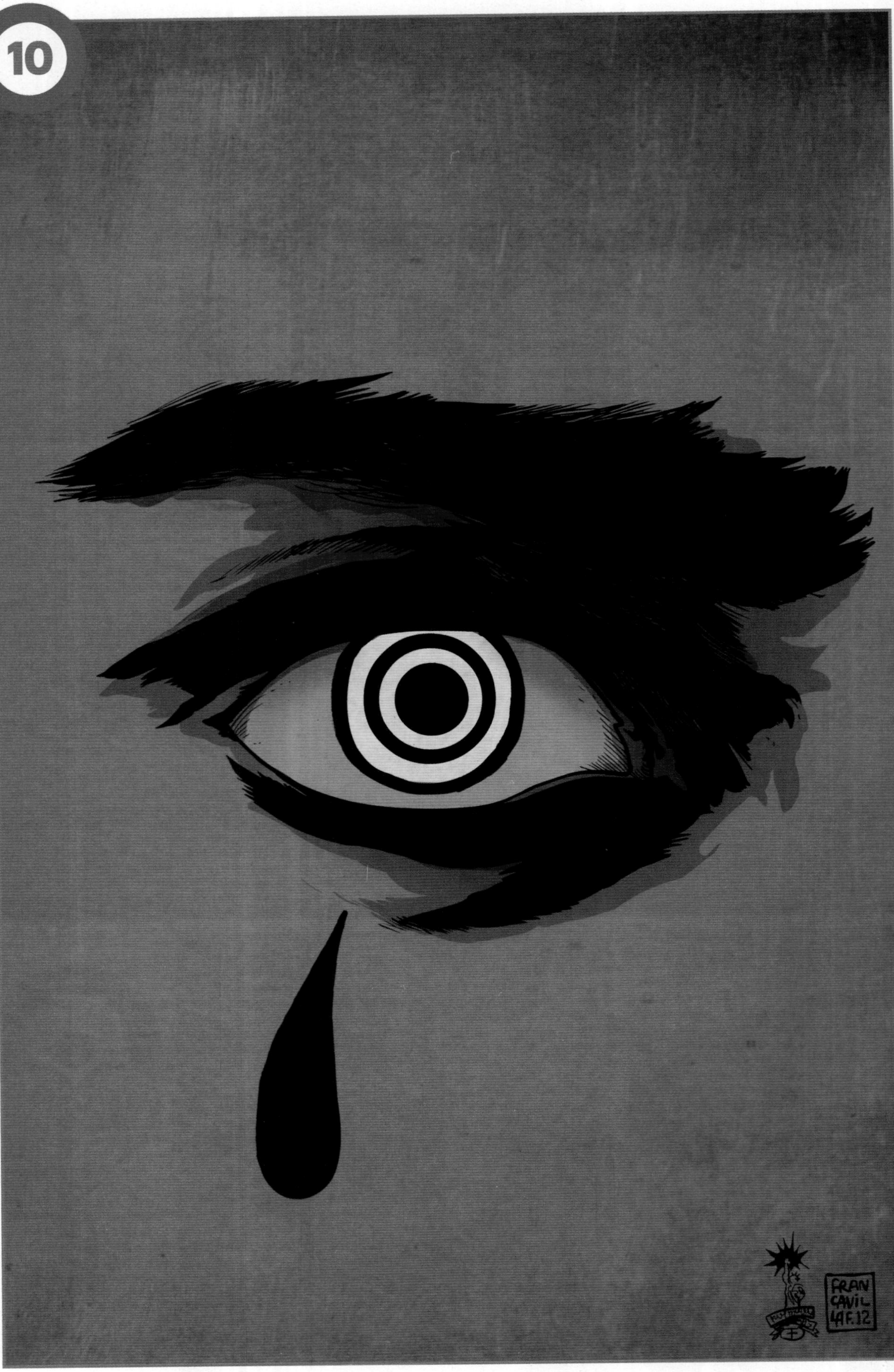
FRAN
GAVIL
14F.12

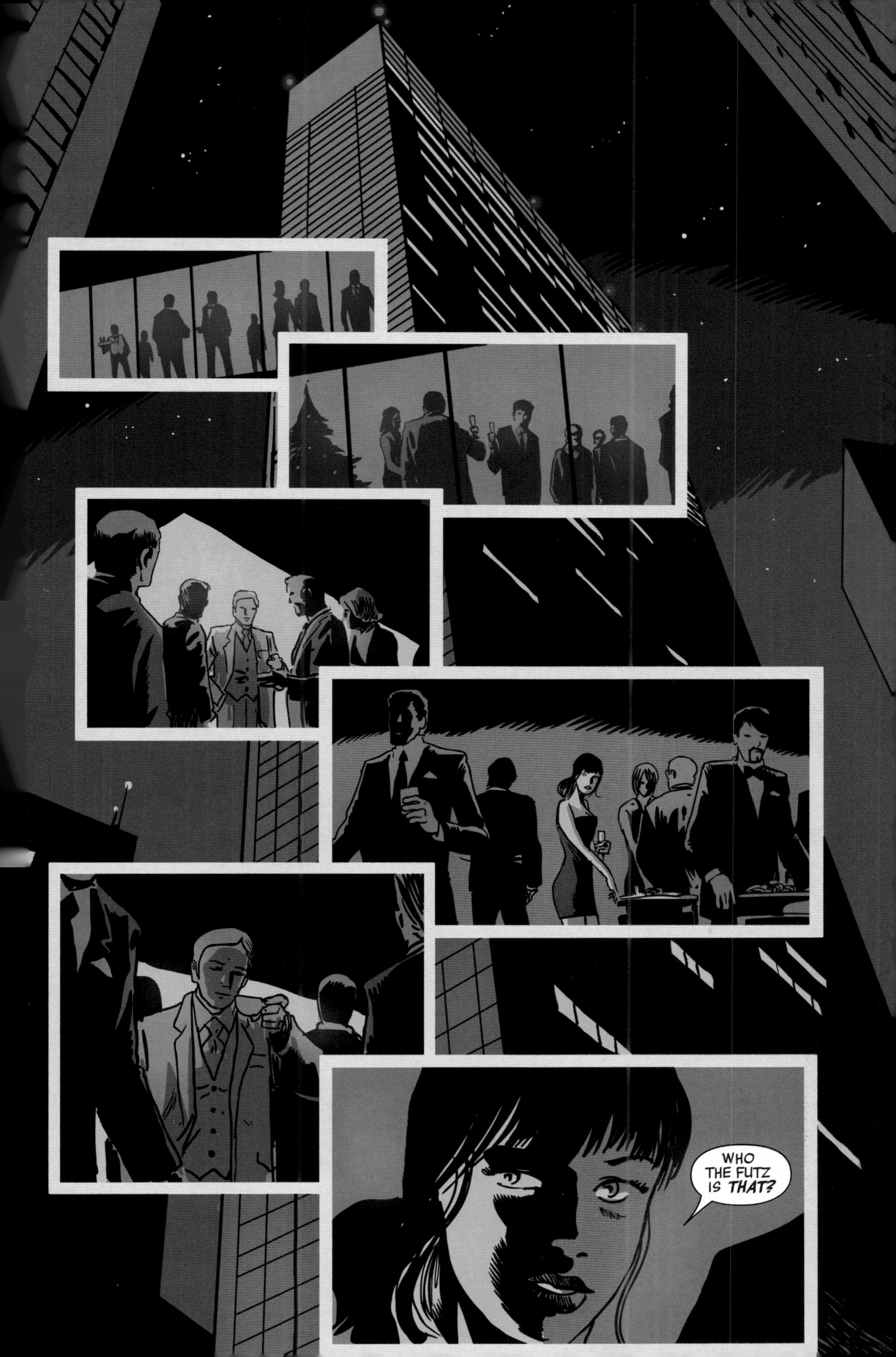
WHO THE FUTZ IS THAT?

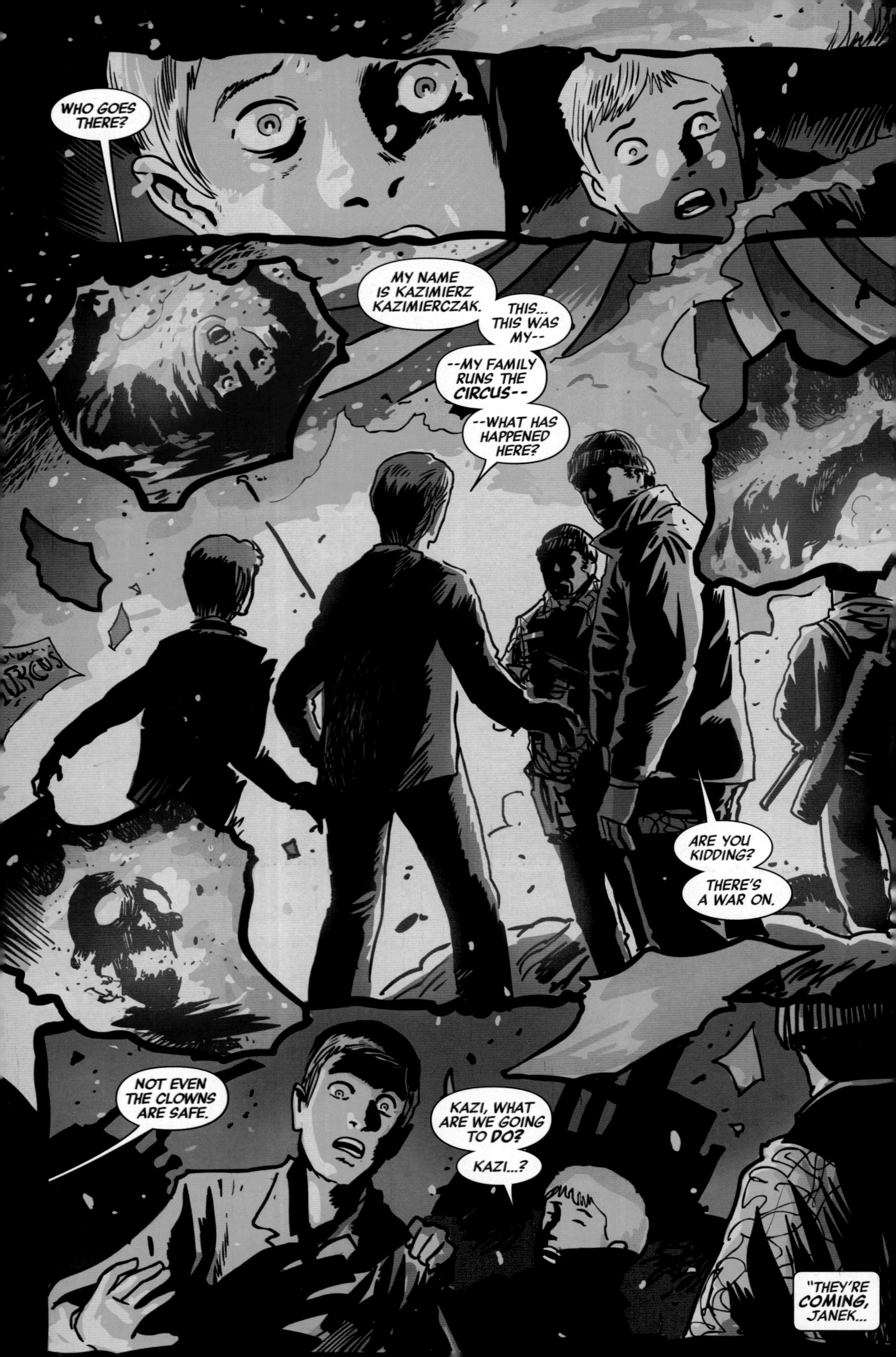
WHO GOES THERE?
MY NAME IS KAZIMIERZ KAZIMIERCZAK.
THIS... THIS WAS MY--
--MY FAMILY RUNS THE CIRCUS--
--WHAT HAS HAPPENED HERE?
CIRCUS
ARE YOU KIDDING?
THERE'S A WAR ON.
NOT EVEN THE CLOWNS ARE SAFE.
KAZI, WHAT ARE WE GOING TO DO?
KAZI...?
"THEY'RE COMING, JANEK...

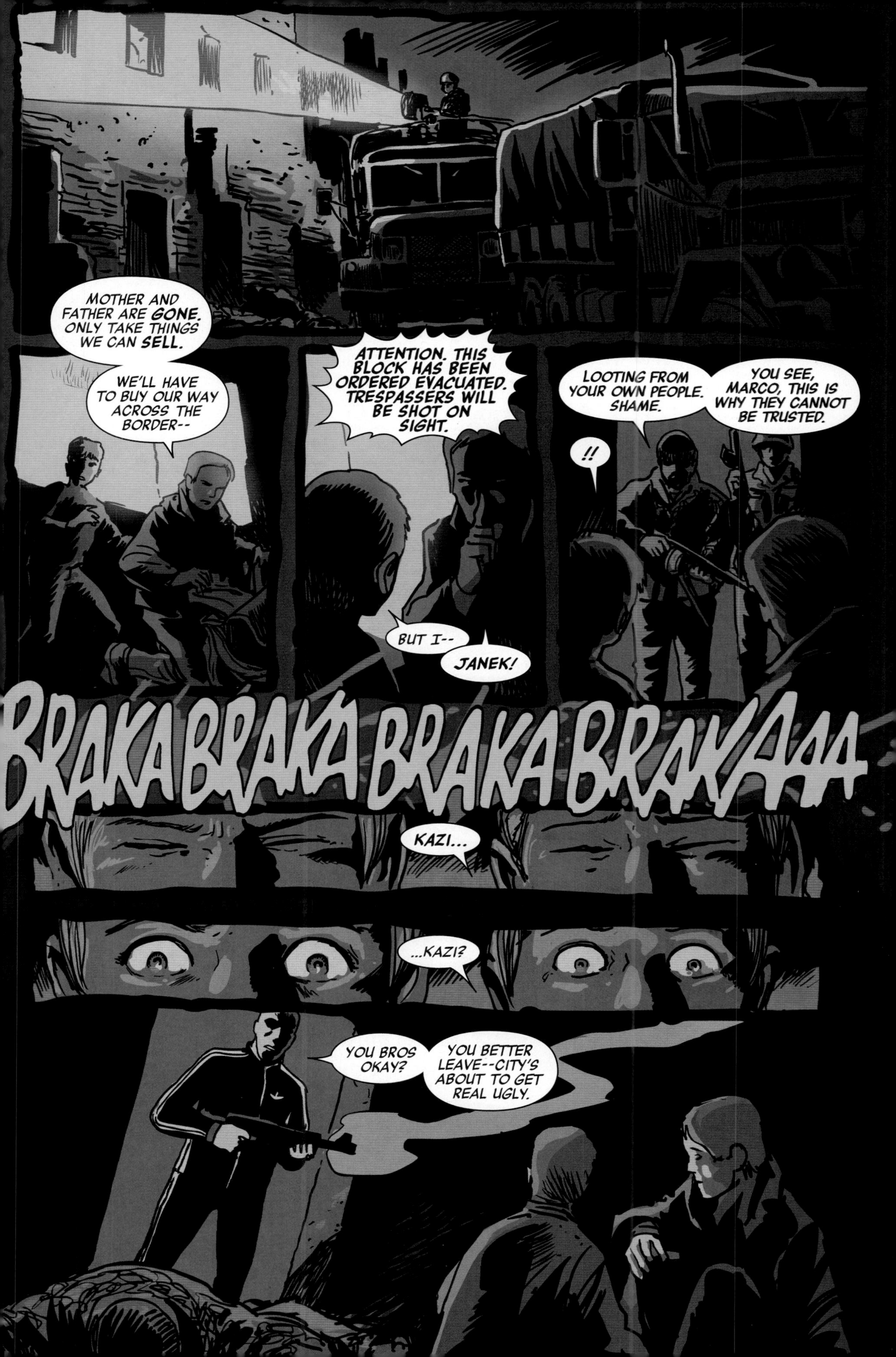
MOTHER AND FATHER ARE GONE. ONLY TAKE THINGS WE CAN SELL.
WE'LL HAVE TO BUY OUR WAY ACROSS THE BORDER--
ATTENTION. THIS BLOCK HAS BEEN ORDERED EVACUATED. TRESPASSERS WILL BE SHOT ON SIGHT.
BUT I--
JANEK!
LOOTING FROM YOUR OWN PEOPLE. SHAME.
YOU SEE, MARCO, THIS IS WHY THEY CANNOT BE TRUSTED.
!!
BRAKA BRAKA BRAKA BRAKAAA
KAZI...
...KAZI?
YOU BROS OKAY?
YOU BETTER LEAVE--CITY'S ABOUT TO GET REAL UGLY.

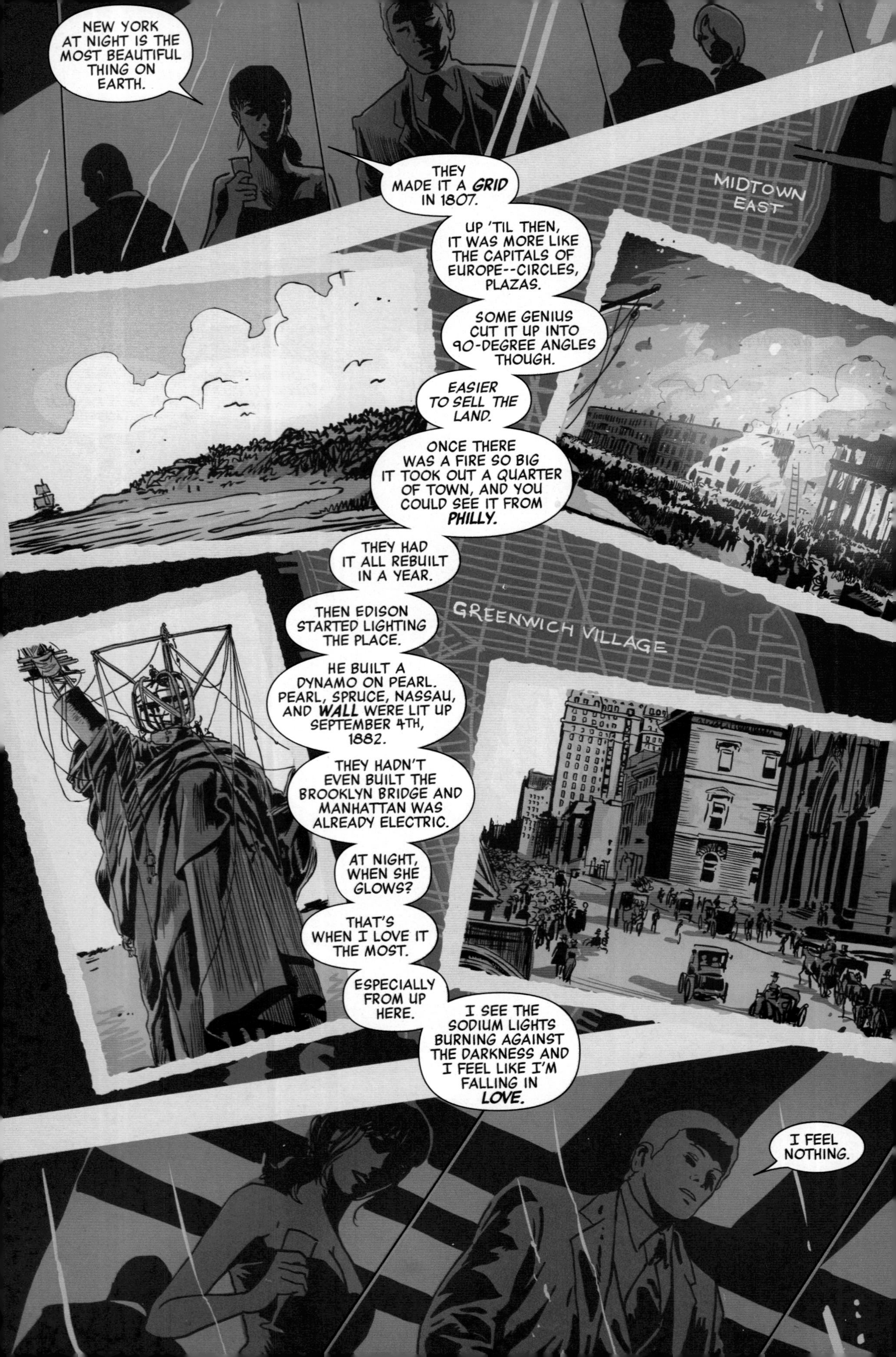
NEW YORK AT NIGHT IS THE MOST BEAUTIFUL THING ON EARTH.
THEY MADE IT A GRID IN 1807.
MIDTOWN EAST
UP 'TIL THEN, IT WAS MORE LIKE THE CAPITALS OF EUROPE--CIRCLES, PLAZAS.
SOME GENIUS CUT IT UP INTO 90-DEGREE ANGLES THOUGH.
EASIER TO SELL THE LAND.
ONCE THERE WAS A FIRE SO BIG IT TOOK OUT A QUARTER OF TOWN, AND YOU COULD SEE IT FROM PHILLY.
THEY HAD IT ALL REBUILT IN A YEAR.
GREENWICH VILLAGE
THEN EDISON STARTED LIGHTING THE PLACE.
HE BUILT A DYNAMO ON PEARL. PEARL, SPRUCE, NASSAU, AND WALL WERE LIT UP SEPTEMBER 4TH, 1882.
THEY HADN'T EVEN BUILT THE BROOKLYN BRIDGE AND MANHATTAN WAS ALREADY ELECTRIC.
AT NIGHT, WHEN SHE GLOWS?
THAT'S WHEN I LOVE IT THE MOST.
ESPECIALLY FROM UP HERE.
I SEE THE SODIUM LIGHTS BURNING AGAINST THE DARKNESS AND I FEEL LIKE I'M FALLING IN LOVE.
I FEEL NOTHING.

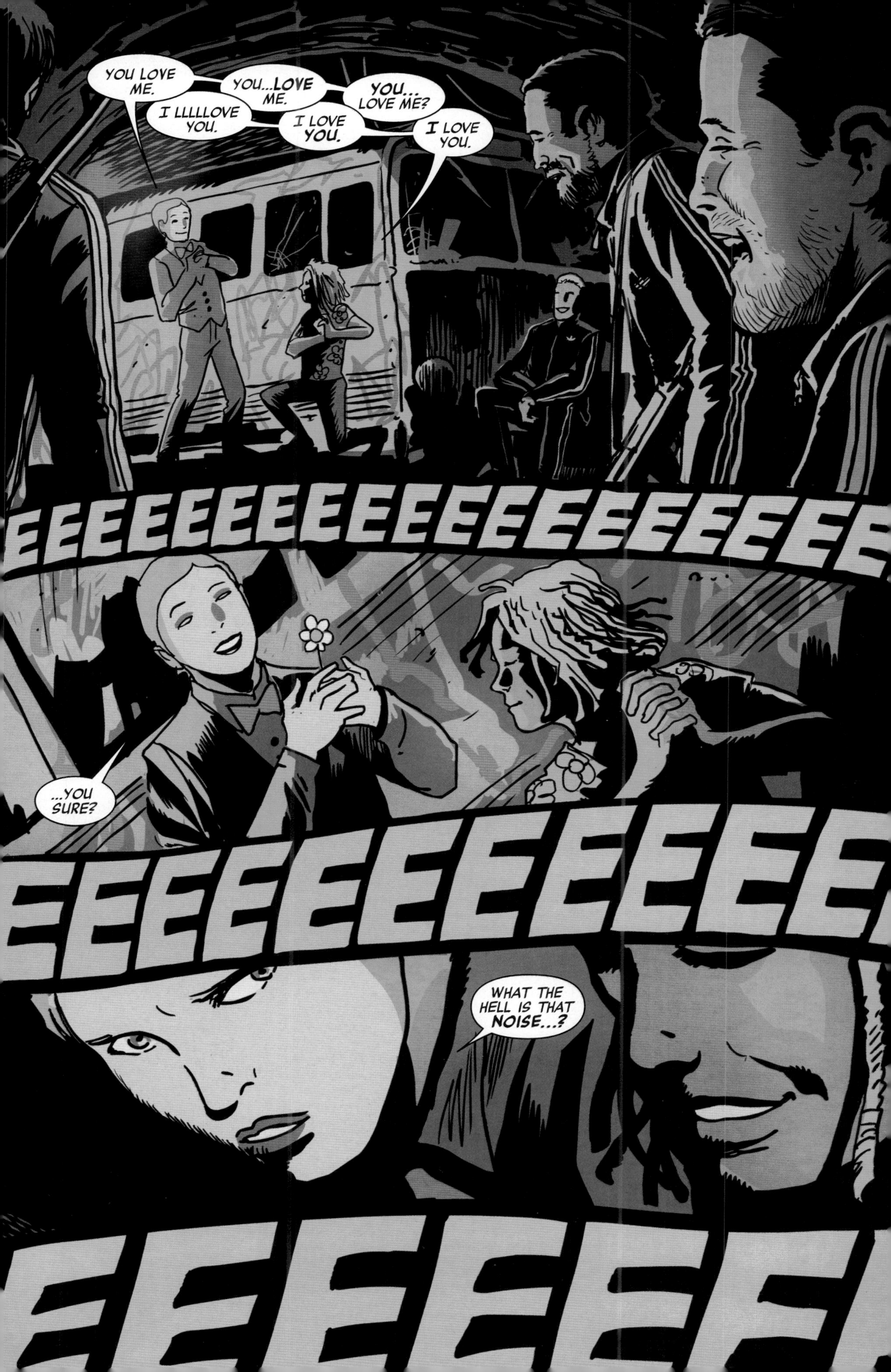
YOU LOVE ME.
I LLLLLOVE YOU.
YOU...LOVE ME.
I LOVE YOU.
YOU... LOVE ME?
I LOVE YOU.
EEEEEEEEEEEEEEEEEE
...YOU SURE?
EEEEEEEEEEEEEE
WHAT THE HELL IS THAT NOISE...?
EEEEEEEE

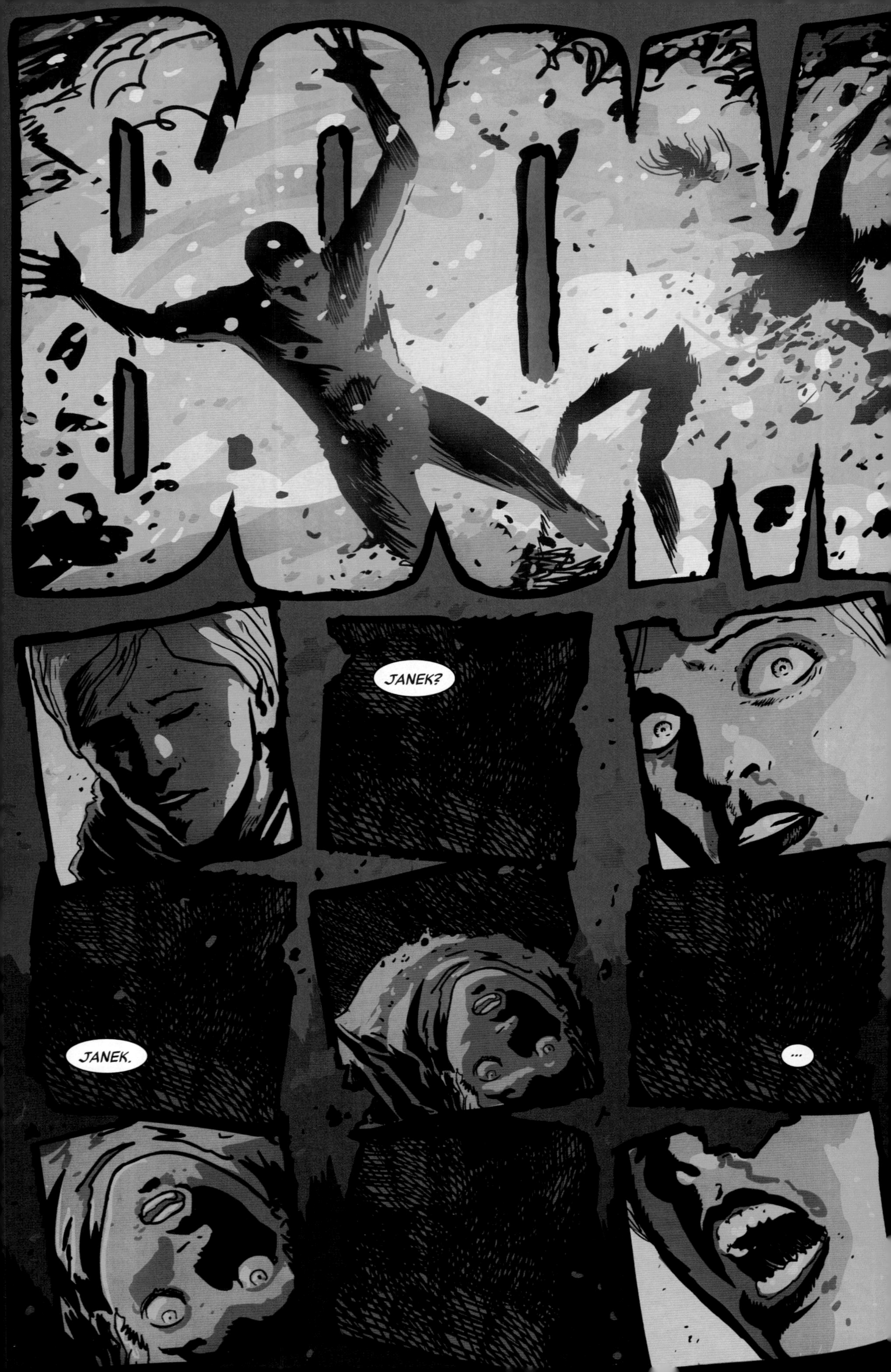
JANEK?
JANEK.
...

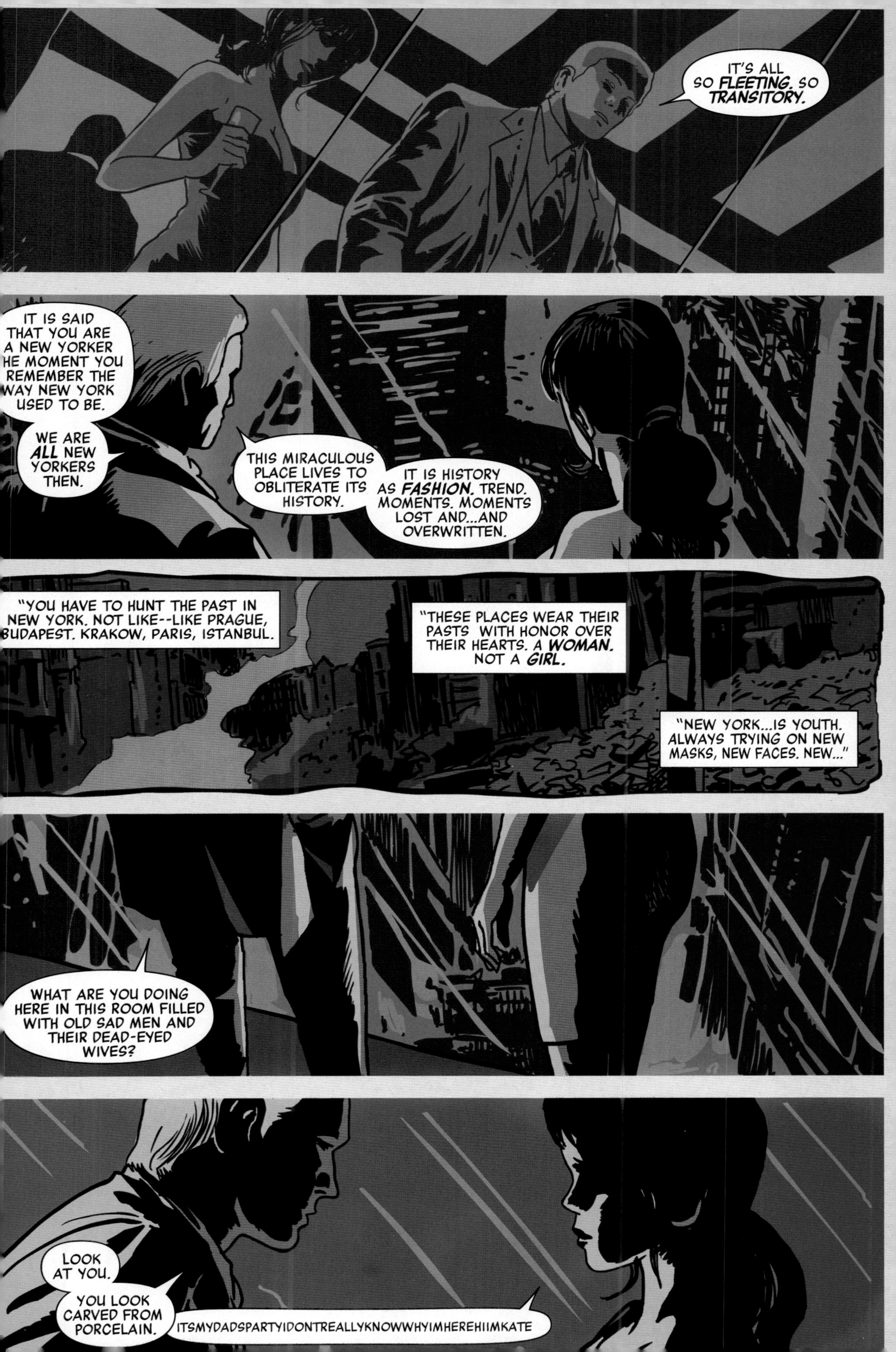
IT'S ALL SO FLEETING. SO TRANSITORY.
IT IS SAID THAT YOU ARE A NEW YORKER HE MOMENT YOU REMEMBER THE WAY NEW YORK USED TO BE.
WE ARE ALL NEW YORKERS THEN.
THIS MIRACULOUS PLACE LIVES TO OBLITERATE ITS HISTORY.
IT IS HISTORY AS FASHION. TREND. MOMENTS. MOMENTS LOST AND...AND OVERWRITTEN.
"YOU HAVE TO HUNT THE PAST IN NEW YORK. NOT LIKE--LIKE PRAGUE, BUDAPEST. KRAKOW, PARIS, ISTANBUL.
"THESE PLACES WEAR THEIR PASTS WITH HONOR OVER THEIR HEARTS. A WOMAN. NOT A GIRL.
"NEW YORK...IS YOUTH. ALWAYS TRYING ON NEW MASKS, NEW FACES. NEW..."
WHAT ARE YOU DOING HERE IN THIS ROOM FILLED WITH OLD SAD MEN AND THEIR DEAD-EYED WIVES?
LOOK AT YOU.
YOU LOOK CARVED FROM PORCELAIN.
ITSMYDADSPARTYIDONTREALLYKNOWWHYIMHEREHIIMKATE

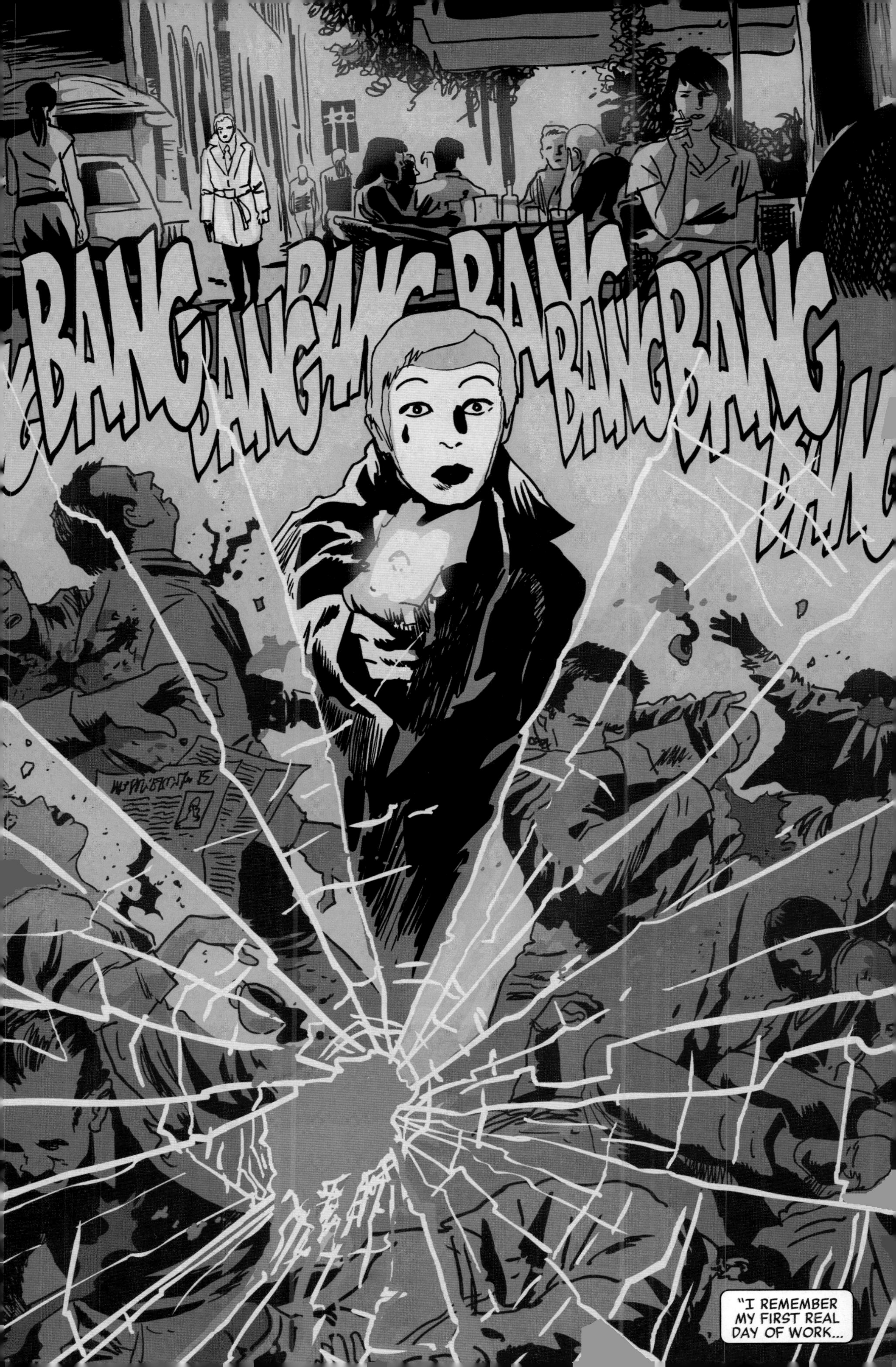
BANG
BANG
BANG
BANG
BANG
BANG
BANG
"I REMEMBER MY FIRST REAL DAY OF WORK...

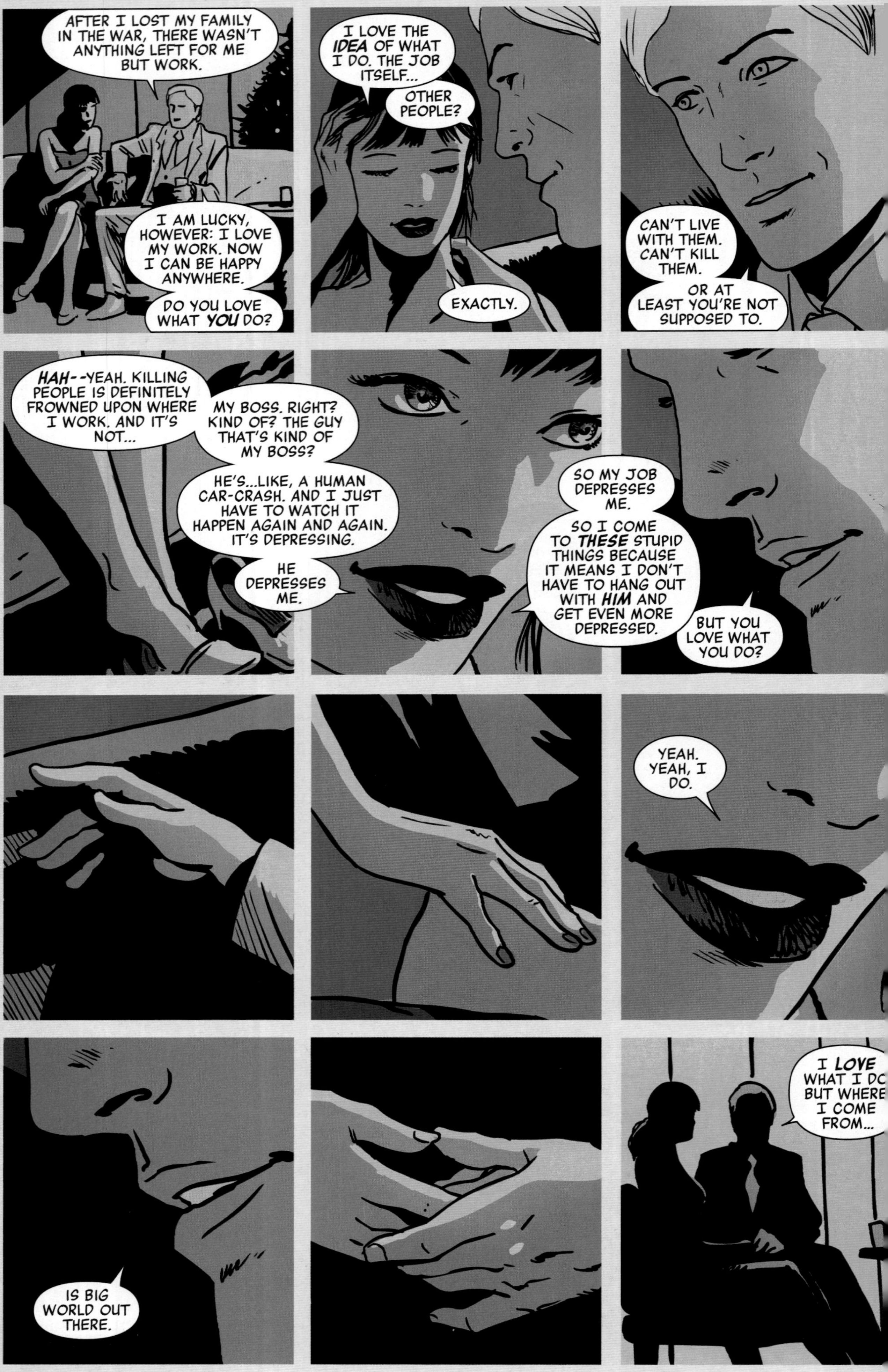

AFTER I LOST MY FAMILY IN THE WAR, THERE WASN'T ANYTHING LEFT FOR ME BUT WORK.
I AM LUCKY, HOWEVER: I LOVE MY WORK. NOW I CAN BE HAPPY ANYWHERE.
DO YOU LOVE WHAT YOU DO?
I LOVE THE IDEA OF WHAT I DO. THE JOB ITSELF...
OTHER PEOPLE?
EXACTLY.
CAN'T LIVE WITH THEM. CAN'T KILL THEM.
OR AT LEAST YOU'RE NOT SUPPOSED TO.
HAH--YEAH. KILLING PEOPLE IS DEFINITELY FROWNED UPON WHERE I WORK. AND IT'S NOT...
MY BOSS. RIGHT? KIND OF? THE GUY THAT'S KIND OF MY BOSS?
HE'S...LIKE, A HUMAN CAR-CRASH. AND I JUST HAVE TO WATCH IT HAPPEN AGAIN AND AGAIN. IT'S DEPRESSING.
HE DEPRESSES ME.
SO MY JOB DEPRESSES ME.
SO I COME TO THESE STUPID THINGS BECAUSE IT MEANS I DON'T HAVE TO HANG OUT WITH HIM AND GET EVEN MORE DEPRESSED.
BUT YOU LOVE WHAT YOU DO?
YEAH. YEAH, I DO.
IS BIG WORLD OUT THERE.
I LOVE WHAT I DO BUT WHERE I COME FROM...

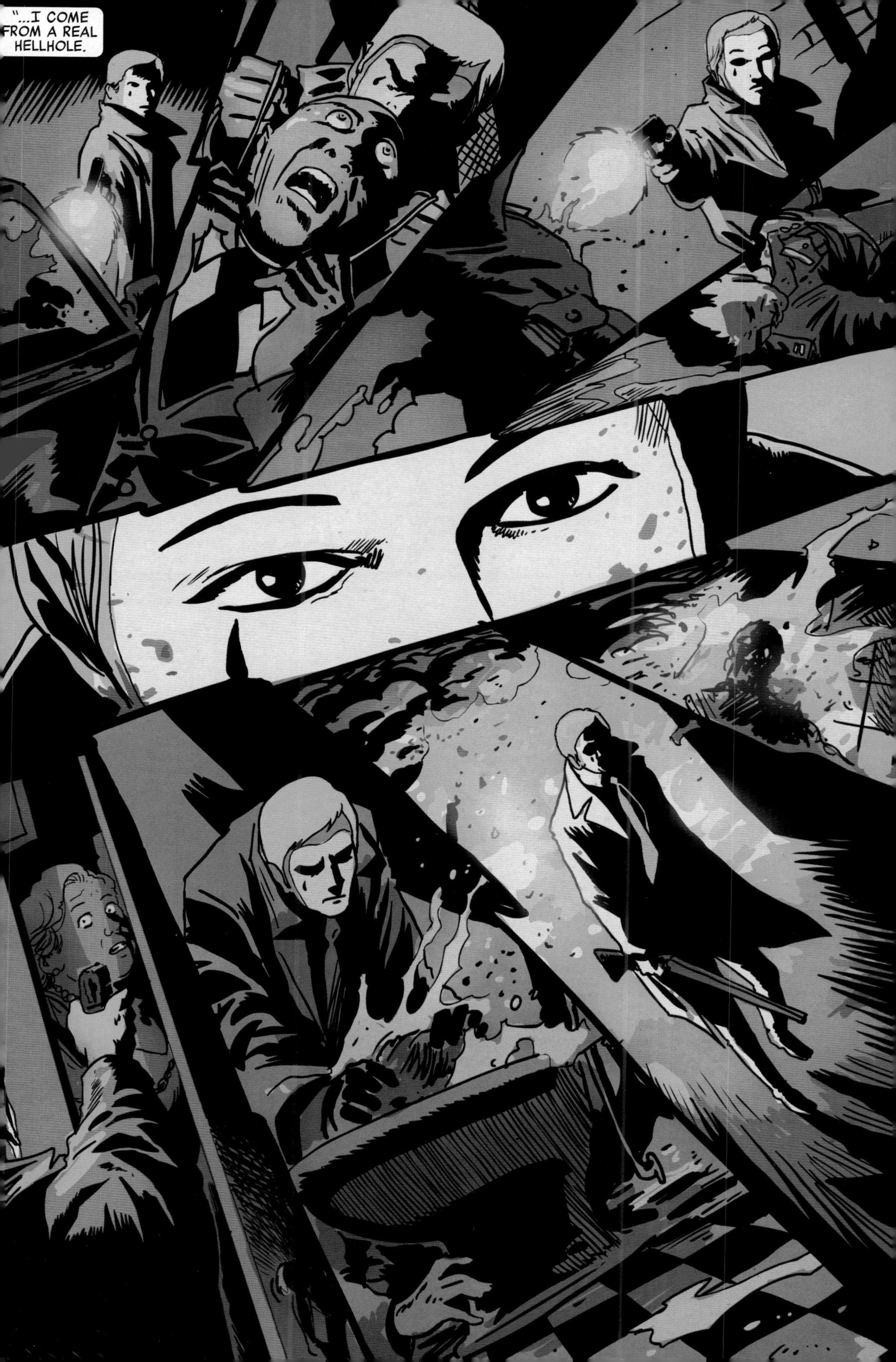
"...I COME FROM A REAL HELLHOLE.

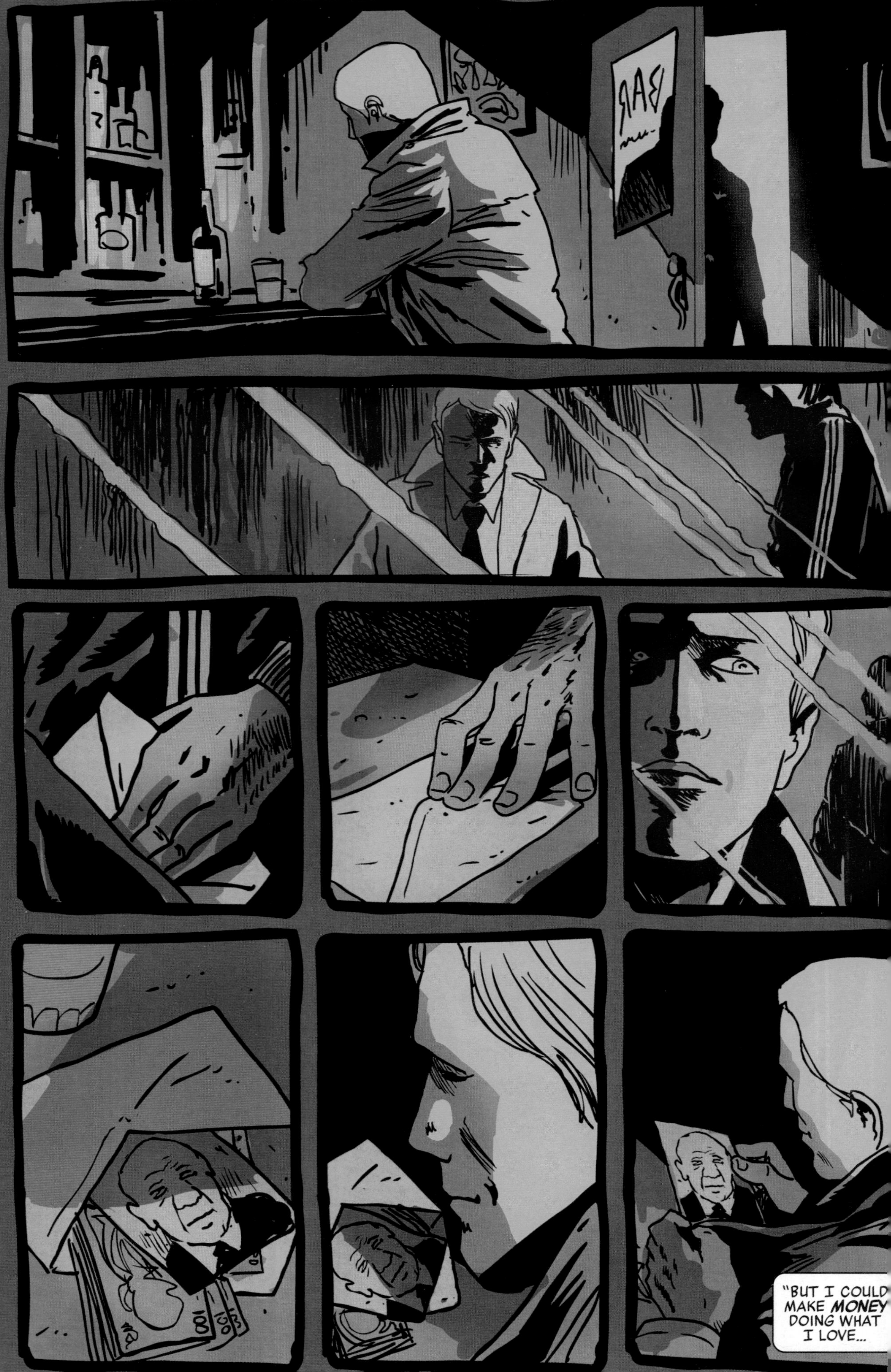
"BUT I COULD MAKE MONEY DOING WHAT I LOVE...

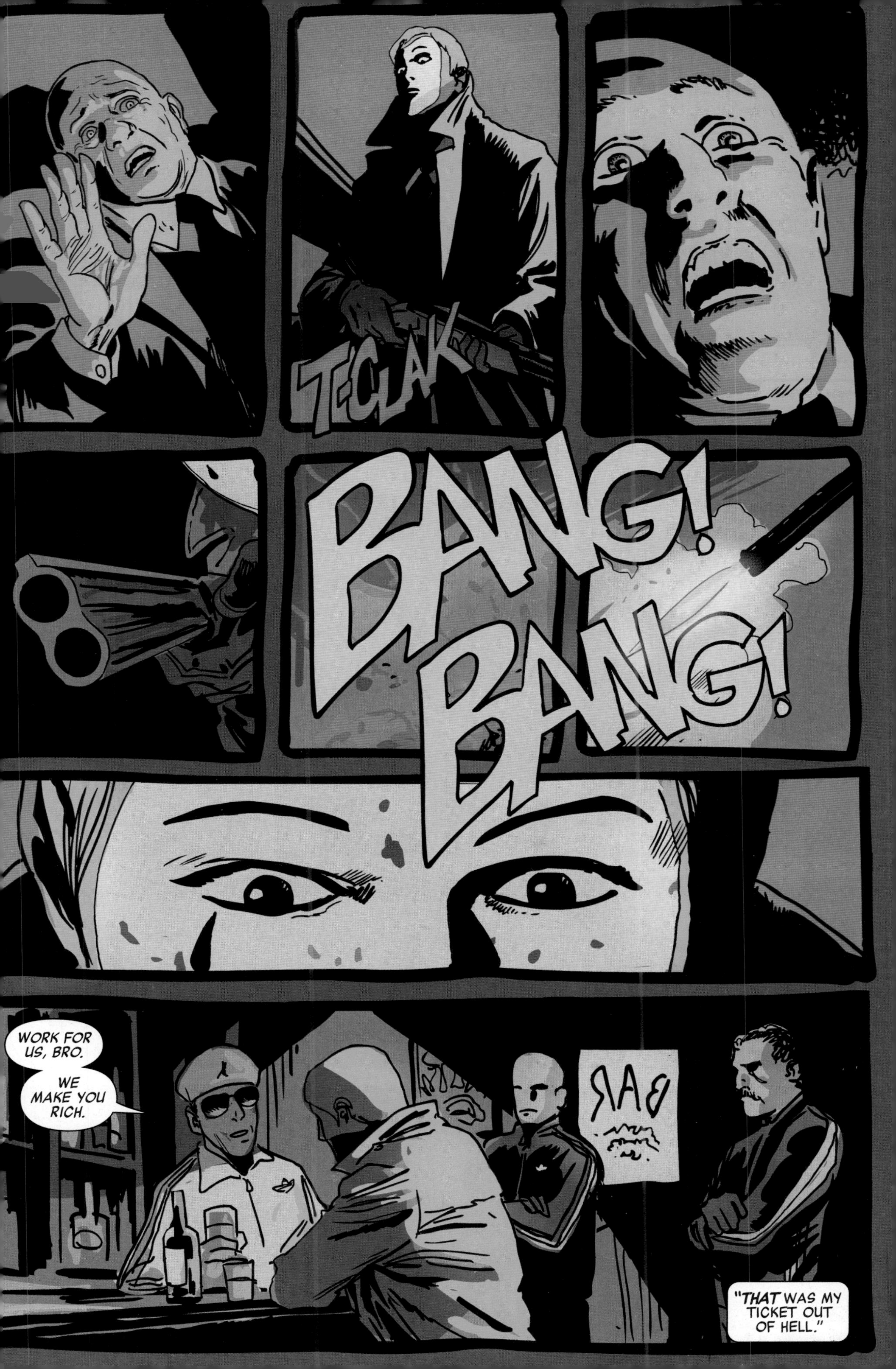

T-CLAK
BANG!
BANG!
WORK FOR US, BRO.
WE MAKE YOU RICH.
BAR
"THAT WAS MY TICKET OUT OF HELL."

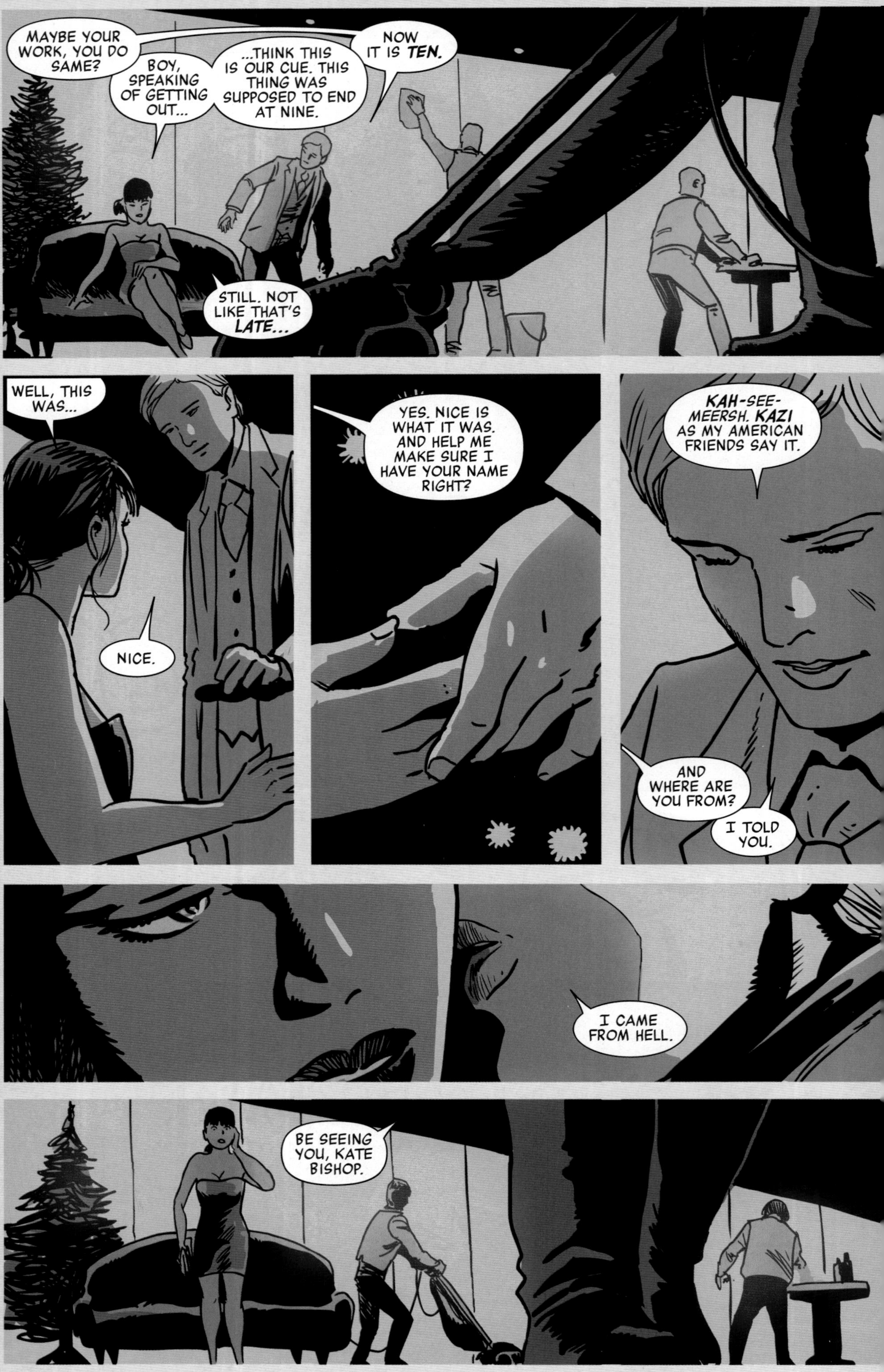
MAYBE YOUR WORK, YOU DO SAME?
BOY, SPEAKING OF GETTING OUT...
...THINK THIS IS OUR CUE. THIS THING WAS SUPPOSED TO END AT NINE.
NOW IT IS TEN.
STILL. NOT LIKE THAT'S LATE...
WELL, THIS WAS...
NICE.
YES. NICE IS WHAT IT WAS. AND HELP ME MAKE SURE I HAVE YOUR NAME RIGHT?
KAH-SEE-MEERSH. KAZI AS MY AMERICAN FRIENDS SAY IT.
AND WHERE ARE YOU FROM?
I TOLD YOU.
I CAME FROM HELL.
BE SEEING YOU, KATE BISHOP.

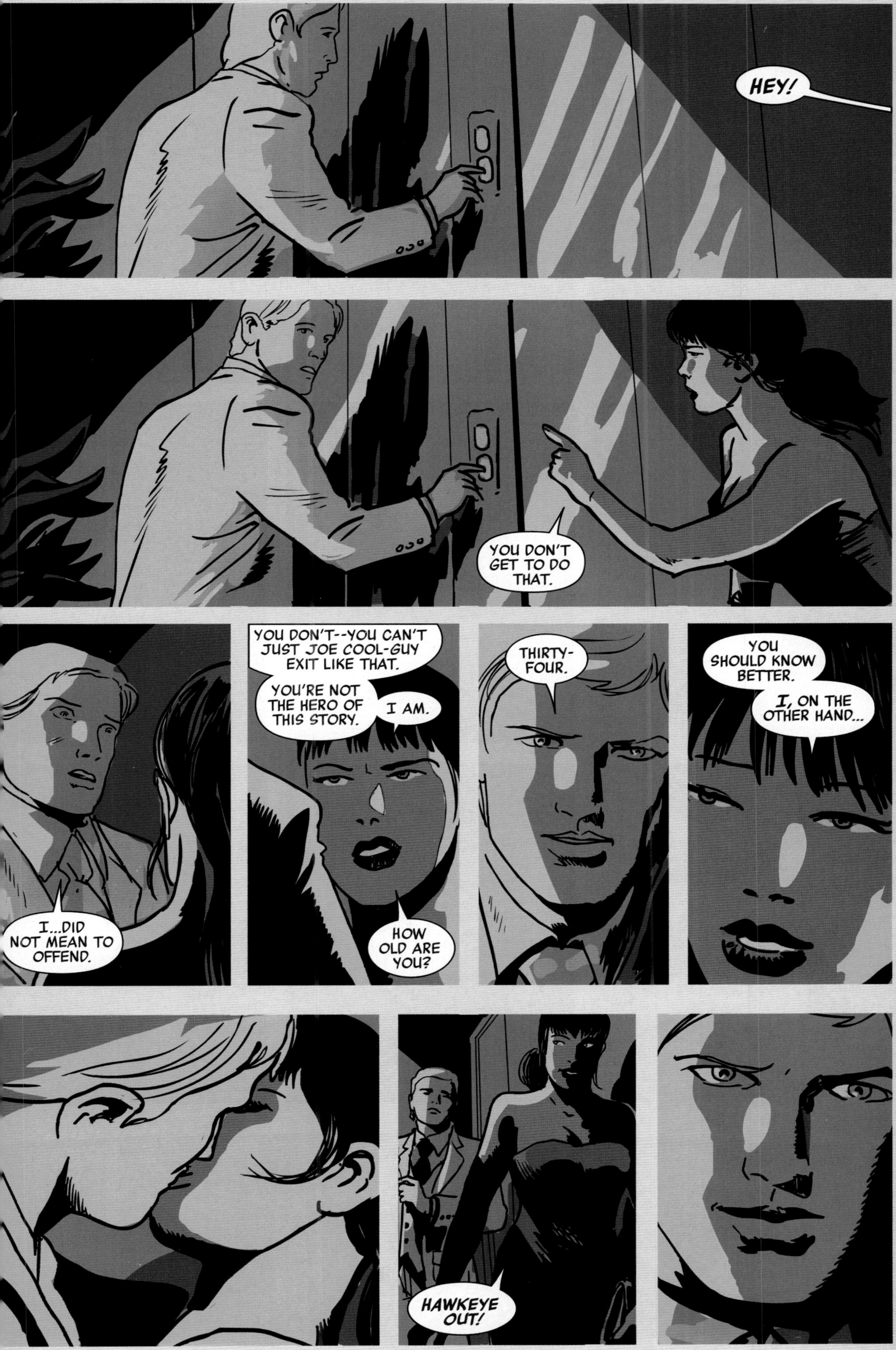
HEY!
YOU DON'T GET TO DO THAT.
I...DID NOT MEAN TO OFFEND.
YOU DON'T--YOU CAN'T JUST JOE COOL-GUY EXIT LIKE THAT.
YOU'RE NOT THE HERO OF THIS STORY.
I AM.
HOW OLD ARE YOU?
THIRTY-FOUR.
YOU SHOULD KNOW BETTER.
I, ON THE OTHER HAND...
HAWKEYE OUT!

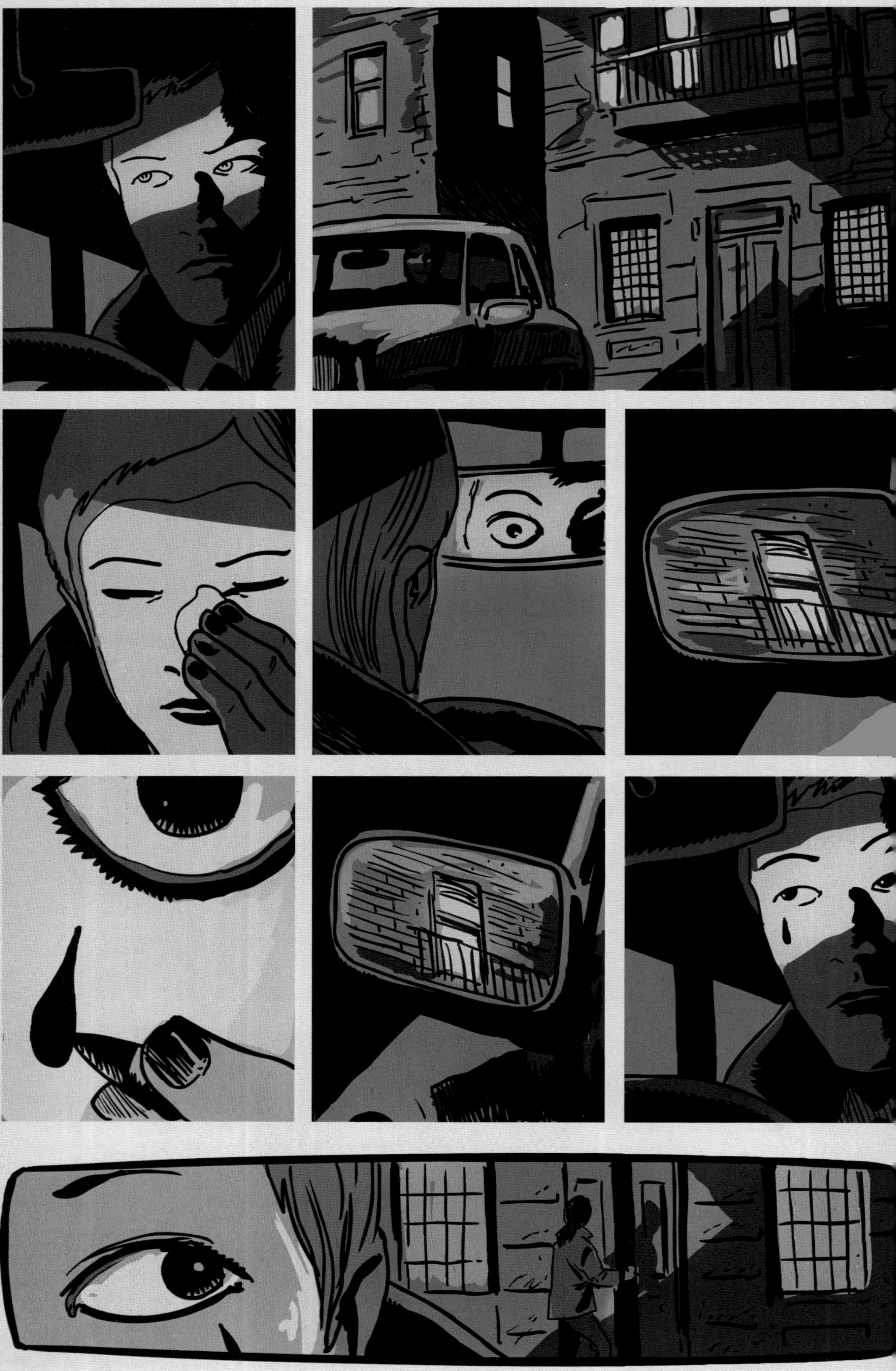

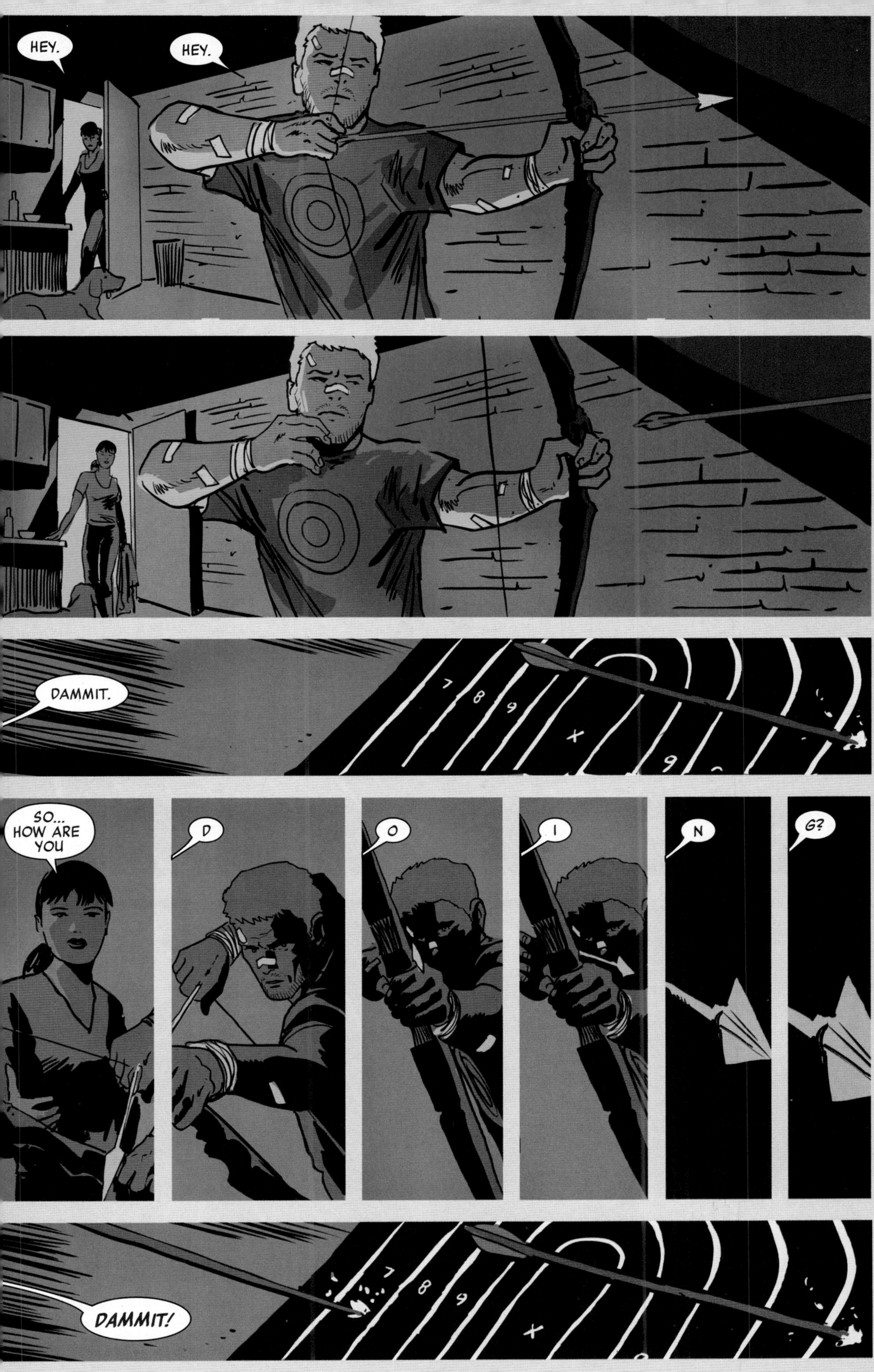
HEY.
HEY.
DAMMIT.
SO... HOW ARE YOU
D
O
I
N
G?
DAMMIT!

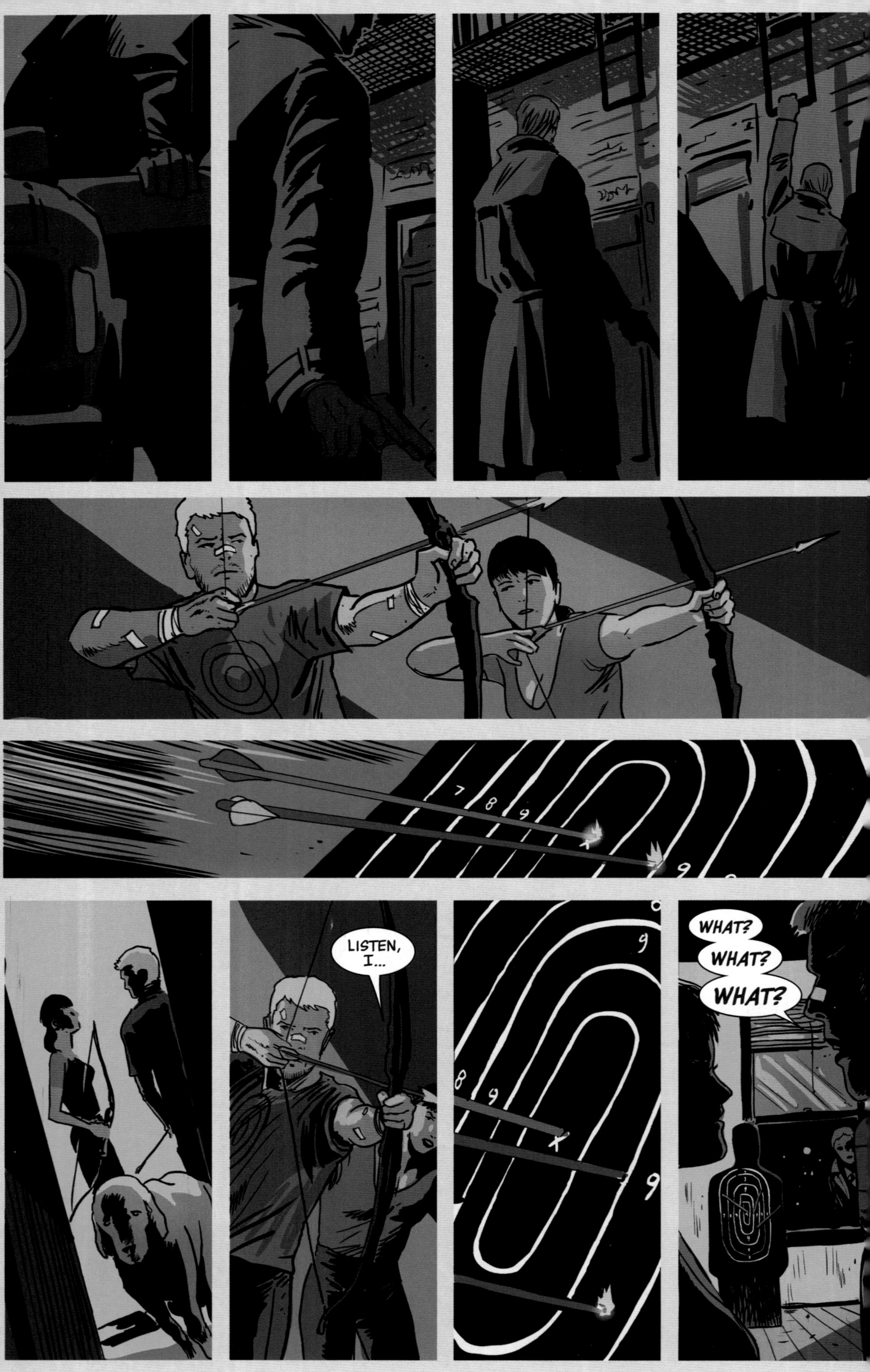
LISTEN, I...
WHAT?
WHAT?
WHAT?

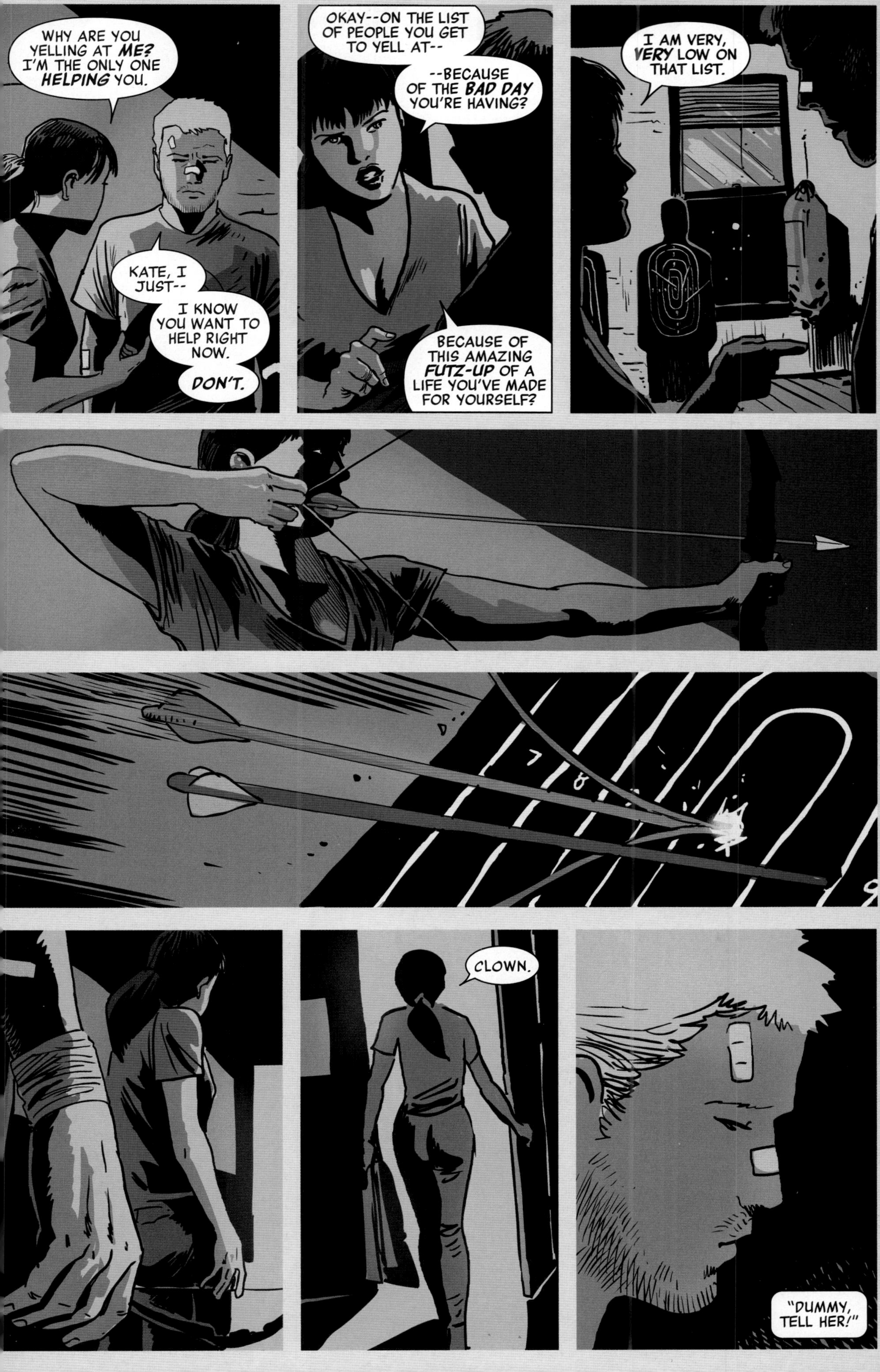
WHY ARE YOU YELLING AT ME? I'M THE ONLY ONE HELPING YOU.
KATE, I JUST--
I KNOW YOU WANT TO HELP RIGHT NOW.
DON'T.
OKAY--ON THE LIST OF PEOPLE YOU GET TO YELL AT--
--BECAUSE OF THE BAD DAY YOU'RE HAVING?
BECAUSE OF THIS AMAZING FUTZ-UP OF A LIFE YOU'VE MADE FOR YOURSELF?
I AM VERY, VERY LOW ON THAT LIST.
CLOWN.
"DUMMY, TELL HER!"

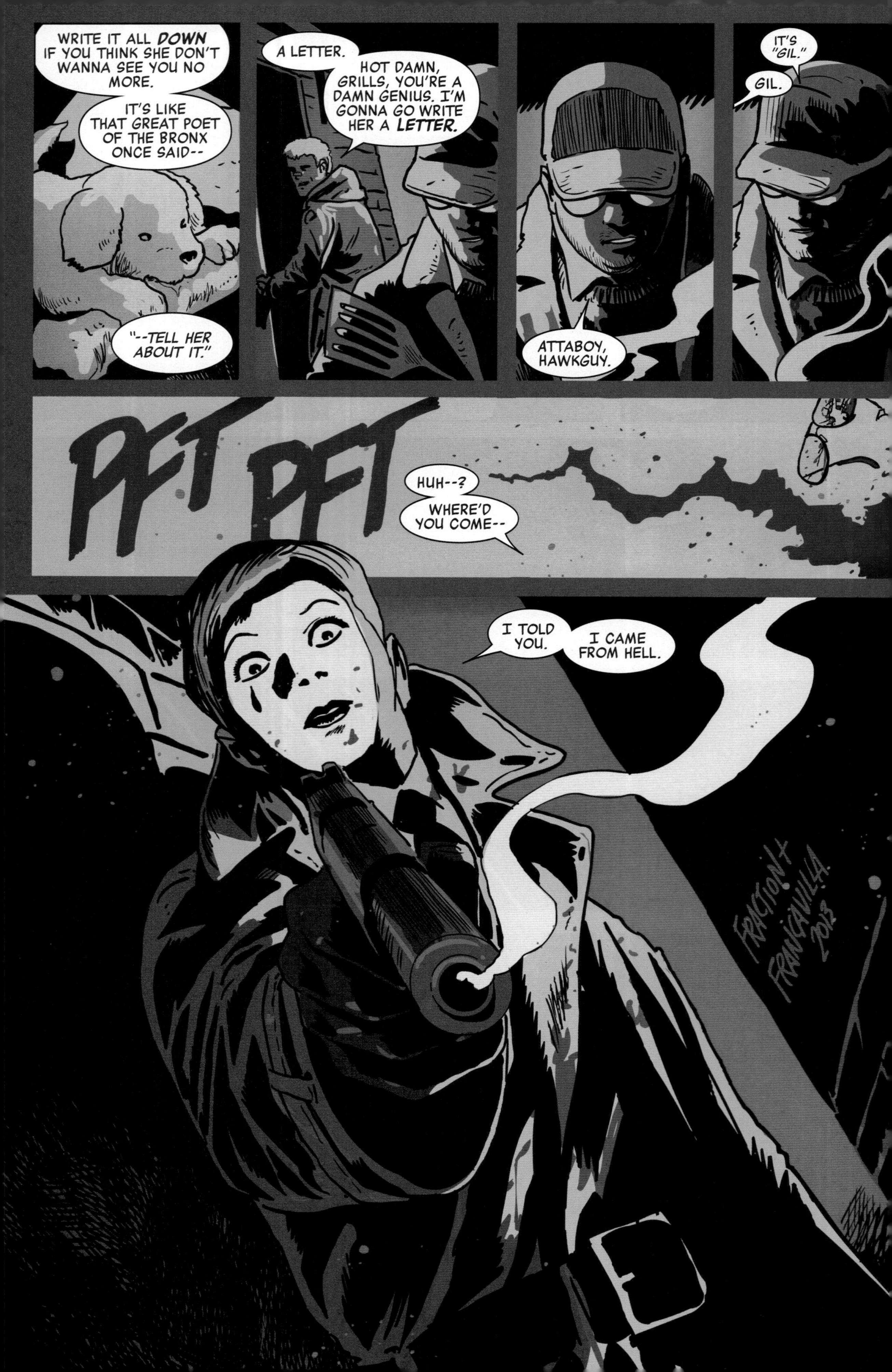

WRITE IT ALL DOWN IF YOU THINK SHE DON'T WANNA SEE YOU NO MORE.
IT'S LIKE THAT GREAT POET OF THE BRONX ONCE SAID--
"--TELL HER ABOUT IT."
A LETTER.
HOT DAMN, GRILLS, YOU'RE A DAMN GENIUS. I'M GONNA GO WRITE HER A LETTER.
ATTABOY, HAWKGUY.
IT'S "GIL."
GIL.
PFT PFT
HUH--?
WHERE'D YOU COME--
I TOLD YOU.
I CAME FROM HELL.
FRACTION + FRANCAVILLA 2013

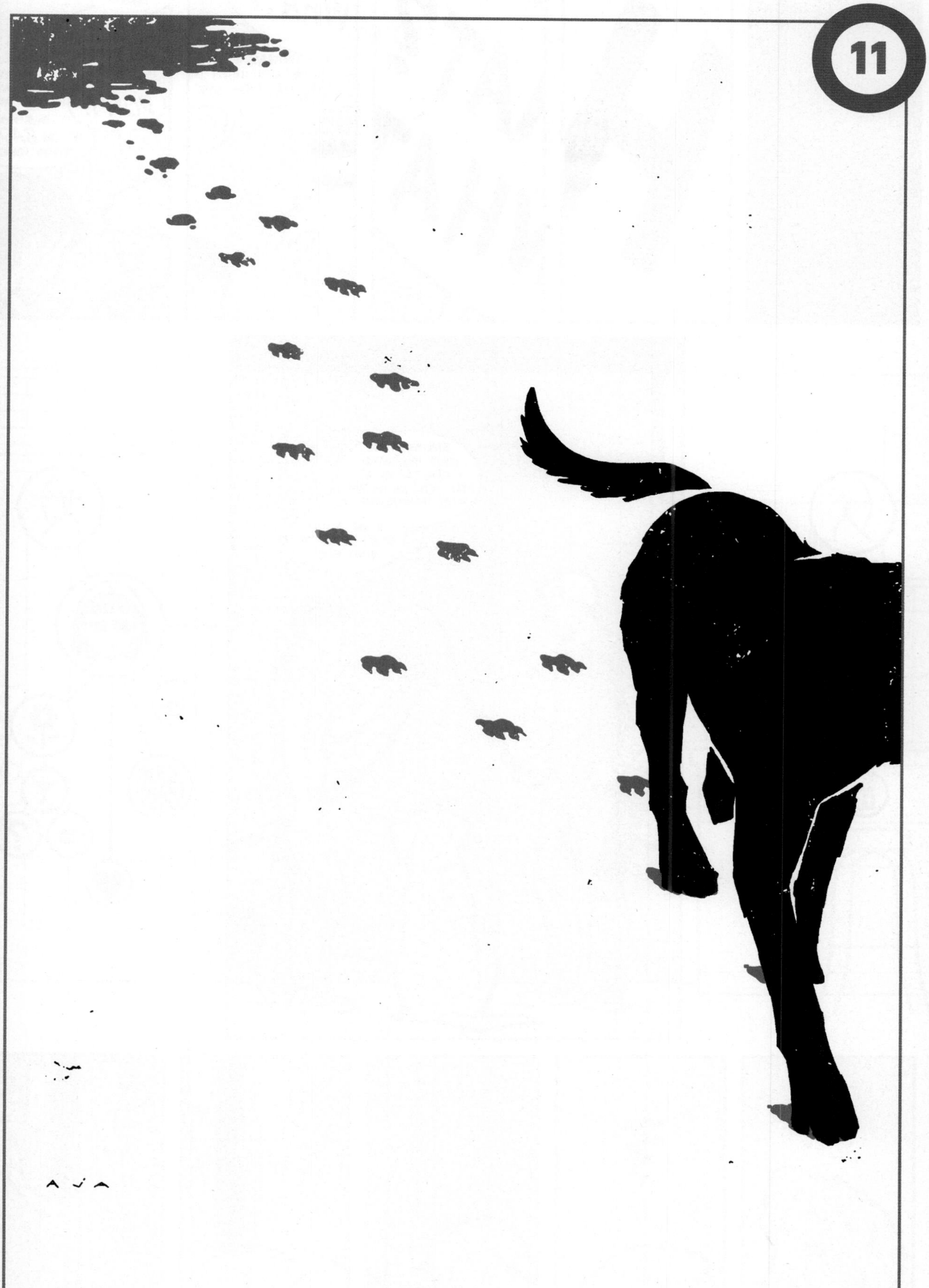

11

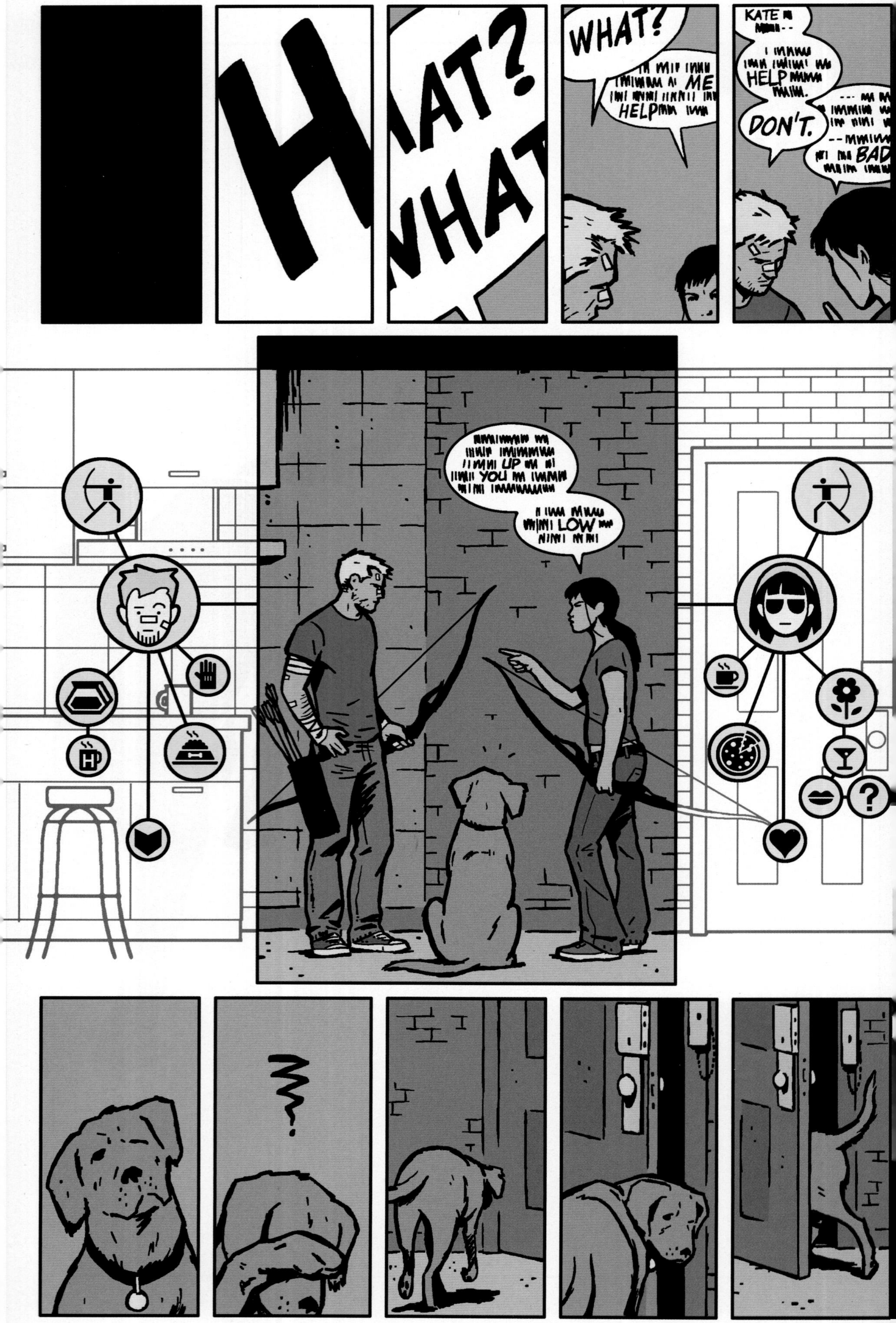
H
HAT? WHAT
WHAT?
ME
HELP
KATE
HELP
DON'T.
BAD
UP
YOU
LOW
?

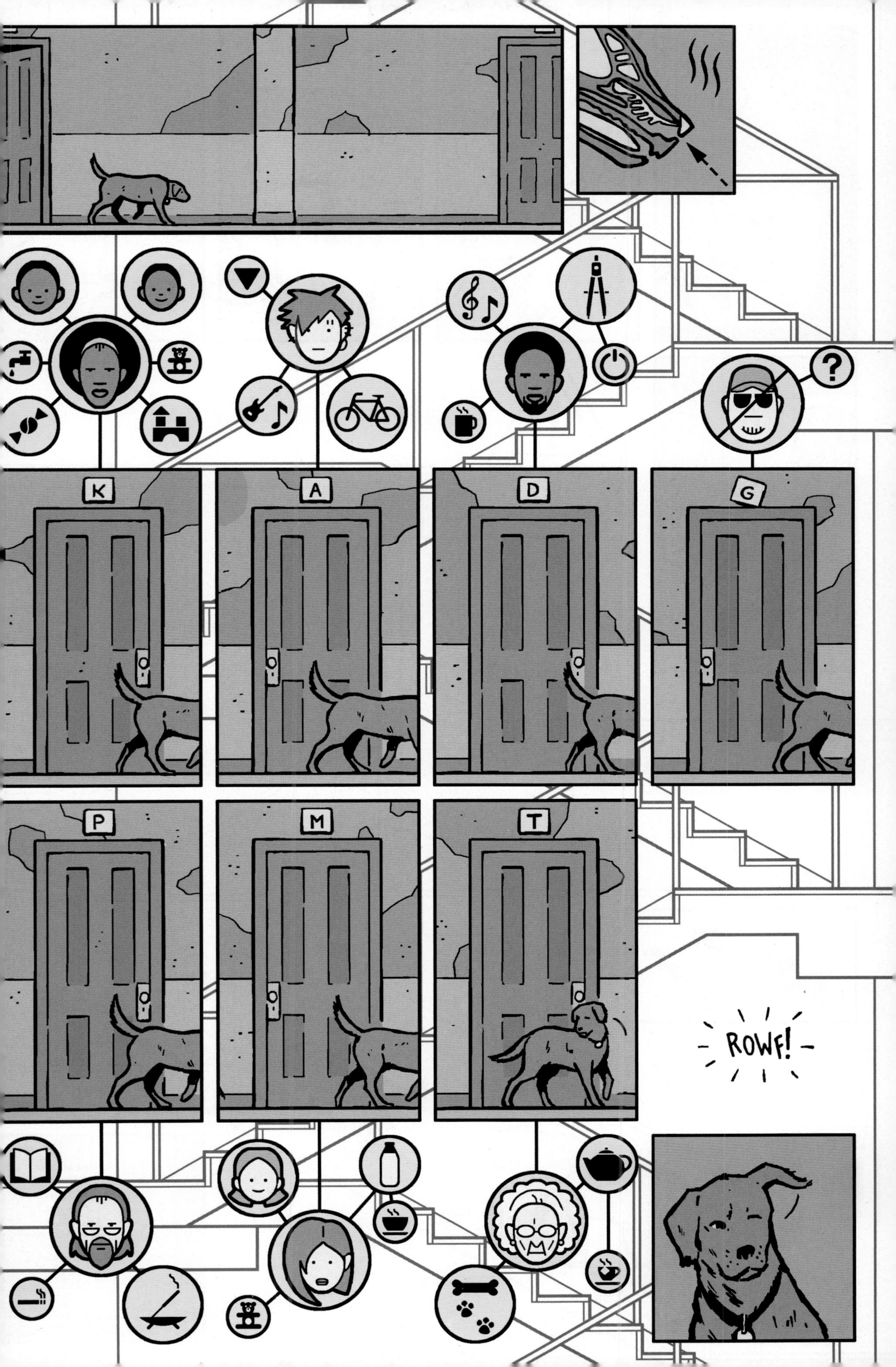
K
A
D
G
P
M
T
ROWF!

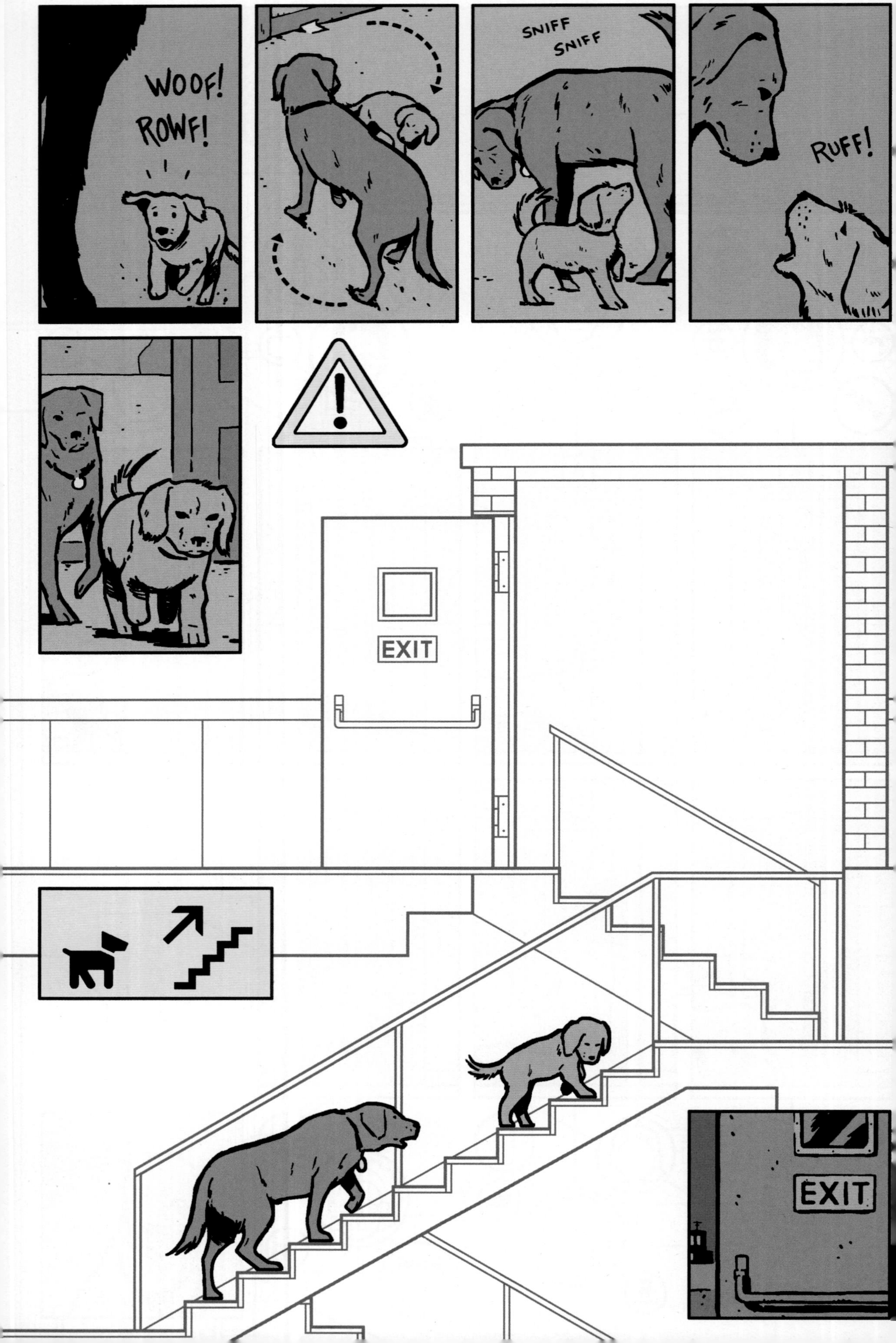
WOOF!
ROWF!
SNIFF
SNIFF
RUFF!
EXIT
EXIT

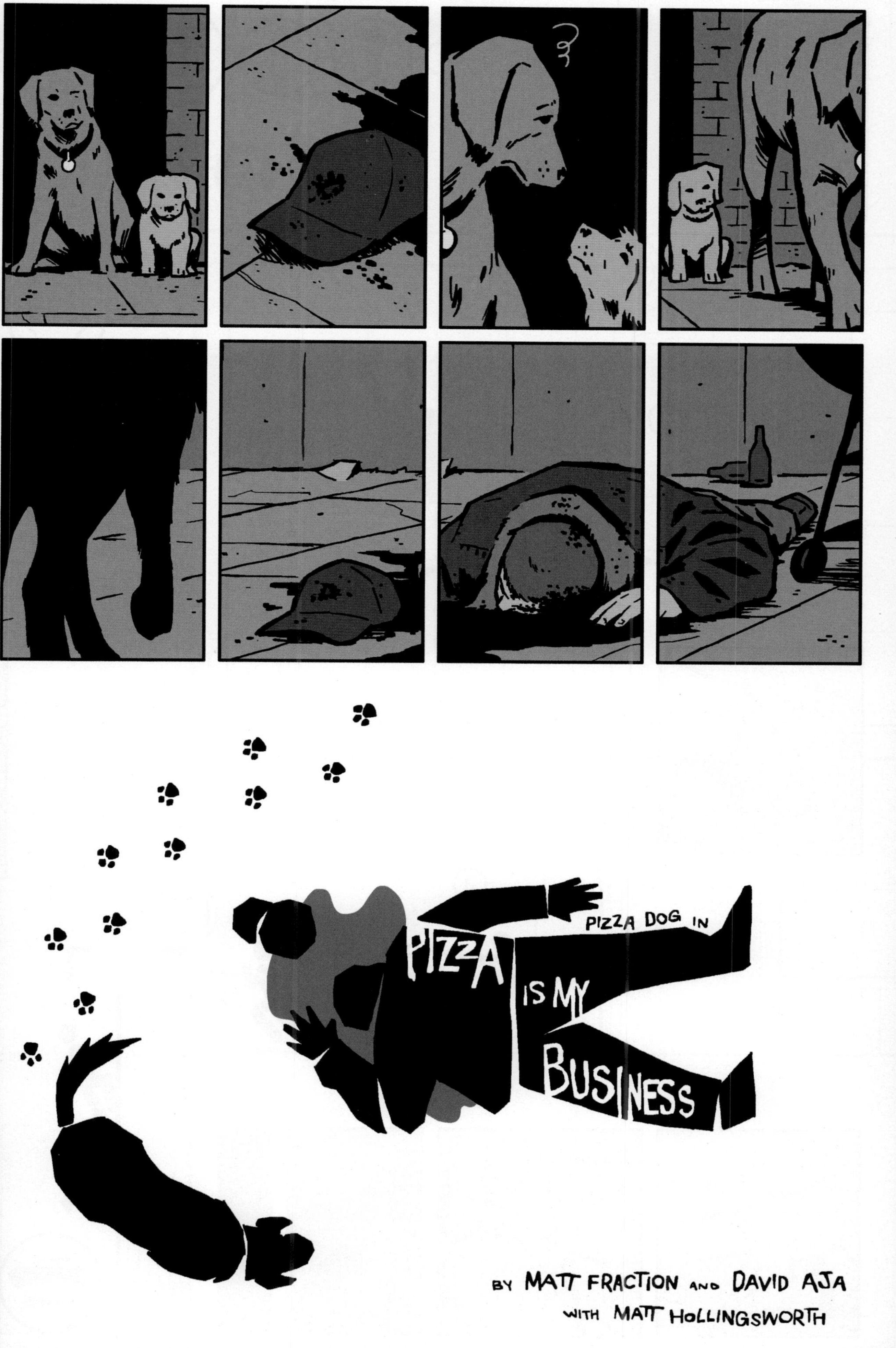
PIZZA DOG IN
PIZZA IS MY BUSINESS
BY MATT FRACTION AND DAVID AJA
WITH MATT HOLLINGSWORTH

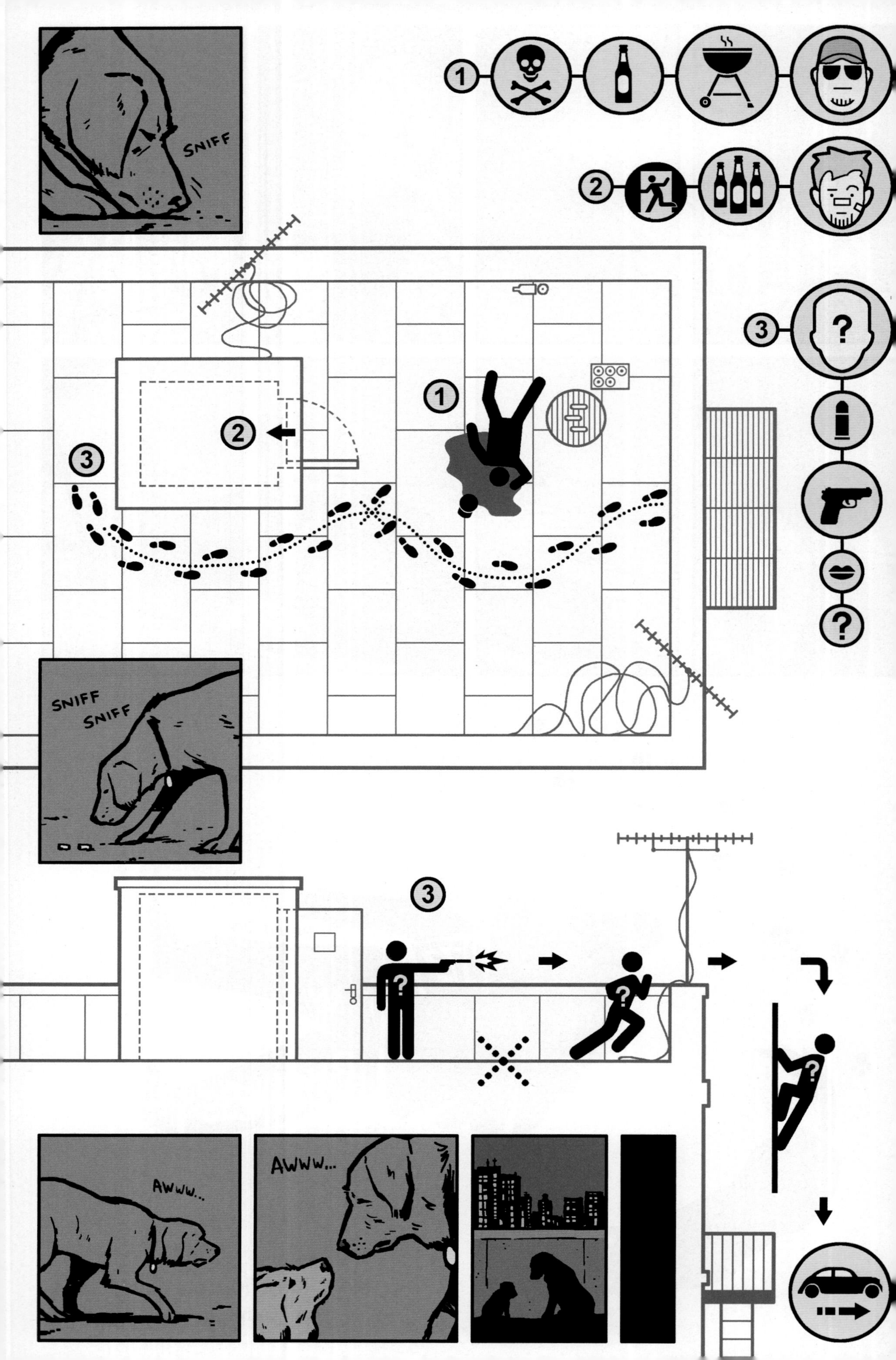
SNIFF
SNIFF
SNIFF
AWWW...
AWWW...

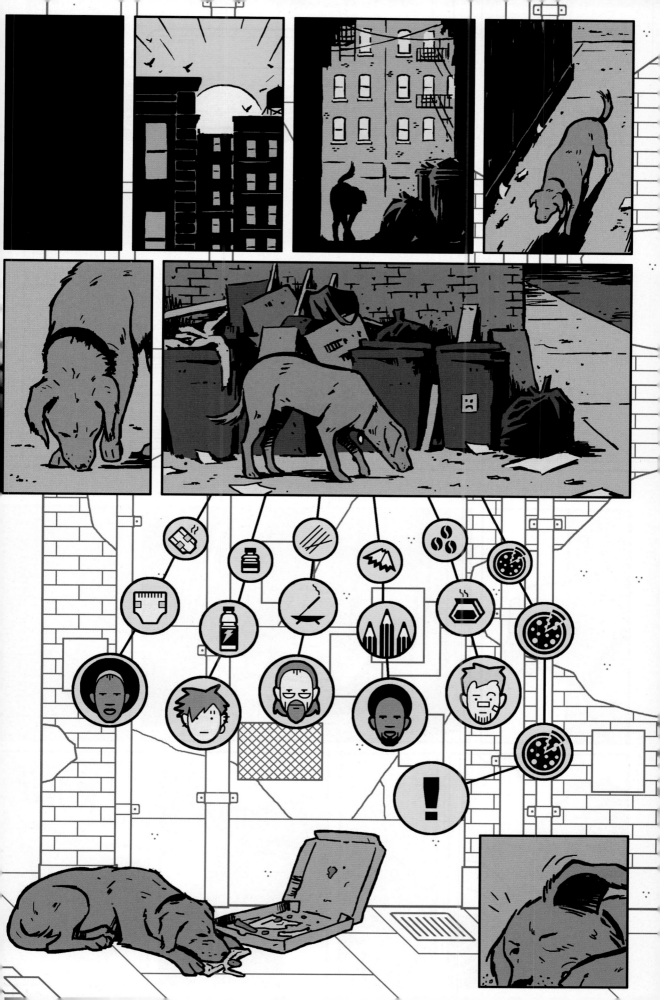

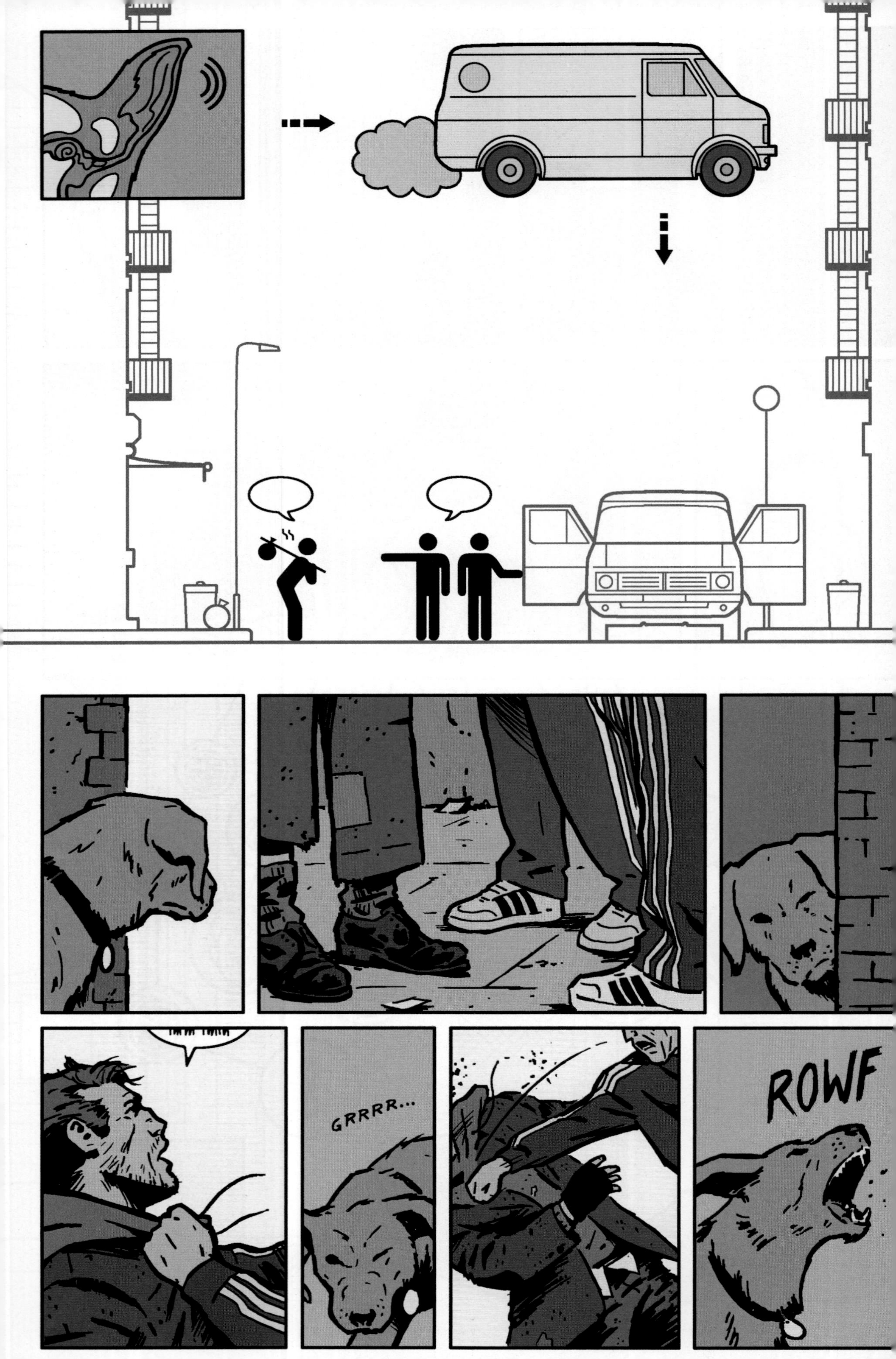
GRRRR...
ROWF

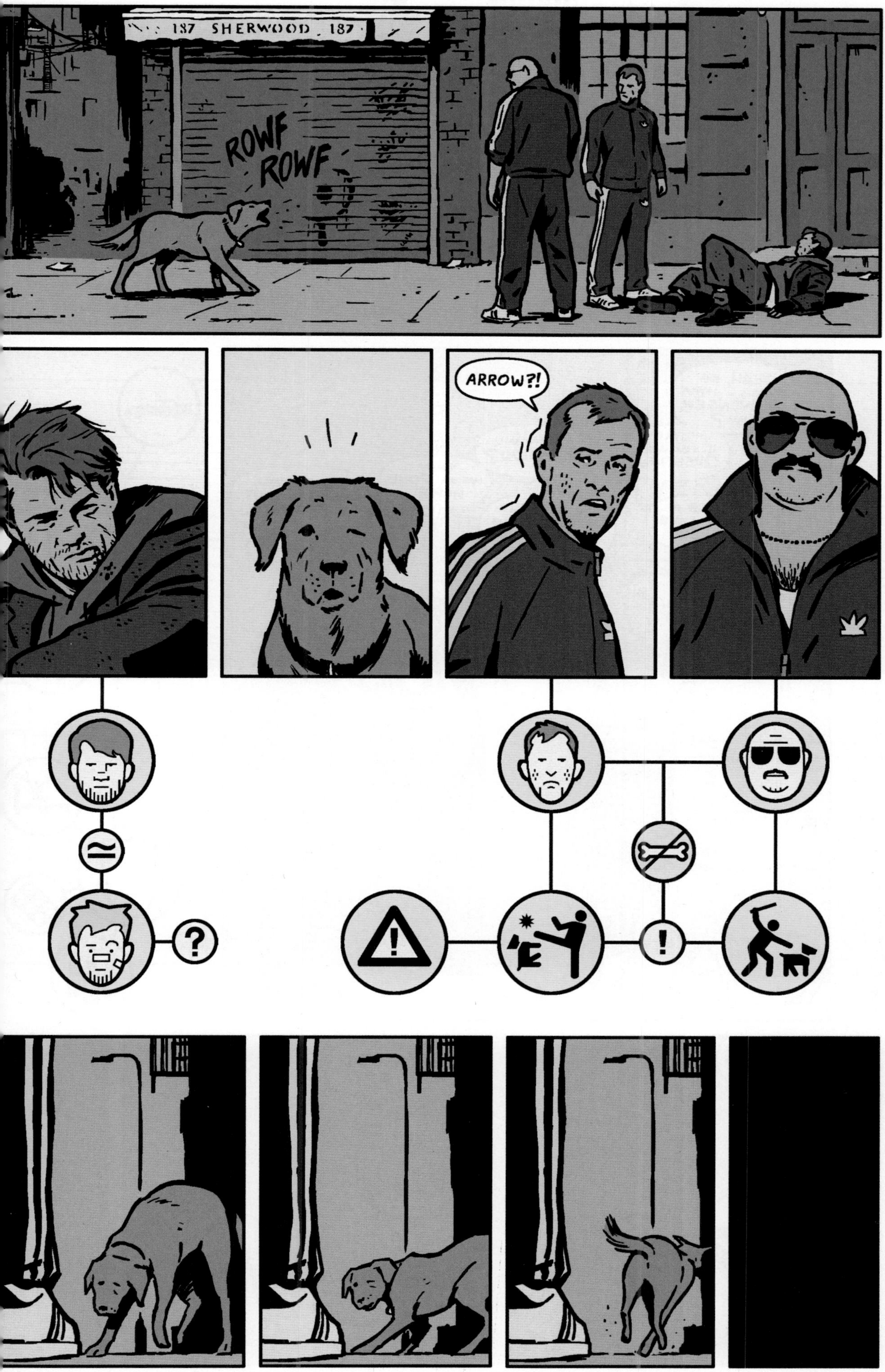
187 SHERWOOD 187
ROWF ROWF
ARROW?!

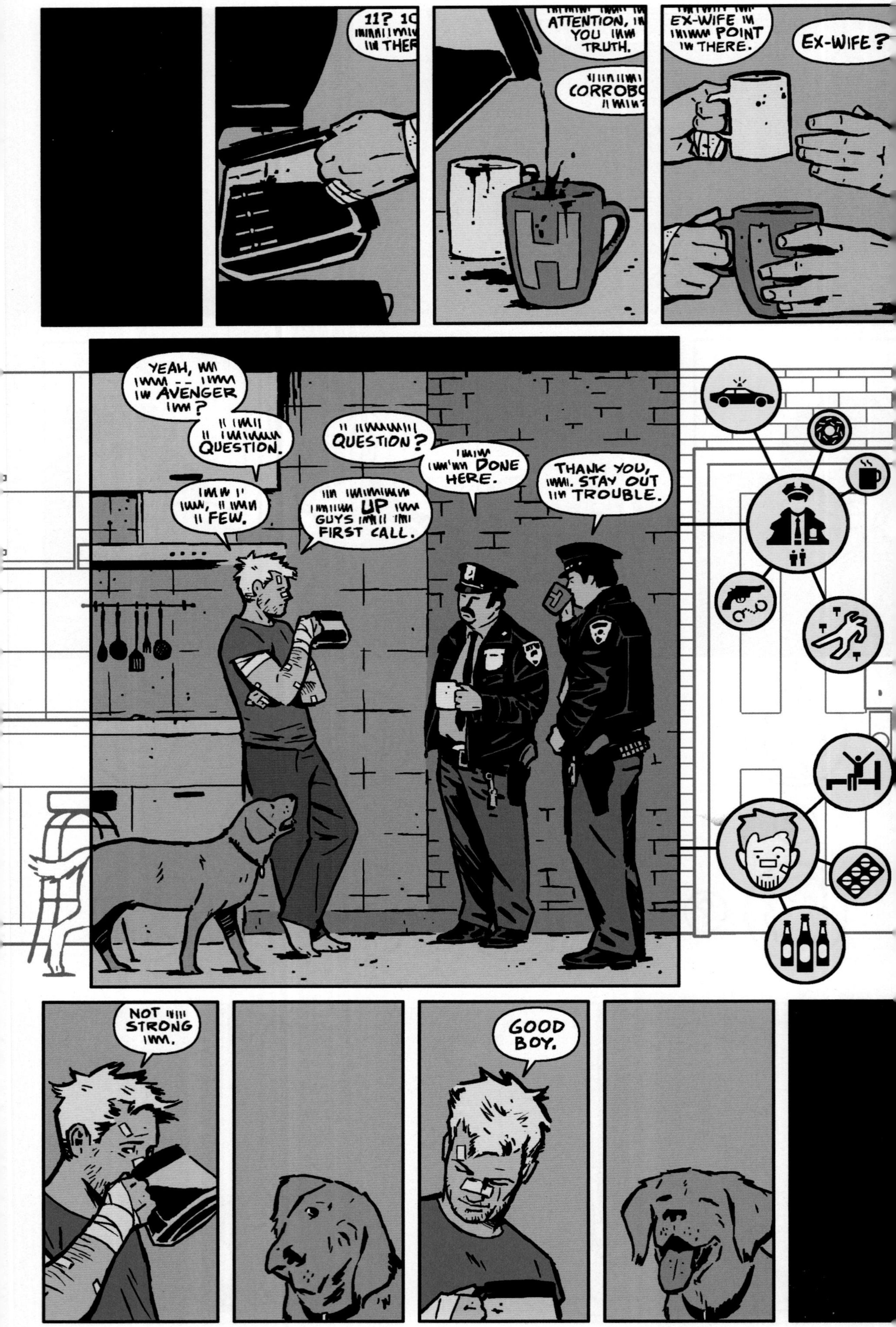

11?
ATTENTION, YOU TRUTH.
EX-WIFE POINT THERE.
EX-WIFE?
YEAH, AVENGER ?
QUESTION.
FEW.
QUESTION?
UP GUYS FIRST CALL.
DONE HERE.
THANK YOU, STAY OUT TROUBLE.
NOT STRONG
GOOD BOY.

WHAT?

I |||||| ||||| COLLAR STAYS.

CURL UP? YOU |||||| |||||| ||||| GU' NI THERE.

COLLAR STAYS.

YES. |||| |||||| COLLAR ST' IM PLACE

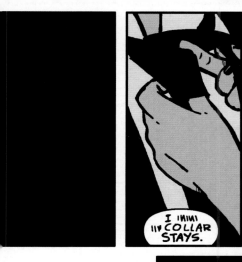

GREAT. NOW I |||||| ||||||||||| IMI WORRY ||||||| I NEVER WORRI|||| |||||| BEFORE.

|||||| ONCE -- ONCE -- I'M |||| IM GET OUT I'M HERE |||||||||| YOU |||||| II TOTAL ||||||, CLINT.

KATE--

KEEP IM EYE IM IM PLACE.

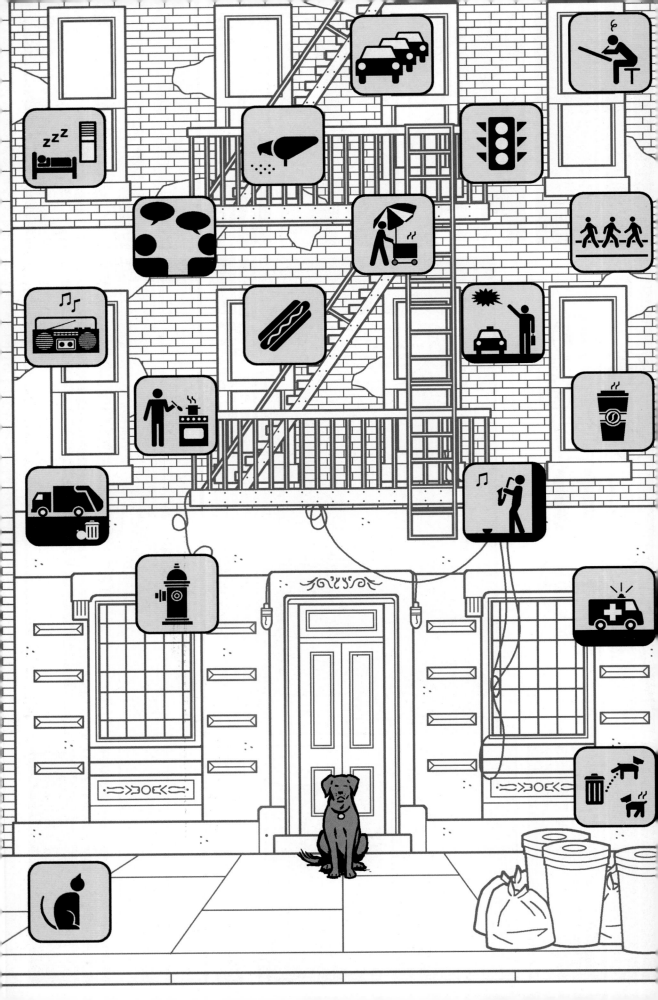

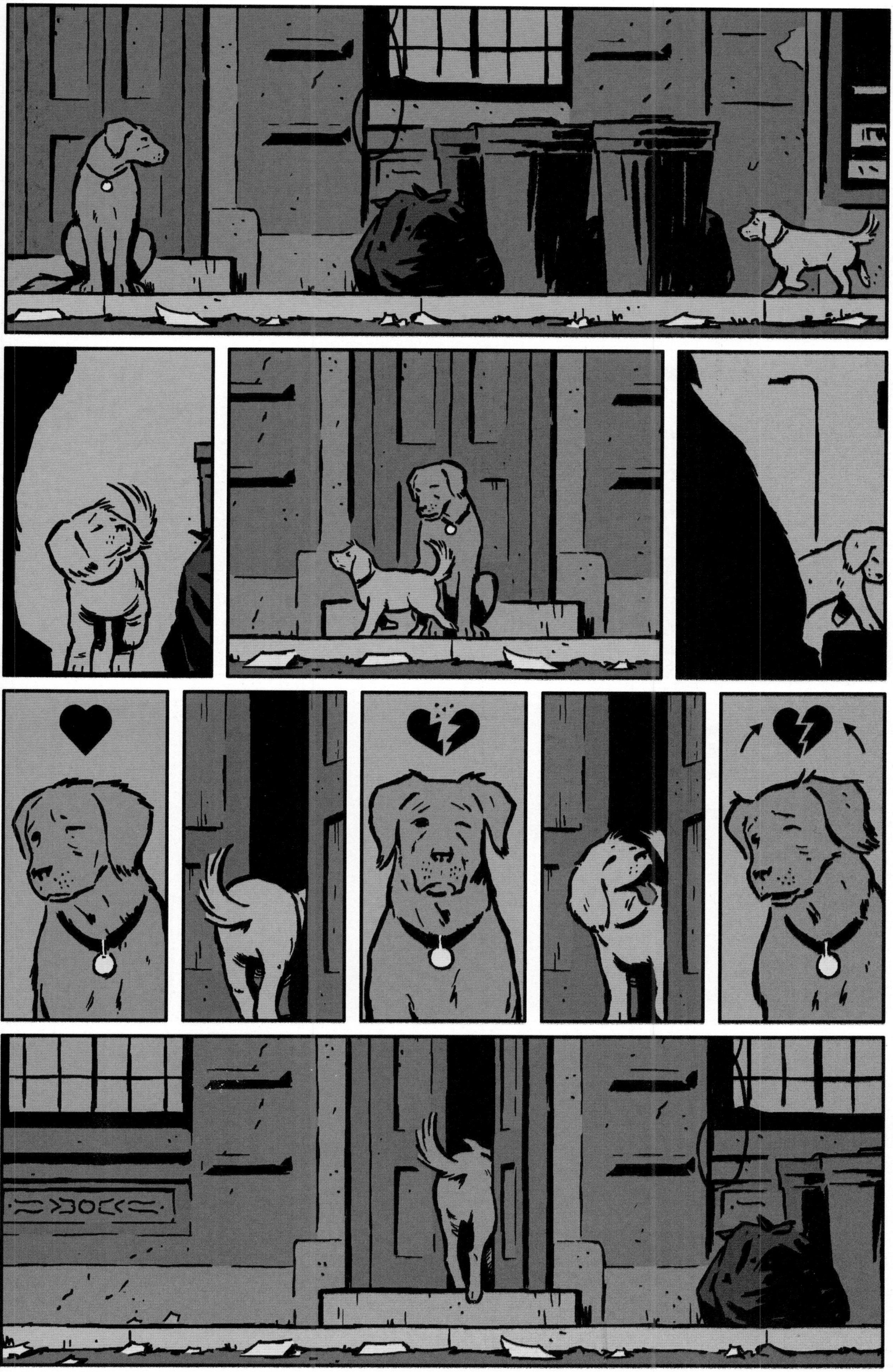

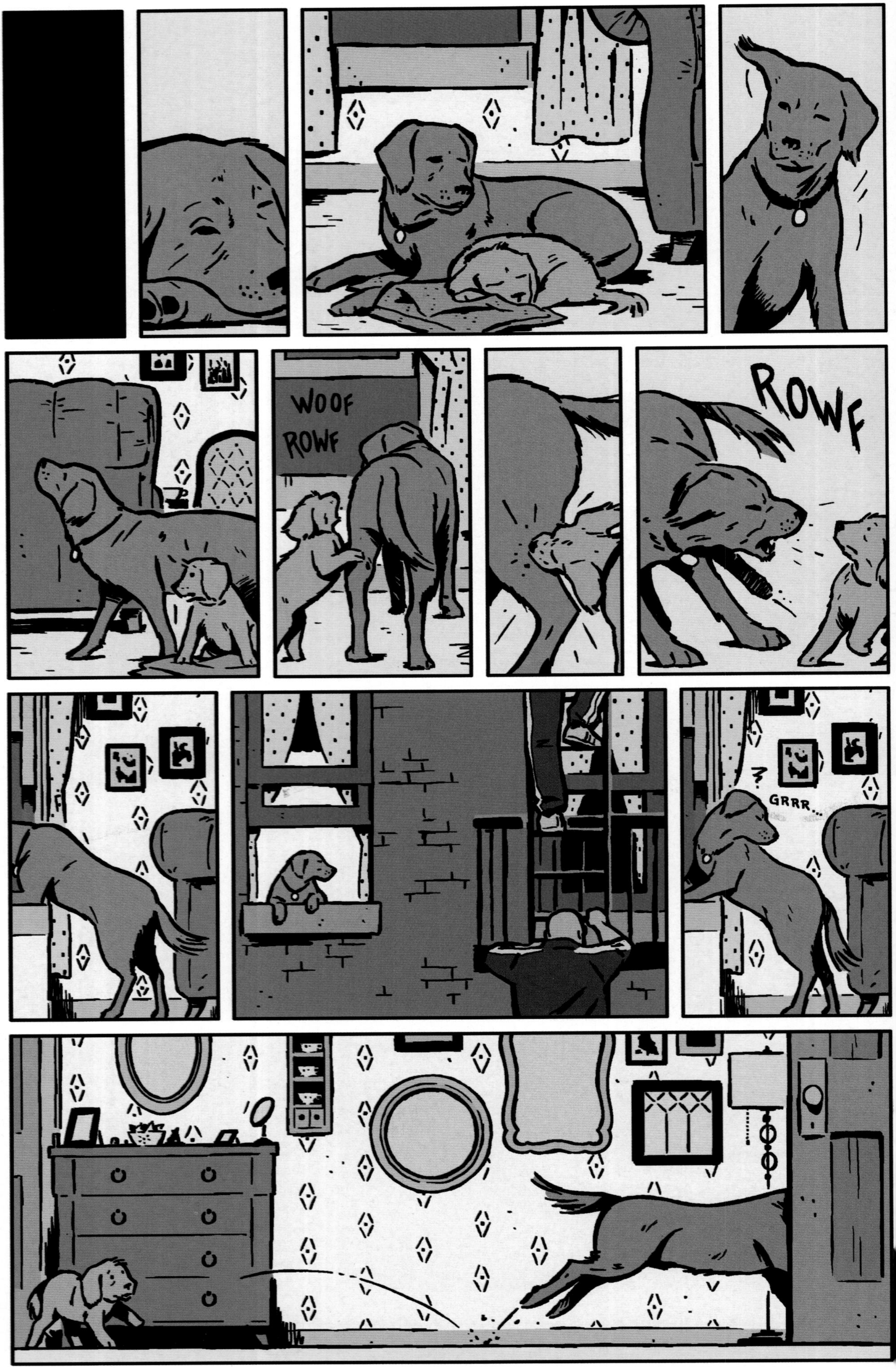
WOOF
ROWF
ROWF
?
GRRR...

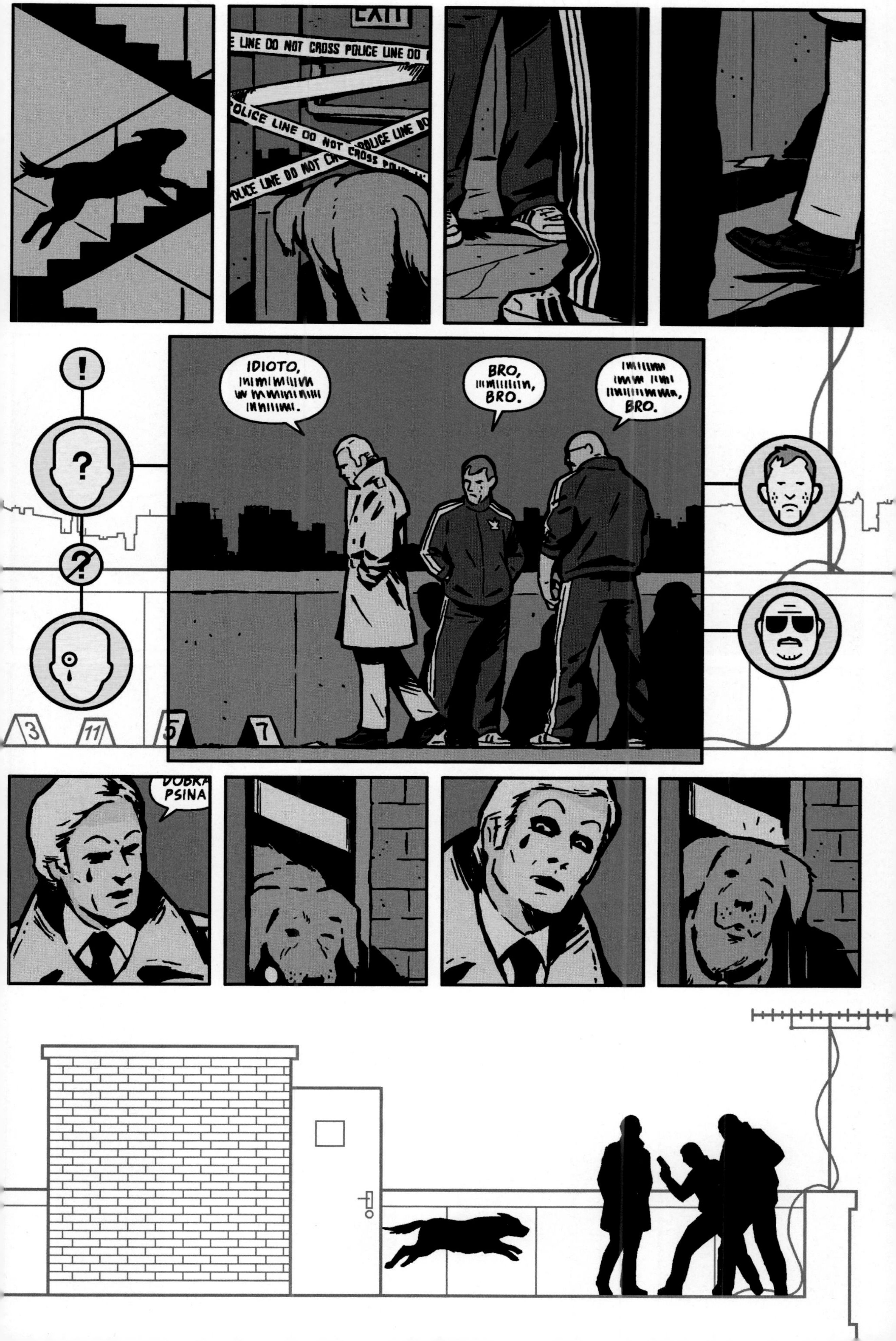
EXIT
POLICE LINE DO NOT CROSS POLICE LINE DO
POLICE LINE DO NOT CROSS POLICE LINE DO
IDIOTO,
BRO,
BRO.
BRO.
3
11
5
7
DOBRA
PSINA

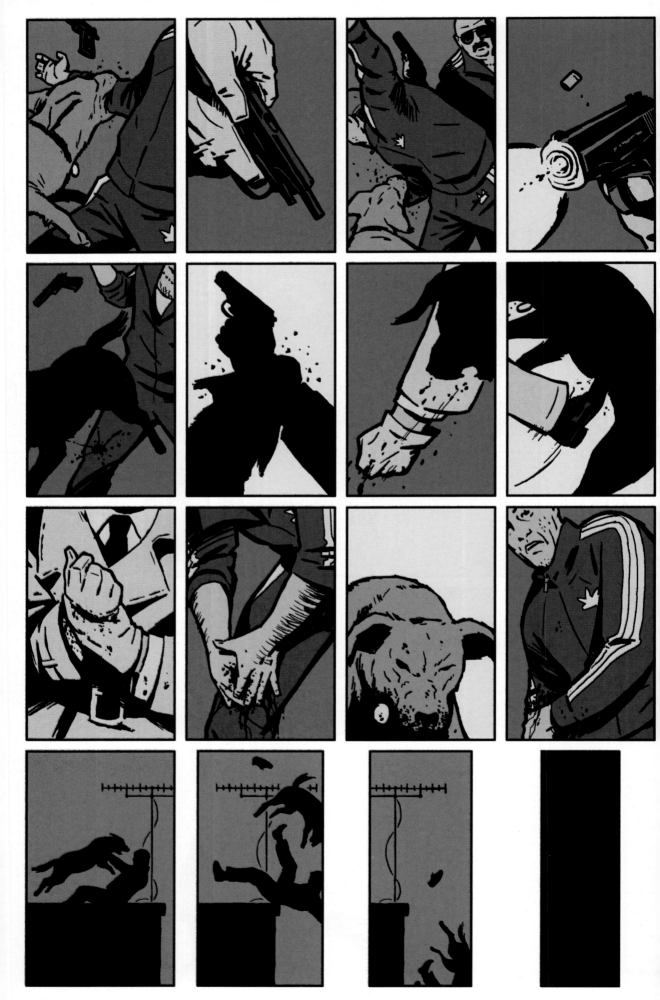

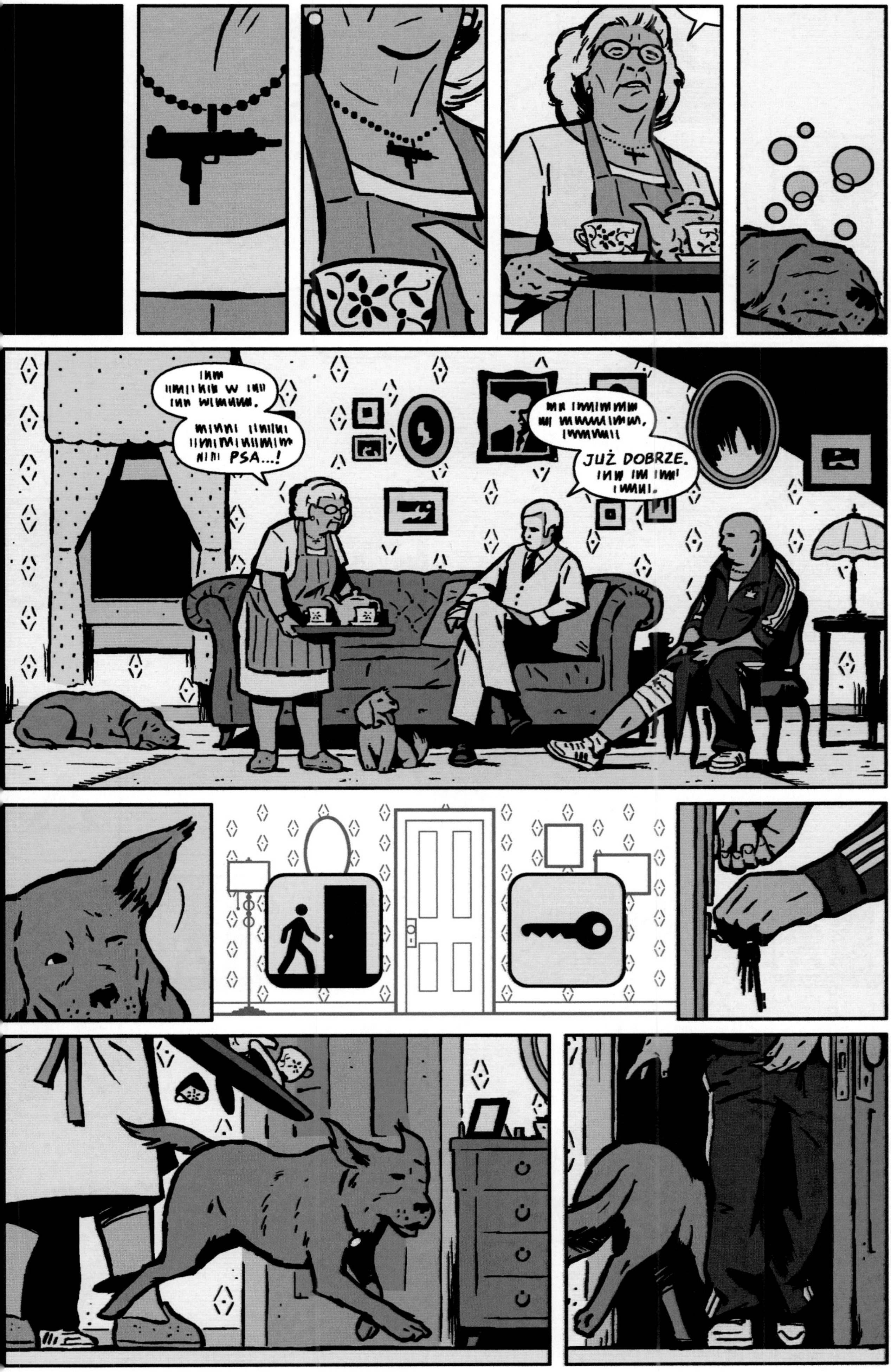
PSA...!
JUŻ DOBRZE.

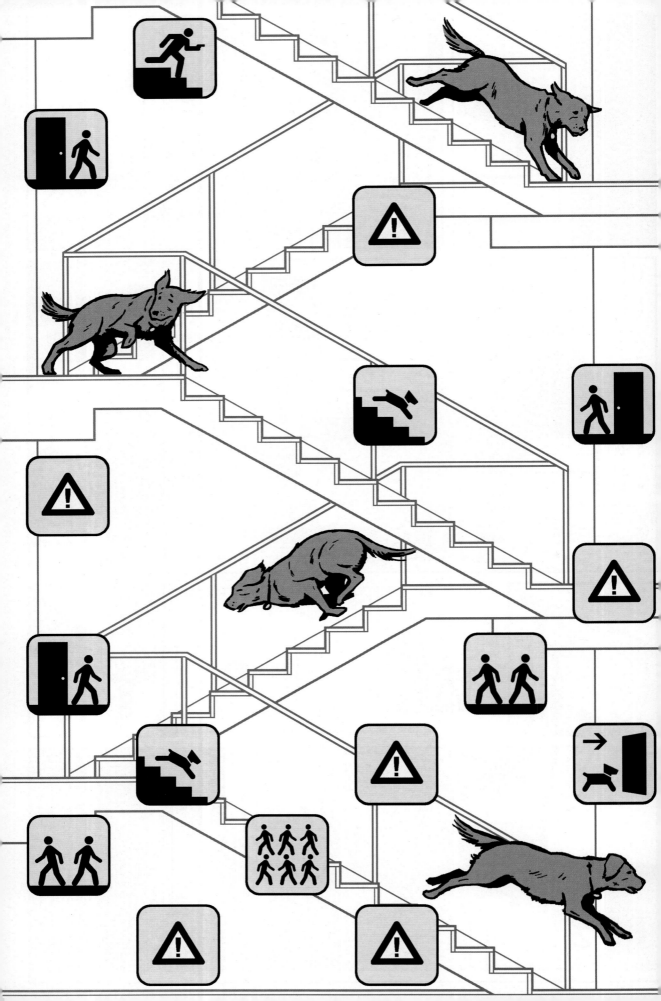

LUCKY

COME.

AWWWW.

GOOD BOY. GOOD.

IM IMMI MI STOP EATIM GARBAGE, BOY. OKAY? OKAY.

IMM'M GO.

COME, IMMMMIV? COME? LUCKY. COME!

LUCKY, PIZZA.

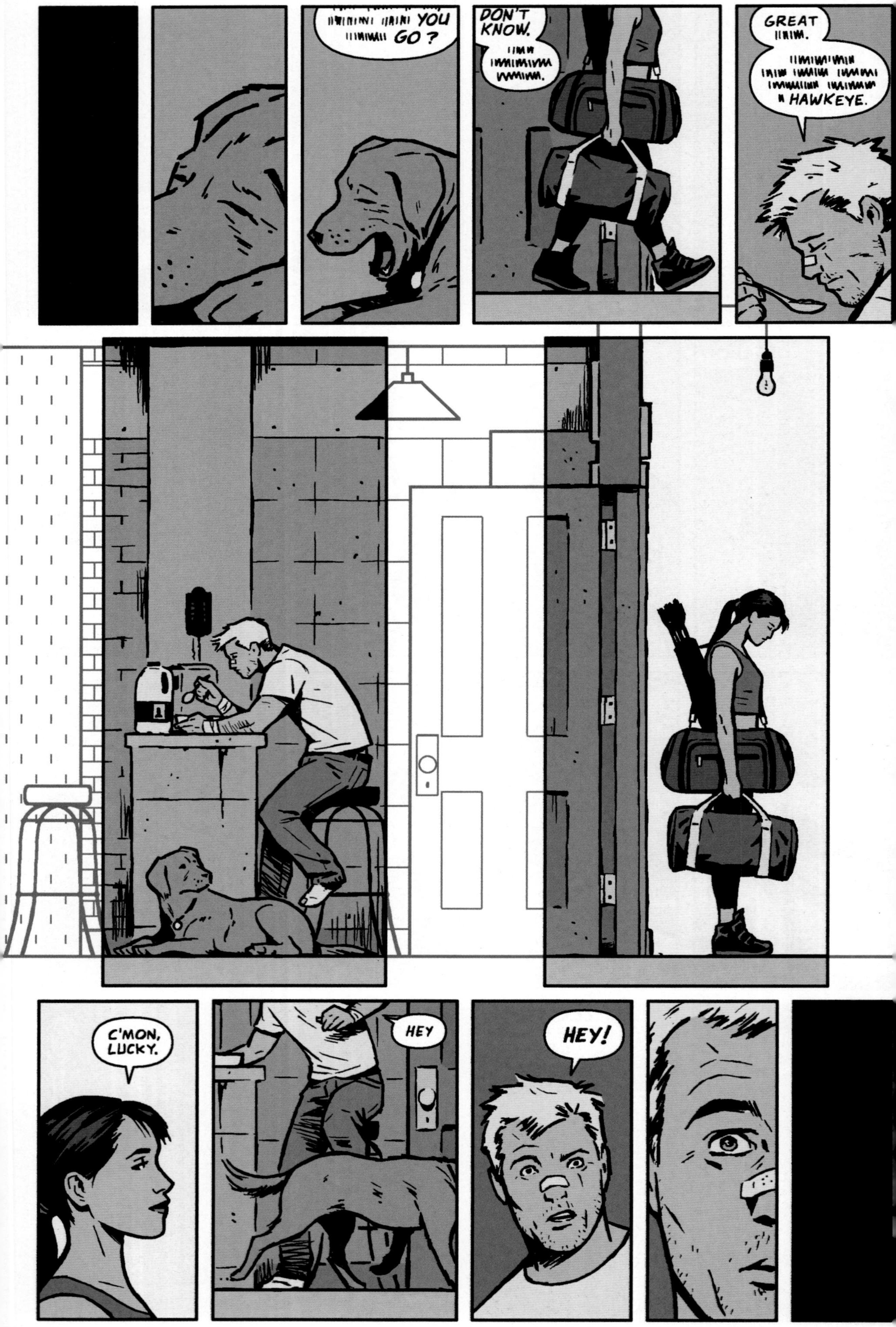
YOU GO?
DON'T KNOW.
GREAT
HAWKEYE.
C'MON, LUCKY.
HEY
HEY!

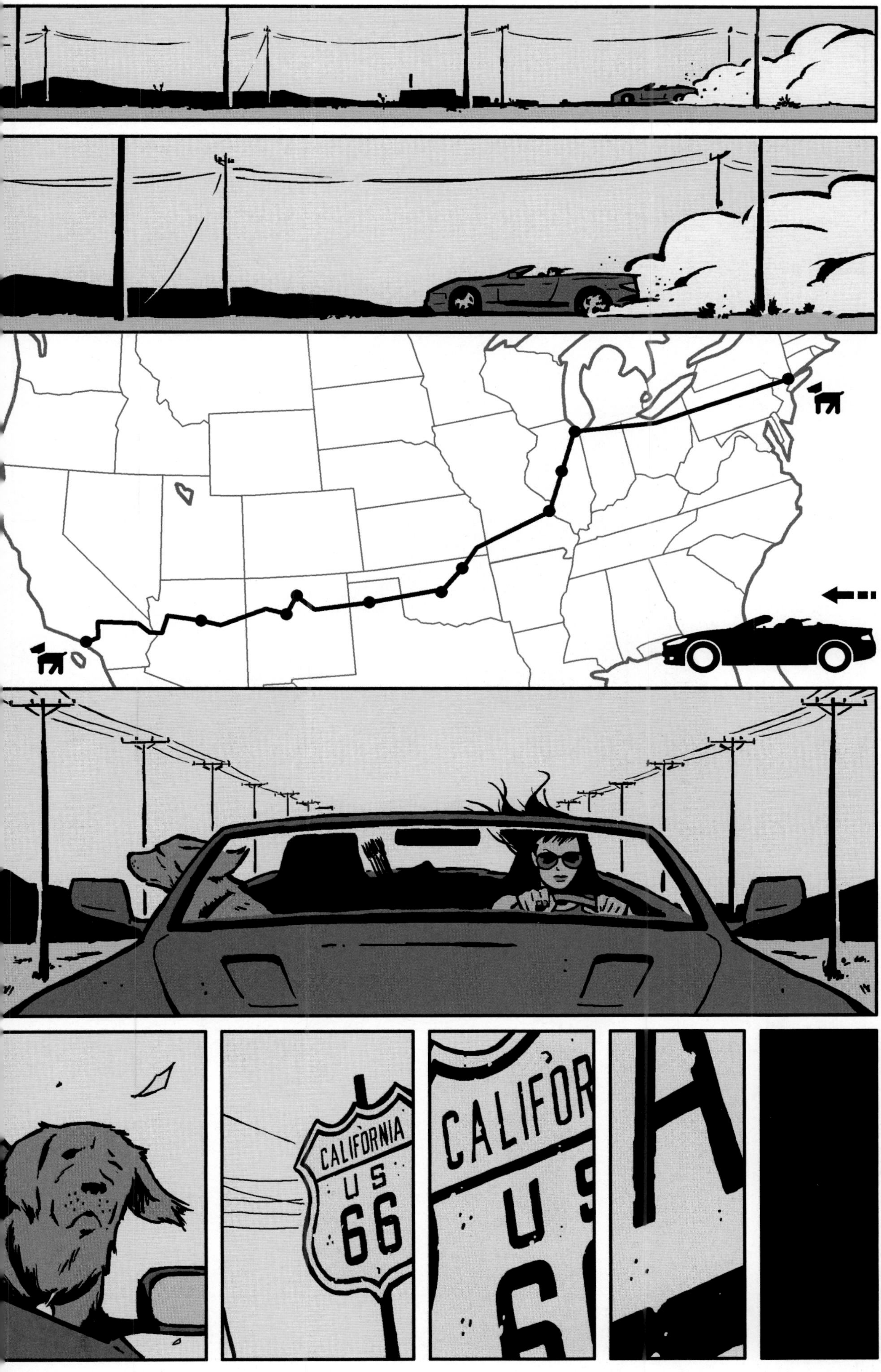
CALIFORNIA
US
66

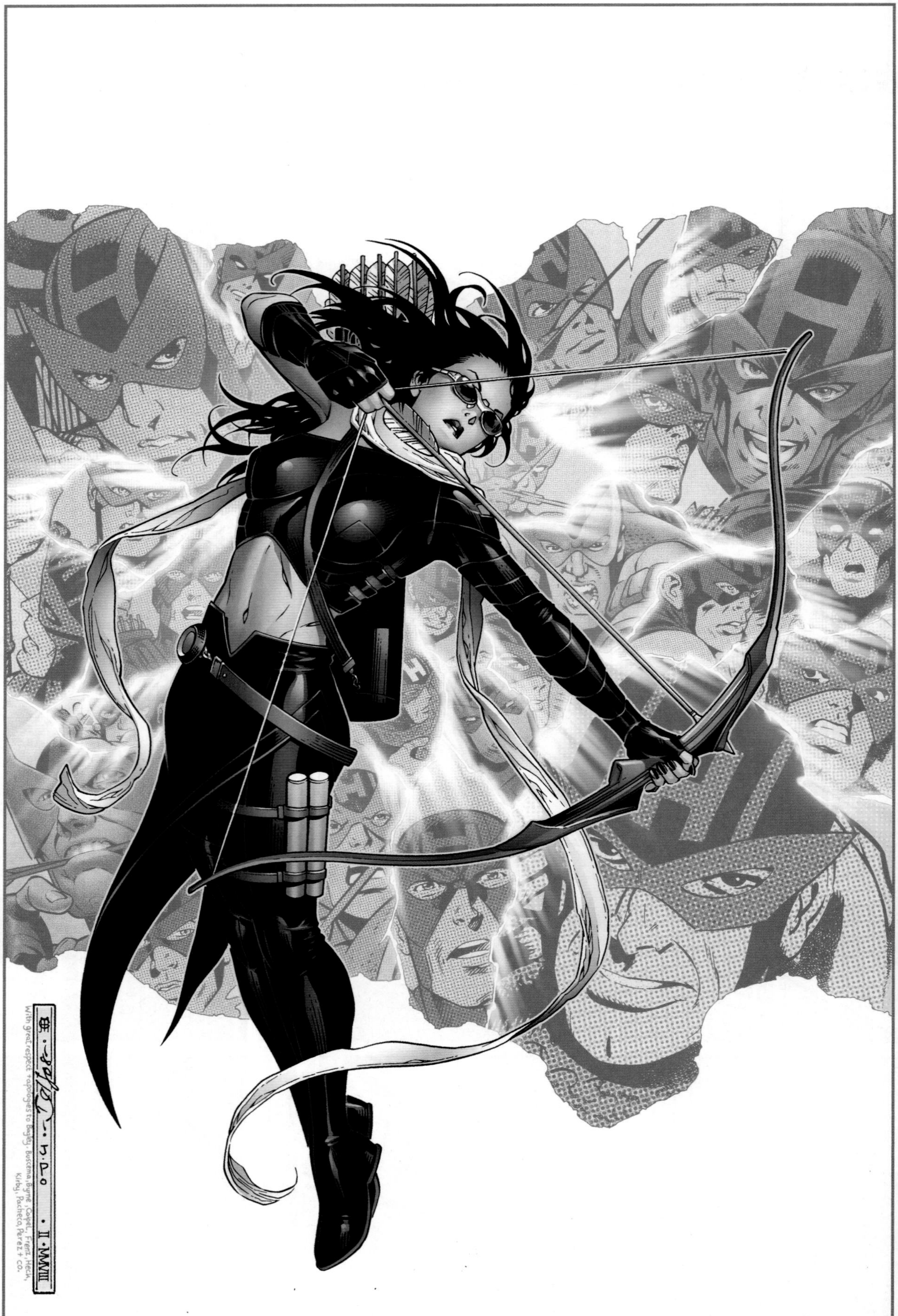

YOUNG AVENGERS PRESENTS #6

**United by friendship and bravery, Patriot, Hawkeye, Wiccan, Hulkling, Stature, Speed and the Vision are the Young Avengers, following in the footsteps of Earth's mightiest heroes! While superhuman registration temporarily caused the team to cease operations, they are ready to return to the streets to take on the threats no single super hero can withstand!**

# YOUNG AVENGERS PRESENTS HAWKEYE

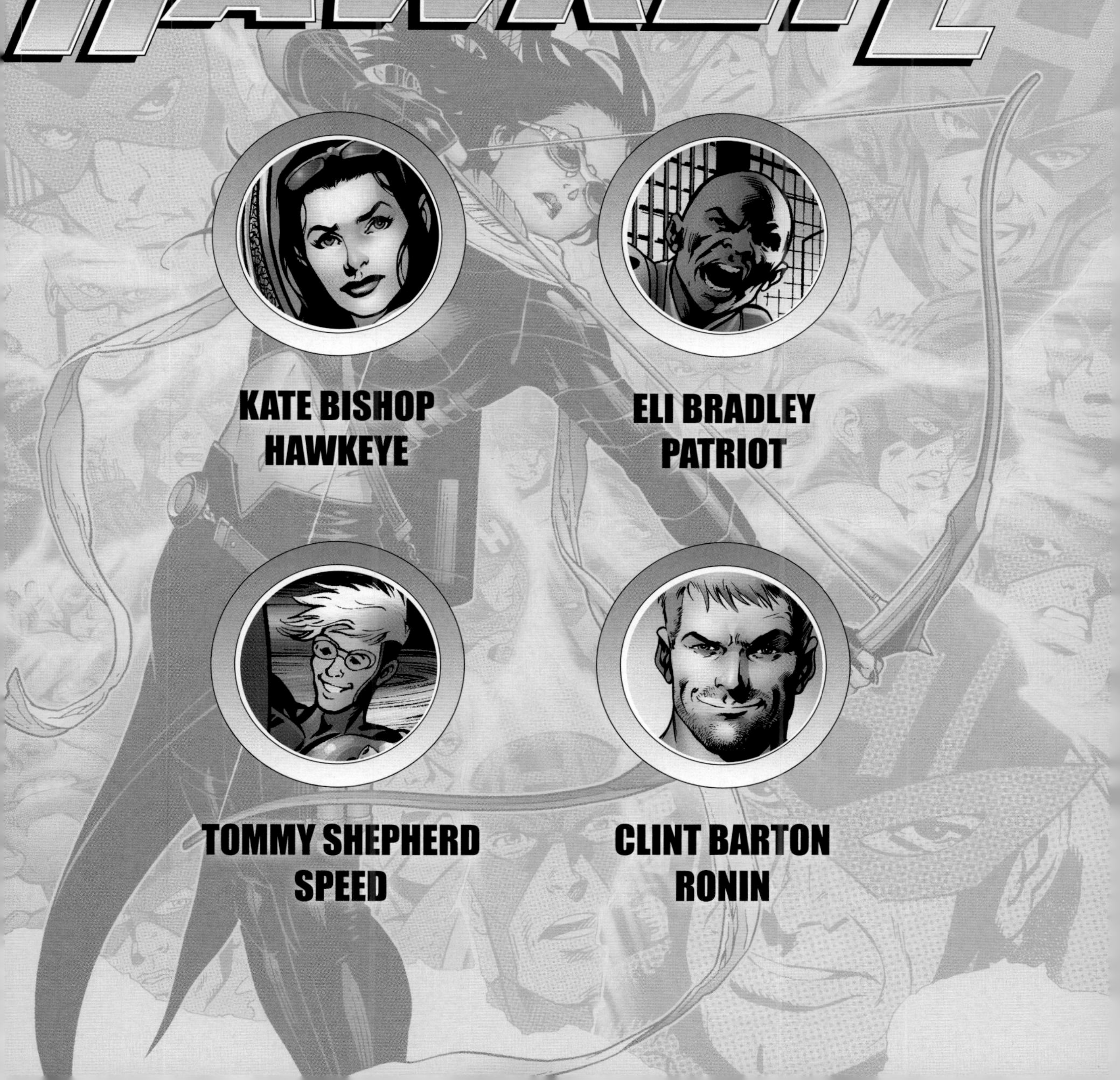
KATE BISHOP
HAWKEYE
ELI BRADLEY
PATRIOT
TOMMY SHEPHERD
SPEED
CLINT BARTON
RONIN

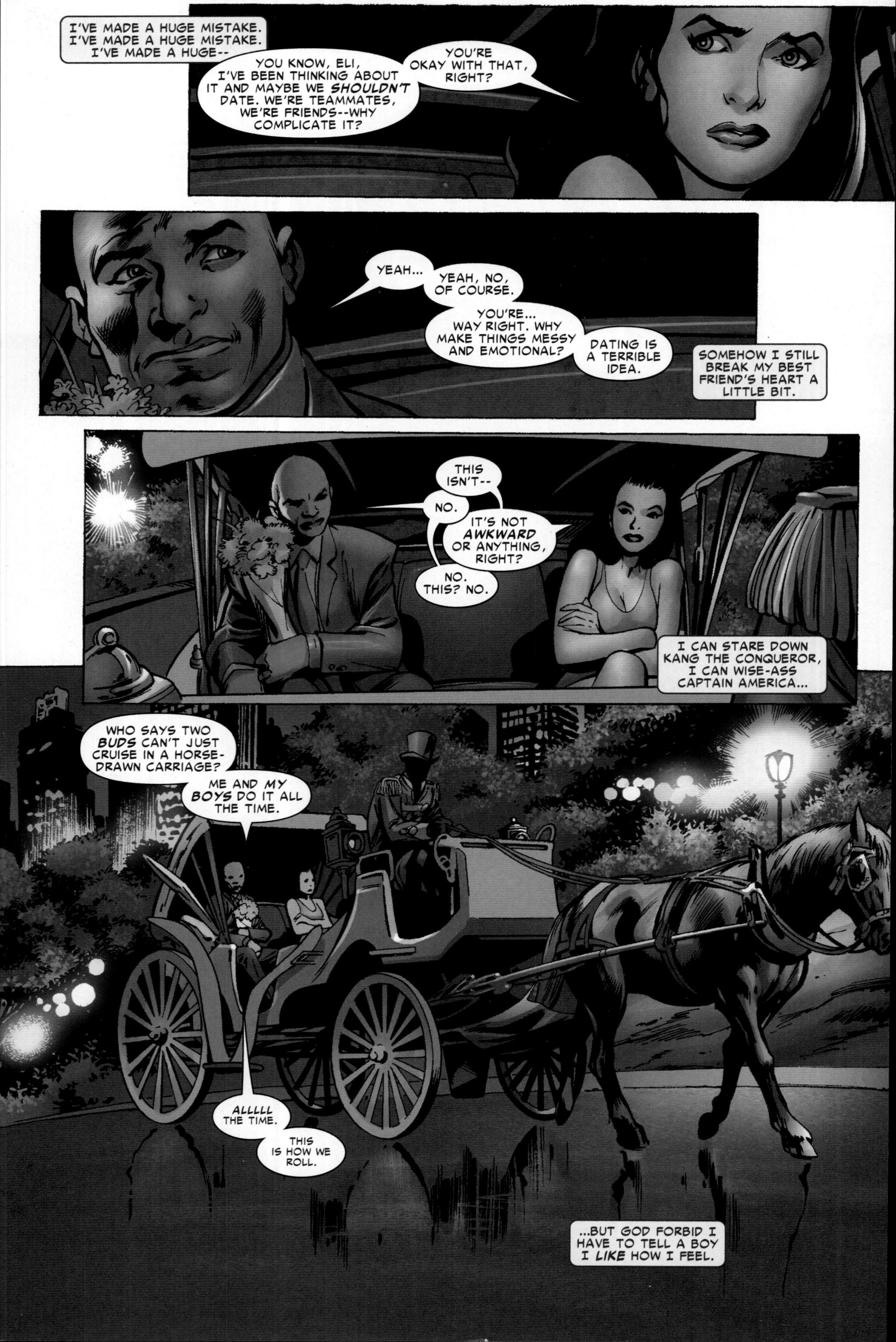
I'VE MADE A HUGE MISTAKE. I'VE MADE A HUGE MISTAKE. I'VE MADE A HUGE--
YOU KNOW, ELI, I'VE BEEN THINKING ABOUT IT AND MAYBE WE *SHOULDN'T* DATE. WE'RE TEAMMATES, WE'RE FRIENDS--WHY COMPLICATE IT?
YOU'RE OKAY WITH THAT, RIGHT?
YEAH...
YEAH, NO, OF COURSE.
YOU'RE... WAY RIGHT. WHY MAKE THINGS MESSY AND EMOTIONAL?
DATING IS A TERRIBLE IDEA.
SOMEHOW I STILL BREAK MY BEST FRIEND'S HEART A LITTLE BIT.
THIS ISN'T--
NO.
IT'S NOT *AWKWARD* OR ANYTHING, RIGHT?
NO. THIS? NO.
I CAN STARE DOWN KANG THE CONQUEROR, I CAN WISE-ASS CAPTAIN AMERICA...
WHO SAYS TWO *BUDS* CAN'T JUST CRUISE IN A HORSE-DRAWN CARRIAGE?
ME AND *MY BOYS* DO IT ALL THE TIME.
*ALLLLL* THE TIME.
THIS IS HOW WE ROLL.
...BUT GOD FORBID I HAVE TO TELL A BOY I *LIKE* HOW I FEEL.

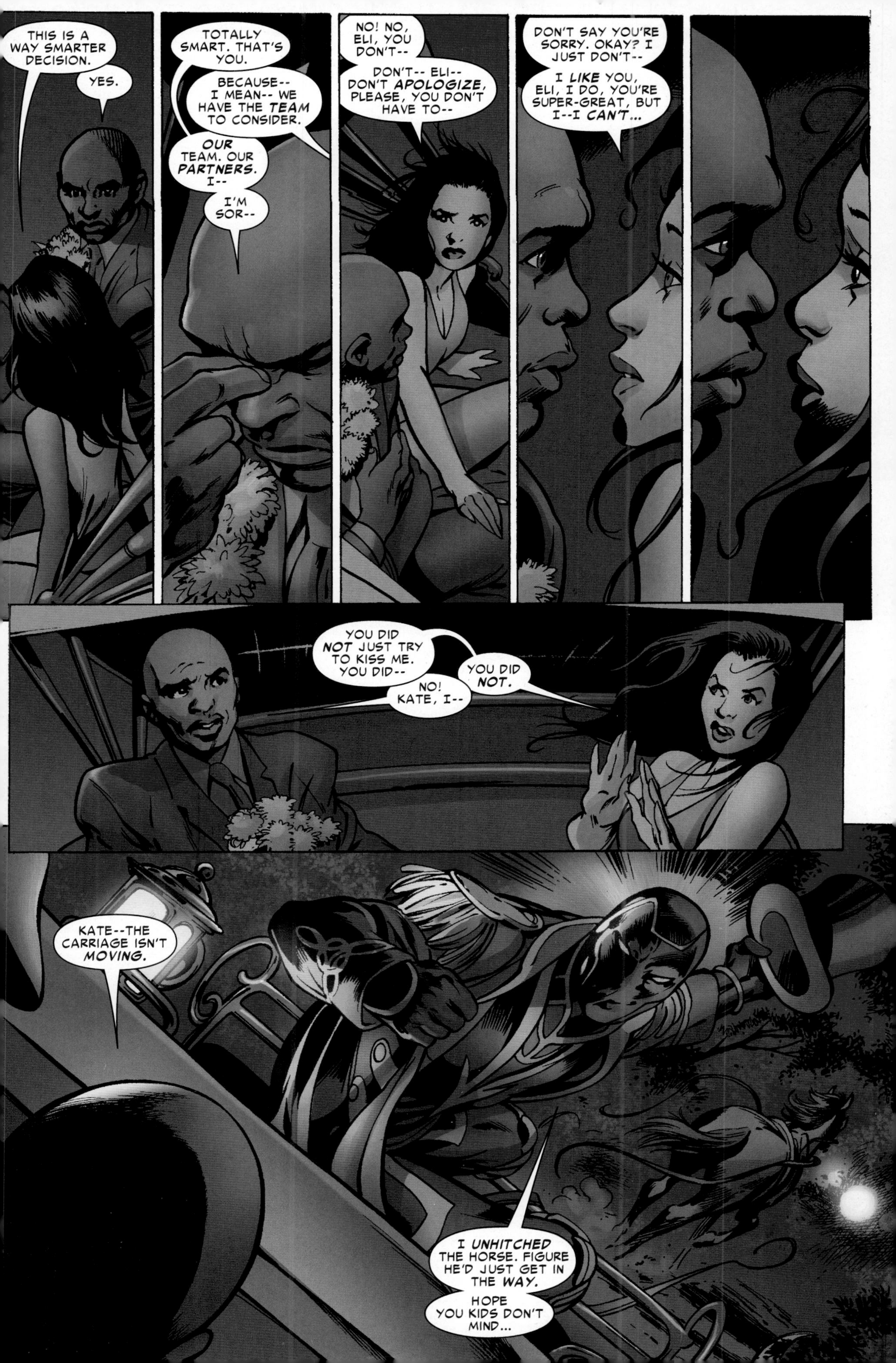
THIS IS A WAY SMARTER DECISION.
YES.
TOTALLY SMART. THAT'S YOU.
BECAUSE-- I MEAN-- WE HAVE THE *TEAM* TO CONSIDER.
*OUR* TEAM. OUR *PARTNERS*. I--
I'M SOR--
NO! NO, ELI, YOU DON'T--
DON'T-- ELI-- DON'T *APOLOGIZE*, PLEASE, YOU DON'T HAVE TO--
DON'T SAY YOU'RE SORRY. OKAY? I JUST DON'T--
I *LIKE* YOU, ELI, I DO, YOU'RE SUPER-GREAT, BUT I--I *CAN'T*...
YOU DID *NOT* JUST TRY TO KISS ME. YOU DID--
NO! KATE, I--
YOU DID *NOT*.
KATE--THE CARRIAGE ISN'T *MOVING*.
I *UNHITCHED* THE HORSE. FIGURE HE'D JUST GET IN THE *WAY*.
HOPE YOU KIDS DON'T MIND...

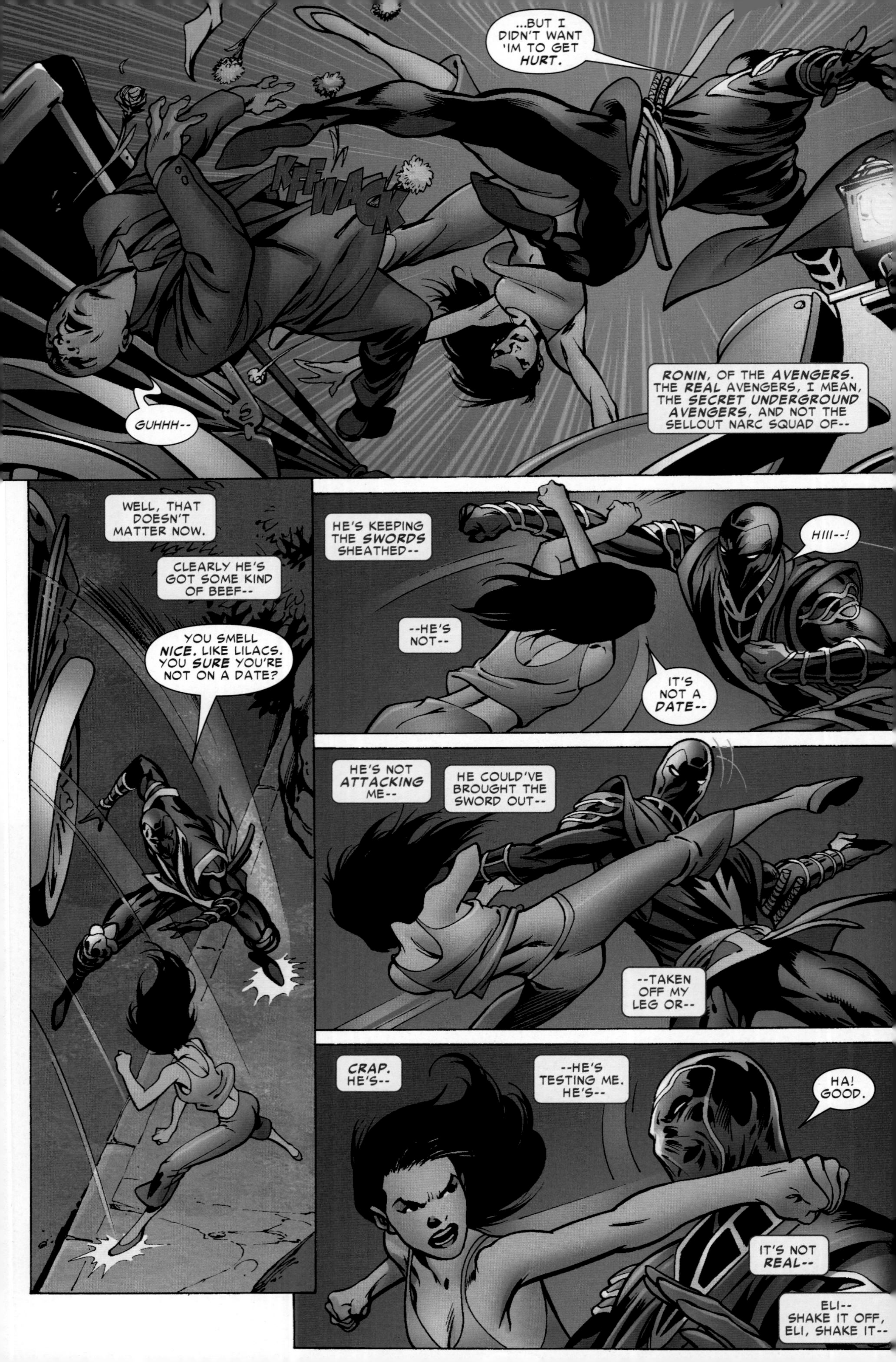
...BUT I DIDN'T WANT 'IM TO GET HURT.
KFFWACK
GUHHH--
RONIN, OF THE AVENGERS. THE REAL AVENGERS, I MEAN, THE SECRET UNDERGROUND AVENGERS, AND NOT THE SELLOUT NARC SQUAD OF--
WELL, THAT DOESN'T MATTER NOW.
CLEARLY HE'S GOT SOME KIND OF BEEF--
YOU SMELL NICE. LIKE LILACS. YOU SURE YOU'RE NOT ON A DATE?
HE'S KEEPING THE SWORDS SHEATHED--
HIII--!
--HE'S NOT--
IT'S NOT A DATE--
HE'S NOT ATTACKING ME--
HE COULD'VE BROUGHT THE SWORD OUT--
--TAKEN OFF MY LEG OR--
CRAP. HE'S--
--HE'S TESTING ME. HE'S--
HA! GOOD.
IT'S NOT REAL--
ELI-- SHAKE IT OFF, ELI, SHAKE IT--

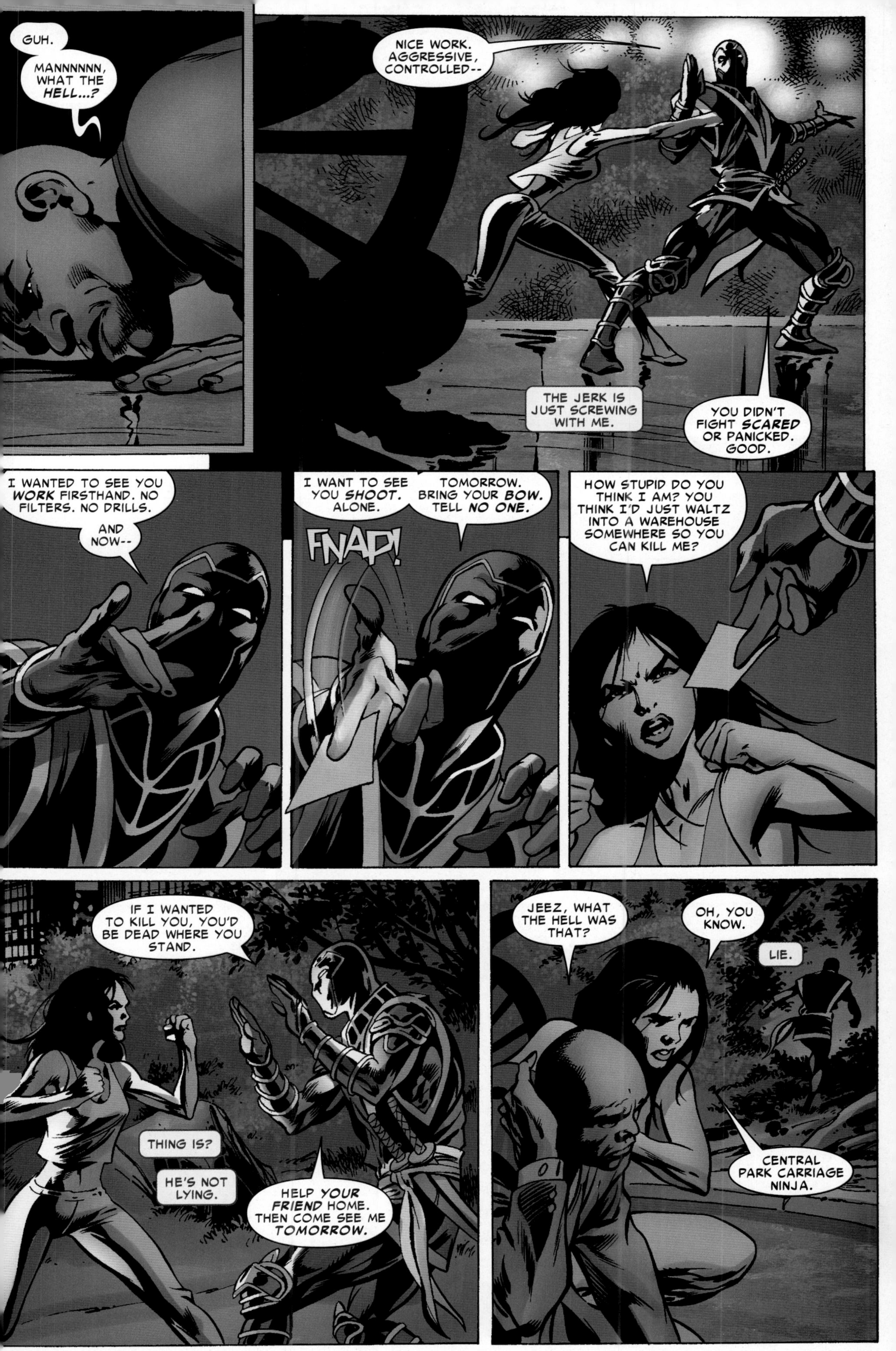
GUH.
MANNNNNN, WHAT THE HELL...?
NICE WORK. AGGRESSIVE, CONTROLLED--
THE JERK IS JUST SCREWING WITH ME.
YOU DIDN'T FIGHT SCARED OR PANICKED. GOOD.
I WANTED TO SEE YOU WORK FIRSTHAND. NO FILTERS. NO DRILLS.
AND NOW--
FNAP!
I WANT TO SEE YOU SHOOT. ALONE.
TOMORROW. BRING YOUR BOW. TELL NO ONE.
HOW STUPID DO YOU THINK I AM? YOU THINK I'D JUST WALTZ INTO A WAREHOUSE SOMEWHERE SO YOU CAN KILL ME?
IF I WANTED TO KILL YOU, YOU'D BE DEAD WHERE YOU STAND.
THING IS?
HE'S NOT LYING.
HELP YOUR FRIEND HOME. THEN COME SEE ME TOMORROW.
JEEZ, WHAT THE HELL WAS THAT?
OH, YOU KNOW.
LIE.
CENTRAL PARK CARRIAGE NINJA.

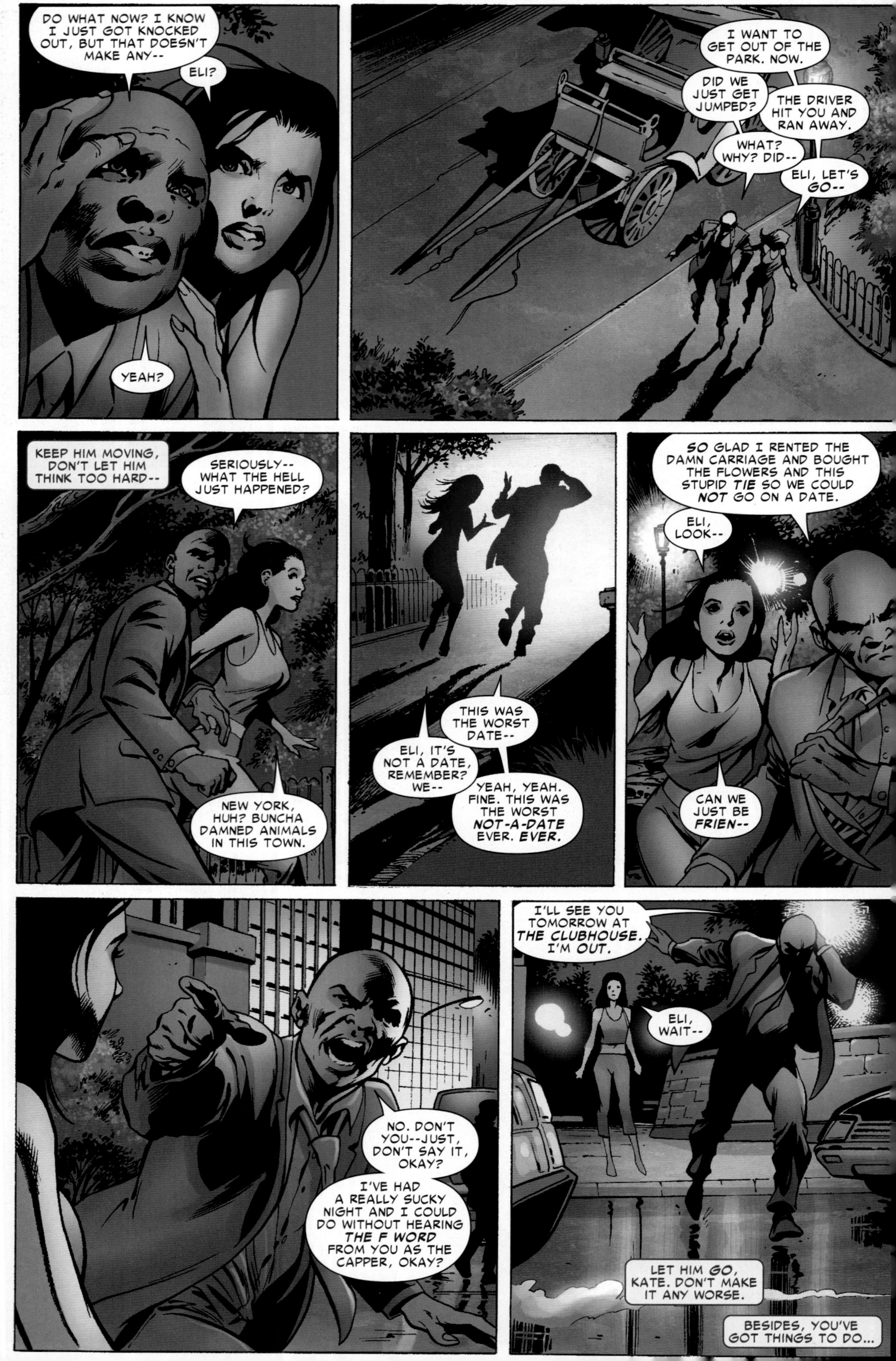
DO WHAT NOW? I KNOW I JUST GOT KNOCKED OUT, BUT THAT DOESN'T MAKE ANY--
ELI?
YEAH?
I WANT TO GET OUT OF THE PARK. NOW.
DID WE JUST GET JUMPED?
THE DRIVER HIT YOU AND RAN AWAY.
WHAT? WHY? DID--
ELI, LET'S GO--
KEEP HIM MOVING, DON'T LET HIM THINK TOO HARD--
SERIOUSLY-- WHAT THE HELL JUST HAPPENED?
NEW YORK, HUH? BUNCHA DAMNED ANIMALS IN THIS TOWN.
THIS WAS THE WORST DATE--
ELI, IT'S NOT A DATE, REMEMBER? WE--
YEAH, YEAH. FINE. THIS WAS THE WORST NOT-A-DATE EVER. EVER.
SO GLAD I RENTED THE DAMN CARRIAGE AND BOUGHT THE FLOWERS AND THIS STUPID TIE SO WE COULD NOT GO ON A DATE.
ELI, LOOK--
CAN WE JUST BE FRIEN--
NO. DON'T YOU--JUST, DON'T SAY IT, OKAY?
I'VE HAD A REALLY SUCKY NIGHT AND I COULD DO WITHOUT HEARING THE F WORD FROM YOU AS THE CAPPER, OKAY?
I'LL SEE YOU TOMORROW AT THE CLUBHOUSE. I'M OUT.
ELI, WAIT--
LET HIM GO, KATE. DON'T MAKE IT ANY WORSE.
BESIDES, YOU'VE GOT THINGS TO DO...

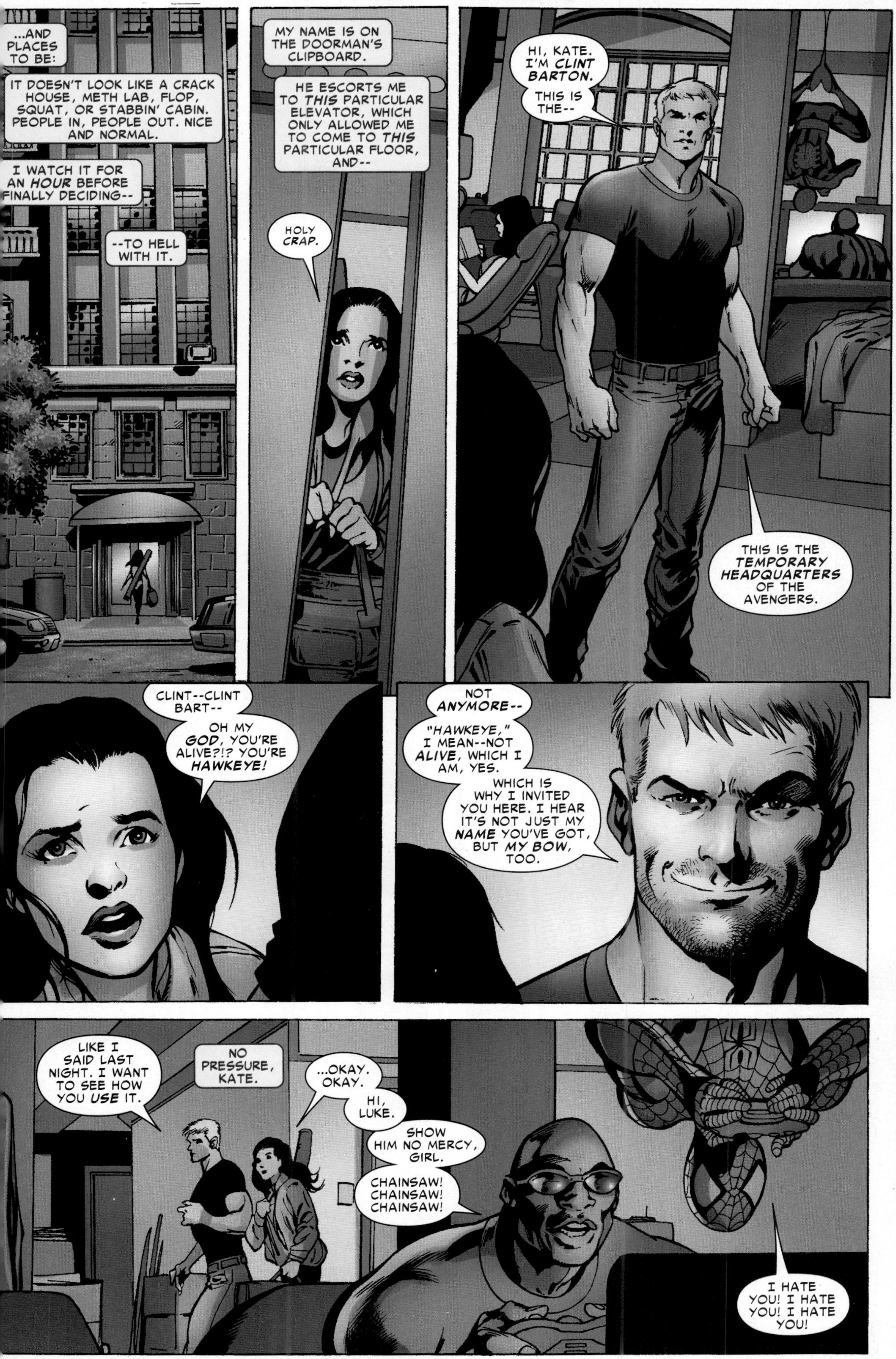
...AND PLACES TO BE:
IT DOESN'T LOOK LIKE A CRACK HOUSE, METH LAB, FLOP, SQUAT, OR STABBIN' CABIN. PEOPLE IN, PEOPLE OUT. NICE AND NORMAL.
I WATCH IT FOR AN HOUR BEFORE FINALLY DECIDING--
--TO HELL WITH IT.
MY NAME IS ON THE DOORMAN'S CLIPBOARD.
HE ESCORTS ME TO THIS PARTICULAR ELEVATOR, WHICH ONLY ALLOWED ME TO COME TO THIS PARTICULAR FLOOR, AND--
HOLY CRAP.
HI, KATE. I'M CLINT BARTON.
THIS IS THE--
THIS IS THE TEMPORARY HEADQUARTERS OF THE AVENGERS.
CLINT--CLINT BART--
OH MY GOD, YOU'RE ALIVE?!? YOU'RE HAWKEYE!
NOT ANYMORE--
"HAWKEYE," I MEAN--NOT ALIVE, WHICH I AM, YES.
WHICH IS WHY I INVITED YOU HERE. I HEAR IT'S NOT JUST MY NAME YOU'VE GOT, BUT MY BOW, TOO.
LIKE I SAID LAST NIGHT. I WANT TO SEE HOW YOU USE IT.
NO PRESSURE, KATE.
...OKAY. OKAY.
HI, LUKE.
SHOW HIM NO MERCY, GIRL.
CHAINSAW! CHAINSAW! CHAINSAW!
I HATE YOU! I HATE YOU! I HATE YOU!

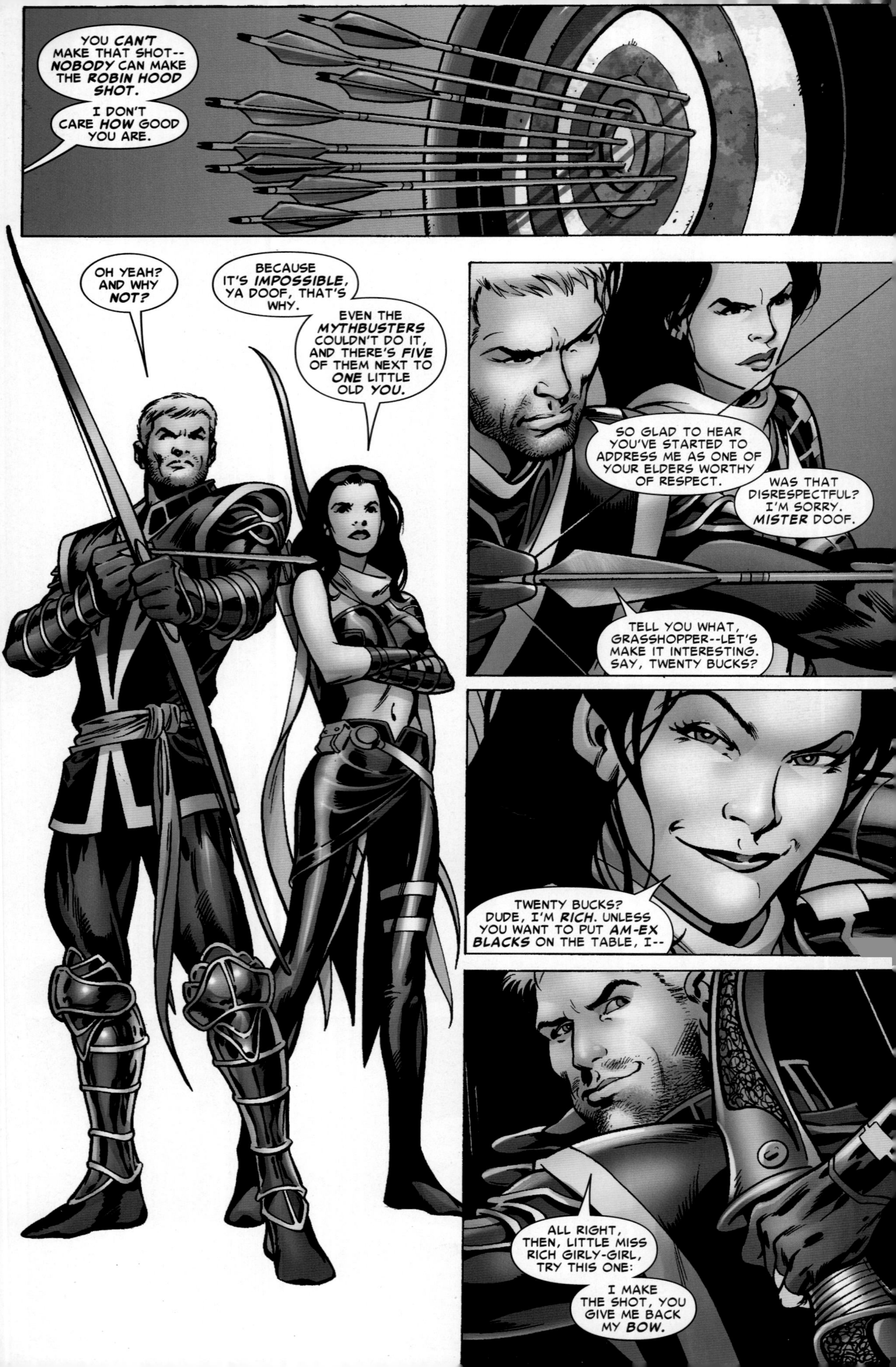
YOU CAN'T MAKE THAT SHOT-- NOBODY CAN MAKE THE ROBIN HOOD SHOT.
I DON'T CARE HOW GOOD YOU ARE.
OH YEAH? AND WHY NOT?
BECAUSE IT'S IMPOSSIBLE, YA DOOF, THAT'S WHY.
EVEN THE MYTHBUSTERS COULDN'T DO IT, AND THERE'S FIVE OF THEM NEXT TO ONE LITTLE OLD YOU.
SO GLAD TO HEAR YOU'VE STARTED TO ADDRESS ME AS ONE OF YOUR ELDERS WORTHY OF RESPECT.
WAS THAT DISRESPECTFUL? I'M SORRY. MISTER DOOF.
TELL YOU WHAT, GRASSHOPPER--LET'S MAKE IT INTERESTING. SAY, TWENTY BUCKS?
TWENTY BUCKS? DUDE, I'M RICH. UNLESS YOU WANT TO PUT AM-EX BLACKS ON THE TABLE, I--
ALL RIGHT, THEN, LITTLE MISS RICH GIRLY-GIRL, TRY THIS ONE:
I MAKE THE SHOT, YOU GIVE ME BACK MY BOW.

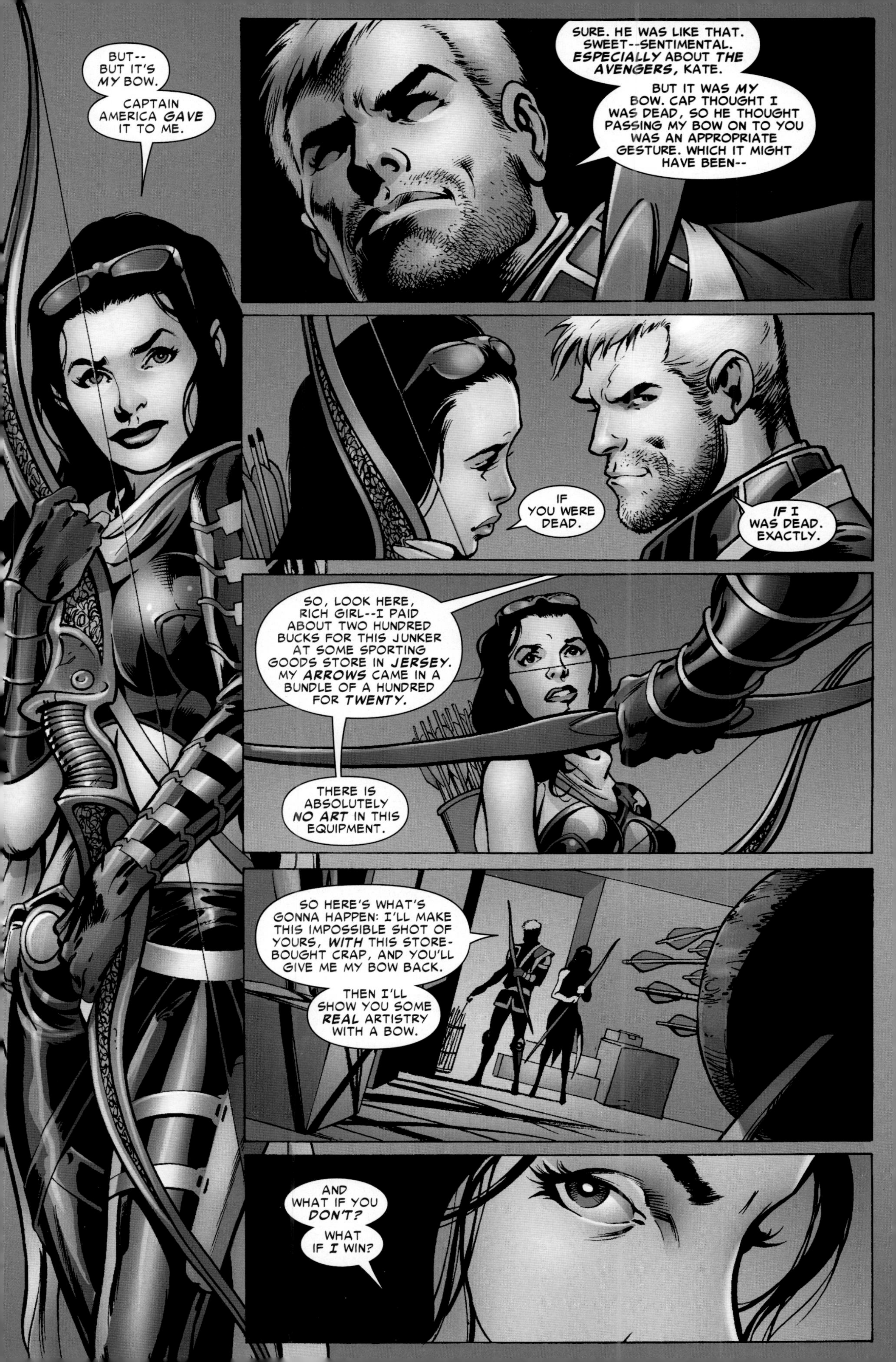

BUT-- BUT IT'S *MY* BOW.
CAPTAIN AMERICA *GAVE* IT TO ME.
SURE. HE WAS LIKE THAT. SWEET--SENTIMENTAL. ***ESPECIALLY*** ABOUT ***THE AVENGERS,*** KATE.
BUT IT WAS *MY* BOW. CAP THOUGHT I WAS DEAD, SO HE THOUGHT PASSING MY BOW ON TO YOU WAS AN APPROPRIATE GESTURE. WHICH IT MIGHT HAVE BEEN--
IF YOU WERE DEAD.
***IF*** I WAS DEAD. EXACTLY.
SO, LOOK HERE, RICH GIRL--I PAID ABOUT TWO HUNDRED BUCKS FOR THIS JUNKER AT SOME SPORTING GOODS STORE IN ***JERSEY***. MY ***ARROWS*** CAME IN A BUNDLE OF A HUNDRED FOR ***TWENTY***.
THERE IS ABSOLUTELY ***NO ART*** IN THIS EQUIPMENT.
SO HERE'S WHAT'S GONNA HAPPEN: I'LL MAKE THIS IMPOSSIBLE SHOT OF YOURS, ***WITH*** THIS STORE-BOUGHT CRAP, AND YOU'LL GIVE ME MY BOW BACK.
THEN I'LL SHOW YOU SOME ***REAL*** ARTISTRY WITH A BOW.
AND WHAT IF YOU ***DON'T?***
WHAT IF ***I*** WIN?

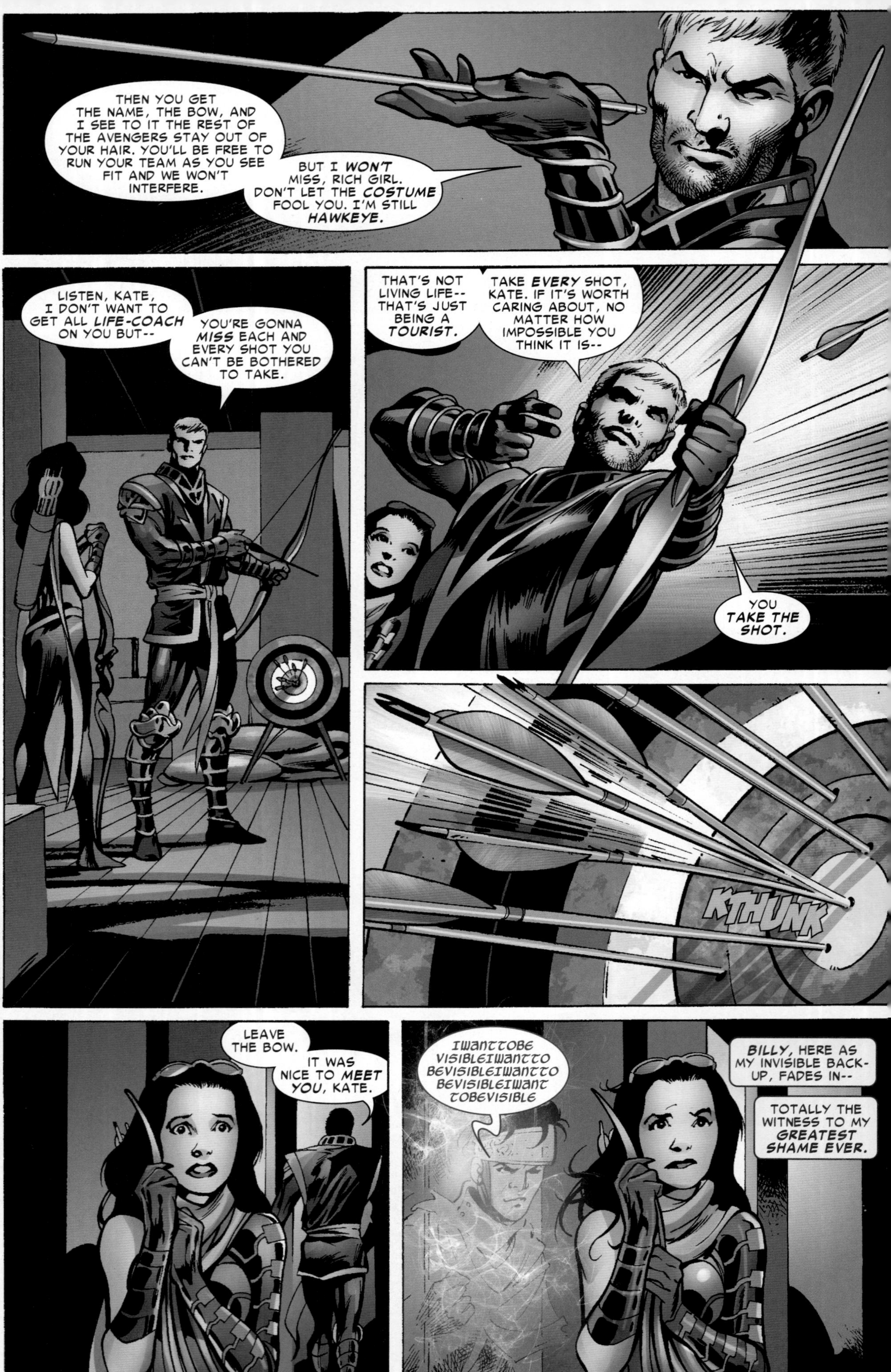
THEN YOU GET THE NAME, THE BOW, AND I SEE TO IT THE REST OF THE AVENGERS STAY OUT OF YOUR HAIR. YOU'LL BE FREE TO RUN YOUR TEAM AS YOU SEE FIT AND WE WON'T INTERFERE.
BUT I WON'T MISS, RICH GIRL. DON'T LET THE COSTUME FOOL YOU. I'M STILL HAWKEYE.
LISTEN, KATE, I DON'T WANT TO GET ALL LIFE-COACH ON YOU BUT--
YOU'RE GONNA MISS EACH AND EVERY SHOT YOU CAN'T BE BOTHERED TO TAKE.
THAT'S NOT LIVING LIFE-- THAT'S JUST BEING A TOURIST.
TAKE EVERY SHOT, KATE. IF IT'S WORTH CARING ABOUT, NO MATTER HOW IMPOSSIBLE YOU THINK IT IS--
YOU TAKE THE SHOT.
KTHUNK
LEAVE THE BOW.
IT WAS NICE TO MEET YOU, KATE.
IWANTTOBE VISIBLEIWANTTO BEVISIBLEIWANTTO BEVISIBLEIWANT TOBEVISIBLE
BILLY, HERE AS MY INVISIBLE BACK-UP, FADES IN--
TOTALLY THE WITNESS TO MY GREATEST SHAME EVER.

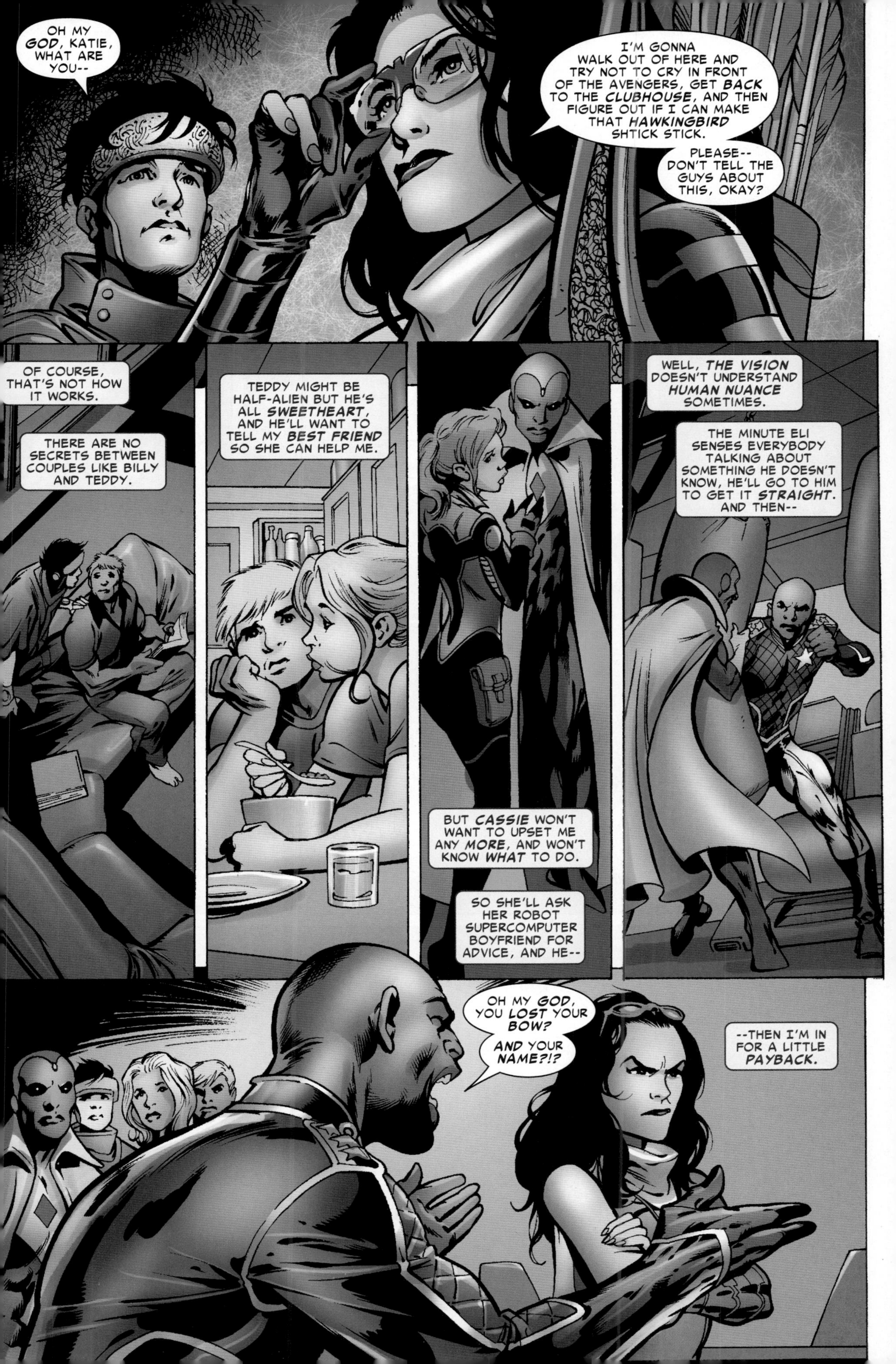
OH MY GOD, KATIE, WHAT ARE YOU--
I'M GONNA WALK OUT OF HERE AND TRY NOT TO CRY IN FRONT OF THE AVENGERS, GET BACK TO THE CLUBHOUSE, AND THEN FIGURE OUT IF I CAN MAKE THAT HAWKINGBIRD SHTICK STICK.
PLEASE-- DON'T TELL THE GUYS ABOUT THIS, OKAY?
OF COURSE, THAT'S NOT HOW IT WORKS.
THERE ARE NO SECRETS BETWEEN COUPLES LIKE BILLY AND TEDDY.
TEDDY MIGHT BE HALF-ALIEN BUT HE'S ALL SWEETHEART, AND HE'LL WANT TO TELL MY BEST FRIEND SO SHE CAN HELP ME.
BUT CASSIE WON'T WANT TO UPSET ME ANY MORE, AND WON'T KNOW WHAT TO DO.
SO SHE'LL ASK HER ROBOT SUPERCOMPUTER BOYFRIEND FOR ADVICE, AND HE--
WELL, THE VISION DOESN'T UNDERSTAND HUMAN NUANCE SOMETIMES.
THE MINUTE ELI SENSES EVERYBODY TALKING ABOUT SOMETHING HE DOESN'T KNOW, HE'LL GO TO HIM TO GET IT STRAIGHT. AND THEN--
OH MY GOD, YOU LOST YOUR BOW?
AND YOUR NAME?!?
--THEN I'M IN FOR A LITTLE PAYBACK.

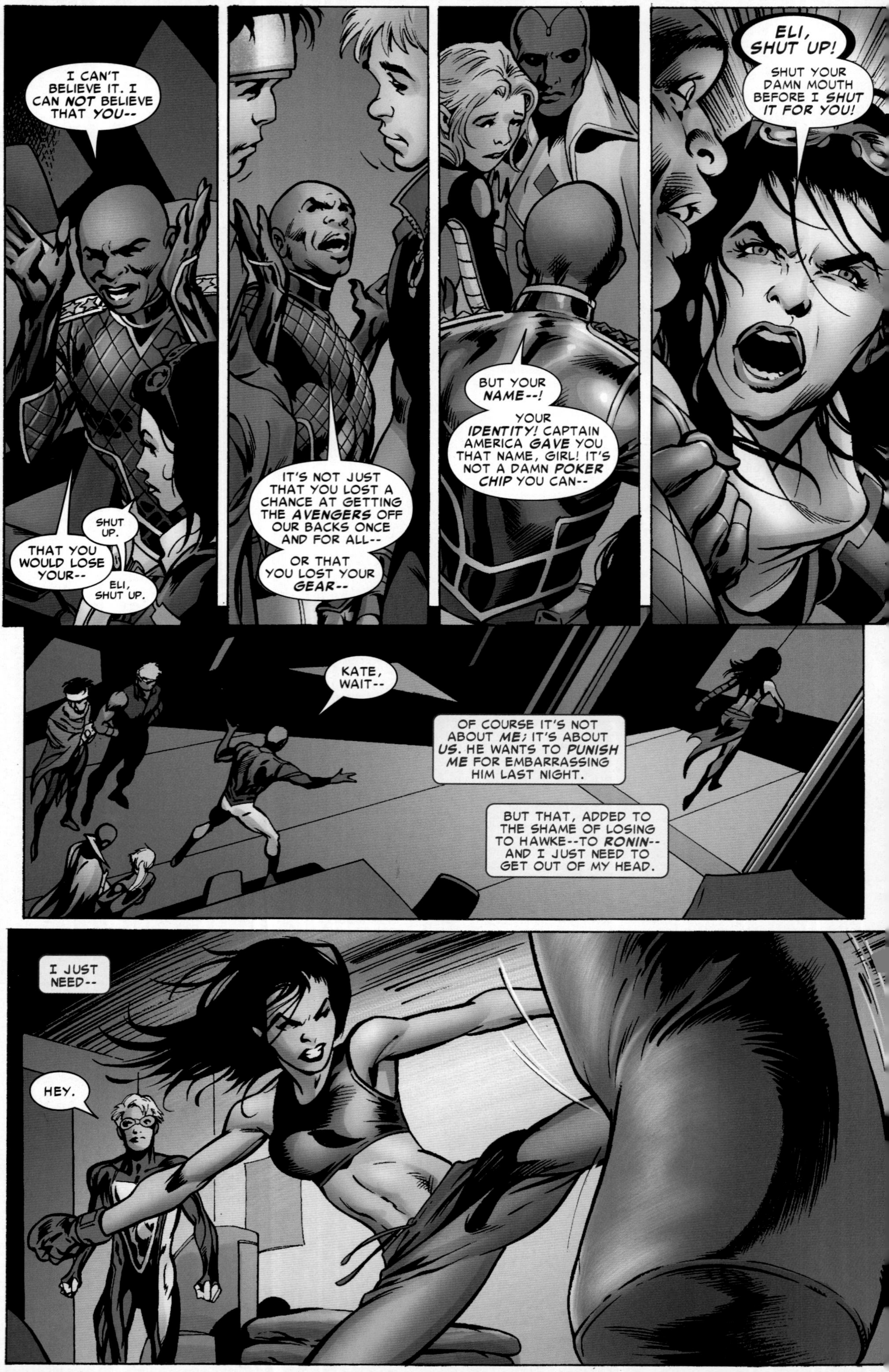

I CAN'T BELIEVE IT. I CAN NOT BELIEVE THAT YOU--
THAT YOU WOULD LOSE YOUR--
SHUT UP.
ELI, SHUT UP.
IT'S NOT JUST THAT YOU LOST A CHANCE AT GETTING THE AVENGERS OFF OUR BACKS ONCE AND FOR ALL--
OR THAT YOU LOST YOUR GEAR--
BUT YOUR NAME--!
YOUR IDENTITY! CAPTAIN AMERICA GAVE YOU THAT NAME, GIRL! IT'S NOT A DAMN POKER CHIP YOU CAN--
ELI, SHUT UP!
SHUT YOUR DAMN MOUTH BEFORE I SHUT IT FOR YOU!
KATE, WAIT--
OF COURSE IT'S NOT ABOUT ME; IT'S ABOUT US. HE WANTS TO PUNISH ME FOR EMBARRASSING HIM LAST NIGHT.
BUT THAT, ADDED TO THE SHAME OF LOSING TO HAWKE--TO RONIN--AND I JUST NEED TO GET OUT OF MY HEAD.
I JUST NEED--
HEY.

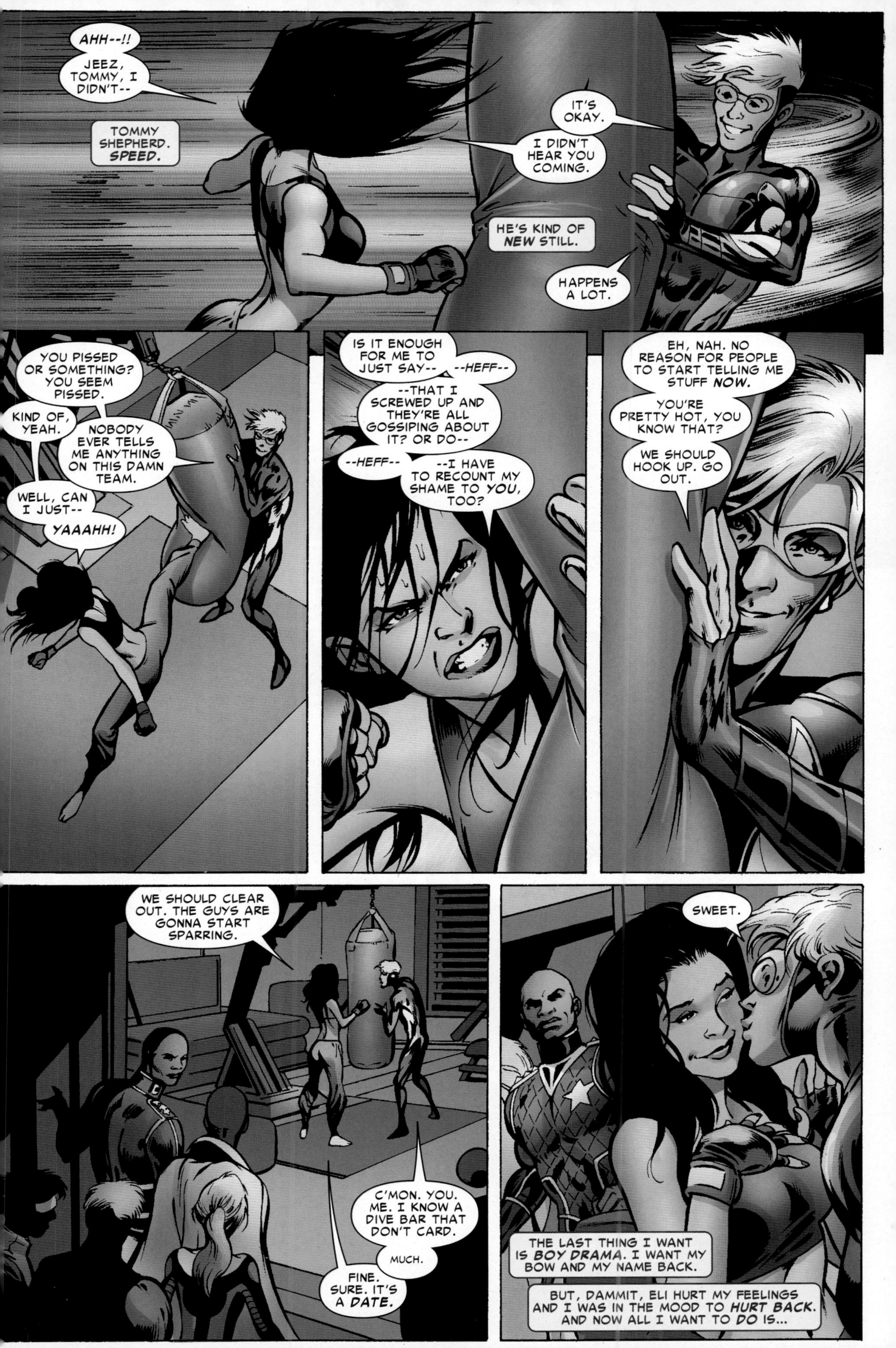
AHH--!!
JEEZ, TOMMY, I DIDN'T--
TOMMY SHEPHERD. SPEED.
IT'S OKAY.
I DIDN'T HEAR YOU COMING.
HE'S KIND OF NEW STILL.
HAPPENS A LOT.
YOU PISSED OR SOMETHING? YOU SEEM PISSED.
KIND OF, YEAH.
NOBODY EVER TELLS ME ANYTHING ON THIS DAMN TEAM.
WELL, CAN I JUST--
YAAAHH!
IS IT ENOUGH FOR ME TO JUST SAY--
--HEFF--
--THAT I SCREWED UP AND THEY'RE ALL GOSSIPING ABOUT IT? OR DO--
--HEFF--
--I HAVE TO RECOUNT MY SHAME TO YOU, TOO?
EH, NAH. NO REASON FOR PEOPLE TO START TELLING ME STUFF NOW.
YOU'RE PRETTY HOT, YOU KNOW THAT?
WE SHOULD HOOK UP. GO OUT.
WE SHOULD CLEAR OUT. THE GUYS ARE GONNA START SPARRING.
C'MON. YOU. ME. I KNOW A DIVE BAR THAT DON'T CARD.
MUCH.
FINE. SURE. IT'S A DATE.
SWEET.
THE LAST THING I WANT IS BOY DRAMA. I WANT MY BOW AND MY NAME BACK.
BUT, DAMMIT, ELI HURT MY FEELINGS AND I WAS IN THE MOOD TO HURT BACK. AND NOW ALL I WANT TO DO IS...

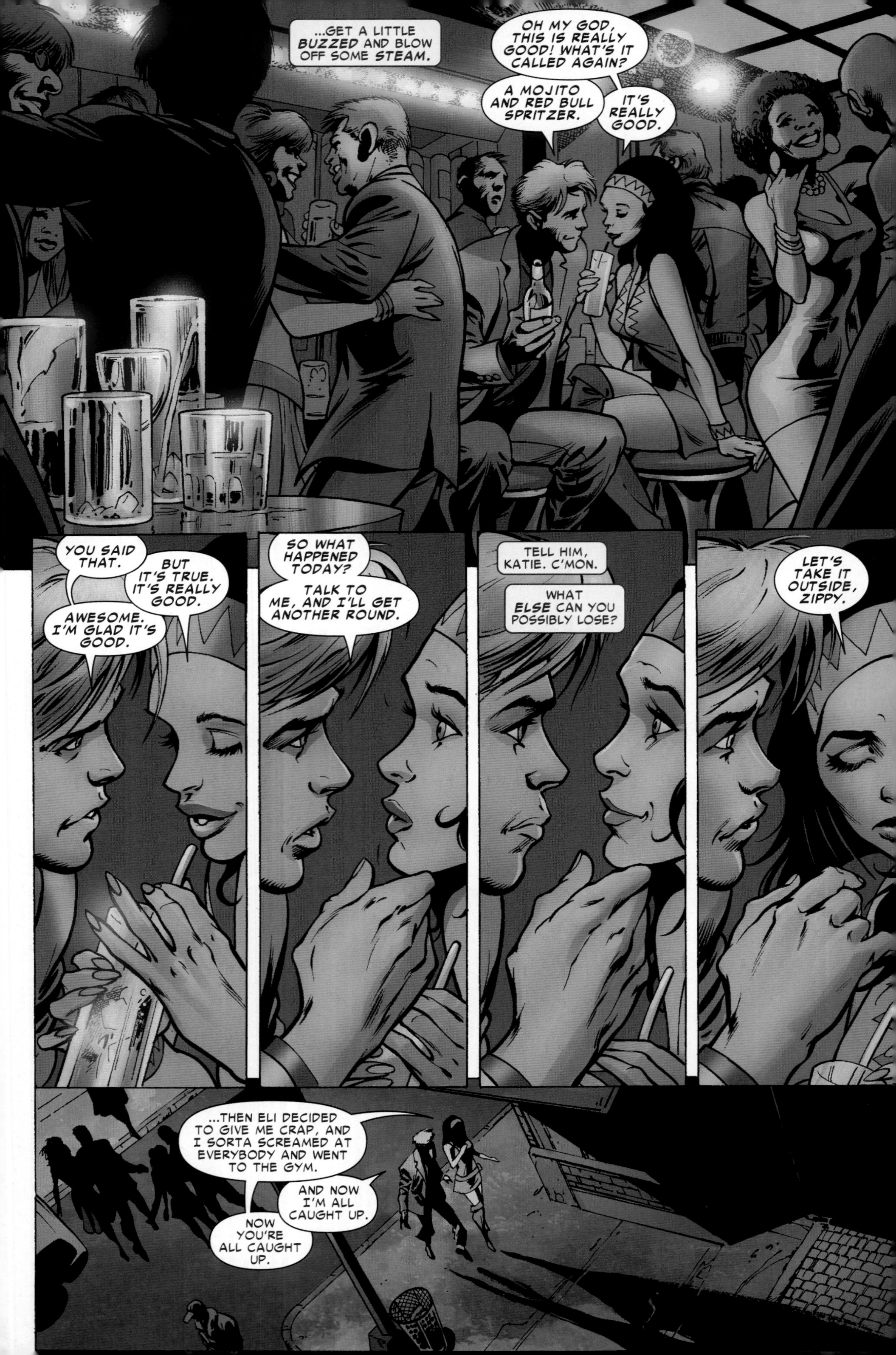
...GET A LITTLE BUZZED AND BLOW OFF SOME STEAM.
OH MY GOD, THIS IS REALLY GOOD! WHAT'S IT CALLED AGAIN?
A MOJITO AND RED BULL SPRITZER.
IT'S REALLY GOOD.
YOU SAID THAT.
BUT IT'S TRUE. IT'S REALLY GOOD.
AWESOME. I'M GLAD IT'S GOOD.
SO WHAT HAPPENED TODAY?
TALK TO ME, AND I'LL GET ANOTHER ROUND.
TELL HIM, KATIE. C'MON.
WHAT ELSE CAN YOU POSSIBLY LOSE?
LET'S TAKE IT OUTSIDE, ZIPPY.
...THEN ELI DECIDED TO GIVE ME CRAP, AND I SORTA SCREAMED AT EVERYBODY AND WENT TO THE GYM.
NOW YOU'RE ALL CAUGHT UP.
AND NOW I'M ALL CAUGHT UP.

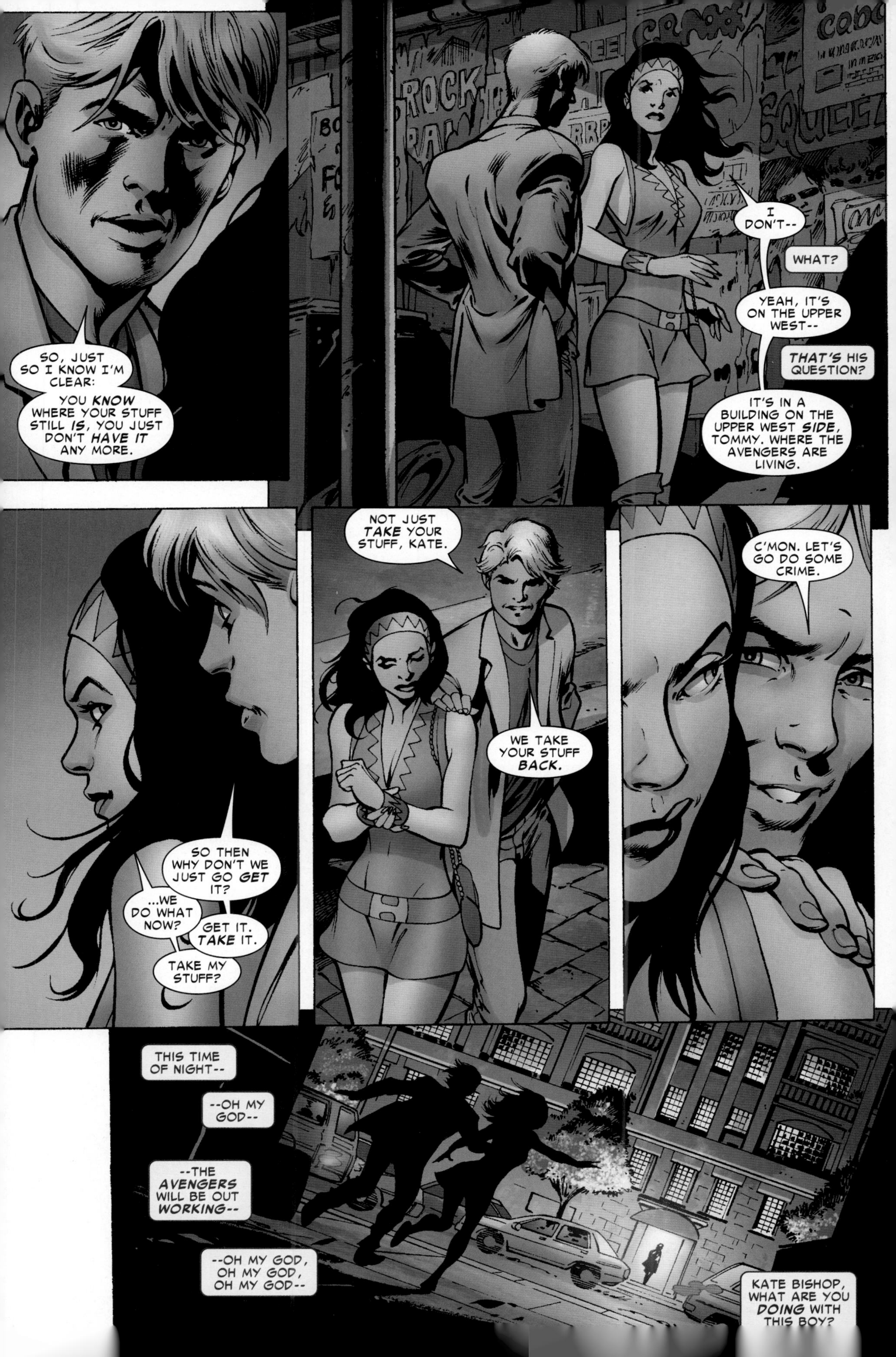
SO, JUST SO I KNOW I'M CLEAR:
YOU KNOW WHERE YOUR STUFF STILL IS, YOU JUST DON'T HAVE IT ANY MORE.
I DON'T--
WHAT?
YEAH, IT'S ON THE UPPER WEST--
THAT'S HIS QUESTION?
IT'S IN A BUILDING ON THE UPPER WEST SIDE, TOMMY. WHERE THE AVENGERS ARE LIVING.
SO THEN WHY DON'T WE JUST GO GET IT?
...WE DO WHAT NOW?
GET IT. TAKE IT.
TAKE MY STUFF?
NOT JUST TAKE YOUR STUFF, KATE.
WE TAKE YOUR STUFF BACK.
C'MON. LET'S GO DO SOME CRIME.
THIS TIME OF NIGHT--
--OH MY GOD--
--THE AVENGERS WILL BE OUT WORKING--
--OH MY GOD, OH MY GOD, OH MY GOD--
KATE BISHOP, WHAT ARE YOU DOING WITH THIS BOY?

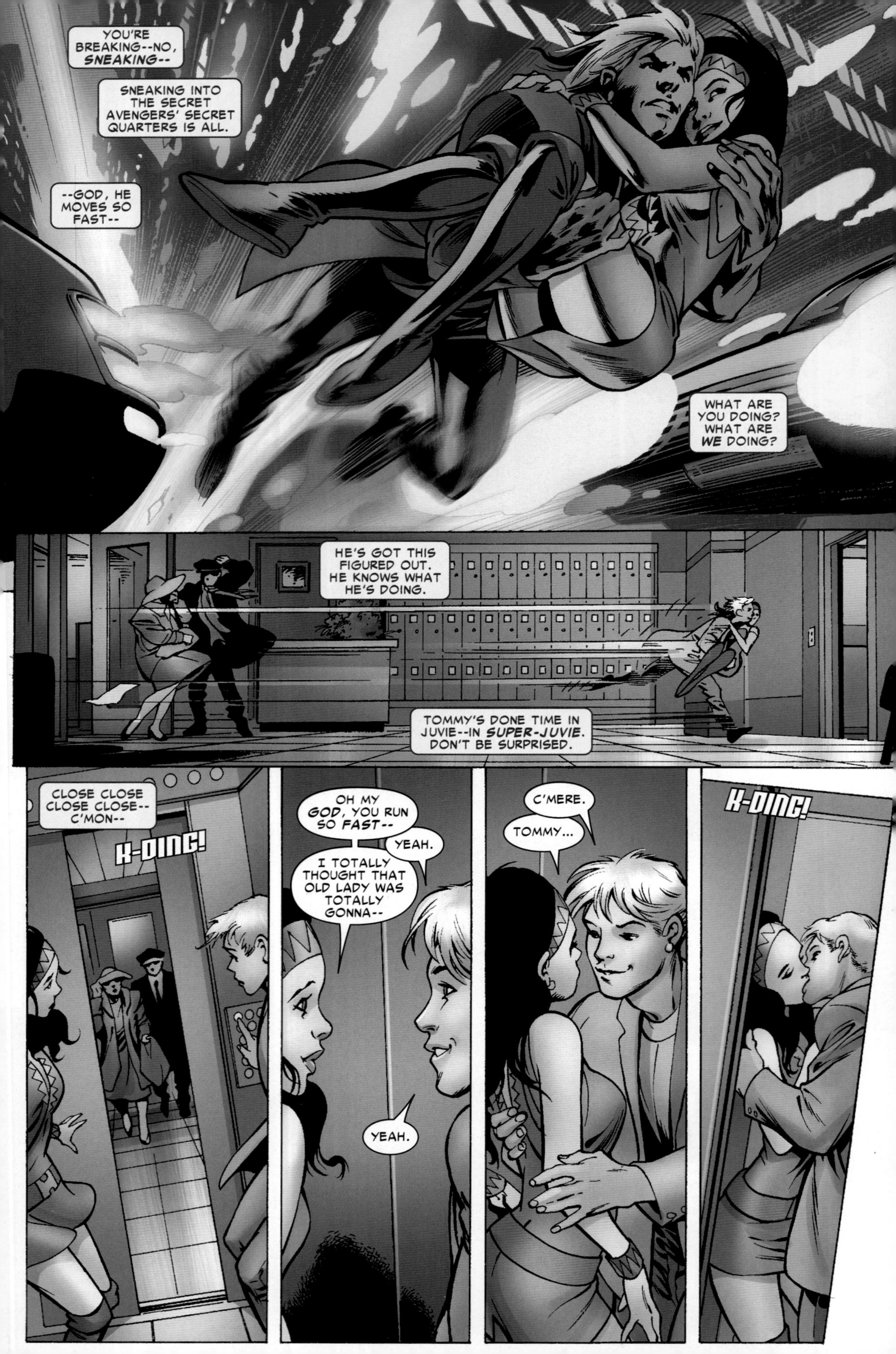
YOU'RE BREAKING--NO, SNEAKING--
SNEAKING INTO THE SECRET AVENGERS' SECRET QUARTERS IS ALL.
--GOD, HE MOVES SO FAST--
WHAT ARE YOU DOING? WHAT ARE WE DOING?
HE'S GOT THIS FIGURED OUT. HE KNOWS WHAT HE'S DOING.
TOMMY'S DONE TIME IN JUVIE--IN SUPER-JUVIE. DON'T BE SURPRISED.
CLOSE CLOSE CLOSE CLOSE-- C'MON--
K-DING!
OH MY GOD, YOU RUN SO FAST--
YEAH.
I TOTALLY THOUGHT THAT OLD LADY WAS TOTALLY GONNA--
YEAH.
C'MERE.
TOMMY...
K-DING!

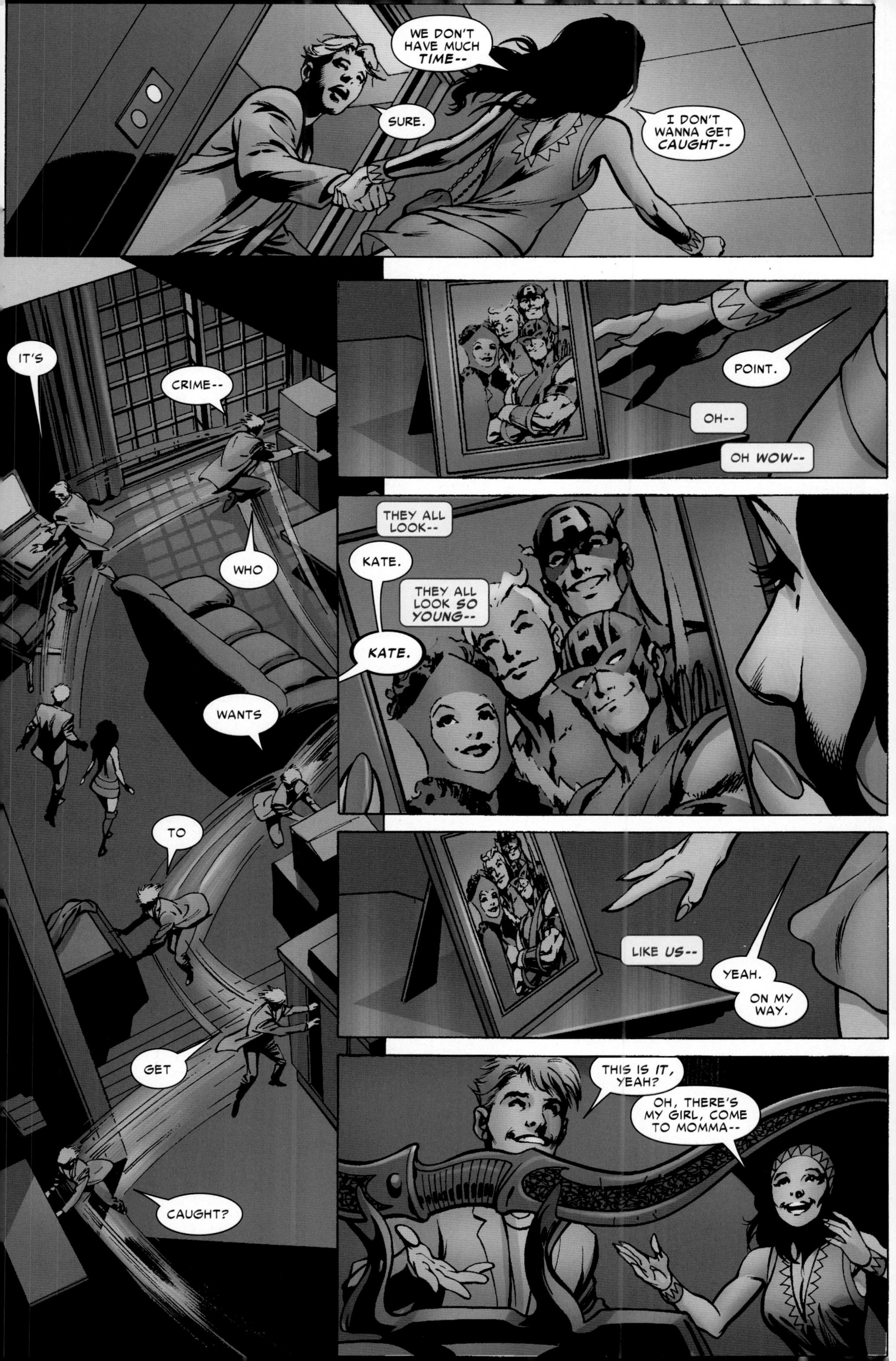

WE DON'T HAVE MUCH TIME--
SURE.
I DON'T WANNA GET CAUGHT--
IT'S
CRIME--
WHO
WANTS
TO
GET
CAUGHT?
POINT.
OH--
OH WOW--
THEY ALL LOOK--
KATE.
THEY ALL LOOK SO YOUNG--
KATE.
LIKE US--
YEAH.
ON MY WAY.
THIS IS IT, YEAH?
OH, THERE'S MY GIRL, COME TO MOMMA--

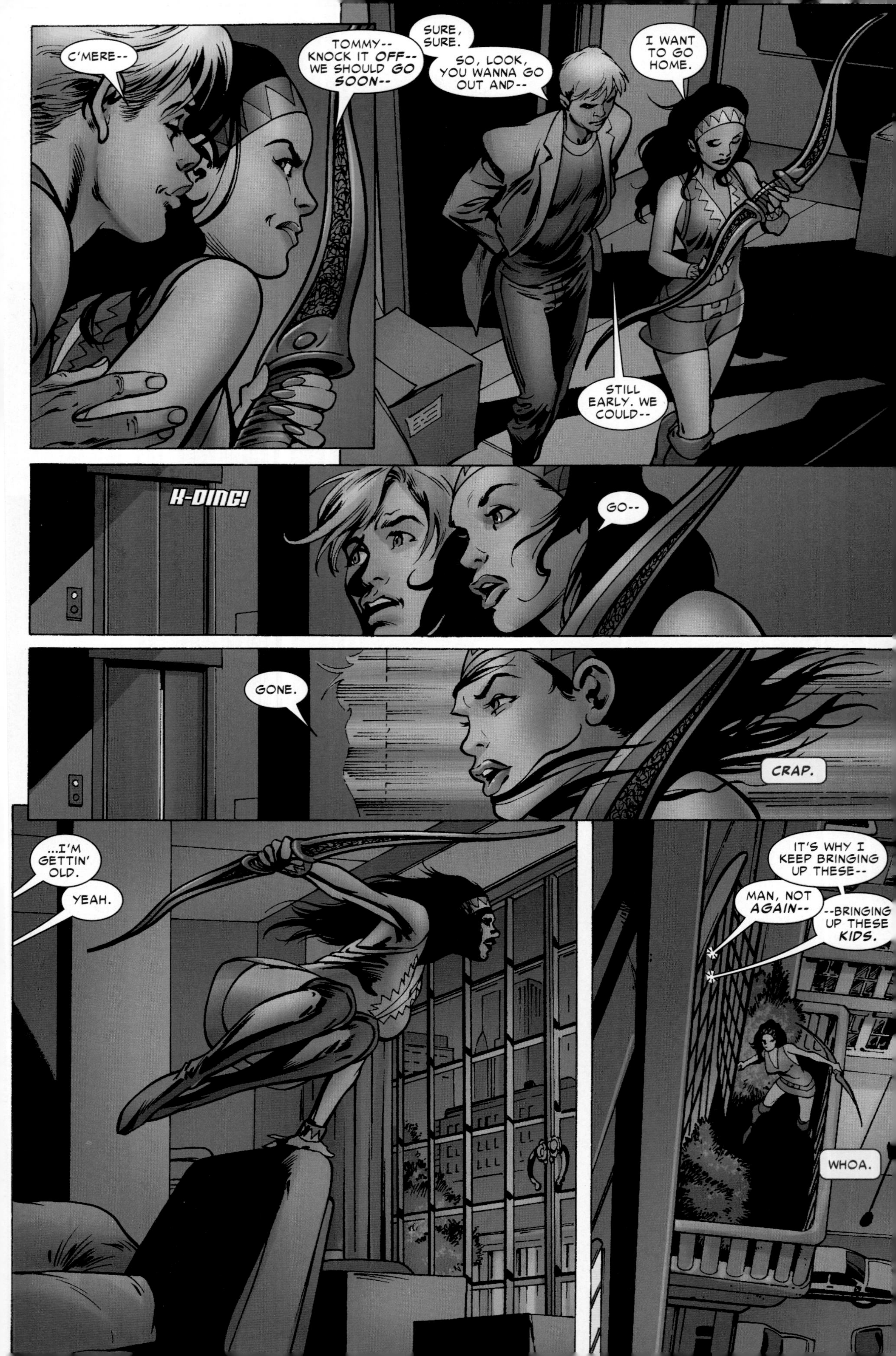

C'MERE--
TOMMY--
KNOCK IT OFF--
WE SHOULD GO
SOON--
SURE,
SURE.
SO, LOOK,
YOU WANNA GO
OUT AND--
I WANT
TO GO
HOME.
STILL
EARLY. WE
COULD--
K-DING!
GO--
GONE.
CRAP.
...I'M
GETTIN'
OLD.
YEAH.
IT'S WHY I
KEEP BRINGING
UP THESE--
MAN, NOT
AGAIN--
--BRINGING
UP THESE
KIDS.
WHOA.

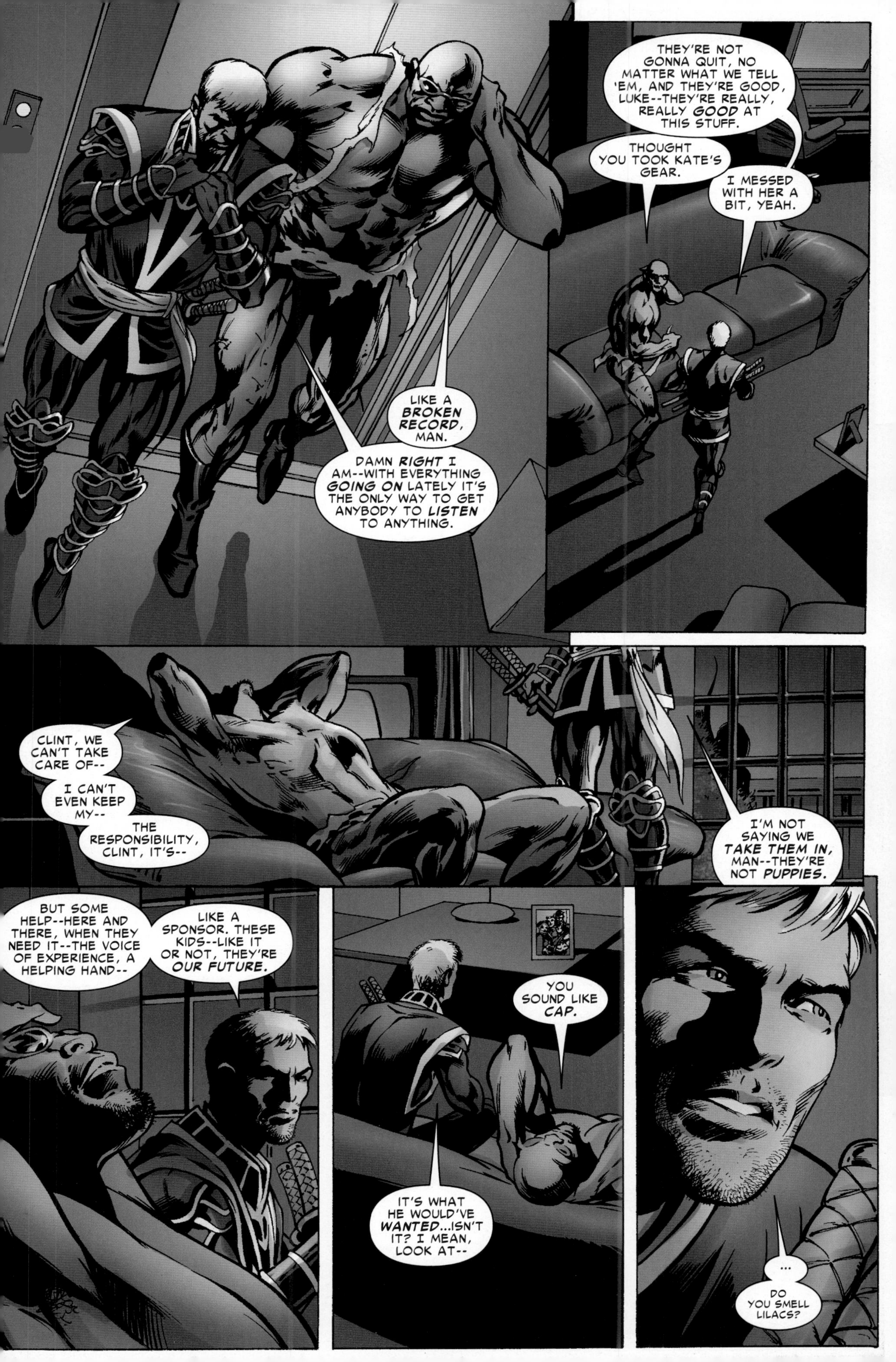
LIKE A BROKEN RECORD, MAN.
DAMN RIGHT I AM--WITH EVERYTHING GOING ON LATELY IT'S THE ONLY WAY TO GET ANYBODY TO LISTEN TO ANYTHING.
THEY'RE NOT GONNA QUIT, NO MATTER WHAT WE TELL 'EM, AND THEY'RE GOOD, LUKE--THEY'RE REALLY, REALLY GOOD AT THIS STUFF.
THOUGHT YOU TOOK KATE'S GEAR.
I MESSED WITH HER A BIT, YEAH.
CLINT, WE CAN'T TAKE CARE OF--
I CAN'T EVEN KEEP MY--
THE RESPONSIBILITY, CLINT, IT'S--
I'M NOT SAYING WE TAKE THEM IN, MAN--THEY'RE NOT PUPPIES.
BUT SOME HELP--HERE AND THERE, WHEN THEY NEED IT--THE VOICE OF EXPERIENCE, A HELPING HAND--
LIKE A SPONSOR. THESE KIDS--LIKE IT OR NOT, THEY'RE OUR FUTURE.
YOU SOUND LIKE CAP.
IT'S WHAT HE WOULD'VE WANTED...ISN'T IT? I MEAN, LOOK AT--
...
DO YOU SMELL LILACS?

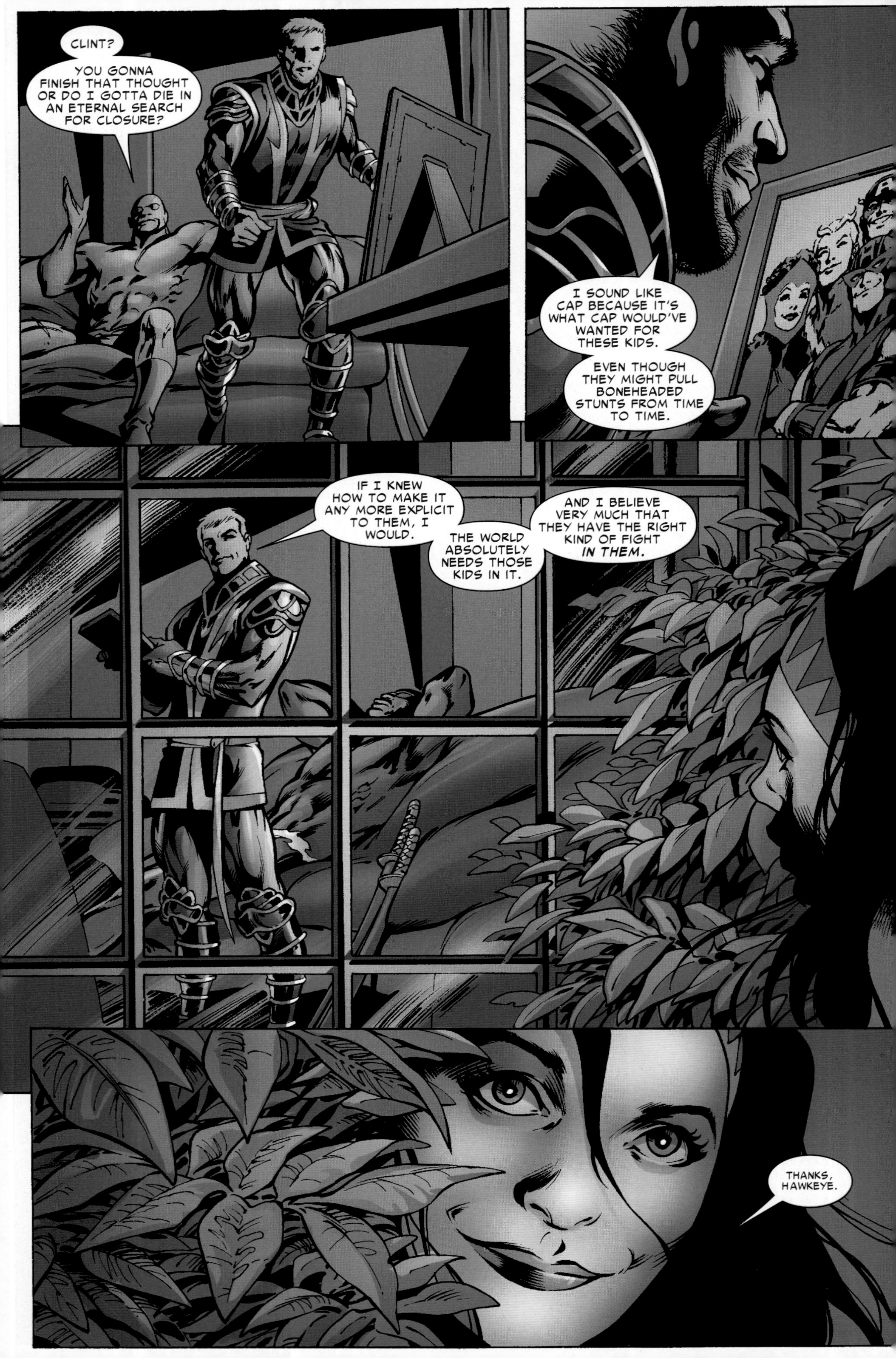
CLINT?
YOU GONNA FINISH THAT THOUGHT OR DO I GOTTA DIE IN AN ETERNAL SEARCH FOR CLOSURE?
I SOUND LIKE CAP BECAUSE IT'S WHAT CAP WOULD'VE WANTED FOR THESE KIDS.
EVEN THOUGH THEY MIGHT PULL BONEHEADED STUNTS FROM TIME TO TIME.
IF I KNEW HOW TO MAKE IT ANY MORE EXPLICIT TO THEM, I WOULD.
THE WORLD ABSOLUTELY NEEDS THOSE KIDS IN IT.
AND I BELIEVE VERY MUCH THAT THEY HAVE THE RIGHT KIND OF FIGHT *IN THEM.*
THANKS, HAWKEYE.

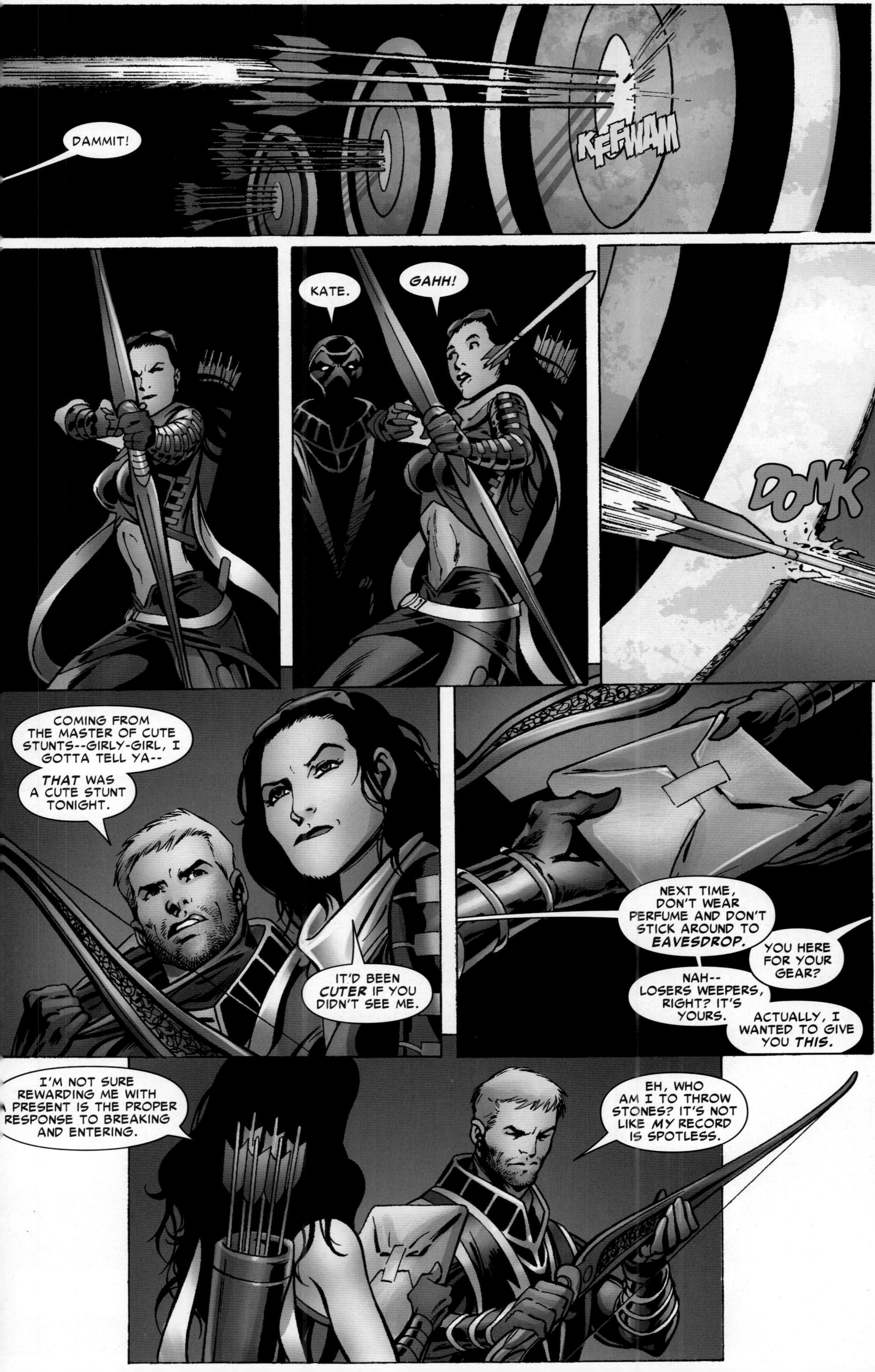
DAMMIT!
KFFWAM
KATE.
GAHH!
DONK
COMING FROM THE MASTER OF CUTE STUNTS--GIRLY-GIRL, I GOTTA TELL YA--
THAT WAS A CUTE STUNT TONIGHT.
IT'D BEEN CUTER IF YOU DIDN'T SEE ME.
NEXT TIME, DON'T WEAR PERFUME AND DON'T STICK AROUND TO EAVESDROP.
YOU HERE FOR YOUR GEAR?
NAH-- LOSERS WEEPERS, RIGHT? IT'S YOURS.
ACTUALLY, I WANTED TO GIVE YOU THIS.
I'M NOT SURE REWARDING ME WITH A PRESENT IS THE PROPER RESPONSE TO BREAKING AND ENTERING.
EH, WHO AM I TO THROW STONES? IT'S NOT LIKE MY RECORD IS SPOTLESS.

YOU'VE MADE IT CRYSTAL CLEAR YOU'RE NOT AFRAID TO STAND UP FOR WHAT YOU BELIEVE--

AND TONIGHT YOU SHOWED ME THAT YOU'LL *KEEP STANDING*, NO MATTER WHAT.

OH, CLINT.

CLINT, I CAN'T ACCEPT THIS.

THE AVENGERS HAVE ALWAYS BEEN ABOUT TRADITION, KATE--ABOUT UNITY, ABOUT FAMILY--

ABOUT *LEGACY*. I KNOW, BECAUSE I GOT TO EXPERIENCE THAT FIRSTHAND. I WAS ONE OF THE *FIRST* AVENGERS THAT PEOPLE DIDN'T BELIEVE IN, DOUBTED, AND DESPISED A LITTLE.

NOW IT'S YOUR TURN.

WE'LL *BE HERE* FOR YOU KIDS.

GO OUT, FIGHT HARD, SCREW UP. SAVE THE WORLD A FEW TIMES. WE HAVE YOUR BACK.

JUST KEEP TAKING THE SHOTS, OKAY?

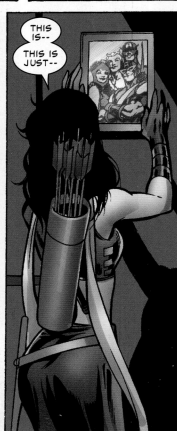

THIS IS--

THIS IS JUST--

...

FOR THE SECOND TIME TONIGHT, I FIND MYSELF SAYING...

THANKS, HAWKEYE.

EVEN THOUGH I'M NOT SURE HE HEARD IT.

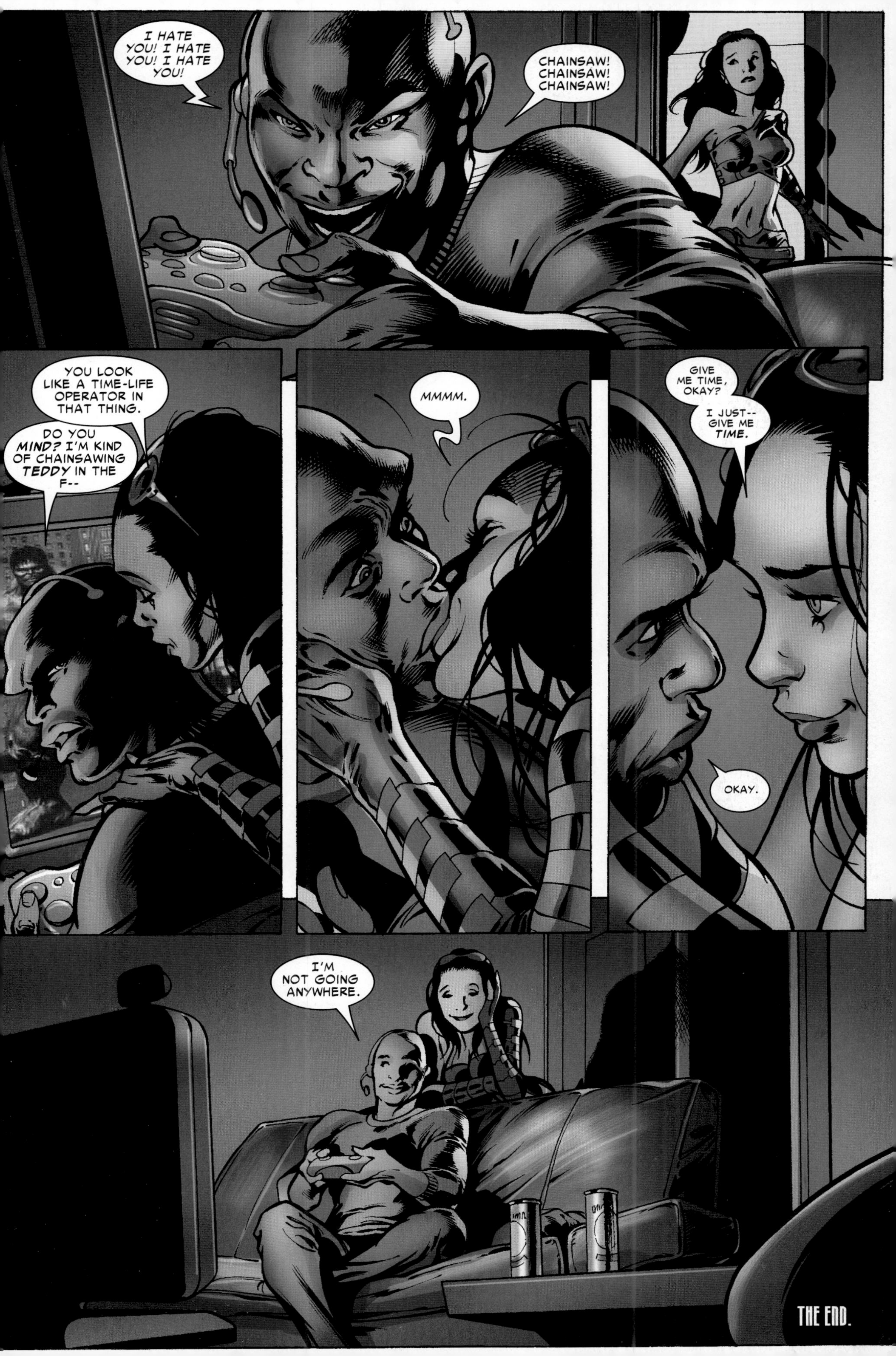
I HATE YOU! I HATE YOU! I HATE YOU!
CHAINSAW! CHAINSAW! CHAINSAW!
YOU LOOK LIKE A TIME-LIFE OPERATOR IN THAT THING.
DO YOU MIND? I'M KIND OF CHAINSAWING TEDDY IN THE F--
MMMM.
GIVE ME TIME, OKAY?
I JUST-- GIVE ME TIME.
OKAY.
I'M NOT GOING ANYWHERE.
THE END.

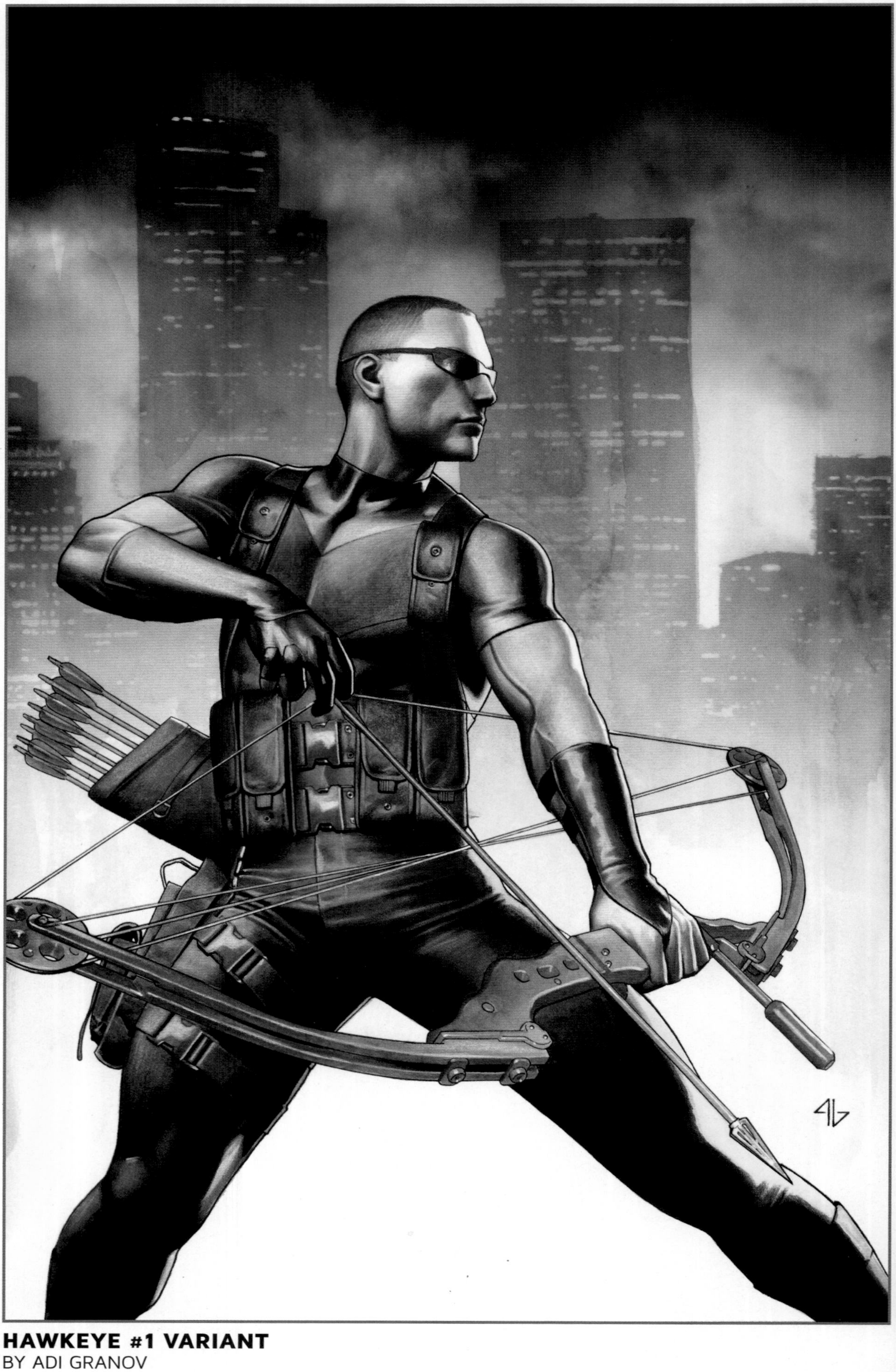

**HAWKEYE #1 VARIANT**
BY ADI GRANOV

# DAVID AJA SKETCHBOOK

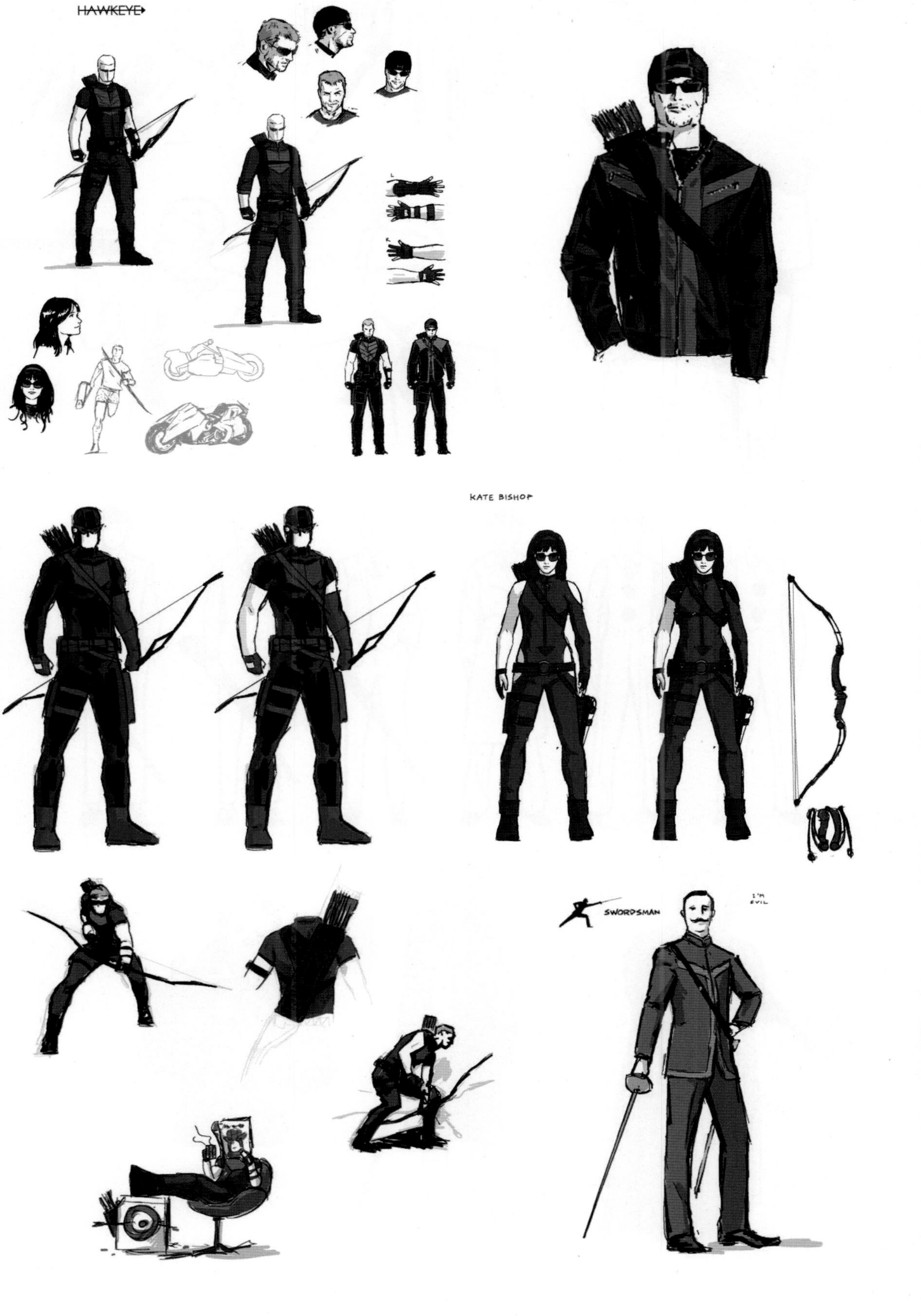
HAWKEYE
KATE BISHOP
SWORDSMAN
I'M EVIL

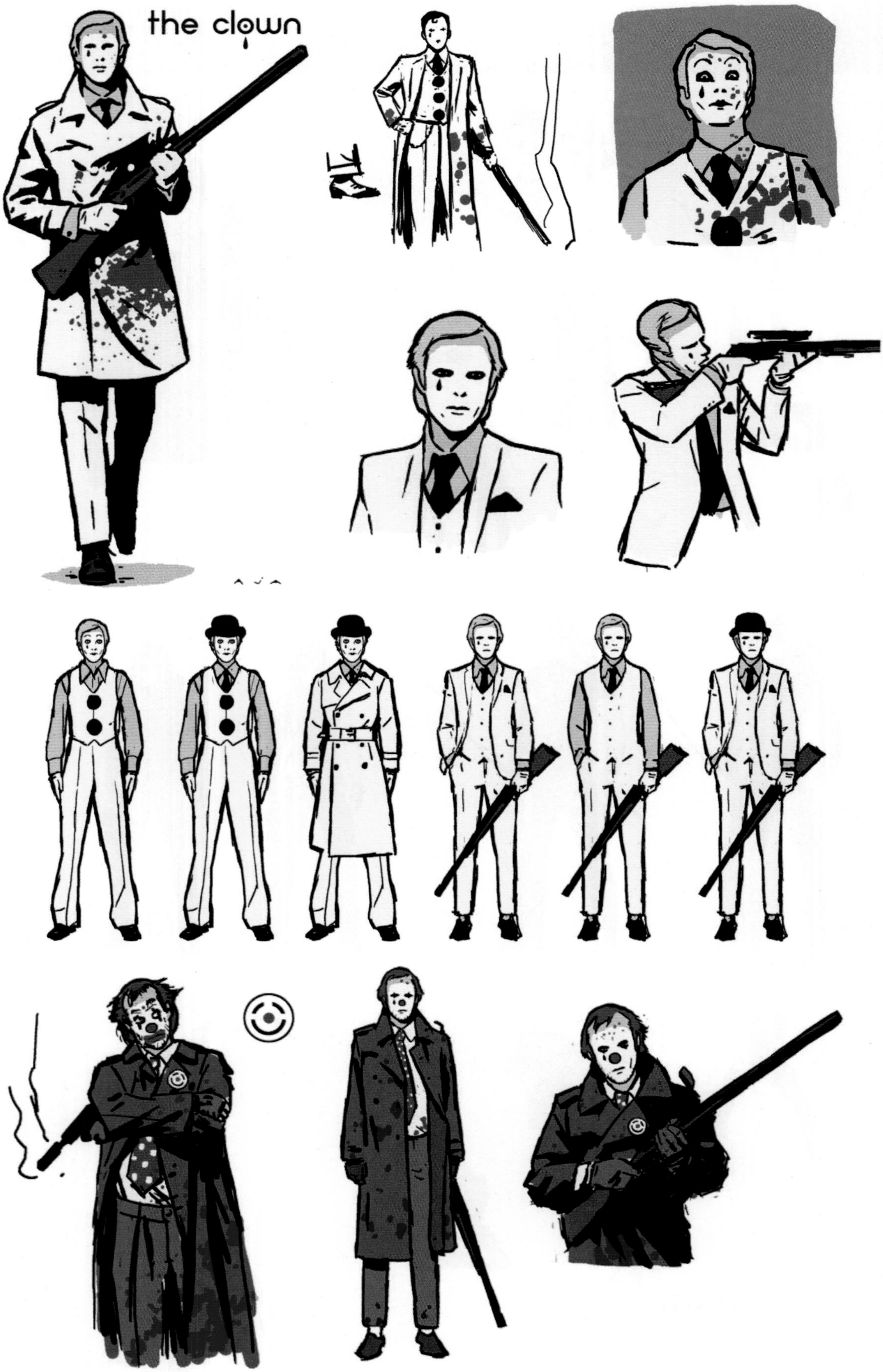

the clown

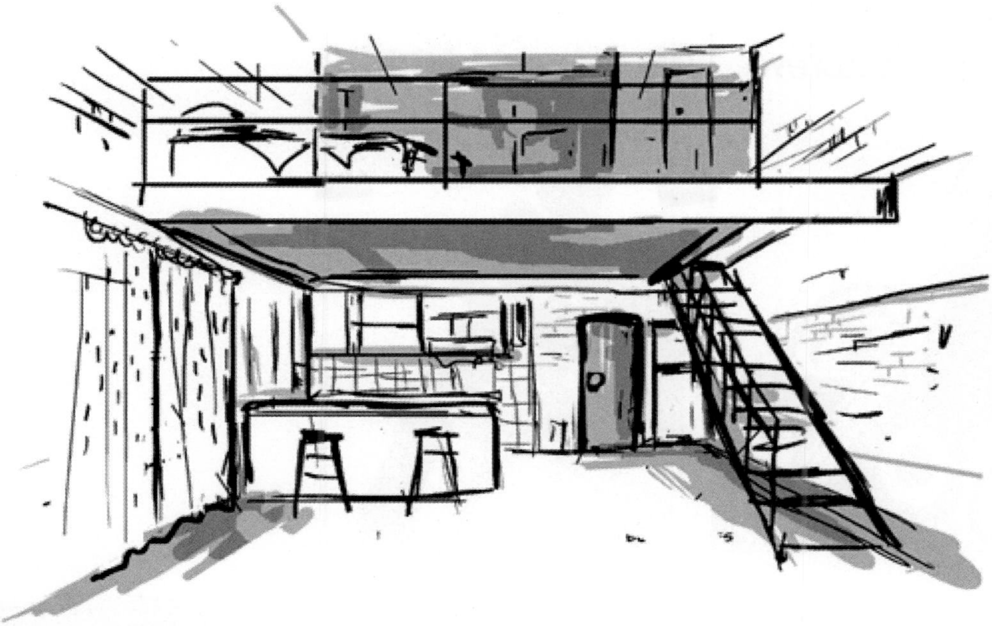

CLINT LOFT

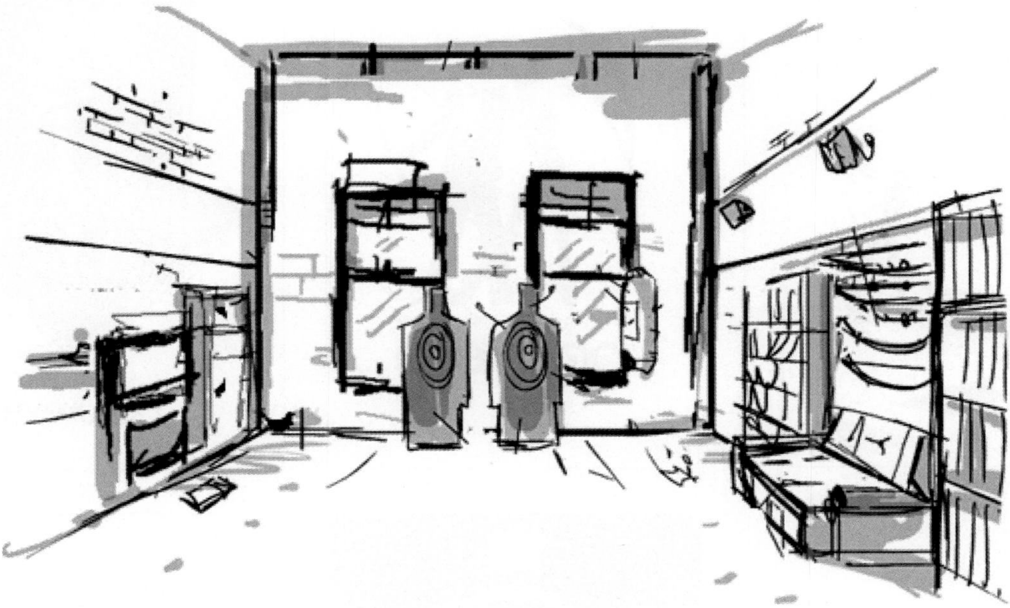

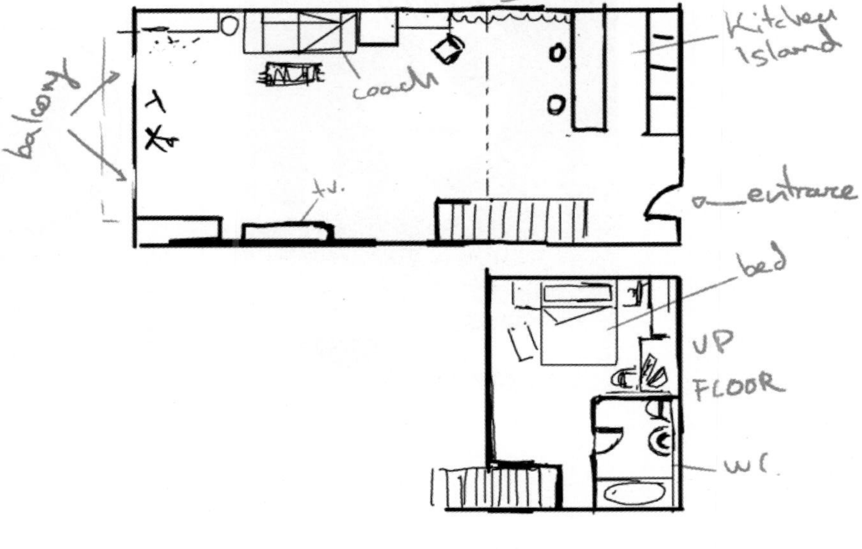
curtain
Kitchen Island
coach
balcony
t.v.
entrance
bed
UP FLOOR
wc

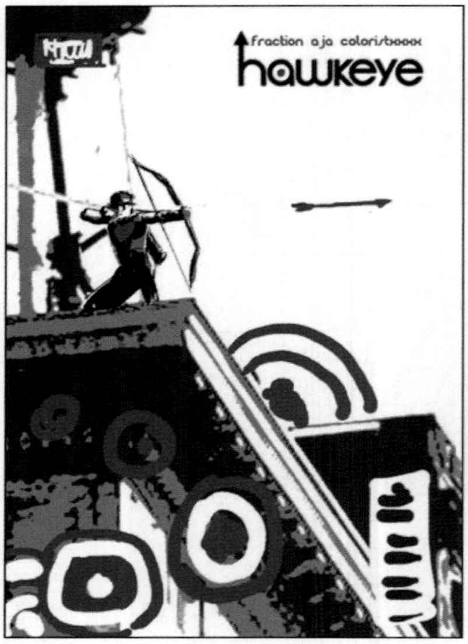
hawkeye

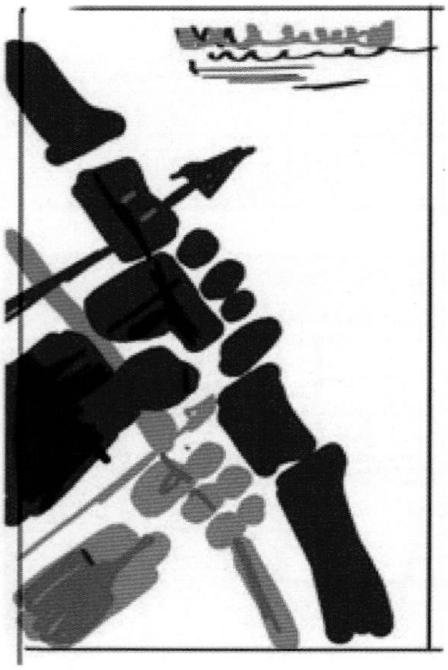

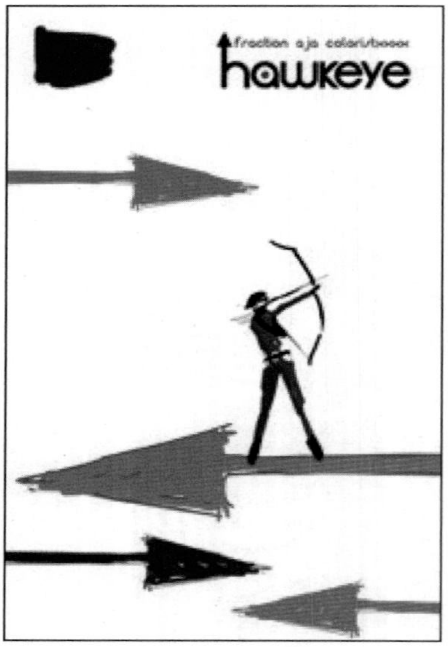
hawkeye

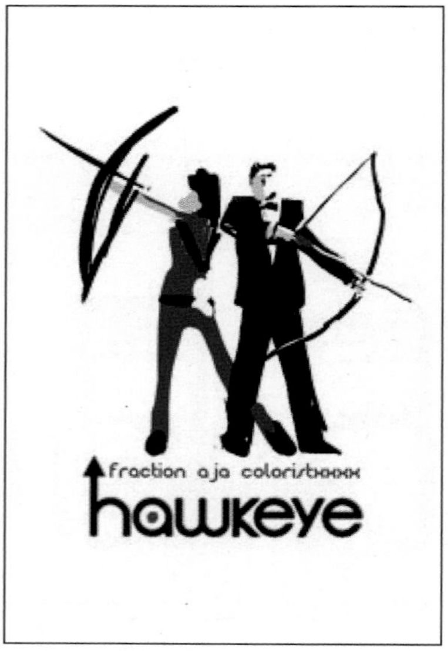
fraction aja coloristxxxx
hawkeye

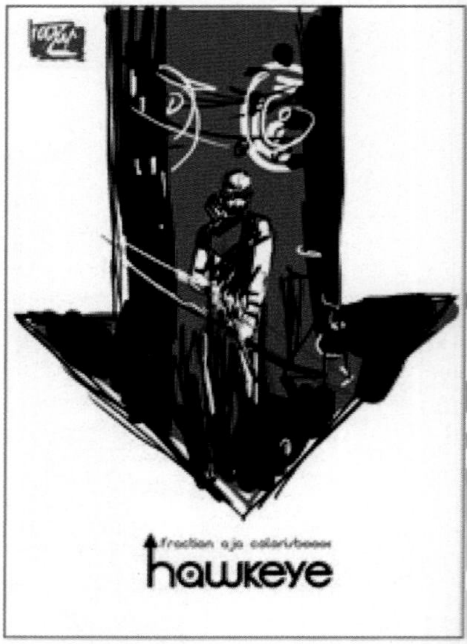
hawkeye

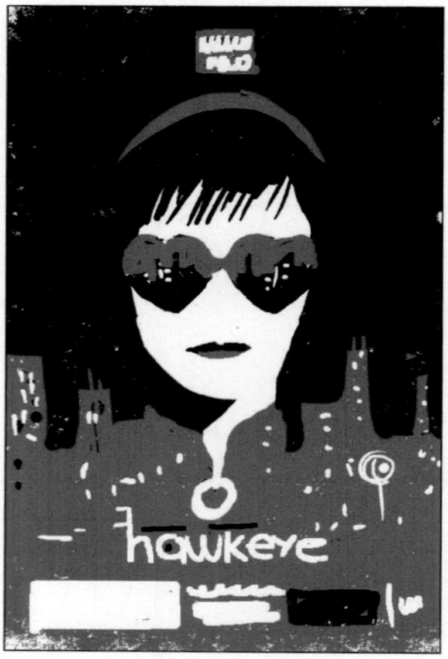
hawkeye

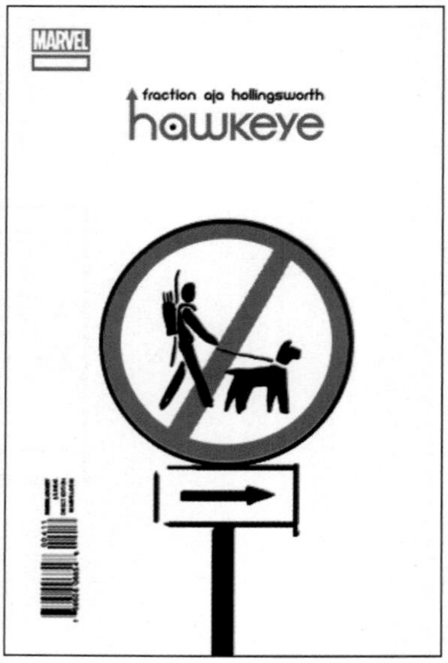
MARVEL
fraction aja hollingsworth
hawkeye

**COVER CONCEPTS**
BY DAVID AJA

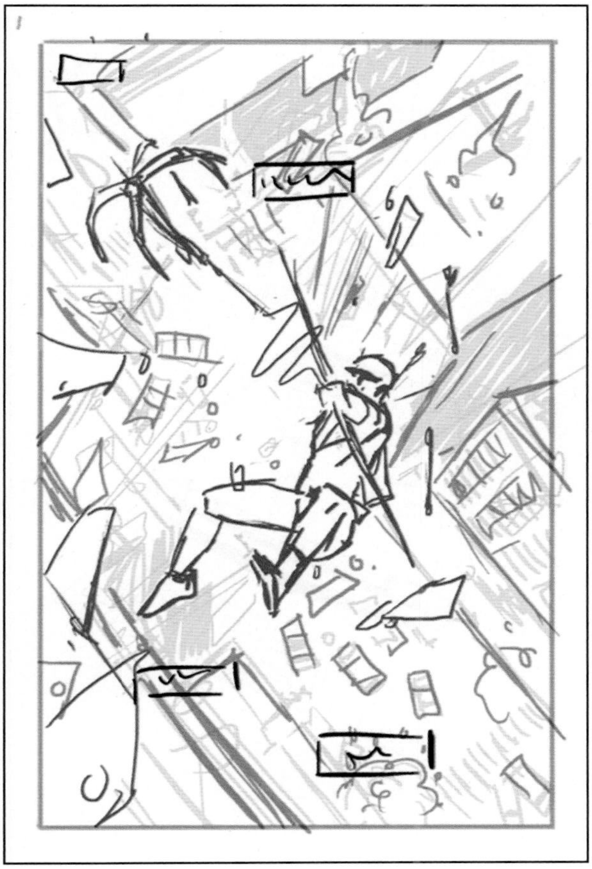

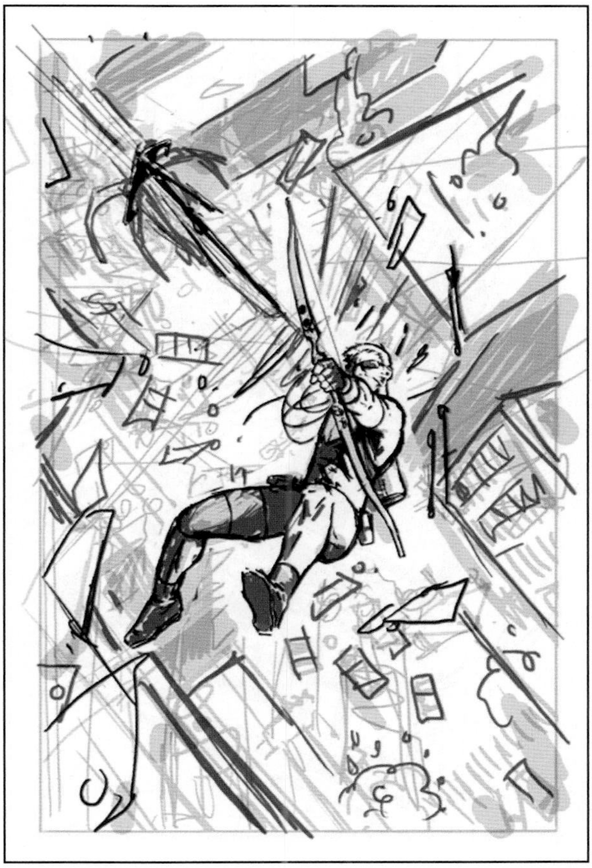

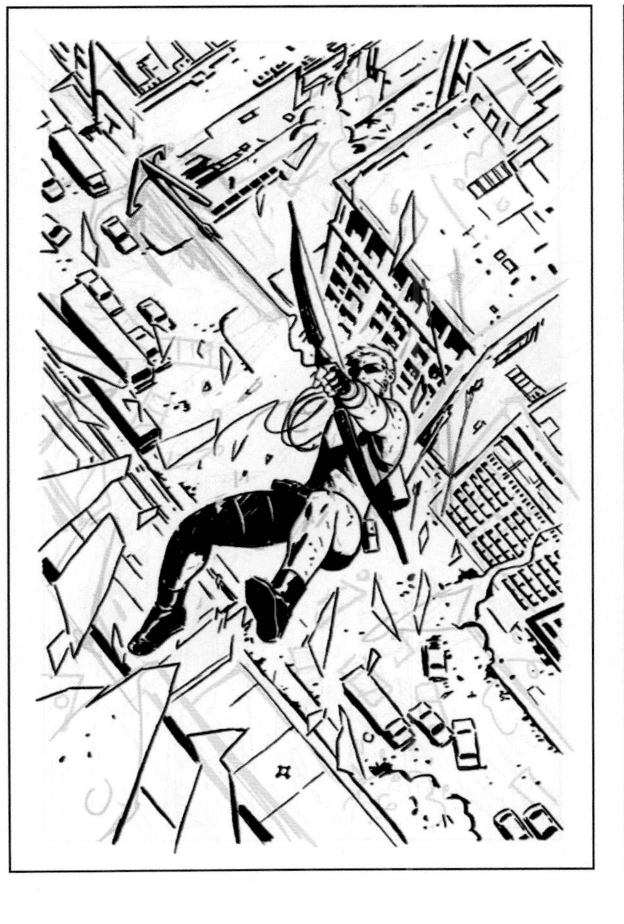

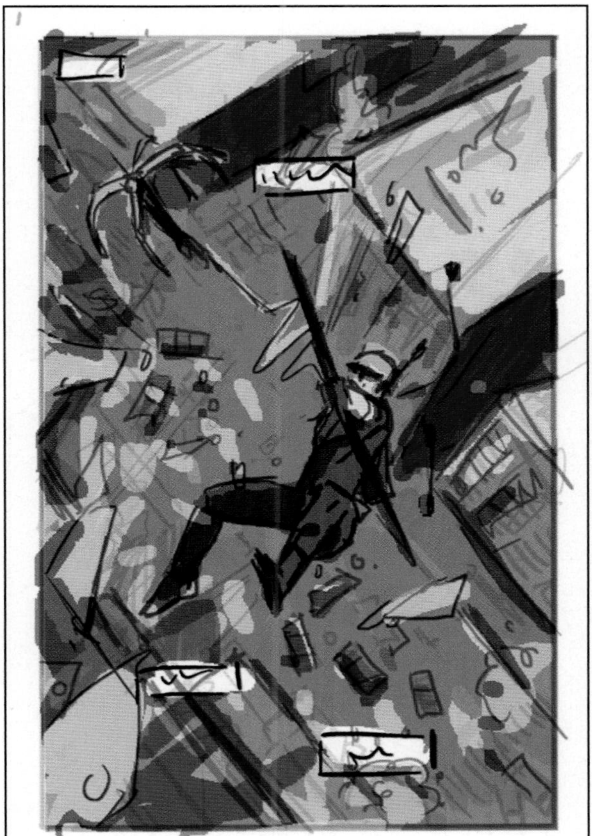

**ISSUE #1, PAGE 1 PROCESS**

CHERRY
CHERRY
CHERRY
CHERRY

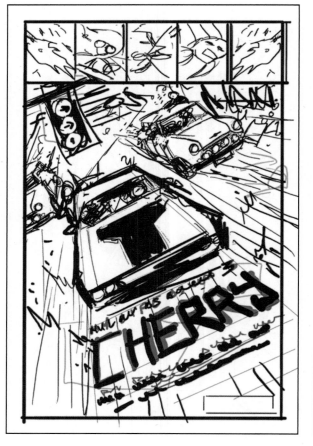

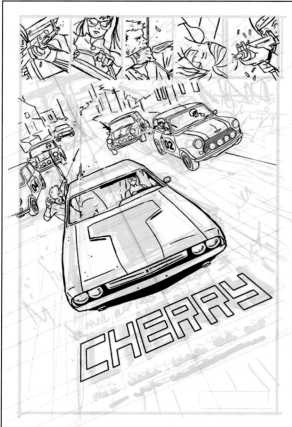

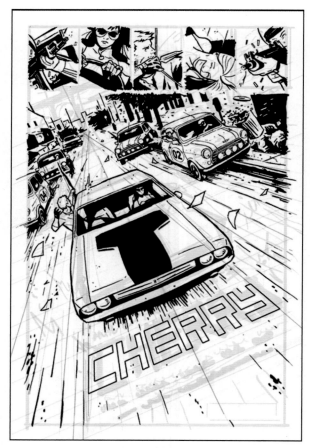

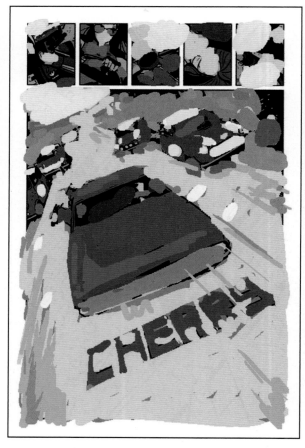

**ISSUE #3, PAGE 1 PROCESS**

WHAT?
DON'T.

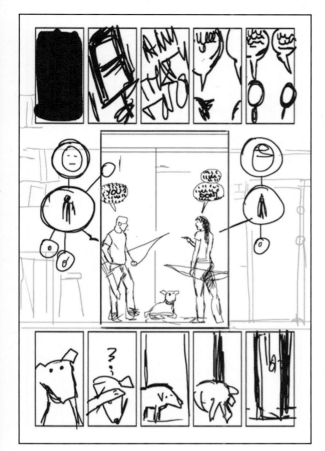

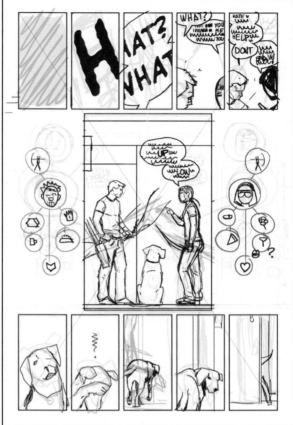

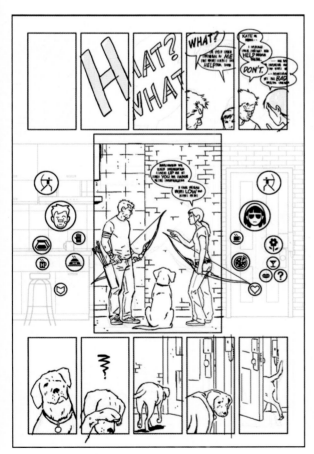

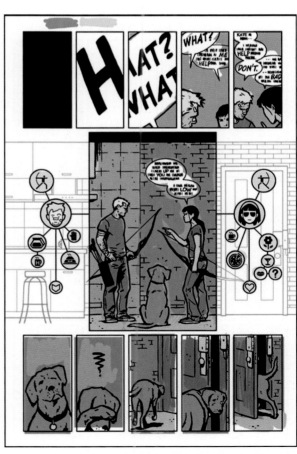

**ISSUE #11, PAGE 1 PROCESS**

**PAGE NINE**

CLINT and CHERRY, lit by Kate's TAILLIGHTS, stare at their wheelman leaving them out to dry.

They look at each other.

CLINT stomps across the street, CHERRY waiting in the shadows. A TRACKSUIT stands outside, not noticing. A couple other STRIPPERS, a few PATRONS mill about the front door of the club. We can all but hear the OONTZ OONTZ music from within.

The TRACKSUIT is bro-ing at one of the strippers as CLINT stomps up, shouting HEY ADIDAS —

— and PUNCHES THE [redacted] out of him, knocking the big guy off his stool.

The guy GETS UP in time for CLINT to HIT HIM BACK TOWARDS THE DOOR with that stool, hard —

ISSUE 8, PAGE 9 LAYOUTS

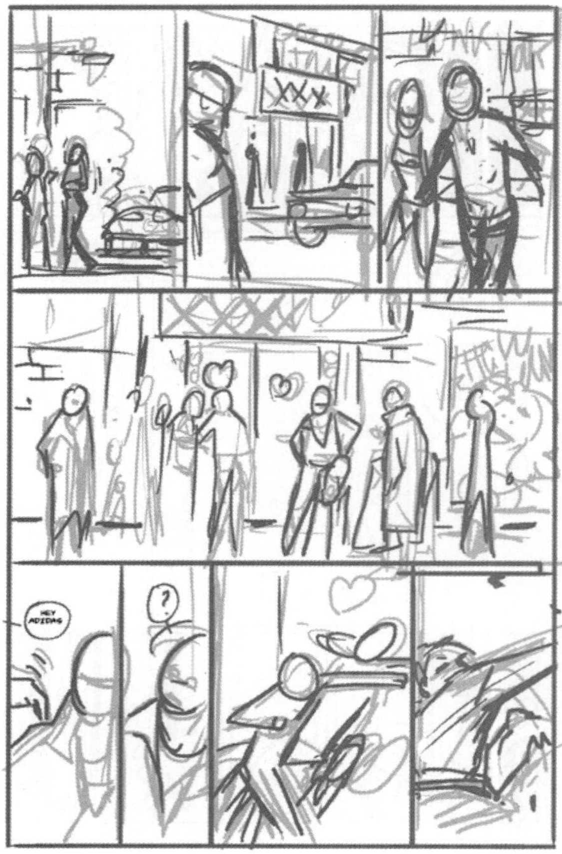
HEY ADIDAS

ISSUE 8, PAGE 9 PENCILS

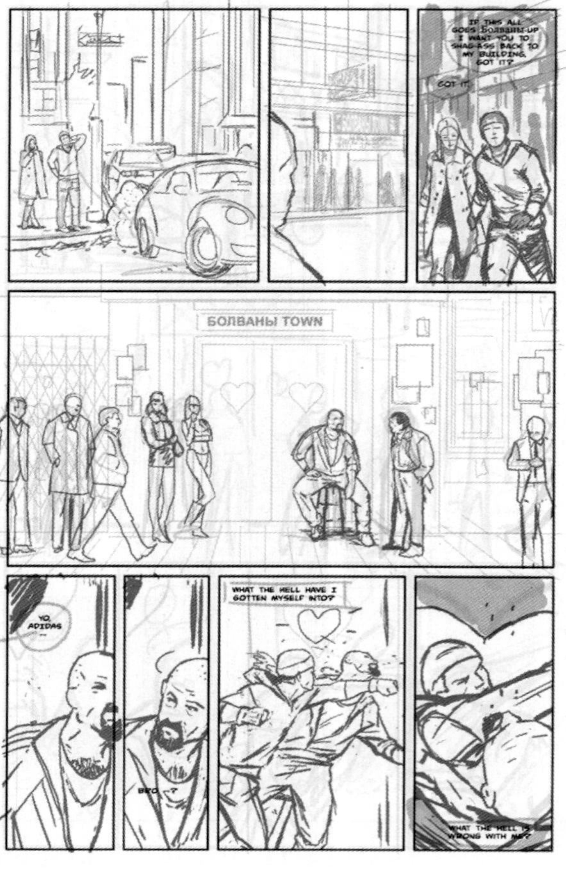
IF THIS ALL GOES БОЛВАНЫ-UP I WANT YOU TO SHAG-ASS BACK TO MY BUILDING. GOT IT?
GOT IT.
БОЛВАНЫ TOWN
YO, ADIDAS
WHAT THE HELL HAVE I GOTTEN MYSELF INTO?
WHAT THE HELL IS WRONG WITH ME?

ISSUE 8, PAGE 9 PARTIAL INKS

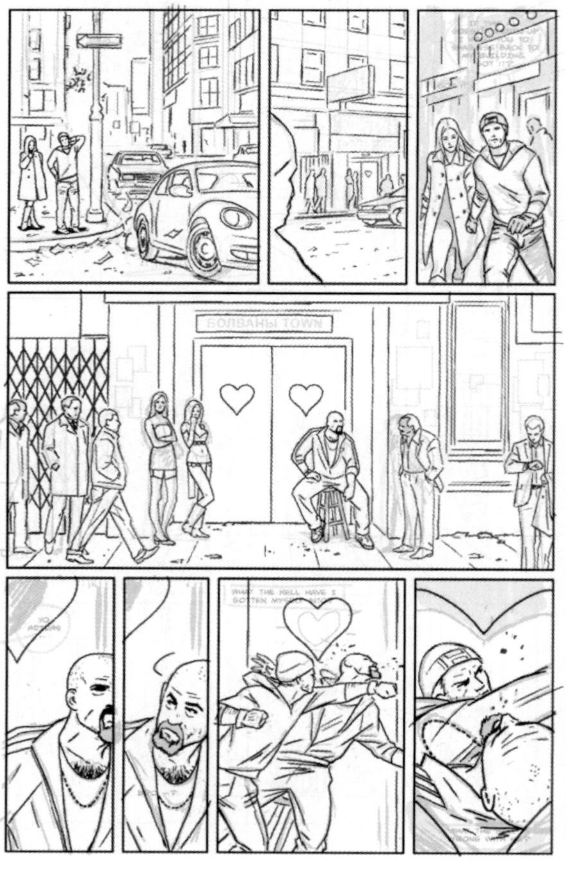
БОЛВАНЫ TOWN

ISSUE 8, PAGE 9 INKS

БОЛВАНЫ TOWN
TEL
ADULTS ONLY

ISSUE 8, PAGE 9 COLORS

БОЛВАНЫ TOWN
TEL
ADULTS ONLY

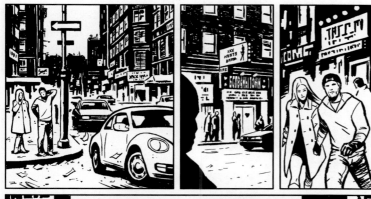

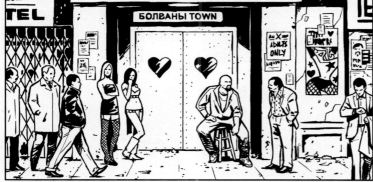

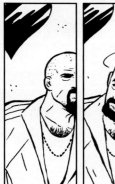

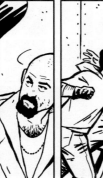

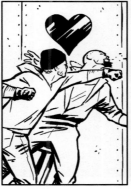

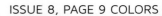

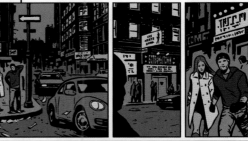

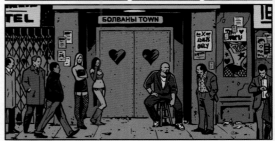

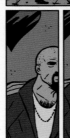

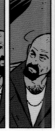

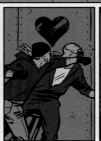

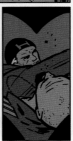

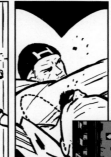

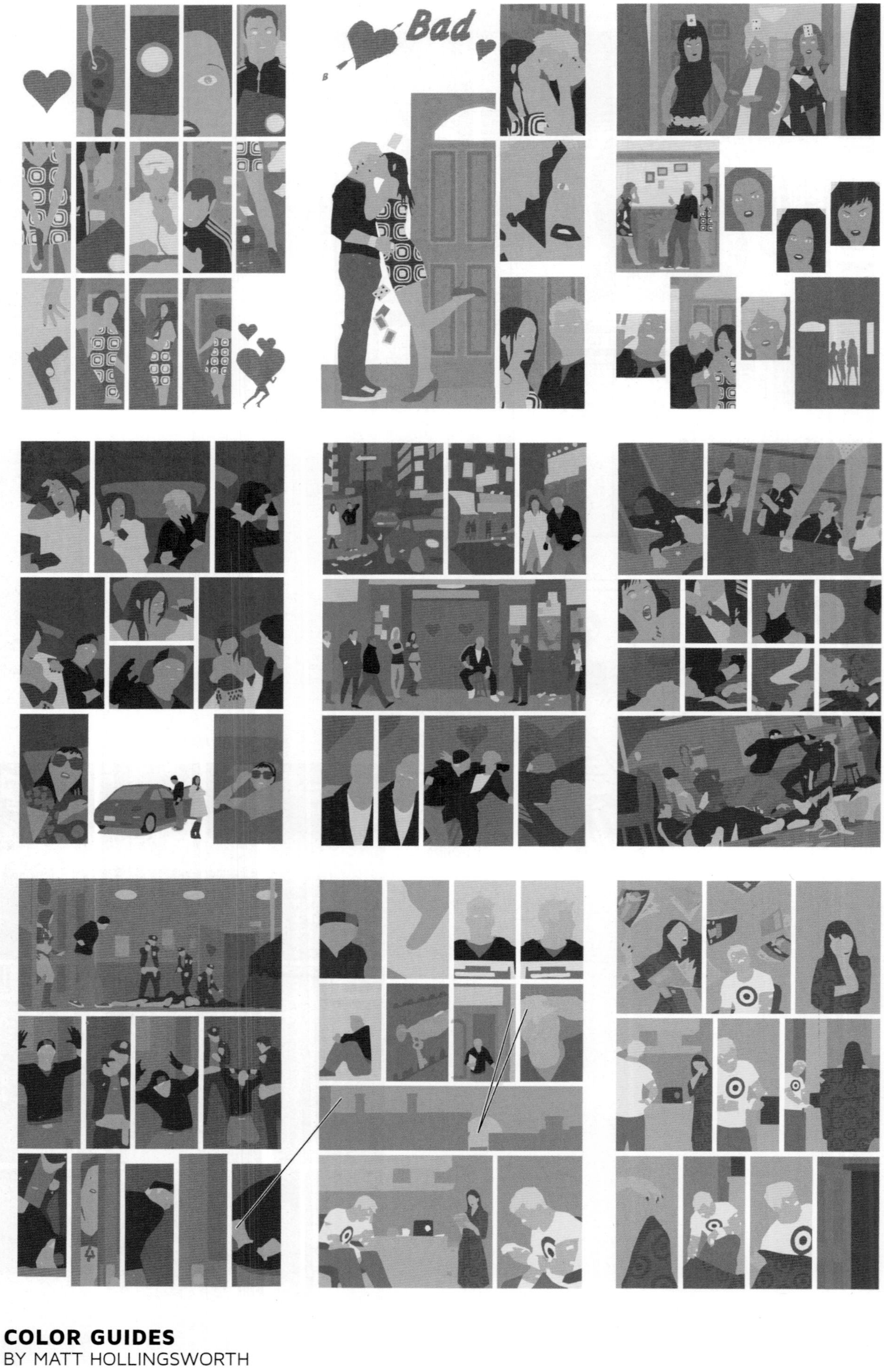
Bad

**COLOR GUIDES**
BY MATT HOLLINGSWORTH

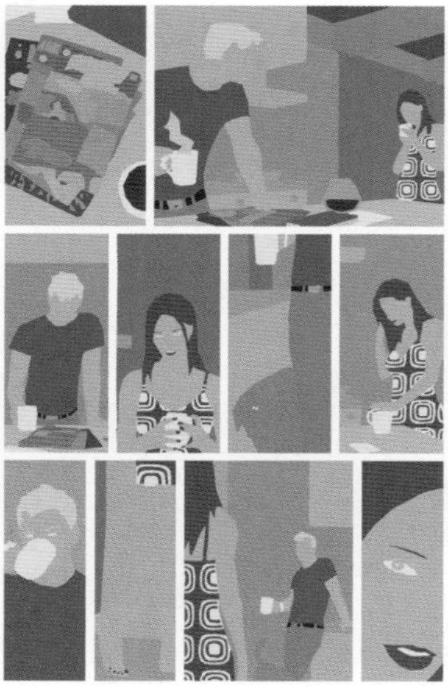

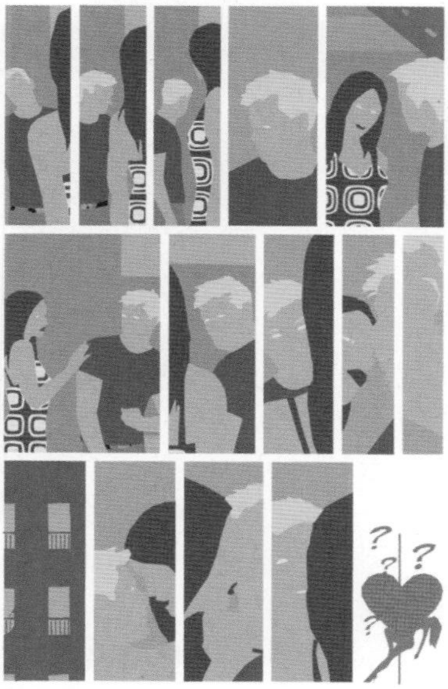

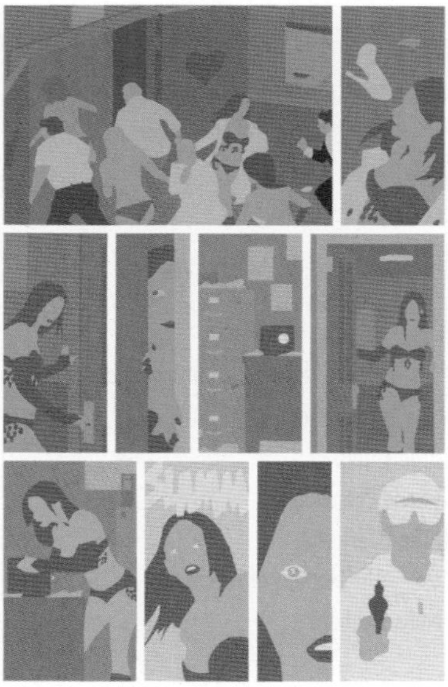

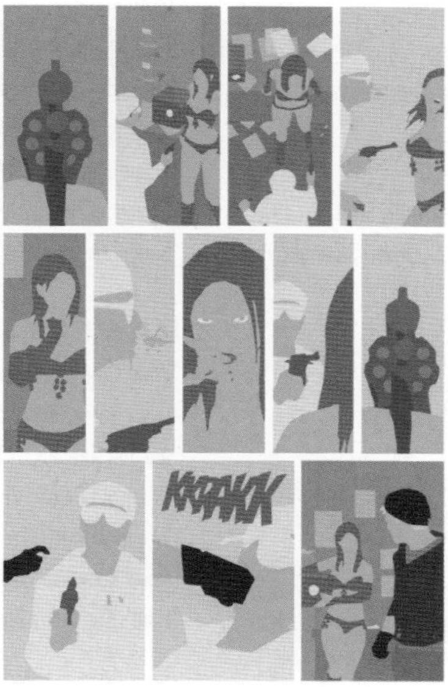
KKRAKK

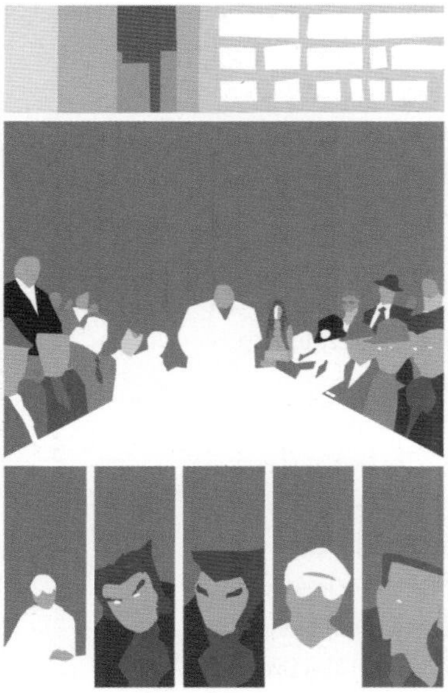

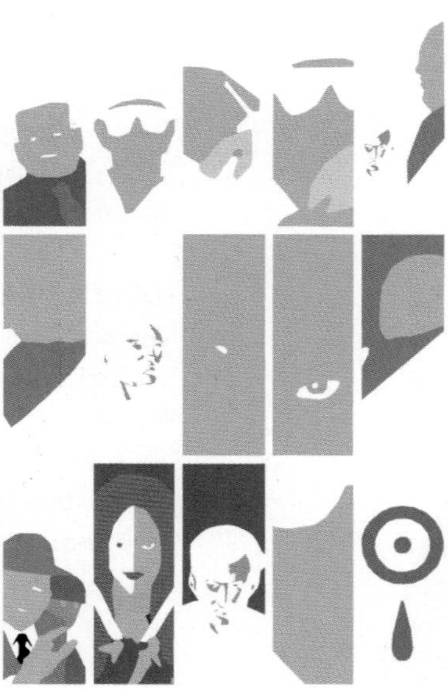

"Hawkeye is colored with minimalism in mind. Generally, as few colors as possible are used across the issue. Colors will reappear on pages across the book. You can see some examples I marked where the flesh tone from one scene is used as the sky color on the following scene and the hair color is carried over to be the color of the sun. The colors sometimes appear different because of the surrounding colors, which affect the way our eyes see that color. Color is a contextual thing.

"The book is colored as one whole unit rather than as separate pages. I work by laying out the entire issue on my second monitor. I pull a page to my main monitor and do a rough layout of the colors I want to use, then put the page back into the layout and pull another page and repeat that. Once I have the basic rough colors laid out for the entire issue, I go back and refine the colors over and over, usually minimizing the amount of colors I have more and more, distilling it down to a pretty minimal amount of colors. I don't often go monochromatic. It's usually a 2-3 color scheme with variations within those colors. I'm constantly looking at the entire issue to see how it's sitting as a whole. I will rough it in and then let it sit for a day or so and see what I think of it with fresh eyes. Well, when time allows, that is!"

— Matt Hollingsworth

# DAVID AJA'S DRAWING PLAYLISTS

## HAWKEYE #1
"Fire Dance" - **Dizzy Gillespie & Lalo Schifrin**
"Summertime" - **Dizzy Gillespie**
"Page 26" - **Fantômas**
"Scorpio" - **Dennis Coffey and The Detroit Guitar Band**
"One Finger Snap" - **Herbie Hancock**
"Page 6" - **Fantômas**
"Ah-Leu-Cha" - **Miles Davis**
"Hang Up Your Hang Ups" - **Herbie Hancock**

## HAWKEYE #2
"String Quartet No. 14 in D minor, I. Allegro" - **Franz Schubert**
"High Society Girl" - **The New Breed**
"String Quartet No. 4, I. Allegro Molto" - **Arnold Schönberg**
"String Quartet No. 8 in C minor, II. Allegro Molto" - **Dmitri Shostakovich**
"The Mad Scientist" - **The Zanies**
"String Quartet No.5, Allegro" - **Béla Bartók**
"String Quartet No. 11 in F minor, III. Recitative: Adagio" - **Dmitri Shostakovich**
"String Quartet No. 11 in F minor, V. Humoresque: Allegro" - **Dmitri Shostakovich**
"The Return of Rübezahl" - **Amon Düül II**
"The End" - **The Ruins**

## HAWKEYE #3
"Have Love, Will Travel" - **The Sonics**
"The Champ" - **The Mohawks**
"Gotta Get Some" - **Bold**
"Greatest Lover in the World" - **Bo Diddley**
"Something Against You" - **The Pixies**
"Titoli Di Testa" - **Guess What**
"Funky Jam" - **Eddie Bo**
"Slow Down" - **The Swingin' Apollos**
"Vanishing Point" - **Michael Z. Gordon and The Routers**
"You're Gonna Miss Me" - **The 13th Floor Elevators**

## HAWKEYE #6
"Secret Code" - **Lalo Schifrin**
Tetris music
"Funky Miracle" - **The Meters**
"Alexander Nevsky: The Battle on The Ice" - **Sergei Prokofiev**
"The Last Stroke of Midnight" - **Dizzy Gillespie and Lalo Schifrin**
"Round Midnight" - **Miles Davis**
"Alexander Nevsky: Waiting" - **Sergei Prokofiev**
"Soulful Christmas" - **James Brown**

## HAWKEYE #8
"What's the Ugliest Part of Your Body?" - **The Mothers of Invention**
"Can't Seem To Make You Mine" - **The Seeds**
"Are You Nervous? - **The Instrumentals**
"Drums A-Go-Go" - **The Hollywood Persuaders**
"Womp Womp" - **Freddie & The Heartaches**
"Nasal Retentive Calliope Music" - **The Mothers of Invention**
"Here's The Rainy Day" - **Freddie Hubbard**

## HAWKEYE #9
"What's the Ugliest Part of Your Body? (Reprise)" - **The Mothers of Invention**
"Black Widow" - **Lalo Schifrin**
"Chemical Marriage" - **Mr. Bungle**
"Unicorn" - **Dizzy Gillespie and Lalo Schifrin**
"Spider" - **Herbie Hancock**
"White Rabbit" - **Jefferson Airplane**

## HAWKEYE #11
"Bloomdido" - **Charlie Parker and Dizzy Gillespie**
"Two Bass Hit" - **Miles Davis**
"Street of Dreams" - **Chet Baker**
"The Dog Breath Variations" - **The Mothers of Invention**
"Splanky" - **Count Basie**
"The Big Noise from Winnetka" - **Bob Crosby**
"We Can Shoot You" - **The Mothers of Invention**
"Leap Frog" - **Charlie Parker and Dizzy Gillespie**
"(Get Your Kicks on) Route 66" - **Nat King Cole**